The Twenties in America

The Twenties in America

Volume 2

Gambling—*Public Opinion*

Editor

Carl Rollyson
City University of New York,
Baruch College

SALEM PRESS
A Division of EBSCO Publishing
Ipswich, Massachusetts
Hackensack, New Jersey

Library of Congress Cataloging-in-Publication Data

The twenties in America / editor, Carl Rollyson.
    p. cm.
    ISBN 978-1-58765-855-6 (set) — ISBN 978-1-58765-856-3 (vol. 1) — ISBN 978-1-58765-857-0 (vol. 2) — ISBN 978-1-58765-858-7 (vol. 3)
    1. United States—History—1919-1933. 2. United States—Social conditions—1918-1932. 3. United States— Social life and customs—1918-1945. 4. Nineteen twenties. I. Rollyson, Carl E. (Carl Edmund)
    E784.T84 2012
    973.91–dc23
                                                                                            2011051370

■ Contents

■ Complete List of Contents

Volume 1

Volume 2

Volume 3

The Twenties
in America

G

■ Gambling

By the early twentieth century, gambling had been officially banned throughout most of the United States. However, illegal gambling was ubiquitous during the Prohibition era of the 1920s, aiding the rise of many organized criminal networks.

Gambling has a lengthy history in North America. Early explorers described indigenous games of chance, and European settlers imported their gambling habits to the continent. As the new nations of the United States and Canada thrived, so did various gambling initiatives, including new games and methods such as gambling machines.

Passage of the National Prohibition Act, known as the Volstead Act, and the Eighteenth Amendment in 1919 resulted in the nationwide prohibition of alcohol. On the heels of Prohibition came attempts to restrict other "sinful" pursuits, including gambling, which was already illegal in most places anyway. For this reason, the Prohibition years, which lasted until 1933, had a dampening effect on legal gambling enterprises, while resulting in tremendous payoffs for individuals willing to break these laws.

Popularization of Illegal Gambling

One of the more publicly visible illegal gamblers was Arnold Rothstein, who ran a New York–based criminal network and owned a number of gambling houses in Manhattan. He was murdered on November 4, 1928, allegedly for refusing to pay a gambling debt. Rothstein had been involved in sports betting, including racetrack activities and the infamous 1919 World Series sports fixing scandal, as well as high-stakes games of chance. All these initiatives were lucrative for Rothstein and his cohorts, despite the fact that many states had enacted laws to ban betting on horse races. Instead of putting a stop to gambling, these legislative initiatives merely pushed it underground, neatly connecting sporting activities, book-

makers, and violence. The public was only occasionally made aware of these activities, generally when the bloodshed became too extreme, such as when Rothstein was shot.

Despite community outrage at these outbursts of violence, novelists continued to romanticize gambling and its practitioners. F. Scott Fitzgerald, for example, based his character Meyer Wolfsheim in *The Great Gatsby* (1925) on Arnold Rothstein. Writers of various media were interested in gambling tales, with occasional stories appearing in the 1920s popular press.

Newspaper and wire services also played a more insidious role in the popularization of gambling. Some types of gambling, such as off-track betting and wagering on sports, required the speedy transmission of data from the location of the activity to the betting shop before a payoff to the winners could occur, creating a new market for organizations skilled in information distribution. During the 1920s, newspapers and wire services were battling for territories and circulation numbers and so were willing to extend their services to gambling enterprises and their clients in their attempts to outdo the competition.

While public slot machines prior to the 1920s had often been designed to look like they dispensed gum or toy prizes rather than cash, Prohibition made such subterfuge unnecessary, as slot machines moved underground to speakeasies, where they no longer needed to be disguised. In many cities, machine gambling and other informal betting arrangements were rampant. Some of these games were associated with certain ethnic groups, such as Mah-Jongg among the Chinese. Similarly, illegal lotteries known as numbers games were played mainly by African and Italian Americans, as such games were especially popular in poorer neighborhoods such as Harlem and Little Italy. Like other forms of illegal gambling, numbers games were usually controlled by organized crime.

During the 1920s, when Las Vegas was still just a small town in the desert, Reno, Nevada, featured legal card rooms where certain games could be played for low stakes. Here as elsewhere, however, illegal clubs

Illegal pin games confiscated during raids on four Chicago area taverns. (Getty Images)

provided additional gambling opportunities for those interested in higher stakes, often combined with alcohol, drugs, and prostitution.

Impact

Gambling during the 1920s was intertwined with illegal enterprises led by violent men, with most profits remaining within these criminal networks and few benefits accruing to the general public. It was not until the following decade, which saw the end of Prohibition, that the legal environment began to relax around gaming enterprises, as legislators saw the benefits of legalizing and regulating gambling, generating tax dollars for the community instead of profits for crime bosses.

Susan J. Wurtzburg

Further Reading

Hyde, Stephen, and Geno Zanetti, eds. *Players: Con Men, Hustlers, Gamblers, and Scam Artists.* New York: Thunder's Mouth Press, 2002. An edited collection of stories about the gambling world, some fictional and some not.

Jones, Karen. "'The Old West in Modern Splendor': Frontier Folklore and the Selling of Las Vegas." *European Journal of American Culture* 29, no. 2 (July, 2010): 93–110. A detailed history of Las Vegas, providing background on how the city became an important gambling destination in the decades following the 1920s.

Reith, Gerda. *The Age of Chance: Gambling in Western Culture.* New York: Routledge, 1999. A broad history of gambling and its cultural importance.

Sasuly, Richard. *Bookies and Bettors: Two Hundred Years of Gambling.* New York: Holt, Rinehart and Winston, 1982. A dated but still useful history of gambling.

Schwartz, David G. *Roll the Bones: The History of Gambling.* New York: Gotham Books, 2006. An extensive, scholarly history of gambling, with information relevant to the 1920s.

Wolcott, Victoria W. "The Culture of the Informal Economy: Numbers Runners in Inter-War Black Detroit." *Radical History Review* 69 (1997): 46–75. Emphasis on 1930s inner-city gambling, but with information on 1920s precursors.

See also: Hobbies and recreation; Horse racing; Nightclubs; Organized crime; Prohibition; "Roaring Twenties"

■ Garbo, Greta

Identification: American film star
Also known as: Greta Lovisa Gustafson
Born: September 18, 1905, Stockholm, Sweden
Died: April 15, 1990, New York, New York

Film actress Greta Garbo began her illustrious career in the silent films of Hollywood in the 1920s. Even before her successful transition to the early "talkies," Garbo's impact in

1920s American film foreshadowed her rise to legend status in the decades to come.

Greta Garbo, born Greta Lovisa Gustafson, began her acting career in Sweden filming department store commercials. She then starred in three Swedish movies, the second of which, *Gosta Berling's Saga* (1924), was a huge commercial success and drew the attention of Metro-Goldwyn-Mayer (MGM) film studio president Louis B. Mayer. In September of 1925, at the age of twenty, Greta Garbo arrived in Los Angeles, California, to work under contract for MGM.

Early U.S. Films

Garbo's first U.S. film was *The Torrent* (1926), directed by Monta Bell, in which she played a woman who leaves her small town in Spain and returns an opera star. Garbo was self-assured and photogenic in this first U.S. performance, and Mayer was so impressed that he asked her to sign a five-year contract with the studio, but she did not feel ready for such a commitment. Her next film, *The Temptress* (1926), was directed by Mauritz Stiller, who had mentored her in Sweden. While Garbo was happy to be working with Stiller, Mayer had problems with his method of directing and fired him. During these first years in the United States, it became clear that Garbo preferred her privacy, and she continued to avoid fans and the press for the remainder of her life.

A turning point in Garbo's career was the film *Flesh and the Devil* (1927), costarring the popular screen actor John Gilbert and directed by Clarence Brown. Garbo and Gilbert had an intense real-life chemistry that translated well to the screen. Their love scenes were passionate, making them the first romantic Hollywood team of the 1920s. The two became engaged in 1927 and went on to star together in several highly successful films. Garbo, however, never showed up for the wedding, and their relationship, both on screen and off, feel apart.

Flesh and the Devil was a huge box-office hit for MGM, making Garbo an instant star with the power to negotiate her salary and selectively choose her movie roles. After bitter negotiations lasting several months, Garbo became the highest-paid actress at the time, earning up to $6,000 a week.

In 1928, Garbo starred in the film *Love*, again with John Gilbert, and it became the studio's most profitable silent film of the 1920s. The 1928 film *The Divine Woman*, directed by Victor Sjöström and costarring

Greta Garbo. (Hulton Archive/Getty Images)

Swedish leading man Lars Hanson, was the first film written expressly for Garbo and is considered one of the most important "lost films"—those of which no known copies remain—of the silent era.

Garbo's next film, *A Woman of Affairs* (1928), marked the actress's move toward more modern roles. This was the first film for which Garbo was dressed by designer Gilbert Adrian, who would continue to costume her and other well-known Hollywood actresses in future films. Garbo continued this trend of portraying modern women in *The Single Standard* (1929), in which she played a girl from San Francisco who yearns for the same freedoms as men.

Talkies

By 1929, studios were primarily making "talking pictures," and the only silent films MGM released that year starred Garbo and Lon Chaney. Garbo's last silent film was *The Kiss* (1929), directed by Belgian Jacques Feyder, in which three men vie for one woman's affection.

Garbo was careful in choosing the right film for her speaking debut, as she was ambivalent about sound films. Her choice was *Anna Christie* (1929), based on a play by Eugene O'Neill about a young Swedish American woman who returns to see her father after being sent away as a young child to live with relatives. Clarence Brown directed this demanding role for Garbo, which the studio marketed with the slogan "Garbo Talks!" Garbo's husky, deep voice matched her strong yet mysterious personality, and the film was a huge commercial success. Garbo's first talkie was MGM's highest-grossing film that year. Garbo was thus able to increase her contract to $250,000 per film, and she was given the final say over her roles, costars, and directors. By the end of the 1920s, Greta Garbo was twenty-seven years old and at the peak of her career.

Impact

Greta Garbo's successful speaking debut in the film *Anna Christie* foreshadowed her continuing success as an actress in Hollywood through the 1930s and early 1940s. Her silent films of the 1920s enabled Garbo to hone her skills as an actress and develop the personality and mystique for which she was known throughout her life.

Sandra Rothenberg

Further Reading

Daum, Raymond. *Walking with Garbo: Conversations and Recollections.* New York: Perennial, 1991. Gives insight into Garbo's private life and life after film through photographs and interviews.

Paris, Barry. *Garbo: A Biography.* New York: Knopf, 1995. A thorough biography by a film critic and journalist.

Swenson, Karen. *Greta Garbo: A Life Apart.* New York: Scribner, 1997. An authoritative biography on Garbo's life.

Vieira, Mark A. *Greta Garbo: A Cinematic Legacy.* New York: Harry N. Abrams, 2005. An excellent study of Garbo's films, with many photographs.

Walker, Alexander. *Garbo: A Portrait.* New York: Macmillan, 1980. Authorized by Metro-Goldwyn-Mayer, including many images and documentary evidence from MGM's archives.

See also: Film; *Flesh and the Devil;* Gilbert, John; Metro-Goldwyn-Mayer (MGM); Talking motion pictures

■ Garvey, Marcus

Identification: Jamaican publisher, black nationalist, and leader within the back-to-Africa movement
Born: August 17, 1887, St. Ann's Bay, Jamaica
Died: June 10, 1940, London, England

Garvey initiated one of the earliest black political movements in the United States and was instrumental in the development of the back-to-Africa movement throughout North America and the Caribbean.

Marcus Garvey began his career as a printer's apprentice in Jamaica, where he became active in the printers' union and helped lead an unsuccessful strike in 1907. After traveling and working throughout Central America and Europe, Garvey returned to Jamaica in 1914 to found the Universal Negro Improvement Association and African Communities League (UNIA-ACL), better known as the UNIA, which educated people of African descent to become economically and politically independent of whites.

Early Successes

In 1916, Garvey relocated to Harlem, New York, and began a yearlong, nationwide speaking tour. During the next several years, Garvey incorporated the UNIA and developed a number of auxiliary associations, each with its own educational focus. He established UNIA branches in the Caribbean, Central America, Canada, and Africa, and started the association's official weekly publication, *Negro World*. Garvey also launched the Black Star Line, a black-owned-and-operated shipping company intended to commercially connect black businesses throughout the world in order to develop an autonomous black economy. Garvey also wanted the Black Star Line to facilitate the back-to-Africa movement, which promoted the return of blacks to their ancestral Africa.

By 1920, the UNIA claimed over two million members and almost one thousand divisions worldwide. *Negro World,* with a circulation of 200,000, was the most popular black newspaper in the United States, and the Black Star Line had assets totaling over $340,000. It was during this year that Garvey focused on the back-to-Africa movement and began working with the government of Liberia to try (ultimately unsuccessfully) to secure land on which UNIA members could settle. For Garvey, the mass return migration of blacks to Africa represented the best long-term hope for undoing centuries of white enslavement and oppression.

Controversies and Legal Problems

Garvey's initial success and popularity, however, were short-lived. In April 1922, the UNIA was forced to dissolve the Black Star Line; Garvey had overpaid for dilapidated ships, and although the company was an inspirational symbol of independence to many within the African American community, it was financially unsustainable. Also that year, many African American leaders and newspapers initiated a "Garvey Must Go" campaign after Garvey met briefly with the leader of the Ku Klux Klan (KKK), suggesting afterward that the KKK and the UNIA were similar in that both were racial separatist groups. Another blow came in 1924 when Liberia withdrew its support of Garvey and refused to grant visas to UNIA members.

The U.S. government found Garvey's radical ideas threatening and subversive, so the Bureau of Investigation (later the Federal Bureau of Investigation) began monitoring his activities. In the fall of 1920, Garvey was indicted for criminal libel for an article published in the *Negro World*. The charges were dropped, however, after a retraction was printed. In 1921, Garvey was denied reentry into the United States when the State Department temporarily rejected his visa on the grounds of "political and race agitation." Garvey was arrested again in January 1922 and indicted on a charge of mail fraud for selling Black Star Line stock through the U.S. mail. In June of 1923, Garvey was convicted and sentenced to five years in prison; following unsuccessful efforts to appeal his sentence, he was sent to federal prison in Atlanta, Georgia, in February 1925.

On November 18, 1927, President Calvin Coolidge commuted the remainder of Garvey's sentence, and he was deported to Jamaica two weeks later. Garvey then lived in London, England, for a short time before returning to Jamaica, where he again incorporated the UNIA. Garvey believed that the UNIA should be headquartered where he lived, though leaders within the North American organization disagreed. Garvey did not gain much support in Jamaica, and without his leadership, the UNIA splintered into competing groups. In 1933, the UNIA halted publication of *Negro World*.

Garvey moved back to London in 1935 and lived there until his death in 1940. On November 10, 1964, Garvey's body was returned to Jamaica, and he was declared the country's first national hero.

Impact

Although Garvey's dream of a large-scale return of blacks to Africa did not materialize, his influence on black nationalism and anticolonialism inspired many blacks in the United States and around the world, and "Garveyism" became a term for the set of beliefs he espoused for the uplift of the global African diaspora. Members of the Black Power movement of the 1960s and 1970s consider Garvey an inspiration, and many within the Nation of Islam and the Rastafarian movement regard him as a prophet.

Monica C. Reed

Further Reading

Akpan, M. B. "Liberia and the Universal Negro Improvement Association: The Background to the Abortion of Garvey's Scheme for African Colonization." *The Journal of African History* 14, no. 1 (1973): 105–127. Provides background information and relevant political history surrounding the Liberian withdrawal of support for the UNIA and Garvey's back-to-Africa movement.

Cronon, E. David, and John Hope Franklin. *Black Moses: The Story of Marcus Garvey and the United Negro Improvement Association.* Madison: University of Wisconsin Press, 1960. Comprehensive biography focusing on the rise and fall of the UNIA and race relations in general during the 1920s.

Grant, Colin. *Negro with a Hat: The Rise and Fall of Marcus Garvey.* New York: Oxford University Press, 2010. Biography concentrating on Garvey's rise and fall in the United States from the early 1900s through the 1920s.

Grant, Otis B. "Social Justice Versus Social Equality: The Capitalistic Jurisprudence of Marcus Garvey." *Journal of Black Studies* 33, no. 4 (March, 2003): 490–498. Evaluates the cultural and economic ideas of Garvey as they relate to the legal system of the 1920s.

Lawler, Mary, and John Davenport. *Marcus Garvey: Black Nationalist Leader.* New York: Chelsea House Publications, 2004. Biography aimed at young adults, with a concentration on Garvey's back-to-Africa movement.

See also: African Americans; Great Migration; Hoover, J. Edgar; Universal Negro Improvement Association (UNIA)

■ Gehrig, Lou

Identification: American baseball player
Also known as: Henry Louis Gehrig; Iron Horse
Born: June 19, 1903, New York, New York
Died: June 2, 1941, Bronx, New York

Lou Gehrig, known as the Iron Horse, was one of the greatest players in the history of baseball. His unprecedented streak of 2,130 consecutive games played for the New York Yankees started on June 1, 1925, and didn't end until he was unable to play on May 2, 1939. He died at the age of 36 of amyotrophic lateral sclerosis (ALS), now referred to as Lou Gehrig's disease.

Lou Gehrig was born to a poor family in New York City, the only one of four children to survive past infancy. Gehrig's mother, Christina, encouraged him to get an education, so he attended Columbia University on a football scholarship in 1921. Gehrig also played baseball at Columbia in 1922 and was discovered by baseball scout Paul Krichell, who signed Gehrig to his first contract with the New York Yankees in 1923. For most of the 1923 and 1924 seasons, Gehrig played in the minor leagues at Hartford, where he excelled. During each of these two seasons, Gehrig was called up for a brief stint with the major-league team, where he hit well in his few at-bats, with a .423 average in 1923 and a .500 average in twelve at-bats in 1924.

In 1925, Gehrig became a full-time Yankee. On June 1, 1925, Yankee first baseman Wally Pipp had a headache and missed the game. Gehrig started as a pinch hitter and then proceeded to play in 2,130 consecutive games for the team, becoming a star at the plate and in the field. Often in the shadow of teammate Babe Ruth, Gehrig won the league's most valuable player award in 1927. His career statistics are exceptional, with a .340 batting average, 1,995 runs batted in, 493 home runs, and a major-league record of 23 grand-slam home runs. He played in seven World Series, winning six, and carried a .361 career batting average in the fall classic. In contrast to Babe Ruth, Gehrig was a modest man, and he was considered an excellent role model for young people. Gehrig's uniform number was the first to be retired in professional baseball on July 4, 1939, when he was honored at Yankee Stadium.

Lou Gehrig. (Getty Images)

Impact

In the decades since his career ended, Gehrig has served as an American symbol of strength and perseverance both as an athlete and in his struggle with ALS, the disease that is often known by his name. The feats of early professional athletes like Gehrig and Ruth helped establish professional sports as a major entertainment industry and mainstay of American culture.

Douglas A. Phillips

Further Reading

Frommer, Harvey. *Five O'clock Lightning: Babe Ruth, Lou Gehrig, and the Greatest Team in Baseball, the 1927 New York Yankees.* Hoboken, N.J.: John Wiley & Sons Inc., 2008.

Kashatus, William C. *Lou Gehrig, A Biography.* Westport, Conn.: Greenwood Press, 2004.

Robinson, Ray, II. *Iron Horse: Lou Gehrig in his Time.* New York: W.W. Norton, 2006.

See also: Baseball; New York Yankees; Ruth, Babe; Sports

■ General, The

Identification: A silent film about the theft of a train during the Civil War
Directors: Clyde Bruckman and Buster Keaton
Date: 1926

The General showcases the diverse acting, writing, and directing talents of Buster Keaton, one of the brightest comedy stars of the 1920s. The movie, which premiered just as talking pictures were coming into vogue, proved a critical and commercial failure at the time of its release. The unfavorable reaction to The General *adversely affected Keaton both personally and professionally.*

The General is based on historical events. In 1862, Union commandos stole the titular locomotive in Georgia and rode it north, pursued by Confederates. During the hundred-mile chase, the Northerners sabotaged rails, burned bridges, and cut telegraph lines between Atlanta and Chattanooga, two Confederate strongholds targeted in Union campaign plans. Deep in enemy territory and running out of fuel, the men abandoned the train and fled but were rounded up and put on trial. Several were hanged as spies, and the rest were imprisoned.

Keaton adapted the events of the incident as a vehicle for his unique brand of visual comedy. In the movie, he plays Johnnie Gray, engineer of the General. Johnnie tries to enlist in the Confederate infantry to please his girlfriend, only to be refused, as he is more valuable in his current occupation. When the train is then stolen with Johnnie at the controls and his estranged girlfriend onboard, he gives chase, recaptures the General, rescues the girl, and heads south, followed by a trainload of angry Yankees. He arrives home in time to alert the Confederate command to imminent attack. An accidental hero, Johnnie is made an officer and regains his girlfriend's affections.

The General gave Keaton ample opportunity to display his trademark deadpan expression, maintained even in the midst of a series of physically demanding stunts. He used the train and track themselves as props, leaping and climbing all over the locomotive, taking pratfalls over railroad ties, and performing last-second switchovers to avoid head-on collisions. He also employed numerous train-related objects, including an axe, the cowcatcher, a mobile cannon, and the boxcars and their contents, for humorous sight gags. One highlight of the movie is a spectacular scene in which a real locomotive crashes through a burning bridge into a river.

Impact

Despite Keaton's best efforts, *The General* was a costly flop: too dramatic for slapstick, too flippant for drama. His judgment in question, Keaton soon lost creative control of his independent productions and became a studio player. In the 1930s, he sank into alcoholism while suffering through two painful divorces. No longer in demand for the lead roles that had made him famous, he played mainly support and cameo roles for the remainder of his career. Modern critics consider *The General* a silent-film gem, however, and the Library of Congress entered it into the National Film Registry in 1989.

Jack Ewing

Further Reading

Smith, Imogen Sara. *Buster Keaton: The Persistence of Comedy.* Chicago: Gambit, 2008.
Sweeney, Kevin W., ed. *Buster Keaton: Interviews.* Jackson: University Press of Mississippi, 2007.

See also: Film; Metro-Goldwyn-Mayer (MGM); Talking motion pictures; Vaudeville

■ Gentlemen Prefer Blondes

Identification: A comic novel about a 1920s gold digger who charms wealthy men
Author: Anita Loos
Date: 1925

Anita Loos's novel about the exploits of an attractive blond woman satirizes male-female relations. It also highlights the excesses of the Roaring Twenties, poking fun at the veil of respectability in post–World War I American society.

Screenwriter Anita Loos wrote *Gentlemen Prefer Blondes* after watching her friend, journalist H. L. Mencken, fawn over an attractive but unintelligent woman with blond hair. In 1924, the story was serialized in *Harper's Bazaar* magazine. The 1925 book spawned a Broadway musical, a Hollywood film, and the song "Diamonds Are a Girl's Best Friend."

Written in diary form, the book chronicles the life of socialite Lorelei Lee. The wealthy blond from Little

Rock, Arkansas, writes at the request of "Button King" Gus Eisman, a married businessman with "a friendly interest in educating a girl." Eisman, a Chicago manufacturing mogul in the post–World War I economy, monitors Lorelei's progress on outings to supper clubs, theatrical productions, and stylish society in New York and abroad.

Lorelei's diary describes Prohibition-era luxuries and amusements, praising fancy hotels, Cartier jewelry, filmmaker D. W. Griffiths, alcoholic judges, and rich lords. She claims to be an old-fashioned girl among modern flappers; Lorelei prizes refinement and tries to teach manners to her wisecracking hometown companion, Dorothy. Men vying for Lorelei's company pay for the Arkansas duo's champagne cocktails, lavish shopping excursions, and European tours.

The subtitle of the novel, *The Illuminating Diary of a Professional Lady*, hints that Lorelei may be exchanging sexual favors for the financial support of her male admirers, but Lorelei keeps the tone of the diary sweet, flattering, and seemingly innocent.

Impact

Lorelei's entry into high society is a comic exaggeration of 1920s reality, featuring class distinctions, social mores, and gender roles that had become blurred in the aftermath of World War I. Popular as a 1925 book character, and subsequently played by Carol Channing in the 1949 stage musical and Marilyn Monroe in the 1953 film, Lorelei Lee has become America's prototype for the material girl.

Gentlemen Prefer Blondes was lauded by novelist Edith Wharton and translated into fourteen languages. It remains an ironic testament to 1920s consumerism and expensive living, mocking romance and the American social elite of its time.

Wendy Alison Lamb

Further Reading

Gourley, Catherine. *Flappers and the New American Woman: Perceptions of Women from 1918 through the 1920s.* Minneapolis, Minn.: Twenty-First Century Books, 2008.

Loos, Anita, Cari Beauchamp, and Mary Anita Loos, eds. *Anita Loos Rediscovered: Film Treatments and Fiction.* Berkeley: University of California Press, 2003.

See also: Flappers; Griffith, D. W.; Literature in the United States; Marriage and dating; Mencken, H. L.; Nightclubs; Prohibition; "Roaring Twenties"

■ Gershwin, George

Identification: American composer and pianist
Born: September 26, 1898, Brooklyn, New York
Died: July 11, 1937, Hollywood, California

George Gershwin is best remembered for his talents as both a classical and popular music composer. His music has been performed in concert halls, on Broadway, on television, and in films, and has been recorded by numerous artists.

Born Jacob Gershowitz, George Gershwin was one of four children born to Russian Jewish immigrants Morris and Rose Gershowitz. All the Gershwin children exhibited musical talent. Gershwin's parents bought a piano for his older brother, Ira, to play, but it was George who became fascinated with the instrument and who began studying it seriously. Gershwin's piano teacher and mentor, Charles Hambitzer, introduced him to the diverse repertoire of the classical canon, as well as to modern composers such as Arnold Schoenberg. Gershwin also studied with noted composers Henry Cowell, Rubin Goldmark, Wallingford Riegger, and Joseph Schillinger.

Gershwin left school at age fifteen to become a "song plugger"—a pianist who promotes sheet music by playing it for customers in music stores—on Tin Pan Alley in Manhattan, while simultaneously recording piano rolls and composing. He published his first song at the age of seventeen and achieved commercial success in 1919 with the song "Swanee." That same year, he composed the music for the musical *La La Lucille*, his first complete score.

Gershwin worked with several lyricists, but it was his collaborations with his older brother Ira for which he is best remembered. Together, they wrote the songs for many popular 1920s musicals, including *Lady, Be Good* (1924), *Strike Up the Band* (1927), and *Funny Face* (1927).

In 1924, bandleader Paul Whiteman commissioned Gershwin to compose a piece for piano and jazz band. Gershwin completed the commission in three weeks, and *Rhapsody in Blue*, orchestrated by Ferde Grofé, became one of his best-known works. Gershwin continued to incorporate popular music into his compositions, as evidenced in the evocative tone poem *An American in Paris* (1928) and the "I Got Rhythm" variations (1934).

George Gershwin. (Getty Images)

Impact

Gershwin would continue writing Broadway musicals, classical pieces, and opera into the 1930s, eventually moving into film scores before his early death in 1937 at age thirty-eight of a brain tumor. A remarkable pianist and composer, Gershwin produced a large body of work of enduring popularity. He is perhaps best remembered for his ability to synthesize the classical and jazz genres into a unique brand of concert music that is distinctly American.

Anastasia Pike

Further Reading

Ewen, David. *George Gershwin: His Journey to Greatness.* New York: Ungar Publishing, 1956.

Jablonski, Edward. *Gershwin.* New York: Doubleday, 1987.

Pollack, Howard. *George Gershwin: His Life and Work.* Berkeley: University of California Press, 2006.

See also: Broadway musicals; Classical music; Jazz; Music, popular; *Rhapsody in Blue;* Tin Pan Alley

■ Gila Wilderness Area

At the urging of conservationist Aldo Leopold, the U.S. Forest Service designated a portion of the Gila National Forest as the world's first official wilderness area in 1924. Leopold's vision of a roadless recreation area was in stark contrast to then-ongoing efforts to improve road access to U.S. National Park sites, and it set a precedent that would later provide the foundation for a system of federally designated wilderness areas.

Historical records show that the Gila Wilderness was once populated by wolves, grizzly bears, river otters, and the now-extinct Merriam's elk. The area was also home to the ancient cliff-dwelling Mogollon people and, later, the nomadic Chiricahua Apache. The region of southwestern New Mexico that contains the present-day Gila National Forest became part of the United States in 1848 under the terms of the Treaty of Guadalupe Hidalgo, which ended the Mexican-American War. Later, when other western areas were experiencing an influx of settlers following the Civil War, the area's rugged terrain contributed to its continued isolation. The Gila River Forest Reserve was established in 1899; in 1905, it was renamed the Gila Forest Reserve, and management was subsequently transferred to the newly established U.S. Forest Service. In 1907, the official designation changed from forest reserve to national forest.

In 1921, New Mexico forester Aldo Leopold wrote a paper called "The Wilderness and Its Place in Forest Recreational Policy." Leopold conceived of wilderness as a relatively undisturbed natural area large enough for a "two weeks' pack trip," and felt that while wilderness lands should be open to hunting and fishing, they should remain free of roads, buildings, and "other works of man."

In October 1922, Leopold submitted a plan to district forester Frank Pooler recommending the creation of a wilderness area within the Gila National Forest, in which the construction of roads and permanent buildings would be banned. Two years later, on June 3, 1924, Pooler signed a recreation management plan that set aside 755,000 acres as designated wilderness.

At the end of the decade, a sudden increase in the deer population caused Pooler to approve the construction of the North Star Mesa Road to provide better access for hunters. The road divided the Gila Wilderness, separating over 200,000 acres from the rest of the land. Legislation passed in 1980 would officially designate this land as the Aldo Leopold Wilderness Area.

Impact

The creation of the Gila Wilderness Area signified the birth of the modern wilderness movement. In 1929, the Forest Service enacted the L-20 Regulations, which would establish seventy-five protected "primitive areas," comprising more than 14 million acres, over the next ten years. In 1964, Congress passed the Wilderness Act, making the Gila Wilderness part of the new National Wilderness Preservation System. The area now consists of nearly 560,000 acres.

Thomas A. Wikle

Further Reading

Murray, John A. *The Gila Wilderness Area: A Hiking Guide.* Albuquerque: University of New Mexico Press, 1988.

Roth, Dennis Morrow. *The Wilderness Movement and the National Forests.* 2d ed. College Station, Tex.: Intaglio Press, 1995.

Vale, Thomas R. *The American Wilderness: Reflections on Nature Protection in the United States.* Charlottesville: University of Virginia Press, 2005.

See also: Automobiles and auto manufacturing; National Parks of the United States

---

■ Gilbert, John

Identification: American film actor
Also known as: John Cecil Pringle
Born: July 10, 1897, Logan, Utah
Died: January 9, 1936, Hollywood, California

After Rudolph Valentino, John Gilbert was regarded as the heartthrob of the silent film era. However, after a dispute with Louis B. Mayer, he was not cast in many talking pictures, although he did appear in some films in the 1930s.

John Cecil Pringle was born to an actor with a traveling company and the company's elocutionist. After his mother died when he was a teenager, John lived with his stepfather, Walter B. Gilbert, whose surname he adopted, and attended a military academy in Cali-

fornia. Working in a stock company in Spokane, Washington, he managed to get an unaccredited role in director Thomas H. Ince's film *The Coward* (1915). He soon picked up more minor parts in a large number of films but interrupted his career in 1918 to enlist in the U.S. Army.

Returning to the film industry after the war, Gilbert joined the Fox Film Corporation in 1921, where he wrote and directed the film *Love's Penalty.* In the following year, he starred as Edmond Dantes in *Monte Cristo.* After he signed on with Metro-Goldwyn-Mayer (MGM) in 1924, he accumulated major roles in some very important films. In 1926, after the death of Rudolph Valentino, Gilbert became the great romantic actor of the era. He played the lead role in the 1925 film *The Big Parade*, which was one of the most successful films in the silent movie era. In *Love* (1927), based on Leo Tolstoy's novel *Anna Karenina*, Gilbert played Count Vronsky opposite actor Greta Garbo. He also starred in *The Cossacks* (1928), a film adaption of Tolstoy's novel *War and Peace.*

Gilbert made his talking picture debut in *The Hollywood Revue* (1929). His first feature-length talking film was the disastrous *His Glorious Night* (1929), best known for the high-pitched quality of Gilbert's voice. His career never recovered.

Impact

John Gilbert was an example of a rags-to-riches film star during the era of silent motion pictures. Although he did appear in a number of other films during the 1930s, his career crashed with the advent of talking pictures. By his last film appearance in 1934, Gilbert had divorced his fourth wife and was suffering badly from alcoholism. He lost his fortune just before his death in 1936 at age thirty-eight.

Justin Corfield

Further Reading

Fountain, Leatrice Gilbert. *Dark Star: The Untold Story of the Meteoric Rise and Fall of Legendary Silent Screen Star John Gilbert.* New York: St. Martin Press, 1985.

Gronowicz, Antoni. *Garbo: Her Story.* London: Penguin Books, 1991.

Shipman, David. *The Great Movie Stars: The Golden Years.* Boston, Mass.: Little, Brown, & Co., 1995.

See also: Film; Garbo, Greta; Metro-Goldwyn-Mayer (MGM); Talking motion pictures

■ Gipp, George

Identification: American college football player
Born: February 18, 1895, Laurium, Michigan
Death: December 14, 1920, South Bend, Indiana

George Gipp became the first nationally known football star at the University of Notre Dame in the years following World War I. Succumbing to streptococcal pneumonia in his senior year, the young athlete was immortalized in the popular rallying cry "win one for the Gipper," an expression attributed to the dying Gipp himself.

George Gipp was raised in the Upper Peninsula mining region of Michigan, graduating from Calumet High School in 1916. Offered a baseball scholarship at Notre Dame, the six-foot-two Gipp learned to supplement his income playing pool and poker at a local hotel and became equally notorious for his gambling habits as for his football prowess.

Gipp first came to the attention of future football coach Knute Rockne in October 1916, when he drop-kicked a sixty-two-yard field goal in a freshman football game. His most noted achievements came during the period from 1918 to 1920, during which time he led the team in most offensive categories. An indifferent student, Gipp's nonacademic activities were generally overlooked by Rockne. Gipp scored twenty-one touchdowns playing with the football varsity, a significant total for the time, and he completed half of his 187 passes. His career total of 2,341 yards gained remained a school record until 1978.

Gipp was already ill when he played against Northwestern late in November 1920 on a cold, wet Saturday. The following week, Gipp entered the hospital with streptococcal pneumonia, an often deadly disease in the days before antibiotics. On his deathbed, Gipp allegedly asked Rockne, "When the team is up against it, when things are going wrong and the breaks are beating the boys—tell them to go in … and win just one for the Gipper." Rockne invoked the request in a victory over Army in 1928. The phrase was also used by Ronald Reagan, first in the 1940 movie biography of Rockne and later at the 1988 Republican National Convention. Whether Gipp actually made the request is difficult to ascertain. There is little evidence to suggest he ever used the nickname Gipper, Rockne was not present at the time of Gipp's death, and no witnesses ever corroborated the story.

George Gipp. (Collegiate Images/Getty Images)

Impact

Two weeks prior to his death, Gipp had been named in sportswriter Walter Camp's All-America squad, the first Notre Dame football player to be so honored. Gipp became the symbol of Notre Dame for two generations of college football fans. Many of his sports records lasted until the 1980s. The phrase "Win one for the Gipper" became one of the most famous lines in college sports history and remains part of the American vocabulary.

Richard Adler

Further Reading

Cavanaugh, Jack. *The Gipper: George Gipp, Knute Rockne, and the Dramatic Rise of Notre Dame Football.* New York: Skyhorse, 2010.

Sperber, Murray A. *Shake Down the Thunder: The Creation of Notre Dame Football.* Bloomington: Indiana University Press, 2002.

See also: Football; Four Horsemen of Notre Dame; Rockne, Knute; Sports

■ Girl Scout cookies

While the first Girl Scout cookies were sold during World War I, it was in the 1920s that sales truly started to take off. Soon, Girl Scout troops across the country were selling cookies to help raise money.

The first known cookie sale in the Girl Scouts took place in Muskogee, Oklahoma, in 1917, when the Mistletoe Troop sold cookies at a local high school as a way to raise money for the troop's activities. Their cookie sale was a success, and in July of 1922, Florence E. Neil, a local Girl Scout director in Chicago, Illinois, published an article in the Girl Scout magazine *The American Girl,* suggesting that all troops should sell cookies as a way to raise money. In her article, Neil provided a simple sugar cookie recipe for the girls to use and calculated that twenty-five to thirty-five cents would buy enough ingredients for six or seven dozen cookies, which could then be sold for twenty-five to thirty cents per dozen.

Neil's idea took off, and soon over two thousand girls were selling cookies. By 1929, nearly every Girl Scout troop was using cookie sales to help bring in funds. Troops began making their own recipes and swapping them with one another to increase sales. The girls would bake the cookies, wrap them in wax bags, and sell them door-to-door, in the course of which they would learn to create, market, and sell a product, as well as how to handle the money that was brought in. Toward the end of the decade, some local councils started to hire commercial bakers to make the cookies, but this practice did not become widespread until the 1930s.

Impact

Girl Scout cookies continued to gain popularity over the years, and in 1936, the Girl Scout organization started to officially license commercial bakers to produce the cookies. Today, the Girl Scouts use large national bakeries, one of which, ABC Bakers, was among the first companies licensed in 1936. Each licensed baker is allowed to produce up to eight cookie flavors each year, with three of those flavors being mandatory: peanut butter sandwich cookies, shortbread cookies, and Thin Mints. From its humble beginnings of girls going door-to-door with homemade sugar cookies, selling Girl Scout cookies has become a $700 million enterprise, by far the biggest and most successful fundraiser for the Girl Scouts of America.

Kristen Pavka

Further Reading

Degenhardt, Mary, and Judith Kirsch. *Girl Scout Collectors' Guide: A History of Uniforms, Insignia, Publications, and Memorabilia.* Lubbock: Texas Tech University Press, 2005.

Proctor, Tammy M. *Scouting for Girls: A Century of Girl Guides and Girl Scouts.* Santa Barbara, Calif.: Praeger, 2009.

Smith, Andrew F. *Encyclopedia of Junk Food and Fast Food.* Westport, Conn.: Greenwood Press, 2006.

See also: Bubble gum; Eskimo Pie; Food trends

■ Gish, Dorothy

Identification: American film and stage actor
Born: March 11, 1898, Massillon, Ohio
Died: June 4, 1968, Rapallo, Italy

Although Dorothy Gish spent her life in the shadow of her more acclaimed older sister, Lillian, she was nevertheless one of the groundbreaking stars of silent films.

Dorothy Gish became a stage actor when she was only four, after her father deserted her family in New York City. She befriended another child actor, Mary Pickford, who introduced Dorothy and Lillian to film director D. W. Griffith. Beginning in 1912, the sisters appeared in Griffith's films.

Dorothy was directed by her sister in the box-office success *Remodeling Her Husband* (1920), one of her more notable comedies. Following the suicide of her close friend and frequent costar Robert Harron, Dorothy married James Rennie, her costar in *Remodeling Her Husband.* The sisters made their final appearances in a Griffith film in 1921 with *Orphans of the Storm.* Dorothy gave perhaps her greatest performance, playing a young blind woman struggling to survive amid the turmoil of the French Revolution.

Dorothy's considerable versatility became evident in the films she made after leaving Griffith's company. She played a country girl who becomes a flapper to win her sweetheart in *The Country Flapper* (1922), a

Cuban dancer in *The Bright Shawl* (1923), and a young woman killed by her lover in *Romola* (1924). In her final film with her sister, Dorothy played a telephone operator in *Night Life of New York* (1925). Dorothy's other 1920s film roles included the Irish girlfriend of an Italian flower vendor in *The Beautiful City* (1925), a domineering wife in *Clothes Make the Pirate* (1925), the lover of the king of England in *Nell Gwyn* (1926), a dancer opposite comedian Will Rogers in *Tiptoes* (1927), and the mistress of King Louis XV in *Madame Pompadour* (1927). Several of these films demonstrate Dorothy's comic talents, which she discussed in a 1925 *Ladies Home Journal* article "And So I Am a Comedienne."

Dorothy made her Broadway debut in 1928 in the play *Young Love*, starring opposite her husband, under the direction of future film director George Cukor. She went on to concentrate on stage work, including seventeen more Broadway productions, while appearing in only four additional feature films after 1930.

Impact

Dorothy Gish was devoted to her more famous sister and content to let Lillian command the spotlight. Dorothy was more outgoing than her reserved sister, and Griffith claimed she understood his direction more quickly, though she was not the perfectionist Lillian was. Dorothy's obvious wittiness, however, made her superior to her sister in comedy, with some authorities calling her one of the most brilliant comic performers in silent films.

Michael Adams

Further Reading

Gish, Lillian, and Ann Pinchot. *The Movies, Mr. Griffith, and Me.* Englewood Cliffs, N.J.: Prentice-Hall, 1968.

Golden, Eve. *Golden Images: Forty-One Essays on Silent Film Stars.* Jefferson, N.C.: McFarland, 2001.

Menefee, David W. *The First Female Stars: Women of the Silent Era.* Westport, Conn.: Praeger, 2004.

See also: Film; Flappers; Gish, Lillian; Griffith, D. W.; *Orphans of the Storm;* Pickford, Mary; Rogers, Will

---

■ Gish, Lillian

Identification: American film, stage, and television star
Born: October 14, 1893, Springfield, Ohio
Died: February 27, 1993, New York, New York

Lillian Gish was one of the first stars of silent films. In a career of almost ninety years, she went on to establish herself as one of America's most revered actors.

Lillian Diana Gish was only six when her acting career started. After her father left her family, she went on the stage with her mother and younger sister, Dorothy. But her distinguished career began in 1912 when fellow actor Mary Pickford, already famous in silent films, introduced her to renowned film director D. W. Griffith. Both Gish sisters appeared in Griffith films, but Lillian's poignancy and delicate beauty made her the ideal Griffith heroine. She first attracted attention as the ravished maiden in his epic *The Birth of a Nation* (1915), and later brought audiences to tears as the abused child in *Broken Blossoms* (1919). By the next decade, she was a major attraction with *Way Down East* (1920) and *Orphans of the Storm* (1921), a drama of the French Revolution featuring both Gish sisters. So great was Griffith's admiration for Lillian that he encouraged her to direct her sister Dorothy in *Remodeling Her Husband* (1920). Although she benefited from the experience, Lillian realized that she preferred acting to directing.

Lillian Gish. (Hulton Archive/Getty Images)

In the days before stunt artists performed difficult cinematic feats, Gish subjected herself to all manner of dangers in the pursuit of her art. She once performed on an ice floe, with her hair trailing in the frigid water. When she appeared in the King Vidor film *La Bohème* in 1926, she starved herself for several days before her death scene, which was so realistic that the crew feared she had actually died.

Gish also performed in several notable films that were not directed by Griffith, including *The White Sister* (1923), *Romola* (1926), *Annie Laurie* (1927), and *The Wind* (1928). For most of her roles, she played a fragile maiden in distress, with few opportunities to demonstrate her theatrical versatility.

Impact

Although Gish believed that silent pictures were a truly universal art form, her expressive voice enabled her to transition well into talking pictures. Critics applauded her for advancing film acting as a unique art form. She frequently returned to the stage, where she received good reviews. In later years, she took character roles in films, most notably in *The Night of the Hunter* (1955). At ninety-three, she gave her last film performance in *The Whales of August* (1987). Her television work was also acclaimed. In 1953, she led the cast of the television show *The Trip to Bountiful*, which some critics felt signaled television's coming-of-age as an artistic medium.

Allene Phy-Olsen

Further Reading

Affron, Charles. *Lillian Gish: Her Legend, Her Life.* New York: Scribner, 2001.

Gish, Lillian, and Ann Pinchot. *The Movies, Mr. Griffith, and Me.* New York: Prentice-Hall, 1968.

See also: Film; Gish, Dorothy; Griffith, D. W.; *Orphans of the Storm*

■ *Gitlow v. New York*

The Case: U.S. Supreme Court ruling on the free speech clause of the First Amendment and its application to the states

Date: Decided on June 8, 1925

The U.S. Supreme Court ruled that the free speech clause of the First Amendment was binding upon the states but that

the clause did not protect speech that might have harmful effects.

During the Red Scare of 1919 to 1920, Benjamin Gitlow, a founding member of the Communist Labor Party, was arrested for publishing a manifesto that advocated revolution. Despite a lack of evidence demonstrating any effect of this publication, Gitlow was convicted of violating New York's 1902 Criminal Anarchy Law, which made it a felony to promote the violent or illegal overthrow of government. Two state appellate courts upheld the statute over challenges on free speech grounds. Gitlow, represented by American Civil Liberties Union lawyers Walter Pollak and Walter Nelles, appealed to the U.S. Supreme Court.

The case addressed two important matters. Speaking for the majority, Justice Edward Sanford declared that free speech—a fundamental liberty protected by the First Amendment from abridgement by Congress—was also protected by the due process clause of the Fourteenth Amendment from impairment by the states. Second, the justices held that the state statute did not violate the due process clause. They maintained that the constitutional protection for free speech does not grant an absolute, unrestricted right to speech, spoken or published; rather, a state could punish speech that may be detrimental to the public good or advocates illegal action. Furthermore, as the effects of such speech cannot be anticipated, a state cannot be expected to defer action against such utterances until they create an imminent danger to the state. Two justices dissented, Oliver Wendell Holmes Jr. and Louis D. Brandeis, opining that because the speech in question represented a minority view, it was unlikely to incite immediate revolution and therefore should not be prohibited.

Impact

The application of the free speech clause to the states seen in *Gitlow v. New York* was a watershed decision in civil liberties cases: Today, most provisions of the Bill of Rights have been found to be binding upon the states. The Gitlow case also redefined the scope of the "clear and present danger" test, by applying a wartime doctrine during a time of peace and by accepting the legislative judgment of the harmful potential of the speech instead of scrutinizing the facts independently to see whether a danger existed. The line of cases that permitted government to suppress subversive speech that might have harmful effects—

of which *Gitlow v. New York* is illustrative—came to an end in 1969, when the justices held in *Brandenburg v. Ohio* that the free speech clause protected the advocacy of illegal action unless such advocacy was intended and likely to produce "imminent lawless action."

Richard A. Glenn

Further Reading

Kersch, Kenneth I. *Freedom of Speech: Rights and Liberties Under the Law*. Santa Barbara, Calif.: ABC-CLIO, 2003.

Stone, Geoffrey R. *Perilous Times: Free Speech in Wartime from the Sedition Act of 1798 to the War on Terrorism*. New York: Norton, 2005.

See also: American Civil Liberties Union (ACLU); Censorship; Civil rights and liberties; Darrow, Clarence; Holmes, Oliver Wendell, Jr.; Red Scare, The; Supreme Court, U.S.

■ Goddard, Robert

Identification: American physicist and inventor
Born: October 5, 1882, Worcester, Massachusetts
Died: August 10, 1945, Baltimore, Maryland

Robert Goddard designed and launched the world's first liquid-fueled rocket and developed techniques for steering rockets in flight.

Robert Hutchings Goddard was born in Worcester, Massachusetts, to a local businessman and a housewife. Goddard's father encouraged his growing interest in science, showing him how to generate static electricity on the carpet and buying him a telescope and a microscope. Science fiction writer H. G. Wells's book *The War of the Worlds* (1898) motivated the sixteen-year-old Goddard to think about space travel. Later, he read scientist Sir Isaac Newton's writings on motion and recognized that Newton's third law applied to the propulsion of rockets in space. While a student at South High School in Worcester, Goddard submitted an article discussing the possibility of space travel to the periodical *Popular Science News*.

Education and Research

Goddard entered the Worcester Polytechnic Institute in 1904, serving as a laboratory assistant in the physics department. His gunpowder rocket experiments produced clouds of smoke in the basement of the physics building, interesting the faculty in his work. After receiving a bachelor's degree in physics in 1908, he taught in Worcester for one year. Several years after he completed his graduate studies in physics in 1911 at Clark University in Worcester, Goddard was appointed to the school's physics faculty. Beginning in 1915, he conducted experiments demonstrating that a rocket could work in a vacuum. Goddard later published the results of his study in the periodical *Popular Science Monthly*.

Goddard's research was expensive. He requested funds from the Smithsonian Institution, submitting a proposal titled "A Method of Reaching Extreme Altitudes," which developed the mathematics of rocket propulsion. The Smithsonian awarded him five thousand dollars to continue his work. His proposal suggested a rocket could send a spacecraft to the Moon. Later, the Smithsonian published Goddard's proposal, attracting press attention. In 1920, *The New York Times* ran an article titled "Believes Rocket Can Reach Moon," ridiculing Goddard for saying a rocket would have nothing to push against in space.

Liquid-Fueled Rockets

Goddard began experimenting with liquid-fueled rockets in 1921. He tested his first liquid-fueled rocket engine in November 1923 and launched the world's first liquid-fueled rocket on March 16, 1926, from a field in Auburn, Massachusetts. The flight lasted only two-and-a-half seconds, as Goddard's design was not stable. The rocket climbed forty feet, and then it flew nearly horizontally before hitting the ground.

Liquid-fueled rockets could achieve higher efficiency than solid-fueled rockets because liquid fuel burned hotter. They had first been proposed by scientists Hermann Oberth, in Germany, and Konstantin Tsiolkovsky, in Russia. Unlike solid-fueled rockets, invented by the Chinese and used for centuries, engineering a liquid-fueled rocket was challenging. Two liquids had to be pumped at a constant rate into a combustion chamber. Liquid oxygen was very cold, but the combustion chamber was very hot. It was Goddard who pioneered wrapping the pipes that delivered liquid oxygen around the combustion chamber and exhaust nozzle, cooling them. Goddard's tests demonstrated that liquid-fueled rockets could be successfully constructed.

Robert Goddard standing next to rocket-launching platform. (Time & Life Pictures/Getty Images)

Goddard also addressed the problems of guidance and stability in his work, successfully employing gyroscopes to control steering vanes in the rocket exhaust. On July 17, 1929, Goddard launched the first rocket to carry a scientific payload, which is a collection of documentation and measurement tools such as barometers and cameras.

In 1929, the famed transatlantic aviator Charles Lindbergh heard about Goddard's research and sought funds for Goddard. But corporate money was scarce after the stock market crash in October 1929. However, Lindbergh convinced the Guggenheim family to provide $100,000 to support Goddard's research for four years. With this funding, Goddard moved his research to Roswell, New Mexico.

Impact

In his 1920 letter to the Smithsonian Institution, Goddard predicted that spacecraft could photograph the moon and planets, messages could be sent to other civilizations by inscribing metal plates on spacecraft, solar energy could be used on spacecraft, and ion exhaust could be used to propel rockets. Not only did his work anticipate future scientific developments, but Goddard's engineering actually contributed directly to these achievements. The liquid-fueled rockets and guidance systems he designed in the 1920s led to ballistic missiles and rockets that launched the first satellites and carried humans into space. Goddard also proposed an ablative heat shield that is now used to return spacecraft and missile warheads to Earth.

Between 1926 and 1945, Goddard flew thirty-four rockets, which reached altitudes of up to 1.6 miles, at speeds of up to 550 mph. But Goddard kept the designs secret, fearing they would be stolen. Shortly before his death from cancer in August 1945, Goddard examined a German V-2 rocket captured during World War II. He was convinced that German scientists had stolen his ideas for propulsion and guidance.

George J. Flynn

Further Reading

Clary, David. *Rocket Man: Robert H. Goddard and the Birth of the Space Age.* New York: Hyperion Books, 2004. A biography detailing Goddard's personal and scientific life.

Farley, Karin C. *Robert H. Goddard.* Englewood Cliffs, N.J.: Silver Burdett Press, 1991. An account of Goddard's life, intended for a high school audience.

Goddard, Robert. *Rockets.* Mineola, N.Y.: Dover, 2002. Reprints Goddard's work on liquid-propelled rockets and ways to reach high altitudes.

Lehman, Milton. *Robert H. Goddard: Pioneer of Space Research.* New York: Da Capo Press, 1988. Well-illustrated account of Goddard's achievements.

Lomask, Milton, and Al Fiorentino. *Robert H. Goddard: Space Pioneer.* Champaign, Ill.: Garrard, 1972. A brief illustrated account of Goddard's life, intended for younger readers.

See also: Lindbergh, Charles; Rocketry

■ Gold Diggers of Broadway

Identification: A musical comedy film about the lives of Broadway showgirls
Director: Roy Del Ruth
Date: 1929

Gold Diggers of Broadway *was the second all-color, all-talking film ever released after* On with the Show, *another Warner Bros. film from earlier that same year. Embodying the carefree spirit of the 1920s on the eve of the Great Depression, it remained America's highest-grossing film until 1939.*

Gold Diggers of Broadway is Warner Bros.' second film adaptation of Avery Hopwood's play *The Gold Diggers* (1919), the first being a 1923 silent film with the same name as the play. Robert Lord adapted the story, De Leon Anthony is credited with the titles, and Joseph Burke and Al Dubin wrote the music and lyrics, respectively.

The plot revolves around Broadway showgirls Ann (Ann Pennington), Jerry (Nancy Welford), and Mabel (Winnie Lightner) and their gold-digging pursuit of the men of their dreams. The film opens with musical numbers from the Broadway production in which the showgirls appear, including one of the film's two most memorable songs, "Painting the Clouds with Sunshine," performed by guitarist and singer Nick Lucas.

After the evening's performance, Ann, Jerry, Mabel, and Nick embark on an evening of drinking and carousing, now joined by Blake (Albert Gran), a lawyer; Stephen (Conway Tearle), a businessman; and Stephen's nephew, Wally (William Bakewell). Mabel pursues Blake for most of the evening, while Jerry turns her attentions to Stephen, initially in an attempt to convince him to let Wally marry one of the other showgirls. During their night out, Nick performs the other well-known song of the film, "Tiptoe Through the Tulips." After a rapid series of dramatic events, each woman ultimately lands the man she covets, and the story concludes with the following evening's performance, which includes another rendition of "Tiptoe Through the Tulips" and the extravagant closing number "Song of the Gold Diggers."

Impact

Gold Diggers of Broadway was highly influential, both technically and culturally. Its use of sound and Technicolor represents the culmination of the technological advancements that had been made throughout the 1920s, making the film a groundbreaking product for its time. It also demonstrates the complexities of gender relations in the late 1920s, showcasing the balancing act of enjoyment and desperation in the pursuit of love and money. Unfortunately, while the soundtrack has survived, the film itself is now mostly lost, with only the last two reels and some earlier fragments known to still exist.

Eric Novod

Further Reading

Barrios, Richard. *A Song in the Dark: The Birth of the Musical Film.* New York: Oxford University Press, 1995.
Bradley, Edwin M. *The First Hollywood Musicals: A Critical Filmography of 171 Features, 1927 Through 1932.* Jefferson, N.C.: McFarland, 2004.

See also: Broadway musicals; Film; Talking motion pictures; Warner Bros.

■ Gold Rush, The

Identification: A silent film about a lonely tramp who searches for companionship while others search for gold
Director: Charles "Charlie" Chaplin
Date: 1925

After his highly praised but not widely popular domestic drama A Woman of Paris *(1923), Charlie Chaplin returned to comedy with* The Gold Rush. *The film was a critical and commercial success and is the work that Chaplin himself said he wished to be remembered for the most.*

The Gold Rush is a period piece, inspired by illustrations and tales of the exhilaration and dangers of nineteenth-century prospecting in California and Alaska. It is also a principled, although not moralizing, commentary on historical and contemporary materialism, greed, and cruelty. But what makes it a classic is the extraordinary comic performance of Chaplin in his familiar guise as the Little Tramp. Alongside the physical skills that make him such an entertaining spectacle, this character also possesses deeper qualities of imagination, resiliency, emotional honesty, determination, and bravery that help him achieve the most basic and important human goals: survival and security, not profit; love and friendship, not status; and dignity, not fame or popularity.

The Tramp journeys to the Yukon for the Klondike gold rush; once there, he wanders through an inhospitable environment, encountering harsh weather, snarling murderers such as Black Larsen (Tom Murray), smiling bullies such as Jack Cameron (Malcolm Waite), and the painful indignity of the indifference of saloon-hall women. Chaplin's comic strategy is to transform what he can and accommodate himself to what he cannot. In two of the film's most celebrated sequences, he turns a boot into a Thanksgiving meal and dinner rolls on the end of forks into dancing legs. He also forges a cautious friendship with Big Jim McKay (Mack Swain), who, driven mad with hunger, had at one point wanted to eat him, and ends up in the arms of Georgia (Georgia Hale), who earlier had looked right through him.

Impact

The Gold Rush helped Chaplin maintain his enormous popularity in the 1920s as a comedian representing the common person: downtrodden, disadvantaged, and isolated, but nonetheless buoyant, resourceful, sympathetic, and ultimately successful. While the Tramp is primarily associated with physical comedy, *The Gold Rush* continues Chaplin's development away from simple, albeit enjoyable, slapstick and sight gags, toward a comedy that incorporates pathos, emotional insight, and thoughtful commentary on our desires, values, and social institutions.

Sidney Gottlieb

Further Reading

Robinson, David. "*The Gold Rush.*" In *Chaplin: His Life and Art.* Rev. ed. London: Penguin, 2001.

Vance, Jeffrey. "*The Gold Rush.*" In *Chaplin: Genius of the Cinema.* New York: Harry N. Abrams, 2003.

See also: Chaplin, Charlie; Circus, The; Film; United Artists

---

■ Goldwyn, Samuel

Identification: Polish American film producer
Also known as: Schmuel Gelbfisz
Born: August 17, 1879, Warsaw, Poland
Died: January 31, 1974, Los Angeles, California

One of the founders of the American motion picture business, Samuel Goldwyn was a fiercely competitive executive who insisted on bringing to his films the best writers and production values available. He was as autocratic as other studio moguls but remained independent, preferring to concentrate on one or two important films each year rather than follow the mass-production model of his competitors.

Born Schmuel Gelbfisz to a Hasidic Jewish family in Warsaw, Goldwyn moved to Birmingham, England, in 1895. He worked odd jobs and stayed with relatives, one of whom anglicized his name to Samuel Goldfish. After a few years, he managed to acquire enough money for passage to North America. Goldwyn arrived in Canada at the end of 1898 and crossed into the United States early the following year. After a brief stay in New York City, he settled in Gloversville, New York, and began working in the garment industry, first in a glove factory and later as a salesperson. By 1904, he had established himself as a leading figure among New York glove dealers and moved his business to New York City.

Early Career

In 1910, Goldwyn married Blanche Lasky, daughter of Jesse Lasky. In 1913, he and Blanche's brother, vaudeville producer Jesse L. Lasky, established the Jesse L. Lasky Feature Photoplay Company. Goldwyn divorced Blanche in 1915 but remained in business with Lasky. The next year, their company merged with Adolph Zukor's Famous Players to form what would ultimately become Paramount Pictures.

After repeated quarrels with Zukor, Goldwyn resigned from the company and formed the Goldwyn Pictures Corporation with theater producers Edgar and Archibald Selwyn. They devised the name by combining Selwyn and Goldfish, which Goldwyn was still known by at the time, though he would soon legally change it. Once again, Goldwyn eventually fell out with his business partners and left Goldwyn Pictures, which would later become Metro-Goldwyn-Mayer (MGM). Goldwyn himself was never part of MGM; he established his solo venture, Samuel Goldwyn Productions, in 1923.

Samuel Goldwyn Productions

While Goldwyn's contemporaries worked on several projects at once, designating some films as special "A" productions and others as cheap "B" productions, he concentrated on one film at a time, hiring the best writers, directors, and actors and selling the public on the idea that they could always count on his films being first rate. In 1925, he signed a contract with United Artists, of which his friend Charlie Chaplin was part owner, giving the company exclusive rights to distribute his films.

Although many of Goldwyn's greatest successes came in the 1930s, he produced the film classic *Greed* in 1924 and had several popular successes during the decade as well, including *The Dark Angel* (1925), *The Winning of Barbara Worth* (1926), and *Bulldog Drummond* (1929). A superb spotter of talent, Goldwyn cast Gary Cooper in one of his first important roles in *Barbara Worth*; the film also featured another Goldwyn contract player, Ronald Colman, whose later performance in *Bulldog Drummond* would earn him an Academy Award nomination for Best Actor. Many of Goldwyn's romantic films in the 1920s starred Colman opposite Vilma Bánky, a pairing that would set the standard for later romantic screen couples such as Clark Gable and Jean Harlow or Dana Andrews and Gene Tierney.

The formula that Goldwyn established in the 1920s for sumptuously produced major motion pictures continued to bear fruit after the close of the decade, resulting in such award-winning films as *Wuthering Heights* (1939) and *The Best Years of Our Lives* (1946). Goldwyn continued to produce films until the end of the 1950s, his last one being *Porgy and Bess* (1959), which unfortunately was plagued with difficulty during production and poorly received upon release.

Impact

Samuel Goldwyn was instrumental in building the careers of numerous Hollywood stars even as he defied the star system by using his contract players sparingly, although he would sometimes loan them out to other studios. His work in film prior to 1920 laid the groundwork not only for his success in the 1920s but also for other independent producers like Edward Small and, later, David O. Selznick. Dubbed "Mister Malaprop," Goldwyn remains famous for using expressions such as "include me out" and "a verbal contract isn't worth the paper it's written on," which he may or may not have actually said.

Carl Rollyson

Further Reading

Berg, A. Scott. *Goldwyn: A Biography*. New York: Riverhead Books, 1998. A comprehensive biography written with complete access to Goldwyn's archives.

Booker, M. Keith. *Historical Dictionary of American Cinema*. Lanham, Md.: Scarecrow Press, 2011. Includes a biographical entry on Goldwyn emphasizing the evolution of his film company.

Easton, Carol. *The Search for Sam Goldwyn: A Biography*. New York: Quill, 1989. A critical account of Goldwyn's life.

Epstein, Lawrence J. *Samuel Goldwyn*. Boston, Mass.: Twayne, 1981. Studies Goldwyn's attitudes toward art and the industry through the lens of his films.

Gabler, Neal. *An Empire of Their Own: How the Jews Invented Hollywood*. New York: Anchor Books, 1989. A revealing look at the early days of Hollywood, touching on the uneasy relationship Goldwyn and others had with their background and identity.

Marx, Arthur. *Goldwyn: A Biography of the Man Behind the Myth*. New York: W. W. Norton, 1976. Includes discussion of Goldwyn's role in the movie industry and accounts of specific productions.

See also: Chaplin, Charlie; Colman, Ronald; Film; Metro-Goldwyn-Mayer (MGM); United Artists

■ Golf

Golf became a national pastime in the United States in the 1920s. During this decade, American golf associations established their rules and produced some of the sport's greatest practitioners and personalities, who in turn made the sport very popular in American society.

With the rise of leisure time during the 1920s, many Americans took an interest in sports, forming leagues to play and clubs to promote games like golf. Although golf societies such as the United States Golf Association (USGA) and the Professional Golfers' Association of America (PGA of America) had been founded in the late nineteenth century and early twentieth century, several features defining American golf were established in the early 1920s.

Changes to the Sport

At this time, American golf associations chose new types of sports equipment that would become international standards decades later. For example, American associations set new regulations on golf clubs, allowing steel as well as wood shafts to be used in golf club construction. They also set different weight limits on golf balls, expanding on the golf rules established in Great Britain.

Walter Hagen during a golf match. (Getty Images)

With Americans' increased interest in the sport, practice ranges were opened for both amateur and professional golfers, although most courses were limited to male patrons. The first of these practice courses appeared in Pinehurst, California. Advertisers quickly realized the potential revenue the expanding popularity of golf could generate and helped establish magazines dedicated to golf, such as *The Professional Golfer of America*. Other developments included the introduction of irrigated fairways, first installed in Dallas, Texas. New golf tournaments appeared, offering cash prizes, which helped professionalize the sport. The Texas Open (now called the Valero Texas Open), the Walker Cup Match, and the Louisiana Open (the oldest U.S. professional golf tournament) were all established during this decade.

Famous Golfers

Along with advancements in golf equipment and competitions, leading golfers captured America's attention during the 1920s. Walter Hagen won the Open Championship in 1922 and opened a golf equipment company under his own name. In 1925, Jesse Sweetser became the first American golfer to win the British Amateur Championship. American amateur golfer Bobby Jones won both the British Open and U.S. Open in 1926.

Both women and African Americans established their place in the sport during the 1920s. Women played separate tournaments. The United States Senior Women's Golf Association was founded in 1923, followed by the Women's Trans-Mississippi Golf Association in 1927. By the end of the decade, nine separate amateur women's golf tournaments were held each year. Important women golfers included Glenna Collett Vare, Joyce Wethered, and Dorothy Campbell Hurd. Vare, also known as the "Queen of American Golf," took the Women's Amateur title in 1922. Hurd won three USGA Women's titles between 1924 and 1928. Wethered was one of the most notable woman golfers of the 1920s, winning five English Ladies' Championships in a row and accumulating four other women's titles by 1924.

African Americans and other ethnic minority groups in the United States had less success than women did in establishing a presence in the golf community. However, some African American golfers were able to demonstrate their skill in U.S. Opens and PGA tournaments if they were registered as American Indian rather than African American. One such golfer was John Shippen Jr., who played in six U.S. Opens and was posthumously granted membership to the PGA of America.

Impact

American golf developed significantly during the 1920s. Along with the establishment of an American version of official golf rules, women golfers and African American golfers became increasingly involved in professional golf tournaments. The rise of golf celebrities set new athletic standards as well as new fashion trends. The American apparel designed for the sport in the 1920s is still a recognized form of golf attire in the twenty-first century: plus fours in baggy, lightweight material, blazers and Argyle sweaters matched with fancy colors, and two-toned shoes.

R. L. Smith

Further Reading

Dawkins, Marvin P., and Graham Charles Kinloch. *African American Golfers During the Jim Crow Era.* Westport, Conn.: Praeger, 2000. Discusses the presence of African American golfers from 1890 on and the segregation that prevented them from formal participation.

Elliot, Alan, and John Allan May. *The Illustrated History of Golf*. New York: Gallery Books, 1990. Provides a comprehensive history of the game, discussing its early stages, major golf courses, and international development.

Gabriel, Mike. *The Professional Golfers' Association Tour: A History*. Jefferson, N.C.: McFarland, 2001. A comprehensive history of the PGA Tour and the touring professionals who contributed to its success, including Walter Hagen and Bobby Jones.

Hudson, David L. *Women in Golf: The Players, the History, and the Future of the Sport*. Westport, Conn.: Praeger, 2008. Discusses the development of women's golf and the professionalizing of the sport.

Kirsch, George B. *Golf in America*. Urbana: University of Illinois Press, 2009. A social history of golf examining stereotypes of its players, its popularity among the upper and middle classes, and classic heroes of golf.

Murray, Peter. *Golf*. New York: Murray Books, 2008. An introduction to the sport, including the history of the game, instructions on how to play, and descriptions of major tours, resorts, and leading players.

Peper, George. *The Story of Golf*. New York: TV Books, 1999. Provides a history of golf, with information on its evolution, equipment, early masters, and milestone events.

See also: Advertising in the United States; African Americans; Hobbies and recreation; Jones, Bobby; Women's rights

■ Gompers, Samuel

Identification: American labor leader
Born: January 27, 1850, London, England
Died: December 13, 1924, San Antonio, Texas

Samuel Gompers led the American Federation of Labor (AFL) from the late nineteenth century until his death. An advocate of craft unionism, Gompers's approach ignored many workers and left organized labor vulnerable to business pressure by the time of his death.

Samuel Gompers's family immigrated to the United States in 1863 and settled in New York. As an adult, Gompers became a cigar maker and joined the Cigar Makers' International Union (CMIU), soon turning to union organizing. When the AFL was established in 1886, Gompers became its first president and would continue in this capacity until his death in 1924.

Gompers emphasized an approach to unionization that organized workers with similar skills (craft unionism) rather than organizing a labor union across a whole industry (industrial unionism). He tended not to support radical approaches such as socialism. An admirer of Woodrow Wilson, Gompers supported the American war effort during World War I and was critical of labor leaders who opposed the war, such as William D. Haywood. He expected that the labor movement would continue to gain strength after the war, but the anti-Communist period known as the First Red Scare, coupled with employer hostility, led to attacks on organized labor that continued throughout the 1920s.

Maintaining Power

Gompers's increasing conservatism was seen in his opposition to a 1919 steelworkers' strike. He feared that a victory by unskilled workers in the steel industry would shift the balance in the labor movement; this attitude continued to persist for many years after his death. The collapse of the steelworkers' strike and the U.S. government's prosecution of the international labor union Industrial Workers of the World (IWW) left Gompers the main labor leader in the United States at the beginning of the 1920s. Along with his allies, Gompers denounced rising younger leaders such as John L. Lewis, the head of United Mine Workers (UMW), as Communist sympathizers.

By 1920, Samuel Gompers had developed an organization within the AFL that enabled him to control much of the organized labor in the United States. He and his supporters often labeled opponents as "Reds," and he used his control over the AFL organization, which interlocked with the leadership of many of its constituent unions, to freeze out opponents. Gompers often played one union head against another to ensure that no other union leader would challenge him. He also maintained a close working relationship with some political leaders derived from his backing of presidential candidates such as Woodrow Wilson.

When Gompers died in 1924, the leadership of the AFL unions was still subservient to him, with the exception of Lewis, an arrangement that did not produce a strong leader to take his place. William Green, who succeeded Gompers, was not a very capable leader.

The Decline of Organized Labor

Although Gompers was the preeminent labor leader in the United States, he presided over a movement that was in decline. The Red Scare and a growing economy weakened organized labor during the 1920s, but Gompers's ideology and leadership also greatly contributed to the decline. He did little to support unionism for female or African American workers, considering them unskilled and unworthy of organizing. Gompers and his fellow craft union leaders (with the exception of Lewis in the UMW) opposed industry-wide organization, so some increasingly important industries received no support from the AFL leadership. As industries such as the textile industry cut back on production in the early 1920s, unions lost membership, and when they went on strike, they were usually defeated by managements that often enjoyed support from the U.S. government.

As the AFL became weaker domestically, Gompers supported efforts at international organization with the Pan-American Federation of Labor (PAFL) that tried to forge alliances with unions in Latin America. Gompers was at a meeting of the organization in Mexico City when he collapsed from a combination of heart failure, diabetes, and renal failure. At his request, he was rushed back to the United States so that he could die on American soil. With his death, the PAFL also went into decline.

Impact

Gompers played a very decisive role in helping to strengthen organized labor in the United States in the late nineteenth and early twentieth centuries. However, he also laid the groundwork for labor unions' relative weakness in the 1920s and early 1930s. His disdain for any form of what he considered radicalism alienated potential allies, and his tendency to ignore the rise of mass labor industries meant that many workers remained unorganized for a long time. Gompers's authoritarian control of the labor movement set a style for union leadership that was open to abuse, ignored new ideas, and even led to corruption. Although he did not live to see the full impact of what his leadership had produced, Gompers must have been aware of the increasingly marginalized position that organized labor held by 1924. A dynamic, resourceful leader as a young man, Samuel Gompers

had become authoritarian and rigid by 1920, a situation that would condemn the American worker to a bleak period throughout the 1920.

John M. Theilmann

Further Reading

Albert, Peter J., and Grace Palladino, eds. *The Last Years, 1922–24*. Vol. 12 in *The Samuel Gompers Papers*. Urbana: University of Illinois Press, 2010. Includes Gompers's writings and papers from his final years.

Bernstein, Irving. *The Lean Years: A History of the American Worker, 1920–1933*. Chicago: Haymarket, 2010. A classic treatment of the American worker during the 1920s.

Buhle, Paul. *Taking Care of Business: Samuel Gompers, George Meany, Lane Kirkland, and the Tragedy of American Labor*. New York: Monthly Review Press, 1999. A collective biography of leaders of the AFL, taking a critical stance on Gompers.

Livesay, Harold C. *Samuel Gompers and Organized Labor in America*. Prospect Heights, Ill.: Waveland Press, 1993. A short biography of Samuel Gompers.

Zieger, Robert H., and Gilbert J. Gall. *American Workers, American Unions: The Twentieth Century*. 3d ed. Baltimore: Johns Hopkins University Press, 2002. Contains a chapter on labor unions in the 1920s.

See also: American Federation of Labor (AFL); Communism; Haywood, Big Bill; Red Scare, The; Unionism

---

■ Graham, Martha

Identification: American dancer, choreographer, and teacher
Born: May 11, 1894, Allegheny, Pennsylvania
Died: April 1, 1991, New York, New York

In the early 1920s, Martha Graham completed her education as a dance student. She went on to start her own ballet company, synthesizing elements from classical and folk dance into her unique style. Graham is known for her provocative, angular, and athletic approach to dance that contrasted strongly with the fluidity of traditional ballet movements. Her innovations would influence the vocabulary of modern dance throughout the twentieth century.

Born in a suburb of Pittsburgh, Martha Graham moved with her family to Santa Barbara, California, in

1908. In 1911, she saw her first dance performance in Los Angeles by dancer Ruth St. Denis and was fascinated. Five years later, Graham successfully auditioned for Ruth St. Denis and Ted Shawn's Denishawn School of Dancing and Related Arts, where she studied ballet as well as American and world folk dances, particularly absorbing rhythmic elements of the folk dances into her distinctive language of dance. Graham starred in her first major production, *Xochitl* (1920), in which she played the title part of a Native American girl to much critical acclaim. After graduating from Denishawn, Graham joined a vaudeville dance troupe, the Greenwich Village Follies. Graham was hired at the George Eastman School of Design in 1925, but she left in 1926 to found and direct the Martha Graham Center of Contemporary Dance in New York City, an institution that continues to teach and perform ballet in the twenty-first century. There, Graham gained recognition for her unique approach to dance as she increasingly broke away from the traditional themes and movements of classical ballet.

From the mid- to late 1920s, Graham continued to develop and teach her experimental approach to dance. She developed sharp, sometimes violent movements; sexually suggestive body language; and symbolic gestures. In particular, her theory of contraction and release in relationship to the dancers' alternating muscle movements coalesced at this time. During the 1920s, Graham choreographed and danced in over twelve ballets, including *Revolt* (1927) and *Immigrant* (1928), which were seminal works in the development of her style. *Heretic* (1929) is considered one of her first masterpieces; its minimalistic staging and avant-garde costuming were elements that Graham retained as her technique matured.

Impact

Martha Graham's distinctive approach to dance and choreography helped to define the development of modern dance throughout the twentieth century. She continued to teach dance and perform on stage into her seventies, and she continued choreographing works until her death in 1991.

Joanna R. Smolko

Further Reading

Graham, Martha. *Blood Memory*. New York: Doubleday, 1991.

Horosko, Marian. *Martha Graham: The Evolution of Her Dance Theory and Training*. Rev. ed. Gainesville: University Press of Florida, 2002.

Stodelle, Ernestine. *Deep Song: The Dance Story of Martha Graham*. New York: Schirmer Books, 1984.

See also: Art movements; Dance and choreography; Denishawn School of Dancing and Related Arts; Vaudeville

---

> ### The Eastman School of Music
>
> Feeling that she was destined to be an "artist," which in her view translated as "worker," Martha Graham left Broadway in 1925 to teach and, more importantly, to learn in the newly created dance department of the Eastman School of Music in Rochester, New York. Founded by George Eastman, the inventor of the Kodak camera and a patron of the arts, the Eastman School became the launching pad for Graham's creative genius. Once she was given autonomy, she threw out the old, standardized modes of teaching dance and began to experiment with and through her students. In 1929, beginning with her former Eastman students, Graham established her own company, the Martha Graham Center of Contemporary Dance.

■ Grand Ole Opry, The

The Grand Ole Opry is one of the longest-running broadcasts in the history of radio. Since its beginning in 1925, the Opry has showcased the biggest stars in country, bluegrass, and gospel music.

With the rise of music-recording technology, traditional country music became more widely accessible during the 1920s. Early country music performers, notably the Carter Family and Jimmie Rodgers, contributed to the spread of country music through their recordings, but it was radio shows such as the Grand Ole Opry that were chiefly responsible for popularizing country music on a national level.

Originally known as the WSM Barn Dance, the Grand Ole Opry premiered November 28, 1925. The program was broadcast from Studio A of WSM in the National Life and Accident Insurance Building at

Seventh Avenue North and Union Street in Nashville, Tennessee. The one-hour broadcast went on air immediately following the NBC Music Appreciation Hour, which featured classical music. Initially, the program featured local amateur performers with a limited live audience. The first performer on the program was a fiddler named "Uncle" Jimmy Thompson. Other early performers included Fiddlin' Arthur Smith, the Crook Brothers, the Possum Hunters, the Fruit Jar Drinkers, and "Uncle" Dave Macon.

In December 1927, the program moved to a larger studio to accommodate a growing live audience and expanded to a three-hour time slot; the program also adopted its iconic name then. Program director and announcer George "Judge" Hay introduced the December 10 broadcast by saying that the previous hour had featured grand opera but that for the next three hours, he would present "grand ole opry," and the label stuck.

As the show's live audience continued to grow, the Grand Ole Opry moved to various venues throughout Nashville, including the Ryman Auditorium. In 1974, the show moved to a custom building known as the Grand Ole Opry House, which was originally part of the theme park Opryland USA. The Opry House stills hosts Opry performances even though the theme park was discontinued in 1997.

Impact

The Grand Ole Opry is largely responsible for popularizing country music beyond the southeastern United States. The Grand Ole Opry's radio and television broadcasts expanded the country music fan base across the United States and the world, also disseminating musical styles that developed out of country music, such as rockabilly, gospel, and bluegrass music. The Opry remains the standard-bearer for country music, with a membership spanning historical musicians Ralph Stanley, Little Jimmy Dickens, and Johnny Cash, as well as contemporary stars Carrie Underwood and Brad Paisley.

Eric S. Strother

Further Reading

Escott, Colin. *The Grand Ole Opry: The Making of an American Icon.* New York: Center Street, 2006.

Oermann, Robert K. *Behind the Grand Ole Opry Curtain: Tales of Romance and Tragedy.* New York: Center Street, 2009.

Wolfe, Charles K. *A Good-Natured Riot: The Birth of the Grand Ole Opry.* Nashville: Vanderbilt University Press, 1999.

See also: Carter Family; Music, popular; Radio; Rodgers, Jimmie

■ Grange, Red

Identification: American college and professional football player
Also known as: Galloping Ghost; Harold Edward Grange
Born: June 13, 1903, Forksville, Pennsylvania
Died: January 28, 1991, Morton, Illinois

A charter member of both the College Football Hall of Fame and the Pro Football Hall of Fame, Red Grange helped popularize football across America while legitimizing the fledgling National Football League.

A high school gridiron sensation at Wheaton Community High School in Illinois, Harold Edward "Red" Grange did not initially intend to play football when he entered the University of Illinois in 1922. Grange changed his mind, however, and in his first varsity season in 1923, he was named a college All-American. Over the next couple seasons, Grange gained recognition nationwide and helped college football to emerge as a game of interest across the United States. At the completion of his college career, Grange, dubbed the "Galloping Ghost" by Chicago sportswriter Warren Brown, had played in 20 games, ran 3,362 yards, caught 14 passes for 253 yards, and completed 40 out of 82 passes for 575 yards.

After Grange signed with the Chicago Bears of the National Football League (NFL) in 1925 for a reported $3,000 per game plus a percentage of the gate, the credibility and popularity of professional football began to rise. To capitalize on Grange's fame, George Halas, player-coach of the Bears, arranged a nationwide tour for the Bears to play in exhibition games. With Grange on the roster, the Bears attracted a large number of fans, many of whom simply wanted to see Grange perform. His presence also attracted the interest of major sportswriters, who began to turn their attention to professional football in earnest.

After a dispute with the Bears, Grange left the NFL and helped form the short-lived American Football

Red Grange. (Getty Images)

League (AFL) in 1926. While playing for the AFL's New York Yankees, Grange sustained a knee injury that benched him for the 1928 season. In the meantime, the AFL folded, and the Yankees joined the NFL. In 1929, Grange returned to the Chicago Bears, where he finished his pro career in 1934. As a pro, he played in 96 games, ran for 569 yards on 170 carries, caught 16 passes for 288 yards, and scored 21 touchdowns.

During his professional football career, Grange also starred in two silent movies: *One Minute to Play* (1926) and *Racing Romeo* (1927). In addition, products that included teddy bears and candy bars were named after him.

Impact

Red Grange emerged as the first superstar of the NFL, raising the profile of professional football. He was the first football player to have a personal representative to negotiate playing agreements and the first professional athlete in team sports whose pay reflected the number of fans he attracted to the games. His name consistently appears on lists of the greatest college and professional football players in history.

Alvin K. Benson

Further Reading

Carroll, John Martin. *Red Grange and the Rise of Modern Football.* Urbana: University of Illinois Press, 1999.

Poole, Gary Andrew. *The Galloping Ghost: Red Grange, an American Football Legend.* Boston: Houghton Mifflin, 2008.

See also: Football; Gipp, George; National Football League; Rockne, Knute; Sports

■ Grauman's Chinese Theatre

Grauman's Chinese Theatre is an elaborate structure whose grand opening in 1927 was the one of the most extravagant in American motion picture history. Its best-known feature is the Forecourt of Stars, where the handprints and footprints of the icons of motion picture industry are captured in concrete. The theater is one of Hollywood's key tourist attractions, bringing in over four million visitors each year, and remains in high demand for film premieres.

On May 18, 1927, showman Sid Grauman opened the doors to the fourth of his famous Los Angeles theaters, Grauman's Chinese Theatre, to a crowd of thousands lining Hollywood Boulevard to see the arriving celebrities. Immediately preceding its first premiere, director Cecil B. DeMille's *The King of Kings*, Grauman staged a live prologue entitled, "Glories of the Scriptures," which featured a Wurlitzer organ and sixty-five-piece orchestra. The theater officially opened to the public the following day.

In 1926, after securing a lease on property along Hollywood Boulevard, Grauman began planning with architect Raymond Kennedy to realize his dream theater. Designed with an opulent Chinese theme, the theater features artifacts imported from China, including pagodas and temple bells. Several of the statuary pieces that decorate the interior of the theater were produced on site by Chinese artisans. Among the theater's immediately recognizable attributes are the high curved walls, enormous stone dog statues known as Heaven Dogs, and lotus-shaped fountains.

Grauman's Chinese Theatre is best known for the Forecourt of the Stars, a cement courtyard that contains the footprints, handprints, and signatures of Hollywood celebrities. Accounts differ as to how this tradition first began; actor Norma Talmadge, Mary

Pickford's dog, and Grauman himself have all been credited with having walked through wet cement, thereby inspiring the idea to create concrete slabs specifically for that purpose. Among the first stars to make their mark in the cement were actors Mary Pickford and Douglas Fairbanks. The novelty quickly became a tradition that attracts millions of visitors each year.

Impact

Grauman's Chinese Theatre went on to host the Academy Awards ceremony three times during the mid-1940s. In 1968, the iconic building was designated a historic landmark and has since been renovated several times. The theater continues to hold film premieres and serve as a physical link with the rich and storied past of the American motion picture industry. Its famous cement imprints—from actor John Wayne's fists to comedian Harpo Marx's harp—are part of American popular culture and offer visitors a tangible reminder of the Hollywood of yesteryear.

Amanda J. Bahr-Evola

Further Reading

Beardsley, Charles. *Hollywood's Master Showman: The Legendary Sid Grauman.* New York: Cornwall Books, 1983.

Gomery, Douglas. *Shared Pleasures: A History of Movie Presentation in the United States.* Madison: University of Wisconsin Press, 1992.

Williams, Gregory Paul. *The Story of Hollywood: An Illustrated History.* Malden, Mass.: Blackwell, 2005.

See also: Academy Awards; Architecture; Fairbanks, Douglas, Sr.; Film; *King of Kings, The;* Movie palaces; Pickford, Mary

---

■ *Great Gatsby, The*

Identification: A novel describing the moral decadence of the 1920s and the corruption of the American Dream
Author: F. Scott Fitzgerald
Date: 1925

Widely considered a classic of American literature, F. Scott Fitzgerald's masterpiece The Great Gatsby *employs a love story to evoke the ostentatious, degenerate materialism of the 1920s, an era that Fitzgerald dubbed "the Jazz Age."*

Framed by the innocent midwestern perspective of narrator Nick Carraway, the story of Jay Gatsby captures the wild extravagance, economic prosperity, and moral depravity of the 1920s. Through the novel's love triangle, Fitzgerald depicts the failure of the American Dream, a uniquely American spirit of optimism deriving from the right to "Life, Liberty, and the pursuit of Happiness" articulated in the Declaration of Independence and emphasizing success through hard work and constant reinvention of self.

This ethos is personified in the novel by Jay Gatsby, a poor soldier who falls in love with the shallow, upper-class New York beauty Daisy Fay, who represents Gatsby's sought-after ideal. When Gatsby leaves to serve overseas in World War I, Daisy marries Tom Buchanan, a wealthy heir and dilettante. After the war, Gatsby devotes himself to accumulating wealth in order to win Daisy. Having made his fortune by dubious means, Gatsby buys an estate in nouveau riche West Egg, on the north shore of Long Island, across a small bay from Daisy's home in East Egg, the seat of old money. At his opulent mansion, Gatsby throws lavish parties to attract Daisy's attention and to acquire friends. Although Gatsby and Daisy do finally come together, Tom confronts Gatsby, and tragedy rapidly ensues, signaling the death of the American Dream embodied in Gatsby's rags-to-riches life story. Ultimately, Gatsby is unable to escape his lower-class background or buy the companionship and love he desires.

Impact

Like Fitzgerald's earlier novels, *This Side of Paradise* (1920) and *The Beautiful and the Damned* (1922), *The Great Gatsby* deftly portrays American society of the 1920s, holding it up for moral critique. Although the novel was not initially well received, since the 1940s it has risen to iconic stature as a representation of the loneliness and tragedy lurking beneath the veneer of carefree pleasure with which the decade is associated.

Deborah D. Rogers

Further Reading

Berman, Ronald. "America in Fitzgerald." *Journal of Aesthetic Education* 36, no. 2 (2002): 38–51.

Bruccoli, Matthew J., and Scottie Fitzgerald Smith. *Some Sort of Epic Grandeur: The Life of F. Scott Fitzgerald.* Second rev. ed. Columbia: University of South Carolina Press, 2002.

Prigozy, Ruth, ed. *The Cambridge Companion to F. Scott Fitzgerald.* Cambridge, England: Cambridge University Press, 2002.

See also: Fitzgerald, F. Scott; Fitzgerald, Zelda; Literature in the United States; *Tales of the Jazz Age; This Side of Paradise*

■ Great Migration

The Great Migration brought about a massive redistribution of the African American population throughout the United States. It transformed black ways of life, art, and institutions, as well as the demographics and cultures of many American cities.

In the late nineteenth century, following Reconstruction, thousands of black southerners migrated to other regions of the country, seeking a better life. A majority of these migrants moved to rural areas and continued to work in agriculture. These early population shifts were decidedly different from the Great Migration of the 1920s, which involved much larger numbers of African American migrants to urban areas.

Causes and Demographic Changes

In 1910, about 90 percent of the African American population lived in the South, and 60 percent worked in agriculture. A majority were sharecroppers, tenant farmers who contracted to give a portion of their crops as rent to the landowners whose fields they worked. By 1920, the promise of a decent living through sharecropping had given way to the reality of a corrupt, exploitive system that was little better than slavery. Sharecroppers were forced to purchase supplies they needed on credit from plantation stores at exorbitant prices, creating a cycle of debt that increased with each passing season. In addition, comprehensive and openly discriminatory Jim Crow laws in the South had created a highly segregated social system that was enforced through legal as well as extralegal means, including lynching and other forms of violence.

Grinding poverty and an almost total lack of educational or occupational opportunities motivated black southerners to relocate, and the cities of the industrial North became increasingly attractive destinations. World War I brought about labor shortages in the North as the supply of European immigrant labor decreased along with the native-born white male labor force after the United States entered the war in 1917. Job opportunities previously closed to African Americans thus opened, and many black southerners moved to northern cities for work. The Immigration Acts of 1921 and 1924 restricted immigration, particularly from southern and eastern Europe, further stimulating the demand for labor and quickening the Great Migration.

By 1920, black southerners were hearing firsthand from earlier migrants and from black newspapers about jobs, salaries, and living conditions in the North that were far superior to those in the South. As a result, around one million African Americans moved north during the 1920s, causing black population explosions in many urban centers. Between 1920 and 1930, the black population in Detroit grew by nearly 300 percent, in New York by 115 percent, and in Chicago by 114 percent. By 1930, more than 20 percent of the country's black population lived in the North.

Cultural and Political Effects

In cities with large influxes of black migrants in the 1920s, a uniquely African American urban culture developed and thrived. Jazz and modern forms of blues music emerged. The birth of modern jazz is sometimes attributed to trumpeter Louis Armstrong's migration from Louisiana to Chicago in 1922. "Race records," black music recordings sold to black consumers, became a booming industry, and jazz music inspired new popular dances and permeated the nation's culture during the decade that became known as the Jazz Age. New York City's Harlem neighborhood, the largest African American enclave in 1920s at 200,000 residents, generated breakthroughs in black literature and art in a cultural movement that came to be known as the Harlem Renaissance.

These cultural developments led to expanded social and political consciousness among urban African Americans. Black migrants continued to endure hardships and discrimination in the North, but in different ways than in the Jim Crow South. Although discrimination against blacks was not codified in the law, many African Americans living in the North experienced de facto segregation, often only finding employment in the least desirable jobs and housing in the least desirable neighborhoods. However, the black vote, suppressed in the South despite constitutional protections, was taken up enthusiastically by the large and growing urban black populations in the North to try to better their situation. Black churches and advocacy organizations such as the National Urban League, the National Association for the Advancement of Colored People, and the Universal Negro Improvement Association became centers for political mobilization and social activism.

Impact

The Great Migration was a pivotal event in twentieth-century African American history. It nationalized the black population, establishing a more politically active, proud, and self-assured black population in the urban industrial North. By the late 1920s, only 42 percent of African American men were farm workers, and black entrepreneurs owned more than seventy thousand businesses. The number of black teachers, professional training institutions, and hospitals had increased dramatically, and by 1930 the black literacy rate had topped 80 percent. The Great Migration laid the groundwork for a more racially and culturally diverse country and a more inclusive American democracy.

Jack Carter

Further Reading

Arnesen, Eric. *Black Protest and the Great Migration: A Brief History with Documents.* New York: Bedford/St. Martin's, 2002. Analyzes the causes of the Great Migration and the origins of black political organization using period publications.

Harrison, Alferdteen. *Black Exodus: The Great Migration from the American South.* Jackson: University of Mississippi Press, 1992. Focuses on the cultural and socioeconomic effects on both the areas of origin and destination.

Sernett, Milton C. *Bound for the Promised Land: African American Religion and the Great Migration.* Durham, N.C.: Duke University Press Books, 1997. Explores the role of the Great Migration in transforming black churches into centers for social activism.

Trotter, Joe William Jr., ed. *The Great Migration in Historical Perspective: New Dimensions of Race, Class, and Gender.* Bloomington: Indiana University Press, 1991. A collection of essays examining the role of black social networks in spurring the exodus from the South.

Wilkerson, Isabel. *The Warmth of Other Suns: The Epic Story of America's Great Migration.* New York: Random, 2010. Discusses the history of the Great Migration through the stories of a number of individual African Americans who made the trek.

See also: African Americans; Civil rights and liberties; Demographics; Harlem Renaissance; Jazz; Jim Crow in the U.S. South; Migrations; Racial discrimination; Urbanization

---

■ Great Mississippi Flood of 1927

The Event: A disastrous flood engulfing millions of acres in seven states and leaving hundreds of thousands homeless

Date: April 1927

Place: Mississippi River drainage basin

One of the worst flood disasters in U.S. history, the 1927 flood displaced 700,000 people, carried off tens of thousands of domestic animals, and covered some 16.5 million acres of land, washing away large swaths of seeded and growing crops. Evacuation and rescue efforts saved over 300,000 lives, but at least 246 people, and perhaps as many as 500, died.

The Mississippi River and its tributaries form a funnel-shaped drainage basin that draws from two Canadian provinces and thirty-one states, a region exceeding 1.2 million square miles. The formation of the Mississippi River Commission in 1879 and the implementation of the Flood Control Act of 1917 had facilitated levee building, the closure of natural outlets along the river, and the draining of lowlands. These steps contributed to the region's commercial development but left it vulnerable to the vagaries of the weather.

A Roaring Flood

In late 1926 and early 1927, torrential rains affecting eleven states filled rivers to record levels. Winding 1,100 miles from Missouri to the Gulf of Mexico, the Lower Mississippi River had reached flood stage at Cairo, Illinois, by January 1. Heavy seasonal rains in March on the Ohio, Missouri, and Tennessee Rivers increased the size of the impending disaster.

Desperate efforts were made to fortify levees along the Mississippi and its larger tributaries. Despite assurances from the U.S. Army Corps of Engineers that the levees would hold, more than one million acres

Army Corps of Engineers attending the flood. (Getty Images)

were covered by April 9. As the deluge continued, the Mississippi River rose so high that portions of the waterway reversed and flowed back into its tributaries.

On April 16, a government-built levee failed just south of Cairo, Illinois, and flooded some 175,000 acres. The greatest levee break occurred on April 21 at Mounds Landing, a dozen miles from Greenville, Mississippi, when a surge of water nearly three-quarters of a mile wide and more than a hundred feet deep burst through the levees, a quantity double that of Niagara Falls. The overflow covered an area 50 miles wide and 100 miles long, increasing fears that the lower Mississippi Delta would be inundated. Anxious leaders in New Orleans, Louisiana, authorized breaching the Poydras levee south of the city in order to lower the level of the river. Dynamiting of the levee commenced on April 29 and resulted in the flooding of Saint Bernard Parish.

Rescue Operations

In the aftermath of the April 21 Mounds Landing levee break, over 185,000 people were forced to evacuate, and many were trapped by floodwater; some thirteen thousand people, primarily African Americans, remained stranded on remnants of the levee because plantation owners feared that rescued sharecroppers would leave the land for good. President Calvin Coolidge appointed Secretary of Commerce Herbert Hoover to head a regional relief committee in cooperation with the Red Cross. However, when Hoover visited Greenville, he chose to leave the mistreated sharecroppers in the hands of the local officials.

As news of the enormity of the flood spread, volunteers, equipment, and donations poured in from all over the nation, and an estimated thirty-three thousand people went to work in the rescue and recovery effort. Spotters in airplanes located survivors clinging to trees and rooftops and sent watercraft to rescue them. As many as 330,000 people were saved from the rising waters, and 154 Red Cross camps provided food and shelter. Receding floodwaters remained high for months, with 1.5 million acres left underwater as late as July 1.

At its greatest extent, the flood covered 27,000 of the 35,000 square miles of lowlands that had previously been protected by levee systems. The federal government's levees-only policy had contributed immeasurably to the violence of the flood, incurring losses of some $347 million.

Impact

Although relief workers provided care for African American flood victims, these sharecroppers (who comprised the majority of the agricultural labor force) were held by armed guards in unhealthy Red Cross camps, forced to work in the recovery effort, and later made to return to plantation owners. Additional misery may have been caused by the decision to flood Saint Bernard Parish, which modern historians maintain was unnecessary, as the floodwaters would probably have dispersed before reaching New Orleans. The aftermath of the flood contributed to the ongoing mass migration of southern laborers seeking employment in the industrial North, and after being largely ignored by Republican policymakers, a majority chose to support the Democratic Party. Nationwide calls for increased federal funding of flood prevention measures on the Lower Mississippi led to the Flood Control Act of 1928 and its allocation of an unprecedented $325 million for the creation of spillways and channels in addition to levee repairs.

Margaret A. Koger

Further Reading

Barry, John M. *Rising Tide: The Great Mississippi Flood of 1927 and How It Changed America*. New York: Simon & Schuster, 1997. A comprehensive study of methods used to control the river and protect the Mississippi Delta, along with additional analysis of the political and cultural repercussions of the flood.

Bearden, Russell E. "Arkansas' Worst Disaster: The Great Mississippi River Flood of 1927." *Arkansas Review: A Journal of Delta Studies* 34, no. 2 (2003): 79–97. Describes the damage and suffering caused by flooding along the Arkansas River, White River, and other Mississippi tributaries.

Daniel, Pete. *Deep'n As It Comes: The 1927 Mississippi River Flood*. Fayetteville: University of Arkansas Press, 1996. Details the experiences of flood victims through photographs, firsthand accounts, and newspaper reports.

Percy, William Alexander. *Lanterns on the Levee: Recollections of a Planter's Son*. Baton Rouge: Louisiana State University Press, 1973. A memoir describing the author's experience as the head of the Flood Relief Committee in Greenville, Mississippi. Originally published in 1941, this later edition contains an introduction by noted novelist Walker Percy, the author's nephew and adopted son.

Spencer, Robyn. "Contested Terrain: The Mississippi Flood of 1927 and the Struggle to Control Black Labor." *Journal of Negro History* 79, no. 2 (Spring, 1994): 170–181. Reveals the adverse treatment of African American refugees by the Red Cross, National Guard, federal officials, and plantation owners that contributed to the breakup of the peonage system.

See also: African Americans; Elections of 1928, U.S.; Great Migration; Hoover, Herbert; Natural disasters; Racial discrimination

---

■ *Greed*

Identification: A silent film about the corrupting effects of money
Director: Erich von Stroheim
Date: 1925

Greed was director Erich von Stroheim's most famous and controversial film. This epic is best known for its extraordinary production costs and tensions between director and studio over its length.

In this silent film based on Frank Norris's novel *McTeague: A Story of San Francisco* (1899), the title character McTeague (Gibson Gowland), a San Francisco dentist, marries Trina (ZaSu Pitts), who has just won five thousand dollars in a lottery and adds to her fortune by hoarding most of her husband's income. McTeague loses his business when Marcus Schouler (Jean Hersholt), Trina's former suitor, discovers that he has no dental license, and the couple end up living in squalid quarters, Trina hoarding all the while. Crazed by his need for money, McTeague kills her and flees to Death Valley, pursued by Marcus.

Most of von Stroheim's films tended to be moralistic, with wealthy characters leading lives of extravagance. Although the protagonists of *Greed* come from a different social class, the director's message is the same. With the crass, vulgar McTeague and Trina destroyed by their love for gold, von Stroheim aimed to depict a grittier realism than in his previous films and to comment on the recklessness of the 1920s.

Greed began as a Goldwyn Pictures project, but Goldwyn merged with Metro Pictures and Louis B. Mayer Productions to form Metro-Goldwyn-Mayer (MGM) during the production, which cost a then-staggering $585,000. Recently fired by Universal's Irving Thalberg because of his extravagance, von Stroheim filmed on location for nine months. The director was zealously devoted to his vision of perfection, assembling a rough cut more than nine hours long. He edited it down to about four hours but refused to cut it further. Von Stroheim sought the help of fellow director Rex Ingram, who reduced it to just over three hours. MGM, now under the control of Thalberg, finally released a 140-minute version, reportedly edited with the aid of screenwriter June Mathis. Many characters were eliminated during the extensive editing, leaving only McTeague, Trina, and Marcus, and causing lapses in continuity. Legend has it that MGM melted down most of von Stroheim's unused footage to salvage silver from the negative.

Greed was one of the most famous Hollywood box-office failures of the silent era, despite all the changes ordered by Thalberg. The uncut version is a legendary lost film, though even the truncated version is widely considered a masterpiece. In 1991, *Greed* was selected for preservation by the Library of Congress's National Film Registry, and in 1999, Turner Entertainment attempted to create a more complete four-hour version by adding still photographs of lost scenes.

Michael Adams

Further Reading

Brownlow, Kevin. *The Parade's Gone By....* Berkeley: University of California Press, 1997.

Koszarski, Richard. *The Man You Loved to Hate: Erich von Stroheim and Hollywood.* New York: Oxford University Press, 1983.

Lennig, Arthur. *Stroheim.* Lexington: University of Kentucky Press, 2007.

See also: Film; Goldwyn, Samuel; Griffith, D. W.; Metro-Goldwyn-Mayer (MGM)

■ Griffith, D. W.

Identification: American film director
Born: January 22, 1875, Floyds Fork, Kentucky
Died: July 23, 1948, Hollywood, California

D. W. Griffith was one of the most prolific and influential filmmakers prior to the 1920s, revolutionizing the art of filmmaking. During the 1920s, Griffith gained public recognition for his contributions to cinema, though his commercial viability as a filmmaker waned.

By the mid-1910s, David Wark Griffith had already established his reputation as an exceptional filmmaker, having directed over four hundred films for the American Mutoscope and Biograph Company and perfected continuity editing and the use of varied framing in cinematography to emphasize emotion. His 1915 Civil War epic, *The Birth of a Nation*, was the greatest financial success of his career, while the far more costly *Intolerance* (1916) became the first of many financial failures.

Way Down East (1920), a melodrama starring Lillian Gish, was the only 1920s film by Griffith to turn a significant profit. Poor business management resulted in overspending on film production and promotion throughout the decade. In 1923, Griffith lost $571,645 on the construction of sets for a film meant

D. W. Griffith. (Hulton Archive/Getty Images)

to star renowned blackface actor Al Jolson, who had not signed a written contract and left the country for Europe. Griffith's 1924 Revolutionary War drama, *America*, would only recoup its production costs years after its release with a reissue and the selling of portions of the film as stock footage.

Unable to obtain further bank loans for the independent production of his films, Griffith turned to the studios. Griffith signed with Adolph Zukor at Paramount Pictures in June 1924, an arrangement that would end after disappointing returns on two W. C. Fields collaborations and *The Sorrows of Satan* (1926). In 1927, Griffith signed with Joseph Schenck of the Art Cinema Corporation, who would retain script approval rights as well as the rights to Griffith's stock in United Artists, the distribution company that Griffith had cofounded with actors Charlie Chaplin, Mary Pickford, and Douglas Fairbanks in 1919. The three films Griffith directed for Schenck between 1927 and 1929 all performed poorly, both critically and financially. Before the contract expired, Griffith directed two sound films, *Abraham Lincoln* (1930) and *The Struggle* (1931), both unsuccessful as well.

Impact

Despite the turmoil that plagued Griffith's career in the 1920s, the filmmaker gained increasing recognition for his immense contributions to cinema and continued to be honored throughout the following decade. The Friars, a theatrical club, held a dinner in honor of Griffith in 1921. He received a special Academy Award in 1936 and was named the first Honorary Life Member of the Director's Guild of America in 1938, but further offers from studios to direct never materialized. Griffith's signature film techniques eventually became industry standards employed in nearly all film and television productions.

Jef Burnham

Further Reading

Barry, Iris. *D. W. Griffith: American Film Master*. New York: Museum of Modern Art, 2002.

Henderson, Robert M. *D. W. Griffith: His Life and Work*. Reprint. New York: Garland, 1985.

Schickel, Richard. *D. W. Griffith: An American Life*. Reprint. New York: Limelight Editions, 1996.

See also: Chaplin, Charlie; Fairbanks, Douglas, Sr.; Fields, W. C.; Film; Gish, Dorothy; Gish, Lillian; Jolson, Al; *Orphans of the Storm;* Pickford, Mary; United Artists

■ Gross national product of the United States

The gross national product (GNP) is an economic indicator showing the total value of a nation's output of goods and services produced in one year. Changes in the demand for these goods and services is the principal cause of fluctuations in output and employment. Following the recession of 1920–1921, the GNP of the United States rose steadily for the rest of the decade, corresponding to improvements in technology and productivity, as well as increases in disposable (after-tax) income.

Although official estimates of the gross national product (GNP) have long been an important economic indicator, such data were not available to Americans in the 1920s. However, retrospective data for that decade have since been calculated.

The GNP is most fundamentally a measure of the value of a nation's output. The total or aggregate demand is determined by multiplying data on the quantities of individual products by the price of each. For instance, in 1920, the nominal GNP was estimated at $91.5 billion, representing expenditures on goods and services by households, businesses, and the government, as well as the value of exports. Compared to 1958 (when the data for the 1920s were compiled), prices in 1920 were 65.4 percent of those in 1958, on average. Dividing $91.5 billion by 65.4 percent yields $140 billion, the estimated value of 1920 output at 1958 prices, or "real" GNP. Estimates of real GNP are chiefly used to compare different years. Thus, although the 1921 nominal GNP was only $69.6 billion, price declines accounted for much of this seemingly huge decrease from the previous year; the real output in 1921 was $127.8 billion in 1958 prices, representing a much smaller decline from 1920. By 1923, with continuing low prices, the real GNP had reached $165 billion, even though the nominal GNP was still lower than in 1920.

"GNP per capita" is a way of measuring economic growth on the individual level, calculated by dividing the total real GNP by population. In 1920, the real GNP per capita was $1,315 in 1958 prices; by 1929, this had risen to $1,671, a 27 percent improvement over 1920.

The Recession of 1920–1921

According to the National Bureau of Economic Research (NBER), the American economy reached a business cycle peak in January 1920, followed by a brief but painful recession that ended in July 1921. The nominal GNP data indicate that total spending on current output fell by about 24 percent from 1920 to 1921, though the real GNP declined only about 9 percent during this period. The federal deficit had reached a record $13 billion in fiscal year 1919. Federal spending was sharply cut, while tax revenues were raised in an effort to eliminate the deficit in fiscal year 1920. The Federal Reserve took steps to tighten credit. Then, in 1921, export sales declined from $8.7 billion to $4.6 billion. Households' disposable income declined from $71.5 billion to $60.2 billion, leading to decreased consumer spending. The principal effect of the economic downturn was to reduce prices, which fell by as much as 18 percent, with the biggest impact on crop prices.

Recovery began in mid-1921, and for the rest of the decade, the national economy enjoyed relatively high employment and stable prices. Mild cyclical recessions occurred in 1924 and 1927, but both were relatively brief. According to the NBER, another business-cycle peak occurred in August 1929. However, the onset of the Great Depression in November, 1929, does not show in the 1929 GNP figures.

GNP and the Flow of Incomes

All the money spent to buy the current output of goods and services becomes income, with a portion going to households, a portion to government, and some retained within business firms. Thus, in 1920, about $6 billion of the GNP represented funds set aside by business to cover depreciation of capital equipment. Another $4 billion went to the government in indirect business taxes. Deducting these two items leaves about $79 billion of national income. Of this, $2.6 billion was retained by business as undistributed corporate profits. Income taxes on persons and corporations took another $4 billion. Adding in interest and transfer payments by government yields the total of disposable personal income: $71.5 billion. Between 1920 and 1929, the nominal GNP rose roughly 12.6 percent. Disposable personal income rose somewhat more, by 16.5 percent, because income tax rates were reduced. National income represents the factor costs of the inputs that produce national output.

For the decade of the 1920s, 60.5 percent of national income went to employee compensation. Another 17.6 percent was the income of unincorporated

businesses, including farmers, shopkeepers, doctors, and lawyers. Much of this was really labor income. The remainder consisted of property incomes—rental income of persons (7.6 percent), corporate profits (8.2 percent), and net interest (6.2 percent).

Households' disposable incomes reflect mostly the subtraction of personal taxes from personal incomes. Government transfer payments are added in, but they were not very large in the 1920s, since no Social Security or unemployment compensation existed yet. Household spending to buy consumer goods and services correlates closely with the amount of disposable income, which in turn tends to follow closely the variations in the nominal GNP. This interaction of income and expenditures is often referred to as a "circular flow." All money spent for the GNP becomes income, but not all income is spent. Variations in the GNP can thus be traced to variations in the "propensity to spend" of households, businesses, and government. After the end of World War I, the expenditures of the U.S. federal government were severely cut back, reducing the incomes of government workers (including all the soldiers and sailors) and those who sold things to the government. They in turn reduced their consumption spending, thereby curtailing the incomes of another set of people. However, this deflationary tendency was somewhat offset by tax reductions, which raised disposable incomes and helped support higher consumption spending.

GNP, Economic Growth, and Consumer Welfare

Estimates of the real GNP provide information about the growth of output in the economy from year to year. Between 1920 and 1929, the real GNP increased from $140 billion to $203.6 billion, about 45 percent. Part of this reflected a larger population and labor force. Between 1920 and 1930, the civilian labor force increased from 42.4 million to 48.8 million, an increase of 16 percent. In addition, labor productivity increased in both agricultural and nonagricultural activities. Between 1919 and 1929, farm output per man-hour rose about 16 percent, and productivity in the nonfarm sector increased about 25 percent. Greater capital and technological innovations accounted for much of the increase. Applications of electric power were spreading through the economy, and the efficiency of electricity generation improved greatly. Automobiles, trucks, and tractors became much more common, and the highway system expanded to keep pace.

The increase in labor productivity brought an increase in the demand for labor and in real wages and real household incomes. Estimated annual earnings of full-time workers rose from $1,342 in 1920 to $1,425 in 1929. Because prices were substantially lower in 1929, real wages increased about one-fourth, nearly matching the approximately 27 percent increase in the real GNP per capita.

Some elements in the GNP do not directly increase the consumption welfare of households. The GNP includes the gross value of capital goods, which do not contribute much to productivity until they are used. Production of military goods and services does not directly benefit consumers. Nevertheless, there is a relatively close correlation between the real GNP and many other measures of personal welfare, particularly indicators of physical health such as infant mortality and life expectancy. And higher productivity makes possible increased leisure time; for example, manufacturing workers' average weekly hours declined from forty-seven in 1920 to forty-four in 1929. Growth of the real GNP does not account for the improvement in consumer welfare resulting from the spread of new products, such as radios and electric refrigerators and improvements in existing products such as automobiles.

Impact

Aggregate demand for goods and services, as measured by the gross national product, took a sharp dip in 1920 and 1921, leading to sustained agricultural depression and numerous bank failures in the 1920s. Outside of farming, however, recovery came quickly, and the remainder of the decade was characterized by economic growth and stable prices until the beginning of the downswing in mid-1929.

Paul B. Trescott

Further Reading

Atack, Jeremy, Peter Passell, and Susan Lee. *A New Economic View of American History: From Colonial Times to 1940*. 2d ed. New York: Norton, 1994. Includes a concise overview of the macroeconomic developments of the 1920s.

Carson, Carol S. "The History of the United States National Income and Product Accounts." *Review of Income and Wealth* 21, no. 1 (June, 1975): 153–181. Describes the invention of gross national product concepts and provides data, mainly from the 1930s and 1940s.

Kuznets, Simon, Lillian Epstein, and Elizabeth Jenks. *National Income and Its Composition, 1919–1938*. New York: Columbia University Press, 1941. A pioneering study of the conceptualization and measurement of national income elements.

Romer, Christina. "World War I and the Postwar Depression: A Reinterpretation Based on Alternative Estimates of GNP." *Journal of Monetary Economics* 22, no. 1 (July, 1988): 91–115. An analysis of the relatively neglected depression of 1920 and 1921, providing useful insights for understanding the Great Depression.

Sutch, Richard. "National Income and Product." In *Historical Statistics of the United States: Millennial Edition*, edited by Susan B. Carter. New York: Cambridge University Press, 2006. A readers' guide to the relationships among the various components of the GNP.

See also: Agricultural Marketing Act of 1929; Agriculture in the United States; Income and wages; Recession of 1920–1921; Unemployment

■ Group of Seven

The Canadian landscape painters known as the Group of Seven set out to create a distinct Canadian style of painting and to explore and document the Canadian wilds. Their work arose from and contributed to the growth of Canadian nationalism during the 1920s.

The original members of the Group of Seven were A. Y. Jackson, Franz Johnston, Franklin Carmichael, Lawren Harris, Arthur Lismer, Frederick Varley, and J. E. H. MacDonald. They often socialized and discussed Canadian art at the Arts and Letters Club of Toronto, expressing their frustration that Canadian artists still relied on European techniques and evaluation models. The Group decided to form their own society to create distinctly Canadian modern art and to educate Canadians about who they were as a nation. By devoting their talent to portraying the full range of the country's landscape, they sought to advance the development of Canadians' national pride, which had begun to increase during World War I.

The members of the Group of Seven embarked on group sketching expeditions all over Canada, traveling by canoe, going on daylong hikes, and sleeping under the stars. Strongly influenced by post-Impressionist French painters such as Vincent van Gogh and Paul Gauguin, they painted in vigorous Expressionist style characterized by heavy impasto (a thick layering of paint), brilliant colors, bold summarization, and surface patterning. The group aspired to capture on canvas the Canadian Shield, an area of stone that stretches almost two million square miles from Newfoundland to the Rocky Mountains and from the Great Lakes northward. They were especially interested in the distinct light of the northern countryside as well as the vivid array of colors displayed each autumn. Since the artists frequently painted together, their painting style developed along analogous lines.

When the Group of Seven held their first public exhibition at the Toronto Art Gallery on May 7, 1920, their vibrant images shocked the art world. In comparison to idyllic scenes in European style, their work seemed primitive and crude, with their portrayal of rocks, snow, trees, and even buildings, in vermilion, deep orange, and mauve. Many artists did not think the Canadian landscape merited painting; few believed the movement would last. Nevertheless, as the decade progressed, the Group of Seven came to be distinguished as pioneers of a new Canadian art movement. Over the next twelve years, the Group of Seven held seven increasingly successful art shows together, launching more than forty other exhibitions throughout North America.

Impact

The Group of Seven created a Canadian art tradition and developed Canadians' sense of national identity by empowering them to discover the beauty of their country. The group's influence became so broad that they no longer needed to remain together. Their final collective exhibit was in 1931. Some members of the group went on to join the artists' collective known as the Canadian Group of Painters, which became active in the 1930s.

Chrissa Shamberger

Further Reading

Mellen, Peter. *The Group of Seven.* Toronto: McClelland and Stewart, 1981.

Murray, Joan, and Lawren Harris. *The Best of the Group of Seven.* Toronto: McClelland and Stewart, 1993.

Silcox, David P. *The Group of Seven and Tom Thomson.* Toronto: Firefly Books, 2011.

See also: Art movements; Canadian nationalism

■ Grove, Lefty

Identification: American baseball player
Also known as: Robert Moses Grove
Born: March 6, 1900, Lonaconing, Maryland
Died: May 22, 1975, Norwalk, Ohio

Over the course of a seventeen-year career in the major leagues, Grove became one of the most successful left-handed pitchers of all time. He was inducted into the Baseball Hall of Fame in 1947 and elected by popular vote to the Major League Baseball All-Century Team in 1999.

Robert Moses "Lefty" Grove was signed by the Baltimore Orioles, a minor International League team, in 1920. During the five seasons he spent with the Orioles, his team won the league pennant each season, and he led the league in strikeouts four times. When his contract was sold in 1925 to the Philadelphia Athletics of the American League, the price was $100,600, the most that had ever been paid for a player, topping the rumored $100,000 that the New York Yankees had paid to sign Babe Ruth.

Lefty Grove. (Getty Images)

Grove's first year with the Athletics was in some ways his rockiest; he led the American League in strikeouts, but for the first and only time, he lost more games (twelve) than he won (ten). He also gained a reputation as an angry man who was hard to get along with, punching walls and lockers and publicly blaming his teammates for losses. His record improved in 1926, when he had the highest earned run average (ERA) in the major league for the first of nine times. In 1928, he twice managed to pitch a perfect inning, striking out three batters with nine pitches; he was the first major-league pitcher to accomplish this feat twice in one season, and only two other pitchers have managed it since. During Grove's time with the Athletics, his team won the league pennant three times and the World Series twice, in 1929 and 1930. Grove was traded to the Boston Red Sox following the 1933 season, and he continued to play for them until his retirement in 1941.

Impact

With a career record of 300 wins and 141 losses, Grove ranks as one of the most successful pitchers in major-league history; over his entire professional career, including his time in the minor leagues, he achieved a record of 421 wins and 179 losses, the highest-winning percentage in the history of baseball. Grove led the American League in strikeouts seven times, in ERAs nine times, and in games won twice, and he was named Most Valuable Player in 1931.

Cynthia A. Bily

Further Reading

Kaplan, Jim. *Lefty Grove: American Original.* Cleveland, Ohio: Society for American Baseball Research, 2000.

Remy, Jerry, and Cory Sandler. *Red Sox Heroes: The RemDawg's All-Time Favorite Red Sox, Great Moments, and Top Teams.* Guilford, Conn.: Lyons Press, 2010.

Sullivan, George. *Pitchers: Twenty-Seven of Baseball's Greatest.* New York: Simon & Schuster, 1999.

See also: Baseball; Ruth, Babe; Sports

H

◾ Hair dryers

Many inventions of the 1920s helped to improve day-to-day living by introducing new and efficient ways of doing things. Among these inventions was the handheld hair dryer, developed in 1920. Though not very popular at first, it paved the way for today's lightweight and efficient hair dryers.

Until the late nineteenth century, women used vacuum cleaners to dry their hair by either plugging a special vacuum attachment or the vacuum hose itself into the exhaust end of the machine and using the warm air to blow their hair dry. By 1890, French hair salon owner Alexandre F. Godefoy invented a bulky, but stationary, hair-drying machine that women would sit beneath. Godefoy most likely used vacuum cleaner technology for his machine, but heat was probably generated through an attachment to gas-stove piping.

At the turn of the century, hair dryers were still stationary and cumbersome, but they were now powered by electricity and had moved from the salon to the home. In the early 1920s, engineers at the Racine Universal Motor Company and Hamilton Beach Manufacturing, both of Racine, Wisconsin, teamed up to develop a small universal motor to power the household appliances being invented and marketed by the two companies. This new motor revolutionized the national small-appliance market because it ran on alternating (AC) and direct (DC) currents, both of which were in use in the United States at the time. After inventing the hugely successful electric blender, the two companies began developing the handheld hair dryer by adding little more than a wooden handle and heat coils to the small universal motor.

Initially, these new hair dryers were not popular. These early models were manufactured primarily of steel and zinc, weighed almost two pounds, making them heavy to use, and had a dangerous tendency to overheat. In fact, hundreds of women were electro-cuted when they dropped their hair dryers in water. Efficiency was another problem early on, since the dryers produced only 100 watts of heat, which was not sufficient to dry hair quickly.

Impact

The handheld hair dryer is one of several inventions of the 1920s powered by the universal motor, a significant innovation that helped to modernize American culture. Although initially unpopular, the handheld dryer eventually became a staple household appliance. Its technology has remained much the same as it was in the 1920s, but with the development of plastics, more efficient motors, and government safety regulations, present-day versions are lightweight, powerful, and much safer to use.

Macey M. Freudensprung

Further Reading

Gordon, Bob. *Early Electrical Appliances.* Oxford, England: Shire Publications, 2010.

Hillman, David, and David Gibbs. *Century Makers: One Hundred Clever Things We Take for Granted Which Have Changed Our Lives Over the Last One Hundred Years.* New York: Welcome Rain, 1999.

Sherrow, Victoria. *Encyclopedia of Hair: A Cultural History.* Westport, Conn.: Greenwood Press, 2006.

See also: Electrification; Hairstyles; Inventions

◾ Hairstyles

While men's hairstyles in the 1920s did not undergo a drastic change from previous short hair fashions, women's changing hairstyles in the 1920s symbolized a paradigm shift in the role women played in society. The "flapper" style embraced women's growing freedom to define their femininity. Short, "bobbed" hair was a reflection of this freedom.

Taking inspiration from the Art Deco movement, women's hairstyles of the 1920s moved away from the heavier, more elaborate styles of the Victorian era to reflect an interest in all things futuristic. In the Edwardian era (from 1901 to 1910), women's fashion shifted toward a more relaxed attitude regarding appearance; as the feminist movement developed, waistlines were lowered, and the corset gradually disappeared. By the 1920s, it had become fashionable for women to look boyish, both in dress and in hairstyle. Men's hair was worn generally short, combed smooth with hair products such as brilliantine, and kept off of the face with a middle or side part.

Society and Women's Fashion

Women's hairstyles in the 1920s were closely related to women's changing status in society. Since World War I, women had been increasingly working outside of the home; in 1920, they gained the right to vote and had greater access to birth control, thanks to the creation of the American Birth Control League. Long hair had previously been the only option in women's hair fashions; in fact, it had been the norm to purchase hairpieces or extensions to make hair appear even longer. The advent of bobbed hair and flapper fashion created a dramatically different aesthetic in the 1920s.

The flapper craze popularized a look consisting of straight, knee-length dresses, a chest-diminishing, sleeveless top, and, most importantly, cropped hair. All of these worked together to create an androgynous appearance, for which women compensated by wearing heavy makeup. The look was encouraged by another phenomenon of the era: the burgeoning motion picture industry. Suddenly, the latest fashions were no longer communicated only through images in magazines; examples of the latest styles were visible on motion picture screens, displayed by some of the most beautiful celebrities. Film stars Clara Bow and Louise Brooks helped to popularize the fashions and hairstyles that came to be associated with the 1920s.

The Bob

At the very beginning of the 1920s, wigs, called "transformations," were extremely popular; they helped women to create fashionable and difficult styles involving ringlets and multiple partings. Around the same time, Irene Castle, a fashionable ballroom dancer, styled her hair in what is believed to have been one of the first bob cuts. As the bob grew in popularity, it developed many variations, including the Orchid (cropped close to the nape of the neck,

parted in the middle, and worn long and curled on sides), the Coconut (clipped above the ears, with a bang cut above the eyebrows), and the Moana (left unparted, with a small sideburn and the rest combed back from the face and behind the ears). The Garçonne bob was also known as the Eton Crop, another iconic look of the era that was popularized by dancer Josephine Baker. The Eton Crop and the Shingle, another boyish crop, were popular cuts for women who were on the cutting edge of fashion.

Other changes in hair fads of the 1920s included the increased use of hair dye and "finger curls," rows of tiny ringlets meant to inject a more feminine appearance into the androgynous style that had become the rage. Many fashionable movie stars combined finger curls with the short bob, which also became an iconic look of the era.

Soon, short hair on women became the subject of religious sermons, news columns, and literature. American writer F. Scott Fitzgerald immortalized the bobbed hairstyle in his short story "Bernice Bobs Her Hair" (1920), and his character Daisy in *The Great Gatsby* (1925) is famous for her Eton Crop, a style that reemerged in the 1960s when actor Mia Farrow played Daisy in the movie version. Fitzgerald's wife, Zelda, is also known to have adopted the bob hairstyle before it became fashionable, and she was often the inspiration for his work.

Impact

Women who adopted the shorter hairstyles of the 1920s faced widespread criticism. Many women cut their hair before discussing it with their husbands, and as a result, men were forced to deal not only with their wife's new appearance but also with the fact that she had made the decision on her own. In addition, religiously conservative areas of the United States and Europe found the shorter styles cause for concern, since the flapper phenomenon was associated with sexual promiscuity and alcohol consumption, which was illegal at the time.

The hairstyles of the 1920s persisted throughout the twentieth century and into the twenty-first century; it may even be said that the bob never went out of fashion entirely.

Shannon Oxley

Further Reading

Corson, Richard. *Fashions in Hair: The First Five Thousand Years.* 3d ed. London: Peter Owen Limited,

2005. Presents a history of men's and women's hairstyles from ancient Egypt to the twentieth century, including illustrations.

Gourley, Catherine. *Flappers and the New American Woman: Perceptions of Women from 1918 Through the 1920s.* Minneapolis, Minn.: Twenty-First Century Books, 2008. Discusses the lives of early-twentieth-century American women, including historical photographs, source notes, and suggestions for further reading.

Moore, Lucy. *Anything Goes: A Biography of the Roaring Twenties.* New York: Overlook Press, 2010. Addresses social, political, and economic changes occurring during the 1920s, with information about notable historical figures, jazz music, and flapper culture.

Sherrow, Victoria. *Encyclopedia of Hair: A Cultural History.* Westport, Conn.: Greenwood Press, 2006. Discusses the significance of hairstyles throughout human history, including illustrations.

See also: Bobbed hair; Fashions and clothing; Film; Flappers; Women's rights

■ Halibut Treaty of 1924

The Treaty: Canadian-American agreement to conserve and rebuild Pacific halibut fisheries

Date: Signed on March 2, 1923; ratified on October 22, 1924

The Halibut Treaty set a precedent for fishery management in international waters. It also demonstrated Canada's growing autonomy in foreign affairs, as it was the first international treaty to be signed by Canada independently of Great Britain and influenced later changes to British imperial policy.

In October 1919, Canada proposed a treaty that would prohibit halibut fishing between November 15 and February 15 in order to arrest the growing depletion of the stock. The U.S. government rejected the proposal for a number of reasons, among them provisions concerning port privileges and tariffs on fish.

In 1922, Canada again proposed a closed season on halibut fishing. Violators would be tried by either the U.S. Department of Commerce or the Canadian Department of Marine and Fisheries. The proposal also called for the establishment of the International Pacific Halibut Commission (IPHC) to conduct a study and offer recommendations for halibut preservation. The United States accepted these terms, with the provision that any halibut "incidentally" caught during the closed season could be used as food for the ship's crew.

Two problems threatened passage of the treaty. First, the U.S. Senate ratified it with an amendment stating that no inhabitant of any other part of the British Empire should engage in Pacific halibut fishing. Canadian prime minister William Lyon Mackenzie King objected, as this would require Britain's approval, thus undermining Canada's intention to negotiate an independent treaty. He persuaded the administration of President Calvin Coolidge to resubmit the treaty to the U.S. Senate without the amendment. Second, the British government wished to be listed as a contracting party and cosign the agreement. King argued that the treaty involved a North American concern that did not affect British interests. After Canada threatened to establish separate diplomatic representation in Washington, D.C., Britain yielded; the preamble stated the treaty's purpose without mentioning contracting parties, and Canadian minister of marine and fisheries Ernest Lapointe and U.S. secretary of state Charles Evans Hughes signed it alone.

As the halibut catch further declined, the IPHC developed new regulations for the administration of the treaty, which were enacted in 1931. The closed season, now beginning on November 1, could be shortened or suspended with joint Canadian-American approval. Area-based restrictions were also implemented to increase the fish stock. Later treaties kept catch levels below population growth, both preserving the fish and making the fishery more profitable.

Impact

The treaty allowed the Pacific halibut population to rebound significantly, in addition to helping pave the way for independent Canadian-American diplomatic relations. It also influenced Britain's adoption of the Statute of Westminster (1931), which granted greater autonomy to the dominions of the British Commonwealth.

Dean Fafoutis

Further Reading

Thistle, John. "'As Free of Fish as a Billiard Ball of Hair': Dealing with Depletion in the Pacific Halibut

Fishery, 1899–1924." *BC Studies* 142/143 (Summer/Autumn 2004): 105–125.

Wigley, Philip G. *Canada and the Transition to Commonwealth: British-Canadian Relations, 1917–1926.* Cambridge, England: Cambridge University Press, 1977.

See also: Canada and Great Britain; Canadian nationalism; Foreign policy, U.S.; King, William Lyon Mackenzie

---

■ *Hallelujah!*

Identification: An early film musical about a sharecropper trying to live an honest life while lusting after a beautiful but devious young woman
Director: King Vidor
Date: 1929

A project personally developed by film director King Vidor, Hallelujah! was the first mainstream Hollywood studio film to feature an all-black cast. Shot in Tennessee and Arkansas, this innovative combination of location footage and emerging sound techniques introduced actor Nina Mae McKinney to audiences and earned Vidor an Academy Award nomination for Best Director.

Intending to make a film depicting "real Negro folk culture" for Metro-Goldwyn-Mayer Studios (MGM), Vidor was unable to sell the idea to studio chairman Nicholas Schenck until Vidor offered to invest his entire salary in a dollar-for-dollar deal for the project. To keep within budget, Vidor shot silent footage on location and then added dialogue and sound effects in the studio. Vidor also sought "unknown" stage actors from New York and Chicago who could be paid less but who also contributed believable performances. Vidor cast *Show Boat* understudy Daniel L. Haynes in the lead role as sharecropper-turned-preacher Zekiel "Zeke" Johnson and selected seventeen-year-old Nina Mae McKinney, a Broadway chorus girl in the show *Blackbirds of 1928*, to play Chick, the juke-joint dancer who leads Zeke astray. (Vidor's initial preference for well-known performers Paul Robeson and Ethel Waters would undoubtedly have increased the budget.)

Vidor faced numerous obstacles making such an ambitious "all-talking" picture, but the results were impressive, blending a stunning visual style with credible dialogue and musical numbers. Extras hired from a

Nina Mae McKinney starred in the MGM film Hallelujah! *(Getty Images)*

Tennessee Baptist church added authenticity to a baptismal scene, and Vidor's use of traditional spirituals added a redemptive quality to material considered unsavory by Schenck, who was concerned with exhibitors' reactions, particularly in the South.

Impact

Hallelujah! was embraced by popular white journalists, but the reaction of the black press was mixed. Vidor's portrayals of African Americans were based on stereotypes, resulting in characters either portrayed as idealists or animalistic, but his sincere intentions provided a step forward, creating a model for subsequent all-black musicals. Despite being banned by the Southern Theatre Foundation, the film was booked in some southern venues. The first African American to play the female lead in a major studio release, Nina Mae McKinney signed a five-year contract with MGM but worked primarily in Europe as a dancer and actor, playing a major role as the wife of

Bosambo (Paul Robeson) in the British epic *Sanders of the River* (1935).

Scott Allen Nollen

Further Reading

Bogle, Donald. *Toms, Coons, Mulattoes, Mammies, and Bucks: An Interpretive History of Blacks in American Films.* 4th ed. New York: Continuum, 2001.

Friedman, Ryan Jay. *Hollywood's African American Films: The Transition to Sound.* Piscataway, N.J.: Rutgers University Press, 2011.

Jones, G. William. *Black Cinema Treasures: Lost and Found.* Denton: University of North Texas Press, 1997.

See also: Academy Awards; African Americans; Jim Crow in the U.S. South; Metro-Goldwyn-Mayer (MGM); Racial discrimination; Robeson, Paul; *Show Boat;* Talking motion pictures; Vidor, King

■ Hall-Mills murder case

The Event: The double murder of Reverend Edward Hall and Eleanor Mills, a member of his church choir
Date: September 14, 1922
Place: New Brunswick, New Jersey

The double murder of Edward Hall, a married Episcopal priest in New Brunswick, New Jersey, and Eleanor Mills, a choir member in Hall's church, attracted widespread news coverage, including verbatim transcripts of their love notes to each other. In 1926, Hall's wife and her two brothers were indicted but were never convicted, ensuring the case's continued infamy as an unsolved crime.

The bodies of Reverend Edward Hall, aged forty-one, and Eleanor Mills, aged thirty-four, were discovered on the morning of September 16, 1922, on property surrounding an abandoned farm in New Brunswick, New Jersey. Reverend Hall had been rector of the Episcopal Church of St. John the Evangelist in New Brunswick, where Mills sang in the church choir and served as an informal assistant to Hall. They were found lying side by side under a crab apple tree, neatly dressed, with his arm, positioned after death, under her shoulder, and her hand resting on his thigh. Each had been shot with a .32 caliber pistol—

Hall once, Eleanor three times—and Eleanor's throat had been cut. Love letters that Mills had written to Hall were found with the bodies.

Neighbors and parishioners knew the pair had been romantically involved for years. Hall's wife, Frances, was related to the wealthy and powerful Carpender family and possibly the Johnson family of Johnson & Johnson medical supply founders. Eleanor's husband, James Mills, was a school janitor. Both denied any knowledge of the affair.

The investigation uncovered hundreds of witnesses, including servants in the Hall home and many citizens of New Brunswick, who claimed to have been near the murder scene. Frances Mills and her brothers William "Willie" Stevens and Henry Stevens were indicted and tried in September 1926. William Stevens was developmentally disabled and lived with Frances and Edward Hall; Henry Stevens was an accomplished marksman. Although Frances Hall and her two brothers had the means and the motive for the murders, there was not enough evidence to convict them.

Impact

The Hall-Mills case became notorious for the authorities' inability to solve it despite its having occurred in a relatively small community of thirty thousand inhabitants, the wealth of physical evidence available, and the hundreds of witnesses interviewed. It drew national attention and was one of the most reported on trials in U.S. history, surpassed only by the Lindbergh kidnapping case in the 1930s. The Hall-Mills case was never officially solved, generating speculation for decades afterward and leading to several books on the subject.

Maureen Puffer-Rothenberg

Further Reading

Katz, Hélèna. *Cold Cases: Famous Unsolved Mysteries, Crimes, and Disappearances in America.* Santa Barbara, Calif.: Greenwood Press, 2010.

Kunstler, William M. *The Hall-Mills Murder Case: The Minister and the Choir Singer.* New Brunswick, N.J.: Rutgers University Press, 1980.

Tomlinson, Gerald. *Fatal Tryst: Who Killed the Minister and the Choir Singer?* Lake Hopatcong, N.J.: Home Run Press, 1999.

See also: Crimes and scandals; Newspapers, U.S.

■ Hammerstein, Oscar, II

Identification: American lyricist and writer
Also known as: Ockie; Oscar Greeley Clendenning
Hammerstein II
Born: July 12, 1895, New York, New York
Died: August 23, 1960, Doyelstown, Pennsylvania

A lyricist of successful operettas and musicals, Oscar Hammerstein's collaboration with composer Jerome Kern on Show Boat *(1927) revolutionized musical theater; by the 1940s, Hammerstein's lyrics and books (the words used in a musical), combined with the music of partner and collaborator Richard Rodgers, dominated and transformed musical theater.*

Oscar Hammerstein II was born into a theatrical family as the son of theater manager William Hammerstein, the nephew of successful Broadway producer Arthur Hammerstein, and the grandson of famous opera promoter Oscar Hammerstein. Despite this background, Oscar's father steered him away from a career in theater, and in 1912, he entered Columbia University to study law. He joined the Columbia University Players as a performer and eventually a writer of lyrics for the university's Varsity Shows.

After William's death in 1914, Oscar worked as a stage manager for many of his uncle's shows and was soon contributing songs, scenery sketches, and story concepts to most every production. In 1919, his first play, *The Light*, was produced but ran for only four performances. He continued work on lyrics and librettos and collaborated with respected composers Otto Harbach, Vincent Youmans, Jerome Kern, and Herbert Stothart to create the successful operettas *Wildflower* (1923), *Rose-Marie* (1924), *Sunny* (1925), *The Desert Song* (1926), and *New Moon* (1928).

In 1927, Hammerstein wrote the book and lyrics for *Show Boat*, the landmark musical based on Edna Ferber's best-selling novel of the same name, which cemented his career and reputation as a lyricist. *Show Boat* was the first of several Hammerstein musicals treating serious social problems, ranging from marital conflicts to racism. Hammerstein continued to collaborate on musicals and operettas with various composers throughout the 1920s and 1930s but did not see huge success again until partnering with Columbia University acquaintance and composer Richard Rogers in the early 1940s. With Hammerstein as lyricist and book writer, the pair produced a

Oscar Hammerstein II. (Time & Life Pictures/Getty Images)

string of hugely successful Broadway musicals, including *Oklahoma!* (1943), *Carousel* (1945), and *South Pacific* (1949). Later film adaptations of these musical hits also enjoyed a great deal of success.

Impact

Through collaboration with many of the great composers of his day, Oscar Hammerstein II helped create a new genre of musical theater: the musical play. By combining musical comedy with operetta, Hammerstein transformed musical theater, influenced future generations of lyricists and librettists, and earned thirty-four Tony Awards, fifteen Academy Awards, two Pulitzer Prizes, and two Grammy Awards.

Betty Richardson

Further Reading

Citron, Stephen. *The Wordsmiths: Oscar Hammerstein 2nd and Alan Jay Lerner.* New York: Oxford University Press, 1995.
Fordin, Hugh. *Getting to Know Him: A Biography of Oscar Hammerstein II.* New York: Da Capo Press, 1995.

Hammerstein, Oscar Andrew. *The Hammersteins: A Musical Theatre Family*. New York: Black Dog & Leventhal, 2010.

See also: Broadway musicals; Ferber, Edna; Hart, Lorenz; Kern, Jerome; Romberg, Sigmund; *Show Boat*

■ Hammett, Dashiell

Identification: American fiction writer
Born: May 27, 1894, St. Mary's County, Maryland
Died: January 10, 1961, New York, New York

Dashiell Hammett was the most influential pioneer of the hard-boiled school of detective fiction that emerged in the 1920s. His stories and novels transformed the genre by shifting its focus from drawing-room puzzles to gritty real-life settings, in which the motives and actions of the purported heroes are often difficult to distinguish from those of the criminals they pursue.

In 1922, when lingering health issues from a bout of Spanish influenza and tuberculosis made it impossible for Hammett to continue working as an operative for the Pinkerton National Detective Agency, he turned to mystery writing, using his experience as a detective for reference. He published his short stories in the pulp magazines of the day, notably *Black Mask*, which became closely associated with the tough style exemplified by Hammett's work. His early stories are narrated by the unnamed Continental Op, a character who moves easily, if warily, among the underworld figures he investigates, adhering to a personal code of conduct whose connection to the law is tenuous at best. The Op served as a model for later hard-boiled detective characters, including Hammett's own Sam Spade.

After gaining some acclaim for his short stories, Hammett started writing novels. His first was *Red Harvest*, published in February 1929, and featured the Continental Op. Just a few months later, he published *The Dain Curse*, also starring the Op. His most famous work is *The Maltese Falcon* (1930), which introduced the world to private eye Sam Spade. Hammett's prose style is clipped, lean, and rich in observational detail. Thematically, his stories reveal the author's view that social institutions tend to corruption and the individual must rely on his own moral convictions to guide him, qualities that make his work comparable to that of Ernest Hemingway and other writers of the Lost Generation.

After *The Maltese Falcon*, Hammett published only two more novels and a handful of stories in his lifetime. Instead, he wrote for movies, radio, and the stage, and created a comic strip called *Secret Agent X-9*. Later in his life, he would become involved with Communism and left-wing activism.

Impact

As novelist Raymond Chandler famously wrote, "Hammett gave murder back to the kind of people that commit it for reasons, not just to provide a corpse." In doing so, he helped establish a style that would inspire such stalwarts of the genre as Chandler, John D. MacDonald, Robert B. Parker, and Walter Mosley, among many others. His influence also extends to movies, radio, and television, where the tough, hard-boiled detective remains a staple of American popular culture.

John C. Hajduk

Further Reading

Hammett, Dashiell. *Complete Novels: Red Harvest, The Dain Curse, The Maltese Falcon, The Glass Key, The Thin Man*. New York: Literary Classics of the United States, 1999.

_____. *Crime Stories and Other Writings*. New York: Literary Classics of the United States, 2007.

Johnson, Diane. *Dashiell Hammett: A Life*. New York: Random House, 1983.

See also: Book publishing; Comic strips; Hemingway, Ernest; Literature in the United States; Lost Generation; Magazines

■ Hardin, Lillian

Identification: American pianist, composer, singer, and bandleader
Also known as: Lil Armstrong, Lil Hardin Armstrong, Lil Hot Miss
Born: February 3, 1898, Memphis, Tennessee
Died: August 27, 1971, Chicago, Illinois

Lillian Hardin was one of the first women to be a part of a major jazz band. She performed, composed, and arranged music for some of the leading jazz orchestras from New Orleans. Hardin had significant influence in shaping jazz trumpeter Louis Armstrong's career.

Hardin was an educated and talented jazz pianist. She studied at Fisk University but decided to abandon her college career when she discovered the music that surrounded her while living in Chicago. She encountered the rhythmic and colorful jazz music of pianist Jelly Roll Morton as he played at Jones's Music Store in Chicago, where she worked as a sheet music demonstrator. Deeply influenced by Morton's jazz style, Hardin incorporated elements from his playing into her own; joined various all-male, African American jazz bands at the age of twenty; and soon became known as Lil Hot Miss.

Hardin first met Louis Armstrong while playing at Dreamland with King Oliver's Creole Jazz Band. She was not attracted to him at first, but she soon realized his musical potential and became romantically interested in him. Hardin and Armstrong were married on February 24, 1924. Hardin was very influential in Armstrong's career. She convinced him to leave the Creole Jazz Band to begin a solo career and helped him make more fashionable wardrobe choices. Hardin formed a band named Lil's Dreamland Syncopators, featuring Armstrong as the lead trumpet player.

Hardin was involved in producing the first recording of King Oliver's Creole Jazz Band. She and Armstrong also recorded together with Okeh Records. Hardin made sure that Armstrong was the featured trumpet player in the recording session. She organized a band called the Hot Fives, which was one of the most successful jazz bands in early jazz history. Hardin later promoted the group as Louis Armstrong and the Hot Fives.

Throughout her career, Hardin composed major songs that featured both her and Armstrong. Some of these songs include "Just for a Thrill" (1936), "Struttin' With Some Barbeque" (1927), "King of the Zulus" (1926), and "Lonesome Blues" (1926).

Impact

Lillian Hardin is considered one of the most prominent women in early jazz. She is known as one of the world's greatest jazz pianists. However, she is best known for the impact she had on Louis Armstrong's musical career and for her compositions that were covered by later musicians, including Ringo Starr and Ray Charles.

Monica T. Tripp-Roberson

Further Reading

Dickerson, James L. *Just for a Thrill: Lil Hardin Armstrong, First Lady of Jazz.* New York: Cooper Square Press, 2002.

Terkel, Studs. *And They All Sang: Adventures of an Eclectic Disc Jockey.* New York: New Press, 2006.

See also: Armstrong Louis; Jazz; Morton, Jelly Roll; Music, popular; Oliver, Joe "King"

■ Harding, Warren G.

Identification: Twenty-ninth president of the United States
Born: November 2, 1865, Blooming Grove, Ohio
Died: August 2, 1923, San Francisco, California

Warren G. Harding led the United States into the 1920s and contributed to an era of peace and prosperity. He was widely honored at his premature death, but subsequent scandals concerning the malfeasance of some of his appointees and sensationalized allegations about his personal life severely damaged his reputation. Years of bad press have resulted in Harding being regarded as one of the weakest presidents in American history.

Warren Gamaliel Harding was born on a farm, the eldest of eight children. He graduated from Ohio Central College at the age of sixteen and moved to Marion, Ohio, where he briefly tried teaching, selling insurance, and studying law before forming a partnership to buy a local newspaper, the *Marion Daily Star.* By 1886, Harding was sole owner of the paper, which he turned into a popular success.

Early Political Career

Harding, a gregarious man who made friends easily, had a gift for public speaking. He was elected to the Ohio state senate as a Republican in 1899 and served two terms before becoming lieutenant governor. When he was denied the Republican gubernatorial nomination in 1906, he bided his time and won the nomination in 1910. His success was tempered by the fact that the Republican Party was divided between conservatives and Progressives, however, and Harding was ultimately defeated by the Democratic incumbent.

Harding aligned himself with the conservatives in the Republican Party rather than the Progressives, and gave the speech at the 1912 Republican National Convention nominating Ohio native son William

---

Harding Eulogizes the Unknown Soldier

President Warren G. Harding's funeral speech at the burial of an unidentified U.S. World War I soldier at Arlington National Cemetery on November 11, 1921, highlighted the contributions of the United States during that war and provided Americans with a symbol of the war's casualties. In his speech, Harding solemnly expressed Americans' appreciation and reverence for the Unknown Soldier as a symbol of the sacrifices Americans and their allies had made. Although the soldier's origins were unknown, Harding remarked, his commitment to the United States and his sacrifices were understood by many. Harding told those who had lost family members in the war that paying tribute to the Unknown Soldier might give families comfort, and he vowed to secure peace. The following day, an international disarmament and peace conference began, and many of those attending had been in Washington, D.C., during the Armistice Day holiday. Touched by the ceremony for the Unknown Soldier and by Americans' sincere response to the war, empathetic allies were more willing to cooperate in planning disarmament strategies.

Howard Taft for a second term as president. Two years later, he successfully ran for the United States Senate. Harding's affability proved a valuable asset in the clubbish atmosphere of the Senate, where he was popular with his colleagues but failed to distinguish himself as a legislator or take a leading role on any issue. In 1916, Harding chaired the Republican National Convention and delivered its keynote address. So broad was his intraparty appeal that former president Theodore Roosevelt pondered making Harding his running mate in a potential 1920 presidential campaign.

Apostle of Normalcy

Harding's friends in Ohio first suggested he run for president in 1919. Harding was initially receptive to this talk because he thought it would strengthen his prospects for reelection to the Senate. When it appeared that the 1920 convention might deadlock over the large field of Republican front-runners, his candidacy became more serious. As an uncontroversial senator from an electorally crucial state, he was the ideal compromise candidate, and after some extended backroom negotiations, he became the official Republican presidential nominee.

Harding waged one of the most successful presidential campaigns in history. He adopted the strategy of fellow Ohioan William McKinley, staying home and speaking to hundreds of thousands of visitors from his front porch, while surrogates traveled the country and campaigned on his behalf. He took advantage of public weariness with the Woodrow Wilson administration and postwar economic dislocation, calling for a "return to normalcy." This meant a renewed focus on peace and prosperity, relying on such time-tested conservative Republican principles as limited government, lower taxes, and higher tariffs. Harding also held out the promise of a return to a more traditional America through his support of immigration restriction and his coolness toward Wilsonian internationalism.

The campaign was a spectacular success, winning Harding 404 electoral votes to Democrat James M. Cox's 127. He received 60.3 percent of the popular vote, then the largest ever majority. In addition, the Republicans gained sixty-three seats in the House of Representatives and ten seats in the Senate.

Domestic Policy

Harding did not want to be an activist president like Theodore Roosevelt or Woodrow Wilson. Hoping to act as a mediator between power bases in Congress, the judiciary, and the Republican Party, he appointed a cabinet of the "best minds," among them Charles Evans Hughes as secretary of state, Andrew Mellon as secretary of the treasury, Herbert Hoover as secretary of commerce, and Henry C. Wallace as secretary of agriculture. He also appointed former president William Howard Taft as chief justice of the United States. Harkening back to the example of the nineteenth century, Harding saw his role as limited and largely ceremonial; during the course of his presidency, however, difficulties with Congress would lead him to take a more forcible role in promoting his policies.

Harding took immediate steps to combat the postwar economic recession. In 1921, he signed legislation to create the Bureau of the Budget, which, under the leadership of Charles G. Dawes, brought efficiency to the executive budgeting process and dramatically reduced government spending. Harding and Mellon persuaded Congress to reduce tax rates, while the Fordney-McCumber Tariff of 1922 raised duties on foreign goods. Farmers benefited from the Packers and Stockyards Act of 1921, which prohibited unfair practices in the packing industry, and the Capper-Volstead Act of 1922, which afforded agricultural cooperatives certain exemptions from antitrust laws. As a result of Harding's policies, the economy had recovered by the fall of 1922.

In August 1921, Harding created the Veterans' Bureau to administer benefits to World War I veterans; in November of that same year, he signed the Sheppard-Towner Act, which funded child health programs in individual states. He denounced discrimination against African Americans and called for an antilynching bill, though this legislation would be blocked repeatedly by southerners in the Senate, and released Americans who had been imprisoned by the Wilson administration during the Red Scare of 1919, among them Socialist Party leader Eugene Debs. Harding also supported the Immigration Act of 1921, which restricted immigration to the United States.

Foreign Policy

Once in office, Harding took steps to end the state of war between the United States and its World War I opponents, still officially ongoing due to the Senate's rejection of the Treaty of Versailles. A congressional joint resolution ending the war was signed by Harding on July 2, 1921, followed by individual treaties with Germany, Austria, and Hungary. In addition, the Harding administration resolved an old dispute with Colombia by compensating it for the loss of Panama with a payment of $25 million.

The most important diplomatic initiative of Harding's presidency was the Washington Naval Conference, which lasted from November 12, 1921, to February 6, 1922. The goal of the conference was to prevent an expensive naval arms race and resolve disputes between the powers in eastern Asia. The conference resulted in a number of treaties, including agreements limiting the tonnage of capital ships and establishing a building ratio between the great powers, an agreement by the United States, Great Britain, France, and Japan to respect one another's possessions in the Pacific, and a nine-power pact guaran-

teeing the independence and territorial integrity of China.

Death and Scandal

Despite Republican losses in the 1922 midterm election, Harding remained a popular and effective president, and he looked forward to reelection. Early in 1923, when he learned that Charles R. Forbes, head of the Veterans' Bureau, had been defrauding the government, he fired Forbes and began cleaning up the agency. While on a speaking tour in the West, however, Harding died suddenly of a heart attack.

After Harding's death, the public learned of the unsavory activities of a group of influence peddlers known as the Ohio Gang. Albert B. Fall, the former secretary of the interior, was discovered to have accepted bribes to lease naval oil reserves at Teapot Dome in Wyoming to private oil companies. Attorney general Harry Daugherty was accused of corruption but never convicted.

Impact

Warren G. Harding's memory was tarnished by association with the Ohio Gang, though he had not been involved in their activities. Allegations of an extramarital affair and an illegitimate child completed the ruin of Harding's reputation, and a collection of sensationalized contemporary accounts of his administration solidified its low standing in history. While Harding's policies laid the foundation for the unprecedented prosperity of the 1920s, his death prevented him from defending himself against the negative view of his presidency that emerged from the popular press.

Daniel P. Murphy

Further Reading

Dean, John W. *Warren G. Harding.* New York: Times Books, 2004. A sympathetic biography written by a key figure in the Watergate scandal.

Murray, Robert K. *The Harding Era: Warren G. Harding and His Administration.* Minneapolis: University of Minnesota Press, 1969. Corrects many myths and highlights the achievements of the Harding administration.

_____. *The Politics of Normalcy: Governmental Theory and Practice in the Harding-Coolidge Era.* New York: W. W. Norton, 1973. An overview of Harding's Normalcy Program that argues for its influence on the prosperity and politics of the 1920s.

Russell, Francis. *The Shadow of Blooming Grove: Warren G. Harding in His Times.* New York: McGraw-Hill, 1968. A detailed biography that focuses on Harding's personal failings.

Trani, Eugene P., and David L. Wilson. *The Presidency of Warren G. Harding.* Lawrence: Regents Press of Kansas, 1989. A critical analysis of the Harding presidency.

See also: Cox, James M.; Daugherty, Harry M.; Dawes, Charles G.; Elections of 1920, U.S.; Forbes, Charles R.; Hoover, Herbert; Mellon, Andrew; Recession of 1920–1921; "Return to Normalcy"; Teapot Dome scandal; Washington Naval Conference

■ Harlem Renaissance

The African American cultural movement known as the Harlem Renaissance provided new directions for many African Americans as they sought to discover the sources of their identity in art, literature, and music during the 1920s and 1930s.

By the end of the nineteenth century, African Americans in the United States had lived through several decades of alterations in their social, economic, and cultural identity. Many pre–World War I cultural perceptions of African Americans were tied to popular minstrel shows, spirituals, and emerging forms of blues and jazz. Historians suggest that World War I, which brought thousands of rural African Americans north for wartime jobs, affected northern cities' demographic composition and emerging attitudes toward what pioneers of the Harlem Renaissance called the "New Negro."

By the first two decades of the twentieth century, African American identity had already been somewhat shaped by contributions from social reformer Frederick Douglass and political leader Booker T. Washington. Probably the most widely recognized African American figure of the immediate pre–World War I era was Harvard graduate W. E. B. Du Bois, whose 1903 book *The Souls of Black Folk* greatly influenced the following generation. As head of the National Association for the Advancement of Colored People (NAACP) after 1910 and founder of its main publication, *The Crisis*, Du Bois encouraged African Americans to claim their deserved social, economic, and political rights. In addition to his politically ori-

ented writings, Du Bois's name is associated with the production of theatrical presentations called "pageants," involving dramatic scenes of the African American historical experience, as well as highly idealized images and symbols. Du Bois's early message would soon be echoed by others seeking to add cultural and intellectual dimensions to their evolving African American identity.

Alain Locke, often called the "Father of the Harlem Renaissance," was also a Harvard graduate and was appointed assistant professor of English at Howard University in Washington, D.C. Within a short time, he became a primary spokesperson for artists and authors who lacked a forum for discussing their aesthetic goals. Many of the ideas in Locke's 1925 landmark work, *The New Negro*, can also be seen in his early writings, which support cultural pluralism in American society. These views hold that distinct ethnic groups make valuable contributions to the total cultural matrix of North and South America and to the entire world. Locke's declaration of his adherence to the Baha'i Faith in 1918 further exemplified his search for intercommunal values.

Although the ideas broached by Locke and his followers represented a rather high level of discourse, the founders of the Harlem Renaissance welcomed all cultural expression, considering popular art forms such as traditional African American music and stage presentations to be equally valid aspects of their cultural identity.

Until he moved to New York in 1924, Locke frequented a small group of intellectuals in Washington, D.C., who called for a "search for fulfillment by the black self in America." Among these intellectuals was the writer Jessie Redmon Fauset. Like Locke, Fauset left Washington for New York, where her 1924 book *There Is Confusion* placed the political issue of racism in a new cultural context and set the stage for meetings of what became known as the Writers' Guild of New York. By the mid-1920s, the collective work of African American thinkers and artists was becoming known as the Harlem Renaissance, and although led by the African American community in the Harlem neighborhood of New York, contributors to the movement worked in other northern and midwestern cities as well.

Early Productions

Immediately after World War I, it seemed that progress toward interracial harmony would fail unless efforts were made to redefine the social position of African Americans, especially following the violence of the 1919 Chicago race riots. This redefining began to develop most noticeably in the fields of literature, music, and theater.

In 1920, black actor Charles Gilpin performed in the Provincetown Playhouse production of the Eugene O'Neill play *Emperor Jones.* The publishing company Harcourt, Brace, and Company released Jamaican American poet Claude McKay's poetry collection *Harlem Shadows* in 1922, calling national attention to the social destitution and moral humiliation in large urban ghetto communities like Harlem. McKay's language reflected not only bitterness but also an undercurrent of what would become an essential part of the Harlem Renaissance: pride in an African American cultural heritage that was not dependent on white perceptions.

An important sounding board for such ideas was the official publication of the National Urban League, *Opportunity, A Journal of Negro Life,* first edited by University of Chicago sociology graduate (and future president of Fisk University) Charles S. Johnson. *Opportunity* tried to serve the needs of promising black writers by introducing their works to established white publishing houses.

Several major black musicians and dancers became internationally famous for their performances at the Cotton Club, a nightclub on Lenox Avenue and West 142nd Street, which opened in 1927. One of the Cotton Club's most famous performers was pianist and bandleader Duke Ellington, who played there between 1927 and 1930. Two other performance venues became known for their musical revues: the Savoy Ballroom, which would become famous for swing music and dancing, and the Apollo Theater on 125th Street. The Apollo became greatly significant to the Harlem Renaissance in the late 1920s, when, under a new name, it hosted more serious artists and vocalists. Some very famous African American singers, including Ella Fitzgerald and Billie Holiday, made their debuts at the Apollo. Other entertainers who rose to fame during the 1920s portion of the Harlem Renaissance include dancer and singer Josephine Baker and jazz pianist Fats Waller.

Harlem Renaissance playwrights produced a number of significant stage performances addressing African American experience in new ways. Although known for his poetry, writer Langston Hughes also made notable contributions to African American

Jessie Redmon Fauset was one of the best-known women authors of the Harlem Renaissance. (© Corbis)

theater, such as his work *Mule Bone: A Comedy of Negro Life* (1930). Probably the most outstanding Harlem Renaissance playwright of the 1920s was North Carolina–born Willis Richardson. Richardson made his earliest theatrical contributions in Washington, D.C., where he directed the Little Theater Group. This theater company devoted itself to the grassroots cultural goals of the Harlem Renaissance by bringing original African American plays to local community schools and churches. Richardson's first well-known play, *The Chip Woman's Fortune,* was the first African American play staged on Broadway, opening at the Frazee Theater in 1923.

Throughout his career, Richardson maintained close contact with the periodical *The Crisis,* publishing articles on African American drama. Both *The*

Crisis and its rival, *Opportunity*, drew attention to Richardson's work by granting him "first prizes," publicizing other black playwrights' work as "runners-up."

Richardson's contribution to the Harlem Renaissance was so significant that Locke included his 1925 play *Mortgaged* in *The New Negro*, an anthology of African American writing from the Harlem Renaissance. Richardson sought to portray the experiences of common African American people who were as deserving of respect and dignity as any other segment of society.

Major Figures

Langston Hughes was a highly influential poet of the Harlem Renaissance. In 1921, one of his most famous poems, "The Negro Speaks of Rivers," was printed, and he published his first volume of collected poetry in 1926 while he was still a student at Lincoln University. Hughes's poetry sought to replicate traditional African American rhythms and was sometimes labeled "jazz poetry." Also in 1926, Hughes published an important essay in the periodical *The Nation* entitled "The Negro Artist and the Racial Mountain," discussing the artistic and political principles that contributed to the developing Harlem Renaissance.

Perhaps the best-known woman author of the Harlem Renaissance was Fauset, who graduated from Cornell University in 1905 and received a master's degree from the University of Pennsylvania. Fauset's service as literary editor of *The Crisis* between 1919 and 1926 provided her with an important channel for communicating not only her fiction but also her ideas concerning perceptions of African American women. Her groundbreaking 1924 novel *There Is Confusion* discusses issues of identity experienced by light-skinned African Americans, as does her 1928 best seller *Plum Bun.*

Around the same time his poetry collection *Harlem Shadows* was published, McKay also released a Russian-language volume that placed him in the ranks of radical political authors associated with the Harlem Renaissance: *Negry v Amerike.* This general description of African American life was later translated as *The Negroes in America* and published in the United States in 1979. The book had definite ideological objectives regarding such issues as African Americans' relationship to the U.S. labor movement, but it also described black artistic contributions in American society.

McKay served as a coeditor of the radical newspaper *The Liberator* until 1922, occasionally contributing work for publication. One of McKay's early radical poems in *The Liberator*, "If We Must Die," became an enduring symbol of African American defiance in the face of the racial violence that struck Chicago in 1919. However one may judge McKay's ideological radicalism, there is no doubt that *Harlem Shadows* and his novels *Home to Harlem* (1928) and *Banjo* (1929) were meant to instill strong feelings of pride in African American identity.

Marcus Garvey, another important Harlem Renaissance intellectual, was a Jamaican American writer and advocate of African American rights. Some of his early twentieth-century projects included the founding of the nationalist organization Universal Negro Improvement Association (UNIA), the African Communities (Imperial) League (ACL), and the industrial manufacturing venture known as the Negro Factories Corporation. Garvey's vision of African Americans' return to Africa was also influential to the development of the Rastafarian movement in 1930s Jamaica.

Support from Outside Sources

Several key publishers invested time and financial support to Harlem Renaissance artists in the 1920s, helping many black authors establish lasting reputations. Equally important were sources of personal encouragement given by white artists who supported the causes reflected in the work of African American artists.

A prime example of the latter can be seen in the work of writer Carl Van Vechten, whose literary career began in the years before and after World War I, when he served as dance and music critic for *The New York Times.* Although his literary and musical interests were varied, Van Vechten took a particular interest in the careers of emerging Harlem Renaissance artists, especially that of Hughes. This interest in African American art and culture led him to write about Harlem life in the mid-1920s in the novel *Nigger Heaven* (1926). Although members of the black intellectual middle-class society portrayed in the book led similar lives to their white contemporaries on the surface, Van Vechten indirectly suggests that the book's protagonists (an idealistic writer and his fiancée) will inevitably face insurmountable dilemmas because of racism. While Van Vechten's work may not have communicated hope to oppressed African Americans or presented possible solutions to racial conflict, his novel indicates growing white interest in the lives of African Americans.

White encouragement and patronage of the Harlem Renaissance became problematic, however. Du Bois and other influential African American intellectuals found white contemporaries exhibited a worrying appetite for representations of black primitivism, which led many black artists and authors to seek artistic independence.

Impact

Because of redefined patterns of cultural expression pursued by artists in the Harlem Renaissance, African Americans were able to overcome some racial stereotypes, to a degree. During the Harlem Renaissance, African American thinkers, writers, artists, and performers made important contributions to the artistic and intellectual heritage passed on to American society. Nevertheless, African Americans continue to confront major challenges in social, economic, and political status in the twenty-first century.

Byron Cannon

Further Reading

Du Bois, W. E. B. *The Souls of Black Folk: Essays and Sketches.* Chicago: A.C. McClurg, 1903. Recognized as one of the important forerunners of the "new spirit" guiding supporters of the Harlem Renaissance.

Gray, Christine Rauchfuss. *Willis Richardson, Forgotten Pioneer of Afro-American Drama.* Westport, Conn.: Greenwood Press, 1999. A biography of one of the best-known dramatists of the Harlem Renaissance.

Kramer, Victor A., and Robert A. Russ, eds. *The Harlem Renaissance Re-examined.* Rev. ed. Troy, N.Y.: Whitson, 1997. A collection of articles by different specialists, covering a variety of helpful topics.

Krasner, David. *A Beautiful Pageant: African American Theatre, Drama, and Performance in the Harlem Renaissance, 1910–1927.* New York: Palgrave Mac-Millan, 2002. Deals with major figures, themes, and representative musical and theatrical productions from the heyday of the Harlem Renaissance.

Locke, Alain L., ed. *The New Negro.* New York: Touchstone, 1997. A compendium of contributions to the ideas and goals of the Harlem Renaissance, edited by one of the movement's most prominent representatives.

Wintz, Cary. *Harlem Speaks: A Living History of the Harlem Renaissance.* Naperville, Ill: Sourcebooks MediaFusion, 2007. Features essays on people and themes involved in the Harlem Renaissance, including historical audio material and photographs.

See also: Armstrong, Louis; Baker, Josephine; Cotton Club; Du Bois, W. E. B.; Ellington, Duke; Garvey, Marcus; Hughes, Langston; Jazz; Literature in the United States; Nightclubs; Waller, Fats

---

■ *Harp Weaver and Other Poems, The*

Identification: A book of poetry
Author: Edna St. Vincent Millay
Date: 1923

This collection won a Pulitzer Prize in poetry for Millay and helped her reach the apex of her appeal as a woman poet of the 1920s. The volume includes many of her celebrated sonnets expressing a woman's consciousness of fleeting love and her efforts to connect with a world that is larger than the personal circumference of her romantic involvements.

"The Harp Weaver," the title poem in Edna St. Vincent Millay's 1923 collection of sonnets and other poems, is a ballad reflecting the poverty of a young boy, now a man, who recalls how his mother created a world of beauty in spite of their dire circumstances. The woman's weaving of bright, beautiful clothes is seen by some as a metaphor for her youthful energy that inspires her son even as she exhausts her own life. The simple rhyming of this ballad reflects the tone of other Millay poems that were celebrated in the 1920s for their attention to the domestic and romantic lives of women.

Millay's sonnets and other poems in the collection are traditional in form, but they reject conventional notions of women as ignorant, poorly educated, or dependent on men for fulfillment. A strong undercurrent of the poet's own life informs this volume, including allusions to her suitors and to people who may have interfered with her writing, such as the figure in "The Concert," who "would put yourself/Between me and my song." Further themes addressed in the collection include restlessness, beauty, death, maturation, romantic relationships, physical attraction, and sacrifice.

Millay's collection *The Harp Weaver and Other Poems* was published the same year that she married Dutch entrepreneur Eugen Jan Boissevain, who helped her maintain her literary career, go on public reading tours, and read her poetry on the radio.

Impact
The Harp Weaver and Other Poems is hailed as expressing the strong, independent spirit of a woman poet. Millay's work inspired a new generation of women writers in the 1920s, including Sara Teasdale, Elinor Wylie, and Amy Lowell, and rivaled the work of her male counterparts. In 1923, Millay became the first woman to be awarded a Pulitzer Prize in poetry.

Carl Rollyson

Further Reading
Brittin, Norman A. *Edna St. Vincent Millay.* Rev. ed. Boston: Twayne, 1982.

Epstein, Daniel Mark. *What My Lips Have Kissed: The Loves and Love Poems of Edna St. Vincent Millay.* New York: Henry Holt, 2002.

Milford, Nancy. *Savage Beauty: The Life of Edna St. Vincent Millay.* New York: Random House, 2004.

See also: Literature in the United States; Lowell, Amy; Poetry; Teasdale, Sara; Wylie, Elinor

■ Hart, Lorenz

Identification: American lyricist
Born: May 2, 1895 , New York, New York
Died: November 22, 1943 , New York, New York

Lorenz Hart was one of the greatest lyricists in the history of Broadway and Hollywood musicals. With his composing partner, Richard Rodgers, he contributed lyrics to songs in many successful shows.

Lorenz Hart was born Lorenz Milton Hart to German-Jewish immigrants Max and Frieda Hart (anglicized from Hertz) on New York City's Upper West Side. At summer camp and later at Columbia University, he acquired a love for amateur theater. He soon put his avocation to use working for the Schuberts, who were famous theater impresarios. Hart's task was to translate German language works into English for possible productions on the New York stage. Around 1919, he met composer Richard

Rodgers, and they entered into one of the most famous musical partnerships in American theatrical history, working together exclusively for the next twenty years. Rodgers wrote the music for their many revues and musicals, while Hart supplied song lyrics. The first show to which they contributed songs was *Poor Little Ritz Girl* (1920).

Partnership in the 1920s
Rodgers and Hart's numerous classic songs included "Where or When," "There's a Small Hotel," "Manhattan," "My Funny Valentine," "Isn't It Romantic," "Blue Moon," "With a Song in My Heart," and "Bewitched, Bothered, and Bewildered." However, they were largely unsuccessful in getting their songs into shows during the first half of the 1920s and even considered splitting up. The success of their musical revue *The Garrick Gaieties* revived their careers in 1925, and they were very productive in the latter half of the 1920s. During that time, the team wrote for musicals in which Hart's witty and often complexly rhyming lyrics (as in the song "Thou Swell") were highly praised. Their shows from the late 1920s included *The Girl Friend* (1926), *Peggy-Ann* (1926), *A Connecticut Yankee* (1927), *Present Arms* (1928), *Spring Is Here* (1929), and *Simple Simon* (1930). These tended to be lighthearted productions, although later critics and theater historians have pointed out that Hart's lyrics may have reflected his personal struggles with body image and closeted homosexuality. Despite this, or perhaps because of it, Rodgers and Hart proved to be among the leading theater personalities in the latter 1920s. Although not all their shows had long runs, each one produced at least one memorable song that seemed to capture both the sophistication and the pleasure-bent spirit of the Jazz Age.

Hollywood and Broadway
With the advent of talking motion pictures, Hollywood attracted many Broadway personalities, among them Rodgers and Hart. In 1929, they were featured in a movie short called *Makers of Melody,* in which they demonstrated their work methods. Unlike the Gershwin brothers and other musical collaborators who worked in the movies, they did not produce particularly memorable film scores, with the exception of the music for the film *Love Me Tonight* (1932). Rodgers and Hart returned to the theater in the mid-1930s, with such hits as *On Your Toes* (1936), *Babes in Arms* (1937), and particularly their darkest musical,

Pal Joey (1940), showing them to have matured as artists.

By the time of his final show, *By Jupiter* (1942), which opened in the year before his death, Hart had been the lyricist for almost thirty Broadway and London musicals as well as nearly ten motion pictures. In his last years, Hart's alcoholism made him an increasingly unreliable collaborator, often disappearing for days. A frustrated Rodgers sought out a new collaborator, Oscar Hammerstein II, forming a partnership that would prove very successful in coming years, while Hart experienced a decline in his health, in his career, and in the public eye.

Impact

The Broadway musical stage in the 1920s and 1930s was enriched by the clever, complex lyrics of Lorenz Hart, which still resonate with twenty-first-century audiences. Before his work, musicals had tended to be frivolous, forgettable productions with little or no lasting influence on their times. Hart's work as a lyricist was perhaps only matched by songwriter Cole Porter, and Hart is still very much honored for his contributions to the maturation of musical comedy. The best Rodgers and Hart shows continue to be revived and performed, along with a large number of their songs that have become enduring classics.

Roy Liebman

Further Reading

Hart, Dorothy. *Thou Swell, Thou Witty: The Life and Lyrics of Lorenz Hart.* New York: Harper & Row, 1976. A biography written by Hart's sister-in-law, including newspaper clips, magazine articles, and photographs from Hart's career and life.

Hart, Lorenz. *The Complete Lyrics of Lorenz Hart.* Edited by Robert Kimball and Dorothy Hart. New York: Knopf, 1986. Presents Hart's song lyrics.

Keyser, Herbert H. *Geniuses of the American Musical Theatre: The Composers and Lyricists.* New York: Applause Theatre and Cinema Books, 2009. Includes a section on Hart, along with twenty-seven other biographies of Broadway songwriters and lyricists.

Marx, Samuel, and Jan Clayton. *Rodgers and Hart: Bewitched, Bothered, and Bedeviled: An Anecdotal Account.* New York: Putnam, 1976. Offers an account of the Rodgers and Hart songwriting partnership of the 1920s, 1930s, and 1940s.

Nolan, Frederick W. *Lorenz Hart: A Poet on Broadway.* New York: Oxford University Press, 1994. A biography of Hart featuring reminiscences by Hart's contemporaries in musical theater, including performers such as Gene Kelly, as well as Hart's songwriting partner, Richard Rodgers.

See also: Broadway musicals; Hammerstein, Oscar, II; Music, popular; Talking motion pictures

---

■ Haywood, Big Bill

Identification: American labor leader
Also known as: William D. Haywood
Born: February 4, 1869, Salt Lake City, Utah
Died: May 18, 1928, Moscow, Soviet Union (now Russia)

A leading force in the Industrial Workers of the World (IWW), Big Bill Haywood organized workers in various industries throughout the early twentieth century. However, in the years after World War I, widespread distrust of labor movements and leftist political groups made the United States an inhospitable place for prominent activists. In 1921, Haywood fled to the Soviet Union, where he remained until his death later in the decade.

William Dudley "Big Bill" Haywood worked as a labor organizer throughout much of his life, serving as a leader of the Western Federation of Miners before cofounding the inclusive Industrial Workers of the World in 1905. During World War I, Haywood, like many other leftists, spoke out against U.S. involvement in the war. He was arrested on charges of sedition and espionage in 1917 and was eventually sentenced to twenty years in prison. However, prior to the start of his sentence in 1921, Haywood left the United States and sought refuge in the newly formed Soviet Union.

Haywood's influence on the labor movement had been sharply curtailed by the time he fled to the Soviet Union. He was no longer a member of the executive committee of the IWW, which itself had nearly collapsed due to legal and social opposition. By the 1920s, his leadership was more symbolic than real in the U.S. labor movement, with some labor activists accusing him of cowardice for fleeing the country. Despite this, the Soviet government welcomed him with open arms.

In November of 1921, Haywood began to organize an American worker-run industrial colony in western

Big Bill Haywood. (Getty Images)

Siberia. The project quickly became a disappointment, as few American workers traveled to the Soviet Union to join the colony and those who did found appalling conditions. With his health deteriorating, Haywood returned to Moscow in 1922 and remained there for the remainder of his life, growing increasingly disillusioned with the Soviet Union.

Impact

Once a prominent labor leader, Big Bill Haywood declined in influence during the 1920s as federal prosecution of leftist leaders sent him into exile. Despite this, Haywood's legacy, the Industrial Workers of the World, survived the subsequent decades, carrying the philosophy and goals of industrial labor activism into the twenty-first century.

John M. Theilmann

Further Reading

Carlson, Peter. *Roughneck: The Life and Times of Big Bill Haywood.* New York: W.W. Norton, 1983.

Dubofsky, Melvyn. *We Shall Be All: A History of the Industrial Workers of the World.* Reprint. Urbana: University of Chicago Press, 2000.

Haywood, William D. *Bill Haywood's Book: The Autobiography of William D. Haywood.* New York: International Publishers, 1929.

See also: Communism; Gompers, Samuel; Palmer raids; Red Scare, The; Soviet Union and North America; Unionism

■ Health care

Following the end of World War I, the United States experienced an economic boom that affected mainstream society as well as nearly all industries. While the strong economy allowed for lifestyle excesses that were often unhealthy, it also spurred the creation of treatments for the major illnesses. Throughout the decade, the delivery of health care improved dramatically, and health insurance plans began to develop, improving the quality and availability of medical care.

The health care challenges and improvements of the 1920s were largely caused by the social and economic changes of the decade. In much of the United States, the period was one of overall prosperity, and constitutional amendments prohibiting alcohol and enfranchising women drastically altered American society. In addition, a move toward urban living brought large numbers of people into the cities. These social changes created new challenges in the realm of health care, for while much of the young, urban population was increasingly conscious of physical appearance and caloric consumption, smoking and drinking were common. As alcohol was prohibited, the liquor sold in speakeasies was at times of suspect origin and could be physically harmful. This new culture's increasing sexual promiscuity also contributed to an increased risk of disease. Despite these new challenges in health care, the widespread prosperity of the period allowed for the development of new hospitals and new treatments, with major medical advances occurring during the period.

Delivery of Health Care

The delivery of medical care in the 1920s varied with location. For the first time in history, more Americans lived in the cities than in the country, and it became advantageous to centralize health care in hospitals and clinics. Hospitals were much less common in the country because people had to travel too far to use them. Consolidating medical services improved the accessibility and quality of care, but medical care costs began to increase as well. Although wages lost while ill were generally considered to be more costly than medical care itself in 1920, this was no longer the case later in the decade. The demand for physicians also increased as rising urban populations necessitated more medical facilities. Despite this, the number of licensed physicians and accredited medical schools, operating under the guidelines set by the American Medical Association (AMA) early in the century, decreased. This further exacerbated the problem of rising medical costs, with the decreased supply and increased demand for medical personnel causing costs to exceed the level that most people could pay.

In an attempt to ease this financial burden, President Calvin Coolidge initiated a research study that became the Committee on the Costs of Medical Care (CCMC). The committee eventually recommended voluntary insurance, but this proposed solution was not supported by the AMA or the American public. Although federal efforts failed, private insurance began to develop near the end of the decade. These early insurance systems focused on large businesses as sources of people to insure. Worksites offered large groups of prospective buyers of insurance, and since employees who missed work effectively cost their employers money, businesses had a vested interest in their employees' health. Although individuals paid for their own insurance in the beginning, employers eventually began to lessen the cost by enrolling employees in group insurance plans funded through payroll deductions. In 1928, General Motors began to provide insurance to 180,000 employees in conjunction with the Metropolitan Life Insurance Company, becoming one of the first employers to provide such health care benefits. Although the primary purpose was to provide for lost wages due to illness or disability, some funds contributed directly to health care costs.

The first health maintenance organization (HMO) was founded in Los Angeles, California, in 1929 by the Ross-Loos Medical Group. Doctors Donald E. Ross and H. Clifford Loos believed that coordination of medical care within a group would improve the quality of the care and that prepayment for services would limit the out-of-pocket cost. Under this plan, employees of the Los Angeles Department of Water and Power were initially insured for $1.50 per month. Preventive care, including vaccination and prenatal care, was a primary focus of this insurance plan. The same year, the first prepaid hospital plan was developed at the Baylor Hospital in Dallas, Texas. Teachers working in Dallas public schools were offered up to twenty-one days of hospital care for six dollars per year. This Baylor Plan would go on to evolve into the Blue Cross system over the course of several decades.

Innovations in Treatment

One of the most important medical breakthroughs in the 1920s did not take place in the United States but had a profound effect on people throughout the world. In 1921, Frederick Banting and his colleagues at the University of Toronto in Canada isolated and purified insulin. In the next year, they successfully tested the substance and confirmed that regular doses of insulin enabled people with diabetes to properly process glucose, thus obtaining the energy needed by the body. The pharmaceutical company Eli Lilly began mass-producing insulin for use throughout North America soon afterward. This discovery allowed for the treatment of diabetes, a condition that had previously been fatal.

Polio, a disease causing the paralysis of muscles, was one of the major infectious diseases of the 1920s. The specific muscles affected varied, and polio was particularly deadly when it paralyzed the muscles used for breathing, particularly the diaphragm. At Children's Hospital in Boston in 1928, an iron lung, a type of ventilator, was used to treat this form of polio for the first time. When treated with an iron lung, the patient was placed in a chamber that covered all but the patient's head. Air was pumped in and out to change the pressure around the body and force air in and out of the lungs. The iron lung was widely used for polio patients into the 1950s, when the development of a successful polio vaccine virtually eliminated the disease in the United States.

A new challenge for hospitals in the United States was created by the rapidly increasing number of automobiles in use, an effect of the nation's overall prosperity. Although these automobiles had engines capable of high speeds, they continued to resemble early automobiles and horse-drawn carriages, frequently having open or cloth tops and lacking seatbelts or other safety mechanisms. This design and the general absence of driving regulations resulted in many injuries and deaths. The injured were taken to hospitals, where doctors were not prepared for such trauma. Additionally, those injured in automobile accidents often had no way to pay for their emergency medical care. Hospitals consequently supported automobile insurance requirements, and in the mid-1920s, Massachusetts became the first state to require insurance for all automobiles.

Disease Prevention

In the 1920s, the leading cause of death in the United States was infectious disease, and antibiotics that could cure such diseases were not yet available for much of the decade. Penicillin was developed by Alexander Fleming in Scotland in 1928, but it would not become widely available for nearly twenty years. With no effective treatments for these diseases, the focus was on prevention in the form of vaccines, which encouraged the body to become immune to a disease through the injection of an inactive form of the bacteria or virus. Throughout the decade, effective vaccinations were developed for diphtheria, pertussis, tetanus, tuberculosis, and scarlet fever. This preventive therapy was particularly beneficial to children, who were most susceptible to these diseases.

Another major disease prevention strategy focused on improving nutrition. Vitamins were first identified as substances needed in the diet early in the century, and they were named with letters as they were discovered. Vitamins D and E, among others, were discovered in the 1920s. Vitamin D was found to cure or prevent rickets, a disorder causing the bones to harden insufficiently. Vitamin E was later found to be an antioxidant that protects the body, although it was not shown to cure or prevent any specific disease. Progress was also made in the mineral needs of the diet. In the previous decade, iodine deficiency had been identified as the cause of goiter, an enlargement of the thyroid gland causing swelling in the neck that was common in the inland areas of the United States. In the 1920s, iodine was added to table salt, and the prevalence of goiter decreased significantly. This interest in and better understanding of vitamins and minerals led to the foundation of the American Institute of Nutrition in 1928.

Although many Americans became interested in nutrition, body image, and health during the 1920s, new foods and an increasingly urban lifestyle presented further challenges. Consumption of sweet soft drinks, candy, and ice cream rose dramatically, particularly at popular social venues such as soda fountains. Fast-food restaurants, including White Castle and A&W, also became widely popular. The consumption of high-calorie foods that were introduced in the 1920s created new health concerns that continued into the future.

Impact

The economic prosperity of the 1920s brought about many advancements in the United States, including in the area of health care. The numbers and quality of hospitals increased over the course of the decade, while many diseases were prevented by immunizations and improved nutrition. New medical treatments transformed diseases that had once been fatal into manageable conditions. The various health insurance programs created during the period made medical care more affordable, and many such programs continued to evolve throughout the subsequent decades. However, the stock market crash of 1929 put an end to the economic growth that helped medicine progress during the 1920s, impeding the development of health care in the United States for a number of years.

Bradley R. A. Wilson

Further Reading

Cooper, Thea, and Arthur Ainsberg. *Breakthrough: Elizabeth Hughes, the Discovery of Insulin, and the Making of a Medical Miracle.* New York: St. Martin's Press, 2010. An account of the development of purified insulin, focusing on 1919 through 1922.

Kennedy, Michael. *A Brief History of Disease, Science, and Medicine: From the Ice Age to the Genome Project.* Mission Viejo, Calif.: Asklepiad Press, 2004. A history of health and health care that discusses the major diseases of the 1920s.

Murray, John E. *Origins of American Health Insurance: A History of Industrial Sickness Funds.* New Haven, Conn.: Yale University Press, 2007. A discussion of the development of health insurance in the United States, including the early insurance plans and prepayment plans of the 1920s.

Starr, Paul. *The Social Transformation of American Medicine: The Rise of a Sovereign Profession and the Making of a Vast Industry.* New York, Basic Books, 1982. A detailed history of medicine, with several chapters covering topics relevant to the 1920s.

Stevens, Rosemary. *In Sickness and in Wealth: American Hospitals in the Twentieth Century.* Rev. ed. Baltimore: Johns Hopkins University Press, 1999. An exploration of the evolution of hospitals in the United States, featuring a section on the 1920s.

See also: Band-Aids; Baylor Plan; Cancer; Food, Drug, and Insecticide Administration, U.S.; Insulin; Iron lung; Polio; Sexually transmitted diseases; Vitamin D discovery

■ Hearst, William Randolph

Identification: American newspaper magnate
Born: April 29, 1863, San Francisco, California
Died: August 14, 1951, Beverly Hills, California

William Randolph Hearst was among the most influential media figures in the United States during the 1920s, presiding over a publishing empire that produced newspapers, magazines, and books. Throughout the decade, Hearst also successfully established himself in the fields of radio and film, though his long-held political ambitions were thwarted.

Born into a wealthy mining family, William Randolph Hearst first established his newspaper empire in the 1880s. His newspapers pioneered so-called yellow journalism, using blaring headlines and sensationalist stories to sell copies and influence public opinion. Hearst actively managed the reporting style and editorial tone of his newspapers, maintaining a populist perspective and an increasingly America-first attitude concerning foreign affairs as relations among European powers deteriorated in the 1910s. By the 1920s, Hearst's newspaper empire had reached its zenith, including numerous newspapers based in major cities. In addition, he owned the national news agency International News Service, a book publishing business, and several national magazines, including *Harper's Bazaar*, *Good Housekeeping*, *Cosmopolitan*, and *Town and Country*. Recognizing the future of communications, Hearst began to purchase radio stations in 1928. He had also formed his own motion picture company, Cosmopolitan Productions, late in the previous decade, and it went on to produce several major films over the course of the 1920s.

Political Aspirations

While Hearst was a dedicated business executive, he also had political aspirations. He represented New York in the U.S. House of Representatives from 1903 to 1907, but he was defeated in mayoral and gubernatorial elections that same decade. In the 1920s, however, Hearst resumed his attempts to gain political influence. His 1922 attempt to become governor of

William Randolph Hearst. (NY Daily News via Getty Images)

New York was unsuccessful, the Democratic nomination and office going instead to Al Smith, as was his effort to secure the Democratic senatorial nomination the same year. In his final bout of political ambition, he embarked on a campaign to influence the Democratic Party's presidential nomination in 1924, widely promoting his favored candidate and waging war against political rivals in his newspapers. This attempt, too, was unsuccessful. While Hearst's influence over the media was a powerful tool, it had engendered animosity against him over the years, effectively sabotaging his political career. His widely known extramarital relationship with the film star Marion Davies and reputation for extravagance further hampered his political aspirations.

Hearst Castle

As a powerful figure in the entertainment industry, Hearst regularly entertained for the Hollywood set and other celebrities, including writers, aviators, and even politicians. Much of his entertaining was done at his 240,000-acre estate in coastal California, near San Simeon. The construction of Hearst Castle, as the estate was commonly known, had begun in 1919 and continued throughout the 1920s under the supervision of architect Julia Morgan. The estate contained hundreds of rooms, indoor and outdoor swimming pools, lush gardens, and the world's largest private zoo. A collector of art and antiquities, Hearst filled the castle with paintings, rare books, antique architectural elements, and classical statuary.

Events at Hearst Castle were very popular with celebrities and were discussed at length in the media. Sometimes, however, Hearst's parties received public attention for negative reasons. On November 15, 1924, Hearst hosted a party on his opulent yacht, the *Oneida*, in celebration of film producer Thomas Ince's birthday. Various movie stars were in attendance, including actors Charlie Chaplin and Marion Davies. Ince became ill during the party, dying the next day of a heart ailment. Although Ince's death was ruled natural, rumors of foul play abounded, reflecting Hearst's somewhat questionable public reputation.

Impact

With the onset of the Great Depression, Hearst's vast media empire and personal holdings became a financial drain. Undergoing significant reorganization during the Depression, the Hearst Corporation nevertheless survived the period, enduring into the next century. After Hearst's death, his estate at San Simeon was donated to the state of California, becoming one of its leading tourist attractions. His legacy further endures through Orson Welles's classic film *Citizen Kane* (1941), which features a protagonist based loosely on Hearst and a fictionalized version of Hearst Castle.

Howard Bromberg

Further Reading

Davies, Marion. *The Times We Had: Life with William Randolph Hearst.* Reprint. New York: Ballantine Books, 1985. A memoir written by Hearst's longtime companion Marion Davies and featuring anecdotes about his life during the 1920s.

Kastner, Victoria, and Victoria Garagliano. *Hearst's San Simeon: The Gardens and the Land.* New York: Harry N. Abrams, 2009. An illustrated history and tour of Hearst's estate written by its official historian.

Nasaw, David. *The Chief: The Life of William Randolph Hearst.* New York: First Mariner Books, 2001. An in-depth portrait of Hearst that describes the contrast between Hearst's personal life, in which Nasaw presents him as shy and ambivalent, and his business empire.

Pizzitola, Louis. *Hearst Over Hollywood: Power, Passion, and Propaganda in the Movies.* New York: Columbia University Press, 2002. A discussion of Hearst's pioneering efforts in movie production.

Procter, Ben H. *William Randolph Hearst: The Later Years, 1911–1951.* New York: Oxford University Press, 2007. An account of the last half of Hearst's life, including the 1920s, that recounts Hearst's influence in the media as well as his thwarted political aspirations.

See also: Chaplin, Charlie; Elections of 1924, U.S.; Hearst Castle; Ince, Thomas H.; Magazines; Newspapers, U.S.; Radio; Smith, Alfred E.; Talking motion pictures

■ Hearst Castle

An estate located in coastal California, Hearst Castle consists of a mansion, also commonly known as the castle, as well as guesthouses and expansive grounds. Built for the wealthy newspaper publisher William Randolph Hearst and designed by architect Julia Morgan, the castle was one of the premier destinations for celebrities of the 1920s, serving as host to writers, politicians, and Hollywood legends.

In the late 1910s, newspaper publishing magnate William Randolph Hearst inherited 250,000 acres of land along a remote stretch of the California coast between San Francisco and Los Angeles, near San Simeon. The property included a large, rocky hill that Hearst called La Cuesta Encantada, or the Enchanted Hill. In 1919, Hearst began to collaborate closely with architect Julia Morgan, who designed a multibuilding estate to be set atop the hill. The centerpiece of this estate was the main residence, Casa Grande, which was surrounded by guesthouses, pools, and gardens. The construction of the estate was ongoing throughout the 1920s.

The Grounds

The grounds of the estate consist of 123 acres and encompass three guest cottages, outdoor and indoor swimming pools, elaborate gardens, statuary, tennis courts, and Casa Grande. The first of Morgan's buildings to be constructed, the guest cottages each contain at least ten rooms and are of Spanish Renaissance design. Known as Casa Del Sol, Casa Del Mar, and Casa Del Monte, the cottages were named for the view from their respective windows: the sunset, the ocean, and the mountains. The outdoor swimming pool, named after the Roman god Neptune, was constructed beginning in 1924 and boasts marble flooring and Greco-Roman architecture. Another noted feature of the grounds was the 2,000-acre zoo, first established in 1923. Animals were of interest to Hearst, and he amassed a significant collection of nonnative and exotic animals to occupy his menagerie and large grazing enclosures. While the zoo would be dismantled over the course of the following decades, some of its animals and their offspring made the estate grounds their permanent home.

The Castle

Construction of the main residence, Casa Grande, began in 1922. Casa Grande consists of more than one hundred rooms and is of Mediterranean Revival design, mixing Spanish Renaissance, Gothic, and other styles. While some of the architectural elements were designed by Morgan to resemble such styles, many are European antiques. For example, the main entrance features stone and grillwork from a fifteenth-century Spanish convent. The castle serves as a backdrop for Hearst's extensive art collection, and many of the rarest pieces are showcased in the largest room of the residence, known as the Assembly Room.

Much of the interior is decorated in the dramatic Gothic style. Hearst conducted most of his business in the vast Gothic study on the third floor, which features an ornate barrel-vaulted ceiling. The library houses four thousand books, many of which are rare editions, as well as Hearst's collection of classical pottery. Casa Grande is complete with a private cinema in which, during Hearst's lifetime, first-run films were viewed twice nightly for staff and for guests. The castle's kitchen and pantry were designed to accommodate the large number of guests invited to the estate.

Guests

Hearst entertained at the castle often and lavishly, with many influential figures of the 1920s gracing the guest list. Guests were drawn from all spheres of influence and included powerful Hollywood producers such as Louis B. Mayer, cultural icons such as Charles Lindbergh, and numerous film stars. Evenings at the castle adhered to a relatively fixed schedule. Dinner was a formal affair, with guests first gathering in the Assembly Room to amuse themselves at the grand piano or with games. Hearst would enter dramatically and circulate among the guests until dinner was announced. Since the journey to the estate was lengthy, most guests stayed overnight. The equipment, facilities, and clothing necessary to enjoy sports or recreation were available to guests. Feeding the zoo animals was a popular pastime, and entertainment frequently consisted of masquerade balls or theatrical productions based upon guest participation.

Impact

Work on the estate continued into the 1940s, with several areas of the castle undergoing remodeling or other alterations. In 1957, Hearst Castle was donated to the state of California, becoming a state park and museum offering tours to the public. With its intact furnishings and art collections, the estate serves as a window into Hearst's world and the culture, politics, and society of the 1920s.

Amanda Bahr-Evola

Further Reading

Kastner, Victoria, and Victoria Garagliano. *Hearst Castle: The Biography of a Country House.* New York: Henry N. Abrams, 2000. An illustrated examination of the creation and maintenance of the castle, including discussion of Hearst's powerful position in American society of the 1920s.

Lewis, Oscar. *Fabulous San Simeon: A History of the Hearst Castle.* San Francisco: California Historical Society, 1958. A historical narrative of Hearst's estate.

Loe, Nancy E. *Hearst Castle: The Official Pictorial Guide.* Santa Barbara, Calif.: Companion Press, 1991. Contains images of the castle and its contents, detailed context for the images, and a timeline of the construction.

Longstreth, Richard W. *Julia Morgan, Architect.* Berkeley, Calif.: Berkeley Architectural Heritage Association, 1986. A biography of the estate's architect.

Winslow, Carleton M., Jr., Taylor Coffman, and Nickola L. Frye. *The Enchanted Hill.* Los Angeles: Rosebud Books, 1980. Features biographical information about Hearst and detailed photographs, as well as a chronology, glossary, and guide to the estate collections.

See also: Architecture; Hearst, William Randolph; Newspapers, U.S.

■ Hemingway, Ernest

Identification: American writer
Born: July 21, 1899, Oak Park, Illinois
Died: July 2, 1961, Ketchum, Idaho

Ernest Hemingway was an author and journalist known for his characteristically minimalist style of prose. Rising to prominence in the 1920s, he published several of his most notable works during the period, including the novels The Sun Also Rises *and* A Farewell to Arms. *An expatriate living in Paris for much of the decade, Hemingway chronicled the lives and anxieties of the lost generation.*

Raised in Oak Park, Illinois, Ernest Miller Hemingway defied the wishes of his parents, who encouraged him to enroll in college, and took a position as a cub reporter with the *Kansas City Star* shortly after the United States entered into World War I. Hemingway joined the Red Cross in 1918 and was stationed as an ambulance worker in Italy. Within two months of his arrival, he was severely wounded, an experience he would recapture in his 1929 novel *A Farewell to Arms*.

In 1921, Hemingway married Hadley Richardson, and the two moved to Paris not long after. Paris in the 1920s was partly characterized by its large American expatriate community and its flourishing artistic community. There, Hemingway worked as a foreign correspondent for the *Toronto Star*, further developing his clear, reportorial prose. A letter of introduction from writer Sherwood Anderson, along with his natural inquisitiveness and charisma, gave Hemingway access to Paris literary and artistic circles, and he met and befriended such luminaries as writers Gertrude Stein, Ford Madox Ford, and Ezra Pound. Hemingway offered his short fiction to these writers for criticism and became a volunteer editor for Ford's influential small literary magazine *The Transatlantic Review*.

Early Stories

As Hemingway made contacts with the Paris literati, he quickly became known and respected for his work ethic as well as the minimalist aesthetic of his early stories. In 1923, he published a small print run of *Three Stories and Ten Poems*. The following year, he published a limited run of a short collection

Ernest Hemingway. (AP Photo)

of vignettes and very brief sketches titled *in our time*. Hemingway was able to secure publication of a full book of stories in 1925. Again titled *In Our Time*, the collection was published by Sherwood Anderson's publisher, Boni & Liveright, and contained new stories, some that had originally appeared in various magazines, two stories from *Three Stories and Ten Poems*, and the entirety of *in our time*. Although the book did not gain widespread popularity, other writers and critics praised the innovative techniques and realism of the stories. While stories such as "The End of Something" and "The Three Day Blow" address relationships in a realistic and lucid light, others such as "Soldier's Home" and "Big Two-Hearted River" focus on the difficulty faced by combat veterans reintegrating into peacetime life. A number of the stories feature protagonist Nick Adams. Based at least partly on Hemingway himself, Adams would go on to appear in many short stories throughout Hemingway's career.

The Sun Also Rises

Although the novella *The Torrents of Spring* (1926) was Hemingway's first piece of long fiction published, it was written after the completion of *The Sun Also Rises*.

Encouraged by his friend and fellow expatriate writer F. Scott Fitzgerald, Hemingway sought to end his contract with Boni & Liveright and instead seek publication with Charles Scriber's Sons, Fitzgerald's publisher. Since *Torrents* was primarily a satirical parody of Boni & Liveright's star author Sherwood Anderson, the two hoped that Boni & Liveright would reject the book, thereby breaking Hemingway's contract and freeing him to publish with Scribner's. The ploy worked, and Scribner's published both *The Torrents of Spring* and *The Sun Also Rises* in 1926.

The Sun Also Rises is considered by many to be one of the foremost chronicles of the lost generation. The term "lost generation" itself was coined by Hemingway's epigram in the prefatory pages; he attributes the quote to writer Gertrude Stein. Additionally, some of the characters and events that occur in the novel are based loosely on people and occurrences from Hemingway's life, and the book gained initial notoriety as a roman à clef.

The novel is narrated by World War I veteran and foreign correspondent Jake Barnes, an American expatriate in Paris. With several friends, he makes a trip to Spain, where he divides his time between fishing in the mountains and attending the festival and bullfights in Pamplona. He is in love with Brett Ashley, a former nurse from England. Each has been wounded by the war; Jake, physically wounded, is impotent, and Brett, who lost the love of her life in the war, must constantly make men love her in order to feel secure. Jake's acquaintance and traveling companion Robert Cohn, who has also fallen in love with Brett, represents an absurd and outdated way of life through his romantic pursuit of her.

Published eight years after the end of World War I, the novel captures the lives of expatriate Americans and Europeans striving to overcome the war's legacy and make sense of their lives. While completing the novel and editing galleys, Hemingway's life in some ways reflected those of his characters, as his first marriage disintegrated. In 1927, he married fellow expatriate Pauline Pfeiffer.

Men Without Women and *A Farewell to Arms*

While the success of *The Sun Also Rises* made Hemingway a renowned novelist, he continued to publish short stories throughout the 1920s. In addition to appearing in various magazines, several of his most famous stories were published in the 1927 collection *Men Without Women*. These stories include "Hills Like White Elephants," a brief study in modernist symbolism about a pregnant woman trying to decide whether to abort her unborn child, and "In Another Country," in which the wounded narrator, likely Nick Adams, goes through physical rehabilitation. "Now I Lay Me" further explores Nick's inability to adjust to postwar life. Hemingway expanded upon many of these stories' themes and ideas in *A Farewell to Arms*, published in 1929.

Another semiautobiographical novel, *A Farewell to Arms* tells of an American, Frederic Henry, who serves in the Italian ambulance corps during World War I. Frederic meets a young Scottish nurse, Catherine Barkley, with whom he falls in love after he is badly wounded. Initially, Frederic is naïve and without purpose, while Catherine, having lost her fiancé early in the war, is pragmatic and realistic. After the Italian defeat at Caporetto, Frederic deserts, making his own "separate peace," and he and Catherine flee to Switzerland. The novel, ultimately tragic in tone, represents Frederic's initiation into the fallen and shattered postwar, modern world.

Impact

The years following World War I saw the publication of many literary works chronicling the war and its impact on people and society, including John Dos Passos's *Three Soldiers* (1921), Erich Maria Remarque's *All Quiet on the Western Front* (1928), and Robert Graves's *Good-Bye to All That* (1929). The works of Ernest Hemingway, too, defined this postwar period, bringing to light the anxiety and alienation felt by the lost generation. Hemingway's sparse language, understated dialogue, laconic delivery, minimalist style, and modernist sensibilities, as demonstrated in these works, became incredibly influential in the 1920s and the following decades. In light of his contributions to the field of literature, Hemingway was awarded the Nobel Prize in 1954.

Scott D. Yarbrough

Further Reading

Baker, Carlos. *Hemingway: The Writer as Artist.* 4th ed. Princeton, N.J.: Princeton University Press, 1980. A critical analysis of Hemingway's work that includes some biographical details.

Conrad, Winston. *Hemingway's France: Images of the Lost Generation.* Emeryville, Calif.: Woodford Press, 2000. A narrative of Hemingway's time in France, accompanied by historical photographs.

Hemingway, Ernest. *A Moveable Feast.* New York: Scribner, 1964. A memoir of Hemingway's life in Paris in the 1920s.

Reynolds, Michael S. *Hemingway: The Paris Years.* Reprint. New York: W.W. Norton, 1999. A biography focusing on Hemingway's career and personal life during the early and mid-1920s.

Wagner-Martin, Linda, ed. *Ernest Hemingway: Seven Decades of Criticism.* East Lansing: Michigan State University Press, 1998. A collection of critical essays on Hemingway's works, some written by his 1920s contemporaries.

See also: Anderson, Sherwood; *Farewell to Arms, A;* Fitzgerald, F. Scott; Literature in the United States; Lost Generation; Pound, Ezra; Stein, Gertrude; *Sun Also Rises, The*

■ *Hester v. United States*

The Case: U.S. Supreme Court decision establishing the open fields doctrine that clarified and redefined an individual's rights under the Fourth Amendment to privacy and unreasonable searches and seizures

Date: Decided on May 5, 1924

In this Prohibition-era case, the Supreme Court ruled that the protection of the Fourth Amendment to unreasonable searches and seizures of "'persons, houses, papers, and effects' is not extended to open fields."

After the passage of the Eighteenth Amendment, which made the sale, manufacture, and transportation of alcohol illegal, the demand for alcohol increased sharply, and illegal distilleries proliferated in order to provide alcohol to individuals and speakeasies (illegal bars). The widespread and lucrative trade in illegal alcohol prompted officials to increase efforts to enforce Prohibition laws. Investigations included observation of and surprise visits to suspected distilleries.

Law enforcement officers visited the family property of Mr. Hester to investigate possible violations of Prohibition laws. The officers observed Hester selling illegal alcohol outside a house and began to approach him. Hester ran across his family's open field, smashing bottles as he went. He was apprehended, the broken bottles were recovered, and the officers

identified the contents as illegal alcohol. Mr. Hester was convicted of concealing illegal distilled alcohol, and he appealed on the contention that law enforcement did not have a search or arrest warrant, which rendered the evidence inadmissible under the Fourth Amendment.

Hester's appeal made its way to the Supreme Court, which ruled against him, citing that limits to the protections of the Fourth Amendment to people in their "persons, houses, papers, and effects" do not extend to open fields. The police, therefore, did not need a search warrant, and Hester's conviction was upheld.

Impact

Hester v. United States defined and limited the scope of unreasonable searches and seizures under the Fourth Amendment. The Supreme Court clarified that the words "persons, houses, papers, and effects" did not apply to open fields, and therefore law enforcement did not need a warrant before observing and ultimately arresting Hester for possessing and concealing alcohol. Later cases involving the open field doctrine have helped to further clarify the limits of the Fourth Amendment by defining "reasonable expectations of privacy" for outdoor activities. The debate is ongoing, with technological innovations such as telescopic lenses, aerial photography, and thermal imaging continuing to push the limits of privacy.

Eric T. Bellone

Further Reading

Clancy, Thomas K. *The Fourth Amendment: Its History and Interpretation.* Durham, N.C.: Carolina Academic Press, 2008.

Sinclair, Andrew. *Era of Excess: A Social History of the Prohibition Movement.* New York: Harper & Row, 1964.

See also: Bathtub gin; Hoover, J. Edgar; Organized crime; Prohibition; "Roaring Twenties"; Speakeasies

■ Historiography

While the 1920s was not a time of great innovation in U.S. historiography, a large number of important historical works were published during the decade, including new perspectives on the study of the history and the causes of World War I.

Many of the historiographical concerns of the 1920s were continuations of ideas and controversies of earlier periods. Frederick Jackson Turner's frontier thesis, which emphasized the positive impact of the American frontier experience, remained a major paradigm. While the decade saw an increase in African American historians, most white historians tended to minimize the issue of race, and very few of them were critical of the Jim Crow segregation laws in the southern states. Having lived through the destructive war in Europe, a significant number of historians became preoccupied with the problem of how and why the war had begun.

Causes of World War I
During the early years of the decade, most American historians held that Germany and the Austro-Hungarian Empire were solely responsible for the outbreak of the war, while the Allies were defenders of democracy and opponents of brutal aggression. The noted historian Carlton Hayes, for instance, published *A Brief History of the Great War* (1920), which emphasized the nefarious impact of Prussia's extreme militarism and nationalism. However, Hayes argued that the nationalism of other countries also contributed to the "international anarchy" of the time and accused author and propagandist John Buchan and others of creating a climate of "Germanophobia."

By the late 1920s, a large number of academic articles and books were proposing a revisionist interpretation that blamed all participating counties more or less equally. This change was due in part to the view that the victors had been overly harsh in their treatment of Germany and to the explosion of new information from governmental archives and memoirs. The most scholarly and influential work of moderate revisionism was Sidney B. Fay's *The Origins of the World War* (1928), which argued that the public had been given "a great deal of silly propaganda" during the war and the "greatest single underlying cause of the War was the system of secret alliances." Because of their conflicting goals and suspicions of one another, members of each alliance "felt bound to support each other, even in matters where they had no direct interest."

Numerous historians took issue with Fay's analysis. Bernadotte Schmitt wrote a number of scholarly articles arguing that German leaders pushed the Austro-Hungarian Empire into making demands on Serbia, thereby precipitating the war. He won the Pulitzer Prize in history for his 1930 masterpiece *The Coming of the War, 1914*. Fay reviewed the book favorably in the *Journal of Modern History*, finding that Schmitt minimized the millenarianism and mistakes of the Allies but conceding that the matter could be a question of perspective.

This polite disagreement was not the norm, however, and historical debates on the causes of World War I were often heated and polemical. One of the most extreme examples of revisionism was Oklahoma senator Robert Latham Owen's *The Russian Imperial Conspiracy, 1892–1914* (1926), which placed almost all of the blame on the czar's government. Similarly, revisionist historian Harry Elmer Barnes believed that he had been "taken in" by Allied propaganda and wrote *The Genesis of the World War* (1926) in response, in which he argued that the war was primarily the result of a Franco-Russian plot to destroy Germany.

The historical debate over the causes of World War I was politically significant. In arguing that all the powers were responsible for the war, revisionist writers such as Fay and Barnes rejected the validity of Article 231 of the Treaty of Versailles, which blamed Germany for the war and thus provided justification for the large reparations that Germany was required to pay. These revisionists also suggested that U.S. participation in the war had been a mistake, a view that would promote the cause of isolationism during the subsequent decade.

The New History
In his book *The New History* (1912), James Harvey Robinson insisted that historians should concentrate on the study of social conditions, cultural changes, and economics, rather than facts about great leaders, political events, and wars. An unapologetic presentist, Robinson believed that historians should promote Progressive reform and borrow liberally from the methods and theories of sociology, anthropology, and political science. He had a reputation for criticizing Christianity and conservative traditions, while praising science and the idea of world government. In 1929, fellow professional historians recognized the impact of his work by electing him president of the American Historical Association.

The well-known historian Charles A. Beard generally agreed with Robinson's point of view, though he rarely used the term "new history." A self-described socialist, Beard was clearly influenced by Marxist theory of class conflict; he argued that the conflict between northeastern industrialists and planters in the South had been the principal cause of the Civil War. In 1919, Beard joined Robinson and other like-minded intellectuals to establish the New School, which would have no grades, no degrees, and no administration. This utopian experiment ended in 1921, when the school's founders left and it was converted into an adult education center.

Another leading figure of the new history movement was archaeologist and historian James Henry Breasted, the first American to earn a Ph.D. in Egyptology. He originated the term "Fertile Crescent" and was one of the earliest American scholars to consider the Middle East as a key part of the foundation and development of Western civilization. Breasted spent much of the 1920s traveling and acquiring antiquities for the Art Institute of Chicago and the Oriental Institute of the University of Chicago. He was elected president of the American Historical Association in 1928.

Race and the South

The two most prominent African American historians of the decade were W. E. B. Du Bois and Carter G. Woodson. Du Bois, the first African American to earn a Ph.D. from Harvard, spent most of the decade in political activism, but he found time to write two major books: *Africa: Its Place in Modern History* (1930) and *Africa: Its Geography, People, and Products* (1930). Woodson is often called the "father of black history"; he began the *Journal of Negro History* in 1916, founded the African American publishing company Associated Publishers in 1920, and in 1926, established Negro History Week, now better known as Black History Month. He was an enthusiastic collector of original African American documents and published at least eight books during the 1920s, including *History of the Negro Church* (1921), *The Negro in Our History* (1922), *Free Negro Owners of Slaves in 1830* (1924), *Negro Makers of History* (1928), and *African Myths and Proverbs* (1928).

Most white historians of the period tended to ignore or minimize the African American perspective, and many were sympathetic to the so-called Dunning School. A proponent of white supremacy, historian William A. Dunning strongly criticized the Radical Republicans' attempts to improve conditions for African Americans during Reconstruction, the period from 1863 to 1877. He defended the Jim Crow system of racial segregation and maintained that African Americans had proven themselves incapable of the

responsibilities of equal citizenship. Important books in the Dunning tradition include Thomas Staples's *Reconstruction in Arkansas, 1867–1874* (1923), E. Merton Coulter's *Civil War and Readjustment in Kentucky* (1926), and Claude Bowers's *The Tragic Era* (1929).

The most prominent of the pro–southern white historians was Ulrich B. Phillips, whose 1928 article "The Central Theme of Southern History" claimed that the desire to maintain regional racial dominance had kept white southerners united for centuries. Phillips did much pioneering research in archives, plantation records, and unpublished manuscripts. In *Life and Labor in the Old South* (1929), he contended that slavery, while economically ineffective, remained a valid means of racial control. In his view, slavery had been a benevolent institution and slaveholders had helped to "civilize" the slaves by providing them with housing, food, medical care, and security in their old age.

Other Prominent Historians

One of the most influential works of the decade was Vernon Louis Parrington's *Main Currents in American Thought* (1927), which won the Pulitzer Prize for historical writing in 1928. The three volumes divide U.S. intellectual history into three phases—Calvinistic pessimism, Romantic optimism, and mechanistic pessimism—and focus on the fortunes of democratic idealism throughout these phases. Parrington admitted to being "liberal rather than conservative, Jeffersonian rather than Federalist," viewing the nation's history as a battle between capitalist oppressors and hardworking farmers and laborers.

The 1920s saw a number of other important works in the field of social and cultural history. John Franklin Jameson, an avid collector of primary documents and one of the founders of the American Historical Association, wrote *The American Revolution Considered as a Social Movement* (1926), which provoked considerable debate. Carl L. Becker, a liberal writer with a taste for irony, published three major works: *The Declaration of Independence: A Study in the History of Political Ideas* (1922), *Our Great Experiment in Democracy* (1924), and *The Spirit of '76* (1926). Frederick Jackson Turner, famous for his thesis about the impact of the frontier experience on U.S. culture and institutions, won a Pulitzer Prize for his essay collection *The Frontier in American History* (1921). Charles Homer Haskins published two major works, *The Rise of Universities* (1923) and *The Renaissance of the Twelfth*

Century (1927), asserting that certain important social changes in medieval Europe had been overlooked.

A number of young historians launched distinguished careers during the 1920s. Harvard professor Arthur Schlesinger's *New Viewpoints in American History* (1922) included the influential essay "The Significance of Jacksonian Democracy," which challenged Turner's frontier thesis by focusing on the democratic movement in industrialized eastern cities; in 1927, he began editing the twelve-volume *History of American Life*, the last volume of which would be published in 1944. Will Durant, an outstanding popularizer of philosophy and history, published the first edition of his *Story of Philosophy* in 1925. Allan Nevins, an extremely prolific author of narrative accounts, published at least six books during the decade, while the similarly prolific Samuel Eliot Morison published the first edition of his *Oxford History of the United States* (1927).

Impact

The 1920s was not a decade of spectacular new theories or interpretations in the field of historiography, but rather a period of maturity and consolidation. The study of social history, especially the African American experience, became more prominent than in earlier periods. When writing about race relations, the majority of white historians appeared to hold conservative views and tolerate the existence of racial segmentation in the South; in other areas, however, the most influential historians of the decade tended to sympathize with Progressive ideology. Despite the strong emphasis on social history, topics relating to war and politics were not neglected, and the decade's most bitterly contested historical controversy was about which countries and leaders were most responsible for the outbreak of World War I.

Thomas Tandy Lewis

Further Reading

Adler, Selig. "The War-Guilt Question and American Disillusionment, 1918–1928." *Journal of Modern History* 23, no. 1 (March, 1951): 1–28. Reviews a selection of articles and books on who was responsible for World War I.

Banner, James M., Jr., ed. *A Century of American Historiography*. New York: Bedford/St. Martin's, 2010. A collection of fifteen historiographical essays about major topics in U.S. history.

Hofstadter, Richard. *The Progressive Historians: Turner, Beard, Parrington*. Reprint. Chicago: University of Chicago Press, 1979. A standard historiographical work with substantial material about the 1920s.

Novick, Peter. *That Noble Dream: The "Objectivity Question" and the American Historical Profession*. New York: Cambridge University Press, 1998. Examines the longstanding debate about whether historians can and should attempt to describe the past objectively.

Smith, John David. *Slavery, Race, and American History: Historical Conflict, Trends, and Method, 1866–1953*. Armonk, N.Y.: M. E. Sharp, 1999. A collection of essays about the history and historiography of U.S. race relations, including several essays devoted to the 1920s.

Thorpe, Earl E. *Black Historians: A Critique*. New York: Morrow, 1971. Essays about the careers and challenges of major African American historians.

See also: Du Bois, W. E. B.; Durant, Will; *Frontier in American History, The;* Negro History Week; Reed, John; Social sciences; *Ten Days That Shook the World*

■ Hobbies and recreation

The prosperity of the 1920s gave Americans the chance to devote more time to recreation and leisure, opening up the pursuit of a wide variety of hobbies and other pastimes, including movie watching, road trips, and sports.

The 1920s, also called the Roaring Twenties or the Jazz Age, was a decade characterized by prosperity. As the economy developed and the middle class grew wealthier, many Americans wanted to put the horrors and privations of World War I, labor problems, and a deadly influenza epidemic behind them and enjoy their lives. The increase in American recreation at this time was greatly influenced by three major developments that became popular leisure pursuits: motion pictures, radio, and automobiles.

Movies and Radio

Going to the movies was one of the most popular entertainment activities outside of the home. During the 1920s, movie studios produced more than seven hundred full-length films per year. This necessitated the creation of more movie theater chains, such as Loews, Metro-Goldwyn-Mayer (MGM), and United Artists. The motion picture theater buildings became increasingly luxurious and elegant and were called "movie palaces." Many theaters continued to combine live vaudeville acts with newsreels, shorts, and feature films that were changed weekly. The developing motion picture industry also helped create movie stars, such as Rudolph Valentino, who became famous for his role in *The Sheik* (1926), and Walt Disney's animated character Mickey Mouse, who first appeared in *Plane Crazy* (1928), the same year Disney-based toys made their debut.

Film producer Walt Disney's creations have become some of the most recognizable icons of American popular culture. It was Disney who perfected the concept of licensing his characters and products to toy companies. Disney merchandised toys that were based on both cartoon and live-action characters in his films and television programs, creating a mass-marketing blueprint that remains successful in the twenty-first century.

In 1920, Pittsburgh radio station KDKA transmitted the first commercial radio broadcast, initiating one of the most popular sources of entertainment, eventually influencing most of the population. By the mid-1920s, telephone lines made simultaneous live broadcasting (known as networking) possible, relaying baseball games, concerts, and commercial programs around the nation. The radio became a family entertainment, as families could gather around it for nightly broadcasts. By 1929, more than six hundred stations regularly broadcast commercial programs to more than twelve million households, which amounted to over 40 percent of all American homes.

The Impact of the Automobile

More than any other invention, the automobile made it possible for Americans to expand their opportunities for leisure. The 1920s brought changes to the automotive industry and infrastructure projects that made the automobile a more accessible means of transportation for many Americans. More individuals were able to purchase an automobile on installment plans, and cars were now available in many price ranges. With the Federal Highway Act of 1921, road construction dramatically increased to more than ten thousand miles of road per year, and a national highway numbering system began, expanding in 1925 to include local road and directional signs. In addition, the first automobile tunnel, the Holland Tunnel, opened in 1927 to connect Manhattan and New Jersey.

Auto vacations soon involved sightseeing, with visits to newly emerging pastimes such as amusement parks, circuses, traveling chautauquas (adult education initiatives), national parks, and sporting events. In turn, the growing number of travelers created the need for many hospitality services and businesses, such as service stations, roadside camps, diners, and drive-in restaurants. Grocery chains expanded, and by 1929, advertising billboards became permanent fixtures on highways.

For many rural inhabitants, driving one's car to Sunday worship services served as a form of recreation and socialization, while large tent revivals and traveling chautauquas served as forms of leisure for others; some of the revival meetings led by evangelists Billy Sunday and Aimee Semple McPherson gained nationwide media attention.

Amusement parks continued to flourish in the 1920s, with more than fifteen hundred parks reported to be in operation at the beginning of the decade. Popular amusements at these parks included Ferris wheels, merry-go-rounds, roller skating, dancing, shooting galleries, arcades, and sideshows. At the best-known 1920s amusement park, Coney Island in New York City, the Cyclone roller coaster was added in 1927, and daily attendance at the park was estimated at 800,000.

Traveling circuses, once a popular form of rural entertainment, went into decline. To stay in business, one circus, Ringling Brothers, merged with the Barnum and Bailey Circus in 1919 to become the largest circus of its time and continued to perform at outdoor sports stadiums and county fairs, as did other independent, smaller circuses. The decline of both the circus and the chautauqua was due mainly to the rise of movies, radio, and the automobile.

Professional and Amateur Sports

One of the most popular leisure activities in the 1920s was sports. It is reported that by 1929, amateur baseball leagues had 241,766 players, while another 300,000 reported participated in American Legion teams. Interest in the national pastime grew through the exploits of baseball celebrities such as Babe Ruth, whose career was carefully followed in newspapers, magazines, and radio. Meanwhile, cities provided baseball fields for youth to play in nonleague sandlot games; larger cities such as Chicago and San Francisco were actually unable to meet the demand for enough fields for those who wanted to play. At the

Fred Astaire and his sister Adele playing a game of Mah-Jongg. (Hulton Archive/Getty Images)

college level, over 10 percent of enrolled students played either intercollegiate or intramural baseball. In fact, baseball was ranked fourth among collegiate sport participation as more students took part in basketball, football, and tennis.

An African American baseball league was first formed in 1920, known as the National Negro Baseball League, with teams in Kansas City, Indianapolis, Dayton, Chicago, Detroit, and St. Louis. A rival league, known as the Eastern Colored League, was established in 1923, with teams in cities including Philadelphia, Brooklyn, Baltimore, and Atlantic City. A world series was held between the two leagues from 1924 to 1927, but the leagues faced financial difficulty and folded. A new Negro National League was later formed in 1933, and the Negro American League was formed in 1937.

Amateur sports grew in popularity as more municipalities and colleges expanded their playing facilities and recreation areas to accommodate the growing demand for sports facilities. The athlete who characterized the true spirit of 1920s amateurism was golfer Bobby Jones, a national hero whose charismatic appeal sparked an interest in golf, both in amateur participation in the sport and in the construction of new courses.

An important side effect of the popularity of sports was the reintroduction of daylight saving time. Setting their clocks one hour ahead during the summer gave Americans an extra hour of daylight for recreation and leisure activities.

Fads and Toys

Many fads swept the nation during the 1920s. Among the most popular were dance marathons, Mah-Jongg, crossword puzzles, miniature golf, yo-yos, model electric trains, roller skating, and parlor games. The game of Mah-Jongg took the country by storm after 1922, when American engineer Joseph Babcock modified the rules of the ancient Chinese game. Within one year, more than 1.5 million sets were sold, and Mah-Jongg clubs sprang up around the country.

Another fad that achieved national popularity was the crossword puzzle, originally carried in only a few newspapers. In 1924, Simon & Schuster published the first collection of crossword puzzles bound in a book, with a pencil attached for convenience. Within one year, the book sold one million copies, and the fad continued to grow.

Social dancing was enjoyed by people of all ages and was offered at community centers, social clubs, fraternal lodges, public parks, private country clubs, and homes, often with just a phonograph or radio for music. Public dancing was also available at resorts, hotels, and commercial dance halls. The dominant dance craze of the period was the Charleston, first introduced in 1923 and danced to jazz music, which also became extremely popular in the 1920s

Dolls with dollhouses and miniature kitchen appliances gained popularity throughout the 1920s, introducing a new merchandising bonanza. In 1923, Beatrice Alexander obtained a small business loan to establish the Alexander Doll Company in New York City, where it quickly earned a reputation for its elegant Madame Alexander dolls. Also in 1923, Alexander worked with the toy company FAO Schwartz to advertise her Alexander dolls in their national catalog. By the end of the 1920s, Alexander was one of the nation's most successful entrepreneurs. Contemporaries and competitors of Alexander included doll companies such as E.I. Horsman and Effanbee, as well as manufacturers such as Schoenhut and Steiff, who produced the Patsy doll in 1924.

The Playground Movement and National Parks

The U.S. federal government emphasized recreation development in parks and community centers in conjunction with the Playground and Recreation Association of America; the government advocated planned activities with supervised leadership, known as the playground movement. At this time, urban streets still served as playgrounds where many young children engaged in street games such as leapfrog, hopscotch, and baseball. Public parks did not exist in rural areas.

For many Americans, open recreation areas were found in the national parks and forests that existed in twenty-six states and became popular destinations for camping, hunting, and fishing. These parks included more than seventeen hundred campgrounds

and twelve hundred hotels. During this decade, total visitation rose from approximately 920,000 visitors in 1920 to 31.7 million visitors in 1929; the most popular parks were Yosemite, Yellowstone, Mt. Rainier, Platt, and the Rocky Mountains. Recreation in these open spaces included fishing, hunting, and hiking. By 1929, 6.9 million hunting licenses and 5.3 million fishing licenses had been issued to national parks visitors.

Hiking and fishing were especially popular year-round activities in the national parks. Hiking clubs were established, such as the Municipal Hiking Club of Minneapolis, founded in 1920; by 1928, it had sponsored over eighty separate hikes with nearly 4,200 participants. Other such clubs operated in San Francisco, Portland, Seattle, and portions of the Northeast. Similar fishing clubs and organizations also started. Some organizations, including the Izaak Walton League, the Sierra Club, and the Audubon Society, lobbied the U.S. Congress to protect wilderness areas from development.

Impact

After the end of World War I, the 1920s saw a reduced workweek that allowed more time for recreation and leisure and a new appreciation for these activities as important and healthy uses of time. By the end of the decade, with the growth of urban populations and the increasing importance of the automobile and the mass media, Americans were spending more money on commercial recreation. Sports activities and road trips also shaped the physical landscape, both in urban and wilderness areas across the United States. These cultural and physical changes would continue to influence American life throughout the remainder of the twentieth century.

Martin J. Manning

Further Reading

Cross, Gary S. *A Social History of Leisure Since 1600.* State College, Pa.: Venture, 1990. Discusses the dilemmas of leisure and public policy in the 1920s.

_____, ed. *Encyclopedia of Recreation and Leisure in America.* Farmington Hills, Mich.: Charles Scribner's Sons, 2004. Presents chiefly historical perspectives in the fields of American and cultural studies, sociology, recreation, sports, and leisure studies.

Giamatti, A. Bartlett. *Take Time for Paradise: Americans and Their Games.* New York: Bloomsbury,

2011. Explores the concepts of leisure as ritual, self-betterment, faith, home, and community.

Giordano, Ralph G. *Fun and Games in Twentieth-Century America: A Historical Guide to Leisure*. Westport, Conn.: Greenwood Press, 2003. Chronologically identifies the most popular games, sports, and hobbies of American social groups ranging from the working class to the wealthy.

Scott, Sharon M. *Toys and American Culture: An Encyclopedia*. Westport, Conn.: Greenwood Press, 2010. Documents America's shifting cultural values as symbolized by the nation's favorite playthings, also discussing the individuals, organizations, companies, and publications that gave them form.

See also: Baseball; Dances, popular; Disney, Walt; Fads; Film; Movie palaces; Ringling Bros. and Barnum & Bailey Circus; Sports

■ Hockey

With the inception and growth of the National Hockey League and its introduction as an Olympic event, the 1920s saw the transformation of ice hockey from an emerging Canadian pastime to a major professional sport that was popular and respected throughout North America.

During the 1920s, ice hockey grew as a popular sport in Canada and the northern United States. As the newly founded National Hockey League (NHL) entered the decade, its future as the dominant league in professional hockey was uncertain. The Pacific Coast Hockey Association (PCHA), a league in Western Canada and the U.S. Pacific Northwest, and the Western Canada Hockey League (WCHL) competed with the NHL for control, but both were eventually disbanded and their players absorbed by NHL teams.

The National Hockey League Expands
In 1920, the NHL was made up of four teams: the Toronto St. Patricks, the Ottawa Senators, the Montreal Canadiens, and the Hamilton Tigers. At that time, representative teams from several leagues, such as the PCHA and the WCHL, competed against the NHL champion for the Stanley Cup, the trophy presented to the overall winner of the season.

Much of the early 1920s was dominated by the Ottawa Senators, who won three of the decade's first

four Stanley Cups. The NHL's first scoring stars included Montreal's Newsy Lalonde, Ottawa's Cy Denney, Hamilton's Joe Malone, and Toronto's Cecil "Babe" Dye, while Montreal's Georges Vézina was one of the league's best goaltenders. The NHL games were so well attended and the stars so popular that, by 1924, the league added two more teams, the Montreal Maroons and its first U.S. team, the Boston Bruins. In 1925, the NHL expanded again, adding the New York Americans and the Pittsburgh Pirates. The Hamilton Tigers by this point had disbanded.

In 1925, the WCHL's Victoria Cougars won the Stanley Cup, a first for a non-NHL team. By 1926, the WCHL had changed its name to the Western Hockey League (WHL) but disbanded shortly thereafter, leaving the NHL as the dominant and most popular hockey league in North America. That same year, the NHL added two additional teams, the Chicago Blackhawks and the Detroit Cougars, and in 1927, the Toronto St. Patricks were renamed the Toronto Maple Leafs. The now ten-team league was made up of two groups, the Canadian and American Divisions, which would remain the format for the rest of the decade. During the 1920s, the NHL would grow and become profitable, establishing hockey as a major sport throughout much of North America.

Other Hockey Leagues and Tournaments
Competitive hockey was also gaining popularity during the 1920s among minority groups in North America. The Colored Hockey League (CHL) was started in Nova Scotia in 1894 after many African Americans fled to Canada with the passage of the 1850 Fugitive Slave Law. The NHL's white-only rule forced many descendants of escaped slaves to form their own league. Some sports historians believe that the CHL was responsible for introducing features of the game that would later be adopted by the NHL, such as the slap shot and goaltenders going down to the ice to make a save.

Women's hockey also grew during the 1920s as leagues sprang up in every Canadian province. PCHA owner Frank Patrick considered starting a national women's league, and in 1921, he held a three-team championship alongside the PCHA season, but it only lasted one year. Regional women's leagues thrived throughout Canada, however, and the number of women's collegiate hockey leagues grew yearly in the United States.

Ice Hockey and the Olympics

Ice hockey was introduced as an Olympic event in the 1920 Antwerp Summer Games. A seven-team tournament resulted in Canada winning the first gold medal, the United States the silver, and Czechoslovakia the bronze. With the first Winter Olympic Games, held at Chamonix, France, in 1924, ice hockey became a permanent Olympic sport, with the now-familiar Olympic hockey format: an initial round-robin tournament followed by a medal round consisting of the four best teams competing against one another. Canada repeated its gold-medal performance in the 1924 Games and again in the 1928 Games held at St. Moritz, Switzerland.

Impact

By the end of the 1920s, ice hockey had grown quickly from its initial roots. With the popularity of the game increasing and the rise of the professional game's first superstars, hockey joined baseball, basketball, and football as a major national sport. Rule changes in 1929 saw a dramatic increase in scoring that only added to the sport's popularity.

Steven L. Danver

Further Reading

Fosty, George Robert, and Darril Fosty. *Black Ice: The Lost History of the Colored Hockey League of the Maritimes, 1895–1925.* Halifax, N.S.: Nimbus, 2008. Chronicles the history of the Colored Hockey League (CHL) and the hardships and trials of black Canadians in the late nineteenth and early twentieth centuries.

McFarlane, Brian. *Brian McFarlane's History of Hockey.* Urbana, Ill.: Sagamore, 1997. Written by renowned hockey broadcaster and television commentator. Chronicles hockey's origins and provides a year-by-year history with discussion of rule changes and memorable games.

_____. *Proud Past, Bright Future: One Hundred Years of Canadian Women's Hockey.* Toronto: Stoddart, 1994. Details the history of women's hockey in Canada, beginning with Lady Stanley, daughter of Stanley Cup benefactor Lord Stanley.

McKinley, Michael. *Hockey: A People's History.* Toronto: McClelland & Stewart, 2009. Provides history and little-known hockey facts and accompanies a television series by the same name.

Wright, Marshall D. *The National Hockey League, 1917–1967: A Year-by-Year Statistical History.* Jefferson, N.C.: McFarland, 2010. A statistical history of the first fifty years of hockey providing information on players and regular-season and playoff games.

See also: African Americans; Canadian minority communities; Olympic Games of 1920 (Summer); Olympic Games of 1924 (Winter); Olympic Games of 1928 (Winter); Sports

■ Holland Tunnel

Connecting the New York City borough of Manhattan to Jersey City, New Jersey, the Holland Tunnel was the world's longest and widest underwater vehicular tunnel from the time it opened in 1927 until 1950. It was also the first to feature a ventilation system that pumped in fresh air while venting car and truck exhaust.

In 1906, the New York State Bridge and Tunnel Commission and the New Jersey Interstate Bridge and Tunnel Commission began planning a bridge over the Hudson River that would link Manhattan with Jersey City. In 1913, however, considerations involving the design and projected cost of the bridge led the commissioners to approve the construction of a tunnel beneath the river instead. Clifford Milburn Holland was appointed chief engineer of the project in 1919.

The actual construction of the tunnel began on March 31, 1922, with Milton H. Freeman serving as resident engineer and Ole Singstad as design engineer. In 1924, Holland suffered a nervous breakdown due to stress and left New York for a sanatorium, where he succumbed to heart disease on October 27 of that year. His death came only two days before crews digging from opposite ends of the tunnel met in the middle. Holland's measurements proved to be so precise that the two sections were aligned to within three-fourths of an inch of each other.

Freeman stepped into Holland's position but died shortly afterward of pneumonia; he was replaced in turn by Singstad, who oversaw the project until its completion. President Calvin Coolidge formally opened the tunnel, now named the Holland Tunnel in honor of the late engineer's contribution to the project, on November 12, 1927.

The completed tunnel consisted of two tubes, each one over eight thousand feet long and carrying two lanes of traffic. It featured a revolutionary duct system designed by Singstad that drew in fresh air while venting vehicle exhaust. The project had cost $48.5 million to complete.

Impact

The Holland Tunnel expedited the transportation of goods between Manhattan and New Jersey and spared motorists the often inordinate delays involved in ferry service. Acquired by the Port of New York Authority (now the Port Authority of New York and New Jersey) in 1930, it served as a model for similar projects around the world and remained the longest underwater vehicular tunnel on the continent until the opening of the Brooklyn-Battery Tunnel over twenty years later. The tunnel was designated a National Historic Civil and Mechanical Engineering Landmark in 1984.

Grove Koger

Further Reading

Gillespie, Angus K. *Crossing Under the Hudson: The Story of the Holland and Lincoln Tunnels.* New Brunswick, N.J.: Rutgers University Press, 2011.

Mysak, Joe, and Judith Schiffer. *Perpetual Motion: The Illustrated History of the Port Authority of New York and New Jersey.* Los Angeles: General Publishing Group, 1997.

Petroski, Henry. *Engineers of Dreams: Great Bridge Builders and the Spanning of America.* New York: Knopf, 1995.

See also: Detroit-Windsor Tunnel; Science and technology; Transportation

■ Hollywood Bowl

In the 1920s, when the movie industry was in its infancy and Los Angeles was not yet considered a major center of American culture, the Hollywood Bowl amphitheatre served as a showcase for a variety of performing arts, from classical music to avant-garde modern dance.

Modeled on the amphitheatres of ancient Greece and Rome, the Hollywood Bowl took its name from a feature of the southern California landscape: a large, bowl-shaped area surrounded by hills in a section of Bolton Canyon known as Daisy Dell. Because of its natural acoustic properties, Daisy Dell had been a popular location for musical events even before civic

Hollywood Bowl pictured in 1928. (AP Photo)

leaders decided to build a permanent stage at the site. Construction began in 1921, and the Hollywood Bowl's first official season opened on July 11, 1922, with a performance by the Los Angeles Philharmonic, a symphony orchestra that was then only three years old.

Initially, the Hollywood Bowl had no band shell above the stage and no built-in seating, just wooden benches set out on the steep hillside in front of the stage. In 1926, architect Myron Hunt, creator of Pasadena's Rose Bowl stadium, designed a permanent hillside seating area as well as the first band shell structure, which was demolished after one season. Newly designed shells were constructed in 1927 and 1928 by Lloyd Wright, son of celebrated architect Frank Lloyd Wright, but ultimately these were demolished as well. A fourth shell design by the firm of Elliott, Bowen and Walz was erected in 1929, giving the stage its final distinctive look, though it has since undergone several renovations and acoustical improvements. With a seating capacity of more than seventeen thousand, the Hollywood Bowl remains the largest natural amphitheatre in the United States, and its band shell structure has become a Los Angeles icon.

Impact

The quality and variety of performances at the Hollywood Bowl, which included dance recitals, operas, and other theatrical productions, as well as symphony orchestra concerts, helped 1920s Los Angeles achieve a reputation as a city of cultural importance. Live performances, radio broadcasts, and recordings would later bring the Los Angeles Philharmonic international acclaim, and, in subsequent decades, numerous movies and television shows would feature scenes set at the Hollywood Bowl.

Karen Manners Smith

Further Reading

Henken, John, and Michael Buckland, eds. *The Hollywood Bowl: Tales of Summer Nights.* Los Angeles: Balcony Press, 1996.

Smith, Catherine Parsons. "Founding the Hollywood Bowl." *American Music* 11, no. 2 (Summer, 1993): 206–242.

_____. *Making Music in Los Angeles: Transforming the Popular.* Berkeley: University of California Press, 2007.

See also: Architecture; Art movements; Classical music; Dance and choreography; Music, popular; Wright, Frank Lloyd

■ Hollywood sign

The Hollywood sign was constructed as a billboard designed to attract those moving into the area in the 1920s. The sign quickly became a world-famous landmark, synonymous with the American motion picture industry and serving as a physical representation of celebrity, wealth, and power.

In 1923, a fifty-foot-tall sign spelling "Hollywoodland" was erected as an advertisement for a real estate development in the Hollywood area of Los Angeles. The development investors heading the sign project were noted film director Mack Sennett and newspaper publisher Harry Chandler. The sign's construction involved sheet metal panels, scaffolding, pipes, and telephone poles dragged up Mount Lee. Originally, there was also a large dot positioned one hundred feet below the sign. The dot and the letters glowed with four thousand lightbulbs, whose replacement and maintenance necessitated the attention of a full-time caretaker who lived in a cottage near the sign.

The sign was visible for 25 miles, and it quickly became a local landmark. As the 1920s progressed, the sign came to be a tourist attraction and later achieved notoriety in 1932 as the suicide site of young actor Lillian Millicent "Peg" Entwistle, who allegedly climbed a workman's ladder to the top of the *H* and jumped to her death.

By 1939, the Hollywoodland real estate development had failed, and the sign was no longer maintained. Due to the sign's dilapidated state, the City of Los Angeles Parks Department decided to tear it down. The Hollywood Chamber of Commerce saved it from demolition, however, agreeing to repair the "Hollywood" part of the sign and to remove the "land" letters. After this initial improvement, the sign underwent various restorations and repairs, often supported by celebrities. In 1978, the original sign was demolished and replaced with a sign that was 4 stories high, 450 feet long, 480,000 pounds, and anchored by 194 tons of concrete. The Hollywood Sign Trust was created in 1992 to maintain and secure the sign, which was outfitted with an around-the-clock surveillance system.

Impact

Much has changed in the film industry since the birth of Hollywood, but the Hollywood sign continues to serve as a tangible reminder of the formative years of the Los Angeles motion picture industry during the 1920s and an expression of the glamour, fame, and fortune associated with Hollywood society and the motion picture industry.

Amanda J. Bahr-Evola

Further Reading

Braudy, Leo. *The Hollywood Sign: Fantasy and Reality of an American Icon.* New Haven, Conn.: Yale University Press, 2011.

Wallace, David. *Lost Hollywood.* New York: St. Martin's Press, 2002.

See also: Architecture; Chandler, Harry; Film; Housing; Sennett, Mack

■ Holmes, Oliver Wendell, Jr.

Identification: American lawyer and judge
Born: March 8, 1841, Boston, Massachusetts
Died: March 6, 1935, Washington, D.C.

Oliver Wendell Holmes Jr.'s legal writing and thirty-year career on the U.S. Supreme Court cemented his reputation as one of the most famous, controversial, and revered justices in American history. He greatly influenced the course of twentieth-century American constitutional law.

After graduating from Harvard Law School in 1866, Holmes practiced law for a time, devoting his evenings to philosophy and legal research. He believed that "the life of the law has not been logic; it has been experience," a principle developed in his book *The Common Law* (1881). Holmes was a state supreme court judge for twenty years before his 1902 appointment to the U.S. Supreme Court, where he served until 1932.

The "Great Dissenter," so called due to his frequent disagreements with the Court's decisions, was known for both his deference to state legislation and his support for free speech. Many of his opinions follow his dissent in *Lochner v. New York* (1905), in which he defended a law that prohibited bakers from working more than sixty hours each week by arguing that the U.S. Constitution does not uphold the principles of free market economic theory.

In *Schenck v. United States* (1919), Holmes wrote the now-famous opinion that speech can be abridged when, and only when, it poses a "clear and present danger." His commitment to free speech deepened throughout the 1920s, culminating in his dissenting opinion in *United States v. Schwimmer* (1929) that the Constitution protects "freedom for the thought that we hate."

Holmes was no social reformer, frequently disdaining "the crowd" and less concerned with justice than with following the rules. He believed that judges should not allow their own views to dictate constitutional policy, and that barring express constitutional prohibition and with sufficient public support, state legislatures should be able to act as they saw fit.

For Holmes, life was fundamentally about action and struggle. His service in the Civil War was the central, glorious experience of his life, and he considered force to be the ultimate principle of law and politics. His social Darwinist tendencies occasionally crept into his addresses and his writings, such as in *Buck v. Bell* (1927), when, writing for the Court, he upheld a law providing for compulsory sterilization of the "feeble-minded." Holmes argued that if a state could ask its "best citizens" to sacrifice themselves in war, it could surely sterilize "those who already sap the strength of the State."

Impact

As a Supreme Court judge, Holmes's interpretation of the law was one in which the state enjoys latitude in economic regulation while remaining subject to strict limits on its power to abridge civil liberties, in accordance with his reading of the Constitution. Nevertheless, his fundamental attitudes belied his reputation as a Progressive.

Thomas M. J. Bateman

Further Reading

Holmes, Oliver Wendell. *The Common Law.* Reprint. Boston: Little, Brown & Co., 2009.

White, G. Edward. *Justice Oliver Wendell Holmes: Law and the Inner Self.* New York: Oxford University Press, 1993.

See also: *Adkins v. Children's Hospital; Buck v. Bell; Gitlow v. New York; Meyer v. Nebraska; Olmstead v. United States;* Supreme Court, U.S.

■ Home furnishings

Home furnishings of the 1920s reflected the major technological, social, economic, and cultural trends sweeping the United States and Canada. Widespread prosperity, mass production, and electricity in the home led to more appliances, leisure time, and home entertainment products. Toward the end of the decade, Art Deco style and the modernist movement influenced interior decoration and the design of household items.

Often called the Roaring Twenties, the 1920s was a time of prosperity, rapid economic growth, optimism, and consumerism in North America. World War I had ended, leaving a booming peacetime economy in its wake. The United States and Canada became urbanized as large populations shifted to metropolitan centers. The modern white-collar job became the norm, and increasing numbers of women worked outside of the home. Flappers epitomized the modern woman and contributed to the fashionable opulence of the era.

Technological progress created household appliances or gadgets that helped working women. After World War I, domestic plumbing expanded throughout North America, so most homes had bathrooms and indoor plumbing by the 1930s. During the 1920s, electricity became widely available; two-thirds of all American homes had electricity by 1924. Mass production and the moving assembly line lowered production costs, so products became more affordable to more consumers. New types of electrical products were constantly being created. The development of low-cost building materials led to new designs, while a futuristic machine aesthetic cropped up in interior design and home furnishings.

Design Styles

The most popular suburban house of the 1920s was the affordable, single-family bungalow, typically less than two stories tall, with a pitched roof and large porch. Early bungalows featured built-in cabinetry, hardwood floors, wood paneling, and furnishings in Craftsman style, which was the North American version of the Arts and Crafts movement popular in England during the late nineteenth and early twentieth century. Craftsman homes had Victorian-style bathrooms with pedestal sinks, claw-foot tubs, porcelain-tiled floors, and pull-chain toilets. Later in the decade, bungalow bathrooms had modern low-tank toilets and enclosed bathtubs.

Between 1908 and 1940, the retail firm Sears, Roebuck and Company sold over seventy thousand Modern Homes construction kits through its mail-order catalog. These affordable kits, which included all the materials needed to build a home, peaked in sales during the 1920s. Sears also sold interiors kits that included furniture, wallpaper, paint, curtains, carpets, linoleum, and appliances for these homes.

In contrast to earlier Victorian homes, the typical 1920s home was smaller, with fewer rooms. Apartments became increasingly popular. Dining rooms were also smaller and featured built-in cupboards and alcoves. Bedrooms favored traditional styles of earlier centuries with the addition of the latest mattress technology. The Murphy bed, a pivot bed that could fold into its own wall closet, became very popular, as did the Pullman Davenport sofa bed.

The flapper lifestyle epitomized the romantic, idyllic, exotic, and flamboyant interior designs of the decade. Flapper decor included a variety of furniture styles, including Gothic, Federal, Cottage, Empire, Chippendale, and Elizabethan. Walls were paneled or painted in muted greens, taupes, and blues, while floors were made of wood, tile, or linoleum. Factory-made but lavish Oriental rugs were widely popular. Fringe and ostrich feathers from flapper fashion also appeared in home furnishings of the period.

The Art Deco movement began in Europe in 1925 and spread to North America later in the decade, influenced by ancient Egyptian and African art, cubism, futurism, neoclassicism, and modernism. Its linear

Art Deco

The Art Deco style was introduced at the 1925 Exposition internationale des arts décoratifs et industriels modernes. This style emphasized a basic geometrical structure, typically including repeating lines, rounded corners, steps, and symmetry. Rich colors, black, and metallics were used frequently. Stylized sun rays, animals, and foliage were common motifs. Materials included chrome, glass, and Bakelite, a chemically resistant plastic. Natural materials such as silver, rock crystal, ivory, and jade also were popular.

symmetry, geometric forms, and purely decorative designs were a contrast to the earlier Art Nouveau style, which favored asymmetrical organic forms, and the Craftsman style, which contained elements from folk decoration. Typical Art Deco interiors had mirrored furniture, exotic woods, high-gloss lacquered finishes on inexpensive woods, chairs with wood inlay, and leathers dyed in reds and oranges. Wall clocks, radios, chandeliers, lamps, and furniture often had luxurious accents or embellishments of jewels or semiprecious stones such as jade, ivory, and onyx.

The post–World War I modernist design movement used the new mass-production techniques and manufactured materials such plate glass, tubular metal, and concrete to make form follow function, which represented a central theme for the style. Classic geometry and utilitarian simplicity were the new "machine age" aesthetic. In 1925, inspired by bicycle handlebars, designer Marcel Breuer created the celebrated Model B3 chair, later known as the Wassily Chair. Mass-produced in both folding and non-folding versions beginning in the late 1920s, this revolutionary chair was constructed of bent, chromium-plated tubular steel and canvas. Later versions replaced canvas with leather. In 1926, Dutch architect Mart Stam designed the first cantilever chair, which is a chair without back legs, and it became a popular classic.

Appliances

The mass production of goods, widespread availability of electricity, and aggressive advertising campaigns in the 1920s brought an ever-increasing number of electrical appliances to North American homes. Two-thirds of American homes had electricity by 1924, and over 70 percent of urban homes had electricity by the end of the decade. During the 1920s, Canada became a leading producer of hydroelectric power. As more electrical appliances became available, there was an increasing demand for electricity in homes. Gas and electric stoves were common in Canada by the 1920s, and Canada began manufacturing electric refrigerators in 1925.

In 1922, the U.S. government endorsed the Better Homes Movement, a nationwide campaign that encouraged home ownership, maintenance, improvement, and decoration. This movement helped make household appliances a huge industry. During the 1920s, electric washing machines replaced hand-operated washtubs. In 1921, the appliance company Electrolux introduced its Model V, an easily portable and less bulky vacuum cleaner. In 1927, General Electric introduced its affordable "monitor top" refrigerator, the first widely used refrigerator. The same year, inventor Charles Strite created the first thermostatically controlled automatic pop-up toaster. Although the first commercially viable electric laundry iron had been invented as early as 1905, the 1920s represented an important decade in the history of electric irons: In 1927, Proctor & Schwartz launched the first iron with adjustable temperature control, and it became one of the most popular home appliances of the decade, along with radios.

By 1929, North American households had accumulated a wide variety of laborsaving electrical appliances and gadgets. Homes had heavy-duty electrical systems that could support larger appliances such as washing machines and vacuum cleaners. Popular products relying on home electricity included toasters, percolators, corn poppers, lights, fans, stoves, sewing machines, waffle irons, hotplates, flat irons, and chafing dishes.

Home Entertainment

The late nineteenth century saw the rise of mass-produced pianos for the home. In the early 1900s, the player piano, a self-playing piano with preprogrammed music, became a popular form of home entertainment. With models ranging from foot-powered players to complex motorized mechanisms, player pianos reached their peak during the early 1920s, when they accounted for over half of all piano sales. Phonographs and radios were also becoming more popular and affordable as their technology improved. Following the stock market crash of 1929, player piano sales declined rapidly, and by 1932, player pianos were no longer being manufactured.

Invented by Thomas Edison in 1877, the phonograph was a popular item in North American homes during the 1920s. While piano sales decreased during the decade, phonograph technology and production advanced from 190,000 phonographs sold in 1923 to 5 million in 1929. These records brought jazz, blues, and country music to a broad American audience.

Westinghouse Electric Corporation's radio station KDKA made its historic modern radio broadcast in 1920. Over the course of the decade, radios became the single most popular household product in North America. By 1922, the United States had over six hundred radio stations. By the end of the decade, over twelve million households had radios. By 1929, Canada had eighty-five low-power broadcasting stations offering a variety of programs, but most of the content on Canadian radios was from American productions.

While easily made at home, the early crystal radios produced weak sounds and required headphones. These early radios ran on large batteries that required frequent recharging. Introduced in 1924, the tube radio allowed clearer sounds over long distances. Speakers replaced headphones, and in 1925, Canadian inventor Ted Rogers created the first batteryless radio, which plugged directly into a home's electrical current. The typical radio by the late 1920s had components combined into a single unit or piece of furniture that fit into the budgets and decor of both urban and rural homes.

Impact

Home furnishings of the 1920s reflected the optimism and flamboyant spirit of the flourishing post–World War I economy in North America. The increasing use of electricity and indoor plumbing led to higher construction costs. As a result, new houses were built smaller, with fewer and smaller rooms. Homes included more open interior spaces and had fewer private, single-purpose rooms such as a library, sewing room, or pantry. However, even middle- and lower-class homebuyers could choose from a wide range of popular styles, including traditional, exotic, romantic, and modernist. Mass production and new materials enabled greater varieties of affordable home furnishings, including replicas of expensive classics.

As the market grew for electrical appliances, the 1920s saw the rise of American and Canadian brands such as Bissell, Black & Decker, Frigidaire, General Electric, Hamilton Beach, Hoover, Kitchen Aid, Maytag, Proctor, Sears, Singer, Sunbeam, Tappan, West Bend, and Westinghouse. The radio, the decade's popular new entertainment and communications device, linked rural and urban areas with a shared common experience.

Alice Myers

Further Reading

Abercrombie, Stanley. *A Century of Interior Design, 1900–2000.* New York: Rizzoli International, 2003. Uses a timeline format to describe the most significant developments in twentieth-century furniture, home furnishings, architecture, culture, and technology, with illustrations and an index.

Fiell, Charlotte, and Peter Fiell. *Decorative Art, 1920s.* New York: Taschen, 2000. Describes the decade's design trends and styles in architecture, furniture, interiors, glassware, lighting, ceramics, textiles, and metalware, with illustrations and an index.

Ierley, Merritt. *Comforts of Home: The American House and the Evolution of Modern Convenience.* New York: C. Potter, 1999. Includes vintage illustrations and photographs of appliances and lighting; discusses the importance of comfort in 1920s interior furnishing.

Kyvig, David E. *Daily Life in the United States, 1920–1940: How Americans Lived Through the Roaring Twenties and the Great Depression.* Lanham, Md.: Ivan R. Dee, 2004. Comments on the role of electrical appliances and radios in both rural and urban homes of the 1920s.

Miller, Judith, and Nicholas M. Dawes. *Art Deco.* New York: DK, 2005. Discusses over one thousand pieces of metalware, furniture, glass, ceramics, clocks, and textiles from the 1920s, including full-color illustrations, an index, and appendixes.

Rosenfeld, Lucy D. *Inside Art Deco: A Pictorial Tour of Deco Interiors from Their Origins to Today.* Atglen, Pa.: Schiffer, 2005. Discusses both European and American Art Deco interiors and their influence on later designers. Includes color photographs.

See also: Art Deco; Better Homes in America movement; Bungalows; Electrification; Inventions; Player

pianos; Radio Corporation of America (RCA); Refrigerators; Sears, Roebuck and Co.

■ Homosexuality and gay rights

The gay and lesbian subcultures that thrived throughout the Roaring Twenties allowed homosexuals to be more visible in American society, sparking the establishment of gay rights organizations.

The 1920s was a time of experimentation and change, and while homosexuals were finding greater acceptance, particularly in urban areas, an undercurrent of discrimination and homophobia loomed throughout the decade. The U.S. military classified sodomy as a crime under military law, and suspected homosexuals were given dishonorable discharges. In addition to criminalization, gay men and lesbians were subject to job loss and social ostracism. Despite repressive laws and policies, however, homosexuals developed extensive social networks, as gay and lesbian subcultures began to flourish.

New York City

Aspects of gay culture could be found in most urban areas during the 1920s, but New York City proved to be a gay and lesbian cultural hub. With its many taverns, bathhouses, and neighborhoods such as Greenwich Village, homosexuals found a safe and welcoming refuge from hostility and widespread discrimination. From male beauty contests at Coney Island to the drag balls in Harlem, gay subculture thrived throughout the city. Although the ban on alcohol consumption, known as Prohibition, was in full effect, cabarets and speakeasies owned by homosexuals could be found around Broadway and in Times Square by 1924. While homosexuals enjoyed certain autonomy within the confines of the city's gay subculture, they had to remain cautious as neighborhood crusades, antigay policing, and the criminalization of homosexual behavior led to the arrests of hundreds of men each year. Police raids were not uncommon, especially in establishments linked to prostitution or overt sexual entertainment. Individuals arrested for disorderly conduct or homosexual activities were subject to fines or prison time. News media regularly depicted homosexuals with negative images, thus increasing homophobia and hostile attitudes.

The Harlem Renaissance movement fueled by

The Society for Human Rights

On December 10, 1924, Henry Gerber formed The Society for Human Rights, a nonprofit social justice organization and the first documented gay rights organization in the United States, in an effort to spearhead a U.S. gay rights movement. Gerber wanted the society to help promote social equality and encourage acceptance of "alternative" sexualities. While the society sought to bring together and empower the homosexual community of Chicago, widespread fear inhibited the realization of the society's goals. Although the society did not have an immediate impact on the lives of gays and lesbians living in the 1920s, as the first gay rights and advocacy organization of its kind, the society helped clear a path for future gay and lesbian rights groups and organizations to follow. Although the organization was short-lived, it is said to have inspired the founding in 1950 of the Mattachine Society.

African American literary and artistic works is not always associated with the African American lesbian and gay subculture that originated there. However, the Harlem Renaissance marks an important period in gay and lesbian history. The jazz culture that blossomed in Harlem fostered a bohemian environment in which gay men, lesbians, bisexuals, and cross-dressers found some safety and acceptance. That is not to say that homosexuals in Harlem were protected from criminalization and prosecution, but while other alleged homosexual establishments were subjected to raids in areas such as the Bowery, Harlem remained relatively unaffected. In fact, a homosexual presence can be found in nearly all of the artistic expressions of the Harlem Renaissance.

Henry Gerber and the Society for Human Rights

One of the most defining moments in gay rights history occurred in 1924, when U.S. soldier Henry Gerber returned from Germany and attempted to establish a gay rights organization. Gerber, along with the help of a few friends and a charter from the state of Illinois, founded the Society for Human Rights (SHR) in 1924. However, the society's efforts to gain funding and support proved to be futile, and in mid-1925, it came to an abrupt end amidst scandal and controversy. Until his death in 1972, Gerber continued to be an advocate for homosexual rights, authoring several articles and books promoting gay and lesbian liberation. Gerber's profound role in gay rights history was commemorated in 1981 with the founding of the Gerber/Hart Library in Chicago.

Film and Literature

Broadway, vaudeville, and burlesque theater were popular forms of entertainment in the 1920s and became a vehicle for homosexual innuendo, which was abundant on stages throughout New York City during the decade. However, while Broadway was experimenting with nudity and racy subjects, the New York City Police Department (NYPD) and vice crusaders set out to "clean up" the theater. In February 1927, stage actor Mae West was arrested for obscenity for her Broadway play *Sex*, which depicted prostitution and drag queens. Just two months later, the public obscenity code was extended to include a ban on any play depicting sexual perversion; gay actors and plays discussing gay themes were also banned.

Homosexual literature gained popularity as well. Notable lesbian novels included Virginia Woolf's *Orlando* (1928) and Djuna Barnes's *Ladies Almanack* (1928). However, it was Radclyffe Hall's *The Well of Loneliness* (1928), depicting a female protagonist named Stephen, that began a firestorm of backlash and censorship. The hint of lesbianism made the novel the subject of a famous literary trial, in which the book was ruled obscene and subsequently banned in Great Britain. The United States also sought to ban the book's importation but had little success. Although the NYPD seized hundreds of copies and arrested the distributor, *The Well of Loneliness* was a huge success in the United States, selling more than twenty thousand copies.

Impact

The increased visibility of gay men and lesbians in the 1920s influenced film, theater, literature, and the arts. Henry Gerber's Society for Human Rights laid the foundation for later gay rights organizations. However, by 1930, homosexuals began to face additional scrutiny as the end of Prohibition and the Great Depression led to harsher antihomosexual legislation.

Amanda Bird

Further Reading

Bullough, Vern L., ed. *Before Stonewall: Activists for Gay and Lesbian Rights in Historical Context.* New York: Harrington Park Press, 2003. Contains biographical entries on individuals involved in the gay rights struggle before the 1960s.

Chauncey, George. *Gay New York: Gender, Urban Culture, and the Making of the Gay Male World, 1890–1940.* New York: BasicBooks, 1996. Examines the gay world in turn-of-the-century New York City.

Eaklor, Vicki Lynn. *Queer America: A GLBT History of the 20th Century.* Westport, Conn.: Greenwood Press, 2008. An extensive chronicle of the movements, people, and events that contributed to the gay, lesbian, bisexual, and transsexual history of the twentieth century.

Leider, Emily Wortis. *Becoming Mae West.* New York: Farrar, Straus, Giroux, 1997. Explains how the racy vaudeville star became a critically acclaimed actor.

Schwarz, A. B. Christa. *Gay Voices of the Harlem Renaissance.* Bloomington: Indiana University Press, 2003. Explores the same-sex-oriented literary works produced by Harlem Renaissance writers Countée Cullen, Langston Hughes, Claude McKay, and Richard Bruce Nugent.

See also: African Americans; Film; Harlem Renaissance; Jazz; Prohibition; Speakeasies; Vaudeville; West, Mae

---

■ Hood ornaments

The 1920s in the United States was a decade particularly marked by the growing automobile industry. Leaving behind the plain carriage-style Model T's, new car enthusiasts demanded that beauty be incorporated into even the mechanical aspects of the automobile.

In 1912, the Boyce Motometer Company had developed a thermometer for gauging engine coolant temperatures that the automobile operator could see from the outside of the car. Then, as now, an overheated engine could mean expensive repairs, but judging engine coolant temperature meant opening the hood of a boiling-hot car, which was not a pleasant task. Boyce Motometer's gauge examined the temperature of steam in the engine rather than the temperature of the liquid water, which allowed the placement of the meter to sit over the radiator grille and extend high above the hood of the car. These gauges, usually cast in brass or bronze and plated with chrome, started out as fairly functional radiator caps, but as greater numbers of car manufacturers in the United States and Great Britain emerged during the 1920s, more thought was put into redesigning the radiator cap to add style and flair, as well as individuality, to each new vehicle. Some radiator caps were even plated with alloys of nickel or silver.

At the height of the ornament craze, Boyce Motometer crafted no fewer than three hundred individual styles of hood ornaments, with each design being particularly designed for a single manufacturer and often dedicated to a particular make of car, motorcycle, truck, or even tractor. Familiar styles began to emerge and, even decades later, are immediately identifiable. For example, there is a leaping jaguar hood ornament on Jaguars, a crest and wreath on Cadillacs, a pelican on Packards, and a figurine called the "Spirit of Ecstasy," resembling a woman with wings, on Rolls-Royces. Eventually, the hood ornament ceased to have any functional purpose and became completely decorative.

Impact

The hood ornament, once a necessary cap for the automobile's radiator cooling system, became a cosmetic fixture on 1920s vehicles. In the early twenty-first century, most hood decorations look more like badges than sculptures, while engine and coolant temperatures are now gauged by complex thermometers placed in the dashboard. Although hood ornaments lost their original function and became more standardized over time, all such devices recall an era of greater diversity and individuality in car manufacturing.

Julia M. Meyers

Further Reading

Crandall, Larry. "The Spirit of Ecstasy." *Tampa Bay Magazine* 14, no. 2 (March/April, 1999): 133.

Einstein, Arthur W. *"Ask the Man Who Owns One": An Illustrated History of Packard Advertising.* Jefferson, N.C.: McFarland, 2010.

Hinckley, James, and Robinson, Jon G. *The Big Book of Car Culture: The Armchair Guide to Automotive Americana.* St. Paul, Minn.: Motorbooks, 2005.

See also: Automobiles and auto manufacturing; Auto racing; Inventions; Model A Fords

■ Hoover, Herbert

Identification: Thirty-first president of the United States
Born: August 10, 1874, West Branch, Iowa
Died: October 20, 1964, New York, New York

President Herbert Hoover took office shortly before the 1929 stock market crash and the Great Depression of the 1930s. Due to his ill-timed accession to the nation's highest office, he is consistently regarded as one of the lowest-ranking presidents in U.S. history, and his positive contributions are often overlooked.

Herbert Hoover's mother was a teacher, and his father was a blacksmith. His Quaker upbringing provided a religious influence that would last throughout his life, teaching him that hard work and diligence were qualities to be prized and rewarded. By the time Hoover was eight years old, both his parents had died, leaving him to be raised by his uncle in Oregon. He spent his spare time assisting the bookkeeper in his uncle's real estate office, an experience that convinced him to pursue a career in accounting; he later changed his mind, however, and decided to study engineering instead.

Hoover was among the first class of students to enter Stanford University. While there, he met Lou Henry, his future wife, who was studying geological engineering. Following his graduation in 1895, Hoover worked for several years as a mining engineer in Australia and then moved to China in 1899, shortly after his marriage to Henry. He later operated mines in Russia, Burma, and Japan and regularly contributed articles to mining journals. In 1909, he wrote the book *Principles of Mining*, a volume that combined his interests in engineering and accounting. By this time, he was recognized as a distinguished engineer at the top of his field.

Because Hoover's consulting firm managed mines for numerous corporations, he was in an ideal position to standardize their accounting and management functions. This standardization made comparability of operations and financial statements possible, which led to greater efficiency in operations. Hoover's philosophy throughout his mining career was the elimination of waste.

Herbert Hoover. (Getty Images)

Moving into Government Service

Hoover's mining days ended with the beginning of World War I, when he began his career in public service. By this time, his mining interests had made him a wealthy man. He served first as administrator for Belgian relief and then, starting in 1917, as head of the United States Food Administration, both positions making him a household name in Europe. Hoover's goals as the U.S. food administrator were to stabilize prices while ensuring ample supplies of wheat, meat, corn, and poultry. He popularized the concept of "meatless Mondays," encouraging the people at home to reduce their consumption and thus provide more rations for soldiers overseas. Hoover's work allowed the United States to weather the war and its aftermath without the food riots and hyperinflation experienced by other countries. His emphasis on efficiency of operations was as evident in government as it had been in his mining days; one commentator stated that Hoover could squeeze more out of a dollar than anyone else in Washington.

Following the war, Hoover headed up the American Relief Administration (ARA), which supplied food and other assistance to war victims in Central Europe. In response to the Russian famine of 1921, he oversaw the passage of the Russian Famine Relief Act of 1921, which authorized the ARA to provide aid to the Soviet Union as well.

From 1921 to 1928, Hoover served as secretary of commerce in the Harding and Coolidge administrations, presiding over the booming business of the Roaring Twenties. He made the fairly new Department of Commerce business-friendly, seeing it as the hub of the nation's growth, in contrast to the adversarial position taken by the three preceding presidential administrations. As secretary, Hoover preached the concept of efficiency, with emphasis on convincing manufacturers to standardize parts and supplies. He expanded the role and responsibility of the Department of Commerce by taking over functions previously performed by other agencies. As a result, he was sometimes called the "secretary of commerce and assistant secretary of everything else" and was often more visible than even the presidents under whom he served. Hoover was also asked by President Calvin Coolidge to head the relief efforts of the Great Mississippi Flood of 1927, which sent nearly a million people to refugee camps for several months. Some say that it was his work in the flood areas that made him a viable candidate for the presidency.

An Unlucky President

Herbert Hoover was viewed as a statesman rather than a politician, having never been elected to office before running for president in 1928; he was widely known and extremely popular, however, and few other presidents have been as well qualified for the job as he was. Unfortunately, his luck ran out shortly after he took over the job in 1929. The stock market crashed in October of that year, a worldwide economic depression followed, and Hoover spent the next three years of his presidency trying to restore some normalcy to the economy. He met with industry leaders, tried to balance the government budget, and attempted to increase production and consumption, all to no avail. Although Congress continued to support him, the general public did not, and the charismatic New York governor Franklin Delano Roosevelt easily won the election in 1932.

Hoover spent the last thirty years of his life trying to defend himself from the blame leveled at him by a disheartened populace. He wrote numerous autobiographical books explaining his positions. Although he was virtually ignored during the twelve-year presidency of Roosevelt, President Harry S. Truman rekindled the government's relationship with Hoover in the late 1940s when he asked the former president to head a study of government efficiency and effectiveness. The success of the study, dubbed the Hoover Commission, led to the convocation of a second commission under President Dwight D. Eisenhower in the 1950s, also led by Hoover.

Impact

As a mining engineer, Hoover's focus on cost accounting and management efficiency took a jumbled industry and made it profitable, while his work in Washington prior to his presidency earned him a great deal of respect and acclaim. Industry as a whole benefited from his popularization of efficiency measures and standardization of production. Later in his life, his involvement in the Hoover Commission restored some of his previous political standing. Thus, disregarding his presidency, Hoover is remembered as a contributor to the public welfare who improved the efficiency and effectiveness of both business and government. However, this legacy is often overshadowed by the fact that he had the misfortune to be in office when the stock market crashed and the Great Depression began.

Dale L. Flesher

Further Reading

Barry, John M. *Rising Tide: The Great Mississippi Flood of 1927 and How It Changed America.* New York: Simon & Schuster, 1998. Argues that Hoover's handling of the 1927 Mississippi River flood led to his election.

Burner, David. *Herbert Hoover: A Public Life.* Newtown, Conn.: American Political Biography Press, 2005. A scholarly biography with much emphasis on Hoover's years of public service.

Clements, Kendrick A. *The Life of Herbert Hoover: Imperfect Visionary, 1918–1928.* New York: Palgrave Macmillan, 2010. Covers Hoover's time as the secretary of commerce and the public philosophy he developed for dealing with the problems of the United States.

Lester, Paul Martin. *On Floods and Photo Ops: How Herbert Hoover and George W. Bush Exploited Catastrophes.* Jackson: University Press of Mississippi, 2010. A more critical view of how Hoover may have exploited the opportunities presented him by the Great Mississippi Flood of 1927.

Nash, George H. *Master of Emergencies, 1917–1918.* Vol. 3 in *The Life of Herbert Hoover.* New York: W. W. Norton, 1996. Explains how Hoover became famous, with emphasis on his relief work following the famine in Belgium.

Smith, Richard Norton. *An Uncommon Man: The Triumph of Herbert Hoover.* New York: Simon & Schuster, 1984. A detailed biography by a former director of the Herbert Hoover Presidential Library and Museum.

Sobel, Robert. *Herbert Hoover at the Onset of the Great Depression, 1929–1930.* Philadelphia: J. B. Lippincott, 1975. A short volume covering the first year of Hoover's presidency.

See also: Agricultural Marketing Act of 1929; Coolidge, Calvin; Elections of 1928, U.S.; Great Mississippi Flood of 1927; Harding, Warren G.; Recession of 1920–1921; Russian Famine Relief Act of 1921

■ Hoover, J. Edgar

Identification: Director of the Bureau of Investigation, later the Federal Bureau of Investigation
Born: January 1, 1895, Washington, D.C.
Died: May 2, 1972, Washington, D.C.

In 1924, President Calvin Coolidge appointed J. Edgar Hoover director of the Bureau of Investigation (BOI), the predecessor agency of the Federal Bureau of Investigation (FBI). He is credited with creating the FBI and making it the crime-fighting arm of the United States government that it is today.

John Edgar Hoover was born on January 1, 1895, in Washington, D.C. He obtained a law degree from George Washington University in 1917 and took a position as a law clerk with the Department of Justice. Hoover rose through the ranks quickly, and in August of 1919, he began working as the head of the new General Intelligence Division at the Bureau of Investigation.

General Intelligence Division Chief
In 1919 and 1920, the first Red Scare raids brought to light the anticommunist sentiment brewing in the United States. During these raids, the U.S. government focused on identifying Bolshevik sympathizers inspired by the Russian Revolution of 1917. One series of raids, called the Palmer raids after Attorney General Alexander Mitchell Palmer, was orchestrated in thirty-three cities throughout the United States within a twenty-four-hour period. Their purpose was to target members of the Union of Russian Workers and the Communist Labor Party and enforce the Anarchist Exclusion Act of 1918, which required the deportation of noncitizens who supported anarchism. Following mass arrests, 249 noncitizens were deported to Russia, not all as a result of the raids; for example, deportees Emma Goldman and Alexander Berkman, whom Hoover considered to be "two of the most dangerous anarchists in this country," had been imprisoned in 1917 for encouraging resistance to military conscription. It was during this time that Hoover began cataloging people and organizations involved in radical and otherwise suspicious activities.

Bureau of Intelligence Director
In 1921, Hoover was promoted to assistant director of the BOI. On May 10, 1924, in an effort to rid the bureau of corruption, Attorney General Harlan Fiske Stone named Hoover acting director. Hoover took over on the heels of accusations that the previous director, William J. Burns, was indirectly involved in the Teapot Dome scandal, in which Secretary of the Interior Albert Fall was found guilty of bribery for leasing land in Wyoming to an oil company in return for kickbacks; Burns was accused of dispatching employees from his own private detective agency to pay the jurors in Sinclair's trial for information. As a result, Burns resigned as director of the BOI, and Hoover stepped in. Coolidge made Hoover's appointment permanent a month later.

As director, Hoover inherited command of 441 special agents and about 200 other staff. Throughout the 1920s, in an effort to ensure consistent congressional appropriations to support and run the BOI, he worked to establish the bureau's importance to the U.S. government. Hoover developed a system for documenting fingerprints during these early years.

Hoover played a large role in laying the groundwork for the creation of the Federal Bureau of Investigation in 1935. One main goal of Hoover's agency was to fight public enemies such as John Dillinger, Al Capone, Charles "Pretty Boy" Floyd, Kate

"Ma" Barker and her sons, and Bonnie Parker and Clyde Barrow, all of whom emerged during the 1920s and 1930s in connection with bootlegging and organized crime. Hoover was the first director of the FBI, holding this position until his death in 1972 at age 77. He served as BOI and FBI director under eight presidents, from Calvin Coolidge to Richard Nixon.

Impact

Hoover's legacy is a mixed one. While he played a large role in forming the FBI as it stands today, his image is tainted by many facts and rumors. Many people feel he abused his authority by investigating and spying on individuals he believed to be subversive radicals, by illegally wiretapping phone lines, and by maintaining a list of about twelve thousand Americans he believed to be disloyal to the United States. These excesses eventually led to the establishment of a ten-year term limit for future FBI directors.

On the other hand, J. Edgar Hoover built the FBI into the foremost law enforcement agency of its time. Today, it employs more than thirty-five thousand people, based either at FBI headquarters or in the numerous field offices and resident agencies throughout the country, who fight domestic crime using criminal investigation and intelligence-gathering techniques. Two days after his death, President Richard Nixon signed Public Law 92–520, which officially named the FBI headquarters in Washington, D.C., the J. Edgar Hoover Building.

Eileen M. Ahlin

Further Reading

Breuer, William B. *J. Edgar Hoover and His G-Men.* Westport, Conn.: Praeger, 1995. A laudatory biography that focuses on the 1920s and 1930s.

Hack, Richard. *Puppetmaster: The Secret Life of J. Edgar Hoover.* Beverly Hills, Calif.: New Millennium Press, 2004. A critical account of both Hoover's lengthy career and his private life.

Powers, Richard G. *G-Men: Hoover's FBI in American Popular Culture.* Carbondale: Southern Illinois University Press, 1983. Examines the popular image of the FBI and Hoover's role in creating that image.

Raptopoulos, Kilby, and Walker, Jeffrey T. "J. Edgar Hoover and the FBI." In *Icons of Crime Fighting: Relentless Pursuers of Justice,* edited by Jeffrey Bumgarner. Westport, Conn.: Greenwood Press, 2008. An overview of Hoover's contributions to law enforcement.

Theoharis, Athan G. *The FBI and American Democracy: A Brief Critical History.* Lawrence: University Press of Kansas, 2004. Takes a close look at the darker side of the FBI.

See also: Coolidge, Calvin; Crimes and scandals; Palmer raids; Teapot Dome scandal

---

■ Hopper, Edward

Identification: American artist
Born: July 22, 1882, Nyack, New York
Died: May 15, 1967, New York, New York

Known for his bold use of light and color, Edward Hopper was one of America's most important realist painters. Hopper was trained as an illustrator, taught himself engraving, and later focused solely on oil and watercolor painting. He was famous for creating haunting images of buildings and people that seem to depict tension without movement.

When the 1920s began, Hopper was living in a sky-lighted studio on the upper floor of a cold-water walk-up building in Greenwich Village, which suited his self-sufficient and frugal manner. He supported himself by doing illustrations for magazines and advertising, although he hated the work. Artistically, he was beginning to make a name for himself as a print-maker and would produce more than sixty etchings before devoting himself fully to painting in 1923.

The Young Artist

As a young man, Hopper spent a year studying at the Correspondence School of Illustrating in New York City, having been encouraged by his parents to find a commercial outlet for his artistic skill. Unsatisfied, he then transferred to the New York School of Art, where he learned painting and drawing from artists such as Robert Henri, one of the founders of American realism and a member of the gritty Ashcan School movement. After finishing his studies, Hopper made three trips to Europe between 1906 and 1910, primarily to Paris. His work from this period shows the influence of the Impressionists, particularly Edgar Degas. Hopper was deeply affected by his time abroad and would always have a love of French culture and language, though he would never travel there again;

he later said that it took him ten years to get over Europe.

Success as a Painter

Starting in 1912, Hopper would spend his summers in New England, making oil paintings of picturesque towns and coastal scenes. He sold his first painting, *Sailing*, for $250 at the landmark 1913 Armory Show, but it would be ten years before he sold another. He had his first solo show in January 1920, exhibiting sixteen paintings at the Whitney Studio Club in New York City. In the summer of 1923, while painting near Gloucester, Massachusetts, Hopper reconnected with a fellow student of Henri's from the New York School of Art, Josephine "Jo" Verstille Nivison.

A watercolor painter herself, Nivison encouraged Hopper to make more use of watercolors in his work. The two often painted together and visited each other's studios in New York. Nivison was scheduled to participate in a group exhibition at the Brooklyn Museum that autumn, and she convinced the curator to include some of Hopper's paintings as well. They were very well received; critics raved about his work, and the museum bought one of his watercolors, *The Mansard Roof*, for $100.

Hopper and Nivison married the following summer, on July 9, 1924. Both over forty years old, they made for an unusual couple, with Nivison barely over five feet tall and Hopper having topped six feet at the age of twelve. Nivison later served as a model in several of Hopper's paintings.

A Mature Style

In 1925, Hopper received his last payment for his illustrations and turned to painting full time. His mature style, a blending of what he learned in Paris, what he learned from Henri, and the influence of John Sloan, another Ashcan School painter, had come to the fore during his third solo exhibition, which was displayed at the Frank K. M. Rehn Gallery in early 1924. Rehn's would remain Hopper's gallery for the remainder of his career.

Hopper's style continued to mature throughout the rest of the decade. In 1925, he painted *House by the Railroad*, one of his most celebrated works and the first ever painting to become part of the New York Museum of Modern Art's permanent collection. Additional paintings completed by Hopper during the 1920s, such as *Houses of Squam Light* (1923), *Night Windows* (1928), and *Lighthouse at Two Lights* (1929),

---

Edward Hopper and Frank K. M. Rehn

In an uncharacteristically bold move, Edward Hopper took some of his watercolors to Frank K. M. Rehn, an art dealer in New York, in 1924. Impressed by the works, Rehn not only became Hopper's first dealer but also arranged a one-man show in his gallery. All eleven watercolors that were shown, as well as five additional pieces, were sold. The show was also a critical success. Aside from illustrations and prints, Hopper had sold only two other paintings up to that point: *Sailing* (1912 or 1913), an oil, at the Armory Show in New York in 1913 and *The Mansard Roof* (1923), a watercolor, to the Brooklyn Museum in 1923. After 1924, Hopper had the financial freedom to give up illustrating and devote himself entirely to his art.

---

further established his recognizable style and considerable reputation, which would only increase over the next thirty years.

Impact

In 1961, when first lady Jacqueline Kennedy chose ten paintings to display at the White House that would represent American art, Hopper's *Houses at Squam Light* was one of them. The film director Alfred Hitchcock himself credited Hopper for influencing his classic films *Psycho* and *Rear Window*, and one can easily see similarities between the house near the Bates Motel in *Psycho* and Hopper's *House by the Railroad*. The "Hopperesque" style, which influenced not only filmmakers but playwrights, novelists, dancers, and advertisers as well, emerged and was refined in the mid- to late 1920s.

Randy L. Abbott

Further Reading

Goodrich, Lloyd. *Edward Hopper*. New York: Harry N. Abrams, 1993. Presents an overview of Hopper's best-known paintings, etchings, and illustrations.

Hanson, Anne Coffin. "Edward Hopper, American Meaning and French Craft." *Art Journal* 41, no. 2 (Summer, 1981): 142–149. Argues that Hopper belonged to an international tradition that was largely based in France.

Levin, Gail. *Edward Hopper: An Intimate Biography.*

New York: Knopf, 1995. Focuses largely on the relationship between Hopper and his wife Jo, who was herself an artist.

Marker, Sherry. *Edward Hopper*. North Dighton, Mass.: JG Press, 2005. Contains color plates of many of Hopper's urban and country scenes.

See also: Art movements; Museum of Modern Art (MoMA)

■ Hornsby, Rogers

Identification: American baseball player
Also known as: The Rajah
Born: April 27, 1896, Winters, Texas
Died: January 5, 1963, Chicago, Illinois

During the 1920s, Babe Ruth's hitting exploits may have captured the spotlight in professional baseball's American League, but it was Rogers Hornsby's hitting that dominated the National League. Hornsby, who played second base for the St. Louis Cardinals for twelve years, is often regarded as the greatest right-handed hitter in major-league history. His .424 batting average for the 1924 season set a National League record for the twentieth century.

In September 1915, the St. Louis Cardinals purchased Rogers Hornsby's contract from a minor-league team in Denison, Texas. Very inexperienced, Hornsby showed the promise and discipline to become a solid hitter. In 1917, he led the league in triple hits, and in 1919, his .318 batting average (representing the number of hits divided by the number of times at bat) was the second highest in the league. From 1920 to 1925, Hornsby led the National League in hitting, with his average exceeding .400 during three seasons. In 1922 and 1925, Hornsby became one of two major-league players in the twentieth century to capture baseball's "Triple Crown" by leading in home runs, runs batted in, and batting average. Hornsby also won the National League's Most Valuable Player award in 1925 and 1929.

During the 1925 midseason, Hornsby became a player-manager for the Cardinals, and in 1926, he guided the team to its first World Series appearance, defeating Babe Ruth and the powerful New York Yankees. That December, a salary dispute sent Hornsby to the New York Giants in a controversial trade. In 1928, he joined the Boston Braves, became their

manager, and won his seventh National League batting title. The following year, his last in the major leagues, Hornsby led the Chicago Cubs to the World Series, which they lost to the Philadelphia Athletics.

Hornsby was an intense player who shunned alcohol and tobacco and refused to watch movies or read newspapers for fear of damaging his eyesight. He also expected the same dedication from his fellow players.

Impact

Hornsby's nickname, "The Rajah," was indicative of the awe he inspired as a ferocious line-drive hitter. He was instrumental in leading the St. Louis Cardinals out of mediocrity, and in the 1920s, no other National League player had a higher batting average or had accumulated more hits, doubles, home runs, and runs batted in than Hornsby. During the twentieth century, his lifetime batting average of .358 was second only to Ty Cobb's .367 in 1911. Hornsby's achievements were recognized in 1947 when he was inducted into the Baseball Hall of Fame.

M. Philip Lucas

Further Reading

Alexander, Charles C. *Rogers Hornsby: A Biography.* New York: Henry Holt, 1995.

D'Amore, Jonathan. *Rogers Hornsby: A Biography.* Westport, Conn.: Greenwood Press, 2004.

Golenbock, Peter. *The Spirit of St. Louis: A History of the St. Louis Cardinals and Browns.* New York: Harper-Collins, 2001.

See also: Baseball; Cobb, Ty; Landis, Kenesaw Mountain; New York Yankees; Ruth, Babe; Sports

---

■ Horse racing

Horse racing has always been an important part of American culture. In the 1920s, it furnished Americans who had just endured World War I with an exciting recreational activity.

During the 1920s, horse racing was one of the most popular sports in the United States, with more than three hundred racetracks open throughout the country. The opportunity to wager was one of the main attractions of horse racing; bets could be placed on the horses both on and off the track. Known as the golden age of sports, the 1920s was a decade of sports heroes; the hero of horse racing was the horse known as Man o' War.

Man o' War

Man o' War raced only as a two-year-old and three-year-old. He started twenty-one times, set five American records and two world records, and won all the major stake races except the Sanford Stakes and the Kentucky Derby. His owner, Sam Riddle, did not enter Man o' War in the Kentucky Derby, believing the distance of one and a quarter miles to be too great for a three-year-old's stamina in the early morning, which was when the race began. In the Sanford Stakes, the race was started before Man o' War was in position, which led to him being boxed in. Man o' War won both the Preakness Stakes and the Belmont Park races, but Riddle's decision about the Kentucky Derby kept him from being a Triple Crown Winner.

Retired at the end of his three-year-old season, Man o' War became a stud on Riddle's farm, where he proved a remarkable sire. From 1925 to 1929, the horses Man o' War sired dominated the rosters of horses chosen as champions in their respective categories: Florence Nightingale and Maid at Arms were chosen as Champion Three Year Olds in 1925, and Edith Cavell became a champion in 1926, as did Bateau in 1928. In 1926, Crusader was the American Champion Three-Year-Old and Horse of the Year. In 1929, Bateau also earned the honor of Champion Handicap Female. Man o' War's colt Clyde Van Dusen won the 1929 Kentucky Derby.

Other Great Horses of the 1920s

While Man o' War dominated the 1920s both as a competitor and as a sire, many other outstanding horses raced during the decade, including Exterminator, Mad Hatter, Mad Play, Reigh Count, and Bateau. In appearance, Exterminator was the exact opposite of Man o' War. Both horses were big, with Man o' War at 16.2 hands and Exterminator at 16.3 hands; however, in contrast to the well-muscled, well-proportioned Man o' War, Exterminator was big boned, gaunt, and said to resemble a goat. His appearance earned him nicknames such as Old Bones and the Hatrack. In 1918, he was purchased by Willis Sharpe Kilmer as a workout companion for Sun Briar, a racer intended for the Kentucky Derby. When Sun Briar was eliminated by a lameness caused by ringbone,

Exterminator, who was eligible for the Kentucky Derby, became the Kilmer entry. He won the race by a length. Exterminator continued to race throughout the 1923 season. He won a total of thirty-three stake races—a record for a North American thoroughbred—and was named Horse of the Year in 1923. Throughout his racing career, Exterminator always carried more weight than his competitors, frequently raced against younger horses, and was so successful that Riddle refused to put Man o' War in a match race against him.

Two half-brothers of Man o' War, Mad Hatter and Mad Play, were also exceptional horses of the 1920s. Mad Hatter won the 1921 and 1922 Jockey Club Stakes, while Mad Play won the 1924 Belmont Stakes by one and one-half lengths and finished third in the Preakness Stakes. In 1928, Reigh Count dominated racing, winning six stake races, including the Kentucky Derby. Bateau, a filly sired by Man o' War, was an exceptionally strong race mare able to compete against male horses. In 1929, she won three major handicap races, including the Suburban Handicap at Belmont Park.

Impact

Horse racing made a significant impact on the 1920s as it responded to the American taste for entertainment, excitement, and opportunities to gamble. Man o' War, Exterminator, and other racehorses gave fans and the general public heroes to admire and support. The thoroughbreds of the 1920s strongly influenced the sport itself. Reigh Count, Count Fleet, and Count Turf formed one of only two three-generation dynasties of Kentucky Derby winners. As a sire, Man o' War left one of the greatest legacies in American horse racing: All of the Official American Champions from 1984 to 2009 traced bloodlines back to him.

Shawncey J. Webb

Further Reading

Bowen, Edward L. *Man O' War: Thoroughbred Legends.* Lexington, Ky.: Eclipse Press, 2003. Discusses Man o' War's accomplishments and importance to racing, also describing the people involved in his career and breeding.

Boyd, Eva Jolene. *Exterminator: Thoroughbred Legends.* Lexington, Ky.: Eclipse Press, 2002. The story of a horse that won the Kentucky Derby and received three Handicap Championships and Horse of the Year honors.

Faversham, Rommy. *Great Breeders and Their Methods: Samuel Riddle, Walter Jeffords, and the Dynasty of Man o' War.* Neenah, Wis.: Russell Meerdink, 2005. Analyzes the policies of Riddle and his associates who have been criticized for ruining Man o' War's stud career.

Lefcourt, Blossom, and Eric Rachlis, eds. *Horse Racing: The Golden Age of the Track.* San Francisco: Chronicle Books, 2001. Photographic coverage of thoroughbred racing, which is represented as a sport enjoyed by all social classes.

Simon, Mary. *Racing Through the Century: The Story of Thoroughbred Racing in America.* Irvine, Calif.: BowTie Press, 2002. Presents an overview of exceptional horses, people, and major events of 1920s horse racing.

See also: Gambling; Hobbies and recreation; Man o' War; Sports

Harry Houdini. (NY Daily News via Getty Images)

■ Houdini, Harry

Also known as: Ehrich Weiss, Erik Weisz
Identification: American magician, escape artist, stunt performer, and actor
Born: March 24, 1874, Budapest, Hungary
Died: October 31, 1926, Detroit, Michigan

Harry Houdini was considered by many to be the most significant magician of the early twentieth century. The name Houdini became interchangeable with death-defying stunts, which included escaping from handcuffs while fully submerged underwater and escaping after being buried alive.

Harry Houdini, born Erik Weisz, began his magic career as a teenager at Coney Island. After joining the Welsh Brothers Circus with his wife, aspiring local singer Wilhelmina Beatrice "Bess" Rahner, Houdini became an authority on escaping from handcuffs. Although he made a small name for himself, Houdini was not satisfied with his notoriety, so he and Bess moved to Europe, where he escaped police restraints after jumping into freezing rivers handcuffed. After returning to the United States in the early 1900s, Houdini established himself as an international celebrity. His notable escape performances included the handcuff challenge, milk can escape, Chinese water torture cell, suspended straitjacket escape, and buried-alive escape. In addition to his showmanship

exploits, Houdini became a passionate actor, film director, author, and pilot.

During the 1920s, Houdini ventured into motion pictures, producing and acting in the films *The Man From Beyond* (1921) and *Haldane of the Secret Service* (1923). Apart from working on films and continuing to perfect his buried-alive and Chinese water torture escape acts, Houdini focused his 1920s career on exposing spiritualists as frauds.

In October 1926, a McGill University student, who happened to be a boxer, took Houdini up on his offer that he could withstand any blow above the waist. The next day, despite not feeling well, Houdini completed his show at Garrick Theater in Detroit, Michigan. Afterward, he was rushed to the hospital with a high fever. When the doctors operated, they discovered his appendix had burst, causing peritonitis, a fatal disease in the days before antibiotics. Houdini died on October 31, 1926, at age fifty-two.

Impact

After Houdini's untimely death, his brother and former partner Theodore Hardeen received most of his artifacts and paraphernalia, and over five thousand books from Houdini's personal collection were donated to the Library of Congress. An avid collector, Sidney Hollis Radner, bought much of Houdini's estate and founded the Houdini Museum in Appleton, Wisconsin. Houdini's influence on performance is clearly seen in the work of twenty-first-century magicians, including self-proclaimed fans David Copperfield and David Blaine.

Natalie Dorfeld

Further Reading

Brandon, Ruth. *The Life and Many Deaths of Harry Houdini.* New York: Random House, 2003.

Kalush, William, and Larry Sloman. *The Secret Life of Houdini: The Making of America's First Superhero.* New York: Atria Books, 2006.

See also: Europe; Film; Spiritualism; Vaudeville

■ Housing

The years following the end of World War I saw the beginnings of a modern American identity. It was a period of widespread cultural turmoil, as the United States became an industrial nation rather than an agricultural one, and housing had to adapt to accommodate these changes.

The 1920s was a time of exuberance and innovation, in which many people sought to free themselves from the rigid Victorian era and rebelled against traditional social mores. These were the years of flappers, jazz, and bootleggers, all of which represented a spirit that would last until the stock market crash of 1929. One of the major contributors to the great crash was the collapse of the real estate market in the years leading up to it. Housing starts, defined as the number of new, privately owned housing units on which construction has already begun, peaked in 1925 at 937,000; they then declined to 750,000 in 1928, before falling to 330,000 in 1930 and less than 100,000 in 1933. Real estate values fell at the same pace.

Urbanization

At the end of World War I, veterans were welcomed home with parades and celebrations. Most of them, however, were concerned about finding a job and a place to live. Before 1914, housing shortages were not a problem, and the majority of Americans rented their homes instead of buying them. Residential construction decreased during the war, however, causing a shortage of about one million dwellings in the United States. By 1920, for the first time in American history, there were more people living in cities than on farms. Farming had become difficult and expensive, and an estimated six million farmers or children of farmers moved to the cities during the 1920s.

The country's housing problem was mainly a city problem. Before World War I, middle-class families had tended to avoid apartments, feeling that they were unsuitable homes in which to raise families. Little more than ten years later, the single-family house was in decline, and huge apartment blocks were springing up in all the major cities. The average house size in 1925 was smaller than before the war, about three and a half rooms, because urban families were smaller and rents were high. Wartime emergency housing laws had been passed to control rents, but this provided little relief.

Urban professions such as city planning became prominent at this time, focused on understanding cities in the context of the nation's agricultural past and increasingly viewing them as cultural resources whose growth needed to be managed and directed. New plans were developed for the vast majority of American cities, with architects specifically turning their attention to the problem of urban overcrowding. Zoning, introduced in 1916, soon became an effective method of enforcing city plans. Planners advocated designs that featured principles such as low-density planning, in which buildings are spaced apart and automobile use is encouraged, and clustered housing design, in which homes are grouped in a single area in order to create a shared open space.

Racial Factors

Throughout the 1920s, African Americans continued to migrate from the rural South to the more urban North, becoming in just one generation an urbanized rather than an agricultural people. Due to segregation and high housing costs, black ghettos soon formed in the hearts of the cities, with Harlem in New York City being perhaps the most significant of the era. Until 1920, Harlem had been almost all white; by 1925, it was almost entirely black. The building boom at the turn of the century had left the inner city with blocks of large, empty apartments,

R. Buckminster Fuller

In the 1920s, engineer and inventor Buckminster Fuller conceived of prefabricated multifamily living structures that he called "Lightful Towers," consisting of modular, self-sufficient units supported by a central beam or mast that would be transported and dropped in place by air. This concept later evolved into the better-known Dymaxion House, a single-family domed dwelling designed to be cheap, portable, and efficient. Fuller considered everything as a potential building material. In the early 1920s, he and his father-in-law developed the Stockade Building System, a method of forming resilient, lightweight bricks from fiber and plaster. His 1929 Dymaxion House prototypes were constructed of aluminum, the strength and durability of the lightweight metal making it ideal for his unconventional approach to home design.

once the homes of large upper-middle-class white families. The black families moving in could not afford living quarters that large, so many divided the rooms into smaller living spaces in order to take in lodgers. Landlords, both black and white, many unethical, made a fortune on rent while disregarding upkeep and maintenance, turning blocks of buildings into slums. At the time, African Americans were earning only half as much income as their white counterparts but were often charged as much as 50 percent higher rent.

Urban Development
During the 1920s, many cities began important construction projects, such as the Holland Tunnel connecting Manhattan to New Jersey. These projects made it easier for people to move to the suburbs, where more space and larger homes could be had for the same price as a small city apartment. The resulting exodus of middle-class families from the cities had the effect of depleting city funds for maintenance and improvements. City governments tore down old and neglected tenements but did not have the authority to replace them with public housing, which most people considered undesirable.

The growth and overcrowding of cities continued, prompting increasing numbers of people to move away from them. With automobiles becoming increasingly affordable and hard-surfaced roads and

highways being built, the suburbs were an increasingly attractive option for those who could afford the move. Efforts were made to make housing affordable for the growing working and middle classes, and wide suburban lots eliminated the need to build vertically.

Design and Innovation
The 1920s were a time of transition away from popular nineteenth-century styles of housing, such as row houses and factory houses, to the detached single-family houses more common today. Politicians and business leaders were at the forefront of a campaign to improve the standards of affordable low-cost housing. In 1921, the American Institute of Architects sponsored a "small house competition," in which architects were charged with designing smaller homes using new materials and building methods. The designs had to be attractive, convenient, low maintenance, and economical for a family of modest means and no servants.

The Art Deco style was first exhibited at the 1925 Exposition Internationale des Arts Décoratifs et Industriels Modernes in Paris. In the 1920s, a look to the technology of the future was at odds with the traditional home, which was seen as warm, cozy, and established; the Art Deco house was an attempt to reconcile the traditional with the modern. Predicated upon the beauty of simplicity and straight lines, Art Deco housing design flourished in cities and towns across the United States throughout the 1920s, although this style was even more common in commercial buildings and large apartment complexes. Designers inspired by the movement often used specific motifs and materials appropriate to the particular region. Many examples of Art Deco architecture in the American West, for example, feature designs based on the art of the American Indians who originally inhabited the area.

Plan books for the construction of houses, which provided instructions and detailed blueprints, now included designs for the bungalow. Often referred to as the California bungalow, this style had been introduced in the previous century and remained popular throughout the 1920s. Bungalows featured a simple, cozy design, usually one or one and a half stories and accented by a front porch, and were often constructed from local materials. Popular styles included the craftsman style, typical of the Arts and Crafts movement, with features such as exposed rafters and an exterior stone chimney; the Dutch colonial revival, featuring a hooded entrance and a roof with two slopes on either side; and the Spanish mission, also known as Spanish colonial revival, characterized by stucco siding and flat or low-pitched roofs. These could all be built with local materials and lent themselves to individual styles of interior finishes and furnishings. Bungalows were mainly built in the new suburbs that surrounded the inner core of many cities. As automobiles became more affordable and increased in numbers, bungalow tracts accommodated them with garages.

Impact

The 1920s saw the beginning of suburban developments and a population shift to the cities. Smaller houses became popular during this time, embodying the desire of American architects to break with the established European styles while still maintaining tradition. These smaller houses could be built in many styles and were well suited to illustrating the ingenuity and originality of American architects.

Jo Ann Collins

Further Reading

Bayer, Patricia. *Art Deco Architecture: Design, Decoration, and Detail from the Twenties and Thirties.* New York: Thames and Hudson, 2001. Covers the sources of the Art Deco style, its worldwide spread and popularity during the 1920s, and its later revival.

Breeze, Carla. *American Art Deco: Modernistic Architecture and Regionalism.* New York: W. W. Norton, 2003. A photographic survey of American Art Deco buildings, emphasizing regional variances.

Building Age Publishing Corporation. *Beautiful Bungalows of the Twenties.* Mineola, N.Y.: Dover, 2003. Reproduction of a 1923 collection of contemporary bungalow designs, including floor plans and other dimensional details

Light, Jennifer. *The Nature of Cities: Ecological Visions and the American Urban Professions, 1920–1960.* Baltimore: Johns Hopkins University Press, 2009. Examines the development of city planning as a profession and how cities were shaped by agrarian concerns.

Loizeaux Lumber Company. *Classic Houses of the Twenties.* New York: Dover, 1992. Reproduction of a 1927 plan book, including illustrations and floor plans for many different styles of houses.

Powell, Jane, and Linda Svendsen. *Bungalow: The Ultimate Arts and Crafts Home.* Salt Lake City: Gibbs Smith, 2004. Discusses the architecture and philosophy of the Arts and Crafts movement.

Tinniswood, Adrian. *The Art Deco House: Avant-Garde Houses of the 1920s and 1930s.* New York: Watson-Guptill, 2002. Provides detailed overviews of the features of the Art Deco home, plus photographs of examples from all over the world.

See also: Architecture; Art Deco; Better Homes in America movement; Bungalows; Cities

---

■ Hubble, Edwin Powell

Identification: American astronomer
Born: November 20, 1889, Marshfield, Missouri
Died: September 28, 1953, San Marino, California

Edwin Hubble proved that the universe consists of more than just the Milky Way galaxy. He also showed that the universe is expanding, which led to the theory that it must be expanding from a central point; this in turn gave rise to the big bang theory, a model that describes the origins of the universe.

Edwin Powell Hubble graduated from the University of Chicago in 1910 with a degree in mathematics and astronomy, although his father had wanted him to study law. He then attended Oxford University on a Rhodes scholarship, where, in deference to his then-ill father, he studied law and Spanish rather than astronomy. Hubble returned to the United States in 1913 after his father's death and spent a year teaching Spanish, physics, and mathematics at New Albany High School in Indiana. The following year, he enrolled in graduate school at the University of Chicago and began working at the Yerkes Observatory. He received his Ph.D. in astronomy in 1917.

Before graduation, Hubble had received a job offer at the Mount Wilson Observatory in California, but upon his graduation, he enlisted to serve in World War I instead. He rose to the rank of major before being discharged in 1919. He then started work at Mount Wilson Observatory, home of the 100-inch Hooker telescope, then the largest telescope in the world. Hubble's work there was only

Edwin Powell Hubble. (Time & Life Pictures/Getty Images)

briefly interrupted during World War II, when he served in a scientific capacity at Aberdeen Proving Grounds in Maryland, for which he was given the Legion of Merit award.

The Discovery of Galaxies
Hubble's graduate work at Yerkes was focused on photographic observations of nebulae, which at the time referred to any large, cloudlike astronomical object. Earlier astronomers had disagreed on whether these were gas clouds or collections of stars, possibly separate from our own galaxy. At the beginning of Hubble's career, most astronomers believed the universe to be one single galaxy, and those who speculated otherwise could not prove it.

In 1923, Hubble used the Hooker telescope to make detailed measurements of some nebulae. In particular, he observed some cepheids, which are variable stars that grow brighter and dimmer over a set period. Using data on the brightness of certain cepheids and the length of their cycles, Hubble determined that the nebulae were in fact large systems of stars that could not be within the Milky Way. Hubble's findings were initially met with resistance, but by the end of the decade, most astronomers had accepted the fact that the universe included millions of galaxies.

Hubble's Law
Hubble also created a system of classification for galaxies, called the Hubble sequence. The sequence divides galaxies into two main shapes, spiral and elliptical, with an intermediate shape known as lenticular; when Hubble first published this sequence in 1926, the existence of lenticular galaxies was purely theoretical, but it has since been confirmed. The spiral galaxies comprise two subcategories: regular and barred. Only about 3 percent of galaxies do not rotate about a central nucleus, and Hubble called these "irregular" galaxies. Hubble's system further subdivides each category, describing galaxies by content, distance, shape, and brightness.

While working on the classification sequence, Hubble noticed that the light being emitted from other galaxies showed an increase in wavelength, a phenomenon known as redshift that occurs when a light source is moving away from its observer. Hubble later determined that the redshifts roughly correspond to the distance between galaxies. In 1929, he stated what is now known as Hubble's law: The more distant a galaxy is from Earth, the faster it appears to be receding.

Impact
Edwin Hubble's work caused a drastic shift in the way astronomers, other scientists, and the general public viewed the universe. The static universe became a vast, expanding one. Physicist Albert Einstein's theory of relativity, introduced in 1917, required space to be able to expand or contract; this conclusion, troubling to Einstein at the time, was verified by Hubble's work. In addition, Hubble's law has helped astronomers determine the age of the

universe, and his work supported the development of the big bang theory. The Hubble sequence of galaxy classification continues to be used by astronomers. The impact of Hubble's work was recognized by the scientific community with the launch of the Hubble Space Telescope in 1990.

Linda Eikmeier Endersby

Further Reading

Christianson, Gale E. *Edwin Hubble: Mariner of the Nebulae.* New York: Farrar, Straus and Giroux, 1995. A highly detailed account of Hubble's life, covering both his professional and intellectual successes and his more personal failings.

Datnow, Claire L. *Edwin Hubble: Discoverer of Galaxies.* Rev. ed. Great Minds of Science. Berkeley Heights, N.J.: Enslow, 2008. This short book is aimed at younger audiences and supplies the basics of Hubble's life and work.

Glass, Ian S. *Revolutionaries of the Cosmos: The Astro-Physicists.* New York: Oxford University Press, 2006. Contains a chapter on Hubble that provides an account of his life and family as well as his work.

Nussbaumer, Harry, and Lydia Bieri. *Discovering the Expanding Universe.* New York: Cambridge University Press, 2009. Puts the discovery of the expanding universe in context with the work of several other astronomers and argues that Hubble should not receive sole credit.

Sharov, Alexander S., and Igor D. Novikov. *Edwin Hubble: The Discoverer of the Big Bang Universe.* Translated by Vitaly Kisin. New York: Cambridge University Press, 2005. The first complete account of Edwin Hubble's life and work, this book places his work in the larger context of the field of astronomy. Originally published in Russian in 1993.

See also: Astronomy; Science and technology

■ Hughes, Charles Evans

Identification: American lawyer, judge, and government official
Born: April 11, 1862, Glens Falls, New York
Died: August 27, 1948, Osterville, Massachusetts

As secretary of state from 1921 to 1925, Charles Evans Hughes hosted the Washington Conference of 1921 and 1922, in which he negotiated naval disarmament treaties and counseled the United States to abstain from aggression in eastern Asia.

The son of a conservative Baptist minister, Charles Evans Hughes graduated from Brown University and then completed a law degree at Columbia University in 1884. For the next twenty-two years, he practiced law in New York City, except for the two years that he was a law professor at Cornell University. Hughes was a significant figure in the Progressive movement characterizing early twentieth-century American politics. He served as governor of New York from 1907 to 1910 and as associate justice of the U.S. Supreme Court during the next six years. Hughes resigned from the Supreme Court in 1916 in order to run for president as the Republican candidate, but he lost to Democratic candidate Woodrow Wilson.

Secretary of State

During the election of 1920, Hughes supported Republican Warren G. Harding, who won the presidency. Shortly after the election, President Harding named Hughes head of the State Department, a position he held for the next four years. Since Harding had limited knowledge about international relations, Hughes was allowed a particularly free hand in foreign policy.

As Hughes entered office, the British and Japanese were competing for naval supremacy in Asia. Fearing that the competition might escalate and threaten U.S. interests in Asia, the Senate passed a resolution to hold a conference to discuss the issue. Encouraged by the British government, Hughes seized the opportunity to invite eight interested powers to send representatives to Washington, D.C. Despite the U.S. Navy's opposition, the Washington Naval Conference began on November 12, 1920, with Hughes's dramatic speech announcing that the U.S. would destroy thirty ships and challenging Great Britain and France to make similar cuts.

During the conference, diplomats agreed to sign several important treaties. In the Five Power Treaty, the United States, Britain, Japan, France, and Italy agreed to reduce existing naval vessels and to set a tonnage ratio for aircraft carriers, battleships, and cruisers. Another Five Power Treaty outlawed poison gas and applied rules of war to submarines. The Four Power Treaty specified that the United States, Britain, France, and Japan would respect one another's territorial acquisitions. Finally, in the Nine Power Treaty, the countries with Asian interests endorsed the territorial independence of China and its equal trading rights.

In 1922, Hughes signed the Hughes-Peynado Agreement, which ended the U.S. occupation of the Dominican Republic. A firm defender of U.S. interests, he also helped advance a nonintervention good neighbor policy toward Latin American countries. He also played a significant role in passing the Rogers Act of 1924, which merged the diplomatic and consular services, thereby increasing the number of appointments based on merit. Although unsuccessful in his attempt to convince the French to significantly reduce German reparations, he was instrumental in gaining approval of the Dawes Plan of 1924, which softened the burden of yearly payments and achieved the withdrawal of French troops from German soil.

Legal Profession and Supreme Court Service

In 1925, after President Calvin Coolidge was elected to a full term, Hughes resigned from his position as secretary of state in order to return to his law practice. Recognized as one of the nation's foremost lawyers, he became president of the American Society of International Law, serving from 1925 to 1929, and during these years, he argued over fifty cases before the U.S. Supreme Court. In 1926, New York governor Alfred Smith appointed Hughes to lead a state reorganization commission, which centralized services under the authority of the state governor. From 1926 to 1930, moreover, he served as a member of the Permanent Court of Arbitration. During the years 1928 to 1930, he was a judge at the Permanent Court of International Justice at The Hague, as well as a delegate to the Pan-American Conference on Arbitration and Conciliation. As cofounder of the National Conference of Christians and Jews in 1927, he opposed extremist organizations such as the Ku Klux Klan (KKK).

In 1928, many moderate and conservative Republicans tried to convince Hughes to run for president, but he declined. In 1930, President Herbert Hoover appointed him chief justice of the Supreme Court, a position he held until his retirement in 1941.

Impact

Charles Evans Hughes was a hardworking and intelligent administrator. Most historians rank him as one of the more outstanding secretaries of state in U.S. history. He has often been criticized for not attempting to achieve U.S. membership in the League of Nations, but his moderate isolationism was in conformity with public opinion at the time.

Thomas Tandy Lewis

Further Reading

Glad, Betty. *Charles Evans Hughes and the Illusions of Innocence: A Study in American Diplomacy.* Urbana: University of Illinois Press, 1966. Discusses Hughes's moderate isolationism, legalistic-moralistic approach, and sensitivity to public and political opinion.

Hughes, Charles E. *The Autobiographical Notes of Charles Evans Hughes.* Edited by David J. Danelski and Joseph S. Tulchin. Cambridge, Mass.: Harvard University Press, 1973. Features a narrative that Hughes dictated from 1941 to 1945, with a helpful introduction and commentary.

Patterson, Thomas, et al. *American Foreign Relations: A History Since 1895.* 6th ed. Boston, Mass.: Houghton Mifflin, 2005. Provides a useful summary of U.S. foreign relations during the 1920s and other periods.

Perkins, Dexter. *Charles Evans Hughes and American Democratic Statesmanship.* Westport, Conn.: Greenwood Press, 1978. A mostly favorable account of Hughes's foreign policy.

Pusey, Merlo John. *Charles Evans Hughes.* New York: Garland, 1979. A scholarly biography written by a respected historian who had intimate contact with Hughes.

See also: Asia; Elections of 1920, U.S.; Europe; Foreign policy, U.S.; Harding, Warren G.; Isolationism; League of Nations; Supreme Court, U.S.; Washington Naval Conference

■ Hughes, Howard

Identification: American aviator, business executive, and filmmaker
Born: September 24, 1905, Houston, Texas
Died: April 5, 1976, Houston, Texas

Howard Hughes became famous in the late 1920s as an independent film producer for making the big-budget film Hell's Angels *and began a series of highly publicized love affairs that provided source materials for tabloids for the next several decades. His early interest in flying, already evident in the 1920s, would eventually lead him to become an aviation pioneer.*

Howard Hughes. (Hulton Archive/Getty Images)

Howard Robard Hughes Jr. was born to Allene Gano, the daughter of a Dallas judge and granddaughter of a Confederate general, and Howard R. Hughes Sr., who invented the two-cone roller bit, which allowed oil wells to be drilled through granite. The device proved to be very successful and lucrative: Over the next ten years, over 75 percent of all oil wells used the bit, and Standard Oil alone leased fifteen thousand of them. The drill bit business provided the revenue stream that his son later used to go into the film industry, airplane manufacturing, and other businesses.

Early Years
Howard built his own radio transmitter when he was eleven years old. At twelve, he motorized a bicycle using parts taken from a steam engine and built an intercom system for the family mansion. Howard was an indifferent student but liked mathematics and mechanical engineering. He took his first flying lesson when he was fourteen and audited math and aeronautical engineering courses at the California

Institute of Technology in 1923. In 1928, he obtained a pilot's license.

Hughes's mother died during surgery in 1922, and his father died of a heart attack in 1924, leaving him 75 percent of the estate. Hughes was declared an emancipated minor when he turned nineteen, enabling him to take possession of his inheritance. Hughes dropped out of Rice University shortly after his father's death and married Ella Rice, a member of Houston's social elite, in 1925. They moved to Los Angeles, where he hoped to become a film producer. Unfortunately for Ella, Hughes never intended to keep his marriage vows and conducted highly publicized affairs with film stars, including Joan Crawford, Jean Harlow, and Billie Dove, who was also married. As a result, the couple divorced in 1929, and Ella was awarded a $1.25 million settlement, payable over five years.

Film Career
Hughes's first movie, *Swell Hogan*, was so bad that it was never released and cost him eighty thousand dollars. Fortunately for Hughes, his next two films, *Everybody's Acting* (1926), a romance between a rich young man and an actress, and *Two Arabian Knights* (1927), were profitable. *Two Arabian Knights*, in which two American soldiers (William Boyd and Louis Wolheim) escape from their German captors and have a series of adventures with an Arabian princess, won director Lewis Milestone the first Academy Award for Best Director of a Comedy Picture. Hughes's next films also enjoyed greater success. *The Racket* (1928), a crime drama based on the life of Al Capone featuring Wolheim and directed by Milestone, was both a commercial and critical success. Based on a popular novel of the time, *The Mating Call* (1928) concerns a marriage of convenience that leads to love.

Inspired by the Academy Award–winning *Wings* (1927), Hughes was able to combine his interests in flying and filmmaking when he spent $4.2 million to make the World War I flying film *Hell's Angels* (1930), then the most expensive film ever made. Hughes originally filmed it as a silent movie, but after the success of *The Jazz Singer* (1927), he decided to add dialogue to all the scenes and replace the female lead with Jean Harlow, one of his many mistresses. Although Hughes had hired over twenty World War I pilots to fly the more than forty World War I aircraft in the film, he decided to fly one himself but crashed it, breaking several of his bones and suffering a concussion. By contemporary standards, the film was a commercial success, bringing in gross earnings of $2.7 million, but this still represented a substantial financial loss for Hughes.

Impact

Hell's Angels made Howard Hughes a major player in Hollywood and film actor Jean Harlow a superstar. Hughes later produced controversial films such as *Scarface* (1931) and *The Outlaw* (1943), starring Jane Russell, and bought the Radio-Keith-Orpheum (RKO) movie studio in 1948.

In the 1930s, Hughes launched his first serious aviation endeavors: He founded the Hughes Aircraft Company in 1932, which built the Hughes H-1 Racer and the H-4 Hercules cargo plane, also known as the "Spruce Goose." As a pilot, he set several flight records. Also a successful business executive, Hughes went on to buy a controlling interest in Trans World Airlines (TWA) in 1940.

Thomas R. Feller

Further Reading

Brown, Peter Harry, and Pat H. Broeske. *Howard Hughes: The Untold Story*. Cambridge, Mass.: Da Capo Press, 2004. Presents a biography of Hughes.

Dietrich, Noah, and Bob Thomas. *Howard: The Amazing Mr. Hughes*. Greenwich, Conn.: Fawcett, 1972. A memoir by Hughes's business manager.

Hack, Richard. *Hughes: The Private Diaries, Memos, and Letters*. Beverly Hills, Calif.: Phoenix Books, 2006. Presents biographical information about Hughes.

Thomas, Tony. *Howard Hughes in Hollywood*. Secaucus, N.J.: Citadel Press, 1985. A biography of Hughes, with emphasis on his filmmaking career.

Wynne, H. Hugh. *The Motion Picture Stunt Pilots and Hollywood's Classic Aviation Movies*. Missoula, Mont.: Pictorial Histories, 1987. An illustrated study of aviation films, including *Hell's Angels*.

See also: Academy Awards; Aviation; Capone, Al; Film; Talking motion pictures; *Wings*

■ Hughes, Langston

Identification: African American poet and writer
Also known as: James Mercer Langston Hughes
Born: February 1, 1902, Joplin, Missouri
Died: May 22, 1967, New York, New York

Through his poetry and other writings, Langston Hughes, the "Poet Laureate of Harlem," helped to interpret the African American experience in the United States from the 1920s through much of the 1960s. Hughes was also a major contributor to the Harlem Renaissance, the African American cultural movement of the 1920s and 1930s centered in New York City.

James Mercer Langston Hughes was born in Joplin, Missouri, in 1902. His parents separated when he was young, and Hughes was raised in Lawrence, Kansas, by his maternal grandmother after his father left the family and moved to Mexico and his mother moved throughout the country in search of work. After his grandmother's death in 1914, Hughes joined his mother in Cleveland, Ohio, and attended Central High School, graduating in 1920. After graduation, Hughes lived with his father in Mexico and then relocated to New York City in 1921 to study engineering at Columbia University. Hughes left Columbia after one year and in 1923 spent time traveling throughout Africa. In 1929, with the help of a scholarship, he attended Lincoln University in Pennsylvania and graduated with a bachelor of arts degree in 1929.

Langston Hughes' *The Weary Blues*

The Weary Blues (1926), Langston Hughes's first published volume of poetry, demonstrates Hughes's determination to present the many sides of African American life. The poems address romantic love, African heritage, and the social aspects of race and color. In doing so, the poems raise the experiences of common people to the level of art. Hughes grounded his poems in a blues aesthetic, utilizing the rhythms, structure, and themes of blues and jazz music. The poem "The Weary Blues" depicts jazz life through the observations of a person sensitive to the conditions of performance, who comments:

> Droning a drowsy syncopated tune,
> Rocking back and forth to a mellow croon,
> I heard a Negro play.
> Down on Lenox Avenue the other night
> By the pale dull pallor of an old gas light.

Major Works

In 1921, Hughes published his first play, *The Gold Piece*, and his signature poem, "The Negro Speaks of Rivers," both of which appeared in the magazine *Brownie's Book* (geared toward African American children) and *The Crisis* (published by the National Association for the Advancement of Colored People, or NAACP). "The Negro Speaks of Rivers" is said to present a metaphor of the journey of all Africans, linking the power and endurance of rivers to the struggle of blacks throughout history. Hughes dedicated the poem to W. E. B. Du Bois, the African American scholar and civil rights activist who founded the NAACP in 1909.

In 1923, Hughes worked for a shipping company and traveled to Africa. After six months and a brief stay in France, Hughes relocated to Washington, D.C., to be closer to his mother. While in Washington, Hughes found work as a busboy in a local hotel and had the opportunity to present several of his poems, including "The Weary Blues," to the poet Vachel Lindsay. Lindsay was impressed and introduced Hughes to various publishers. Hughes's first collection of poems, *The Weary Blues,* was published in 1926. An avid lover of music, Hughes combined the musical elements of jazz and blues with poetry, an uncommon technique at the time that was well received by critics and the public.

Hughes's second collection, *Fine Clothes to the Jew* (1927), addressed the everyday struggles of urban blacks in Harlem. Because of the collection's title as well as its crude depiction of blacks, it was not commercially successful and was condemned by many black critics and many in the Jewish community. Hughes would continue to write poems, plays, and books addressing the challenges of race, class, and the daily struggles of African Americans.

Major Influences

Among the writers who influenced Hughes were African American poet Paul Lawrence Dunbar and Chicago poet Carl Sandburg, whom Hughes referred to as his "guiding star." Dunbar's poetry taught Hughes the impact of incorporating black dialect into his own work, while Sandburg's poetry inspired Hughes with its working-class references and modern free-verse style. Music, especially jazz and blues, was extremely influential in the emerging culture of the Harlem Renaissance and was a recurring element in Hughes's poetry, which reflected not only the cadence, flow, and sound of music, but also mirrored the style and themes of jazz and blues. Hughes's bittersweet perspective on urban life is felt in blues music, while the free and loose style of many of his poems resembles the improvisational feel of jazz.

Impact

Although the Harlem Renaissance faded after the 1930s, Langston Hughes and his poetry and prose have had a lasting impact. Hughes's work, unlike most of the professional writing of the 1920s, portrayed the realistic elements of the lives and stories of black America. Whether addressing the music, laughter, or suffering of urban blacks, Hughes used his personal experience to meld with the experiences of the common person in order to create culturally important and commercially successful poetry, short stories, and books.

Diana Pardo

Further Reading

Feinstein, Sascha. *Jazz Poetry: From the 1920s to the Present.* Westport, Conn.: Praeger, 1997. Provides historical and biographical information on jazz-related poetry and poets from the 1920s through the early 1990s.

Hughes, Langston. *The Big Sea.* New York: Hill & Wang, 2001. Autobiographical account of Hughes's life in Europe and Harlem during the 1920s.

Hughes, Langston. *I Wonder as I Wander.* New York: Hill & Wang, 1999. Autobiography of Hughes's life during the 1930s as he traveled the world.

Rampersad, Arnold. *1902–1941: I, Too, Sing America.* Vol. 1 in *The Life of Langston Hughes.* New York: Oxford University Press, 2002. Biography chronicling Hughes's life from his birth through his most prolific years as a writer. Hughes's political activism is also covered.

_____. *1941–1967: I Dream a World.* Vol. 2 in *The Life of Langston Hughes.* New York: Oxford University Press, 2002. Concluding volume of the biography that follows Hughes from the 1940s through the 1960s, exploring his declining career and feelings of alienation from younger African American writers.

Williams, Ella O. *Harlem Renaissance: A Handbook.* Bloomington, Ind.: AuthorHouse, 2008. Chronicles the literature, art, theater, and music of Harlem, New York, from 1910 to 1940.

See also: African Americans; Du Bois, W. E. B.; Harlem Renaissance; Lindsay, Vachel; Literature in the United States; Poetry

■ Hurston, Zora Neale

Identification: African American anthropologist and writer
Also known as: Zora Neal Lee Hurston
Born: January 7, 1891, Notasulga, Alabama
Died: January 28, 1960, Fort Pierce, Florida

While the Great Migration from the rural South to the urban North provoked major social and demographic changes, Zora Neale Hurston used social science, literary talent, and a unique personal openness to capture isolated and small-town African American cultures. Her formal education and most intensive fieldwork largely took place during the 1920s and 1930s and resulted in a variety of creative and anthropological enterprises that inspired future generations. Hurston is identified with the Harlem Renaissance, the black cultural movement of the 1920s and 1930s, which gave her an audience for her cultural studies, short stories, novels, and plays.

Zora Neale Hurston grew up in Eatonville, Florida, an all-black town that was the first U.S. black town to incorporate. After her mother's death in 1904 and her father's remarriage soon after, Hurston worked as a wardrobe girl to a repertory company touring the South.

In 1918, Hurston entered Howard University and was admitted to the university literary society. Hurston's writing was noticed by Charles S. Johnson, founder of *Opportunity* magazine, who then published her short story "Drenched in Light" (1924). Hurston moved to New York City in 1925 and won the *Opportunity* literary contest for her second short story, "Spunk." These stories and the subsequent novel *Color Struck* (1926) were based on Hurston's observations of the folk life she witnessed while growing up in Eatonville and soon drew the attention of Annie Nathan Meyer, founder of Barnard College, who offered Hurston a scholarship. While at Barnard, Hurston wrote a paper that prompted Columbia University professor and noted anthropologist Franz Boas to invite Hurston to study with him.

Hurston as Anthropologist
Boas's national influence and Hurston's gifts as a writer and her intense interest in black folk history invited mentorship, patronage, and fellowship opportunities for Hurston. Boas encouraged Hurston to return to Eatonville and gather and record the folk culture there as an extension of African oral storytelling. Among her projects in the 1920s, Hurston interviewed Kossola Cudjo Lewis, last remaining survivor of the American slave ship, the *Chlotilde*. Hurston also traveled to the West Indies and the Caribbean, studying and recording the various African subcultures she encountered. She absorbed New Orleans voudon rituals, and in the West Indies and the Caribbean, she took photographs and recorded local songs, dances, and ceremonies.

Hurston as Ethnographer and Writer
The late 1920s probably was Hurston's most prolific collection period. With Hurston's growing reputation as an ethnographer (one who studies and records human cultures), the fieldwork became the wellspring for other endeavors and for different takes on anthropology. Hurston emerged as a folklorist who presented the local language, culture, and dialect in a lively yet relatable way. The sermons, songs, and artifacts of everyday life that she gathered entered into her commercially published fiction and nonfiction and became the basis of many of her most important writings of the 1930s. Hurston's first novel, *Jonah's Gourd Vine* (1934), was praised for its vibrant use of folklore; *Mules and Men* (1935) was the first study of African American folklore by a woman; and *Tell My Horse* (1937) was the first significant study of Caribbean folklore.

The last decade of Hurston's life brought declining influence and recognition. Her writing was often criticized during the Civil Rights movement of the 1950s and early 1960s for not addressing racism and racial oppression. Hurston, unable to support herself as an aging writer, took jobs as a librarian and a domestic worker. She died in 1960 in a welfare home, without resources, and was buried in an unmarked grave. In 1973, African American novelist Alice Walker located the Florida cemetery where Hurston was buried and placed a headstone near the presumed grave.

Impact
At the time of her death, Hurston's stories and books were out of print. Thanks to the revival work of Alice Walker in the 1970s, Hurston's writing continues to

invite discovery and discussion. The legacy of Zora Neale Hurston is vast: she wrote four novels, two books of folklore, an autobiography, and many stories, plays, and articles. The Library of Congress contains several hundred songs, stories, and instrumentals recorded by Hurston and her collaborators, as well as thirty minutes of silent footage she taped during the 1920s.

Lynn C. Kronzek

Further Reading

Bloom, Harold, ed. *Zora Neale Hurston.* New York: Chelsea House, 2008. A biography written for young adults, including black-and-white photographs.

Boyd, Valerie. *Wrapped in Rainbows: The Life of Zora Neale Hurston.* New York: Scribner, 2004. Chronicles Hurston's life from birth through death and addresses her work as an anthropologist and her influence on the Harlem Renaissance.

Hemenway, Robert E. *Zora Neale Hurston: A Literary Biography.* Urbana: University of Illinois, 1980. A biography focusing on Hurston's influence on the Harlem Renaissance, her research of black culture, and her politics. Includes a foreword by Alice Walker.

Hurston, Zora Neale. *Mules and Men.* New York: Harper Perennial Modern Classics, 2008. A reprint of Hurston's 1935 collection of black folklore.

_____. *Their Eyes Were Watching God.* New York: Harper Perennial Modern Classics, 2010. A reprint of Hurston's popular and widely read 1937 novel.

Plant, Deborah G. *Zora Neale Hurston: A Biography of the Spirit.* Westport, Conn.: Praeger, 2007. Concentrates on Hurston's creative and intellectual contributions and artistic vision.

See also: African Americans; Civil rights and liberties; Great Migration; Harlem Renaissance; Hughes, Langston; Literature in the United States; Racial discrimination; Social sciences; Toomer, Jean

■ *I'll Take My Stand*

Identification: Major commentary on Southern agrarianism written by twelve well-known Southern writers, historians, professors, and playwrights
Authors: Twelve Southerners
Date: 1930

A collection of essays, I'll Take My Stand: The South and the Agrarian Tradition *is said to have been one of the most succinct, well-written, and meticulously defined statements of the Southern agrarian tradition in response to the growing industrial process in the United States. The book served as a summation of what traditional Southern culture and values meant to Southerners, especially in light of the social and economic changes during the 1920s.*

Known by a variety of names, including the Twelve Southerners, the Vanderbilt Agrarians, or the Tennessee Agrarians, this highly educated group published a resounding outline of what Southern agrarian tradition, culture, and lifestyle meant to them individually, as well as to the region and the nation. As outlined in its introduction, *I'll Take My Stand* confronted such modernist tendencies as industrialism, growing wealth within business, and the rapid proliferation of urban centers in the United States. Arguing that American tradition resided in the region's rural and agrarian traditions, these individuals wanted to maintain Southern values while eschewing the excesses of industrialization and urbanization. While supporting the standards and lifestyle of Southern traditionalism (to the point, some believe, of defending racial segregation), these writers were also vocal in their intense hatred of communism and fascism. Over time, and as the United States continued to develop and prosper, most of the Twelve Southerners waivered in their commitment to Southern cultural traditions and values.

Perhaps one of the most common threads among the Twelve Southerners was their connection to Nashville and Vanderbilt University and their participation in an earlier literary group and magazine called *The Fugitive.* The Twelve Southerners included Donald Davidson, Henry Blue Kline, John Gould Fletcher, Andrew Nelson Lytle, Herman Clarence Nixon, Lyle H. Lanier, Frank Lawrence Oswley, John Crowe Ransom, John Donald Wade, Allen Tate, Robert Penn Warren, and Stark Young. While they were individually accomplished and well known in their fields, it was their collective statement of support for the Southern agrarian principles that cemented their names and ideas together. In the end, however, the majority of these Southern agrarians adjusted their earlier ideas to conform more to the direction in which the country was growing.

Impact

The Twelve Southerners' book *I'll Take My Stand* demonstrated the growing tensions within American society between the modernist industrial world of the 1920s and the nostalgic recreation of an older way of life. It was a most powerful and potent expression of beliefs from some of the best-known authors and scholars of the South.

Michael V. Namorato

Further Reading

Carlson, Allan. *The New Agrarian Mind: The Movement Toward Decentralist Thought in Twentieth-Century America.* New Brunswick, N.J.: Transaction, 2004.
Murphy, Paul V. *The Rebuke of History: The Southern Agrarians and American Conservative Thought.* Chapel Hill: University of North Carolina Press, 2001.

See also: Agriculture in the United States; Fugitive Poets; Literature in the United States; Poetry; Revenue Acts of 1924, 1926, and 1928; Southern Agrarians

■ Immigration Act of 1921

The Law: U.S. federal law establishing immigration quotas

Also known as: Emergency Quota Act, Johnson Quota Act, Per Centum Law

Date: Enacted on May 19, 1921.

The Immigration Act of 1921 established annual immigrant nationality quotas for the first time in the United States. However, the restrictions seemed inadequate to many Americans, who felt that too many immigrants still managed to enter the United States. Pressure continued for stronger restrictions, lower quotas, and tighter borders, resulting in the Immigration Act of 1924.

For three centuries, immigration to North American had been essentially unrestricted. Although anti-immigrant sentiments were not unknown in American history, with a few exceptions these popular moods generally passed before manifesting in legal restrictions. However, a large influx of immigrants from southern and eastern Europe between 1880 and 1920 sparked a backlash culminating in significant immigration restrictions in 1921.

Background

U.S. efforts to control immigration began in the mid-1870s with the introduction of restrictive legislation against Asians, motivated primarily by popular opposition to the influx of Chinese laborers on the West Coast. In the first two decades of the twentieth century, animosity was directed against not only Asians but newcomers from southern and eastern Europe, or anyone whose customs, language, and religion were different from those of the descendants of northern European and British immigrants who made up the bulk of American society. Congress also blocked entry to anarchists and communists on political grounds, and to criminals and people with mental or physical disabilities on grounds of genetic undesirability.

The last significant piece of immigration legislation passed before 1921 was the Immigration Act of 1917, which, over President Woodrow Wilson's veto, barred the immigration of a variety of categories of persons deemed undesirable, along with anyone from a sweeping stretch of southern and eastern Asia and the South Pacific, referred to in the law as the "Asiatic barred zone." The law also established a literacy test for prospective immigrants.

Postwar Social Conditions

Immigration slowed during World War I, but the end of the war reopened the floodgates. In 1920, over

A cartoon showing Uncle Sam enforcing the Immigration Act of 1921. (Getty Images)

800,000 immigrants arrived in the United States. Postwar communist revolts in Europe provoked the first Red Scare from 1919 to 1920, as conservative Americans sought to stave off this latest threat to their way of life. In addition, the United States experienced an economic recession in 1920 and 1921, contributing to the nativist and isolationist worldview of Americans who wished to protect their jobs from immigrant competition. As a result of all these developments, anti-immigration organizations became increasingly influential in U.S. politics during the early 1920s.

The white supremacist Ku Klux Klan was one of the most widespread and active of these groups, distilling anti-immigrant, anti-black, anti–Roman Catholic, and anti-Semitic sentiment. Most Americans were less extreme, but they were ambivalent about accepting Roman Catholics, Jews, and Asians into mainstream society. Another group, the Immigration Restriction League (IRL), called for race-based immigration restrictions with limits on southern and eastern Europeans, who, according to restrictionists, would corrupt American democracy. Catholics and radicals were especially mistrusted.

Crafting the Legislation

Amid the rising tide of anti-immigrant sentiment, Congress assembled in 1921 to craft an immigration law seen as necessary to preserve American society and culture from foreign corruption. Washington congressman Albert Johnson chaired the House Committee on Immigration and Naturalization, which favored an immigration quota according to which the number of immigrants from any one country would be capped at a percentage of people from that country already living in the United States. The 1910 census was favored as the baseline for calculating these numbers, because quotas under that census would allow a greater proportion of northern and western Europeans, whom many Americans preferred to southern and eastern Europeans or Jews trying to escape post–World War I persecution.

A competing bill was introduced in the Senate by William Dillingham of Vermont. Although less anti-Semitic and more receptive to business and agricultural interests that relied on cheap immigrant labor, the Senate recognized the national mood and therefore also favored the implementation of immigrant quotas by nationality. Dillingham's bill maintained restrictions on Asians and did not restrict immigration within the Western Hemisphere, an aspect of the bill favorable to American business and agriculture. Using the 1910 census as a frame of reference, the Dillingham bill set a quota of 5 percent, meaning the number of immigrants admitted annually from a given country could equal no more than 5 percent of the number of people from that country in the U.S. population as of 1910. After an amendment to reduce the 5 percent quota to 3 percent (a number still regarded as too high by those who favored complete exclusion), the House and Senate passed the bill by wide margins, and President Warren G. Harding signed it into law.

Impact

The Immigration Act of 1921 was a watershed in U.S. immigration law, representing the first immigration quota and the first numerical limit on immigrants from Europe. According to the breakdown of the U.S. population in 1910, the annual ceiling for all immigration allowed in 1921 was set at 357,802 immigrants, less than half the number admitted in 1920. The proportion of southern and eastern Europeans admitted to the United States each year fell drastically under the law to less than half the annual total.

In this sense the law achieved its goals, although it was considered only a stopgap measure, and its provisions would be tightened still further in 1924.

John H. Barnhill

Further Reading

Daniels, Roger. *Guarding the Golden Door: American Immigration Policy and Immigrants Since 1882.* New York: Hill and Wang, 2004. Discusses the history of U.S. immigration policy, beginning with the Chinese Exclusion Act of 1882.

Gerstle, Gary. *American Crucible: Race and Nation in the Twentieth Century.* Princeton, N.J.: Princeton University Press, 2001. Presents an analysis of twentieth-century American society, noting the impact of nationalism, prejudice, and immigration policy on American history.

Higham, John. *Strangers in the Land: Patterns of American Nativism, 1860–1925.* New York: Atheneum, 1966. Presents a history of nativism, nationalism, and immigration restriction in the United States.

Zolberg, Aristide. *A Nation by Design: Immigration Policy in the Fashioning of America.* Cambridge, Mass.: Harvard University Press, 2006. Discusses U.S. immigration policy from the eighteenth to the twenty-first century, focusing on immigration restriction, types of migration, and the sociopolitical factors influencing immigration policy.

See also: Anti-Semitism; Demographics; Eugenics movement; Harding, Warren G.; Immigration Act of 1924; Immigration to the United States; Ku Klux Klan; Racial discrimination; Red Scare, The

---

■ Immigration Act of 1924

The Law: U.S. federal law tightening immigration quotas
Also known as: Johnson-Reed Act
Date: Enacted on May 26, 1924

The act established permanent numerical limitations on immigration to the United States and set precedents for immigration policy for the rest of the twentieth century. The immigration act grew out of a desire not only to reduce the number of immigrants allowed to settle in the United States but also to limit the number of immigrants of certain nationalities, particularly those from eastern and southern Europe, as well as Asian countries.

The 1924 Immigration Act, also known as the Johnson-Reed Act, was the culmination of reactions against the increasing influx of immigrants from eastern and southern Europe in the late nineteenth and early twentieth centuries. The act, passed by the U.S. Congress and signed into law by President Calvin Coolidge in May 1924, drew from the Immigration Act of 1921, tightening and making permanent the numerical restrictions in U.S. immigration policy. Though earlier laws had restricted the immigration of migrants from Asian countries and sick or impoverished immigrants, the 1924 act established that the federal government would place numerical caps on the number of visas it issued to prospective immigrants each year and that the government would apportion the visas differently, based on national origins.

Origins of the Act

In the mid-nineteenth century, immigrants to the United States came predominantly from northern and western Europe. By the end of the century, however, there were increasing numbers of migrants from eastern and southern Europe, many of whom were Italian or Slavic Catholics or eastern European Jews. The first decades of the twentieth century saw record-setting numbers of immigrants arriving from Europe, the flow only temporarily interrupted by World War I. There was a growing sense among American Protestants of European descent that the new immigrants from eastern and southern Europe were culturally and perhaps racially too foreign to assimilate into the American population. The interest in maintaining the ethnic and cultural composition of the country, increasing fears of political radicalism such as anarchism and communism, and anti-Semitism combined to create the cultural and political climate in which the U.S. Congress passed immigration restriction.

Provisions of the Act

The Immigration Act of 1921 had placed an annual cap on the number of immigrants from any given country, set at 3 percent of the number of people from that country already living in the United States at the time of the 1910 census. The 1924 law went further, lowering the cap to 2 percent, and backdating the standard of measurement to the 1890 census—a time when the number of U.S. residents from countries such as Italy and Poland was even lower. In contrast, the quotas for Great Britain, Ireland, and

Germany were comparatively high, as those nationalities were well represented in the 1890 census.

Additional provisions in the law phased out the percentage calculations entirely over a period of years: By 1929, the total number of immigrants granted admission annually from countries outside the Western Hemisphere was capped at 150,000, with the number from each country set as a proportion of the total U.S. population in 1920. In addition, the act barred entry to immigrants who could not become citizens; as previous laws had made most Asians ineligible for U.S. citizenship, the 1924 law effectively banned Asian immigration to the United States.

Visas issued to those emigrating from the countries of the Western Hemisphere, such as Canada and most Latin American countries, were not restricted. One reason that the act did not limit emigration from the Western Hemisphere was that lawmakers understood that farmers in the southwestern United States needed seasonal laborers from Mexico. Certain other people were also exempted from the quota provisions. These nonquota exemptions included wives and unmarried children of U.S. citizens, ministers, professors, and college students. For the first time, the act also required all immigrants, even those from the Western Hemisphere, to obtain visas and photographs.

Impact

The impact of the 1924 immigration act was a further drastic reduction of overall immigration to the United States, particularly from the countries of Eastern and Southern Europe. The limit of 150,000 visas per year that the act eventually put in place meant that immigration from most countries, including even Germany and Ireland, went down by as much as 50 percent. Over 800,000 people immigrated to the United States in 1920; following implementation of the Immigration Act of 1921, that number fell to around 350,000, and the 1924 law again more than halved that number.

The act established that the federal government would numerically limit immigration, and it ended the relatively unhindered European immigration that had characterized American immigration history. Subsequent U.S. immigration policies would revise the discriminatory measures of the 1924 act but would retain the concept of numerical limitations on annual immigration. The act was a result of Americans' fears about the ability of foreigners to assimilate into American society, and their desire to resist the perceived cultural, religious, and ethnic fragmentation of the United States.

Jonathan Keljik

Further Reading:

Daniels, Roger. *Guarding the Golden Door: American Immigration Policy and Immigrants Since 1882.* New York: Hill and Wang, 2004. Discusses the history of U.S. immigration policy, beginning with the Chinese Exclusion Act of 1882.

Gerstle, Gary. *American Crucible: Race and Nation in the Twentieth Century.* Princeton, N.J.: Princeton University Press, 2001. Presents an analysis of twentieth-century American society, noting the impact of nationalism, prejudice, and immigration policy on American history.

Ngai, Mae. *Impossible Subjects: Illegal Aliens and the Making of Modern America.* Princeton, N.J.: Princeton University Press, 2004. Offers a history of immigration to the United States, focusing on the relations among immigration restriction, illegal aliens, and multiculturalism.

Zolberg, Aristide. *A Nation by Design: Immigration Policy in the Fashioning of America.* Cambridge, Mass.: Harvard University Press, 2006. Discusses U.S. immigration policy from the eighteenth to the twenty-first centuries focusing on immigration restriction, types of migration, and the sociopolitical factors influencing immigration policy.

See also: Anti-Semitism; Coolidge, Calvin; Demographics; Immigration Act of 1921; Immigration to the United States; Ku Klux Klan; Racial discrimination

■ Immigration to Canada

The 1920s was a period of intense xenophobia in Canada. Public opinion favored government policies that limited immigration to Canada. As the economy began to recover from the brief post–World War I recession of the early 1920s, nonwhite and Jewish immigrants found themselves facing increasingly severe restrictions.

In the period following World War I, the combination of heightened xenophobia and Canada's depressed economy led to public pressure for restrictions on non-British immigrants. Admission was denied to all persons deemed "enemy aliens" during World War I, as well as to central and eastern Europeans, the latter on the basis that they would resist assimilation into mainstream Canadian culture. To tighten immigration controls, the Canadian government imposed a sizable landing fee on all immigrants in 1921; limited the pool of admissible immigrants to agriculturalists, farmworkers, and domestics in 1923; and, in 1925, instated the requirement that all potential immigrants pass a medical examination.

As the economy began to recover in the early 1920s, Canadian policymakers came under growing pressure to relax immigration restrictions on agricultural and industrial workers. Officials strove to entice more British immigrants, and the landing fee was lifted for all European immigrants in 1922. In 1923, the list of admissible immigrants was extended to include British subjects moving from the United States, Newfoundland, Ireland, New Zealand, Australia, and South Africa, as well as white American citizens, none of whom were required to have a passport in order to immigrate.

British and European Immigrants

The Canadian government initiated various schemes under the Empire Settlement Agreement to attract British immigrants. The 3,000 Families Scheme promoted the settlement of British families on farms in Canada by offering government-assisted passage, the sale of land on a credit basis, low-interest long-term repayable loans for the purchase of farm equipment and stock, and agricultural training and supervision. The government also sought to attract more farmworkers by offering ten thousand unemployed British miners reduced transportation rates and guaranteed jobs harvesting wheat in western Canada. Other efforts included schemes targeted at British women and children to serve as domestic workers and farm laborers, respectively, providing such incentives as passage assistance, job training, and guaranteed standard wages.

Restrictions on non-British European immigrants, including Germans and their wartime allies, were also lessened in 1923. Self-sufficient immigrants from the "preferred" countries of northern and western Europe were granted admission, while immigrants from the nonpreferred countries of southern and eastern Europe were permitted entry only if they fulfilled an occupational need.

The Canadian National Railway and the Canadian Pacific Railway had a vested interest in easing immigration controls, as more immigrants would mean more rail traffic. In 1924 and 1925, they negotiated with the government for permission to recruit agriculturalists and farmworkers from nonpreferred European countries. Under the terms of the Railway Agreement, displaced Germans and Mennonites came to Canada as farmers and agricultural workers, as did Poles, Ukrainians, Hungarians, and Romanians. Many were skilled and semiskilled workers who later sought employment in Canada's growing industrial centers.

The permit system, instituted in 1926, also facilitated large-scale immigration of southern and eastern Europeans. The Canadian government issued permits to employers who needed workers, allowing the admission of immigrants to fill open positions. Applicants who satisfied job requirements and passed medical exams were granted immigration visas.

Black, Jewish, and Asian Immigrants

Immigration restrictions remained in place for blacks, Jews, and Asians throughout the 1920s. Virtually no immigration from Africa or the Caribbean took place, as people from British African and Caribbean countries did not enjoy the same advantages as other British subjects. Immigration officers held wide discretionary powers and could easily prevent immigration from British colonies that were considered nonwhite. African Americans, too, were turned away at the border. Black immigration to Canada during the 1920s was reported to constitute fewer than five hundred people. Similarly, fewer than eight hundred South Asians were admitted to Canada in the 1920s due to the continuous-journey regulation of 1908, which made immigration from India virtually impossible.

Jewish refugees facing political, social, and economic persecution in eastern Europe were largely denied admission to Canada. Jews were subject to immigration approval on a case-by-case basis via the permit system, and the government instructed the railways to deny applications to Jewish farmers in the belief that they would not remain farmers once they arrived. In 1927, the Canadian Jewish Colonization Society convinced the government to allow thirty Jewish farming families to immigrate on special conditions: They had to hold valid passports, arrive from their country of origin (which excluded Jewish refugees forced to flee their home countries), and pass the medical examination. Every member of the family also had to be literate, a condition not required of any other immigrants to whom the Railway Agreement applied. By 1930, only eighteen Jewish families had been allowed entrance under these terms. The Canadian Jewish community also campaigned for the admission of one thousand Jewish orphans from the Ukraine, but although the community promised to pay all the costs involved in the settlement of the orphans, the government only agreed to admit 150 of them. Near the end of the 1920s, most new Jewish immigrants had either been sponsored by Canadian relatives or granted progressively more restrictive special permits, as all other routes were effectively blocked.

Though Chinese immigration to Canada had already been limited by a series of increasingly prohibitive regulations, it was all but ended by the Chinese Immigration Act of 1923. Also known as the Chinese Exclusion Act, it banned Chinese people from entering Canada unless they were merchants, students, diplomats and their staff, or Canadian-born or long-term residents who had traveled abroad, and the movements of the latter group were very strictly controlled. Potential immigrants who met these conditions were required to apply for a visa in Hong Kong, which was often refused; even when the visa was granted, admission upon arrival in Canada was not guaranteed. Until the act was repealed in 1947, fewer than fifty Chinese immigrants were allowed to enter the country. In 1922, the Canadian government had also sought to limit Japanese immigration through diplomatic negotiations, as a result of which the Japanese government agreed to reduce the number of visas issued to its citizens for travel to Canada from 400 per year to 150.

Deportations

The government frequently used deportation as a way to rid Canada of foreign-born criminals, alcoholics, and political activists, as well as those who were sick, disabled, homeless, or reliant on public charity. This included people who had lost their jobs, suddenly become ill, or experienced an occupational accident that caused a permanent disability. On average, the 1920s saw the deportation of more than seventeen hundred people per year.

Impact

Between 1921 and 1931, Canada accepted an

astounding 1,166,000 immigrants, which was a testament to the growth and vibrancy of the Canadian economy during the Roaring Twenties. From 1920 to 1923, an average of 100,000 immigrants entered the country each year. This increased to 120,000 for the next three years and then to 160,000 for the rest of the decade. These immigrants were primarily British subjects, Americans, and Christian Europeans, as Jews, blacks, and Asians were severely restricted or even prohibited from entering the country. Deportation was used as a means of removing previously accepted immigrants who were considered to have become "undesirable." Following the collapse of the Canadian economy in 1929, virtually all immigration was halted, while deportations continued.

Kelly Amanda Train

Further Reading

Avery, Donald H. *Reluctant Host: Canada's Response to Immigrant Workers, 1896–1994.* Toronto: McClelland & Stewart, 1995. An exploration of immigration and the Canadian economy's need for immigrant labor.

Hawkins, Freda. *Critical Years in Immigration: Canada and Australia Compared.* 2d. ed. Montreal: McGill-Queen's University Press, 1991. A comparison of Canadian and Australian immigration policies from 1900 to 1986.

Kelley, Ninette, and Michael Trebilcock. *The Making of the Mosaic: A History of Canadian Immigration Policy.* 2d. ed. Toronto: University of Toronto Press, 2010. A detailed exploration of Canadian immigration policy from the end of the fifteenth century to the present.

Knowles, Valerie. *Strangers at Our Gates: Canadian Immigration and Immigration Policy, 1540–2006.* Rev. ed. Toronto: Dundurn Press, 2007. An analysis of Canadian immigration policy from the sixteenth century to the present.

Tulchinsky, Gerald. *Branching Out: The Transformation of the Canadian Jewish Community.* Toronto: Stoddart, 1998. Examines the establishment of the Canadian Jewish community via immigration policies between the 1920s and the 1990s.

See also: Anti-Semitism; Canadian minority communities; Chinese Immigration Act of 1923; Jews in Canada

■ Immigration to the United States

The era of mass immigration ended in the 1920s, not to resume until the 1960s. Immigration controls changed the nature of the American population by reducing immigration totals and restricting immigrants from some countries while encouraging those from others.

The United States had historically been open to immigrants since the country's independence. Between 1820 and 1920, the United States accepted the immigration of 5.5 million Germans, 4.4 million Irish, and 3.25 million Russians. Total immigration between 1880 and 1920 amounted to over 23 million people. The Immigration Act of 1907 required immigrants to enter the country through an official port of entry, such as Ellis Island in New York City.

Background

Although there were periodic episodes of anti-immigrant sentiment, particularly during economic downturns, the federal government had placed virtually no restrictions on immigration before the late nineteenth century, leaving immigration control to the various states. The first federal restriction in 1875 blocked Asian contract laborers, convicts, and prostitutes. In 1882, President Chester Arthur signed the Chinese Exclusion Act, which suspended Chinese immigration to the United States. Subsequent restrictions pertained to paupers, criminals, and the mentally disabled. The wave of immigrants coming through Ellis Island between 1881 and 1920 had to prove their identity, answer questions, pass a physical examination, and have a sponsor who was a U.S. citizen. These were the only restrictions at the time, and only the sick, the impoverished, and those without sponsors were turned back. The rules set a precedent for immigration regulation, and they contributed to the differentiation between legal and illegal immigrants.

The late nineteenth and early twentieth centuries were a period of large-scale immigration to the United States. Between 1880 and 1924, over two million eastern Europeans, two million Jews, and over two million Italians came to the United States. Between 1900 and 1910, Italian immigration averaged about 200,000 entries a year. During the following decade, even with World War I disrupting immigration, an

U.S. Congress Creates Border Patrol

The United States Border Patrol was created in 1924 to curtail illegal immigration from Latin America and Canada. In its first year of operation, Border Patrol staff reported turning back fifteen thousand aliens seeking illegal entry, but an estimated one hundred thousand farmworkers successfully evaded the border guards. In 1926, in an attempt to improve the Border Patrol's success rate, Congress doubled the number of officers and made the agency a permanent part of the Bureau of Immigration and Naturalization. The most significant impact of the creation of the U.S. Border Patrol was that it made illegal entry into the United States much more difficult than it ever had been before, as a government agency now had the authority to arrest and deport illegal aliens.

average of 200,000 Italian immigrants arrived annually. Poles and other eastern Europeans also immigrated in large numbers. The new immigrants were predominantly Roman Catholic, along with large numbers of eastern European Jews.

Eugenicists like Madison Grant articulated a growing concern among Americans about this newer wave of immigration, arguing that older immigrants shared American values of thrift and industry, were more skilled, and were in other ways superior to the new immigrants, who were considered unskilled and uneducated, often inherently so. Grant and Charles Davenport of the Eugenics Record Office—a center in New York for the then-popular study of the genetic improvement of society—advised Congress on the risk of immigrants changing American society for the worse. The rising wave of immigration also worried labor advocates, who wanted to restrict the entry of foreigners who might compete for American jobs.

The 1920s also saw a rebirth of the white supremacist organization called the Ku Klux Klan (KKK), which catered to American fears of communists and ethnic and religious minorities. By 1924, the KKK had accumulated over two million members who were opposed to African Americans, labor unions, Roman Catholics, and Jews. Immigrants were natural targets because they tended to cluster in urban neighborhoods where they could maintain their language, tradition, and customs.

Finally, immigrants from earlier waves also mistrusted the new immigrants. Under pressure from

all directions, Congress passed laws to limit immigration by specific ethnic groups.

Restrictions

The administration of President Warren G. Harding passed an emergency stopgap measure in the Immigration Act of 1921, also known as the Emergency Quota Act, which slowed the flood of immigrants. This 1921 law more than halved the rate of immigration, down to approximately 350,000 a year, limiting immigrants from each nationality to 3 percent of their numbers in the U.S. population as recorded in the 1910 census.

President Calvin Coolidge then signed the Immigration Act of 1924, which tightened the 1921 measure and made it permanent, while reducing immigration quotas to 2 percent of the 1890 census figures. Furthermore, the law provided for the replacement of this quota system with an overall cap on immigration of 150,000, implemented in 1929, with each nationality's proportion of the total to equal their proportion in the U.S. population in 1920. The 1924 act succeeded in reducing southern and eastern European immigration, and it also barred entry entirely to South and East Asians. Exemptions were established for spouses and children, professors, ministers, college students, and people from countries in the Western Hemisphere (that is, Canada and Latin America).

Motivated by anti-Asian sentiment on the West Coast, the Asian Exclusion Act was a subsection of the Immigration Act of 1924 that justified a blanket ban on immigration from Asia by reference to a 1906 law that restricted U.S. citizenship to blacks and whites only; the 1924 law clarified that immigration to the United States was open only to people who were eligible for citizenship, thus excluding Asians. A Japanese man, Takao Ozawa, had mounted a legal challenge to the 1906 law, arguing that Japanese people were white, but in *Takao Ozawa v. United States* (1922), the U.S. Supreme Court ruled that "white" meant Caucasian only. In a related case, *United States v. Bhagat Singh Thind* (1923), the Court ruled that Asian Indians were Asian and not Caucasian, and therefore also not eligible for U.S. citizenship. This reclassification also stripped American citizenship and land ownership rights from Asian Indians who were already naturalized U.S. citizens. With these decisions at its back, Congress succeeded in essentially halting Asian immigration from 1924 until the repeal of the Asian exclusion provisions in 1943.

Exceptions

Although the 1921 and 1924 acts sharply reduced immigration to the United States for many nationalities, total immigration to the United States remained relatively high until the Great Depression of the 1930s. One reason for the continued influx was that the Immigration Act of 1924 eliminated the 1921 requirement that families be counted in the quota, so after 1924, wives and children could immigrate to the United States regardless of quota ceilings.

Initially, the immigration of people from Latin America—primarily Mexico—was not considered a problem in the same way as immigration from Asia and southern and eastern Europe; in fact, it was regarded favorably by western agricultural interests that needed cheap seasonal labor. This is one reason the Western Hemisphere was exempted from the nationality quotas of 1921 and 1924.

In the latter half of the nineteenth century, Mexican immigration to the United States was relatively low. However, the rise of agricultural irrigation in the Southwest led to increased demand for farm labor, and the Mexican Revolution of 1910 sparked a wave of emigration from Mexico; expanding railroad systems also made migration easy. Although wages were low, the American economy was healthy and the political system was stable, and Mexican immigration exceeded 100,000 per year in the early twentieth century. During the 1920s, around 500,000 Mexicans crossed the border. The migrants moved to the Southwest but also to the upper Midwest for jobs in industry, meatpacking, steel, railroads, and the like.

The U.S. Border Patrol was established in 1924, but it was underfunded, understaffed, and generally ineffective. Practically speaking, there was no effective border control in the 1920s, and so undocumented immigration became a problem during this period. By the end of the decade, the administration of President Herbert Hoover was taking steps to deport or repatriate immigrants from Mexico and elsewhere, as the onset of the Great Depression drove people out of work and made immigrant labor even less welcome in the job market.

Impact

Between 1921 and 1930, over four million people immigrated to the United States. The peak year of the decade was 1921, before the restrictions came into effect; in that year, over 800,000 people immigrated. In contrast, about 500,000 immigrants arrived in the entire decade of the 1930s, a result of both the immigration curbs enacted in the 1920s and the economic impact of the Great Depression.

The 1920s immigration acts changed immigration patterns to the United States in significant ways: The flow of Asians and southern and eastern Europeans was drastically reduced, while a new influx from Mexico began. Immigration policy in the 1920s also reflected a particular period in American racial consciousness: The 1920 census had categories for Chinese, Indian, Japanese, mulatto, negro, and white; Hispanic was not a separate category. In the 1970s, the federal government established four categories: white, black, Asian-Pacific Islander, and Hispanic. The national origins quota system, established in 1921 and made permanent in 1924, remained in effect until 1952, when the quotas were relaxed before being abandoned altogether in 1965.

John H. Barnhill

Further Reading

Daniels, Roger. *Guarding the Golden Door: American Immigration Policy and Immigrants Since 1882.* New York: Hill and Wang, 2004. Discusses the history of U.S. immigration policy, beginning with the Chinese Exclusion Act of 1882.

Gerstle, Gary. *American Crucible: Race and Nation in the Twentieth Century.* Princeton: Princeton University Press, 2001. Presents an analysis of twentieth-century American society, noting the impact of nationalism, prejudice, and immigration policy on American history.

Hernandez, Kelly Lytle. *Migra! A History of the U.S. Border Patrol.* Berkeley: University of California Press, 2010. Discusses the history of the U.S. Border Patrol, with a special focus on its evolution from immigration control to transborder policing.

Ngai, Mae. *Impossible Subjects: Illegal Aliens and the Making of Modern America.* Princeton, N.J.: Princeton University Press, 2004. Offers a history of immigration to the United States, focusing on the relations among immigration restriction, illegal aliens, and multiculturalism.

Zolberg, Aristide. *A Nation by Design: Immigration Policy in the Fashioning of America.* Cambridge, Mass.: Harvard University Press, 2006. Discusses U.S.

immigration policy from the eighteenth to the twenty-first centuries, focusing on immigration restrictions, types of migration, and the sociopolitical factors influencing immigration policy.

See also: Border Patrol, U.S.; Demographics; Eugenics movement; Immigration Act of 1921; Immigration Act of 1924; *Ozawa v. United States;* Racial discrimination

■ In the American Grain

Identification: A collection of twenty-one prose essays about American history
Author: William Carlos Williams
Date: 1925

Considered the most important of Williams's early works, In the American Grain *countered the conventional idea that history is an organized construction based on only one version of a person or story. With its unusual presentation style, the book had a major impact on the literary form as well as historical and cultural understandings of what it means to be American.*

William Carlos Williams's first commercially published volume, *In the American Grain*, was critically disparaged in its first year of publication and quickly cast aside by the publisher as a result. Only D. H. Lawrence defended Williams's attempts to present history in a different way. Fifteen years after its original publication, the book was brought back to literary attention by a new set of critics who saw it more objectively. In the decades following its resurgence in academic study, its chapters have received both individual and collective attention from experts in literary, historical, and cultural areas of study.

In the American Grain is a collection of subjective literary histories that depict American figures, events, and ideals. Williams's reliance on the actual words of many of his sources provides a deep and creative insight into the people, places, and themes depicted, while his method of presentation conveys a sense of his own personal vision as seen in his critically controversial beliefs about his topics. His viewpoint is consistently positive as he makes an effort to encourage readers to discover pleasure in earthly realities.

The first few essays consider issues surrounding the European discovery and exploration of America

by figures such as Leif Ericson, Christopher Columbus, Hernan Cortes, Juan Ponce de Leon, and Samuel de Champlain. The essays then progress chronologically through significant American topics, including the *Mayflower,* Reverend Cotton Mather, pioneer Daniel Boone, Revolutionary War hero George Washington, printer Benjamin Franklin, and slavery, ending with poet Edgar Allan Poe and President Abraham Lincoln. Williams's prose varies in form, sometimes appearing as a first-person narrative, sometimes a fictionalized journal entry, and sometimes a third-person commentary.

Impact
In the American Grain is significant for its literary characteristics as well as its study of history. Williams experiments narratively and linguistically with key pieces of American history and culture, which, though problematic to some readers, nevertheless celebrate the American character while seeking new ways of understanding it. Located firmly in the modernist tradition of the 1920s, the essays show gratitude to the American past while breaking away from established views of politics, social issues, and religion.

Theresa L. Stowell

Further Reading
Conrad, Bryce. *Refiguring America: A Study of William Carlos Williams' "In the American Grain."* Urbana: University of Illinois Press, 1990.
Lowney, John. *The American Avant-Garde Tradition: William Carlos Williams, Postmodern Poetry, and the Politics of Cultural Memory.* Lewisburg, Pa.: Bucknell University Press, 1997.
Pritchard, William H. *Lives of the Modern Poets.* New York: Oxford University Press, 1980.

See also: Historiography; Literature in the United States; *Main Currents in American Thought*

■ Ince, Thomas H.

Identification: American film producer
Born: November 6, 1882, Newport, Rhode Island
Died: November 19, 1924, Hollywood, California

By the early 1920s, Thomas H. Ince was known as one of Hollywood's most innovative film producers, having written and directed dozens of films over the preceding decade. How-

ever, he is remembered almost as well for his death in 1924 under tragic and mysterious circumstances.

Born in 1882, Thomas Harper Ince began making films when the Hollywood motion picture industry was in its infancy. He first acted on screen in 1905 and began directing full-length features in 1910. By 1920, Ince was one of the most influential independent filmmakers in the United States, and his work contributed greatly to the rise of Westerns, films set in the Old West.

As the 1920s continued, Ince found it harder to compete economically with the larger Hollywood studios. Although his movies remained popular, he lacked revenue to distribute them competitively. His luck seemed to have changed in late 1924, however, when he brokered a lucrative deal with William Randolph Hearst, a media entrepreneur and one of the richest men in the country.

On November 16, 1924, Ince joined Hearst and other celebrities in San Diego for a birthday party aboard Hearst's yacht. Under conditions that are still mysterious, Ince became ill while on board and had to be taken ashore by a physician. Although his condition grew steadily worse, Ince never went to a hospital and died within three days.

Thomas H. Ince. (Getty Images)

Almost immediately, rumors spread about Ince's death. Hearst's newspapers, including the *Los Angeles Examiner*, neglected to mention the yacht party, reporting instead that Ince died at home of heart failure. Rival newspapers, including the *Los Angeles Times*, reported that Hearst had shot Ince. According to those accounts, Hearst allegedly feared that his mistress, the actress Marion Davies, was having an affair with actor Charlie Chaplin, both of whom were also guests on Hearst's yacht that weekend. Hearst reportedly had tried to shoot Chaplin, but ended up wounding Ince. Another version of the story was disseminated by San Diego authorities, who offered their opinion that Ince had died of alcohol poisoning.

Impact

Although he made dozens of films, Ince's impact mainly came from his innovative ways of planning and scheduling film production. Like most subsequent filmmakers, Ince realized that films would be less expensive and less time consuming the more rationally the production was planned and scheduled. His innovations include the "shooting script," which remains the standard screenplay format for use during film production. In 2001, the circumstances of his death were dramatized in the film *The Cat's Meow*, directed by Peter Bogdanovich.

Michael R. Meyers

Further Reading

Cerra, Julie Lugo, and Marc Wanamaker. *Movie Studios of Culver City.* Charleston, S.C.: Arcadia Publishing, 2011.

Taves, Brian. *Thomas Ince: Hollywood's Independent Pioneer.* Lexington: University Press of Kentucky, 2011.

See also: Chaplin, Charlie; Film; Hearst, William Randolph

■ Income and wages

Wages, also called labor income, comprise the majority of all income in the United States and Canada. The other principal forms of income in the 1920s were property incomes, such as interest, rents, and dividends. Most incomes were paid by business firms, with their flow being determined by business revenues from the sale of products, work, or other services.

The 1920s began and ended in a state of extreme economic turbulence. Inflation at the end of World War I was followed by a severe deflation, which reduced incomes and wages to a painful extent in 1921. Rapid recovery was followed by nearly ten years of relatively stable prosperity, but this all came to an end in the final months of 1929.

Gross National Product and National Income

The tempo of business is determined by the gross national product (GNP), which measures expenditures to buy currently produced goods and services. All of these expenditures become income of some sort, but indirect business taxes and depreciation allowances are excluded from the national income. Wages and salaries accounted for between 60 and 65 percent of U.S. national income throughout the 1920s, while workers received virtually no fringe benefits and were responsible for their own retirement and health care costs. Income of unincorporated businesses accounted for more than one-sixth of national income, but because this category includes many self-employed workers such as farmers, shopkeepers, doctors, and lawyers, much of this income was really labor income. Income tax rates were very low, and the personal exemption was typically high enough to exempt most workers from tax. Government transfer payments such as pensions and welfare benefits were very small, with the majority of these being veterans' benefits.

At the end of the inflationary surge that accompanied World War I, GNP of the United States reached $92 billion in 1920, generating a national income of $79 billion. The severe postwar deflation dropped GNP to $70 billion in 1921, reducing national income to $64 billion. The economy then resumed an upward trend. By 1926, GNP had reached $97 billion, and by 1929, $103 billion. National income in 1929 was $87 billion, of which 59 percent represented employee compensation and 17 percent represented income of unincorporated enterprises. Corporate profits were an abnormally high 12 percent, while interest and rents accounted for 11 percent.

Canadian GNP was C$5 billion in 1920, with around $4.5 billion of that being national income. The GNP decreased to C$4 billion the following year, and then gradually rose again to C$5 billion by 1925. In 1926, GNP was C$5.4 billion, of which C$4.3 billion was national income. By 1929, these had risen to a GNP of C$6.1 billion and a national income of C$4.7 billion. The Canadian dollar was roughly equal to the U.S. dollar, so the data of the two countries can be compared directly with relative accuracy. In 1929, Canada's national income was slightly more than 5 percent of that of the United States, while Canada's population of 10 million was 8 percent of that of the United States. Thus, per capita incomes in Canada were significantly lower, and it is not surprising that many immigrants to Canada continued on to the United States when they could arrange it.

Employee compensation in Canada accounted for about the same percentage of the national income as in the United States. However, Canada recorded a much higher proportion for the income of unincorporated enterprises, especially farms, amounting to $1.2 billion in 1929, or 25 percent.

Income and Employment by Sector

For many sectors of the U.S. economy, the share of national income paid matched fairly closely with their share of production workers. For instance, manufacturing accounted for 22.8 percent of production workers in 1929 and paid 21.4 percent of the national income from 1926 to 1929. However, agriculture accounted for about one-fifth of production workers in 1929 but paid only 9 percent of national income, reflecting the low level of earnings in farming. Similarly, services accounted for 17 percent of production workers but only 13 percent of national income. Meanwhile, government had 7 percent of production workers and paid 10 percent of the national income, much of this difference reflecting interest on the national debt. The most extreme case was the finance sector, employing only 3.4 percent of production workers but paying 17 percent of national income; this excess did reflect high labor incomes, but it mostly comprised interest, dividends, and profits.

With regard to average annual earnings of full-time workers, those in agriculture earned the least, with the decrease from $528 in average earnings in 1920 to $401 in 1929 reflecting the downward trend of farm prices. Hired laborers on farms received very low pay but often were provided with room and board in addition to their wages. Workers in manufacturing earned an average of about $1,500 in 1929, while construction paid around $1,700. Communications and public utilities increased from $1,238 in 1920 to $1,478 in 1929, as both electric power and telephone service boomed. Rates for services remained low ($912 in 1920; $1,079 in 1929); this industry mainly

---

Old-Age Pensions

The United States continued to apply the nineteenth-century doctrine of laissez-faire at a time when circumstances demanded assistance for retired wage earners. It was no longer realistic to expect that lifelong wage earners could set aside enough money to live comfortably through their retirement years. On March 5, 1923, Montana governor Joseph M. Dixon and Nevada governor James G. Scrugham signed the first old-age pension legislation in the United States. The Montana and Nevada laws did not have much impact within the respective populations of those states, but on a national level, the legislation gave momentum to the old-age pension cause. Ultimately, it took the Great Depression, when many well-to-do elderly citizens lost their savings, to force the U.S. government to devise a federally funded program to ensure income for the elderly. The result was the federal Social Security Act, passed during the Franklin D. Roosevelt administration in 1935.

---

comprised household help, mostly female and often part-time. Booming conditions in markets for stocks and real estate helped the finance sector to achieve the highest rank, with wages of $1,758 in 1920 and $2,062 in 1929. Despite the lack of improvement in several sectors during the decade, workers benefited from full employment and the fact that prices in 1929 were lower than in 1920.

Workers in Canada earned C$4.3 billion of total income in 1926, of which C$2.4 billion represented labor income. In 1926, agriculture accounted for C$0.9 billion of total income but only C$0.2 billion of labor income, the rest being income of unincorporated businesses. In both Canada and the United States, the number of people engaged in farming remained relatively constant, with growth in employment occurring elsewhere. For instance, Canadian manufacturing provided about 25 percent of labor income and 21 percent of total income in 1926.

Workforce Demographics

The U.S. Census data for 1920 and 1930 depict several interesting demographic trends. Over the decade, the number of women in the labor force rose from 8.6 million to 10.8 million, representing an in-

crease from 21 percent of workers to 22 percent. The number of workers over sixty-five years of age increased from 1.6 million to 2 million. Meanwhile, the number of young workers between the ages of sixteen and nineteen actually declined from 4.6 to 4.4 million—a good sign, as this suggested that more were remaining in school, although a federal effort to ban child labor was held to be unconstitutional.

In Canada in 1921, women constituted only 15 percent of the labor force of 3.2 million. By 1931, this had risen to 17 percent of 3.9 million workers. The percentage of young male workers aged fourteen to nineteen dropped from 68 percent to 57 percent, again probably because more of them were staying in school.

Productivity and Wages

Worker productivity was increasing in response to technological improvements and organizational innovations, such as Frederick Winslow Taylor's theory of scientific management. In U.S. manufacturing, productivity improved during the 1920s by over 60 percent. In the farm sector, the increase in productivity was about 20 percent, enabling output to rise even though the number of farmers remained relatively constant. Growing productivity led to an increase in real wages, which are wages adjusted for inflation. In 1920, annual wage incomes in the United States averaged about $1,342 per worker, rising to $1,425 by 1929; however, because prices in 1929 were actually lower than in 1920, real wage incomes improved by about one-fourth. The rise in worker productivity helped boost corporate profits, giving impetus to the escalation of stock prices.

For Canada, index numbers for wages provide a comparison with 1949. The index number for 1949 is 100, with the numbers for other years expressing that year's wages as a percentage of their amount in 1949. Thus, the index number in 1920 was 52.3, meaning that wages in 1920 were 52.3 percent of what they were in 1949. This number fell to 47.7 in 1921 and 44.5 in 1922, and then gradually increased throughout the decade to 48.5 in 1929. Adjustment for price changes, however, indicates that real wages in 1920 were about 56, rising to 58 in 1921, 59 in 1922, and 64 in 1929—an increase of about 14 percent from 1920 to 1929.

Labor Unions

Labor unions did not account for a large proportion

of workers in either the United States or Canada during the 1920s. In the United States, World War I had helped boost union membership to about 5 million in 1920, or about one-eighth of the labor force, but this number dropped sharply during the postwar recession and then leveled off around 3.5 million for the rest of the decade. By 1929, unions accounted for only about 7 percent of the labor force. In Canada, there were 313,000 union members in 1921, roughly 10 percent of the labor force of 3.2 million. Union membership dipped and then rose, ending up about the same: 320,000 in 1931, representing 8 percent of workers. Union membership was extensive in skilled crafts, such as the building trades and railroads, but less common in mass production industries with large firms. Despite certain protections embodied in the Clayton Act of 1914, unions in the United States remained vulnerable to a variety of employer anti-union activities, with violent strikes occurring in the coal mining industry in 1922 and the textile industry in 1929. However, apart from these instances, labor disputes were not a major concern during this period.

In the United States, political pressure from unions did contribute to the adoption of severe restrictions on immigration in 1921 and 1924. The number of immigrants, which had exceeded one million per year prior to the war, dropped to around 300,000 per year in the last half of the decade. Since Canada was exempted from the national-origins-based quotas, it became a way station for many immigrants who hoped to ultimately reach the United States. These immigration restrictions slowed the growth of the labor force and contributed in a small degree to increasing real wages. They also reduced visible poverty, as many of the poorest Americans were immigrants beginning their lives in the New World.

Governmental Factors

In the United States, farm, labor, and business lobbyists contributed to the adoption of the Fordney-McCumber Tariff Act of 1922, which raised most duties on imports. Farm lobbyists actively promoted federal interventions aimed at raising farm prices. The Agricultural Marketing Act of 1929 provided for "stabilization corporations" that could buy up surplus products, an early precursor to the extensive price-support programs to come.

In 1913, the U.S. Congress had passed a constitutional amendment authorizing it to collect a federal income tax, which had emerged as a major revenue source during World War I. However, the exemptions and deductions were such that most families did not pay income tax. At the peak of the tax rate in 1920, 7.3 million families filed income tax returns, of which 5.5 million recorded taxable income, yielding tax liability of $1.1 billion. Tax rates were significantly reduced in the early 1920s, and after 1924, only about 4 million families filed tax returns, yielding around $700 million.

The only significant federal income redistribution program of the 1920s was veterans' benefits. Pensions and related payments to veterans averaged $600 million to $700 million in the 1920s, while employer-financed workmen's compensation payments, chiefly for on-the-job injuries, totaled about $200 million in 1929. State and local governments paid out about $350 million for medical services to the poor.

Defining Poverty

Poverty is an imprecise concept, but scholarly studies place the poverty share in the 1920s as high as 30 to 40 percent. Certainly, the 27 percent of U.S. families that earned $1,000 or less per year in 1929 lived in poverty. (The median family income would have been just over $1,500, and fewer than 2 percent of families had an income above $10,000.) The major components of poverty in the United States can be enumerated as follows:

1. *Recent immigrants.* Throughout the 1920s, the foreign-born population was relatively constant, hovering around 7.7 million.
2. *Rural residents in general and black farmers in particular.* The African American population grew during the decade from 10.5 million to 12 million. Half of these lived on farms, with nearly 2 million more being classed as rural nonfarm residents.
3. *People aged sixty-five and over.* There were virtually no systematic old-age pensions, and most people could not save much during their working lifetimes. The number of older people rose from 4.9 million to 6.6 million over the course of the decade.
4. *Female-headed households.* In 1930, 3.4 million women under the age of sixty-five were widowed or divorced.
5. *The unemployed.* After 1922, the number of unemployed people ranged between 1.5 and 2 million.

These populations alone total around 29 million people, or about one-fourth of the total U.S. population. In addition, those who were sick, injured, or disabled also accounted for a significant segment of the poor population, but there is no simple way to estimate their numbers.

Impact

By the 1920s, per capita average income in the United States was probably as high as in any other major country. The leading European countries had suffered severe loss of productive power as a result of World War I, which did little economic harm to the United States. After emerging from depression in 1922, both the Canadian and the U.S. economies enjoyed full employment, economic growth, stable prices, and a steady increase in labor productivity. Even so, many residents of the United States and Canada lived in poverty, as did most of the rest of the world's population. Perhaps equally important, those who did not face poverty still experienced substantial insecurity with regard to such economic risks as unemployment, family breakups, illnesses, accidents, and old age. Private pension and insurance programs were beginning to develop, but they had not advanced very far. Much of the social safety net would not come into existence until the next decade or after.

Paul B. Trescott

Further Reading

Daugherty, Carroll R. *Labor Problems in American Industry.* New York: Houghton Mifflin, 1933. An overview of labor market conditions, with primary emphasis on the 1920s.

Gup, Ted. *A Secret Gift: How One Man's Kindness—and a Trove of Letters—Revealed the Hidden History of the Great Depression.* New York: Penguin Press, 2010. Includes vignettes describing the hardships of life in the 1920s and early 1930s.

Jones, Jacqueline. *American Work: Four Centuries of Black and White Labor.* New York: W. W. Norton, 1998. Views the comparative status of black and white workers in the broader context of the social history of the United States.

Lebergott, Stanley. *Manpower in Economic Growth: The American Record Since 1800.* New York: McGraw-Hill, 1964. Traces the historical development of wages related to many elements of labor supply and demand, especially labor productivity.

Rosenzweig, Roy, et al. *Who Built America? Working People and the Nation's History.* 3d ed. Vol. 2. Boston, Mass.: Bedford/St. Martin's, 2008. A survey of labor market conditions in the United States from 1877 to the present.

See also: Agricultural Marketing Act of 1929; Gross national product of the United States; Labor strikes; Unemployment; Unionism

■ Indian Citizenship Act of 1924

The Law: Federal legislation granting citizenship to all American Indians born in the United States
Also known as: Snyder Act
Date: Enacted on June 2, 1924

The Indian Citizenship Act was the culmination of a long-standing movement to assimilate American Indian tribes by granting their members full citizenship rights in the United States.

Sponsored by New York representative Homer Snyder, the Indian Citizenship Act of 1924 reflected the nativist impulse of the decade, as advocates argued the bill would finally incorporate "the first Americans" into the political fabric of the nation. Prior to the 1920s, American Indians who maintained tribal affiliations were not considered citizens of the United States. While laws such as the Dawes Act provided mechanisms for Indians to become citizens as early as the 1880s, these generally required individuals to sever ties with their tribe and embrace private property. By the early 1920s, almost two-thirds of American Indians had been granted citizenship through various legal mechanisms. Working against the trend, the Choctaw and other tribes resisted government efforts to grant them citizenship and thereby destroy their tribal governments.

World War I served as the catalyst for a sweeping federal mandate on Indian citizenship. As many as sixteen thousand Indians fought in the war, with 50 to 85 percent of them being volunteers. Many Americans saw this as proof that those Indians who served were ready to surrender their tribal ways and become full-fledged Americans, and on that basis, Congress passed an act in 1919 granting citizenship to all Indian veterans.

By this time, such Progressive-minded Indians as

Seneca anthropologist Arthur C. Parker had spent years arguing for full assimilation into American culture, toward which the granting of citizenship would be a vital step. At the urging of Indian reformers and veterans, Representative Snyder sponsored a citizenship bill in 1924. This legislation moved through Congress alongside the anti-immigrant National Origins Act of 1924 and reflected many of the same nativist impulses; many politicians who favored restricting immigration to keep the nation "100 percent American" also supported granting all Indians citizenship as a fitting symbol of their assimilation. The Indian Citizenship Act signed into law by President Calvin Coolidge in June 1924 stated that all American Indians born in the United States were citizens and that citizenship would not affect their rights to tribal property or other rights.

Impact

The 1924 act finally included American Indians into the body politic of the nation, but not all Indians wanted this status. In later years, the Iroquois Confederacy and other groups would protest Congress's blanket inclusion by refusing to vote or pay taxes, issuing their own passports, and even declaring war on the Axis Powers of World War II on their own terms. Although all American Indians were now U.S. citizens by law, many Western states continued to deny Indian residents the vote and other basic rights.

Mark Edwin Miller

Further Reading

Michaels, Walter Benn. *Our America: Nativism, Modernism, and Pluralism.* Durham, N.C.: Duke University Press, 1995.

Wilkins, David E. *American Indian Politics and the American Political System.* 3d ed. Lanham, Md.: Rowman & Littlefield, 2011.

See also: Civil rights and liberties; Coolidge, Calvin; Immigration Act of 1924; Native Americans; Voting rights; World War I veterans

---

■ Installment plans

An early form of consumer credit that allowed goods to be purchased through the scheduling of regular payments, installment plans signaled a shift from the austerity of the Victorian era to the consumer culture of the twentieth century.

These plans have often been cited as a factor contributing to the Great Depression.

The emergence of the installment plan in the 1920s reflected dramatic changes in the American consumer economy. In the early decades of the twentieth century, a host of consumer goods, including automobiles, radios, phonographs, refrigerators, and washing machines, were introduced to the general public, while simultaneous advances in infrastructure such as new highway systems and electrical grids rendered them increasingly practical. Nevertheless, these goods remained out of reach to most Americans due to their relatively high prices. For example, by the 1920s the average cost of a new Ford Model T, the most inexpensive automobile, was around $300, nearly one-third the average annual salary of a teacher. In an effort to stimulate sales of expensive consumer products, many retailers and financial institutions began extending the option of installment loans to consumers.

Installment plans had been used with great effectiveness for several decades prior to the 1920s, most notably by agribusiness pioneer Cyrus McCormick in marketing his mechanical reapers to American farmers. Yet the use of these plans did not become widespread until after World War I, as businesses scrambled for shares of the emerging automobile, appliance, furniture, and entertainment markets. By the end of the decade, the installment plan had spread to other sectors of the economy, with banks extending home mortgage notes and stockbrokers offering the option of margin trading, in which investors used borrowed funds to purchase stocks. Although many traditionalists deplored these practices, their use proliferated as the American economy transformed from a system focused on the production of necessities to a consumer-based model increasingly dependent upon the purchase of luxury goods and labor-saving devices.

Impact

The widespread use of installment plans during the 1920s created a cycle in which increasing defaults on installment loans and consumers' inability to acquire new loans caused a decline in the manufacture of goods typically purchased on installment plans. This exacerbated the effects of the next decade's Great Depression, leading to layoffs in the manufacturing sector and resulting in further defaults. Nevertheless, installment plans regained popularity after the Depression, and they were a precedent for the development of other forms of consumer credit such as credit cards and home equity loans.

Michael H. Burchett

Further Reading

Allen, Frederick Lewis. *Only Yesterday: An Informal History of the 1920s.* New York: Harper Perennial, 2000.

McElvaine, Robert S. *The Great Depression: America 1929–1941.* New York: Times Books, 1993.

Parrish, Michael E. *Anxious Decades: America in Prosperity and Depression, 1920–1941.* New York: W. W. Norton, 1994.

See also: Automobiles and auto manufacturing; Credit and debt; Electrification; Refrigerators; Stock market crash

■ Insulin

Frederick Banting, Charles Best, James Collip, and John Macleod of the University of Toronto extracted and prepared the first injection of insulin sufficient to treat individuals with diabetes in 1922. While its mode of action was little understood at the time, insulin allowed patients to manage and live with a disease previously considered untreatable and ultimately fatal.

Until 1922, diabetes mellitus, especially type 1, was considered to be a death sentence. The Russian-born physiologist Oskar Minkowski had first demonstrated that removing a dog's pancreas would cause it to develop diabetes in 1889, and he was the first to experiment with pancreatic extracts to counteract the symptoms. Others, including German physician George Zuelzer, Romanian physiologist Nicolae Paulescu, and American biochemist Israel Kleiner, continued to experiment with pancreatic extracts over the following decades. These sometimes relieved diabetic symptoms but invariably were accompanied by toxic effects, now attributable to the impurities in their preparations.

By 1920, methods for measuring blood glucose had improved dramatically, permitting multiple, sequential sampling of animal models and human patients. On May 17, 1921, the young doctor Frederick Banting and his assistant, graduate student Charles

Charles Best (left) and Frederick Banting with one of the first diabetic dogs to receive insulin. (Hulton Archive/Getty Images)

Best, began attempting to isolate insulin, then called isletin, by tying off the pancreatic ducts of dogs. They conducted their experiments in the laboratory of John Macleod at the University of Toronto, who also assisted with funding and experimental design. On the basis of encouraging results, Macleod enlisted the aid of biochemist James Collip, who helped the team purify the insulin sufficiently to permit its first successful test on a human patient on January 23, 1922.

Further clinical trials confirmed the success, and in November 1922, large-scale production was initiated with the assistance of the pharmaceutical firm Eli Lilly and Company, which prepared the insulin from the pancreatic tissue of pigs and cattle. Daily insulin injections could restore severely ill diabetics to relative health, but dosages were not precise, and an overdose could put a patient into a hypoglycemic coma; it was not until 1926 that John Jacob Abel of Johns Hopkins University first crystallized insulin, purifying it enough to permit the administration of precise dosages. Only Banting and Macleod were awarded the 1923 Nobel Prize in Physiology or Medicine for the discovery of insulin, but they shared their award money with Best and Collip.

Impact

Insulin was the first protein to have its amino acid composition sequenced—by Frederick Sanger in 1951. Today, insulin is usually synthesized by molecular engineering and can be administered in either short- or long-acting form, depending on the needs of the patient. The discovery and development of insulin has permitted the treatment of all forms of diabetes, a previously fatal disease that people can now live with for many years.

James L. Robinson

Further Reading

Bliss, Michael. *Banting: A Biography.* 2d ed. Toronto: University of Toronto Press, 1992.

———. *The Discovery of Insulin.* 25th anniversary ed. Chicago: University of Chicago Press, 2007.

See also: Banting, Frederick Grant; Medicine; Nobel Prizes

■ International Business Machines (IBM)

Identification: American information-processing company

Also known as: Computing-Tabulating-Recording Company

Date: Founded on June 16, 1911

Under the leadership of president and chief executive officer Thomas J. Watson Sr., the 1920s provided International Business Machines (IBM) with a decade of steady growth as the company focused on its tabulating machine business, the forerunner of computerized data processing.

In 1911, financier Charles R. Flint merged International Time Recording Company, Computing Scale Company, Bundy Manufacturing Company, and Tabulating Machine Company to form a new conglomerate, Computing-Tabulating-Recording Company (CTR), headquartered in New York City. Most of the manufacturing was spread between Dayton, Ohio

(food scales and equipment); Endicott, New York (time recording equipment); and Washington, D.C., where inventor Dr. Herman Hollerith had located his tabulating machine and punch card system business for the 1890 U.S. Census. Because CTR proved difficult to manage, Thomas J. Watson Sr was hired in 1914.

Watson worked tirelessly to bring unity to CTR's diverse businesses. He instilled values of integrity, teamwork, and loyalty through frequent sales conventions and employee communication, and insisted on intensive product and sales training. The sales force was rewarded for meeting quotas and aspired to be in the company's Quarter Century and Hundred Percent clubs. Watson's framed photograph and THINK slogan appeared in every CTR office.

In 1920, CTR's most profitable products were time recorders, followed by scale equipment and tabulating machine systems. Though tabulating machines, which automated manual computations and stored information on punch cards, were just a small portion of the overall business, Watson recognized the long-term financial gains and cost savings they could provide in all areas of business operations and even government. To compete with a rival company, he assembled a group of engineers to research and develop better tabulators, sorters, and punch cards. CTR introduced the first printing tabulator by 1920 and the first electric key punch by 1923.

On February 14, 1924, Watson renamed CTR to International Business Machines Corporation (IBM). The name reflected Watson's vision of IBM as a worldwide institution, one that was already operating in the United States, Canada, Central and South America, Europe, Australia, and Asia. In 1928, IBM introduced the eighty-column punch card, which quickly became the industry standard. Net earnings more than tripled from $2 million in 1920 to $7 million in 1929, and the number of employees increased during the decade from 2,700 to 6,000.

Impact

Because IBM continued production and investment in tabulating machines even during the Great Depression, it was able to fill the U.S. government's data management order for the new Social Security program. IBM's electric accounting machines eventually proliferated in government, business, and academic organizations, to the point that many could not afford to operate without one. The company's continued investment in computing technology directly contributed to the transformation of worldwide information management.

Sheri P. Woodburn

Further Reading

Maney, Kevin. *The Maverick and His Machine: Thomas Watson Sr. and the Making of IBM.* Hoboken, N.J.: John Wiley & Sons, 2003.

Tedlow, Richard S. *The Watson Dynasty: The Fiery Reign and Troubled Legacy of IBM's Founding Father and Son.* New York: HarperCollins, 2003.

See also: Inventions; Science and technology

■ International trade

The vigorous growth of North American trade helped the European economy to recover from World War I. Export markets continued to be a very important outlet for agricultural products from both the United States and Canada. However, the recession of 1920 and 1921 began with a collapse of international markets for farm products and led to economic protectionism in both North American countries. Capital flowed from the United States to Europe during the decade and contributed to the surplus of U.S. exports.

Aside from military casualties, the United States and Canada had not suffered economic damage from World War I. In fact, both countries had experienced a strong export boom. However, the international economic situation as a whole was still chaotic in 1920. Many cargo ships had been destroyed or worn out. Networks of trading relationships were disrupted. Violence, political upheaval, and hyperinflation persisted in Germany, eastern Europe, and Russia. The pre—World War I gold standard had been suspended, and foreign exchange rates had become unstable.

European countries had liquidated overseas assets and borrowed heavily from foreign sources, particularly the United States, in order to finance the war effort. International finances were therefore muddled by war debts and the reparations imposed on Germany. At this time, the United States shifted from a debtor to a creditor nation. During the 1920s, loans from private investors in the United States were an important source of buying power in the financing of U.S. exports.

The international economic position of the United States in 1920 had not changed much from 1919. Merchandise exports were valued at $8.5 billion, only slightly less than the record level in 1919. Imports were valued at $5.4 billion, a record high level that would not be exceeded until 1947. The export surplus of $3 billion was a net contribution to the gross national product (GNP) and contributed to the inflationary conditions in the United States during the early 1920s. The country's new role as a creditor nation brought about a net investment income of $500 million, setting another record high.

Postwar Recession

In 1920, international markets for farm products began to collapse, reflecting the resurgence of farm production in Europe and the fact that European residents did not have sufficient funds to continue buying extensively from other countries. In 1921, the value of U.S. export sales dropped by nearly one-half to $4.6 billion. In response to the fall of income levels, U.S. imports also declined to $2.6 billion. As a result, the export surplus fell by $1 billion, reducing the GNP by at least that amount and contributing to the painful recession of 1920 and 1921.

Canada also experienced a huge export boom during and immediately after World War I. Merchandise exports in 1920 were valued at C$1.4 billion, about the same as in 1918 and 1919. However, Canadian imports ballooned in 1920, from C$1 billion in 1919 to C$1.4 billion in 1920, greatly exceeding the previous levels. Canada's import surplus contributed to the decline in the foreign-exchange value of the Canadian dollar from US$0.96 in 1919 to US$0.89 in 1920.

Canadian exports and imports both dropped in 1921. However, imports declined more than exports, so Canada's international account on balance helped to buffer the recession of 1920 and 1921.

Farmers in both the United States and Canada were hit hard by a drastic turnaround in international agricultural markets. In the United States, exports constituted 27 percent of farm income in 1920. By the next year, they only amounted to 26 percent of a much smaller income. The proportion then declined further and was only 15 percent by 1929.

The economic downswing of 1920 and 1921 led many countries to increase tariffs and other trade restrictions. In 1922, the U.S. Congress adopted the Fordney-McCumber Tariff, which substantially increased tax rates on imports for the protection of

U.S. agricultural and industrial projects. Many European countries retaliated by increasing their tariff rates in turn. The World Economic Conference of 1927 estimated that U.S. tariffs in 1925 averaged about 37 percent of the value of imports, one of the highest rates in the world. They estimated that Canadian tariff rates averaged about 23 percent. Canadian duties on farm machinery had been reduced in 1922 and 1924. However, additional Canadian protectionism was carried out through antimonopoly and antidumping provisions of tariff laws.

The high-tariff policies of the United States and Canada were unpopular with European countries that needed to export in order to earn the money necessary to meet their war debts to the United States. However, the trade pattern that emerged after the United States recovered from the recession of 1920 and 1921 was quite satisfactory to most Americans. Both exports and imports followed very smooth growth trends from 1922 to 1929, with annual export surpluses of $1 billion or more. U.S. exports in 1922 amounted to $3.9 billion, rising steadily to $4.9 billion in 1926 and $5.3 billion in 1929. U.S. imports rose from $3.2 billion in 1922 to $4.5 billion in 1929. Partly because of the tariff increase, U.S. imports only made up about 5 percent of GNP during most of the decade, resulting in a lower proportion than in earlier years.

World War I shifted the United States' role as an international debtor to an international creditor, and this shift was reflected in the steady rise of international investment income. Net income from international investments rose from $0.3 billion in 1921 to $0.8 billion in 1929. The rest of the world borrowed steadily from the United States' private capital market through bond issues and bank loans. These funds helped to finance the persistent U.S. export surplus. Private foreign lending reached its peak in 1928, exceeding $1.5 billion. Soon after, the U.S. stock market boom diverted funds away from foreign investments, which fell off sharply in 1929. This drop hit the German economy hard, starting a downward cycle. Imports into the United States did not increase greatly in the late 1920s, which aggravated the economic situation in Germany and other European countries.

Content of U.S. Exports and Imports

Farm products made up about half of total U.S. export value in 1920 and again in 1922, before trending

steadily downward to 35 percent in 1929. The value of U.S. farm exports declined from $3.9 billion in 1920 to only $1.8 billion in 1929. The decline was especially strong for wheat and flour; those exports dropped from $821 million in 1920 to only $192 million in 1929. The resulting downward influence on farm incomes led Congress to pass the McNary-Haugen bill, which provided export subsidies for farm products, but President Calvin Coolidge vetoed it twice, once in 1924 and again in 1928. Meanwhile, nonfarm product exports reflected those sectors of the economy that were particularly booming, most notably automobiles and petroleum.

Prominent among U.S. imports were products not produced domestically in significant amounts, such as coffee, tea, sugar, rubber, and silk. Declines in value over the decade arose primarily from declines in price. The quantity of sugar imported was substantially larger in 1929 than in 1920 and 1921, even though the value of imports decreased by four-fifths. The quantity of raw silk imports in 1929 was three times that of 1920, despite the inroads made by the expansion of rayon production. The quantity of crude rubber imported doubled from 1920 to 1929, reflecting the expanded production of automobile tires.

Prohibition, a national ban on alcoholic beverages, went into effect in the United States in January 1920. This generated a large illegal trade in alcohol shipments into the United States, much of it coming through Canada. Canadian liquor exports to the United States rose from 8,000 gallons in 1921 to more than 1 million gallons in 1928.

Canadian Developments

Canada's international position also shifted in response to World War I, and foreign trade played a much larger role in the Canadian economy than in the United States. The country had seen a large import surplus in earlier years, but it developed a small export surplus in the 1920s. As in the United States, imports and exports dropped off sharply in the depression of 1920 and 1921, but afterward they increased steadily, if slowly. Export value dropped from C$1.3 billion in 1920 to C$0.8 billion in 1921, and then it rebounded to $1.3 billion in 1926. Although the Canadian dollar had fallen to US$0.89 in 1920, it recovered to US$0.98 between 1922 and 1924, reaching full parity in 1925. This increase in value made Canadian products more expensive to foreign buyers and contributed to the decline of Canadian exports. Perhaps it was for this reason that exports only amounted to C$1.2 billion in 1929, falling slightly below imports for that year. Nevertheless, Canadian merchandise exports averaged more than one-fifth of GNP in the late 1920s.

World War I had intensified Canada's economic interaction with the United States. The connection was particularly strong for Canadian imports. By 1926, two-thirds of Canadian merchandise imports came from the United States, while only one-sixth came from Great Britain. Canada's export markets were much more diverse. Major Canadian exports to the United States included lumber, wood pulp, paper, and mineral products such as nickel. Nearly half of Canada's exports went to the United States in 1920, but that proportion fell to about 40 percent for the rest of the decade. Canada received a major share of new capital inflow from the United States. By 1926, U.S. investors accounted for 53 percent of Canada's foreign-owned assets, while investors from Britain accounted for 44 percent. Major U.S. corporations established Canadian outposts for industrial activities such as mining, refining, and manufacturing. Canada's growing automobile industry was entirely populated with branches of U.S. firms. The high tariff barriers were a major factor in deterring Canadians from buying heavily taxed cars from south of the border.

International Negotiations

Extensive international economic negotiations in the 1920s centered on the gold standard, foreign-exchange rates, and debts. The leaders of the newly formed U.S. Federal Reserve, especially Benjamin Strong, president of the Federal Reserve Bank of New York, actively promoted a return to the pre–World War I gold standard. Britain made a similar return in 1924, restoring stable exchange rates but condemning the British economy to depression. Following suspension of the gold standard, the British pound had fallen to US$3.38 in February 1920. From this point onward, the pound's value rose in value, reaching US$4.44 in mid-1922 and achieving full pre–World War I parity of US$4.85 in 1925. Appreciation of the pound made U.S. goods cheaper in Britain and British goods more expensive in the United States. Germany's hyperinflation in 1923 led to further negotiations to stabilize the value of the German mark and reduce the burden of German

reparations, payable mainly to the victorious Allies. American banker Charles G. Dawes found his name attached to a 1924 agreement to aid Germany in floating a loan in the United States to support a new currency. Germany enjoyed an interlude of prosperity and a high rate of investment, relying heavily on further loans from U.S. investors. A restructuring of war debt in 1929 named after American industrialist Owen Young resulted in reduced U.S. loans, after which war debts and reparations went into default and were ultimately canceled.

Impact

Both the United States and Canada possessed large areas of fertile land during the 1920s. In consequence, both countries had a natural advantage in exporting agricultural products like cotton and wheat to other countries. Both countries adhered to protectionist policies, using tariffs and other restrictions to deter imports. Protectionism in the United States was reflected in a relatively small proportion of foreign trade to GNP. In terms of economics, Canada was more internationally oriented, however. While both countries industrialized and urbanized rapidly as the early twentieth century unfolded, the U.S. economy progressed much more quickly than the Canadian economy.

Tariff rates in the United States had been reduced under President Woodrow Wilson but were drastically increased in the 1920s. This stance reflected the United States' rejection of internationalism, paralleling the country's refusal to join the League of Nations. Protective tariffs did not help American and Canadian farmers with depressed incomes, however. Both countries were dragged into severe economic recession in 1920 when international markets for farm products collapsed. A similar but more intense shock in 1929 was one of the major forces setting off the Great Depression. In response, U.S. tariff rates were increased still further in the Smoot-Hawley Tariff of 1930.

Paul B. Trescott

Further Reading

Atack, Jeremy, Peter Passell, and Susan Lee. *A New Economic View of American History: From Colonial Times to 1940.* 2d ed. New York: Norton, 1994. Relates the international developments in the global economy following World War I.

Brecher, Irving, and S. S. Reisman. *Canada-United*

States Economic Relations. Toronto: Royal Commission on Canada's Economic Prospects, 1957. A diagnosis of the 1920–1921 boom-and-bust cycle, including extensive data on U.S. investments in Canada, trade, and tariff policies.

Eichengreen, Barry. *Golden Fetters: The Gold Standard and the Great Depression, 1919–1939.* New York: Oxford University Press, 1996. Offers an analytical view of the international economy of the 1920s.

Norrie, Kenneth, and Douglas Owram. *A History of the Canadian Economy.* 3d ed. Toronto: Thomson Nelson, 2008. Discusses the international factors affecting Canada's economic evolution.

Soule, George Henry. *Prosperity Decade: From War to Depression, 1917–1929.* New York: Rinehart, 1989. Gives an overview of trade and finance in 1920s America.

See also: Agriculture in Canada; Agriculture in the United States; Dawes Plan

■ Inventions

The United States witnessed an unprecedented economic boom in the 1920s, built largely upon scientific and technological innovations. Productivity skyrocketed. Salaries increased. Workers, with more disposable income, spent freely on new products and services, which gave rise to a flourishing consumer society.

Although Europe in 1920 was still struggling to recover from the effects of World War I, the United States was poised for change and prosperity. The landscape was becoming more urban, with people moving from farms to increasingly crowded cities, where jobs, higher salaries, and better prospects for the future lay. Additionally, women had entered the workforce during the war and were given the right to vote in 1920, further changing the needs of families and society. The technological innovations introduced during this period combined with these changes to improve the quality of life for most Americans and reshape the national character.

A Nation on the Move

One of the innovations that most influenced the American economy and lifestyle was the automobile. Invented in the late nineteenth century, the automobile came of age in the 1920s with Henry Ford and the Model T. First introduced in 1908, the Ford Model T was a novelty that, at $850, was too expensive for most people, until the automaker invented an improved assembly line production system around 1913. The assembly line made mass production possible, resulting in lower consumer costs. In the early 1920s the price of a Model T fell to $290, or about three months' salary for the average consumer. With Ford's innovative idea of the installment plan, the Model T became affordable for individuals who could pay a portion of the cost up front and then commit to reasonable monthly payments. Around this time, other auto makers began the successful combination of low price and easy payments created by Ford and offered options the Model T did not have, such as windshield wipers, headrests, power steering, convertible tops, and a range of color choices. Ford was forced to discontinue the utilitarian Model T in favor of the more consumer-friendly Model A in 1927. More than fifteen million automobiles were sold by Ford and other U.S. auto manufacturers during the 1920s. By the end of the decade, virtually every U.S. household owned a car.

To accommodate the sudden wave of drivers, federal and state governments embarked on massive campaigns throughout the 1920s to build surfaced, all-weather highways and traffic-bearing bridges. The Federal Aid Highway Act of 1921 provided funding to help state agencies construct a paved, two-lane system of interstate highways. The spike in federally funded construction to create a national highway system motivated improvements on a nineteenth-century invention: the caterpillar or "crawling tractor." In 1923, James D. Cummings and John E. McLeod of Kansas invented the bulldozer by adding a scraping blade to the front of the crawling tractor.

Numerous auto-related products and services were also invented during the 1920s, including traffic lights (1920), garage doors (1921), garage door openers (1926), and glare-cutting sunglasses (1929). Motels, or "motor hotels," appeared along major highways. Prior to 1920, most consumers bought gasoline from hardware stores, but with the increase in automobiles on the road and drivers who wanted convenience, filling stations soon dotted the highways. Car washes, shopping centers, tire and auto parts stores, and an entire petroleum industry that would become a dominant force in American economy were all introduced or greatly expanded during the 1920s.

Cars such as these new Model T's became more affordable during the 1920s. (Hulton Archive/Getty Images)

The affordable automobile of the 1920s and Ford's innovative deferred payment plan also affected the way Americans thought about buying goods and about how they spent their money. The simplicity of buying a car on the installment plan, for instance, transformed the country from a cash-and-carry society to one that grew to embrace the concept of credit. Also, the convenience of low-cost personal transportation allowed workers to move to the suburbs and commute easily to jobs in the cities. Tourism flourished, and the economy improved. Families could travel quickly and easily to restaurants where music played from jukeboxes (invented in 1927) or to sporting events, vacation destinations, movie theaters, and amusement parks.

Electricity and Radio

The electrification of the United States began in the 1880s with the construction of the first commercial power plant. By the 1920s, most municipalities had electric power, which made workplaces brighter, safer, and more efficient. Electrically powered conveyor belts brought tasks to employees at their workstations, which saved thousands of hours of labor and made a range of items cheaper to produce, which in turn lowered the unit cost of the product for consumers.

By 1929, the majority of homes had electricity, and a number of newly invented or improved-upon home appliances had been introduced. The portable Electrolux Model V canister vacuum cleaner (1921) sported twin metal runners for easy mobility when housekeeping. Iceboxes were replaced by refrigerators, with Frigidaire introducing the first unit in 1923. Late in the decade, a small freezer compartment for ice cube trays was included for additional convenience, and Freon replaced more dangerous cooling chemicals. Although Clarence Birdseye invented a method to flash-freeze meat and produce in 1923, it would not be until 1930 that consumers could buy Birdseye products or until they had a freezer compartment large enough to store the food. The Schick electric razor (1923) made shaving fast and safe, and the Toastmaster pop-up toaster (1925) could simultaneously brown both sides of a piece of bread and then eject it after a set period of time. Handheld electric hair dryers, electric clothes irons, garbage disposals, and electric phonographs were all introduced during the 1920s and helped to simplify and enhance the lives of many Americans. Few in rural locations, however, were exposed to these new innovations, as only about one-third of American farms had access to electricity before the end of the decade.

The invention that many believe had the greatest impact on both urban and rural residents was the radio. Radios were much cheaper than cars and more widely available than in-home electricity (as they could run on batteries), and by the end of the decade, virtually every home in the United States had one. The first commercial radio station, KDKA in Pittsburgh, Pennsylvania, debuted in 1920, and within a few years, hundreds of stations were operating across the country. In 1926, the Radio Corporation of America (RCA) developed the first radio network, the National Broadcasting Company (NBC). The Columbia Broadcasting System (CBS), a competing network, was created the following year. Before long, the networks and independent stations were broadcasting a wide variety of news, sports, music, comedy, and dramatic programs. With many radio stations competing for time and consumer attention, radio signals were often weak and noisy. Toward the end of the decade, the Radio Act of 1927 was passed, and the Federal Radio Commission (FRC) was formed to regulate radio and assign frequencies and power levels for each station.

Manufacturers and marketers soon found a way to make the new medium profitable by using radio advertising. The first paid commercial was for a New York real estate developer and aired in 1922. Before long, a new industry was built around broadcast marketing, which in thirty- and sixty-second increments helped introduce the public to newly invented brand-name consumer products such as Band-Aids (1921), Eskimo Pies (1922), Q-tips (1923), Popsicles (1924), Kool-Aid (1927), and Double Bubble bubblegum (1928).

Health and Longevity

The 1920s was also a decade that focused on individual health and physical vitality, and medical inventions and discoveries reflected this. In 1922, vitamin D was discovered to prevent rickets, a debilitating bone disease that affected many children. The same year, scientists discovered vitamin E and its ability to protect human tissue, and insulin was developed to treat diabetes, which until that time had no known cure. By the end of the decade, vaccines against potentially fatal diseases such as diphtheria (1923), whooping cough (1926), tuberculosis (1928), and tetanus (1928) were available, and the first iron lung was used to treat respiratory failure.

Impact

The inventions of the 1920s profoundly affected lifestyles and revolutionized the United States in ways that are still being felt in the twenty-first century. In 1926, for instance, Robert Hutchings Goddard invented and tested the first liquid-fuel rocket, helping to inspire, many believe, the national space program.

Major advancements in transportation have profoundly affected lifestyles. Transportation in the 1920s was transformed thanks to affordable automobiles and the thousands of miles of paved highways that replaced dirt roads. Many modern vehicles are still manufactured through similar mass-production procedures that make use of assembly lines, incorporate much of the basic internal combustion technology of early cars, and are sold on installment plans like those introduced in the early 1920s.

The new and improved home appliances of the 1920s gave consumers time and made life easier. The radio was an immediate success with its affordable cost and ability to bring people together to be entertained. The motion picture industry also introduced its own innovations, and during the 1920s, the industry added sound (1927), color (1922), and 3-D capabilities (1922). Air conditioning was installed in theaters to attract patrons with disposable income and newfound leisure time on their hands.

Medical advances in the 1920s improved the health of individuals, saved untold lives, and helped to bring once-fatal diseases under control. Scientists in later years would expand on the 1920s research to further improve treatments and diagnoses.

Jack Ewing

Further Reading

Berger, Michael L. *The Automobile in American History and Culture: A Reference Guide.* Westport, Conn.: Greenwood, 2001. An annotated collection of essays dealing with the history of the automobile industry and its impact on American society.

Best, Gary Dean. *The Dollar Decade: Mammon and the Machine in 1920s America.* Westport, Conn.: Greenwood, 2003. This work pays particular attention to the life-changing effects of such innovations as the automobile on American society during the 1920s and afterward.

Collins, Tom. *The Legendary Model T Ford: The Ultimate History of America's First Great Automobile.* Iola, Wis.: Krause Publications, 2007. An illustrated examination of the history of the Model T and Henry Ford.

Douglas, Susan J. *Listening In: Radio and the American Imagination.* Minneapolis: University of Minnesota Press, 2004. This history of radio demonstrates how broadcasting innovations have affected American listeners from the beginning of the medium to the present.

Gordon, Bob. *Early Electrical Appliances.* Essex, England: Shire Books, 2010. Describes the first electrical appliances, including early manufacturing problems and marketing techniques, with illustrations.

Hilmes, Michele, and Jason Loviglio, eds. *Radio Reader: Essays in the Cultural History of Radio.* New York: Routledge, 2002. A collection of articles demonstrating the influence of radio on American society and on the television industry.

Miller, Nathan. *New World Coming: The 1920s and the Making of Modern America.* New York: Scribner, 2003. An overview of U.S. history and social conditions throughout the 1920s.

See also: Band-Aids; Bread slicer; Bubble gum; Bulldozer; Cellophane; Eskimo Pie; Hair dryers; Insulin; Iron lung; Kool-Aid; Loudspeakers; Radio; Refrigerators; Rocketry; Talking motion pictures

---

■ Iron lung

The iron lung was the first artificial respirator used to treat patients suffering from respiratory failure or other breathing problems. It helped facilitate the recovery and survival of many patients with serious respiratory difficulties, such as those caused by polio and other diseases.

The iron lung—formally known as the negative pressure ventilator, and also called the Drinker respirator

Louis Shaw and Cecil Drinker's Experiments

The concept of the mechanical respirator reportedly arose from Philip Drinker's observations of physiological experiments carried out by Louis Agassiz Shaw and Drinker's brother, Cecil. The experiments involved placing a cat inside an airtight box, a body plethysmograph, with the cat's head protruding from an airtight collar. Shaw and Cecil Drinker then measured the volume changes in the plethysmograph to identify normal breathing parameters. Philip Drinker then placed cats paralyzed by curare inside the plethysmographs and showed that they could be kept breathing artificially by use of air from a hypodermic syringe connected to the device.

or the tank respirator—was invented by industrial hygienist Philip Drinker and physiology professor Louis Agassiz Shaw, both faculty members at the Harvard University School of Public Health. In 1927, the Consolidated Gas Company of New York was funding research into resuscitation to combat the problem of coal gas poisoning, which was affecting many of their employees; Drinker and Shaw, who were already studying artificial resuscitation, received a $5,000 grant from the company to continue their research. This funding led to the development of a prototype iron lung the following year.

Drinker and Shaw's device was designed to stimulate breathing in patients who were unable to breathe on their own. The patient would be placed in a chamber, after which the air pressure in the chamber would be alternately increased and decreased, thus inducing the chest compression and expansion necessary for respiration. Drinker and Shaw initially tested their device on an anesthetized cat; when it proved successful, they received an additional $2,000 to develop a version large enough to be used on humans. The iron lung was first used to treat a human being at Children's Hospital in Boston, Massachusetts, on October 12, 1928, when a young girl suffering from respiratory failure was successfully resuscitated. The following year saw the first use of an iron lung to save the life of a polio victim, at Brigham Hospital, also in Boston.

Impact

The iron lung was the first truly effective treatment for polio patients in whom advancing paralysis was affecting their ability to breathe. The technology was invaluable during the polio epidemics of the 1940s and 1950s, when it was used in the United States and around the world to keep sufferers alive and breathing. Though iron lungs are rarely used today, they have saved countless lives over the years and have helped lead to further advances in life support techniques.

David M. Brown

Further Reading

Drinker, Philip, Thomas J. Shaughnessy, and Douglas P. Murphy. "The Drinker Respirator: Analysis of Case Reports of Patients with Respiratory Failure Treated from October, 1928, to June, 1930." *Journal of the American Medical Association* 95, no. 17 (October, 1930): 1249–1253.

Silver, Julie K., and Daniel J. Wilson. *Polio Voices: An Oral History from the American Polio Epidemics and Worldwide Eradication Efforts.* Westport, Conn.: Praeger, 2007.

Wilson, Daniel J. *Polio.* Santa Barbara, Calif.: Greenwood Press, 2009.

See also: Health care; Inventions; Medicine; Polio

■ Isolationism

Isolationism influenced all U.S. presidents and Congresses in the 1920s. While a shrunken world required the United States to enter into numerous agreements, it did so unilaterally and always sought to avoid any entanglements that might lead to war.

The roots of American isolationism go back to the pragmatic policies of U.S. presidents George Washington and Thomas Jefferson, who considered it the best way to avoid further conflict with Europe. The United States could pursue such a policy because it was surrounded by weak powers, with most other continents an ocean away. During World War I, this stance was abandoned, but after over fifty thousand American casualties and subsequent disillusionment with European politics, isolationism returned in full force as the prevailing philosophy of the 1920s.

Manifestations of Isolationism

In the 1920s, it became clear to many Americans that the ostensible goal of World War I—to make the world safe for democracy—had not been achieved at all. Many scholars wrote antiwar books arguing that the Allies' motivations for war had been far from noble. Europe seemed to relapse into its old rivalries and hatreds, and the United States was loath to enter any relationships that might lead them into another war.

The U.S. Senate rejected the Treaty of Versailles that ended the war in Europe, despite President Woodrow Wilson's strong support for its passage, due to vigorous opposition to the proposed League of Nations. The antitreaty faction feared that the League would compromise American sovereignty and objected to the idea of committing U.S. forces to an international army. Americans were also frustrated by the failure of Allied European nations to pay off the loans they had contracted during the war. The growing tendency toward isolationism was also expressed economically, via high tariffs imposed on foreign imports, and socially, with the Immigration Acts of 1921 and 1924 severely restricting foreign immigration.

The prevailing American sentiment of the 1920s was that modern wars were too destructive to be fought for any reason other than self-defense and that nothing that happened across the oceans could pose a threat to the Western Hemisphere. In other words, the United States wanted to turn its back on the rest of the world, a sentiment that would grow even stronger in the 1930s. Isolationist beliefs existed in all parts of the country, with several U.S. Senators being the most vocal proponents, notably Senate Committee on Foreign Relations chair Henry Cabot Lodge and his successor, William Borah. The presidents of the 1920s had to heed the nation's sentiments on this issue and try to avoid foreign relationships that would make them appear to be departing from isolationism.

Departures from Isolationism in the 1920s

Despite the declarations by politicians and journalists in support of isolationism, the United States did become involved with world affairs to a considerable extent in the 1920s. However, these arrangements were entered into unilaterally, with every effort made to avoid potentially dangerous entanglements that might lead the nation into another war. This applied particularly to Europe, as the United States was much more directly engaged in Asia and Latin America.

Because Congress had rejected the Treaty of Versailles, which ended World War I in Europe, the United States had to make separate peace agreements with each of the former Central Powers. It also signed the multinational Kellogg-Briand Pact to outlaw war as an instrument of national policy, but no mechanism had been devised to enforce this pact.

To curtail a naval arms race and stabilize relations in the Pacific, President Warren G. Harding held the Washington Naval Conference in 1921. Led by U.S. secretary of state Charles Evans Hughes, the attending delegations signed many important agreements, including the Five-Power Treaty regarding naval limitation. Under the terms of this treaty, the United States and Great Britain were to have the world's two largest navies, followed by Japan, then France and Italy. It also established a ratio for battleships and limitations on other vessels. In addition, the Nine-Power Treaty was signed with the intention to maintain an "open door" to China for all powers and thereby prevent aggression against that nation. Territorial questions in Asia were also addressed, such as the removal of wartime Japanese occupation in some areas and the clarification of postwar arrangements for various Pacific islands.

The United States was deeply involved in Latin America before, during, and after World War I. American military and economic power was clearly manifested in that region throughout the 1920s. Frank B. Kellogg, who served as secretary of state under President Coolidge, was instrumental in the withdrawal of U.S. Marines from Nicaragua and in preventing Mexican expropriation of oil and land. At the same time, however, Kellogg rejected the Roosevelt Corollary to the Monroe Doctrine, which claimed that the United States has a right to interfere in hemispheric affairs even though Europe does not.

Impact

Despite American tariff barriers, economic investment in Europe almost doubled from 1919 to 1929. The American-sponsored Dawes Plan helped settle the problem of war reparations, and the United States continued to support humanitarian efforts such as Russian famine relief, while also maintaining considerable cultural ties with Europe. A significant number of Americans traveled to Europe in the 1920s, with quite a few establishing full-time resi-

dence there, and American music, films, and literature were popular throughout Europe. The U.S. government remained involved in Asia and Latin America throughout the period. Complete isolation from the rest of the world was consequently more an abstract ideal than a practical reality during the 1920s.

Henry Weisser

Further Reading

Bagby, Wesley M. *America's International Relations Since World War I.* New York: Oxford University Press, 1999. Places isolationism in a broader context.

Combs, Jerald A. *From 1895.* Vol. 2 in *The History of American Foreign Policy.* 3d ed. Armonk, N.Y.: M. E. Sharpe, 2008. Contains a chapter on foreign policy in the interwar period.

MacKercher, Brian J. C. *Anglo-American Relations in the 1920s: The Struggle for Supremacy.* Edmonton: University of Alberta Press, 1990. Examines the relationship between the United States and Great Britain in the 1920s.

Spiller, John, et al. "Foreign Policy, 1890–1941." In *The United States, 1763–2001.* London: Routledge, 2005. Includes an essay on "Isolationism in the 1920s and 1930s," plus a discussion of why it was abandoned.

Williams, William Appleman. *The Tragedy of American Diplomacy.* 2d ed. New York: Dell, 1972. Stresses worldwide activity during the 1920s.

See also: Dawes Plan; Europe; Foreign policy, U.S.; Immigration to the United States; International trade; Kellogg-Briand Pact of 1928; League of Nations; Mexico; Soviet Union and North America

■ Izaak Walton League of America

Definition: American environmental conservation organization
Date: Founded in 1922

The Izaak Walton League was one of the first national conservation organizations dedicated to lobbying for legislative protection of the environment. Initially, the League consisted entirely of volunteers who sought to reduce pollution, protect habitats, restore watersheds, and promote conservation as a value for outdoor activity. Within a few years, the organization grew to become the largest conservation group in the United States at that time.

The Izaak Walton League, named for the seventeenth-century British fishing enthusiast and author of *The Compleat Angler* (1653), was founded in 1922 in Chicago, Illinois, by fifty-four fishermen and outdoor enthusiasts. Their initial intent—to preserve and protect fishing habitats—soon expanded to include the protection of all natural wildlife. This new focus would help in the effort to safeguard fish from the effects of water pollution and address the varied interests of its founders, members, and supporters. By 1924, the Izaak Walton League had grown to over 100,000 supporters due in part to the expertise of the founders, many of whom were in advertising and business.

One of the first league conservation efforts was initiated by Will H. Dilg, founding member and the league's first president. In 1924, the Izaak Walton League Fund was established to save starving elk in Jackson Hole, Wyoming. Two years later, the league championed the first federally funded fish and wildlife sanctuary, the Upper Mississippi River National Wildlife and Fish Refuge. During the 1920s, the league continued to work toward controlling water pollution by conducting a national water survey, which determined that three-quarters of U.S. waters in 1927 were polluted, and spearheading the construction of sewage plants near Cedar River in Iowa. *Outdoor America*, the group's publication and one of the first environmentally focused magazines in the country, drew the public's attention to environmental issues of the day while simultaneously increasing league membership.

Impact

The Izaak Walton League was among the first organizations to define conservation in the modern sense of grassroots environmentalism. Although the league peaked in membership and national influence in the 1920s and 1930s, the organization continues to promote the conservation and protection of the country's natural resources in the twenty-first century.

John H. Barnhill

Further Reading

Gottlieb, R. *Forcing the Spring: The Transformation of the American Environmental Movement*. Rev. ed. Washington, D.C.: Island Press, 2005.

Middleton, Julie V. "The Stream Doctor Project: Community-Driven Stream Restoration." *BioScience* 51, no. 4 (April, 2001): 293.

Mongillo, John, and Bibi Booth, eds. *Environmental Activists*. Westport, Conn.: Greenwood Press, 2001.

See also: Air pollution; Hobbies and recreation; Magazines; Natural resources, exploitation of

J

◼ Jannings, Emil

Identification: German American silent screen actor
Also known as: Theodor Friedrich Emil Janenz
Born: July 23, 1884, Rorschach, Switzerland
Died: January 2, 1950, Strobl, Austria

By the 1920s, silent film star Emil Jannings had achieved international fame. At the decade's close, he became the first actor to receive an Academy Award for Best Actor.

At the age of eighteen, Theodor Friedrich Emil Jannings joined the company of German theater director Max Reinhardt. In 1914, he made his debut in a World War I propaganda film, leading the way to more important roles through the end of the decade. His role in film director Ernst Lubitsch's *Madame Dubarry* (1919) made Jannings an international star.

During the 1920s, Jannings became one of the highest-paid and most critically regarded silent film stars. His role in the 1922 film *Othello* led to his being cast in film director F. W. Murnau's motion picture *The Last Laugh* (1922). In this role as an aging doorman who is demoted to washroom attendant, Jannings perfected the so-called Jannings Vehicle, a dramatic role in which a pompous and self-important character is brought low by fate. Jannings went on to perform in two more films for Murnau: *Herr Tartuff* (1925) and *Faust* (1926). In 1927, Jannings starred in the acclaimed film *Variety*, after which Paramount Studios signed him to make Hollywood films.

In 1929, Jannings earned the first Academy Award for Best Actor and received the first Oscar statuette in motion picture history for *The Way of All Flesh* and *The Last Command*. At this time, Jannings was in great demand for dramatic roles.

Returning to Germany after little success in American talking pictures, Jannings played his most renowned role in the motion picture *Der Blaue Engel* (1930; *The Blue Angel*, 1931), which was filmed separately in German and English. In this film, Jannings portrays a man destroyed by obsession as he ruins his

Emil Jannings. (Getty Images)

career and life after falling in love with a cabaret performer. Soon afterward, Jannings embraced Nazism, making several propaganda films; Joseph Goebbels, the minister of propaganda in Germany, even dubbed Jannings "Artist of the State" in 1941. After World War II, the actor retired to Austria, bitter at having been blacklisted from the film industry due to his relationship with the Nazis. Jannings died of liver cancer in 1950.

Impact

A master of emotional expression, Emil Jannings helped define the notion of great film acting. His deeply felt portrayal of tragic characters, both from history and literature, set a standard for dramatic acting. He brought gravity and depth to these roles, showing how men reacted to the harsh twists of fate.

Leslie Neilan

Further Reading

Giesen, Rolf. *Nazi Propaganda Films: A History and Filmography.* Reprint. Jefferson, N.C.: McFarland, 2008.

Isenberg, Noah. *Weimar Cinema: An Essential Guide to Classic Films of the Era.* New York: Columbia University Press, 2009.

Kosta, Barbara. *Willing Seduction: The Blue Angel, Marlene Dietrich, and Mass Culture.* New York: Berghahn Books, 2009.

See also: Academy Awards; Talking motion pictures

■ Japanese American Citizens League

Identification: Japanese American civil rights advocacy organization

Date: Founded in 1929

The Japanese American Citizens League (JACL) is a civil rights organization formed in 1929 by second-generation Japanese immigrants. It encouraged the Japanese community to embrace American customs in an effort to overcome the anti-Japanese movement and discriminatory legislation threatening the livelihood of Japanese immigrants in the United States.

By the early 1920s, over 100,000 Japanese immigrants were residing in the United States. This increase sparked a backlash from the American public, who were concerned that Japanese immigrants would not be loyal to the United States or would take the jobs of native-born Americans. Several state legislatures passed laws aimed at preventing Japanese immigrants from owning land and restricting their ability to lease property. Increasing anti-immigrant sentiment led the U.S. Congress to pass the Immigration Act of 1924, which, among other things, prohibited entry by any immigrant who was not eligible for U.S. citizenship. Because the Naturalization Act of 1790 forbade citizenship to nonwhite persons, the Immigration Act effectively denied any further Japanese immigration into the United States.

In contrast to the first-generation Japanese immigrants, who sought to fit into American society while retaining their heritage and customs, many of the second generation, who were born, raised, and educated in the United States, believed that completely embracing American customs would be the most effective means of stopping the anti-Japanese movement. In 1929, second-generation Japanese Americans Clarence Arai, Saburo Kido, and Thomas Yatabe formed the JACL. In keeping with the principle of total immersion into American society, they limited membership to American citizens only, precluding the participation of first-generation immigrants. Heading into the 1930s, the JACL intended to promote Americanization and conciliation as a means of demonstrating loyalty to the United States. The JACL represented a distinct change in the Japanese community's approach to not only political activism but also its role in American society.

Impact

The JACL was successful, on a limited scale, in obtaining the repeal of discriminatory state legislation and preventing its enactment. In the 1940s, the JACL lost most of its support from the Japanese community when its focus on conciliation led it to promote cooperation with the government internment of Japanese people during World War II. After the war ended, however, the JACL played a key role in successfully fighting for redress and reparations for those who had been imprisoned. In the twenty-first century, the JACL continues to serve as a civil rights advocacy organization for Japanese Americans.

Jenny L. Evans

Further Reading

Hosokawa, Bill. *JACL in Quest of Justice.* New York: W. Morrow, 1982.

_____. *Nisei: The Quiet Americans.* Rev. ed. Boulder: University Press of Colorado, 2002.

Kitayama, Glen. "Japanese American Citizens League." In *Japanese American History: An A-to-Z Reference from 1868 to the Present,* edited by Brian Niiya. New York: Facts on File, 2001.

See also: Asia; Asian Americans; Cable Act of 1922; Civil rights and liberties; Foreign policy, U.S.; Immigration Act of 1921; Immigration Act of 1924; Immigration to the United States

■ Jazz

Jazz came to represent the mood of the period between the end of World War I and the onset of the Great Depression. While the word has assumed a great deal of cultural resonance, it is still primarily a term used to describe a musical style. The roots of jazz can be traced to the last years of the nineteenth century, and although its development continued for a century, the 1920s represented its coming of age as both a popular music style and an art form.

Although sometimes called the Jazz Age, the 1920s initially identified jazz music in a very limited way, but it evolved into a vastly different entity by the end of the decade. Around 1920, most people would have identified jazz with the boisterous, highly charged syncopations of the Original Dixieland Jazz Band (ODJB). Following its migration from New Orleans to its residency at Reisenweber's restaurant in New York, the group launched a series of popular recordings that brought jazz to the attention of the public. Syncopated music using African American elements had been the driving force in American popular music since the ragtime boom of the 1890s, when musicians such as Scott Joplin, James Europe, and Eubie Blake had been important arbiters of the style.

The dual influences of ragtime and blues typified by composer W. C. Handy during the 1910s caused a stylistic shift in popular music and song. Tin Pan Alley composers such as Irving Berlin and George Gershwin rode the crest of the wave with songs that featured syncopation, blue notes (notes with slightly lower pitches), and what were perceived as celebrations of African American life in a sophisticated musical setting. Other musical elements associated with the new jazz trend included fast tempos, animated stage presentation, and the nontraditional use of instruments (growls, squeals, the use of mutes, and extended techniques) to produce highly vocalized sounds. Social dances such as the Charleston and the Lindy Hop developed in tandem with the new music, and fashion and literature further adapted musical and cultural elements related to speed and the abandonment of inhibition. In fact, the word "jazz" was a lightning rod for social commentators of the time, as conservative society regarded it as a synonym for sexual license.

Dance Bands

One of the primary developments in dance band music during the period was the introduction of saxophones into ensembles. Art Hickman's Orchestra, based in San Francisco, is generally credited with being the first to incorporate a saxophone section in its arrangements, as early as 1918. By 1920, virtually all full-sized commercial dance bands had at least two saxophones in addition to two trumpets, a trombone, a rhythm section, and occasionally strings and other woodwinds. All the major music publishers produced stock orchestrations for this ensemble and its variants. The modern dance orchestra lineup—featuring three brass sections, three reed sections, and a rhythm section of bass, piano, and percussion—became standard by the middle of the decade.

One of the decade's most popular bands was led by Paul Whiteman. At the beginning of the 1920s, Whiteman established himself in New York and began making recordings and playing high-profile concerts. His 1920 recording of the song "Wang Wang Blues" was a tremendous hit and featured a small group playing in a style similar to the ODJB. By 1929, he was leading a band as large as twenty-five pieces. Whiteman was always careful to include musicians capable of playing jazz in his bands: cornetist Bix Beiderbecke, saxophonist Frankie Trumbauer, and the Dorsey Brothers were just a few of the jazz musicians whom he featured.

African American dance bands were also crucial to the development of jazz style in the early 1920s. In addition to older-styled theater bands led by Eubie Blake and Wilbur Sweatman, younger bandleaders such as Fletcher Henderson in New York and Doc Cook in Chicago began to incorporate more improvisational elements in their arrangements and to attract attention by featuring their soloists.

Blues and Technology

An important part of the development of jazz in the 1920s was the concurrent popularity of the blues. Mamie Smith's recording of the song "Crazy Blues" in 1920 triggered a popular acceptance of African American blues singers, mostly female, leading to the development of what came to be known as classic blues. While the first wave of singers primarily consisted of stage actors singing blues-influenced

Duke Ellington was one of the leading figures in jazz music. (Michael Ochs Archives/Getty Images)

of recordings. By the mid-1920s, radio was also playing a part in publicizing bands from many U.S. locations, not just large cities such as New York and Chicago.

Gershwin, Armstrong, and Ellington

Three key developments in jazz history occurred around 1924. First, Whiteman produced a concert at the Aeolian Hall in New York, which was loosely organized around the history of jazz. This concert purported to trace the style's development from its primitive beginnings with the ODJB to its success as high art in the music performed by the Whiteman ensemble. At some point in the development of the concert, Broadway composer George Gershwin was asked to compose a concert work using jazz elements. The resulting composition, *Rhapsody in Blue*, received mixed reviews, but it was perhaps the first large-scale attempt to combine American popular and art music. By proving that these popular elements could be incorporated into a concert work, Gershwin and Whiteman provided a level of legitimacy for jazz among devotees of art music.

Meanwhile, at the Roseland Ballroom, Fletcher Henderson's group was featuring some of the best New York–based African American musicians, including saxophonist Coleman Hawkins. After an unsuccessful attempt several years earlier, Henderson managed to convince Louis Armstrong to join his band. Armstrong, a cornet player from New Orleans, had been brought to Chicago by his mentor King Oliver in 1922 to play in a small group of African American jazz musicians from New Orleans. Although he was successful in this group, Armstrong was not extensively featured and played for a limited audience. After joining Henderson, he was exposed to an array of contemporary jazz musicians who marveled at his technical command, blues feeling, and effortless rhythmic flexibility, which came to be known as "swing." Armstrong was a featured soloist on many Henderson recordings during his twelve months with the band, and both white and black players copied his stylistic innovations.

Following his return to Chicago in the fall of 1925, Armstrong inaugurated a series of recordings with

popular music, several traditional singers were recorded and introduced to the larger public by 1923. Notable among these were Ma Rainey, Clara Smith, and especially Bessie Smith, who was billed as the "Empress of the Blues." Often accompanied by small jazz bands, these performers were highly regarded for their singing. This blues influx was an important ingredient in the developing art of jazz improvisation.

Most blues recordings were aimed at regional African American markets. These "race records" were found mainly in urban African American centers, although they were often carried to more remote locations and sought out by anyone with an interest in the style or individual performers. Jazz was perhaps the first popular music that owed much of its development and popularity to the dissemination small New Orleans-styled groups generically called the Hot Five. These recordings codified Armstrong's style (as well as his switch to trumpet) and inspired generations of aspiring players, representing another significant development in the history of jazz. Virtuoso performances in songs such as "Potato Head Blues" and "West End Blues" (also featuring pianist Earl Hines) demonstrated Armstrong's superior musical technique and swing style.

Armstrong's playing influenced the whole style of dance band arranging, as well as individual musicians. Bandleader and arranger Don Redman is often credited with introducing some of Armstrong's figures and rhythmic vitality into his arrangements for Henderson, and late-1920s stock arrangers such as Frank Skinner and Archie Bleyer were influenced by Armstrong as well. Improvised solos grew in importance during this time, as can be seen from their inclusion in published arrangements and recordings.

Stride pianist Duke Ellington's decision to form a band in 1926 marked a third watershed moment in jazz history. His group soon became one of the most distinctive black bands in the country. An extended engagement at the African-themed Cotton Club in 1927 provided Ellington with exposure on radio and recordings. There, he developed his "Jungle Style"—an earthy, growling music style using jazz elements and emphasizing the individual tonalities of his players, especially trumpeter Bubber Miley. During the 1920s, Ellington specialized in creating cameos for his soloists, perfectly tailoring his song structure to the three-minute limit of recording technology. By the end of the decade, Ellington had won acclaim for his innovations in composition, song form, and orchestration.

New Generation

The initial popularity of the jazz style in the late 1910s gave way to the next generation of musicians, who began playing professionally by the early 1920s. These players had been profoundly influenced by the recordings of the ODJB and subsequent groups. Urban locations with large African American communities became incubators of the new musical developments. Because of the opportunities it offered in the manufacturing industry, Chicago had become a destination for many southern blacks, and musicians from places such as New Orleans found a hospitable entertainment scene there as well. Younger white musicians were able to hear music from talented black players such as Armstrong, Oliver, and pianist Jelly Roll Morton. These musicians advanced the ensemble-based New Orleans style, with greater emphasis on fast tempos and improvised solos, and carried these developments into the dance band world in which they made their living. Musicians such as Benny Goodman and Bud Freeman learned their craft in this way and ultimately made their way to New York later in the decade.

Both black and white musicians around the country found inspiration in performances given by touring bands and regional units, as well as from recordings. Called "territory bands," these regional dance groups frequently developed variants to the dominant jazz style in Chicago and New York by using different repertoires, improvisational elements, and instrumentation. One of the most influential regional styles came from Kansas City and the area extending down through Oklahoma and Texas. More blues-based and relatively less sophisticated than eastern styles of jazz, the territory bands of this area emphasized ensemble riffs and longer solos, foreshadowing developments to come in the 1930s. Black players such as pianist Count Basie and trumpeter Hot Lips Page, along with white musicians such as trombonist Jack Teagarden, gained much of their early professional experience in these groups.

Impact

While the word "jazz" is often considered synonymous with improvisational music, it meant both much more and much less in the 1920s. As a cultural entity, jazz represented modes of style, literature, fashion, and morals, as well as music. By the end of the decade, the advances in the music itself and changing cultural focus (hastened by the Great Depression) had considerably reduced the extramusical associations with the word. The music, meanwhile, had developed into a legitimate and recognizable style, with several musicians (notably Armstrong, Gershwin, and Ellington) seen as creative geniuses. The surface elements of the music had been adopted by musicians and composers in other genres, and the contingent development of social dancing led to the Swing era of the 1930s.

John L. Clark Jr.

Further Reading

Berrett, Joshua. *Louis Armstrong and Paul Whiteman: Two Kings of Jazz.* New Haven: Yale University Press,

2004. A discussion of the similarities and differences between two of the primary jazz figures in the 1920s.

Hadlock, Richard. *Jazz Masters of the 1920s*. New York: Macmillan, 1965. A general overview of jazz styles from the 1920s, organized by significant individuals and groups.

Lange, Arthur. *Arranging for the Modern Dance Orchestra*. New York: Robbins Music, 1927. A textbook on the style and music theory behind creating dance band arrangements.

Osgood, Henry Osborne. *So This Is Jazz*. New York: Little, Brown, & Co., 1926. A period discussion on the elements of jazz.

Tucker, Mark, ed. *The Duke Ellington Reader*. New York: Oxford University Press, 1995. A comprehensive look at the world of Ellington, including much information on his first bands.

See also: Armstrong, Louis; Black Swan Records; Dances, popular; Ellington, Duke; Harlem Renaissance; Oliver, Joe "King"; Radio; Smith, Bessie; Whiteman, Paul

---

■ Jazz Singer, The

Identification: A film about a popular jazz singer whose career causes an estrangement from his Jewish cantor father
Director: Alan Crosland
Date: 1927

The Jazz Singer was neither the first film to be exhibited with synchronized sound nor the first to contain spoken dialogue. However, its success marked a watershed between the silent and the sound eras of motion picture history.

Experiments in the use of sound on film were almost as old as movies themselves, but Warner Bros. became the first motion picture company to achieve a lasting success. Using a sound-on-disk technique called Vitaphone to synchronize music and sound effects with the film's action, the company's initial feature offering was the 1926 swashbuckler *Don Juan*, starring John Barrymore. After producing a number of short films, essentially filmed vaudeville acts, Warner Bros. and Vitaphone were ready to take the next step of adding synchronized spoken dialogue to a feature-length film.

A Real-World Analogue

Enormously popular Broadway and vaudeville performer Al Jolson had appeared in the well-received 1926 Vitaphone short film *A Plantation Act*, in which he sang some of his signature tunes, including "April Showers." He was then convinced to star in a film based on the 1925 Broadway play *The Jazz Singer* by writer Samson Raphaelson, adapted from the author's 1922 short story "The Day of Atonement." As recounted by Raphaelson in later interviews, he had been inspired to write the original story after watching Jolson perform on Broadway. Although another popular performer, George Jessel, played the lead in the Broadway production of *The Jazz Singer*, Warner Bros. capitalized on the semiautobiographical aspects of Jolson's own life to provide a background to publicize the film.

The story centers on Jakie Rabinowitz, the son of the respected Cantor Rabinowitz, a Jewish immigrant who dreams that his son will carry on the family tradition and become a cantor himself. Jakie chafes at his father's old-fashioned discipline and embraces the more modern culture of America. After his father angrily drags Jakie home from a saloon, where he had been singing for pennies, Jakie tells his mother that he wants to sing on the stage. Ten years later, Jakie, who has run away from home and changed his name to Jack Robin, is singing in a San Francisco nightclub. There, he impresses performer Mary Dale, who encourages him to come on the road with her. Several more years pass, and Jack, now a big success, is about to costar with Mary in a new Broadway musical. One afternoon, when Jack goes to see his mother, Cantor Rabinowitz enters the apartment just as his son is playing an up-tempo rendition of "Blue Skies" to his mother. The cantor bitterly calls his son "a jazz singer" and forces Jack to leave. On Yom Kippur, the Jewish Day of Atonement, the now bedridden cantor is unable to sing the Aramaic liturgy of the Kol Nidre in the temple but dreams that his son will sing in his place. Despite his mother's pleas, Jack refuses to go to his father and begins the final dress rehearsal of his show. His conscience tears at him, though, and he rushes to the temple. As Cantor Rabinowitz dies, he hears his son singing the Kol Nidre and is happy, thinking that his son will now take his place. The next day, however, Jack opens in the show and sings the song "Mammy" to his loving mother, who watches from the audience and realizes that her son is now where he belongs.

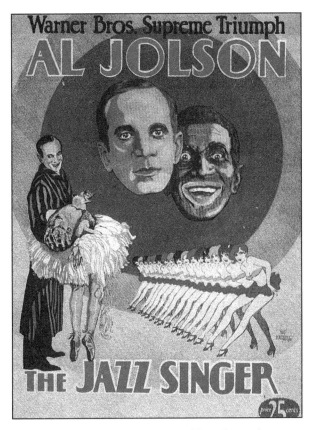

Poster for The Jazz Singer. (Redferns/Getty Images)

The Beginning of the Talkies

The first line of spoken dialogue in *The Jazz Singer* occurs well into the film, when Jolson, as Jack, sings "Dirty Hands, Dirty Face" at Coffee Dan's nightclub. Following strong applause, he cheerfully tells the club's patrons, "Wait a minute, wait a minute, you ain't heard nothin' yet! Wait a minute, I tell ya. You ain't heard nothin'. You want to hear 'Toot, Toot, Tootsie'?" Using a variation of his vaudeville and Broadway catchphrase, Jolson's first line seemed to signal the start of the new sound era. The rest of the film, aside from some casual instructions Jack makes to the band as they prepare to play "Toot, Toot, Tootsie," contains only one additional dialogue sequence, when Jack playfully tells his mother of his plans to buy her a house in the Bronx.

The Jazz Singer proved that sound and dialogue in a film were more than just novelties. Although the story seems maudlin, the dialogue is remarkably natural, and the charismatic entertainer's songs were integral to the picture's success. Within nine months, movie audiences clamoring for more would see films with 100 percent spoken dialogue, beginning with Warner Bros.' *Lights of New York.*

Impact

Following the October 6, 1927, premiere of *The Jazz Singer* and its critical and financial success, Warner Bros. became one of the premiere studios of Hollywood and, for a short time, the industry leader in synchronized sound for motion pictures. The film received an Academy Award nomination for Best Scoring of a Musical Picture, but, more importantly, Warner Bros. received the first ever Special Academy Award for producing *The Jazz Singer.*

The film marked the beginning of Jolson's great success as one of the biggest film stars of the late 1920s, and he appeared in subsequent Warner Bros. films such as *The Singing Fool* and *Mammy.*

Patricia King Hanson

Further Reading

Bradley, Edwin M. *The First Hollywood Musicals: A Critical Filmography of 171 Features, 1927 Through 1932.* Jefferson, N.C.: McFarland, 2004. Provides detailed information about film musicals released in Hollywood between 1927 and 1933, including a section on *The Jazz Singer.*

Carringer, Robert, ed. *The Jazz Singer.* Madison: University of Wisconsin Press, 1979. Presents an edited version of the screenplay for the film.

Eyman, Scott. *The Speed of Sound: Hollywood and the Talkie Revolution, 1926–1930.* New York: Simon & Schuster, 1997. Recounts the evolution of motion pictures from silent films to talking pictures during the late 1920s.

Freedland, Michael. *Jolson: The Story of Al Jolson.* Portland, Oreg.: V. Mitchell, 2007. Offers biographical information about performer Al Jolson, including notes on his theatrical career, personal life, and impact on motion picture history.

Liebman, Roy. *Vitaphone Films: A Catalogue of the Features and Shorts.* Jefferson, N.C.: McFarland, 2009. Details the short and feature films released by the Warner Bros. subsidiary known as Vitaphone.

See also: Film; Jolson, Al; Talking motion pictures; Warner Bros.

■ Jews in Canada

Canadian Jews remained few in number throughout the 1920s, but their experience during the decade is an important element of Canadian and Jewish history. As a group, Jews entered the middle class in increasing numbers. Many Jewish philanthropic and workers' organizations were active. Economic troubles, rising strains of xenophobia, and virulent anti-Semitism also characterized the period, making it a stormy time for this religio-ethnic minority.

At the dawn of the 1920s, over one-quarter of the world's Jewish population lived in English-speaking countries. Most had emigrated from Europe to the United States, but a steadily increasing number made their homes in Canada. Up from just 16,131 individuals in 1901, the Canadian Jewish population had reached 126,198 in 1921—a 682 percent increase in twenty years. Settling throughout the country but concentrating primarily in the Eastern provinces, these Canadian Jews were listed as residents in 695 incorporated cities, towns, and villages across Canada during the decade. They remained a minority of the total Canadian population, hovering between 1.4 and 1.5 percent.

Immigration Restrictions

Immigration remained one of the Jewish population's largest concerns throughout the 1920s. Postwar unrest in Europe, especially in Poland, Ukraine, and the Soviet Union, made relocation to Canada increasingly attractive to European Jews. Canadian immigration laws, however, made the process difficult. Newcomers were only allowed to enter Canada if they traveled directly from their country of origin and carried official passports. A lack of ports in Eastern Europe made it nearly impossible to secure direct transportation to Canada from many of these countries, while for Jews who had sought asylum in more tolerant Western European states, entrance could be denied because of their status as semipermanent residents of countries other than their nation of birth. Potential Canadian immigrants were also required to have at least C$250 cash for a "landing fee." In 1923, Jews were officially categorized by Canadian immigration law as an ethnic group requiring "special permit," making it impossible for them to enter the country except by the individual consent of the authorities. Due to these laws, only 15,800 Jews were welcomed into Canada between 1921 and 1931.

Immigration restrictions were grounded in a sort of Canadian xenophobia, similar to the nativist trends that pervaded the United States during the interwar years. A crippling economic depression during the first half of the 1920s made Canadian citizens skeptical of immigrants, who were believed to steal already-scarce jobs from more deserving native-born Canadian citizens. Many Jews worked for subsistence wages as small storekeepers or laborers in clothing factories, though an increasing number could be considered skilled laborers or professionals. "The struggle for existence engaged our attention so much," one Jewish man claimed, "that we missed a great deal."

Confronting Anti-Semitism

Strong strains of anti-Semitism also characterized Canadian popular sentiment during the decade. Public intellectuals like Father Lionel Groulx denounced Jews on economic, religious, and civil fronts, influencing the elite of his native Quebec and other Canadian provinces. In other areas, the Orange Order, a Protestant unionist organization, criticized both Jews and Catholics with equal rigor. The Native Sons of Canada, founded in 1921 in British Columbia, attempted to encourage Canadian nationalism and support Canadian businesses by excluding perceived "foreigners" such as Jews and Asians. Businesses were also the focus of the "achat chez nous" movement, which was supposedly oriented toward encouraging the patronization of French Canadian establishments but proved more directly a popular boycott of Jewish ones.

Jewish Canadians did not accept these prejudices passively. Since they could not regularly rely on support from their non-Jewish neighbors, many set up mutual aid societies that operated throughout the 1920s. The Arbeiter Ring, the Jewish Labour League Mutual Benefit Society, and the Canadian Workers' Circle, for example, provided economic and social support for newly arrived Jewish immigrants. These federations paired philanthropic functions with union politics and a socialist economic philosophy, effectively organizing Jewish Canadians' lives from the garment factory to the grave. The Canadian Hadassah-WIZO, founded in 1917, remained active throughout the 1920s as a Jewish women's philanthropic organization dedicated primarily to the cause of Zionism. The Young Men's and Women's Hebrew Associations of Canada (YWHA) played an important role as well; Fanny "Bobbie" Rosenfeld, the Canadian relay gold medalist of the 1928 Olympic

Games, had been a YWHA member as a young Jewish woman.

Impact

Exclusivist immigration policies would remain active throughout World War II, excluding many Jews from safe haven in Canada during Hitler's rule in Germany. Anti-Semitism would remain active in the near future as well. Despite these challenges, Canadian Jews were increasingly included in their country's middle class as the twentieth century progressed. At the beginning of the twenty-first century, Canada had the fourth-largest Jewish population in the world.

Rachel E. Grossman

Further Reading

Rosenberg, Louis. *Canada's Jews: A Social and Economic Study of Jews in Canada in the 1930s.* Edited by Morton Weinfeld. Montreal: McGill-Queen's University Press, 1993. Includes comprehensive census data on the geographic spread, economic situation, and vital statistics of Jewish Canadians in the 1920s as well as the 1930s.

Rosenberg, Stuart E. *The Jewish Community in Canada.* 2 vols. Toronto: McClelland & Stewart, 1970–1971. A social and religious history of the Jewish community in Canada.

Schneiderman, Harry, ed. *The American Jewish Year Book.* Philadelphia: Jewish Publication Society of America, 1920–1929. A publication primarily focused on Jews in the United States but includes information about Canadian Jews as well.

Tulchinsky, Gerald. *Canada's Jews: A People's Journey.* Toronto: University of Toronto Press, 2008. An extensive, statistically thorough history of Jews in Canada.

Weinfeld, Morton. "Jews." In *Encyclopedia of Canada's Peoples,* edited by Paul Robert Magocsi. Toronto: University of Toronto Press, 1999. A detailed introduction to Jewish history and life in Canada.

See also: Anti-Semitism; Canadian minority communities; Immigration to Canada; Jews in the United States; Rosenfeld, Fanny "Bobbie"

■ Jews in the United States

The 1920s was both a triumphant and a trying decade for Jewish Americans. While some Jews felt "at home" in America for the first time, many more were hounded by economic troubles, social unrest, and persistent anti-Semitism. Enterprising Jewish Americans were involved in bootlegging and the birth of Hollywood. Their experiences as a group during the 1920s reflect the postwar prosperity as well as the reactionary nativism of the decade.

The Jewish population of the United States was approximately 3.6 million in 1920. Overwhelmingly immigrants prior to the 1920s, native-born American Jews began to account for higher percentages after World War I. The rising middle class, postwar prosperity, and rapid growth of the U.S. economy affected many of them, allowing naturalized American Jews to assimilate almost completely into American society. Assimilation may account for low levels of religious observance during the period. Figures suggest that as few as 23 percent of American Jews were affiliated with a synagogue.

The vast majority of Jews living in the United States during the 1920s still hailed directly from eastern Europe. They settled primarily in such large urban centers as New York and Philadelphia, where overcrowded neighborhoods and industrial jobs awaited. Many labored in clothing manufacture and cigar production. Unions were popular among these working-class Jews: The American Federation of Labor, led by Samuel Gompers, helped many first-generation Jews and other industrial workers fight for better wages, safer working conditions, and shorter hours.

For other American Jews, the entertainment industry offered a path to wealth and prestige. Some found their place on stage, while others became successful in the nascent motion picture industry. Stage performer Fanny Brice of *Ziegfeld Follies* and actor Al Jolson of *The Jazz Singer* (1927) are some of the most well-known figures of the period. Vaudeville performers such as the Marx Brothers were also popular. Their first major movie debuted in 1929. More common were Jewish "moguls," a popular name for the Hollywood studio executives behind major film companies such as Metro-Goldwyn-Mayer (MGM), Warner Bros., and Paramount. Not limited to film, notable Jewish artists of the period also included animator Max Fleischer, writer Gertrude Stein, and composers Aaron Copland, George Gershwin, and Sigmund Romberg.

Anti-Semitism in the United States

The increasingly visible presence of Jews and other minorities in the United States during the 1920s

---

Jews and the Ku Klux Klan

During the 1920s, the Klan saw its role as that of the guardian of the old moral values in a radically changing American environment caused, they believed, by an influx of immigrant Italian, Irish, and Polish Catholics; Russian and Slavic Jews; and Asians. By 1924, Klan membership had grown to between two and five million. Among other activities directed against Catholics, Asian and African Americans, Klan members distributed literature attacking Jews and harassed whites who patronized Jewish businesses.

prompted strong reactions among the American majority. Many did not like the changing face of their country and sought to recreate a lost golden age of predominantly Anglo-Saxon Protestantism. As ethnic minorities, religious outsiders, and often poor workers associated with labor unions, Jews were popular targets of derision and violence. The Emergency Quota Act of 1921 and the Johnson-Reed Act of 1924 were designed to limit immigration from countries where ethnically "undesirable" persons lived, the Jews being just one of many minorities targeted. As a result, many Jews were unable to bring their families to the United States. In addition, Orthodox Judaism struggled to maintain its once-flourishing institutions as the influx of traditionalist Jews from Europe declined.

Other xenophobic trends took hold in the United States during the 1920s. The activities of extremist groups such as the Ku Klux Klan, the anticommunist movement known as the First Red Scare, and legislative acts such as Prohibition were all driven by a desire to restore American racial and spiritual purity. In some cases, anti-Semitism was unabashedly direct. American industrialist Henry Ford produced a publication called the *Dearborn Independent* between 1920 and 1927, which falsely accused Jews of international conspiracy. Jews were also the target of exclusionary measures at universities, resorts, clubs, and hotels. For the most part, nativism took a more subtle form, however. Many in the temperance movement used anti-Semitic beliefs to garner support for the Eighteenth Amendment, which in many ways targeted Jews, who used fermented wine in religious ceremonies and lived in the poor,

working-class urban centers where alcohol consumption was highest. Additionally, some Jews became involved in bootlegging (illicit alcohol trade), including influential crime lord Dutch Shultz. The notoriety of these individuals often drove the anti-Semitism of their neighbors, who saw such activity as proof of Jewish unscrupulousness and dishonesty.

Impact

Trends in the Jewish communities in the United States during the 1920s dramatically changed Jewish life in the country for many decades. Immigration restrictions substantially halted Jewish immigration, later causing serious dilemmas for those trying to escape persecution in Europe during World War II. Anti-Semitism would remain a force for years to come. The inclination toward separation that began with specifically Jewish social clubs and institutions continued to hold influence as American Jews moved into the suburbs, aiding in the development of neighborhoods populated predominantly by Jews. Jewish involvement in film and radio would continue to characterize American popular culture as well.

Rachel E. Grossman

Further Reading

Alexander, Michael. *Jazz Age Jews*. Princeton, N.J.: Princeton University Press, 2001. A portrait of Jewish life in the United States during the 1920s, specifically using the figures Al Rothstein, Felix Frankfurter, and Al Jolson.

Davis, Marni. *Jews and Booze: Becoming American in the Age of Prohibition*. New York: New York University Press, 2011. Offers a perspective on and history of the involvement of U.S. Jews in the alcohol industry and Prohibition's effect on Jewish cultural and national identity in U.S. society.

Hoberman, J., and Jeffrey Shandler, eds. *Entertaining America: Jews, Movies, and Broadcasting*. N.J.: Princeton University Press, 2003. Discusses Jewish involvement in American films and popular culture, including many figures and facts on the 1920s.

Sarna, Jonathan D. *American Judaism: A History*. New Haven, Conn.: Yale University Press, 2004. A history of Jews and Judaism in the United States, including a section on the years between World War I and World War II.

Schneiderman, Harry, ed. *The American Jewish Year Book*. Philadelphia: Jewish Publication Society of America, 1920–1929. Includes statistics, notable events, and other useful information on Jews in the United States for each year of the 1920s.

See also: Anti-Semitism; Immigration Act of 1921; Immigration Act of 1924; Immigration to the United States; Prohibition

---

■ Jim Crow in the U.S. South

Jim Crow laws and social order in the southern United States perpetuated discrimination against African Americans and enforced total segregation of whites and blacks. During the 1920s, black resistance to Jim Crow helped to forge the path toward the Civil Rights movement of the 1950s and 1960s.

Jim Crow was originally the name of a minstrel character that portrayed blacks as unintelligent and foolish. By the late nineteenth century, the phrase "Jim Crow" referred to a series of state laws and codes of social conduct designed to racially segregate African Americans in all areas of life, including housing, education, and public places. Despite the threat of lynching (which was a common tool of intimidation), many African Americans fought Jim Crow rule. Such resistance sometimes resulted in violent, large-scale racial confrontations, as in the Tulsa Riot of 1921.

Following a riot in Elaine, Arkansas, in 1919, five white men were killed and over seven hundred blacks were arrested. The twelve black men who were then tried for the murders were tortured, forced to confess to the crime, and then compelled to testify against one another. The all-white jury found the men guilty, and they were sentenced to death. The National Association for the Advancement of Colored People (NAACP) appealed the verdict, and in *Moore v. Dempsey* (1923), the Supreme Court ruled that it was impossible for the men to have received a fair trial, and all were eventually freed. This ruling dealt a significant blow to the strength of Jim Crow laws.

In 1925, W. E. B. Du Bois, civil rights activist and founder of the NAACP, visited his alma mater, Fisk University in Nashville, Tennessee. Du Bois was disturbed by rumors that the university's white president, Fayette McKenzie, had been running the university in a dictatorial fashion and had received grants from foundations to establish the many restrictive policies and procedures that encouraged students to uphold Jim Crow. After McKenzie

---

Jim Crow and the Great Northern Migration

According to W. E. B. Du Bois, a leading African American intellectual of the period, African Americans who came of age around 1910 were the first generation that did not experience the institution of slavery. Unlike many African Americans who were born during the period of slavery and were accustomed or resigned to their inferior social and economic position, this new generation was less reluctant to seek change. Jim Crow laws, which formalized segregation, discrimination, and racial violence, including lynching, motivated many in this new generation of African Americans to seek better conditions in the North.

---

reneged on several concessions to relax university policy, Du Bois organized student demonstrations to oust him. McKenzie retaliated by summoning campus police, who arrived with riot guns, smashed doors and windows in the men's dormitory, and then beat and arrested six students. University students, supported by Du Bois, responded by organizing a strike that paralyzed the city of Nashville for over two months. McKenzie soon resigned, and the Fisk protest was the first of several future instances where black college students demanded more of a role in their educations.

Impact

Despite the promise of equality for blacks made in the Thirteenth, Fourteenth, and Fifteenth Amendments, Jim Crow flourished in the southern United States throughout the 1920s. Several events during that decade, however, helped to empower blacks and enhance their civil rights and were the precursors to the Civil Rights movement of the 1950s and 1960s.

David M. Brown

Further Reading

Chafe, William, et al. *Remembering Jim Crow: African Americans Tell About Life in the Segregated South.* New York: New Press, 2008.

Packard, Jerrold M. *American Nightmare: The History of Jim Crow.* New York: St. Martin's Press, 2002.

Ritterhouse, Jennifer. *Growing Up Jim Crow: How Black*

and White Southern Children Learned Race. Chapel Hill: University of North Carolina Press, 2006.

See also: African Americans; Civil rights and liberties; Du Bois, W. E. B.; Ku Klux Klan; Lynching; *Moore v. Dempsey;* National Association for the Advancement of Colored People (NAACP); Racial discrimination

---

■ *John Brown's Body*

Identification: A book-length poem about the Civil War
Author: Stephen Vincent Benét
Date: 1928

Published more than sixty years after the American Civil War, John Brown's Body *is an epic poem that recounts the major events of the war and explores its overall effect on the nation through the viewpoints of individuals on either side of the conflict. In a variety of poetic meters and forms, Stephen Vincent Benét chronicles the war from John Brown's raid on Harper's Ferry in 1859 to the assassination of Abraham Lincoln in 1865.*

Acclaimed for its wealth of historical detail and depiction of historical figures ranging from Confederate president Jefferson Davis to Union general Ulysses S. Grant, *John Brown's Body* was Stephen Vincent Benét's attempt to reinterpret the Civil War for readers of his time and succeeding generations. He depicts the war as a redemptive struggle resulting in the reunification of the country and serving as a catalyst for western expansion.

Comparing his poem to a cyclorama, a large panoramic picture arranged in a cylindrical space to provide a 360-degree view of a scene or event, Benét traces the fates of his representative Northerner, Jack Ellyat of Connecticut, and Southerner, Clay Wingate of Georgia, from their initial presentiments of the upcoming conflict to their respective homecomings. As in a cyclorama, the poem comes full circle, beginning and ending with these two fictional characters, whose individual stories reflect the collective destinies of their respective regions. *John Brown's Body* is characterized by realism that is particularly apparent in its depiction of a runaway slave, Spade, who faces nearly as many challenges in the North as he did in the South. Yet, romanticism is evident in the poem's depictions of individual and national reunions.

Melora, the young woman who shelters Ellyat after the Battle of Shiloh and subsequently gives birth to his son, sets out across the country to find her lost love. Their personal reunion at the poem's end and that of Wingate and his childhood sweetheart Sally mirror the restoration of national unity.

Impact

Benét's explicit patriotism stood in stark contrast to the post–World War I disillusionment of many writers of the 1920s, and the blend of realism and romanticism in *John Brown's Body* further endeared it to the reading public. Unusual for a book-length poem, the work was widely popular, selling more than 100,000 copies in its first year of publication. In 1929, *John Brown's Body* received the Pulitzer Prize.

S. Thomas Mack

Further Reading

Fenton, Charles A. *Stephen Vincent Benét: The Life and Times of an American Man of Letters, 1898–1943.* New Haven, Conn.: Yale University Press, 1958.
Izzo, David Garrett, and Lincoln Konkle, eds. *Stephen Vincent Benét: Essays on his Life and Work.* Jefferson, N.C.: McFarland, 2003.
Stroud, Parry E. *Stephen Vincent Benét.* New York: Twayne, 1962.

See also: Historiography; Literature in the United States; Poetry

---

■ *John Keats*

Identification: A biography of the English Romantic poet John Keats
Author: Amy Lowell
Date: 1925

Published more than a century after Keats's death, John Keats *was the first major biography of the English Romantic poet to be written from a female perspective and substantially acknowledge the role of a woman in Keats's life. The work also served as a response to the changing public discourse about sexuality and the increasing role of psychology in the interpretation of relationships between the sexes.*

Amy Lowell, a noted American poet of the 1910s and 1920s, perceived a need for a modern biography of John Keats that reassessed his private life and public persona, both of which, in her view, had been obscured by male commentators. A key area of interest for Lowell was the role of Fanny Brawne, Keats's fiancé, in the poet's life. Lowell believed that Keats's gradual realization of his love for Brawne and her contributions to both his poetry and his character had been overlooked by previous biographers.

Although Lowell was relatively conservative and seemingly unsympathetic to the feminism of the 1920s, *John Keats* provides the first full reading of Keats's relationship with Fanny Brawne, who had traditionally been interpreted and represented as the unworthy companion of a great poet. Despite her great admiration for Keats, Lowell does not spare him from criticism, noting that his prejudices against women only gradually broke down as he fell in love with Brawne, a woman who proved capable of understanding his poetry and identifying with his single-minded devotion to it.

John Keats is in some respects similar to other biographies of the 1920s, many of which explored the intricate psychology of their subjects for the first time. However, while Lowell acknowledged Sigmund Freud's influence on biographers, she was careful not to apply a dogmatic Freudian approach to her interpretation of Keats. Instead, the biography focuses on the female sensibility and demonstrates that an understanding of women such as Fanny Brawne is essential to gauging the mood of Keats's time and the values of his culture.

Impact

Poets, historians, and biographers such as Amy Lowell pioneered new methods of biographical interpretation, expanding upon or overturning earlier accounts with historical evidence often culled from private collections and family archives that previously had been closed to professional writers. Subsequent biographers of Keats, such as Stanley Plumly and Walter Jackson Bate, have paid tribute to Lowell's groundbreaking biography, which remains a vital example of the ways in which 1920s thinkers came to terms with the influence of nineteenth-century values.

Carl Rollyson

Further Reading

Damon, Samuel Foster. *Amy Lowell: A Chronicle, With Extracts from her Correspondence.* Boston, Mass.: Houghton Mifflin, 1935.

Munich, Adrienne, and Melissa Bradshaw, eds. *Amy Lowell, American Modern.* New Brunswick, N.J.: Rutgers University Press, 2004.

See also: Literature in the United States; Lowell, Amy; Psychology, psychiatry, and psychoanalysis

■ Johnson, Jack

Identification: African American heavyweight boxer
Born: March 31, 1878, Galveston, Texas
Died: June 10, 1946, Raleigh, North Carolina

Boxing's first African American heavyweight champion, Jack Johnson served a one-year prison term beginning in 1920 for an alleged violation of the Mann Act. Throughout the remainder of the decade, he struggled to regain his fame and success, hampered by age and the racial discrimination that had impeded his earlier career.

John Arthur "Jack" Johnson rose to prominence as a boxer in the first two decades of the twentieth century, becoming the first African American to win the world heavyweight boxing championship in 1908. Due to his frequent victories against white boxers and highly publicized relationships with white women, Johnson faced a great deal of racial prejudice. In 1913, Johnson was charged and found guilty of violating the Mann Act, a law that prohibited the interstate transportation of women for prostitution or other ostensibly immoral purposes and provided a convenient means of punishing Johnson for his interracial relationships. He fled the United States to avoid sentencing and defended his boxing title from abroad, eventually losing it in 1915 to Jess Willard in a bout in Havana, Cuba.

Johnson returned to the United States to accept his punishment in 1920, serving a brief term in the U.S. penitentiary in Leavenworth, Kansas, where he received preferential treatment due to his celebrity. While in prison, Johnson, a car enthusiast, invented a type of wrench and an automobile theft-prevention device that he went on to patent in 1922. Upon his release, Johnson returned to boxing but was unable to regain his earlier fame or the heavyweight title, as reigning champion Jack Dempsey refused to fight African American challengers. Johnson supported himself with various business ventures throughout the 1920s, including the purchase of a Harlem nightclub.

Jack Johnson. (Hulton Archive/Getty Images)

After a short period of ownership, Johnson sold the establishment to mobster Owney Madden, who renamed it the Cotton Club and transformed it into a whites-only venue featuring black performers. In 1927, Johnson published his autobiography.

Impact

Although Johnson never again achieved success as a boxer, he came to be recognized for his defiance of the racial restrictions of his time, serving as the inspiration for the 1967 Broadway play *The Great White Hope* as well as the 1970 film of the same name. For his achievements in the sport of boxing, Johnson was inducted into the International Boxing Hall of Fame in 1990.

Aaron D. Horton

Further Reading

Kent, Graeme. *The Great White Hopes: The Quest to Defeat Jack Johnson.* Stroud: Sutton, 2006.

Roberts, Randy. *Papa Jack: Jack Johnson and the Era of White Hopes.* New York: Free Press, 1983.

Ward, Geoffrey C. *Unforgivable Blackness: The Rise and Fall of Jack Johnson.* New York: Vintage Books, 2006.

See also: African Americans; Boxing; Dempsey, Jack; Racial discrimination; Sports

■ Johnson, James Weldon

Identification: African American writer and editor, educator, and civil rights activist
Born: June 17, 1871, Jacksonville, Florida
Died: June 26, 1938, Wiscasset, Maine

Known for his work in the fields of education, law, and activism earlier in the century as well as for his writing, James Weldon Johnson remained active throughout the 1920s, becoming a significant figure of the Harlem Renaissance. Johnson served as secretary for the National Association for the Advancement of Colored People (NAACP) throughout the decade and edited several anthologies, calling attention to the literary value of African American poetry and spirituals.

James Weldon Johnson, born James William Johnson, completed his bachelor's degree at Atlanta University in 1894 and entered the field of education, teaching at his former elementary school, Stanton School, and later becoming its principal. He studied law during this time, and in 1898, he became the first African American to be accepted to the Florida bar. Early in the twentieth century, Johnson collaborated with his brother to write a number of songs, including "Lift Every Voice and Sing," which went on to become an anthem of the Civil Rights movement. Johnson was appointed to the position of U.S. consul in Venezuela in 1906 and Nicaragua in 1909. Three years later, he published an anonymous novel, *The Autobiography of an Ex-Colored Man* (1912).

Promoting the Harlem Renaissance

The 1920s proved to be a progressive decade for Johnson, both artistically and politically. Johnson became an influential force in the Harlem Renaissance, actively promoting African American artistic endeavors through his work as an anthologist. He edited the anthology *The Book of American Negro Poetry*, published in 1922, which showcased such early Harlem Renaissance authors as W. E. B. Du Bois, Jessie Redmon Fauset, Georgia Douglas Johnson, and Claude McKay. In the following decade, the collection would be revised to include poets who rose to prominence later in the 1920s, including Langston Hughes, Arna Bontemps, and Countee Cullen. This publication, along with many others during the period, helped to form the lasting legacy of the Harlem Renaissance, chronicling and publicizing the emergence of the African American artistic expression that characterized the era.

Johnson also sought to promote other forms of African American art. Exploring his interest in music, Johnson collaborated with his brother, Rosamond, a composer, to compile *The Book of American Negro Spirituals* in 1925 and *The Second Book of American Negro Spirituals* in 1926. These books called attention to an art form that had largely been neglected in literary contexts.

In addition to editing anthologies, Johnson wrote and published his own works during the period. *God's Trombones*, a collection of poetry, was released in 1927 and went on to win an award from the William E. Harmon Foundation, which celebrated artistic achievements by African Americans, the following year. Also in 1927, *The Autobiography of an Ex-Colored Man* was reprinted under Johnson's name, conclusively proving its status as a work of fiction.

Civil Rights Activism

Johnson was also notable for his contributions to the NAACP during the 1920s. After being a member of the organization for five years, Johnson became the secretary of the NAACP in 1920. While in this position, he worked to end lynching and the overall mistreatment of African Americans. His efforts to expand the reach of the NAACP greatly increased the number of chapters and members during his fifteen years with the organization. In 1925, he received the Spingarn Medal for his exceptional service to the community.

Impact

After resigning from his position with the NAACP in 1930, Johnson pursued a career teaching English at Fisk University. He was appointed the Adam K. Spence Professor of Creative Literature and became the first African American to be a visiting professor at New York University. Johnson published several books throughout the 1930s, including his autobiography, *Along This Way*, in 1933.

Through his many roles, Johnson continually sought to improve the quality of life for African Americans. Johnson's creative endeavors had a lasting influence on African American literature, while his activist work in the 1920s expanded and strengthened the NAACP, which would play a significant role in the Civil Rights movement of the 1950s and 1960s.

Washella T. Simmons

Further Reading

Johnson, James Weldon. *Along This Way: The Autobiography of James Weldon Johnson*. Reprint. New York: Penguin, 2009. Discusses Johnson's life, beginning with his family history and continuing into the early 1930s.

Kostelanetz, Richard. *Politics in the African-American Novel: James Weldon Johnson, W. E. B. Du Bois, Richard Wright, and Ralph Ellison*. New York: Greenwood Press, 1991. Examines the issue of "passing" in James Weldon Johnson's *The Autobiography of an Ex-Colored Man*.

Levy, Eugene D. *James Weldon Johnson: Black Leader, Black Voice*. Chicago: University of Chicago Press, 1976. Explores Johnson's boyhood and moves through adulthood, revealing factors and people that affected Johnson's life and work.

Page, Amanda M. "The Ever-Expanding South: James Weldon Johnson and the Global Color Line." *Southern Quarterly: A Journal of the Arts in the South* 46, no. 3 (2009): 26–46. Focuses on Johnson's time as a U.S. consul in Venezuela and Nicaragua.

Price, Kenneth M., and Lawrence J. Olivier, eds. *Critical Essays on James Weldon Johnson*. New York: G.K. Hall, 1997. Includes essays on Johnson ranging from reviews of *The Autobiography of an Ex-Colored Man* to explorations of Johnson's interactions with Du Bois in the NAACP.

Tate, Ernest Cater. *The Social Implications of the Writings and the Career of James Weldon Johnson*. New York: American Press, 1968. Provides a history of interracial conflict in American history and society and explains the impact of Johnson's upbringing on his views on race.

See also: African Americans; Harlem Renaissance; Literature in the United States; National Association for the Advancement of Colored People (NAACP)

■ Johnson, Judy

Identification: African American baseball player
Also known as: William Julius Johnson
Born: October 26, 1900 (sources vary), Snow Hill, Maryland
Died: June 15, 1989, Wilmington, Delaware

Judy Johnson, a player for several teams in the Negro Leagues, was a third baseman who earned a reputation as a skilled fielder and clutch hitter throughout the 1920s. Although barred from baseball's major leagues due to segregation, Johnson led his team to the Negro League World Series twice during the decade.

William Julius Johnson, the son of the athletic director of the Negro Settlement House in Wilmington, Delaware, inherited his father's love of sports and developed an interest in baseball at a young age. In 1918, he began to play professional baseball as a member of the Bacharach Giants, a team based in Atlantic City, New Jersey. Johnson moved on to the Philadelphia-based Madison Stars in 1919, remaining with the team into the early 1920s.

In 1921, Johnson joined the Hilldale Daisies, also known as the Philadelphia Hilldales, as a third baseman. Due in part to his resemblance to fellow Negro League player Judy Gans, Johnson was nicknamed "Judy." Johnson also played off-season baseball in Cuba during the period, but he experienced his greatest success with Hilldale, participating in the first two Negro League World Series in 1924 and 1925. Although Johnson maintained a batting average of well over .300 throughout the series, Hilldale lost to the powerful Kansas City Monarchs in 1924. The following year, Hilldale defeated the Monarchs in a rematch. An injury in August of 1926 impeded Johnson's productivity as a hitter throughout the 1927 and 1928 seasons, but his batting average recovered by the end of the decade.

Impact

In 1930, Johnson joined the Homestead Grays as a player and manager before briefly returning to Hilldale. He moved on to the Pittsburgh Crawfords in 1932, playing alongside such notable players as James "Cool Papa" Bell, Oscar Charleston, Josh Gibson, and Satchel Paige. Johnson returned to the Negro League World Series in 1935 with the Crawfords before retiring from play the following year. He went on to serve as a coach and scout for various teams, becoming the first African American coach in the major leagues in 1954. For his achievements as a player, manager, coach, and scout, Johnson was inducted into the National Baseball Hall of Fame in 1975.

Mark C. Herman

Further Reading

Lanctot, Neil. *Negro League Baseball: The Rise and Ruin of a Black Institution.* Philadelphia: University of Pennsylvania Press, 2008.

Peterson, Robert. *Only the Ball was White: A History of Legendary Black Players and All-Black Professional Teams.* New York: Gramercy Books, 1999.

See also: African Americans; Baseball; Bell, James "Cool Papa"; Negro League Baseball; Sports

■ Jolson, Al

Identification: American singer and actor
Also known as: Asa Yoelson
Born: May 26, 1886, Sredniki, Kovno, Russian Empire (now Seredzius, Lithuania)
Died: October 23, 1950, San Francisco, California

During the mid-1920s, Jolson, one of the first white singers to perform African American jazz-influenced music for mainstream audiences, became the most popular and highest-paid entertainer in the United States. After headlining several Broadway blockbusters, he began a successful film career starring in the 1927 Warner Bros. production The Jazz Singer, *the first full-length "talking" motion picture.*

Billed as "The World's Greatest Entertainer," Jolson connected directly with his audience like no professional singer before him. He designed what came to be known as the "thrust stage," a platform that allowed him to dance his way into the crowd, and performed his usually flamboyant and sentimental singing style at a more personal, intimate level.

Jolson's repertoire included material from the mid-nineteenth-century era of minstrelsy. Unlike the minstrel-show performers who preceded him, however, Jolson incorporated blackface into his routines, which has been seen by some as an unsubtle physical manifestation of the assimilation of jazz into the predominately white world of successful stage entertainment. His "impersonation" of the black man, which he believed added to the entertainment value of his performance style, is considered offensive and discriminatory by modern standards, but while working on Broadway, Jolson began a career-long fight against racial prejudice, thereby creating work for many African Americans, including good friend and dancer Bill "Bojangles" Robinson. In *The Jazz Singer*, while portraying a cantor's son who becomes a blackface performer, Jolson made a poignant connection between the historic suffering endured by both African Americans and Jews.

Impact

Jolson's fusion of ragtime, jazz, and blues with 1920s popular music began a musical revolution that would influence future performers, including Bing Crosby, Frank Sinatra, and Elvis Presley. Jolson's famous line from *The Jazz Singer*, "You ain't heard nothin' yet!" signaled the end of the era of silent film, and his stand against anti–black discrimination on Broadway helped pave the way for African American performers such as Louis Armstrong and Duke Ellington. Jolson's vocal style influenced countless singers over the ensuing decades, and songs such as "About a Quarter to Nine," "April Showers," and "Toot, Toot, Tootsie" remained popular years after their release.

Scott Allen Nollen

Further Reading

Freedland, Michael. *Jolson: The Story of Al Jolson*. Portland, Oreg.: Vallentine-Mitchell, 2007.

Friedwald, Will. *Jazz Singing: America's Great Voices from Bessie Smith to Bebop and Beyond*. New York: Da Capo Press, 1996.

See also: Armstrong, Louis; Broadway musicals; Crosby, Bing; Jazz; *Jazz Singer, The;* Music, popular; Talking motion pictures; Warner Bros.

■ Jones, Bobby

Identification: American golfer
Also known as: Robert Tyre Jones Jr.
Born: March 17, 1902, Atlanta, Georgia
Died: December 18, 1971, Atlanta, Georgia

Bobby Jones, widely considered the greatest amateur golfer of all time, won thirteen major tournaments within an eight- *year span. In 1930, Jones won the Grand Slam of golf by winning all four major tournaments: the U.S. Open, the U.S. Amateur, the British Open, and the British Amateur. Shortly after retirement from competitive golf in 1930, Jones cofounded Augusta National Golf Club and codesigned the course with golf architect Alister Mackenzie. The course would become the future home of the Masters tournament.*

Robert "Bobby" Tyre Jones Jr. was born in Atlanta, Georgia, to Robert Tyre Jones Sr., a prominent Atlanta lawyer, and Clara Thomas Jones. Bobby suffered from a near fatal digestive ailment as a young child, and at the age of six, moved with his family to their summer home near the East Lake Country Club in Atlanta, where he began golfing. Although he never had formal lessons, Bobby learned the game by following golf professionals and club members around the club's course. At age nine, he won the Atlanta Athletic junior title and would win three additional amateur tournaments in Georgia by the age of fourteen. In 1916, the fourteen-year-old played in the U.S. Amateur tournament, leading during the qualifying round and defeating several former Amateur champions before losing during the third round. It was this tournament that drew national attention to Jones as the "new kid from Dixie."

The Early Years

From 1916 to 1922, Jones participated in eleven national and international tournaments without a victory. Although finishing second in the 1919 U.S. Amateur, the intense, determined, and still very young Jones exhibited a perfectionist attitude, a self-imposed inferiority complex, and frequent temper tantrums. The nadir of his career came at the age of nineteen during the 1921 British Open in St. Andrews, Scotland. In the third round of the tournament, Jones shot an uncharacteristic forty-six for the first nine holes and a six on the tenth hole. After driving the ball into a bunker off the eleventh tee, Jones put the ball in his pocket, effectively and unceremoniously withdrawing from the tournament.

The following year, Jones's game changed as he gained physical strength and emotional maturity. The turning point for Jones came at the 1923 U.S. Open championship, which he won after an eighteen-hole playoff against Bobby Cruickshank. The win would mark an eight-year domination of the game and a series of major-tournament wins.

The Road to the Grand Slam

Between 1923 and his retirement from golf in 1930, Jones won thirteen of twenty-one major tournaments. He won the U.S. Amateur tournament five times, the U.S. Open tournament four times, and the British Open three times. In 1926, Jones won both the U.S. and the British Opens, making him the first golfer to conquer both championships in the same year. Jones's most dramatic moment in a major tournament came at the 1929 U.S. Open when Jones sank a difficult 12-foot putt on the last green to the thunderous roar of the crowd, forcing a playoff with Al Espinosa, who Jones defeated by twenty-three strokes. In 1930, Jones became the first golfer to win the Grand Slam, capturing all four major tournaments in the same year.

Bobby Jones always competed as an amateur rather than as a professional and never took any prize money or played the game as much as other golfers, preferring instead to concentrate on the major tournaments. These choices allowed him to earn a degree in engineering from Georgia Institute of Technology in 1922 and a second degree in English literature from Harvard University in 1924. After attending Emory University Law School in Atlanta for one year, he passed the Georgia bar exam in 1928 and joined his father's law firm, all the while playing in major tournaments and winning many of them.

Impact

Although Bobby Jones retired from competitive golf in 1930 at the age of twenty-eight, he continued his involvement in and support of the game by producing instructional movie shorts, writing articles and books on golf, and designing and endorsing a line of golf clubs through A. G. Spalding & Brothers. Many believe Jones's most significant project during his retirement was his involvement in creating the Augusta National Golf Club in 1930 and the Masters tournament that developed from it in 1934. The Masters, which Jones hosted until 1968, has since joined the British and U.S. Opens as a major tournament and is considered part of the modern-day Grand Slam. These later projects contributed to the professionalization of golf while Jones's earlier record-setting career had helped establish its popularity in the United States.

David L. Porter

Further Reading

Frost, Mark. *The Grand Slam: Bobby Jones, America, and*

Bobby Jones. (Hulton Archive/Getty Images)

the Story of Golf. New York: Hyperion Books, 2004. A history of golf that chronicles Jones's personal and emotional struggles and his domination of professional golf in the 1920s.

Jones, Robert T., Jr. *Golf Is My Game.* Garden City, NY: Doubleday and Company, 1960. An autobiography that includes Jones's instructional guide for playing golf and recounts his competitive golf career.

Keeler, O. B. *The Bobby Jones Story: The Authorized Biography.* Chicago: Triumph, 2003. A biography written by an Atlanta newspaper reporter who knew Jones personally and witnessed all thirteen major championships.

Matthew, Sidney, L. *Portrait of a Gentleman: The Life and Times of Bobby Jones.* Tallahassee, Fla.: Impregnable Quadrilateral Press, 1995. View into Jones's personal and golfing life. Illustrated and with quotes from Jones's writing and journalists who followed his career.

Price, Charles. *A Golf Story: Bobby Jones, Augusta National, and the Masters Tournament.* Chicago: Triumph, 2007. Traces the history of the Augusta National Golf Club, co-designed by Jones and home of the Masters tournament.

See also: Golf; Hobbies and recreation; Sports

K

■ Kahanamoku, Duke

Identification: Hawaiian surfer and Olympic swimmer
Born: August 24, 1890, Honolulu, Hawaii
Died: January 22, 1968, Honolulu, Hawaii

Duke Kahanamoku changed the front-crawl technique used in competitive swimming and is considered the father of modern surfing. He also served as the unofficial ambassador for Hawaii.

Learning from his mother to never be afraid of the water and sharing his family's belief that they came from the water and would return to it someday, young Duke Kahanamoku spent all his free time in the ocean near Waikiki, where he honed his swimming and surfing skills.

In 1911, Kahanamoku participated in an unofficial swim meet and swam the 100-yard freestyle, beating the existing world record. In 1912, he competed in the Olympic trials and easily qualified to compete in the Summer Games that year in Stockholm, Sweden, where he won a gold medal in the 100-meter freestyle and a silver medal with the relay team. The 1920 Summer Games in Antwerp, Belgium, brought two more gold medals, one each in the freestyle and the freestyle relay events. Kahanamoku also won a silver medal in the 1924 Games at the age of thirty-four and competed in the 1932 Games with the water polo team.

During the 1912 Games, Kahanamoku used the "six kicks per cycle" style, which he had learned from older swimmers in Hawaii. Sports writers at the time called the technique "the Kahanamoku Kick," which was an adaptation of the Australian crawl.

With his popularity increasing, Kahanamoku moved to California in the 1920s and took on character roles in Hollywood films. While in California, he also worked as a beach lifeguard and spent time surfing and teaching people to surf. He is responsible for introducing Californians to surfing and be-

coming one of Hawaii's first ambassadors for the sport, starting its widespread appeal.

In 1925, Kahanamoku introduced the surfboard as a lifesaving tool after making a memorable ocean rescue in Newport Beach, California, when a charter fishing boat capsized in rough seas. He used his surfboard to shuttle victims to shore, and of the twelve passengers rescued that day, eight were rescued by Kahanamoku.

Impact

Duke Kahanamoku was the first person to be inducted into both the International Swimming Hall of Fame and the Surfers' Hall of Fame. He is credited with introducing surfing to the United States, Australia and New Zealand, and Europe. His swimming talents and Olympic success provided him opportunities to educate people about Hawaii and surfing. A statue in his honor welcomes visitors to Waikiki Beach.

P. Huston Ladner

Further Reading

Boyd, Duke. *Legends of Surfing: The Greatest Surfriders from Duke Kahanamoku to Kelly Slater.* Minneapolis, Minn.: MVP Books, 2009.

Brennan, Joseph L. *Duke: The Life Story of Hawai'i's Duke Kahanamoku.* Honolulu, Hawaii: Ku Pa'a, 1994.

Hall, Sandra Kimberley. *Duke: A Great Hawaiian.* Honolulu, Hawaii: Bess Press, 2004.

See also: Hobbies and recreation; Olympic Games of 1920 (Summer); Olympic Games of 1924 (Summer); Sports

■ Kane, Helen

Identification: American singer and entertainer
Also known as: Helen Clare Schroeder
Born: August 4, 1904, New York, New York
Died: September 26, 1966, New York, New York

Helen Kane's image as "the Boop-Boop-a-Doop" girl was a very popular feature on the new radio market in the United States during the 1920s, and her style was made immortal by its adoption by Fleischer Studio as the basis for its Betty Boop cartoon character.

Helen Kane grew up in the Bronx neighborhood of New York, and by the early 1920s, she was a professional vaudeville performer, appearing in various stage shows as a singer and kick-line dancer, including touring the Orpheum Circuit with the Marx brothers. Kane's big career break came in 1927 with a show named *A Night in Spain*, in which she incorporated her soon-to-be-famous "boop-boop-a-doop" scat line into the tune "That's My Weakness Now." Kane became an immediate success, and the little-girl-with-sex-appeal delivery style became desirable for Broadway and film alike. In 1928, she appeared in Broadway composer Oscar Hammerstein's *Good Boy*, singing "I Wanna Be Loved by You." The following year, Paramount Pictures signed her as a film actor, and from 1929 to 1931, she appeared in seven motion pictures but was the lead female character in only one, *Dangerous Nan McGrew*.

In 1930, at the peak of Kane's popularity, popular cartoonist Max Fleischer's studio devised a dog-eared parody of Kane, and by 1932, the character's ears had given way to hoop earrings and became known as Betty Boop. In May of that year, Kane sued Fleischer and Paramount for $250,000, claiming unfair competition and wrongful appropriation. The trial lasted two years, and the judge ultimately dismissed Kane's suit. By then, the Great Depression had taken hold of the country, and the lighthearted image Kane presented fell out of favor. Compounding this was the public perception that Kane was imitating Betty Boop.

Kane appeared in a few stage and radio shows in the early 1930s and dropped out of show business entirely in 1935.

Impact

Thanks in part to her signature scat "boop-boop-a-doop" in 1927, Helen Kane's career took off, and Helen Kane dolls and look-alike contests were the norm through the early part of the 1930s. With the creation of the hugely popular Betty Boop character, however, Helen's career waned dramatically. Although Kane appeared on television several times during the 1950s, Betty Boop's cultural influence

and popularity have continued into the twenty-first century.

Jeffrey Daniel Jones

Further Reading

Cullen, Frank, Florence Hackman, and Donald Mc-Neilly. *Vaudeville, Old and New: An Encyclopedia of Variety Performers in America.* New York: Routledge, 2007.

Fleischer, Richard. *Out of the Inkwell: Max Fleischer and the Animation Revolution.* Lexington: University Press of Kentucky, 2005.

"Helen Kane Dead; Boop-A-Doop Girl." *New York Times,* September 27, 1966, p. 47.

See also: Bow, Clara; Flappers; Hammerstein, Oscar, II; Marx Brothers; Talking motion pictures; Vaudeville

---

■ Keaton, Buster

Identification: American comedian and filmmaker
Also known as: Joseph Francis Keaton
Born: October 4, 1895, Piqua, Kansas
Died: February 1, 1966, Los Angeles, California

Next to Charlie Chaplin, Buster Keaton was one of the most important comedic filmmakers in silent film history. His cinematic craft, elaborate visual gags, and trademark deadpan expression made him an iconic symbol of 1920s screen comedy.

Joseph Francis "Buster" Keaton was born into a family of entertainers. His parents performed an acrobatic comedy act before breaking into vaudeville. Buster, a nickname said to have been given to him by escape artist Harry Houdini, was integrated into the act at an early age. Taking the physical comedy and roughhousing from the act in stride, he quickly adopted the blank facial expression that became his lifelong trademark. By his teen years, he emerged as the act's main attraction, constantly honing his improvisational skills and refreshing the gags in his repertoire. By the first time Keaton set foot in a movie studio, he had a well-developed comic persona as well as the ambition and technical audacity to take on the challenges of converting his comic vision to a new medium. His earliest opportunity came as a sidekick to the popular comedian Roscoe "Fatty" Arbuckle, with whom he worked on fifteen shorts over two years

Buster Keaton. (Moviepix/Getty Images)

home life, and the climax of the movie comes when the happy couple must move the misshapen house across some railroad tracks. In *The Playhouse*, Keaton employs multiple exposures to create the illusion that all of the characters in the filmed show—performers, stagehands, even the audience—are him, in an early example of the technical virtuosity that always marked his work. *Cops* portrays an escalating series of comedic misunderstandings between a lovelorn Buster and officers of the law, culminating in his rejection by his lady love despite his risk of life and limb to prove his worth to her.

Moving on to feature-length films, Keaton's work matured as his comedy became more deeply integrated with the stories he chose to film. The twelve movies he made between 1923 and 1929 are marked by consistent comedic brilliance and include several masterpieces of the form, including *Our Hospitality* (1923), *Sherlock Jr.* (1924), *The Navigator* (1924), and *The General* (1926). He proved equally adept at staging vast historical spectacle, as evidenced in *The General*, and smaller-scaled romantic farce, as in *Seven Chances* (1925). The films feature an underdog character contending with overwhelming forces, be they natural (a waterfall, a tornado) or manmade (an ocean liner, a pack of frenzied would-be brides), that require immense resolve and ingenuity to overcome.

Sherlock Jr. is perhaps the quintessential example of Keaton's style and thematic consistency, as a tour de force of accelerating comic momentum building on the premise that in a movie, anything can happen. To accomplish his magic, Keaton depended on intricate planning and his own physical gifts much more than on special effects or camera tricks.

Unlike his contemporary comedians Charlie Chaplin and Harry Langdon, Keaton rarely indulged in sentimentality. His comic persona was one of frenetic stoicism in the face of adversity and feigned indifference when things went well. While his endings often appeared happy, in virtually every instance there were complications on the horizon.

The motion picture industry's transition to sound

before striking out on his own in 1920. He launched his own production studio and spent the next ten years turning out one classic film after another.

1920s Film Career

Keaton's first headlining roles were in a series of two-reel shorts released between 1920 and 1923, including *One Week* (1920), *The Goat* (1921), *The Playhouse* (1921), *The Paleface* (1922), and *Cops* (1922). These films were essentially vehicles for Keaton's brand of increasingly sophisticated physical comedy. In *One Week*, for example, newlywed Buster and his bride construct a build-it-yourself house whose instructions have been sabotaged by a jealous rival. The resulting monstrosity is a cartoonish parody of idyllic was rough on Keaton, and by the early 1930s, his career was in decline. Keaton lost full creative control of his projects when he signed to the film production company Metro-Goldwyn-Mayer (MGM) in 1928. Suffering from the effects of personal setbacks and excessive drinking, the comedian faded into smaller and less prestigious roles. He continued to appear in films of varying quality up until his death, often displaying flashes of his earlier brilliance. Revivals of his silent work in the 1950s helped restore his critical reputation, and video reissues of his films have continued to keep him accessible to new generations of fans.

Impact

Keaton defined a style of film comedy unique to the silent era of the 1920s. His creative physicality made dialogue truly superfluous, and he favored gags and stunts over romance or message, giving his movies a timeless appeal.

John C. Hajduk

Further Reading

Dardis, Tom. *Keaton, The Man Who Wouldn't Lie Down.* New York: Scribner, 1979. A biography oriented to the behind-the-scenes and personal elements of Keaton's life and career.

Keaton, Eleanor, and Jeffrey Vance. *Buster Keaton Remembered.* New York: Harry N. Abrams, 2001. A richly photographed memoir of Keaton's life and career, written by his third wife.

McPherson, Edward. *Buster Keaton: Tempest in a Flat Hat.* New York: Newmarket Press, 2005. A biography with special emphasis on the construction and effects of the elaborate visual gags created for Keaton's classic films.

Robinson, David. *Buster Keaton.* Bloomington: University of Indiana Press, 1969. A critical examination of Keaton's film work, focusing almost entirely on the silent film era of the 1920s.

Sweeney, Kevin W., ed. *Buster Keaton: Interviews.* Jackson: University of Mississippi Press, 2007. Includes conversations with Keaton about his work and life, spanning the entirety of his career.

See also: Arbuckle, Fatty; Chaplin, Charlie; Film; *General, The;* Langdon, Harry; Vaudeville

■ Keller, Helen

Identification: American author, lecturer, and advocate for the disabled
Born: June 27, 1880, Tuscumbia, Alabama
Died: June 1, 1968, Easton, Connecticut

Keller's speaking engagements, vaudeville acts, publications, and role as an advisor for the American Foundation for the Blind (AFB) improved the way 1920s Americans perceived disabled people and gave the AFB much-needed support.

As a nineteen-month-old, Helen Adams Keller contracted an illness that left her deaf and blind. Her personal teacher, Anne Sullivan Macy, who later became her friend and constant companion, proved that she could be educated. Keller attended several educational institutions, including the Perkins School for the Blind, the Horace Mann School for the Deaf, and Radcliffe College, becoming America's first blind and deaf university graduate.

After graduation, Keller, Sullivan, and later another companion, Polly Thomson, traveled across the United States and into Canada, giving speeches. The lecture circuit did not provide the trio with the income they needed to meet their financial obligations, however. They learned that vaudeville would pay them better, and they subsequently joined the Orpheum Circuit in 1920.

Keller left vaudeville in 1924 to campaign for the recently formed AFB. Her addresses reached over a quarter of a million people, and she garnered support from individuals, churches, politicians, and humanitarian groups. In her lobbying and fundraising, Keller pushed to improve learning and employment opportunities for the disabled. Among her accomplishments, Keller successfully lobbied the United States Congress for the creation of reading services for the blind. In 1925, in an address to the Lions Club International Foundation Convention in Cedar Point, Ohio, Keller implored the club to sponsor the AFB's mission, and she won their support.

Keller's active campaign for the AFB took a hiatus in 1927 when Sullivan became too ill to travel. Keller published *My Religion* (1927), a book about Swedish scientist and theologian Emanuel Swedenborg. For the next two years, Sullivan and Nella Braddy Henney, an assistant with Doubleday publishing, worked with Keller on her autobiography *Midstream: My Later Life* (1929).

Impact

Keller influenced presidents, politicians, nonprofit organizations, and individuals. In her early years, she became a socialist and an advocate for human rights, and she helped found the American Civil Liberties Union in 1920. Her work supported the AFB and strongly influenced the mission of the Lions Club. People continue to be amazed at the once-silent girl's impact as an international traveler, performer, writer, and spokesperson for the disabled.

Cynthia J.W. Svoboda

Further Reading

Keller, Helen. *Midstream: My Later Life*. Reprint. New York: Greenwood Press, 1968.

_____. *The World I Live In*. Edited by Roger Shattuck. New York: New York Review Books, 2003.

Lash, Joseph P. *Helen and Teacher: The Story of Helen Keller and Anne Sullivan Macy*. New York: Delacorte Press, 1980.

See also: Vaudeville; Women in college; Women's rights

Frank B. Kellogg. (Getty Images)

■ Kellogg, Frank B.

Identification: American politician and diplomat
Born: December 22, 1856, Potsdam, New York
Died: December 21, 1937, St. Paul, Minnesota

As U.S. secretary of state, Frank Billings Kellogg sought to substitute law for force in settling international disputes. He is best remembered for his work on the Kellogg-Briand Pact of 1928, an antiwar initiative, as well as his policies toward China and Latin America.

By the early 1920s, Frank Kellogg had gained a reputation as a successful antitrust lawyer and a leading member of the Republican Party. After losing his Senate reelection bid in 1922, Kellogg served as a delegate to the Pan-American Conference in 1923 and as ambassador to Great Britain from 1923 to 1925, during which time he helped negotiate the Dawes Plan for collecting German war reparations. His sound reputation and background in foreign affairs led President Calvin Coolidge to appoint Kellogg secretary of state on March 5, 1925.

During Kellogg's tenure as secretary of state, the United States began to move away from interventionism in Latin America, although U.S. military occupations of Nicaragua, Haiti, and other areas continued during the decade. U.S.-Mexican relations were improved, however, and U.S. policy shifted away from using the Monroe Doctrine to justify American interference in hemispheric affairs.

Foreign powers pressured Kellogg to use force to protect their interests in China against antiforeigner violence, while China sought the abolition of extraterritoriality, the exemption of Western nationals from local law. Kellogg demonstrated goodwill toward China by granting it tariff autonomy but refused to end extraterritoriality without protections for foreigners.

Other issues went unresolved. At the Geneva Naval Conference of 1927, differences between Britain and the United States over the tonnage of cruisers undercut Kellogg's effort to advance disarmament initiatives. Kellogg continued to deny any connection between Allied war debts and German reparations, and, bowing to isolationist pressures, did not push for American membership in the World Court.

The Kellogg-Briand Pact of 1928, Kellogg's principal

diplomatic achievement, sought to outlaw wars of aggression. Initially, Kellogg rejected a French proposal for a bilateral agreement, fearful that it represented an entangling alliance. Initially, by suggesting a multilateral treaty, Kellogg hoped to blunt its force, but he eventually embraced the international agreement. The treaty, however, lacked enforcement provisions and ultimately failed to prevent war.

Impact

Restricted in formulating policy by the assertiveness of the Senate, Coolidge's lack of interest in world affairs, and the weight of isolationism in public opinion, Secretary of State Kellogg generally followed established policies. After leaving office on March 28, 1929, Kellogg resumed his law practice and served as a judge on the Permanent Court of International Justice from 1930 to 1935. For his contributions to the Kellogg-Briand Pact, Kellogg received many awards, including the Nobel Peace Prize in 1929.

Dean Fafoutis

Further Reading

Bryn-Jones, David. *Frank B. Kellogg: A Biography*. New York: G. P. Putnam's Sons, 1937.

Ellis, Lewis Ethan. *Frank B. Kellogg and American Foreign Policy, 1925–1929*. New Brunswick, N.J.: Rutgers University Press, 1961.

Ferrell, Robert H. "Frank B. Kellogg." In *American Statesmen: Secretaries of State from John Jay to Colin Powell*, edited by Edward S. Mihalkanin. Westport, Conn.: Greenwood Press, 2004.

See also: Coolidge, Calvin; Dawes Plan; Foreign policy, U.S.; Isolationism; Kellogg-Briand Pact of 1928

■ Kellogg-Briand Pact of 1928

The Treaty: International treaty renouncing war as a method of resolving international disagreements

Also known as: International Treaty for the Renunciation of War as an Instrument of National Policy; Pact of Paris

Date: Signed on August 27, 1928

The Kellogg-Briand Pact committed signatories not to employ war aggressively in their relations with one another or in the resolution of international disputes. For the United States in particular, adherence to the pact represented a small break from its post–World War I isolationism, while allowing Washington simultaneously to appease the growing American peace movement and avoid truly binding commitments to act on the international stage.

After World War I ended, the United States sought to withdraw from the world stage, and an increasing number of Americans questioned their country's participation in that conflict, strengthening and emboldening an existing peace movement. Spearheaded by such diverse figures as American Committee for the Outlawry of War founder Salmon O. Levinson, Carnegie Endowment for International Peace president Nicholas Murray Butler, and international relations scholar James T. Shotwell, the movement advocated outlawing war. By the mid-1920s, the foundations had been laid for the Kellogg-Briand Pact, named for its creators, U.S. secretary of state Frank Kellogg and French foreign minister Aristide Briand, winner of the Nobel Peace Prize for his role in the 1925 Locarno Treaty.

Origins

In March 1927, Shotwell visited Briand, urging the French foreign minister to promote the outlawing of war. Seeing an opportunity to link the United States to France's security system, which then included alliances with Belgium, Czechoslovakia, Poland, Romania, and Yugoslavia, Briand penned an open letter to the American people. In the letter, dated April 6, the tenth anniversary of the United States' entry into World War I, he proposed a Franco-American treaty in which the two signatories would pledge not to go to war against each other. Briand's letter went largely unnoticed until Butler called attention to it in an April 25 letter to the *New York Times*. Immediately, proponents of international peace, as well as staunch isolationists such as Senator William Borah, called for the administration of U.S. President Calvin Coolidge to accept Briand's proposal. Popular support for the measure grew steadily, with enthusiasm mounting after Charles Lindbergh's successful transatlantic flight to Paris in May and culminating in a pro-treaty petition campaign that fall.

Secretary of State Kellogg, who interpreted Briand's proposal as a subtle attempt to entangle the United States in future European conflicts, initially intended to ignore his French counterpart's initiative. Yet, in June, Kellogg accepted a formal draft for a pact of "perpetual friendship" between France and

Washington Disarmament Conference

Beginning on November 12, 1921, representatives from nine countries met in Washington, D.C., to discuss strategies for peace in the Far East—namely, naval disarmament. The major accomplishment of the Washington Disarmament Conference was the Five-Power Treaty, signed by Great Britain, the United States, Japan, Italy, and France on February 6, 1922. This pact called for a ten-year moratorium on the construction of capital, or a navy's largest armored, ships. As a result of the Washington Disarmament Conference, the nine participating countries promised to support the maintenance of peace and the status quo in the Far East. The public regarded the conference as a tremendous success. However, along with other efforts to control arms and the likelihood of war, such as the Kellogg-Briand Pact, it failed to prevent the outbreak of the second, and far more deadly, world war less than two decades later.

the United States; subsequently, he consulted the Senate Foreign Relations Committee, which informed him that while it would approve a general treaty renouncing aggressive war, it would not accept a bilateral treaty. On December 28, 1927, Kellogg therefore offered the counterproposal of a multilateral treaty condemning war as an instrument of national policy.

The Pact and Its Terms

Although Briand was not enthusiastic about a multilateral agreement, especially one that seemed to limit France's ability to resort to war in the name of self-defense, he continued negotiations, eventually accepting Kellogg's proposal in the spring of 1928. On August 27, 1928, diplomats from fifteen nations, including Kellogg representing the United States and Briand representing France, met in Paris and signed the pact as reporters from around the world watched. Ultimately, by November 1929, an additional forty governments had signed on to the pact.

In its final form, the Kellogg-Briand Pact consisted of three short articles. Most importantly, it obliged the signatories to "condemn recourse to war for the solution to international controversies, and renounce it, as an instrument of national policy in their rela-

tions with one another," promising to seek peaceful solutions to all disputes and conflicts, regardless of their origins or nature. The pact identified the United States as the depository for the respective instruments of ratification and charged Washington with responsibility for providing contracting parties with certified copies of the treaty.

Impact

The American peace movement hailed the Kellogg-Briand Pact with great enthusiasm, seeing it as a major step toward perpetual peace, and isolationists and internationalists alike accepted it without significant reservations. The U.S. Senate, while adding caveats about the preservation of the Monroe Doctrine and the right to employ force for the purpose of self-defense, ratified the pact by a vote of eighty-five to one.

Unfortunately, the pact provided no machinery for enforcement, and therefore, its practical impact came to depend upon its adherents' willingness to abide by its terms. Consequently, during the 1930s and early 1940s, when the leaders of Japan, Italy, and Germany—all original signers of the treaty—embarked on wars of aggression and territorial expansion, the pact proved as ineffectual as the previously established League of Nations, offering no deterrent and thus becoming little more than a statement of ultimately unfilled hope.

Bruce J. DeHart

Further Reading

Ferrell, Robert H. *Peace in Their Time: The Origins of the Kellogg-Briand Pact.* New Haven, Conn.: Yale University Press, 1952. Written by an esteemed historian of U.S. foreign policy in the twentieth century.

Josephson, Harold. *James T. Shotwell and the Rise of Internationalism in America.* Cranbury, N.J.: Associated University Presses, 1975.

Louria, Margo. *Triumph and Downfall: America's Pursuit of Peace and Prosperity, 1921–1933.* Westport, Conn.: Greenwood Press, 2000. An analysis of U.S. foreign policy in the 1920s and early 1930s challenging the traditional interpretation of American isolationism. Contains a chapter on Kellogg and his foreign policy.

Miller, David Hunter. *The Peace Pact of Paris: A Study of the Briand-Kellogg Treaty.* New York: G. P. Putnam's Sons, 1928. Includes the background of the treaty negotiations and the full text of the final version.

Steiner, Zara. *The Lights That Failed: European International History, 1919–1933.* New York: Oxford University Press, 2005. Places the Kellogg-Briand Pact in the context of European international relations during the interwar period. Offers interpretation from the perspective of the French.

See also: Foreign policy, U.S.; Isolationism; Kellogg, Frank B.; League of Nations

---

■ Kern, Jerome

Identification: American Broadway composer
Born: January 27, 1885, New York, New York
Died: November 11, 1945, New York, New York

Jerome Kern composed the music for several of the most popular Broadway musicals of the 1920s. His Show Boat *(1927) was one of the decade's biggest successes, signaling the start of a new type of theater and setting the standard for later Broadway shows.*

Jerome Kern began his career while still in high school by writing songs for local musical performances, including a stage adaptation of *Uncle Tom's Cabin.* After a few years of musical training focused on piano, he was getting songs published on New York's Tin Pan Alley, where he also worked as a song plugger, promoting publishers' sheet music by playing their songs in department stores. During this period, he continued to compose new songs for musicals and revues in New York and London. He wrote his first complete score for *The Red Petticoat,* a three-act musical comedy, in 1912. Kern's status as an innovative composer of Broadway music was cemented by a series of groundbreaking musicals he wrote with Guy Bolton and P. G. Wodehouse for the Princess Theatre between 1915 and 1918.

Early Musical Shows

Kern had at least one musical show produced on Broadway each year of the 1920s, though his earlier shows are now largely remembered for only one or two songs. His first big hit was *Sally,* produced by Broadway impresario Florenz Ziegfeld and starring Marilyn Miller in her first musical comedy role. It opened on December 21, 1920, and ran for 570 performances through the 1923–1924 season. *Sally* is a variant of the Cinderella story in which Miller played a dishwasher in a Greenwich Village restaurant who is invited to a party on Long Island. When a visiting dancer fails to arrive, Sally passes herself off as a Russian dancer. Her success is complete when she lands a starring role in the Ziegfeld Follies and marries a socialite. Kern's music for *Sally* experiments with the tempos and harmonies of jazz, including the hit song of the show, "Look for the Silver Lining."

Kern's next big hit, *Sunny,* was another star vehicle for Marilyn Miller, produced by Charles Dillingham. Opening on September 22, 1925, it ran for 517 performances. The show was a milestone in Kern's career, the first of his many collaborations with Oscar Hammerstein II. Miller played Sunny Peters, an American bareback rider performing in a circus in England. While there, she falls in love with Tom, a fellow American, and follows him to the ship on which he will sail back to America. Sunny stows away on the ship and is forced to marry Tom's friend, but they then get divorced and she marries Tom. The show's big hit was the song "Who?"

Show Boat

Inspired by the novel *Show Boat* (1926) by American writer Edna Ferber about life on the Mississippi River showboats of the 1880s, Kern wanted to adapt it as a musical. Ziegfeld agreed to produce the show on the basis of Kern's past successes, while Hammerstein adapted the book and wrote the lyrics. Kern envisioned a new type of musical that would emphasize a dramatically convincing plot and characters; the songs would spring from the events of the story, drive the plot forward, and reveal the inner lives of the characters.

The story takes place on the river showboat *Cotton Blossom.* The captain's daughter, Magnolia, elopes with a gambler to Chicago. Falling into debt, the gambler leaves Magnolia to raise their daughter by herself. She works as a music hall singer until her father convinces her to return to the *Cotton Blossom,* where she is reunited with her husband, and her daughter becomes the star of the boat's show. In addition, *Show Boat* includes subplots dealing with racial issues and was the first Broadway musical to feature a racially integrated cast.

The musical's most popular songs include "Ol' Man River," "Make Believe," and "Can't Help Lovin' Dat Man." The combination of Kern's music with Ziegfeld's usual show-stopping sets, star cast, scene changes, costumes, choruses, and production numbers made *Show Boat* a box-office success. It opened on December 27, 1927, and ran for 572 performances at the Ziegfeld Theatre before going on tour. The show was immediately recognized both for its quality and originality, with a West End production opening in London on May 3, 1928. It is Kern's best-known musical and has been revived countless times since. *Show Boat* proved that the Broadway musical could carry the dramatic weight of opera by using tuneful music to deal with serious, mature, socially relevant subjects. It is the only one of Ziegfeld's shows to have been revived and has twice been adapted to film, in 1936 and 1951.

In 1929 and 1930, Kern went to Hollywood to oversee film versions of *Sally* and *Sunny*, both again featuring Marilyn Miller. The interest in filmed musicals at the time was short-lived, however, and Kern returned to Broadway. Starting in the mid-1930s, he wrote music for many successful Hollywood film musicals. Kern continued writing musicals until 1939, but none matched the success his work during the 1920s.

Impact

Jerome Kern was one of the most successful composers of Broadway musical theater in the 1920s. *Show Boat* became the model for later, more serious Broadway musicals, in which the music was integrated with the drama and the songs served to advance characterization and plot.

Thomas McGeary

Further Reading

Banfield, Stephen. *Jerome Kern*. New Haven, Conn.: Yale University Press, 2006. Discusses and analyzes Kern's compositions in musical terms.

Block, Geoffrey. "*Show Boat*: In the Beginning." In *Enchanted Evenings: The Broadway Musical from "Show Boat" to Sondheim and Lloyd Webber*. New York: Oxford University Press, 2009. Gives attention to the musical aspects of *Show Boat*.

Bordman, Gerald. *Jerome Kern: His Life and Music*. New York: Oxford University Press, 1980. Covers Kern's life in detail and indexes the songs from his shows.

Ewen, David. *The World of Jerome Kern: A Biography*. New York: Holt, 1960. Candid and critical coverage of Kern's career, with contributions from his wife and daughter.

Kreuger, Miles. *Show Boat: The Story of a Classic American Musical*. New York: Oxford University Press, 1977. Documents the creation, production, revivals, and film versions of the musical.

See also: Broadway musicals; Film; Hammerstein, Oscar, II; *Show Boat;* Theater in the United States; Tin Pan Alley; Ziegfeld, Florenz

---

■ King, William Lyon Mackenzie

Identification: Canadian prime minister
Also known as: Mackenzie King
Born: December 17, 1874, Berlin (now Kitchener), Ontario, Canada
Died: July 22, 1950, Kingsmere, Quebec, Canada

As prime minister of Canada during the 1920s, William Lyon Mackenzie King presided over a prosperous decade. In 1926, he successfully survived a constitutional crisis involving the British governor-general and overcame a strong challenge from Conservative leader Arthur Meighen. King's firm leadership helped establish Canada's autonomy within the British Empire.

After he was elected leader of the Liberal Party in 1919 following the death of Sir Wilfred Laurier, King faced severe challenges. The Liberal Party had been torn apart in 1917, when Laurier refused to support a draft during World War I and many Liberal members of Parliament left to form a Union government with the Conservatives. King had supported Laurier during the split, winning Laurier votes in Quebec that helped elect him party leader. King was confident he could bring the Liberal-Unionists back using skills he had honed as a labor mediator, but without alienating his Quebecois followers who strongly resented supporters of conscription. Farmer and labor discontent in western Canada had led to the rise of a loosely structured Progressive Party, and King hoped to bring some of their elected representatives into the Liberal Party as well.

First Administration

King's chance came in the 1921 election, the first in which all Canadian women could vote. His 1919 platform had called for lower tariffs to please farmers, increased railway competition, and better working conditions and public insurance for the sick, elderly, and unemployed. Prime Minister Arthur Meighen, a Conservative intellectual whose sarcastic

William Lyon Mackenzie King. (Time & Life Pictures/Getty Images)

on agricultural machinery were lowered, but few other of the social reform programs he had earlier advocated made it into law.

King presided over a period of increasing economic prosperity, during which Canada's primary economic ties shifted from Great Britain to the United States, as north-south trade and direct investment increased substantially. Prosperity brought with it increased tax revenue for the government, which the fiscally conservative King primarily devoted to reducing the enormous national debt accumulated during World War I.

Constitutional Crisis

King confidently called an election for October 1925 and was shocked when the Conservatives swept the vote with 115 seats, while the Liberals dropped to 100 and the Progressives declined to 22. Since the Conservatives did not have a majority in the House of Commons, King tried to hold onto power. Introducing a bill for old-age pensions won him the support of members of the small Labour Party. Progressives voted with him until a major bribery and corruption scandal erupted in the Customs Department, much of it involving illegal liquor shipments to the United States.

In June 1926, rather than resign when it became clear that most Progressives would support censuring the government over the customs affair, King requested that Governor-General Lord Julian Byng, the representative of the British crown in Canada, dissolve the House and call another election. Byng refused, saying Meighen, who headed the largest bloc of seats, should first have a chance to see if he could govern. King resigned as prime minister and Meighen tried to govern but was hindered by a rule (since repealed) that members appointed to the cabinet had to run for reelection before taking office. Since this would reduce Conservative votes below the number necessary to sustain him in power, Meighen tried to use temporary cabinet appointments to keep his ministers in the House. King offered a resolution claiming that this maneuver made the government illegiti-

wit outmatched King in debates, was contemptuous of King and was certain he would win by focusing his campaign on support of the protective tariff. Meighen was therefore stunned when the Liberals won 118 seats, the Progressives 58, and the Conservatives only 49.

King then formed the first minority government in Canadian history. Though he was unable to convince any Progressive leader to join his cabinet, most voted with King against the Conservatives. King always sought consensus in the cabinet and Parliament, meaning that policies were cautious and incremental, and he did not appear to exert much personal influence on domestic policy. Consequently, import tariffs mate. The Progressives voted with him, bringing down Meighen's government. Byng then granted Meighen the dissolution that he had denied King.

King made the constitutional disagreement the central issue of his campaign, claiming that when the governor-general as representative of the Crown refused a request of the Canadian prime minister, it was an unwarranted direct British intervention into Canadian affairs. He argued this was treating Canada as though it were still a dependent colony, rather than a self-governing dominion. Although constitutional scholars still debate the merits of this argument, at the time, King's appeal to Canadian nationalism won the day: In the 1926 election, the Liberals won 116 seats to the Conservatives' 91. With the support of Liberal-Progressives, King, after being out of office only three months, gained a secure majority for the first time.

Foreign Relations

In the 1920s, Canada claimed independent status in foreign affairs as an autonomous member of the newly named British Commonwealth. Until after World War I, Canada did not have its own foreign policy. It negotiated commercial agreements with the United States and France, but British ambassadors throughout the world spoke for all members of the British Empire on policy issues.

The assertion of a Canadian voice was a bipartisan effort. Prime Minister Robert Borden, a Conservative, insisted that Canada independently sign the Versailles Treaty ending World War I and have its own seat at the League of Nations. His successor and fellow Conservative Meighen effectively opposed renewal of the British-Japanese alliance at the 1921 Imperial Conference, arguing it would offend the United States, and good relations with the United States were a necessity for Canada.

King upheld Canadian autonomy in the 1922 Chanak affair, when the British prime minister requested Commonwealth military support to prevent Turkish troops from occupying a demilitarized zone controlled by Britain and France. King responded that no Canadian military action would be taken without the consent of the Canadian parliament, which was not in session at the time. This time Meighen, showing a lack of appreciation for the growing nationalist sentiment in the country, criticized King, saying Canada should have automatically agreed to the British request.

At the 1923 Imperial Conference, King firmly opposed attempts to formulate a foreign policy binding the British dominions. At the 1926 Imperial Conference, he strongly supported the affirmation of autonomy that led to the 1931 Statute of Westminster, in which the British parliament recognized the complete autonomy of British dominions. In February 1927, Canada sent its first envoy to the United States, receiving full diplomatic status. Ambassadors to France and Japan soon followed.

Impact

King's greatest achievements during his first two administrations as prime minister were more political than social: He rebuilt Canada's Liberals into a national party with significant support in every section of the nation. His conciliatory skills served the Liberal Party well, enabling him to reconcile its French and English wings after the bitter split over conscription during World War I. He also carefully wooed the farm-based Progressives, providing what he could without alienating his supporters in industrial Ontario.

In international affairs, King's stubborn insistence on Canadian autonomy hastened the transformation of the British Empire into the Commonwealth of Nations. His brand of Canadian nationalism combined a strong belief in British ideals and devotion to the monarchy with a firm insistence that foreign policy decisions involving Canada should be made in Ottawa, not London.

King's do-nothing policy at the onset of the Great Depression probably cost him the election of 1930, although he would serve again as prime minister from 1935 to 1948, during which time he held the country together through World War II and finally enacted the social reforms he first proposed in 1919.

Milton Berman

Further Reading

Bothwell, Robert. *The Penguin History of Canada.* Toronto: Penguin Canada, 2007. Contains a chapter on the social and cultural background to King's politics.

Buckner, Philip A., ed. *Canada and the British Empire.* New York: Oxford University Press, 2010. Emphasizes Canada's role in the British Empire and explores Canadian responses to British imperialism.

Dawson, Robert M., and H. Blair Neatby. *William*

Lyon Mackenzie King: A Political Biography. 3 vols. Toronto: University of Toronto Press, 1958. A standard scholarly biography of King.

Graham, Roger. *And Fortune Fled.* Vol. 2 in *Arthur Meighen: A Biography.* Toronto: Clark, Irwin, 1963. Covers Meighen's years as Conservative leader, contrasting with rival King's policies and actions.

Hutchison, Bruce. *The Incredible Canadian: A Candid Portrait of Mackenzie King: His Works, His Times, and His Nation.* Reprint. Toronto: Longmans Canada, 1970. A favorable account of the life of King.

See also: Agriculture in Canada; Canada and Great Britain; Canadian nationalism; Elections, Canadian; Meighen, Arthur

■ King of Kings, The

Identification: A silent film about the life and death of Jesus
Director: Cecil B. DeMille
Date: 1927

Along with DeMille's The Ten Commandments *(1923),* The King of Kings *combined the lavish sets and showmanship of Hollywood with stories purporting to edify motion picture audiences in an effort to deflect criticism of the movie industry on moral grounds in the 1920s.*

One of the first directors of feature films, Cecil B. DeMille turned to the biblical epic in the 1920s as a way to depict love stories with sexually suggestive episodes that would draw large audiences, while still laying claim to a moral higher ground. Thus, *The King of Kings,* shot primarily in black and white, sought to contrast the debauchery of Roman rule with scenes dramatizing the austere and sincere appeal of Jesus and his teachings. Color film segments bookend the film, offsetting the opening scene featuring then-prostitute Mary Magdalene's erotic dance with the closing Resurrection scene.

Interspersing the action with title cards citing or paraphrasing relevant New Testament verses, De Mille created a striking oscillation between the pleasures of the world and the promise of eternal life preached in Jesus's sayings. For audiences of the 1920s, the film's subtext undoubtedly raised concerns about the materialism of American life and the quest for success, with the Judas character modeling the craven opportunist, seeking to exchange the physical pleasure he enjoyed as Mary Magdalene's lover for political power through his relationship with Jesus. The restless, anxious Judas—one of the few clean-shaven characters with a modern-looking haircut—was obviously intended to remind 1920s moviegoers of the perils of worldly ambition.

Also noteworthy is that, at a time when anti-Semitism was widespread in the United States, DeMille attempted to portray only Judas and the Jewish leader Caiaphas, not all Jews, as responsible for Jesus's death. Nonetheless, the film received a mixed reception in the Jewish community, and its stereotyped representation of the Jewish people remains controversial.

Impact

By the 1930s, *The King of Kings* was being shown in church halls, fulfilling the image-boosting goals of a Hollywood rocked by the Fatty Arbuckle scandal and other controversies that had critics calling for censorship. At the same time, DeMille's biblical epics reflected a sincere strain of piety that resulted in many moving enactments of biblical stories. Through this highly successful film, DeMille established both the profitability and the probity of the Hollywood biblical epic, a genre he continued to exploit in *Samson and Delilah* (1949) and his 1956 remake of *The Ten Commandments.* DeMille's work continues to inspire the making of Hollywood spectaculars.

Carl Rollyson

Further Reading

Birchard, Robert S. *Cecil B. DeMille's Hollywood.* Lexington: University Press of Kentucky, 2004.

Eyman, Scott. *Empire of Dreams: The Epic Life of Cecil B. DeMille.* New York: Simon & Schuster, 2010.

See also: Censorship; DeMille, Cecil B.; Film; Grauman's Chinese Theatre; Jews in the United States; Religion in the United States

■ Kirby, Rollin

Identification: American political cartoonist and writer
Born: September 4, 1874, Galva, Illinois
Died: May 9, 1952, New York, New York

Rollin Kirby, the first three-time Pulitzer Prize winner, was a political cartoonist whose illustrations dealt with many salient issues of the 1920s, from American isolationism and the Russian famine to civil rights, the American judicial system, and party politics. He enjoyed a large audience while working for the New York World *newspaper during this time.*

Educated at New York's prestigious Art Students League, Kirby studied painting in Paris before obtaining a position as a magazine illustrator from 1901 to 1910, during which time he worked freelance for such magazines as *Collier's, Harper's,* and *Life.* Kirby was hired as a cartoonist for the *New York Evening Mail* in 1911 and the *New York Sun* in 1912. In 1913, Kirby became the cartoonist for the Pulitzer family's *New York World* newspaper, where he worked for most of his career.

In 1922, Kirby won the first-ever Pulitzer Prize in Editorial Cartooning for his illustration "On the Road to Moscow," which depicted the horrors of the famine in Russia that contributed to the deaths of over five million people. Kirby won the award two more times during the 1920s. His second award was given for his 1925 illustration "News from the Outside World," in which the United States, Russia, and Mexico were portrayed as outcast hobos for not joining the League of Nations. In 1929, he received a third award, this time for "Tammany," a searing indictment of what he considered the hypocrisy of scandal-plagued Republicans who criticized the 1928 Democratic presidential nominee, New York governor Alfred E. Smith, for his association with the state's oft-maligned Tammany Hall political machine.

Impact

Throughout the 1920s, Kirby used his editorial cartoons to decry intolerance and draw attention to social and political issues of the time. He was a staunch supporter of women's rights, contributing cartoons to such magazines as *The Suffragist* and illustrating the injustices women faced with minimum wage and working hours legislation. He was fiercely opposed to Prohibition, creating a popular, foppish-looking character called "Mr. Dry" to personify and satirize the movement. Other favorite targets were the Ku Klux Klan and Christian fundamentalists such as William Jennings Bryan, who fought the teaching of evolution in public schools.

In 1939, Kirby joined the more liberal *New York Post.* Three years later, Kirby returned to drawing for

magazines. Throughout his journalism career, Kirby also occasionally wrote book reviews, news articles, and poetry.

Brian D. Hendricks

Further Reading

Hess, Stephen, and Sandy Northrup. *American Political Cartoons: The Evolution of a National Identity, 1754–2010.* Piscataway, N.J.: Transaction, 2011.

Kirby, Rollin. *Highlights: A Cartoon History of the Nineteen Twenties.* Edited by Henry B. Hoffman. New York: W. F. Payson, 1931.

Press, Charles. *The Political Cartoon.* Rutherford, N.J.: Fairleigh Dickinson University Press, 1981.

See also: Civil rights and liberties; Magazines; Newspapers, U.S.; Voting rights; Women in the workforce; Women's rights

---

■ Knickerbocker Storm

The Event: A devastating and fatal three-day blizzard
Date: January 27–29, 1922
Place: The East Coast of the United States

The Knickerbocker Storm, named for the fatal roof collapse of the Knickerbocker Theatre in Washington, D.C., was a record-setting blizzard, dropping more than 20 inches of snow across much of the upper South and mid-Atlantic region between the afternoon of January 27, 1922, and the early hours of January 29. On January 28 alone, a record 21 inches of snow fell in Washington, the most snow to fall there during a single day in recorded history. Areas hit hardest by the storm included Richmond, Virginia (19 inches total), Baltimore, Maryland (26.8 inches), and Washington, D.C. (28 inches).

The storm was the result of moisture from the Gulf of Mexico reaching an arctic cold front along the eastern seaboard. A high-pressure system in the north and the low-pressure system from the south created perfect conditions for a slow-moving snowstorm that would ultimately cover an estimated 22,000 square miles with over 20 inches of snow. The accumulated snow immobilized much of the area for several days.

The storm took its name from the largest and newest Washington movie house, the Knickerbocker Theatre. Although the storm kept more than half the seats empty, approximately nine hundred theatergoers

Damage caused by the Knickerbocker Storm. (Getty Images)

gathered at the Knickerbocker on the evening of January 28 to see director Frank Borzage's silent comedy *Get-Rich-Quick Wallingford* (1921). Heavy, wet snow accumulated rapidly on the flat roof of the theater, and shortly after 9:00 P.M., without warning, the roof of the theater collapsed under the weight of the snow, splitting down the middle. The roof's collapse knocked down a brick wall and brought the cement balcony down onto the orchestra seating section, killing at least 98 people and injuring 158 others.

Impact

The Knickerbocker Storm is widely considered among the worst natural disasters in the history of Washington, D.C. Many of those killed were prominent citizens, including former congressman Andrew Jackson Barchfeld of Pennsylvania. Investigations found that faulty design was most likely to blame for the roof's collapse. The collapse continued to take its toll in the years to come. In the years that followed, both the architect, Reginald Wyckliffe Geare, and the theater's owner, Harry M. Crandall, were unable to cope with the disaster and committed suicide.

Michael D. Cummings

Further Reading

Compo, Gil, Jeff Whitaker, and Prashant Sardeshmukh. "Bridging the Gap Between Climate and Weather." *Scientific Discovery Through Advanced Computing Review,* no. 7 (Spring, 2008): 50–57.

Fishbein, Gershon. "A Winter's Tale of Tragedy." *The Washington Post,* January 22, 2009, Special.

Kocin, Paul J., and Louis W. Uccellini. *Northeast Snowstorms.* Boston: American Meteorological Society, 2004.

See also: Movie palaces; Natural disasters

■ Koko the Clown

Identification: Animated cartoon character
Also known as: Ko-Ko the Clown
Creator: Max Fleischer
Date: 1919

Koko the Clown was the first animated character created by cartoonist Max Fleischer and his studios. Koko's realistic movement and sometimes surrealistic antics in a combination of animation and live-action film thrilled audiences during the silent era.

Koko the Clown came about when his creator, Max Fleischer, wanted to make a cartoon using his new invention, the rotoscope, a device that allowed animators to trace moving images projected frame by frame onto a screen. Max's brother Dave Fleischer, who also directed the cartoons, dressed up in a clown suit and served as the model for Koko. In 1916, the Fleischer brothers began work on the initial clown series, *Out of the Inkwell,* for Bray Studios, run by Max's friend J. R. Bray. It was not until 1919, however, that the first Koko cartoon was viewed publicly. Critics and audiences enjoyed it immensely, and the clown became a star. In 1921, the Fleischers established their own studio, Out of the Inkwell Films, and continued starring their cartoon clown (first known as Koko in 1923 and renamed Ko-Ko in 1928) in various black-and-white silent series throughout the decade.

The Koko cartoons generally consisted of a combination of live action and animation. Max Fleischer, playing himself, would produce Koko in one of many ways, such as Max pouring an old drawing into his pen and then having the drawing escape to form Koko. Koko would then interact with the world around him, playing with clay (as in *Modeling*) or even roaming around Manhattan as an enormous 100-foot-tall version of himself (as in *Bedtime*). While the plots of these shorts were usually not very complex, the technical innovations and inventiveness of animation kept audiences returning throughout the 1920s.

Out of the Inkwell Films reformed as Fleischer Studios, and the Fleischers switched entirely to making sound cartoons in 1929. At this point, they decided to concentrate on other characters, though Ko-Ko occasionally appeared later in Betty Boop cartoons. His last series was a short-lived color television program that was broadcast from 1961 to 1962.

Impact

Despite his fanciful appearance and the surreal atmosphere of many of his cartoons, Koko the Clown brought a sense of realism to animation, particularly in his movements. Many critics were amazed at the technical prowess of the animation, noting the overall smooth motion and Koko's lifelike body shape. The techniques used in producing these cartoons would influence many other animators, including Walt Disney.

Lisa Scoggin

Further Reading

Crafton, Donald. *Before Mickey: The Animated Film, 1898–1928.* Chicago: University of Chicago Press, 1993.

Fleischer, Richard. *Out of the Inkwell: Max Fleischer and the Animation Revolution.* Lexington: University Press of Kentucky, 2005.

Maltin, Leonard. *Of Mice and Magic: A History of American Animated Cartoons.* Rev. ed. New York: Plume Books, 1987.

See also: Film; Inventions; Science and technology; Talking motion pictures

■ Kool-Aid

Upon its creation in 1927, Kool-Aid became the first powdered soft-drink mix sold nationally in stores. The low-cost beverage mix has remained enduringly popular and has entered the American vocabulary as a generic term.

Although many people use the name "Kool-Aid" to refer to any powdered soft drink, the trademarked drink itself was the result of inventor Edwin Perkins's dedication to an idea. While working in his father's general store in Hendley, Nebraska, at age eleven, Perkins became obsessed with the new Jell-O dessert product. Perkins would later credit his fondness for Jell-O as the driving force behind his desire to get into the prepackaged food business.

By 1920, Perkins had opened his own manufacturing business, Perkins Products, in Hastings, Nebraska. Within two years, the business was producing and selling more than one hundred items, including face creams, medicines, soaps, jelly-making products, and a fruit drink concentrate called "Fruit-Smack." While Fruit-Smack was one of the more popular items, it presented several delivery problems: The weight of the bottles increased shipping costs, and they often broke or leaked.

Perkins's fondness for Jell-O and his company's fruit pectin for homemade jellies helped him realize that Fruit-Smack's long-term success would depend on his ability to repackage the drink as a dry concentrated powder. In 1927, Perkins reintroduced Fruit-Smack as "Kool-Ade," a powdered concentrate sold in one-ounce waxed envelopes and available in six flavors: raspberry, grape, cherry, lemon-lime, orange, and root beer (some histories list strawberry as the original sixth flavor). Consumers only needed to add sugar and cold water to make a pitcher of the finished beverage. Perkins began delivering Kool-Ade to retail outlets, and the product soon proved a major success.

In 1928, Perkins trademarked the Kool-Ade name. Accounts vary as to why the name was later changed to "Kool-Aid." Some say government regulators informed Perkins that "Ade" was reserved for fruit juice products, while others claim a separate party threatened to sue over the name. In either case, Perkins eventually changed the spelling and trademarked the new name in 1934.

Impact

After the stock market crash of 1929, demand for Kool-Aid increased dramatically, making it the centerpiece of Perkins Products. Sold for five cents an envelope beginning in 1933, powdered Kool-Aid provided an affordable option for families seeking a cool drink during the Great Depression. By 1931, Perkins Products had relocated to Chicago, which provided easier access to supplies and more centralized distribution, and refocused its production to food items alone. The popular drink mix was recognized as the official soft drink of Nebraska in 1998 and became the focal point of the Hastings annual summer festival, Kool-Aid Days.

Michael Cummings Jr.

Further Reading

Adams County Historical Society. *The Kool-Aid Story.* Hastings, Nebr.: Adams County Historical Society, 2002.

Smith, Andrew F. *Encyclopedia of Junk Food and Fast Food.* Westport, Conn: Greenwood Press, 2006.

See also: Bubble gum; Eskimo Pie; Food trends

■ Ku Klux Klan

Identification: An extremist organization devoted to white supremacy, Protestant fundamentalism, and nationalism
Also known as: KKK; The Klan
Date: Reestablished in 1915

Dedicated to "100 percent Americanism," the regrouped Ku Klux Klan (KKK) appealed to a Protestant, race-based nationalism and wielded widespread influence in state and national politics during the 1920s.

Resurrected in 1915 following its heroic depiction in the silent film epic *Birth of a Nation* (1915), the Ku Klux Klan enjoyed a resurgence in membership and political influence during the 1920s, when many native-born white Protestant Americans expressed fears of communism, immigrants, and Catholicism and looked to the Klan to represent their desires to control the social norms and political processes in the interest of white Anglo-Americans. The organization's emphasis on traditional American values made

it attractive to people concerned about domestic social changes such as the rise of jazz and the emerging
automobile culture, scientific changes such as Einstein's theory of relativity and Freudian psychology,
and global demographic changes that appeared to
threaten the dominance of white people, both internationally and at home.

The Klan Agenda

Klan rhetoric linked fundamentalist Christianity, patriotism, and traditional values in a seamless fabric of
exclusive Americanism. By 1924, the organization
had as many as eight million dues-paying members,
including those in the auxiliary Women of the Ku
Klux Klan, and for a time, it controlled politics in Indiana, Oregon, and Colorado, as well as across the
South. By allying itself with whatever political party
was in power at the state level, the Klan helped pass
laws that banned the wearing of religious attire by
schoolteachers, a measure directed against Catholic
nuns, and outlawed the teaching of Darwinian biology in the public schools.

The Klan sought to portray itself as just another of
the civic and fraternal organization that were popular in the 1920s. In practice, however, the revived
Klan continued the terrorism and vigilantism of its
Reconstruction-era predecessor. Because Jim Crow
laws and earlier violence had largely subordinated
African Americans in the southern states, Klan rhetoric and activities in the 1920s expanded to target
parochial schools, other racial and ethnic minorities,
union organizers, and bootleggers. An investigation
by the *New York World* newspaper in 1921 linked the
Klan to four homicides, forty-one whippings, and
twenty-seven incidents involving tarring and feath-
ering in pursuit of its aims.

Resurgence and Decline

Marketing itself as the defender of traditional American values and creating financial incentives for its
current members to recruit new members, the ranks
of the Klan swelled throughout most of the United
States. At the same time, its national leaders, William Joseph Simmons and Hiram Wesley Evans,
struggled with one another for sole personal domination of the Klan and its resources. Internally, dis-
unity and disharmony characterized the Klan as an
organization, while stories of hypocrisy, often in-

volving drunkenness and adultery, threatened its
public image.

With members in every state, the Klan was especially influential in Indiana, where its leader David
Curtiss Stephenson controlled the governor's office
and much of the legislature. Over 200,000 Klansmen
and their families attended the "Klonklave in Ko-
komo" on July 4, 1923, a celebration of the Klan's
status in Indiana. However, the Klan did not enjoy
universal support even there: In the spring of 1924,
students from the University of Notre Dame mobbed
Klansmen preparing for a rally and parade. In 1925,
Stephenson was convicted of the rape and murder of
Indianapolis schoolteacher Madge Oberholtzer, tar-
nishing the Klan's image at the state and national
levels as a defender of morals. Klan activity and prominence rapidly subsided. By 1928, national Klan
membership had plummeted to the tens of thousands and Klan influence in politics ceased to be
measurable.

Impact

The Klan has historically reflected the status anxiety
of white Americans when confronted with social
change. Its ability to recruit members and exert social control serves as a measure of the degree to
which Klan beliefs and fears are shared by the larger
mass of white Protestant society. For half a decade
in the 1920s, the Klan controlled state governments
from Texas to Colorado to Indiana and enjoyed major
influence in the Democratic Party at both the state
and national levels. Klan opposition to the Democratic Party's leading presidential candidate, Al
Smith of New York, cost Smith the 1928 presidential
nomination and nearly divided the party. At least
five U.S. senators held Klan membership in the early
1920s. The Klan played a major role in generating
support for the Immigration Act of 1924, which imposed strict quotas on immigration based on national origin.

The Klan's prominence reflected the near-hysteria
that characterized the response of many Americans
to the changes in their world wrought during the
1920s. At the same time, the violent and corrupt
means by which the Klan sought to combat those
changes and the personal hypocrisy of many of its
leaders caused erstwhile supporters to abandon the
organization.

Edward R. Crowther

Further Reading

Chalmers, David Mark. *Hooded Americanism: The History of the Ku Klux Klan.* 3d ed. Durham, N.C.: Duke University Press, 1987. Traces the history of the Klan from Reconstruction to the 1980s.

Horowitz, David A., ed. *Inside the Klavern: The Secret History of a Ku Klux Klan of the 1920s.* Carbondale: Southern Illinois University Press, 1999. A remarkable collection of minutes and pamphlets from an Oregon KKK chapter.

Maclean, Nancy K. *Behind the Mask of Chivalry: The Making of the Second Ku Klux Klan.* New York: Oxford University Press, 1995. Stresses the 1920s Klan connection to the larger social forces operating in the United States.

O'Donnell, Patrick, ed. *Ku Klux Klan America's First Terrorists Exposed: The Rebirth of the Strange Society of Blood and Death.* West Orange, N.J.: Idea Men Productions, 2006. A rich compilation of primary material and contextual analysis.

Wade, Wyn Craig. *The Fiery Cross: The Ku Klux Klan in America.* New York: Oxford University Press, 1998. An accessible account of the Klan from its origins to the end of the twentieth century.

See also: Evangelism; Jim Crow in the U.S. South; Racial discrimination; "Return to Normalcy"

L

■ Labor strikes

Labor strikes in the United States during the 1920s were infrequent as compared to the previous two decades. The largest strikes of the decade involved seamen, coal miners, and railroad shop craftsmen. These strikes helped define the future of the U.S. labor movement, especially with regard to the disappearance of craft unions and the future of the United Mine Workers of America (UMWA).

The 1920s in the United States are generally considered to be years of economic growth and satisfaction, at least until the stock market crashed in October 1929. More Americans were steadily employed, although wages remained low for many workers. The labor upheavals of the previous decades had convinced corporate America of the need to be tough in labor relations. In addition, the post–World War I mood in the country, combined with government and business attempts to minimize the power of labor unions, caused union membership to shrink considerably. The Industrial Workers of the World (IWW) had been effectively destroyed due to relentless attacks on the group's members and leadership by national and local law enforcement, as well as certain elements in the American Federation of Labor (AFL). This left only the AFL as a national union organization. Its dependence on craft unionism rather than the industrial model of other unions exposed the weakness of that model as corporations increased their attacks on organized workers over the course of the decade. The few major strikes that did occur were most often resolved with workers accepting wage cuts and other loss of compensation.

Seamen's, Printers', and Clothing Workers' Strikes

In 1921, industrial production shrank by 15 percent, and the number of factory workers fell by almost 25 percent. The American Shipowners' Association was not the only entity that wanted to cut workers' wages. However, the group's demand that members of two different seamen's unions accept a 25 percent wage cut was met with a strike by the workers that year. On May 1, 1921, members of these two unions walked off their jobs at midnight. The result was the largest work stoppage in American shipping history. More than three hundred vessels were left unattended in New York Harbor alone. The shipping companies responded and, with the assistance of the governmental regulatory agency known as the United States Shipping Board, arrested hundreds of strikers. They then hired strikebreakers and, after fifty-two days, broke the strike. The internal struggles in the aftermath of the strikers' defeat led to a schism within the affected unions, weakening them ever after.

Almost simultaneously, a series of strikes broke out in the printing industry. Hundreds of printing companies had earlier agreed to a forty-four-hour workweek. The strikes began on May 1, 1921, when some companies backed out of the deal. The strikes lasted four years. They cost the International Typographical Union (ITU) approximately $16 million and the International Printing Pressmen and Assistants' Union $1 million in strike benefits, respectively. However, the unions won most of their demands and survived.

Over 100,000 textile workers went on strike in New England in 1928 and ended up reducing the proposed wage cut of 42.8 percent to 22.5 percent. In New York, a similar strike by the Amalgamated Clothing Workers of America saw the union accept a compromise that allowed workers to continue being represented by the union while accepting a 15 percent wage cut. In Gastonia, North Carolina, workers at the Loray Mill went on strike after the company began firing workers on April 1, 1929, for attending a meeting called by organizers from the National Textile Workers Union (NTWU) the day before. The company action led to a vote in favor of a strike. The strike was notable for its interracial character, something almost unheard of in the South at the time. The mayor of Gastonia called in the National Guard on April 3, 1929. On April 19, a gang of around one hundred masked vigilantes destroyed

---

The Great Steel Strike and Its Lessons (1920)

Immediately following the steel strike of 1919, labor leader William Z. Foster published *The Great Steel Strike and Its Lessons* (1920), his personal account of the events in which he emphasized the strike opponents' utter disregard for basic human rights. Foster argued that the workers were helpless in defense of their individual freedoms when confronted with an organized opposition of state police, deputy sheriffs, city officials, company police and detectives, and armed strikebreakers. Local officials nullified the striking workers' civil rights of free speech and assembly without just cause, and state police violated the workers' personal rights. The widespread union defeat had a longstanding impact on union effectiveness throughout the 1920s.

NTWU headquarters. A tent city was constructed outside Gastonia city limits, and armed strikers guarded the encampment. The company resumed production with the support of strikebreakers. On June 7, 1921, a group of strikers went to the mill to urge those inside to join the strike. The strikers were attacked by sheriff's deputies and dispersed. Later that night, the sheriff and four deputies went to the tent city and demanded that the armed guards turn over their weapons. A battle ensued, leaving the sheriff dead and wounding two deputies and several strikers. Eight union organizers and sixty-three strikers were arrested, and some were indicted for murder. Vigilantes roamed the countryside, terrorizing strikers and running them out of the county. One striker, folksinger Ella Mae Wiggins, was killed on September 14, 1929, in an attack on a group of strikers. Seven men were indicted for the murder but were found not guilty in the subsequent trial.

Railroad Strike of 1922

After the enactment of the Transportation Act of 1920, federal operation of the railroads, which had been implemented during World War I, was ended, and the Railroad Labor Board took its place. In essence, this made the federal government the only arbiter of labor and wage issues involving all railroads in the United States. The board's first action in July

1920 was to grant an increase of thirteen cents per hour to all railroad shop employees. Its next action less than a year later, however, essentially decreased wages. Extra pay for working weekends and holidays was also abolished, and some railroad lines began to contract out work to nonunionized companies, paying by the piece instead of an hourly wage. In May 1922, the board heeded the request of the railroad companies and instituted another wage cut. In response, the affected unions sent out over one million strike ballots. The vote was overwhelmingly in favor of a strike.

Railroad workers were organized along a craft union model instead of an industrial model, so only those workers that were affected by the wage cuts and other demanded concessions went on strike. To add to the woes of the affected workers, the leadership of the maintenance-of-way workers unions ignored the majority's vote to strike and merely asked the Railroad Labor Board for a rehearing. Meanwhile, the other 400,000 affected workers—all members of the various unions representing shop craftsmen—walked off the job in July 1922. Despite threats from the Railroad Labor Board to take away their seniority rights, the workers stayed out for three months. In what can only be called a complete surrender to the railroad magnates, federal judge James H. Wilkerson issued an injunction against the striking union members, their leaders, and their attorneys that forbade them from communicating in any way with fellow workers. Union meetings were barred, and unions were forbidden to use their strike funds to support the strike in any way. As a result, the affected unions were destroyed, close to half of the striking workers were deprived of independent union representation, and workers were forced to join company unions if they wanted to keep their jobs.

Coal War

The United Mine Workers of America (UMWA) was the strongest union in the United States in 1920. It had survived the attacks of the previous decade on the labor movement and increased its numerical and political strength exponentially. The federal government had taken over the administration of the industry during World War I and increased miners' wages across the board. In exchange, the unions had agreed not to strike until April 1, 1920. By this time, the wage increases provided during the war were insufficient to meet the rising living costs of the miners. Despite the agreement, 75,000 miners in Illinois disobeyed the instructions of the union leadership and went on strike anyway. The union responded by pulling the charters of twenty-five Illinois locals. In Kansas, a similar scenario prompted UMWA president John L. Lewis to discipline thirty-three locals there.

On May 1, 1920, a strike broke out in Mingo County, West Virginia. Of the over 92,000 soft-coal miners in West Virginia at the time, less than half were unionized. After the miners struck in Mingo, coal company operators called in private detectives from the Baldwin-Felts Detective Agency to evict striking miners from their company-owned homes. Police chief Sid Hatfield of Matewan, West Virginia, sympathized with the miners and tried to stop the Baldwin-Felts men from entering his town. A gun battle ensued. Both Albert and Lee Felts (the Felts of Baldwin-Felts) and four of their men were killed, along with the town mayor, a miner, and a young boy. The governor of West Virginia sent in state troops. Armed skirmishes continued throughout the summer. By this time, over 90 percent of the miners in the area had joined the union. After six people died in a gun battle on August 21, 1920, five hundred federal troops were sent into Mingo County. Legendary labor organizer Mary Harris "Mother" Jones joined the strikers. Meanwhile, the strike continued to spread throughout West Virginia and into Kentucky. Martial law was declared in Mingo County in the spring of 1921. On August 1, 1921, after being acquitted on charges relating to the deaths of Baldwin-Felts agents, Hatfield and Ed Chambers, another participant in the earlier shootout, were gunned down on the courthouse steps by Baldwin-Felts agents. On August 7, 1921, a rally was held in Charleston, West Virginia, protesting the killings. William Blizzard and Frank Keeney, UMWA militants, called on miners to fight. On August 24, 1921, thousands of miners began a march on the county seats of Logan and Mingo counties in West Virginia. After a relatively peaceful beginning, armed battles broke out among miners, national guardsmen, private detectives, and coal company vigilantes. After the union was told that the men could be charged with treason, Keeney urged the miners to return home. However, many stayed on after trains failed to pick them up as promised, and West Virginia state police killed two miners in a raid. On September 1, 1921, President Warren Harding sent in 2,100 federal troops. Although many miners

went home, many others remained and fought what became known to local residents as the Battle of Blair Mountain. Over 1,000 indictments were drawn up against the miners, including 325 for murder and 24 for treason. The only man who was convicted of treason skipped bail. William Blizzard, whom authorities considered the general of the miners' army, was eventually cleared of all charges, as were most of the rest of those indicted.

Impact

The ongoing attacks on the labor movement from industry and government during the early part of the twentieth century finally took their toll on union growth by the early 1920s. In addition, the increasing distance between the militancy of labor's rank-and-file and the conservatism of union leadership led to irreconcilable schisms within various unions, contributing to the overall decline in the numerical and bargaining strength of unions. Furthermore, the failure of the craft union model would lead labor activists to consider other strategies. The strikes of the 1920s and the lessons learned from them influenced the tactics and strategies of labor organizers in the following tumultuous decades, especially the 1930s.

Ron Jacobs

Further Reading

Blizzard, William C. *When Miners March*. Oakland, Calif.: PM Press, 2010. A collection of West Virginia labor newspaper articles on the 1920–1921 miners' strike in Mingo and Logan counties.

Dubofsky, Melvyn. *The State and Labor in Modern America*. Chapel Hill: University of North Carolina Press, 1994. Examines the history of labor, business, and the federal government from the 1870s through 1973 in the United States by decade.

Goldberg, David J. *Discontented America: The United States in the 1920s*. Baltimore: Johns Hopkins University Press, 1999. Challenges the myth of the so-called Roaring Twenties and the idea that all of the United States was a happy and harmonious place, also discussing the weakening of labor unions during the 1920s.

Huber, Patrick. "Mill Mother's Lament: Ella May Wiggins and the Gastonia Textile Strike of 1929." *Southern Cultures* 15, no. 3 (Fall, 2009): 81–110. A biographical sketch of folksinger and labor activist Ella May Higgins, who was killed by vigilantes during the 1929 Gastonia textile workers' strike.

Lens, Sidney. *The Labor Wars: From the Molly Maguires to the Sitdowns.* Garden City, N.Y.: Doubleday, 1973. A survey of U.S. labor history written by an eminent labor historian.

See also: American Federation of Labor (AFL); Haywood, Big Bill; Income and wages; Lewis, John L.; Palmer raids; Railway Labor Act of 1926; Unionism

■ La Follette, Robert M.

Identification: American politician
Born: June 14, 1855, Primrose, Wisconsin
Died: June 18, 1925, Washington, D.C.

A leading Progressive Party political leader who pioneered the direct primary election as a means of nominating party candidates for office, Robert Marion La Follette set a pattern for progressive politics. He developed the "Wisconsin Idea" of government serving a defined public interest through education, infrastructure development, public welfare promotion, protection of labor, and an open political process. La Follette's main goal was to protect Americans' rights from powerful individuals.

The 1920s marked the end of La Follette's long career as a political organizer, first within the Republican Party and then as leader of the Independent Progressive ticket. La Follette had first been elected to U.S. Congress in 1884, taking office as a thirty-year-old. He was a vigorous supporter of the Interstate Commerce Act and the Sherman Antitrust Act, and an early exponent of Native American and African American rights.

From 1901 to 1917, La Follette's reform program had been backed by a loosely defined coalition of consumers and taxpayers. During the post–World War I period, La Follette fought the concentration of economic and political power that knit government agencies with commercial and industrial trusts during the war. La Follette found natural allies in the labor movement and rural organizations such as the Farmers' National Council, the Farmers' Union, the Grange, and the Equity Society. Industry had grown accustomed to the guaranteed profits of War Industries Board contracts, strongly critiqued by La Follette. In the 1920s, he fought to roll back these new monopolistic habits, while business interests fought to keep them.

Robert M. La Follette. (Getty Images)

Conservation and Public Resources
La Follette aligned with conservationists Gifford Pinchot and Harry Slattery to oppose legislation authorizing long-term leases for minerals and for building dams to harness waterpower. He was able to filibuster both bills in 1919, but in 1920, the Mineral Leasing and Water Power acts were both approved by U.S. Congress and signed by President Warren G. Harding.

La Follette had sought the Republican nomination for president in 1912. In 1920, both the newly formed Labor Party and former supporters of Theodore Roosevelt's 1912 Progressive Party wanted to nominate La Follette for president; however, he declined because his supporters could not agree on a common platform.

Opposition to World War I and Labor Support
La Follette and his family had been socially ostracized in 1917, when he opposed U.S. entry into World War I on the side of Great Britain, France, Italy, and Russia. Nevertheless, he won Wisconsin's Republican

presidential primary in 1920. When he ran for Senate reelection in 1922, aides urged him to tone down calls for investigation of war profiteers and to moderate the language of his public appearances. La Follette made no efforts to hide his perspective on World War I, but he won the Republican Party primary with 72 percent of the vote, then swept the general election with 80 percent.

In 1924, he ran for president on the independent Progressive Party ticket, with Democratic senator Burton K. Wheeler of Montana running for vice president. Their ticket was endorsed by the American Federation of Labor (AFL) and secured the votes of many western populists as well as many brands of reform politics. Advocating a public referendum on questions of war and peace, legal protection for collective bargaining, and public ownership of railroads and water resources, La Follette and Wheeler received 4,831,706 votes, amounting to 16.61 percent of the popular total, and they secured Wisconsin's 13 electoral votes. The Progressive Party was not even listed on the ballot in most southern states. La Follette placed third in the election, behind Republican incumbent Calvin Coolidge and Democratic candidate John W. Davis. La Follette died less than a year later.

Impact

Wisconsin's progressive tradition served as a model for electoral reform, education, regulatory commissions, progressive income tax, and consumer protection in many other states. At the end of the decade, *La Follette's Weekly Magazine,* founded by the politician in 1909, became *The Progressive.* Following La Follette's death, his son Robert La Follette Jr. received an interim appointment to the vacant Senate seat, winning three more elections. The independent Progressive Party dominated Wisconsin politics until Robert Jr. sought to return to the Republican Party in 1946, losing the party primary to former judge Joseph R. McCarthy. Thereafter, Wisconsin Progressives, including young La Follette family members, took over the Democratic Party, serving as attorney general and secretary of state.

Charles A. Rosenberg

Further Reading

Fowler, Robert Booth. *Wisconsin Votes: An Electoral History.* Vol. 3. Madison: University of Wisconsin Press, 2008. Presents a history of Wisconsin voting, noting the impact of ethnicity and religious belief on elections, also discussing La Follette's political legacy.

La Follette, Robert M. *La Follette's Autobiography: A Personal Narrative of Political Experiences.* Madison: University of Wisconsin Press, 1960. Covers the politician's career through 1912, offering a helpful introduction to La Follette's work in the 1920s.

Thelen, David P. *Robert M. La Follette and the Insurgent Spirit.* Madison: University of Wisconsin Press, 1976. Focuses on the Progressive movement, insurgency, and La Follette's life and work.

Unger, Nancy C. *Fighting Bob La Follette: The Righteous Reformer.* Chapel Hill: University of North Carolina Press, 2000. Moves from a focus on La Follette's private life to a discussion of his public and political persona, documenting his career as governor and senator.

Weisberger, Bernard A. *The La Follettes of Wisconsin: Love and Politics in Progressive America.* Madison: University of Wisconsin Press, 1994. Discusses the political and activist careers of the entire La Follette family, including Robert's wife and children, focusing on their commitment to political ideals.

See also: Civil rights and liberties; Elections of 1924, U.S.; Farm subsidies; Foreign policy, U.S.; Progressive Party of 1924; Railway Labor Act of 1926; Unionism; Voting rights

---

■ Landis, Kenesaw Mountain

Identification: American commissioner of major-league baseball
Born: November 20, 1866, Millville, Ohio
Died: November 25, 1944, Chicago, Illinois

In November 1920, as an unfolding gambling scandal rocked major-league baseball, Kenesaw Mountain Landis assumed the newly created position of commissioner and restored the sport's image. His banning of the eight Chicago baseball players involved in the "Black Sox" scandal in 1921 helped the sport become more popular after World War I.

As the federal district judge for northern Illinois, Kenesaw Mountain Landis had attracted national attention when he presided over the trials of the Standard Oil Company of Indiana in 1907 and members of the radical Industrial Workers of the World (IWW) in 1918. Major-league baseball appreciated Landis's individualism when he repeatedly postponed ruling on an antimonopoly suit by the Federal League in 1915. The delay doomed the Federal League's chances of survival.

Suffering under an ineffective three-person commission, American and National League team owners approached Landis with an offer to become an impartial arbiter in a new organizational structure. On November 12, 1920, Landis accepted the position of commissioner empowered to protect baseball's interests. His first action was to disregard a jury's verdict of innocence for eight members of the Chicago White Sox who had been accused of taking bribes to lose the 1919 World Series to the Cincinnati Reds. The appearance of guilt was sufficient for Landis to ban "Shoeless Joe" Jackson and seven other players from baseball for life. Landis also banished several other players in the 1920s who had been accused of bribery, forcing baseball team owners to divest themselves of gambling operations. Often criticized for his authoritarian approach, Landis had many defenders who praised his cleansing of baseball's reputation.

Landis's defense of the reserve clause, by which a baseball player was bound to one team until he was traded or retired, quieted labor unrest at the players' expense. When Branch Rickey, general manager of the St. Louis Cardinals, created a farm system to control minor-league teams for player development, Landis vigorously objected. This battle Landis lost, but he continued to defend the freedom of movement of players below the major-league level.

Impact

While his authoritarian style remains controversial, Landis brought order to baseball at a critical time. Elevating the game above corruption and encouraging financial stability, Landis allowed such talented players as Babe Ruth, Rogers Hornsby, and Lou Gehrig to cement baseball as the nation's favorite pastime. Landis's active management proved essential for the difficult Depression and war years that followed, and he was inducted into the Baseball Hall of Fame shortly after his death.

M. Philip Lucas

Further Reading

Burk, Robert F. *Much More Than a Game: Players, Owners, and American Baseball Since 1921*. Chapel Hill: University of North Carolina Press, 2001.
Carney, Gene. *Burying the Black Sox: How Baseball's Cover-up of the 1919 World Series Fix Almost Succeeded*. Washington, D.C.: Potomac Books, 2006.
Pietrusza, David. *Judge and Jury: The Life and Times of Judge Kenesaw Mountain Landis*. South Bend, Ind.: Diamond Communications, 1998.

See also: Alexander, Grover Cleveland; Baseball; Cobb, Ty; Gehrig, Lou; Grove, Lefty; Hornsby, Rogers; New York Yankees; Ott, Mel; Ruth, Babe; Sports

■ Lang, Eddie

American musician
Also known as: Salvatore Massaro; Blind Willie Dunn
Born: October 25, 1902, Philadelphia, Pennsylvania
Died: March 26, 1933, New York City, New York

Eddie Lang, the first great jazz guitarist, established a new musical tradition by employing European string techniques in an improvisational setting. One of the most influential jazz artists of the 1920s, he developed what is now known as the modern guitar method.

Eddie Lang was born Salvatore Massaro, the youngest child of Italian American immigrants in Philadelphia. He inherited a love of music from his father, a guitarist and instrument maker, and studied the violin for over a decade. He also learned how to play guitar and the banjo and was playing all three instruments professionally by the age of sixteen. Early in his career, Massaro took the name of Eddie Lang, a local baseball player, as his stage name. He often played in duets or in larger groups with violinist Joe Venuti, a friend of his from school.

In 1923, Lang played banjo at his first recording session as a member of Charlie Kerr's orchestra. Eventually, he chose the guitar as his main instrument. He performed one of the first recorded jazz guitar solos in 1924, playing both rhythmic accompaniment and highly personalized melodic lines in "Deep Second Street Blues" by the Mound City Blue Blowers, a novelty group that used the human voice and a kazoo to imitate the inflections of jazz trumpet.

Lang's career continued to blossom throughout the 1920s. Based in New York City, he performed and recorded with some of the most important jazz and blues artists of the decade, including guitarist Lonnie Johnson (with whom Lang appeared under the pseudonym Blind Willie Dunn), singer Bessie Smith, trumpeter Louis Armstrong, saxophonist Frankie Trumbauer, and cornetist Bix Beiderbecke. He also continued to perform with his old school friend Joe Venuti.

Lang's career was tragically cut short by his death in 1933 at the age of thirty. He died as a result of unknown complications during a tonsillectomy, which he had intended to improve his voice for speaking roles in films with his friend Bing Crosby.

Impact

Lang is regarded by many as the father of jazz guitar. It was largely due to his influence that the archtop guitar replaced the banjo in jazz, and his work with violinist Venuti had a direct influence on iconic jazz musicians Django Reinhardt and Stéphane Grappelli during the 1930s. Lang's memory continues to be honored with musical events such as the annual Eddie Lang Jazz Festival in his ancestral hometown of Monteroduni, Italy, and Eddie Lang Day in Philadelphia.

John E. Myers

Further Reading

Mairants, Ivor. *The Great Jazz Guitarists, Part 1: The First Jazz Age.* London: Sanctuary, 2001.

Mazzoletti, Adriano. *Eddie Lang: Stringin' the Blues.* Rome: Pantheon, 1997.

Mitchell, Raymond F. *Feeling My Way: A Discography of the Recordings of Eddie Lang, 1923–1933.* Godalming, England: Raymond F. Mitchell, 2002.

See also: Armstrong, Louis; Beiderbecke, Bix; Carmichael, Hoagy; Crosby, Bing; Jazz; Smith, Bessie; Talking motion pictures; Whiteman, Paul

■ Langdon, Harry

Identification: American comedian
Born: June 15, 1884, Council Bluffs, Iowa
Died: December 22, 1944, Los Angeles, California

Known primarily for his ability to pantomime, Harry Langdon transitioned from vaudeville into silent films during the 1920s, producing numerous short and feature-length comedies. Frequently portraying a childlike character whose innocence resulted in misunderstanding and trouble, Langdon proved to be very popular with audiences of the decade.

Harry Langdon. (Moviepix/Getty Images)

Harry Philmore Langdon began his career in show business as a teenager, joining a traveling show and developing an act that he later performed alongside his first wife, Rose. Transitioning from vaudeville into film, Langdon signed with Sol Lesser's Principal Pictures in 1923 and appeared in a series of two-reel silent shorts. The company experienced financial difficulties by the end of the year, and Langdon was released from his contract. However, his skill in portraying a baby-faced innocent had come to the attention of comedy director and producer Mack Sennett, who signed Langdon to a contract.

Langdon rose to fame under Sennett's tutelage, appearing in a series of two- and three-reel comedies in 1924 and 1925, most notably *The First Hundred Years* (1924), *The Luck o' The Foolish* (1924), and *Plain Clothes* (1925). In such films, Langdon always portrayed a naïve, harmless character who never seemed able to avoid conflict in his life. This character was popular with audiences and differentiated Langdon from rival comedians such as Buster Keaton, Harold Lloyd, and Charlie Chaplin.

In 1926, Langdon established his own studio, the

Harry Langdon Corporation, and partnered with the distributor and studio First National Pictures. He went on to make a series of films with writer and director Frank Capra, including *Tramp, Tramp, Tramp* (1926), *The Strong Man* (1926), and *Long Pants* (1927). However, he had a falling-out with Capra during the filming of *Long Pants* and ended their successful relationship by firing him.

Following his break with Capra, Langdon began to direct his own silent films, which were generally unsuccessful. In 1929, Langdon attempted to resurrect his career by signing with producer Hal Roach for a series of short sound films, which also proved unsuccessful.

Impact

While Harry Langdon's style of comedy was not ideal for the new era of talkies, he continued to appear in films throughout the 1930s and early 1940s, typically working with smaller studios such as Columbia Pictures. In 1960, Langdon was posthumously honored with a star in the Hollywood Walk of Fame.

Richard Adler

Further Reading

Everson, William. *American Silent Film.* New York: Da Capo Press, 1998.

Schelly, William. *Harry Langdon: His Life and Films.* 2d ed. Jefferson, N.C.: McFarland, 2008.

Slide, Anthony. *Silent Players: A Biographical and Autobiographical Study of One Hundred Silent Film Actors and Actresses.* Lexington: University of Kentucky Press, 2002.

See also: Chaplin, Charlie; Film; Keaton, Buster; Lloyd, Harold; Talking motion pictures; Vaudeville

■ Langley, John W.

Identification: American politician
Born: January 14, 1868, Floyd County, Kentucky
Died: January 17, 1932, Pikeville, Kentucky

John W. Langley represented the state of Kentucky in the U.S. House of Representatives from 1907 to 1926. He was forced to resign from the House after being convicted in 1924 for conspiracy to transport and sell whiskey in violation of the Eighteenth Amendment and the 1919 National Prohibition Act.

John Wesley Langley, a lawyer, served as a member of the Kentucky House of Representatives during the late nineteenth century before ascending to the U.S. House in 1906. He served several consecutive terms as a Republican and became the chairman of the Committee on Public Buildings and Grounds. However, in 1920, the Eighteenth Amendment and the National Prohibition Act, also known as the Volstead Act, went into effect and prohibited the production, transportation, and sale of alcoholic beverages. The following year, Langley allegedly became involved in a plan to illegally transport fourteen hundred cases of whiskey from the Belle of Anderson distillery just outside of Lawrenceburg, Kentucky, under false pretenses. The alcohol, intended to be for medicinal use, would then be sold for consumption. When the plan was uncovered, Langley was accused of attempting to use his political office to pressure the federal prohibitions director for Kentucky, Sam Collins, into issuing a permit for the transportation of the alcohol.

During the 1924 trial, Collins testified that Langley threatened to destroy him politically if he did not grant the permit, and the other alleged conspirators testified that they had paid Langley to exercise his political influence. Langley was alleged to have a large sum of money in his possession, far exceeding his salary as a public servant, that he could not explain. Although Langley took the stand in his own defense and denied any wrongdoing, he was convicted in May 1924, along with those who had attempted to obtain the illicit whiskey. Langley was sentenced to two years in prison and served eleven months in an Atlanta penitentiary before being paroled in December 1926.

Having resigned from his position in the House, Langley resumed his legal career in Kentucky after his release. His wife, Katherine Gudger Langley, was elected to fill his vacated position and served two terms. Langley was pardoned by U.S. president Calvin Coolidge in 1928, but he continued to assert his innocence throughout the remainder of the decade. In 1929, he published a book, *They Tried to Crucify Me*, in a further attempt to clear his name.

Impact

The controversy surrounding John W. Langley reflected the overall controversy about alcohol consumption in the United States. As Langley's case indicated, there continued to be a market for alcohol despite Prohibition, and legal restrictions contributed to an increase in organized crime and related political corruption. These factors ultimately led to the repeal of Prohibition in 1933.

Camille Gibson

Further Reading

Behr, Edward. *Prohibition: Thirteen Years that Changed America.* New York: Arcade, 2011.

Langley, John W. *They Tried to Crucify Me; Or, The Smoke-Screen of the Cumberlands.* Pikeville, Ky.: Author, 1929.

See also: Crimes and scandals; Organized crime; Prohibition

■ Lardner, Ring

Identification: American writer
Born: March 6, 1885, Niles, Michigan
Died: September 25, 1933, East Hampton, New York

A prolific writer of the 1920s, Ring Lardner was known for works ranging from short stories and newspaper articles to stage plays and films. His distinctive use of vernacular language and satire made his work, particularly his baseball writing, popular with readers of the decade.

Ringgold Wilmer Lardner began his career as a sports reporter in the early twentieth century, writing about baseball and other sports for several newspapers. He began to write fiction during the mid-1910s, publishing sports-related works such as *You Know Me Al* and *The Real Dope*, collections of epistolary stories originally published in the *Saturday Evening Post.* In 1919, Lardner became disillusioned with major-league baseball following the "Black Sox" scandal, wherein eight members of the Chicago White Sox were found guilty for conspiring with gamblers to fix the World Series. Nevertheless, he continued to write about sports and other topics throughout the 1920s, which became his most productive and successful decade.

Short Fiction and Nonfiction

Though he would never abandon the theme of sport and play in his writing completely, Lardner began to write more serious literary works in the 1920s, delving into diverse themes such as family life, marriage, and affluence, drawing on difficulties in his own personal

Ring Lardner. (Gamma-Keystone via Getty Images)

life. In addition to reporting on such major sporting events as the Dempsey-Carpentier boxing match of 1921, Lardner published *The Young Immigrunts* (1920), a sardonic book based on a road trip he took with his family and written from the point of view of his young son, and a collection of short stories, *The Big Town* (1921). In 1922, Lardner published a nonfiction piece titled "Sport and Play," in which he challenged Americans to go outdoors and participate in sports, rather than just be spectators. That same year, Lardner published the short story "The Golden Honeymoon" in *Cosmopolitan.* These and other achievements earned Lardner high accolades from contemporary writers, most notably his friend F. Scott Fitzgerald, whose influence led Lardner into the next phase of his literary career.

In 1924, Fitzgerald asked his editor at Charles Scribner's Sons, Maxwell Perkins, to consider publishing a collection of Lardner's short stories, many of which had appeared in various major magazines.

Perkins agreed, and *How to Write Short Stories (With Samples)* was published later that year. The collection included such stories as "Champion," a tale of a ruthless boxer; "Alibi Ike," about a baseball player given the titular nickname due to his habit of constantly making excuses; and "Some Like Them Cold," about the oftentimes bizarre relationships between men and women. As Fitzgerald had hoped, the collection succeeded in showcasing Lardner as a serious author capable of writing about a wide range of themes not limited to sports. Another collection of short fiction, *The Love Nest and Other Stories*, was published in 1926. This collection included the stories "Haircut" and "A Day with Conrad Green," both of which would come to be widely anthologized. The last collection of fiction to be published in his lifetime, *Round-Up* (1929), collected many of his best-known stories as well as a number of previously uncollected works.

Theater and Film

Lardner's other creative interests included film and stage plays, and he experimented with both forms during the decade. He composed a baseball skit, starring cowboy and vaudeville star Will Rogers, for the popular Ziegfeld Follies in 1922. Other Lardner stage plays included *Elmer the Great* in 1928 and *June Moon* (1929), both based on his own short stories. *June Moon* experienced a moderately successful run on Broadway and would go on to be revived several times in later decades. Lardner broke into the film industry as well during the 1920s, contributing to various films such as *The New Klondike* (1926) and *Fast Company* (1929), based on *Elmer the Great*.

Impact

Lardner's realistic style and satirical humor continued to be popular into the 1930s, and his short fiction and sports articles continued being collected and published in the decades following his death. Some stories went on to become films, including "Champion," which was adapted into a 1949 feature starring Kirk Douglas. For his contributions to the field of baseball writing, Lardner was awarded the J. G. Taylor Spink Award in 1963.

Robert Paul Moreira

Further Reading

Fitzgerald, F. Scott. "Ring." *The New Republic*, October 11, 1933. A eulogy exploring Lardner's legacy.
Lardner, Ring. *Letters of Ring Lardner*. Edited by Clif-ford M. Caruthers. Alexandria, Va.: Orchises Press, 1995. Presents Lardner's letters to his family, friends, and publishers.
Lardner, Ring. *Ring Around the Bases: The Complete Baseball Stories of Ring Lardner*. Edited by Matthew J. Bruccoli. Columbia: University of South Carolina Press, 1992. Includes Lardner's baseball stories as well as a biographical introduction by Bruccoli.
Robinson, Douglas. *Ring Lardner and the Other*. New York: Oxford University Press, 1992. Critiques Lardner's writing in the context of its relation to the philosophical concept of the Other.
Yardley, Jonathan. *Ring: A Biography of Ring Lardner*. Reprint. Lanham, Md.: Rowman & Littlefield, 2001. Details Lardner's life and career from his early life until his death.

See also: Baseball; Fitzgerald, F. Scott; Literature in the United States

---

■ Lasky, Jesse L.

Identification: American film producer
Born: September 13, 1880, San Francisco, California
Died: January 13, 1958, Beverly Hills, California

Jesse Lasky was one of the original movie moguls, whose company was responsible for establishing Hollywood as the center of the motion picture industry.

Jesse Louis Lasky Sr. began his show business career as a vaudeville performer and later producer in New York City. In 1913, excited by the new medium of motion pictures, Lasky partnered with his brother-in-law, Samuel Goldwyn, and his friend and stage director Cecil B. DeMille to form the Jesse L. Lasky Feature Play Company. They moved the operation from New York to California, establishing a studio in a barn in the quiet village of Hollywood, California. In 1914, Lasky's company released *The Squaw Man*, DeMille's first film and the first feature-length film shot in Hollywood. In 1916, the company merged with Adolph Zukor's Famous Players Film Company to form Famous Players-Lasky, with Zukor as president and Lasky as vice president in charge of production.

Famous Players-Lasky produced some of the most important films of the silent era, launching the spectacular career of DeMille, among others, and helping establish Hollywood's star system. Famous Players-

Lasky also pioneered the practice of vertical integration in the film industry, operating film studios as well as buying up theater chains in order to control both production and distribution. Among the company's more notable films was DeMille's 1923 epic *The Ten Commandments*; produced despite Lasky's concerns about cost, the film was the sort of lavish spectacle for which DeMille would come to be known. It was expensive, but it became the studio's crowning achievement of the 1920s. Not long afterward, DeMille left the company after establishing a studio of his own, but he and Lasky remained good friends. Lasky continued to produce films throughout the 1920s, becoming one of the thirty-six founders of the Academy of Motion Picture Arts and Sciences in 1927. Early in the 1930s, Famous Players-Lasky became Paramount Pictures, and Lasky left, involving himself in other film production enterprises into the 1950s.

Impact
Jesse Lasky was a pioneer in the motion picture industry and a key player along with Zukor in shaping what would become Paramount Pictures, the oldest American film studio still operating. The Hollywood barn where *The Squaw Man* was filmed was designated a state historic landmark in 1956; now called the Lasky-DeMille barn, it is home to the Hollywood Heritage Museum.

Patrick Adcock

Further Reading
Birchard, Robert S. *Cecil B. DeMille's Hollywood.* Lexington: University Press of Kentucky, 2004.
Lasky, Jesse Louis. *I Blow My Own Horn.* Garden City, N.Y.: Doubleday, 1957.
Lasky, Jesse L., Jr., and Pat Silver. *The Offer.* Garden City, N.Y.: Doubleday, 1981.

See also: Academy Awards; DeMille, Cecil B.; Film; Goldwyn, Samuel; Metro-Goldwyn-Mayer (MGM); *Ten Commandments, The*

■ Latin America and the Caribbean

When the United States faced multiple problems and economic opportunities in Latin America and the Caribbean during the 1920s, President Woodrow Wilson's ideals of universal democracy and self-determination for all nations were either abandoned or dramatically bent. The three Republican presidents of the decade would employ both direct military intervention and regional law enforcement to protect American interests in the United States' backyard.

World War I brought home the threat of imperial Germany's presence in Latin America, prompting the United States to safeguard the region by increasing its military presence. The Mexican Revolution, which began in 1910, had taught U.S. presidents that chaos in Latin America and the Caribbean could reach the borders of the United States. Since the so-called ABC powers (Argentina, Brazil, and Chile) retained much of their national sovereignty, U.S. military intervention stayed closer to home.

Between the American occupation of Cuba in 1906 and the withdrawal of Marines from Nicaragua in 1928, the United States made fifty armed incursions into Central America and the Caribbean. Starting in 1912, American troops occupied Nicaragua, ostensibly to settle a civil war; however, many Nicaraguans felt the real reason was to protect the U.S.-built and -owned Panama Canal, opened in 1914. Panama itself was split in two by both the canal and the American-leased Canal Zone. American soldiers landed in Honduras in 1924, and again the following year, to protect the interests of the United Fruit Company from local trade unions. The U.S. occupation of Haiti entered its second decade in the 1920s, largely at the behest of the National City Bank of New York, which demanded that the country float a huge foreign loan to pay back its debts. The Dominican Republic saw the U.S. Marines depart in 1924, but not before the American government had placed a lien on the country's revenue until its debts to the United States and several European nations had been paid off. In Cuba, the last American troops stationed there since the end of the American protectorate (1898–1902) withdrew to Guantanamo Bay Naval Base, legally owned by the United States in perpetuity, in 1922, but the hated Platt Amendment to the Cuban Constitution that granted the United States the right to intervene militarily in the island's affairs remained in place.

American Support for Dictators
Following the withdrawal of American troops from several Caribbean and Central American nations, the United States maintained influence over their domestic affairs via proxy rulers or local constables.

U.S. Occupies Haiti

The U.S. occupation of Haiti began in July 1915 following the assassination of the president of Haiti. U.S. president Woodrow Wilson sent the Marines into Haiti to restore order and protect American interests. The United States formulated the Haitian-American Treaty of 1915, in which the United States was given the right to intervene in Haiti at any time and control the economy of Haiti. The occupation lasted from 1915 until 1934, when President Franklin D. Roosevelt withdrew the last of the Marines from the island nation. The lasting impact of U.S. supervision of the Haitian economy was that the majority of domestic societal issues in Haiti were ignored in order to reduce the country's debts, leaving Haiti without many of the social structures it needed to support and improve the lives of its people.

Nicaragua proved an exemplary case. President Calvin Coolidge sent diplomatic envoy Henry L. Stimson to broker a deal with acting president José Moncada: The exit of U.S. Marines from the country would be followed by elections supervised by the United States and the creation of an American-trained National Guard, thereby maintaining the peace and assuring U.S. investors of a stable political climate. Much the same pattern was pursued in the Dominican Republic, where a national police force took over security from the Marines. American forces had carefully groomed a young Dominican officer, Rafael Trujillo, to take command of the police force and transform it into an army, which paved the way for him to seize power in 1930 in a coup supported by U.S. sugar interests.

In nearby Cuba, the political situation proved more difficult for the United States to manipulate. President Mario García Menocal, in office from 1912 to 1920, facilitated the takeover of most Cuban sugar estates by U.S. firms, but his corrupt administration and frequent attempts to rig elections earned him the displeasure of Washington. When Menocal's successor, Gerardo Machado, took power in 1925, he proved even more favorable to Wall Street, granting U.S. businesses concessions not only in sugar but in electricity, transportation, and banking as well. However, his increasingly authoritarian rule and unconstitutional reelection to a six-year term in 1929, combined with the Wall Street crash of that year, signaled a parting of the ways between him and the adminis-

tration of Herbert Hoover, as Cuba drifted toward civil war.

U.S. Economic Penetration
The near-cessation of trade by Great Britain, France, and Germany with Latin America during World War I allowed the United States to push its economic rivals out of the region and turn many local economies into virtual American company towns. In Guatemala during the 1920s, United Fruit was not only the single largest landowner in the country but also its biggest corporate employer. Dictators came and went, but United Fruit's grip remained as strong as ever, to the point that Guatemalan intellectuals and nationalist politicians referred to the company as "The Octopus."

Other nations in Latin America managed to flex some economic muscle, even while U.S. investment continued to pour in. The Mexican Constitution of 1917 granted the nation full sovereignty over its subsoil, but during the 1920s the bulk of oil production remained in the hands of U.S. firms. However, the government of President Plutarco Calles forced them to pay higher royalties and sign a pledge that they would demand no more oil concessions unless authorized by the Mexican government. Brazilian coffee and Argentinian beef, respectively the largest source of wealth for each nation, remained under the control of local landowners, but exportation was geared almost exclusively toward the United States rather than cash-strapped Great Britain, a major prewar trade partner. American imports, from automobiles to ladies' fashions, were much sought after by a small but growing Latin American middle class. This dependence on sales to and imports from the United States undermined the nominal independence of many nations of Latin America and the Caribbean during the American economic boom of the 1920s, and the stock market crash of 1929 decimated economic growth from Cuba to Chile.

Latin American Nationalism
By the 1920s, the United States had to accept that the Mexican Revolution of 1910 could not be reversed, only tamed and contained. General John Pershing's failed 1916 expedition to capture Mexican revolutionary Pancho Villa was the United States' last at-

tempt to use military force to sway the outcome of the revolution; afterward, diplomacy proved a more useful tool. The election of Álvaro Obregón as president in 1920 smoothed relations between the two countries, as the former general used his executive powers to put down the last armed revolts inside Mexico. His successor, Plutarco Elías Calles, pleased the United States with a more pro-business economic policy, but a brutal battle between the Catholic Church and the government over anticlerical legislation rattled U.S.-Mexico relations until American ambassador Dwight Morrow arranged a compromise between the two parties in 1929.

While revolution was winding down in Mexico, another was starting in Nicaragua. General Augusto Sandino and a small faction of the Liberal Party had refused the 1927 deal whereby U.S. forces would exit the country in return for recognition of José Moncada as president. When Sandino and his followers took to the hills and launched a campaign of guerrilla warfare against Moncada, the U.S government sent thousands more Marines to track him down, and the United States was once again at war in Central America. The successful revolution in Mexico, insurrection in Nicaragua, and partial U.S. military withdrawal from Cuba and the Dominican Republic laid the basis for a new kind of Latin American nationalism, from the rabid anti-Americanism of Sandino to the anti-imperialist, though not quite anti-American, version espoused by Brazil's Luís Carlos Prestes and Peru's Víctor Haya de la Torre.

Impact

The withdrawal of most American troops from the Caribbean and Central America during the 1920s meant that the United States had to substitute local constables to maintain political order and protect U.S. businesses. In 1928, the State Department announced that the United States would no longer react militarily to political instability in the region. The Monroe Doctrine would only be invoked in case of an external threat to U.S. lives and property in the Western Hemisphere, a timely and prophetic decree in light of the looming danger posed by Nazi Germany in the following decade.

Julio César Pino

Further Reading

Brewer, Stewart. *Borders and Bridges: A History of U.S.-Latin American Relations.* Westport, Conn.: Praeger Security International, 2006. Examines how American rhetoric about defending democracy in Latin America often clashes with the need to protect U.S. security and economic interests.

Brown, Jonathan C. *Oil and Revolution in Mexico.* Berkeley: University of California Press, 1993. Discusses the most contentious issue in U.S.-Mexico relations during the 1920s, ownership of Mexican petroleum production.

Delpar, Helen. *The Enormous Vogue of Things Mexican: Cultural Relations Between the United States and Mexico, 1920–1935.* Tuscaloosa: University of Alabama Press, 1992. Studies the complex and at times conflicting relationship of the United States and Mexico via film, art, and other cultural imports and exports.

Dosal, Paul J. *Doing Business with the Dictators: A Political History of United Fruit in Guatemala, 1899–1944.* Wilmington, Del.: SR Books, 1993. Dissects how United Fruit became a state within a state in Guatemala, controlling U.S. policy toward Central America.

Hernandez, Jose M. *Cuba and the United States: Interventionism and Militarism, 1868–1933.* Austin: University of Texas Press, 1993. A critical look at how U.S. military intervention in Cuba has fed Cuban anti-Americanism.

Schmidt, Hans. *The United States Occupation of Haiti, 1915–1934.* 2d ed. New Brunswick, N.J.: Rutgers University Press, 1995. Explores why American efforts to bring stability and democracy to Haiti proved unsuccessful.

See also: Coolidge, Calvin; Foreign policy, U.S.; Harding, Warren G.; Hoover, Herbert; Mexico; Wilson, Woodrow

■ Latinos

Latinos played a significant role in the United States during the 1920s, with the country experiencing an increase in Latino immigration that would continue throughout the century. Through contributions to the agricultural and industrial sectors, as well as achievements in athletics and the arts, the Latino population significantly shaped the United States throughout the decade.

It was not until 1930 that the United States Census first counted a segment of the country's Latino population, recording the presence of 1.4 million Mexicans. Therefore, no reliable or thorough information exists about the demographics of this group during the 1920s, although the 1930 census notes that an estimated 700,000 Mexicans had been classified as white in the census of 1920. What is known is that most Latinos living in the United States during the 1920s were Mexican Americans, many of whom lived in southwestern areas that had formerly been part of Mexico, or newly arrived Mexican immigrants. A smaller portion of this population was made up of Spanish-speaking Caribbean immigrants, particularly from Puerto Rico and Cuba, who began arriving in the United States in the aftermath of the 1898 Spanish-American War and subsequent U.S. interventions in the region. These newcomers would establish themselves not only in the traditional Latino strongholds of the Southwest, but also in the industrial centers and farming communities of the Midwest and the East Coast, expanding the distribution of Latino communities nationwide.

Immigration and Migration

Several factors contributed to the increased migration of Mexican nationals to the United States in the 1920s. The need for workers during World War I and the postwar years prompted the recruitment of immigrant labor for agriculture, mining, construction, railroad work, and manufacturing. The Immigration Act of 1917 barred citizens of most Asian countries from immigrating but did not place restrictions on Mexicans or other Latinos. With no head taxes or literacy restrictions in place, these immigrants quickly replaced Asians as the main source of cheap foreign labor, especially in the agricultural field. The more restrictive Immigration Act of 1924 further limited immigration from Asia and southern and eastern Europe, but it did not affect immigration from Latin America. In addition, violent political upheaval was prevalent in Mexico during the 1920s, pushing many to seek employment in the United States.

Because of geographic proximity, U.S. employers and authorities saw Mexicans as transient workers who would eventually return to Mexico and would not alter the American racial, cultural, or social character. However, many of these immigrants stayed in the United States permanently. Between 1920 and 1930, the combined number of Mexican Americans and Mexican-born individuals living in the United States increased to more than one million. A signifi-

cant portion of this population lived in California by the end of the decade, but Mexicans also established important communities in cities such as Chicago, New York, and St. Louis. Despite this, the 1920s also posed obstacles to Latino migration at times. The recession of 1921 led to mass deportations, while the market crash of 1929 and the advent of stricter laws impeded further Mexican immigration.

Puerto Rican migration to the mainland United States during the 1920s was aided by the 1917 Jones-Shafroth Act, which granted U.S. citizenship to all Puerto Ricans. The restrictions placed on immigration from Asia and Europe increased the availability of jobs for Puerto Ricans and further drove migration to the mainland, where New York City became the nucleus of this community. Immigration from Cuba also increased in the 1920s as a result of political instability earlier in the century.

Labor and Civil Rights

Perceptions of Latinos as temporary workers often deprived them of legal, social, and political protections, leading to discriminatory practices based on the racial ideology of the time. Mexican agricultural workers seldom had access to medical care, and their living conditions were far below average. Wages were also lower, with Mexican workers receiving far less than Americans of European descent. Mexicans were also banned from joining most labor unions, as white union members feared these workers might take their jobs. The Ku Klux Klan vigorously persecuted Mexican American workers in the Southwest, and the Texas Rangers, who had fought Mexicans and Mexican Americans on numerous occasions in the previous decade, continued to harass these communities. The creation of the U.S. Border Patrol in 1924 exacerbated the hostile relations between immigrants and authorities.

In spite of low wages and transience, some Latinos succeeded in establishing homes and sending their children to school in the United States. However, access to education remained a major hurdle for both citizens and recent immigrants. In Texas, for example, 40 percent of school-aged Mexican Americans did not have access to education during the 1927–1928 school year. Other issues facing Latinos included the ability to participate in local, state, and federal politics. Would-be voters experienced disenfranchisement due to poll taxes and other methods similar to those used against African Americans. Interference by groups such as the White Man's Primary Association, which worked to maintain white political dominance, further hindered Latino political participation.

To combat adversity and discrimination, Latinos formed *mutualistas*, or mutual aid societies, and established labor unions. The *mutualistas* played a key role in Latino communities, providing support to families during difficult times and often assuming the role of unions. One such *mutualista* developed into the Imperial Valley Workers Union in 1928 and carried out a strike that same year. Other important groups were the Orden Hijos de America, or the Order of Sons of America (OSA), founded in 1921, and the Confederación de Uniones Obreras Mexicanas (CUOM), or the Confederation of Mexican Labor Unions, founded in 1928. These organizations fought for such causes as wage parity, educational equality, and desegregation. The League of United Latin American Citizens (LULAC), which would become the largest Latino civil rights and advocacy group, was founded in 1929. Some Latino workers also managed to join preexisting unions such as the United Mine Workers of America (UMWA), which banned racial and ethnic discrimination in its constitution.

Arts and Popular Culture

A few Latinos achieved popularity in the media, arts, and popular culture of the 1920s. Light-skinned Latino actors such as Mexican-born Ramón Novarro, Dolores Del Río, Gilbert Roland, and Lupe Vélez achieved Hollywood prominence during the era, most often cast as passionate "Latin lover" types in silent films and early sound films. Latino athletes also began to break through during this time. Cuban-born chess player José Raúl Capablanca reigned as world champion from 1921 to 1927, competing in national and international tournaments. Cuba also produced successful baseball players during the decade, including pitcher Adolfo "Dolf" Luque, who played for the whites-only Cincinnati Reds throughout the decade. Meanwhile, fellow Cuban player Martín Dihigo excelled in the Negro Leagues, becoming one of the first Latino players inducted into the National Baseball Hall of Fame.

Impact

Throughout the 1920s, Latinos established a legacy of labor organization and political mobilization that would continue into the next century, producing in-

fluential leaders such as labor and civil rights activist César Chavez. The emerging presence of Latino artists and athletes during this time would also pave the way for the increased participation of Latinos in the arts and popular culture of the United States.

Mauricio Espinoza-Quesada

Further Reading

De León, Arnoldo. *Mexican Americans in Texas: A Brief History.* 3d ed. Wheeling, Ill.: Harlan Davidson, 2009. Provides a comprehensive view of the historical developments affecting one of the largest Latino populations in the United States.

Guerin-Gonzales, Camille. *Mexican Workers and American Dreams: Immigration, Repatriation, and California Farm Labor, 1900–1939.* New Brunswick, N.J.: Rutgers University Press, 1994. Recounts the history of Mexican workers in California and discusses participation in organized labor and the effects of immigration policies.

Ochoa, George. *Atlas of Hispanic-American History.* New York: Facts on File, 2001. A concise yet informative history of Latinos in the United States since Spanish settlement.

Sánchez, George J. *Becoming Mexican American: Ethnicity, Culture, and Identity in Chicano Los Angeles, 1900–1945.* New York: Oxford University Press, 1993. Analyzes identity formation and the Americanization of Mexican Americans.

Sánchez Korrol, Virginia. *From Colonia to Community: The History of Puerto Ricans in New York City, 1917–1948.* Westport, Conn.: Greenwood Press, 1983. Traces the origins and developments of Puerto Rican immigration to the East Coast, as well as settlement and cultural patterns.

See also: Border Patrol, U.S.; Capablanca, José Raúl; Immigration Act of 1921; Immigration Act of 1924; Immigration to the United States; Latin America and the Caribbean; League of United Latin American Citizens; Novarro, Ramón; Racial discrimination

■ Laurel and Hardy

Also known as: Stan and Ollie; The Boys

Officially teamed by motion picture producer Hal Roach in 1927, actors Stan Laurel and Oliver Hardy became a sensation as a comedic duo. They were the first long-running

comedic collaboration to become successful in the twentieth-century Hollywood motion picture industry, enjoying popularity well into the 1930s and 1940s.

Before they were contracted to collaborate with the Hal Roach motion picture studio in 1926, British actor Stan Laurel and American actor Oliver Hardy were already successful comedic entertainers in their own right, having performed individually in many silent films by the mid-1920s. They first appeared together in the motion picture *The Lucky Dog* (1921), but they first starred as an official double act in the 1927 short film *Putting Pants on Philip.*

Similarly to their contemporary comedians Charlie Chaplin and Buster Keaton, Laurel and Hardy performed visual, slapstick comedy, although they developed a unique style in their motion pictures. Their costuming emphasized the contrast in their height and build: Laurel, who was smaller, wore a loose-fitting blazer, while the taller and larger Hardy wore a jacket that was much too tight on him. They both wore bowler hats and dressed their hair to comic effect. One common element of their act was reciprocal property destruction, in which the two parties involved in a dispute would vandalize each other's belongings in an escalating conflict; a later Laurel and Hardy film was even titled *Tit for Tat* (1935). Further gags and thematic motifs in the team's films include pie fights, mud battles, tensions with neighbors, and marital frustrations.

Transition to Sound

Several of Laurel and Hardy's best short films, including *The Battle of the Century* (1927), *You're Darn Tootin'* (1928), *Two Tars* (1928), *Liberty* (1929), and *Big Business* (1929), which costars their frequent collaborator, Scottish comic James Finlayson, were produced during the waning days of the silent film era. While performing in the "talking" two-reel short films Roach released through the Metro-Goldwyn-Mayer (MGM) film studio prior to the end of 1929, the team demonstrated a nearly effortless transition into the new medium of talking pictures. Unlike other comics of the silent era who either refused to work with dialogue (Charlie Chaplin) or became obsolete (Buster Keaton and Harry Langdon), Laurel and Hardy, along with comedian W. C. Fields, became even more successful because of the new technology. Filmgoers had known that Stan and Ollie were amazing pantomimes, but they now

Laurel and Hardy. (Getty Images)

realized that the duo also possessed fine speaking voices and acting abilities.

Although they chose to use the possibilities that sound offered, Laurel and Hardy did not alter their comic style. They still relied on visual technique, using dialogue only when necessary. Since they rarely relied on verbal jokes, but instead stressed sight gags and unorthodox psychological behavior, they made the transition to sound with very few problems. Their motion picture *Unaccustomed As We Are* (1929), costarring actors Edgar Kennedy and Thelma Todd and released in both silent and sound versions, was followed by the film *Double Whoopee* (1929), costarring a very young Jean Harlow. Other Laurel and Hardy pictures included *The Perfect Day* (1929), a study in familial chaos, and *The Hoose-Gow*, in which Laurel and Hardy must perform hard labor while serving jail time. The comedy duo also released five other twenty-minute shorts prior to the close of 1929, as well as dozens of feature-length motion pictures in the 1930s and 1940s.

Impact

Laurel and Hardy excelled into the 1930s, producing many more popular two-reel short films and several successful feature films before the end of the decade. The Stan and Ollie characters, unlike the straightforward clowns that comprised later comedy teams such as the Three Stooges, are richly textured individuals with fully developed personalities. Their worldwide influence has been enormous, and many of their gags, primarily invented by Stan Laurel, were "borrowed" by the likes of later comedic duos Bud Abbott and Lou Costello, Dean Martin and Jerry Lewis, and Jackie Gleason and Art Carney over the ensuing decades. Laurel and Hardy's films, particularly several of their classic two-reelers made during the late 1920s, rank among the twentieth century's cinematic masterpieces.

Scott Allen Nollen

Further Reading

Barr, Charles. *Laurel and Hardy.* Berkeley, California: University of California Press, 1974. Provides an insightful psychological analysis of the characters portrayed by Stan Laurel and Oliver Hardy. Includes illustrations.

Louvish, Simon. *Stan and Ollie, The Roots of Comedy: The Double Life of Laurel and Hardy.* New York: St. Martin's Press, 2002. Focuses on the personal lives of the Laurel and Hardy comedy team.

McCabe, John. *Mr. Laurel and Mr. Hardy: An Affectionate Biography.* London: Robson Books, 2003. First published in 1961, this biography includes reminiscences from Stan Laurel, Oliver Hardy, and their colleagues.

Nollen, Scott Allen. *The Boys: The Cinematic World of Laurel and Hardy.* Jefferson, N.C.: McFarland, 2000. Includes brief biographies of Laurel and Hardy, a critical analysis of their films, and an annotated filmography providing a rating for each title.

Skretvedt, Randy, and Jordan R. Young. *Laurel and Hardy: The Magic Behind the Movies.* Beverly Hills, Calif.: Past Times, 1996. Presents a chronological discussion of the comedic duo's motion pictures, with a special focus on what made many of their feature films less popular than their highly improvised two-reel short films.

See also: Chaplin, Charlie; Film; Keaton, Buster; Langdon, Harry; Metro-Goldwyn-Mayer (MGM); Roach, Hal, Sr.; Talking motion pictures

■ League of Nations

Identification: International peacekeeping organization

Date: Established on January 10, 1920

Created in the ashes of World War I, the League of Nations was an attempt to lessen the likelihood of war in the future. It was the first worldwide peacekeeping organization, but it was hindered by the national interests of some world powers and by the nonparticipation of others.

The League of Nations was created by the Paris Peace Conference in 1919 and was an integral part of the Treaty of Versailles that officially ended World War I for most nations. However, efforts to prevent future war can be traced back another century to the Congress of Vienna (1814–1815), which ended the Napoleonic Wars in Europe and produced the Concert of Europe, in which the major powers agreed to use arbitration to solve disputes before going to war.

Organization and Purpose

The Hague Conferences of 1899 and 1907 had attempted to prevent such a war as World War I from taking place. The horrors of that war intensified the desire and efforts to preserve international peace. Of the four major leaders who met in Paris in January 1919, the most idealistic was U.S. president Woodrow Wilson. Of his Fourteen Points, issued a year earlier, the one he fought the hardest to secure was for a world peacekeeping organization. The other leaders, Georges Clemenceau of France, David Lloyd-George of Great Britain, and Vittorio Orlando of Italy, agreed with the need for such an organization but had less idealistic expectations.

When the Treaty of Versailles was signed on June 28, 1919, one of the major provisions was for the establishment of the League of Nations. It came into existence on January 10, 1920, with its headquarters in Geneva, Switzerland. The headquarters building, the Palace of Nations, was completed around 1937 and was the gift of American business executive John D. Rockefeller Jr.

By 1923, fifty-three nations had joined the League. Germany, which had been deliberately left out, was allowed to join in 1926. The Soviet Union was originally excluded because of its connection to communism, but it joined in 1934. Ironically, the one major world power that never joined the League was the

United States, although a U.S. president had been its first major advocate. Opposition to the League, led by Senator Henry Cabot Lodge, resulted in the rejection of the Treaty of Versailles by the U.S. Senate, which meant League membership for the United States was impossible at the time; isolationist sentiment continued to prevent membership attempts in the future.

The League Covenant established four major bodies with the League. All member nations had equal representation in the Assembly. The Council, which had the most power, originally had four permanent members—Great Britain, France, Italy, and Japan—plus four nonpermanent members elected by the Assembly. The International Court of Justice adjudicated legal questions that were submitted to it, and the Secretariat handled administrative and civil service responsibilities.

The League of Nations was not designed to guarantee a war-free future for the world but to create a process to handle disputes in such a way as to lessen the chance of war. It provided at least three months of arbitration, during which the international conflicts involved might cool down. If a legal question was involved, the court would pass judgment, and if one nation did not accept the decision, economic sanctions could be applied. However, a major weakness for the League was that the French proposal for a League army was rejected, so no military action could be taken to enforce decisions.

Impact

The League of Nations enjoyed some success in solving disputes involving smaller nations. In 1925, a dispute between Greece and Bulgaria was peacefully resolved, as was one between Hungary and Yugoslavia in 1935. The League also left a lasting legacy by granting mandates to help develop new nations. With the breakup of the Ottoman Empire by the Treaty of Versailles, Great Britain was granted mandates for Palestine and Iraq, while France was given Syria and Lebanon. The British mandate for Palestine led to the establishment of Israel after World War II.

Attempts to bolster the League, such as the Washington Naval Conference in 1922 and the Kellogg-Briand Pact of 1928, did little to improve its chances of success.

The League's major failures came when the national interests of major powers were involved. Attempts to sanction Japan after its invasion of Manchuria in 1931 led to the Japanese withdrawal from the League in 1933. Germany also withdrew in 1933 after the rise of Adolf Hitler and the beginning of Nazi aggressive actions. Italy invaded Ethiopia in 1935 and withdrew from the League in 1937. With the German invasion of Poland in 1939, the official beginning of World War II, the League ceased to function. After World War II, in April 1946, the League of Nations was officially dissolved, having been replaced by the United Nations.

Glenn L. Swygart

Further Reading

Burkman, Thomas. *Japan and the League of Nations: Empire and World Order, 1914–1938*. Honolulu: University of Hawaii Press, 2008. Covers Japan's role at the Paris Conference in 1919, the country's involvement in League activities, and the crisis over the Japanese invasion of Manchuria in 1931.

Blanning, Timothy C. W., ed. *Oxford Illustrated History of Modern Europe*. New York: Oxford University Press, 2001. An analysis of the League of Nations, its role in disarmament attempts after World War I, and the failure of those attempts, including photographs of major world leaders of the time.

Davis, Kathryn W. *The Soviets at Geneva: The U.S.S.R. and the League of Nations, 1919–1933*. Westport, Conn.: Hyperion Press, 1977. Details the Soviet involvement in League issues, such as prisoner exchanges, medical work, and labor issues, until the Soviet Union joined the League of Nations in 1933.

Palmer, R. R., and Joel Colton. *A History of the Modern World*. New York: A. A. Knopf, 1965. Puts the League of Nations in the total context of World War I, the Paris Conference, the Treaty of Versailles, and international peace endeavors.

Van Ginneken, Anique H. M. *Historical Dictionary of the League of Nations*. Lanham, Md.: Scarecrow Press, 2006. Discusses the League Covenant, providing a list of members, leaders, budgets, and other basic information.

See also: Dawes Plan; Europe; Foreign policy, U.S.; Kellogg-Briand Pact of 1928; Lodge, Henry Cabot; Washington Naval Conference; Wilson, Woodrow

■ League of United Latin American Citizens

Also known as: LULAC
Identification: Latino American civil rights organization
Date: Founded in 1929.

The League of United Latin American Citizens (LULAC) was the first Mexican American civil rights organization in the United States. It sought acceptance and acculturation for naturalized Mexican Americans, although it rejected immigrant Mexicans because they reinforced the negative stereotype held by many Americans.

Latinos have a long history in the United States. When one-third of Mexico became part of the United States after the Mexican-American war, the 77,000 Mexicans in the annexed territory became Americans but were soon subjected to abuse, discrimination, and the denial of their civil rights. In the 1910s and 1920s, perhaps 90 percent of Mexican immigrants to the United States lacked significant education. Many Mexican Americans were denied the opportunity to learn English and thus could not vote. Public facilities were off limits, as were restaurants and other privately owned facilities. Mexican American immigrants and citizens alike formed mutual aid and other cooperative groups to provide what the dominant society denied them.

After welcoming 73,000 Mexicans to the U.S. workforce during World War I, the United States government restricted Mexican immigration in the 1920s. About 500,000 Mexican nationals and Mexican Americans were deported. Mexican Americans, however, became more prosperous, educated, and urban, and they abandoned cooperative groups, attempting to assimilate to the dominant American culture.

After two years of negotiation, Ben Garza of Corpus Christi, Texas, brought together three Mexican American organizations to form LULAC on February 7, 1929. The organization quickly grew beyond Texas to the rest of the Southwest and eventually had chapters in forty-eight states, Latin America, and Germany. LULAC members were predominantly middle-class Mexican American men who sought to become model Americans. They replaced the old American-based Mexican middle class with an ethnically intentional Mexican American one. Members took their citizenship duties seriously and were highly patriotic. They were also strongly anti-immigrant. The 1927 convention at Harlingen that predated the organization's formal establishment was indicative of the stance LULAC took: The Mexican American minority argued that only U.S. citizens should be members, at which point the immigrant majority left the meeting.

LULAC advocated conservative positions, including hard work, capitalism, individualism, and Americanism. The organization also emphasized American values, choosing the American flag as its official flag and the song "America the Beautiful" as its official song.

Impact

For some LULAC members, Mexican immigrants threatened economic competition. More importantly, because dominant American society tended to stereotype both immigrant Mexicans and naturalized or native-born Mexican Americans as lazy, LULAC's industrious Americanized members backed immigration restriction. LULAC's goal of inclusion was meant for assimilated Mexican Americans only.

John H. Barnhill

Further Reading

Gutiérrez, David G. *Walls and Mirrors: Mexican Americans, Mexican Immigrants, and the Politics of Ethnicity.* Berkeley: University of California Press, 1995.

Montejano, David. *Anglos and Mexicans in the Making of Texas, 1836–1986.* Austin: University of Texas Press, 1987.

Orozco, Cynthia E. *No Mexicans, Women, or Dogs Allowed: The Rise of the Mexican American Civil Rights Movement.* Austin: University of Texas Press, 2009.

See also: Immigration to the United States; Latin America and the Caribbean; Latinos; Mexico

■ League of Women Voters

Also known as: National League of Women Voters
Identification: A nonpartisan volunteer women's organization encouraging women's voting and awareness of political developments
Date: Founded on February 14, 1920

Since its inception, the League of Women Voters has worked to end gender discrimination against women, an agenda

that it advances in a nonpartisan manner. The formation of the league was considered the end of a seventy-two-year women's suffrage movement and the introduction of women into active political participation.

The National League of Women Voters was founded by women's suffrage activist Carrie Chapman Catt to represent the twenty million potential women voters given electoral rights in the Nineteenth Amendment in 1920. (The organization dropped the word "national" from its name in 1946.) The league was an offshoot of the National American Women's Suffrage Association (NAWSA). In fact, the league's informal launch occurred at the NAWSA's 1919 convention in St. Louis, Missouri, when Catt presented her idea for the organization. Its official launch was February 14, 1920, in Chicago, six months before the ratification of the Nineteenth Amendment gave women the right to vote. Maud Wood Park from Massachusetts became the league's first president, though Catt had helped establish the league based on her experiences with the NAWSA. Other women activists involved in the league's formation included Jane Addams, Florence Allen, Mary E. McDowell, Julia Lathrop of Chicago, and Mable Kittredge of New York. A number of men also supported the league's establishment and mission. Catt reportedly hoped that the need for the league might end in about five years, by which time she expected women's impact on established political parties to adequately reflect the female agenda and voice. This did not occur, however, and the league continues to exist in the twenty-first century.

The League of Women Voters developed a structure similar to NAWSA and, more broadly, the United States government, in that the national office brought together affiliated state and local leagues. State league leaders or delegates would then elect the national officers. Communication within the group was facilitated by the NAWSA's popular suffrage publication *Woman Citizen*, known as *Women's Journal* prior to 1920.

The League's Agenda in the 1920s

League of Women Voters president Park advanced the league's agenda for the 1920s despite varying perspectives on how to balance gender equality with protections for women. While women had made substantial economic gains during World War I, their social status as a gender had not improved by the 1920s.

The league used local town surveys and meetings with political candidates as important mechanisms in crafting an agenda. Among the 1920s league agenda items were improved rights for married women, as well as support for women's education, public health, employment, safe working conditions, and minimum wage. Other issues on the league's agenda included child welfare, child labor laws, community improvement, reasonable home prices, morality, human rights, world peace, civic education, improved partisan communication, and voter drives. Working against gender discrimination in the workforce was a priority, as many women who took jobs during the war were being forced to return to domestic work within the home. Many women were relegated to low-skilled, low-pay service and assembly-line work, which many men thought was suitable for "less capable" woman workers. Nevertheless, by the 1920s, increasing numbers of women graduated from college, some even pursuing advanced degrees. Their activism within the league represented an effort to use their intellectual enlightenment for the broader good.

The league's first legislative success was the Sheppard-Towner Maternity and Infancy Protection Act, signed on November 23, 1921, by President Warren G. Harding. It provided over $2.7 million for child care and maternal assistance, which was in fact relatively little when compared to other government provisions of the 1920s. League member Julia Lathrop championed the act with the endorsement of Democratic senator Morris Sheppard, Republican representative Horace Mann Towner, and various political organizations. The law's passage seemed to result in improved prenatal care and decreased infant mortality; nevertheless, it ended in 1929 when Congress did not renew its funding.

Another league victory in the 1920s was the Voigt Act, or "Filled Milk Act," of March 4, 1923, which prohibited the interstate sale of skimmed milk filled with coconut oil as whole milk. In 1920, the Women's Bureau was established in the U.S. Department of Labor, marking another step toward fulfilling the league's workforce agenda.

Obstacles to Activism

Women's political activity slowed after the early victory of women's suffrage in the 1920s. Despite the league's arduous efforts, voter turnout among women

League of Women Voters poster urging women to vote. (Getty Images)

while keeping the league's agenda nonpartisan. Nevertheless, the league was instrumental in getting women elected to state office during this period.

Impact

The efforts of the League of Women Voters in the 1920s helped institute federal social welfare programs through grassroots activism, public education, service learning, and political collaboration. The league's impact reflects its early broad mission to include both male and female political education and to diminish discrimination against women. League of Women Voters chapters still operate in every state, and its credo of "nonpartisan, but political" continues.

Camille Gibson

Further Reading

Andersen, Kristi. *After Suffrage: Women in Partisan and Electoral Politics Before the New Deal.* Chicago: University of Chicago Press, 1996. Recounts the victories and struggles of women in politics after the passing of women's suffrage.

Baker, Paula. "The Domestication of Politics: Women and American Political Society, 1780–1920." *American Historical Review* 89, no. 3 (June, 1984): 620–647. Discusses women's advancements in American politics.

Lemons, J. Stanley. "The Sheppard-Towner Act: Progressivism in the 1920s." *Journal of American History* 55, no. 4 (March, 1969): 776–786. An overview of the Sheppard-Towner Maternity and Infancy Protection Act, including a discussion of its relation to the Progressive movement of the 1920s.

Sharer, Wendy B. *Vote and Voice: Women's Organizations and Political Literacy, 1915–1930.* Carbondale: Southern Illinois University Press, 2004. Analyzes women's political discourse from the early twentieth century.

Stienstra, Deborah. *Women's Movements and International Organizations.* New York: St. Martin's Press, 1994. Explores historical women's initiatives, with particular focus on their influence in the League of Nations and United Nations.

See also: Civil rights and liberties; Elections of 1920, U.S.; Income and wages; Sheppard-Towner Act of 1921; Unemployment; Women in the workforce; Women's rights

remained low during the decade. Some historians attribute this to the insincere gestures of inclusion by the major political parties and their perpetuation of strong racist and patriarchal politics. Within the political parties, men removed assertive women from committees, replacing them with less vocal women. The league was also influenced by feminists such as Anne Martin, who thought that women should be more independent of established political parties, which were unlikely to advance a solid female agenda. Catt's anti-immigrant views, whereby she argued that illiterate male immigrants were a social threat, diminished the league's potential impact in the 1920s. It was also difficult to encourage party participation

■ Leopold-Loeb murder case

The Case: Illinois Circuit Court case involving murderers Nathan Leopold and Richard Loeb
Date: Decided on September 19, 1924

The Leopold-Loeb murder case was largely argued on psychological grounds and led to the increasing use of "alienists" (psychiatrists) as witnesses in criminal cases.

On May 21, 1924, on the south side of Chicago, Illinois, Nathan Freudenthal Leopold Jr., age nineteen, and Richard Loeb, age eighteen, kidnapped fourteen-year-old Bobbie Franks by luring him into a rented automobile. The boy died after being struck on the head with a chisel. The murderers buried the body in a railway culvert and then demanded a ransom of $10,000. However, Franks's body was soon discovered. Leopold had lost his eyeglasses near the railway culvert, and the rented car was easily traced. Loeb, the dominant member of the pair, contacted reporters to offer theories about the crime. The boys immediately became suspects, were soon arrested, and confessed to the murder.

The Motive
Both young men were born to wealth and were academic prodigies. Loeb graduated from the University of Michigan at age seventeen, Leopold from the University of Chicago at eighteen. They had reportedly been reading Russian novelist Fyodor Dostoyevsky's *Crime and Punishment* (1866), the story of a poor but brilliant university student who murders an old pawnbroker for her money. The protagonist believes that he will experience no remorse over what he has done, but he is tortured by guilt until he confesses. Leopold and Loeb decided they would experience no such guilt, so they planned a similar crime to test their theory. The plotters chose a victim who belonged to their families' social group. The press popularized the notion that the boys had killed for the thrill of it, giving the case nationwide notoriety.

The Trial
The Leopold-Loeb trial was held over a period of thirty-three days in July and August of 1924. Public opinion was solidly against the defendants, who were rich, Jewish, and homosexual. Having pled guilty, they were given a bench trial presided over by Circuit Court judge John R. Caverly in Cook County, Illinois.

Leopold's father hired Clarence Seward Darrow as defense attorney; Darrow had a national reputation as a labor and criminal lawyer, although he was more associated with defending lower-class clients than children of privilege. He argued that Leopold acted only out of his psychological and sexual submission to Loeb's dominant personality. Darrow also argued that Loeb's aggressive behavior was the result of his upbringing, especially his childhood exposure to a demanding governess. Darrow made extensive use of alienists (as psychiatrists were then called), who testified as to the Freudian explanations for the defendants' actions. The prosecution responded by securing its own alienists. Darrow attacked societal attitudes and gave an impassioned and eloquent denunciation of capital punishment as his summation. After more than a month of courtroom drama, the boys were sentenced to life imprisonment plus ninety-nine years. That the judge spared their lives was viewed as a significant victory for Darrow.

The Aftermath
The convicted killers were sent to separate institutions at the Illinois State Penitentiary but were eventually reunited in the Stateville prison near Joliet. Leopold was a model prisoner. He was paroled March 13, 1958, on condition that he work as a technician in the Puerto Rican hospital that had agreed to take him and that he would never return to the continental United States. He married on February 5, 1961, was granted complete freedom on March 16, 1963, and died of a heart attack in 1971. On January 28, 1936, Loeb's cellmate James Day killed him in the shower with a straight razor. Day was acquitted on the grounds that he was defending himself against Loeb's sexual advances. Darrow went on to complete his career as a talented defense attorney.

Impact
The Leopold-Loeb trial had a significant effect on jurisprudence and the popular culture. It led to the greater use of psychiatric testimony and furnished a blueprint for defense attorneys to follow in pressing mitigating psychological factors without pleading insanity.

The case popularized the term "thrill killer" and inspired several creative works. In 1928, *Rope*, a stage play by Patrick Hamilton, featured two brilliant young thrill killers. Twenty years later, Canadian actor Hume Cronyn adapted the play as a motion picture, starring actor James Stewart and directed by Alfred Hitchcock. In 1956, Meyer Levin published *Compulsion*, a documentary novel based upon the case. Even though he was not identified by name, Leopold sued the author for $1.5 million, but Levin won the case on First Amendment grounds. *Compulsion* was adapted as a play in 1957 and as a motion picture in 1959. In that production, actor Orson Welles plays Jonathan Wilk, the Clarence Darrow character. "Teen Thrill Killers," produced by A&E television in 2005, prominently features newsreel footage from the Leopold-Loeb trial and is testimony to the continuing interest in the case.

Patrick Adcock

Further Reading

Higdon, Hal. *Leopold and Loeb: The Crime of the Century*. Urbana: University of Illinois Press, 1999. Reflects on the reasons why, despite all the mass murders since, this remains the "crime of the century."

Leopold, Nathan Freundenthal, Jr. *Life Plus Ninety-Nine Years*. New York: Doubleday, 1958. Presents the consequences of the crime and its punishment from the murderers' point of view.

Levin, Meyer. *Compulsion*. New York: Simon & Schuster, 1956. Although framed as a novel, the book is fact-based and is one of the best studies of the Leopold-Loeb murder case.

Payment, Simone. *The Trial of Leopold and Loeb: A Primary Source Account*. New York: Rosen, 2004. A summary of what has been written about the sensational trial.

Rompalske, Dorothy. "Leopold and Loeb: The Murder That Shocked a Nation." *Biography* 6, no. 10 (October, 2002): 26–27. A printed adaptation of the entry from the A&E biographical television series.

See also: Crimes and scandals; Darrow, Clarence; Homosexuality and gay rights; Jews in the United States; Newspapers, U.S.; "Roaring Twenties"

■ Lewis, John L.

Identification: American labor leader
Born: February 12, 1880, Cleveland, Iowa
Died: June 11, 1969, Washington, D.C.

As the president of the United Mine Workers of America (UMWA) and through his leadership within the American Federation of Labor (AFL), John L. Lewis was one of the most powerful U.S. labor leaders of the 1920s.

By 1897, at the age of seventeen, John Llewellyn Lewis had joined his father in the mines, and in 1901, he began traveling throughout the western United States to work in silver, copper, gold, and coal mines. In 1906, Lewis was elected as a delegate to the national convention of the United Mine Workers of America (UMWA), at the time the largest union affiliated with the American Federation of Labor (AFL). In 1909, Lewis settled in Illinois with his wife and children and was appointed state legislative representative for District 12 of the UMWA. It was in this position that he successfully lobbied to pass mine safety and workers' compensation legislation for the state of Illinois. In 1911, Samuel Gompers, founder and president of the AFL, appointed Lewis national legislative representative for the AFL, and in 1917, Lewis was elected vice president of the UMWA. After organizing a mine-operators strike in 1919 and working directly with President Woodrow Wilson to negotiate union demands, Lewis was elected president of the UMWA in 1920, a position he would hold until his retirement in 1960.

Throughout the 1920s, Lewis fought tirelessly for higher wages and improved working conditions for miners amid difficult times in the coal industry. As post–World War I demand for coal declined and more than three thousand mines closed during the 1920s, membership in the UMWA plummeted. Lewis offered several recommendations to boost coal profitability and to secure miners' jobs, including the use of mechanization in the mines to increase efficiency and thereby save jobs. Several union members, angered by the belief that more jobs would be lost to machines, tried unsuccessfully to unseat Lewis in 1930.

Impact

During his forty years as president of the UMWA, John L. Lewis transformed the coal industry by fighting to dramatically increase wages, improve working conditions in the mines, and pass federal safety regulations. Through these efforts and his founding of the Congress of Industrial Organizations (CIO) in 1935, Lewis helped to establish a firm and lasting base for industrial unionization in the United States.

Bernadette Zbicki Heiney

Further Reading

Alinsky, Saul. *John L. Lewis: An Unauthorized Biography.* Whitefish, Mont.: Kessinger, 2007.

Dubofsky, Melvyn, and Warren R. Van Tine. *John L. Lewis: A Biography.* Urbana: University of Illinois Press, 1986.

Zieger, Robert H. *John L. Lewis: Labor Leader.* Boston: Twayne, 1988.

See also: American Federation of Labor (AFL); Coolidge, Calvin; Gompers, Samuel; Income and wages; Labor strikes; Unionism

---

■ Lewis, Sinclair

Identification: American novelist and Nobel laureate
Also known as: Harry Sinclair Lewis
Born: February 7, 1885, Sauk Centre, Minnesota
Died: January 10, 1951, Rome, Italy

Sinclair Lewis's satirical look at American life earned him recognition throughout the 1920s. His novel Arrowsmith *was chosen for the 1925 Pulitzer Prize, which he turned down, and in 1930, he was nominated for and accepted the Nobel Prize for Literature.*

Sinclair Lewis. (Getty Images)

The son of physician and a teacher, Harry Sinclair Lewis earned a bachelor's degree from Yale University in 1908. After graduation, he worked as a reporter, a junior editor, and an advertising manager while honing his craft as a novelist. His first publication, a children's book titled *Hike and the Aeroplane*, was published in 1912. Lewis followed this work with several novels of mild success, including *Our Mr. Wrenn* (1914) and *Free Air* (1919). During this time, he also established himself as a writer of short stories, often contributing to the *Saturday Evening Post.*

Lewis's personal life was somewhat tumultuous. In 1914, Lewis married Grace Livingston Hegger, with whom he had one son, Wells, born in 1917. The marriage ended in divorce in 1928 following a lengthy separation. Later that same year, Lewis married journalist Dorothy Thompson; their marriage would also produce one child and end in divorce.

Best Sellers and Prizes

In 1920, Lewis published his break-out work, *Main Street*, in which he satirically depicts idyllic, small-town America as being small-minded and prejudiced. The novel quickly became a best seller, and Lewis found himself atop the literary world, receiving fan mail from such renowned authors of the time as F. Scott Fitzgerald and Sherwood Anderson. Many reviewers, however, felt the book unfair to the current perception of wholesome and forthright communities dotting the countryside. Although initially recommended for the Pulitzer Prize in Literature for 1921, the award went to Edith Wharton for her novel *The Age of Innocence*. Many believed that *Main Street* did not win due to its controversial subject matter and what some believed to be an unfair take on small-town life.

Lewis's next work, the best-selling novel *Babbitt* (1922), was another satirical attack on society and kept the author in the spotlight. Many critics perceived Lewis's depiction of a businessman with questionable morals and the related themes of hypocrisy and conformity in business as anti-American. Lewis was once again surrounded by controversy and scorned by many. In 1923, his work was again nominated for the Pulitzer Prize, but this time lost to Willa Cather's World War I novel *One of Ours*.

Lewis's next novel, *Arrowsmith* (1925), explored and satirized the medical profession through the eyes of an idealistic physician, and for this work, Lewis was awarded the Pulitzer Prize in 1926, but he refused the prize publicly. Some felt this was a ploy to garner publicity. Others believed Lewis was still bitter from his previous two losses.

Before the decade ended, Lewis published four more novels: *Mantrap* (1926), *Elmer Gantry* (1927), *The Man Who Knew Coolidge* (1928), and *Dodsworth* (1929). While each brought a share of success and criticism, *Dodsworth* became Lewis's greatest literary achievement, earning him the 1930 Noble Prize for Literature.

Although the award was a great honor, many critics felt that the Nobel Prize committee, composed of mainly European academics, awarded the prize to Lewis because of his negative depictions of the United States. Also, many questioned Lewis's refusal of the Pulitzer Prize several years earlier. Nonetheless, Lewis accepted the award but titled his required Nobel lecture "The American Fear of Literature."

Impact

Sinclair Lewis's satirical depictions of American life and clever character development have solidified his place in literary history. While the 1920s saw Lewis garner two Pulitzer Prize nominations, his crowning moment came in 1930 as the first U.S. citizen to win the Nobel Prize for Literature for his 1929 novel *Dodsworth*. Many of Lewis's books continue to find audiences, with such works as *Main Street, Babbitt, Elmer Gantry,* and *Dodsworth* still in print in the twenty-first century.

Michael Cummings

Further Reading

Grebstein, Sheldon Norman. *Sinclair Lewis.* New York: Twayne, 1962. A biography providing detail to Lewis's writings. Each chapter provides an analysis of Lewis's career, with a focus on the 1920s.

Hutchisson, James M. *The Rise of Sinclair Lewis, 1920–1930.* University Park: Pennsylvania State University Press, 1997. Examines components involved in the creation and publication of *Main Street, Babbitt, Arrowsmith,* and *Elmer Gantry,* including the roles of publishers, assistants, and wives in the final versions of each novel.

Lewis, Sinclair. *Minnesota Diary, 1942–46.* Edited by George Killough. Moscow: University of Idaho Press, 2000. Lewis's diary entries during the mid-1940s revealing his inner thoughts and connections to rural Minnesota life.

_____. *"Main Street" and "Babbitt."* New York: Literary Classics of the United States, 1992. The two novels are taken from first-edition reprints. Includes background information on each novel's inception and subsequent publishing and printing, as well as a chronology of Lewis's life and notes for each novel.

Lingeman, Richard. *Sinclair Lewis: Rebel from Main Street.* St. Paul, Minn.: Borealis Books, 2005. A biography drawing on previously uncovered correspondence, diaries, and criticism.

Lundquist, J. *Sinclair Lewis.* New York: Frederick Ungar, 1973. Examines Lewis's writing style as a popular novelist and explores Lewis's viewpoint on the popular perception of American life versus his depiction of it in his work.

Schorer, Mark. *Sinclair Lewis: An American Life.* New York: Dell, 1961. A complete biography of Lewis's life and career.

See also: Anderson, Sherwood; *Babbitt;* Cather, Willa; *Elmer Gantry;* Fitzgerald, F. Scott; Literature in the United States; *Main Street;* Nobel Prizes; Wharton, Edith

■ Lincoln Memorial

The Lincoln Memorial, located on the National Mall in Washington, D.C., was constructed to honor Abraham Lincoln, the sixteenth president of the United States. In the years since its dedication in 1922, the monument has also become a symbolic setting for social and political gatherings.

President Abraham Lincoln was assassinated on April 14, 1865. Plans for a memorial began as early as 1867 when Congress formed the Lincoln Monument Association, but due to a lack of funding, the project was abandoned. In 1901, during the federally funded city improvement and expansion project, a site for the memorial was chosen. Soon after, architect Henry Bacon's Greek temple design was approved, and construction began in 1914 with a budget of $2 million.

The memorial has thirty-six exterior Doric columns, which represent the twenty-five union and eleven seceded states at the time of Lincoln's death. Each state name is inscribed above the columns.

Inscribed into an upper roof structure are the names of the forty-eight states at the time of the memorial's construction. A plaque was later added to commemorate the admission of Alaska and Hawaii as states.

The entire memorial is made from granite, marble, and limestone from across the United States, with the marble statue of a seated Abraham Lincoln in the center. Initially designed to be twelve feet tall, the sculpture was increased to nineteen feet so as not to be out of proportion with the surrounding building. Designed by Daniel Chester French, the statue is composed of twenty-eight pieces of Georgia marble and sits on a marble pedestal that is ten feet high and sixteen feet wide. Lincoln's Gettysburg Address is inscribed on the southern wall of the building beneath the Jules Guerin mural *Emancipation*. Lincoln's second inaugural address is inscribed on the northern wall with *Unification*, another Guerin mural, above it.

The Lincoln Memorial was dedicated on Memorial Day, May 30, 1922, by President Warren G. Harding, with Lincoln's only surviving son, Robert Todd Lincoln, in the audience.

Impact

Since its dedication, the Lincoln Memorial has come to represent more than a tribute to U.S. president Abraham Lincoln. It has been the setting of numerous speeches and rallies and has become a symbol of civil rights and free speech. When African American opera singer Marian Anderson was denied use of Constitution Hall in 1939 because of her race, she instead performed in front of the Lincoln Memorial to a crowd of thousands, and her performance was broadcast over the radio to millions more. The Lincoln Memorial was also the site of Martin Luther King's "I Have A Dream" speech on August 28, 1963. A marker identifies the step he stood on while delivering the speech.

Jennifer L. Campbell

Further Reading

Ashabranner, Brent K., and Jennifer Ashabranner. *No Better Hope: What the Lincoln Memorial Means to America.* Brookfield, Conn.: Twenty-First Century Books, 2001.

Thomas, Christopher A. *The Lincoln Memorial and American Life.* Princeton, N.J.: Princeton University Press, 2002.

See also: Architecture; Mount Rushmore; National Parks of the United States

■ Lindbergh, Charles

Identification: American aviator
Also known as: Lone Eagle; Lucky Lindy
Born: February 4, 1902, Detroit, Michigan
Died: August 26, 1974, Maui, Hawaii

Charles Lindbergh began his aviation career as a barnstormer (stunt pilot) during the 1920s flying-circus phenomenon. In 1927, he became internationally known as the first pilot to successfully complete a nonstop solo transatlantic flight, which dramatically affected the course of aviation technology and commercial air travel.

Charles Augustus Lindbergh was born in Detroit, Michigan, on February 4, 1902, to Charles Lindbergh Sr., a lawyer and congressman, and Evangeline Lindbergh, a science teacher. Raised in Little Falls, Minnesota, Lindbergh showed an early aptitude for mechanics, and at eighteen he entered the University of Wisconsin to study mechanical engineering. He left the university after three semesters to begin flight training at the Nebraska Aircraft Corporation in Lincoln, Nebraska. After buying a surplus World War I Curtiss "Jenny" airplane, Lindbergh spent the next two summers as an airplane mechanic and a stunt pilot on the barnstormer circuit throughout the midwestern United States. In 1924, he enlisted in the U.S. Army Air Service cadet program in San Antonio, Texas, and graduated in 1925 at the top of his class with the rank of second lieutenant. Lindbergh credited the Army with developing his professional flying skills and attitudes.

The Orteig Prize

In 1926, Lindbergh was living in St. Louis, Missouri, and working for Robertson Aircraft Company as their lead airmail pilot. It was during this time that he learned of the Orteig Prize. Raymond Orteig, a French immigrant and New York hotel owner, offered $25,000 to any pilot who could fly nonstop between New York and Paris. Although several before him had died or had been seriously injured attempting the flight, Lindbergh was confident he would have a chance with the right airplane.

The *Spirit of St. Louis*

Lindbergh secured financial backing from several St. Louis businessmen and hired Ryan Aeronautical Company of San Diego, California, to manufacture a modified one-person, single-engine plane with the necessary specifications. The design had to accommodate the extra fuel needed for the trip, while at the same time reducing unnecessary weight to conserve fuel. Lindbergh decided to fly without a radio, parachute, or brakes, and since the plane would be modified to have the fuel tank placed in front of the pilot seat, a front window would not be needed either. Lindbergh also designed special lightweight boots for the trip and replaced the traditional heavy leather pilot's seat with a wicker chair instead. More than three thousand man-hours were spent designing and building the plane, and on May 10, 1927, Lindbergh tested the *Spirit of St. Louis,* named in honor of his financial backers, on a flight from San Diego, California, to New York City. In spite of an overnight stop in St. Louis, the flight broke transcontinental records at just over twenty hours.

Lindbergh waited several days for the weather to clear, and at 7:52 A.M. on May 20, 1927, the *Spirit of St. Louis* took off from Long Island, New York. Within twelve hours, Lindbergh was over the open ocean battling fog, ice, and extreme fatigue. Fifteen hours later, the coast of Ireland was within sight. Lindbergh calculated that he was more than two hours ahead of schedule and about three miles off course. Less than seven hours later, at 10:22 P.M. Paris time, Lindbergh landed the *Spirit of St. Louis* at Le Bourget Field. He had flown over thirty-three continuous hours and over thirty-six hundred miles to complete the first solo transatlantic flight.

Lindbergh was celebrated throughout Europe and was given a ticker-tape parade when he returned to New York. President Calvin Coolidge awarded Lindbergh the country's first Distinguished Flying Cross, and Congress presented him with the Congressional Medal of Honor. The Army promoted Lindbergh to colonel in the Air Corps Reserves.

Impact

Lindbergh's transatlantic flight made him an instant world hero and helped spur the growth of commercial aviation. Shortly after returning to New York, Lindbergh flew the *Spirit of St. Louis* across the United States, visiting every state, giving speeches and riding in parades, which further increased public interest

---

The Landing at Le Bourget

On the evening of May 21, 1927, Charles Lindbergh became the first pilot to fly solo across the Atlantic Ocean when he landed at Paris's Le Bourget Field at 10:22 P.M. He was mobbed by the waiting crowd of thousands and instantly became a hero. The feat was no less than that of man stepping on the moon. Lindbergh later described that landing in his book We *(1927):*

The sun went down shortly after passing Cherbourg and soon the beacons along the Paris-London airway became visible.

I first saw the lights of Paris a little before 10 P.M., or 5 P.M., New York time, and a few minutes later I was circling the Eiffel Tower at an altitude of about four thousand feet.

The lights of Le Bourget were plainly visible, but appeared to be very close to Paris. I had understood that the field was farther from the city, so continued out to the northeast into the country for four or five miles to make sure that there was not another field farther out which might be Le Bourget. Then I returned and spiraled down closer to the lights. Presently I could make out long lines of hangars, and the roads appeared to be jammed with cars.

I flew low over the field once, then circled around into the wind and landed.

---

in air travel. During a goodwill tour of Mexico, Central America, and the West Indies, Lindbergh met Anne Morrow, daughter of the American ambassador to Mexico, whom he married in May 1929. The Lindberghs moved to England during the 1930s to escape the intense media attention brought on by the kidnapping and death of their firstborn child. Lindbergh continued to be involved in aviation throughout his life as a consultant to commercial airlines and various military groups worldwide. He flew missions against the Japanese in World War II and won the Pulitzer Prize for Literature in 1953 for his second autobiography, *The Spirit of St. Louis.* During the 1960s, Lindbergh became a vocal advocate for environmental conservation. He died of cancer at his home in Hawaii in 1972.

Joseph F. Clark III

Further Reading

Bak, Richard. *The Big Jump: Lindbergh and the Great Atlantic Air Race.* Hoboken, N.J.: John Wiley & Sons, 2011. Explores the technological advances in aviation at the time of Lindberg's transatlantic flight and provides information on the other pilots who attempted the trip.

Grant, R. G. *Flight: One Hundred Years of Aviation.* New York: DK, 2007. A history of twentieth-century aviation with photos, diagrams, and archival images.

Hixson, Walter L., and Oscar Handlin. *Charles A. Lindbergh: Lone Eagle.* New York: Longman, 2002. A brief account of Lindbergh's life.

Kessner, Thomas. *The Flight of the Century: Charles Lindbergh and the Rise of American Aviation.* New York: Oxford University Press, 2010. A biography that explores the details of Lindbergh's life in historical context and how 1920s society and culture contributed to his success and fame.

Lindbergh, Charles A. *The Spirit of St. Louis.* New York: Scribner, 2003. An autobiographical account of Lindbergh's historic solo transatlantic flight, originally published in 1952.

Lindbergh, Charles A. *"We."* Guilford, Conn.: Lyons Press, 2002. An autobiographical account of Lindbergh's life from birth through his historic transatlantic flight, written and published within weeks of landing in Paris in 1927.

See also: Air Commerce Act of 1926; Airmail; Air Mail Act of 1925; Aviation; Byrd, Richard E.; Earhart, Amelia; Fokker, Anthony; Science and technology; Transportation; Travel

---

■ Lindsay, Vachel

Identification: American poet
Born: November 10, 1879, Springfield, Illinois
Died: December 5, 1931, Springfield, Illinois

Vachel Lindsay was an eccentric idealist who advocated for poetry as performance art, writing verse intended to be chanted or sung. He gained notoriety by making several journeys across much of the continental United States on foot, during which he would recite poetry in exchange for food and shelter.

Born to a middle-class family and raised in the Midwest, Nicholas Vachel Lindsay briefly studied medicine in Ohio at the behest of his parents. He wanted to be a painter, however, and left college after three years to study art, first in Chicago and then in New York. During his time in New York, Lindsay self-published his poems while working menial jobs and depending on his father for income.

In 1906, he became a troubadour of sorts, walking from Florida to Kentucky and trading theatrical readings of his poetry for hospitality. He followed this with another hike in 1908 from New York City to Ohio and in 1912 from Illinois to New Mexico. He gained recognition during the 1910s when Harriet Monroe published his work in her influential *Poetry* magazine.

Lindsay was well established by 1920, and that year became the first American poet invited to lecture at Oxford University. During the decade, he published eight books of poetry, two books for children, a revised edition of his 1915 book *The Art of the Moving Picture*, and assorted pamphlets. He also contributed poems, articles, short stories, and reviews to prominent magazines such as *The Nation*, *Ladies' Home Journal*, *The New Republic*, and *Collier's*. Lindsay worked as poet-in-residence at Gulfport Junior College in Mississippi from 1923 to 1924, and then moved to Spokane, Washington, where he wrote columns for local newspapers.

Despite his professional success, Lindsay had many personal difficulties. His father died in 1918, his mother in 1922. He suffered a collapse during a poetry recital in 1923 that forced him to cancel the rest of his planned tour, after which both his physical and his mental health continued to deteriorate; he was diagnosed with epilepsy the following year. In 1925, Lindsay married young high school teacher Elizabeth Connor, with whom he had two children, but he was continually plagued with anxieties over finances and family obligations. He and his family returned to Springfield in 1929. Two years later, in poverty and failing health, Lindsay committed suicide by drinking a bottle of lye.

Impact

Lindsay greatly contributed to the revival of poetry as an oral art form, using solid rhythms and a theatrical delivery to appeal to the masses. As one of the "prairie poets" of the early twentieth century, along with Carl Sandburg and Edgar Lee Masters, he idealized the American village as a democratic utopia and helped to popularize the ideals and culture of the Midwest.

Bill Knight

Further Reading

Lindsay, Vachel. *Collected Poems of Vachel Lindsay.* Reprint. Charleston, S.C.: BiblioBazaar, 2009.

Masters, Edgar Lee. *Vachel Lindsay: A Poet in America.* New York: Scribner, 1935.

Monroe, Harriet. *Poets and Their Art.* New York: Macmillan, 1932.

See also: Poetry; Sandburg, Carl

■ Lindy Hop

The first major African American dance form created in the North, the Lindy Hop was central to the popularity of the ballroom scene in Harlem during the late 1920s and became a core element of youth culture. It had a significant impact on the stylistic evolution of jazz music, also influencing many of the changes that furthered the development of swing music.

The Lindy Hop emerged through the blending of several popular dances, including the Charleston, the Breakaway, and the Collegiate. Though the dance likely began to form earlier, the first recorded use of the term "Lindy Hop" occurred in 1928. "Shorty" George Snowden, often credited as the creator of the Lindy Hop, likely developed the dance at either the Savoy Ballroom or the Rockland Palace, which were both major dance venues in Harlem. Snowden is said to have named the dance in honor of aviator Charles Lindbergh's landmark 1927 transatlantic flight, mirroring the newspaper headline "Lindy Hops the Atlantic."

At the end of the 1920s, the dance was still in its infancy and bore a strong resemblance to the upright, bouncy Charleston, as it had yet to adopt the smoother style characteristic of Lindy dancers in the 1930s. The only surviving footage of this early style of Lindy Hop appears in the 1929 film *After Seben* in a sequence featuring three couples, including Snowden, in a nightclub dance contest.

Snowden, his partner Big Bea, and other leading dancers, including "Twistmouth" George Ganaway, danced the Lindy Hop in competitions and as professional touring performers. By the decade's end, the Lindy Hop had begun to eclipse other social dances, becoming the most popular dance in Harlem and spreading nationally as well.

Impact

Dance styles and popular music developed a symbiotic relationship during the 1920s; the Lindy Hop in particular made significant contributions to the evolution of 1920s hot jazz as it developed into the swing music that dominated the 1930s. The dance influenced the smoother rhythmic bassline and the relaxed syncopation that became significant in many styles of jazz. Furthermore, the Lindy Hop helped expand social dancing into a less rigid medium with more room for improvisation, experimentation, athleticism, humor, and individuality. As it became the dominant form of dance at the Savoy Ballroom, the nation's most popular integrated dance venue, the Lindy Hop played a crucial role in the softening of racial tensions during this period.

Christopher J. Wells

Further Reading

Hubbard, Karen, and Terry Monaghan. "Negotiating Compromise on a Burnished Wood Floor: Social Dancing at the Savoy." In *Ballroom, Boogie, Shimmy Sham, Shake: A Social and Popular Dance Reader*, edited by Julie Malnig. Urbana: University of Illinois Press, 2009.

Manning, Frankie, and Cynthia R. Millman. *Frankie Manning: Ambassador of Lindy Hop.* Philadelphia: Temple University Press, 2007.

Spring, Howard. "Swing and the Lindy Hop: Dance, Venue, Media, and Tradition." *American Music* 15, no. 2 (Summer, 1997): 183–207.

See also: African Americans; Charleston, The; Dances, popular; Flappers; Harlem Renaissance; Jazz; Music, popular; Nightclubs; "Roaring Twenties"

■ Lippmann, Walter

Identification: American journalist and political commentator
Born: September 23, 1889, New York, New York
Died: December 14, 1974, New York, New York

Walter Lippmann was an intellectual whose political news career took off during World War I. He continued to flourish as a political commentator for six decades, although his influence was perhaps greatest in the 1920s.

Walter Lippmann. (Getty Images)

Lippmann grew up in an affluent German Jewish home in Manhattan. He graduated from Harvard as a member of the academic honor society Phi Beta Kappa and was a convert to the socialist reform movement that was popular in early twentieth-century America. Brief stints in politics left him convinced that his true calling was journalism.

As Lippmann expounded on his political stance throughout the 1920s, he became increasingly skeptical of most Americans' ability to act as responsible and knowledgeable citizens. His viewpoint was pointedly expressed in his commentary on two highly publicized court cases, the Scopes trial of 1925 and the trial of purported anarchist murderers Nicola Sacco and Bartolomeo Vanzetti. He feared that the 1927 execution of Sacco and Vanzetti would mark a swing to the extreme political left and right for Americans. As American politics underwent a period of degeneration in the 1920s, Lippmann became increasingly politically skeptical.

Lippmann penned eight books between 1920 and 1930. His book *Liberty and the News* explored the relationship among mass media, the formation of public opinion, and democracy. *Public Opinion* (1922) stemmed from his attempt to discover why the policies of President Woodrow Wilson had unfolded so disastrously. The book became a stern indictment of the shortcomings of the American masses, which Lippmann pronounced volatile and impulsive in their collective political outlook. *A Preface to Morals* appeared in 1929 and became very popular, going through six editions in one year and being translated into twelve languages. It was Lippmann's first book to be featured in the national reading group known as the Book of the Month Club. The book proclaims that traditional religion has run its course and that secular humanism, based on aspects of the philosophical perspective of stoicism, is the best hope for modern civilization. Americans snapped up several editions of the book, and Lippmann ended the decade of the 1920s as a well-respected political and cultural pundit.

Impact

Lippmann was a towering figure among political commentators and theorists from the end of World War I until the early 1970s. He championed critical thinking, exposed inconsistencies and errors in mass media, and worked to mediate between news reporting and the general public, contributing greatly to the development of American public opinion in the 1920s. Lippmann's syndicated newspaper column "Today and Tomorrow" won him two Pulitzer Prizes in 1958 and 1962.

Michael Polley

Further Reading

Childs, Marquis, and James Reston, eds. *Walter Lippmann and His Times.* New York: Harcourt Brace, 1959.

Lippmann, Walter. *Public Opinion.* Blacksburg, Va.: Wilder Publications, 2010.

Steel, Ronald. *Walter Lippmann and the American Century.* New York: Vintage Books, 1981.

See also: Foreign policy, U.S.; Return to Normalcy; Sacco and Vanzetti case; Scopes trial

■ Literature in Canada

Canadian literature of the 1920s reflects the writers' efforts to come to terms with a country that was still largely unset-

tled. Canadian writers were primarily preoccupied with defining their own specific regions, though they were also clearly aware of the lingering question of a national identity, an issue further complicated by the fact that Canada comprises two different cultures, one anglophone (English-speaking) and the other francophone (French-speaking).

During the 1920s, a period of growing Canadian nationalist sentiment, many anglophone and francophone Canadian writers explored new subject matter and new means of literary expression distinct from that of their European predecessors. In essence, they began to establish a uniquely Canadian literary voice.

Anglophone Literature

During the nineteenth century, the historical romance was the dominant form of fiction in English-speaking Canada. This began to change early in the twentieth century, when authors started to produce realistic novels that emphasized local settings. In 1908, Lucy Maud Montgomery published *Anne of Green Gables*, set on Prince Edward Island and reflecting the unique character of the Maritime Provinces. Seven more books about her young redheaded heroine followed, including *Rilla of Ingleside*, released in 1921. Over a century after the first novel was published, the series remains in print.

Another popular series of the early twentieth century began with Mazo de la Roche's novel *Jalna* (1927), the story of a fictional estate in rural western Ontario and the family that lives there. The book won the first ever US$10,000 *Atlantic Monthly*-Little Brown Award for Best Novel. Though the sixteen novels set in Jalna contain some sensational plot elements, they all advocate such traditional values as fidelity, propriety, and family loyalty. They are often described as prairie novels and works of social realism.

The Prussian-born author and translator Frederick Philip Grove fled Europe in 1909 to escape crippling debt and settled on a farm in rural Manitoba. His first two books in English, *Over Prairie Trails* (1922) and *The Turn of the Year* (1923), consist of sketches describing his experiences. Though at the time they were admired primarily for their descriptions of nature, it has been suggested that each volume can be read as a short story cycle, united by the theme of survival. Grove's *Settlers of the Marsh* (1925), which is now considered a prairie novel, met with public disapproval at the time due to its hero's marriage to a pros-

titute. By the end of the decade, Grove had published three more novels and a collection of essays and risen to literary prominence.

Another immigrant who achieved fame with a prairie novel was Martha Ostenso. Born in Norway in 1900, she left for the United States with her parents at the age of two. The family lived in South Dakota and Minnesota before immigrating once more, this time to Canada. They made their home in Manitoba, the setting of Ostenso's novel *Wild Geese* (1925), a best seller that won the Dodd, Mead and Company Best Novel of the Year Award.

The movement from romantic fiction to social realism is perhaps best illustrated by the career of another Manitoba writer, Robert J. C. Stead, who published his first book in 1908. Though his early novels all have romantic plots, in the mid-1920s, he began writing works that highlight the spiritual and moral conflicts inherent in life as a pioneer. With *The Smoking Flax* (1925) and his best novel, *Grain* (1926), Stead joined the ranks of prairie realists.

Short Fiction

Most of the short selections that appeared in nineteenth-century periodicals would not meet the twentieth-century definition of a short story. They would be classified as humorous anecdotes, observations, descriptions, animal stories, moralistic tales, or sentimental sketches. By the 1920s, however, under the influence of modernism, writers were producing more carefully crafted short fiction that was less regional in emphasis and more conscious of structure and tone. One such writer, Raymond Knister, was one of the first Canadian authors to have his short stories published by a Paris magazine. He was also the editor of *Canadian Short Stories* (1928), a landmark anthology that reflects the modernist values of its contributors.

The decade also saw the emergence of Morley Callaghan of Toronto, who would become one of the most important Canadian writers of the time. As a young reporter, he had worked briefly with American novelist Ernest Hemingway, who then arranged to have some of Callaghan's short stories published in Paris. Meanwhile, American author F. Scott Fitzgerald saw some of Callaghan's stories in an American periodical and mentioned them to his own publisher, Scribner's. They published Callaghan's first novel, *Strange Fugitive* (1928), and a collection of his short stories entitled *A Native Argosy* (1929).

During the decades that followed, Callaghan produced a number of impressive stories, novellas, and novels that use realistic settings and characters to present moral and spiritual truths.

Poetry

During the last two decades of the nineteenth century, the most influential poets in Canada were the Confederation Poets, members of a group whose work reflects the landscape and the spirit of Canada in both form and substance, rather than simply following English models. Although most of these poets were gone by the 1920s, several remained active. In 1927, Charles G. D. Roberts, who was largely responsible for the formation of the group, published a volume of poetry entitled *The Vagrant of Time*. Also during this decade, his cousin Bliss Carman published several collections of poetry and edited two anthologies. Carman was named Canada's poet laureate in 1928. Two volumes by another Confederation poet, Duncan Campbell Scott, appeared during the 1920s: *Beauty and Life* (1921) and *Poems* (1926).

The 1920s saw the emergence of a new generation of Canadian poets, all of them to some degree influenced by modernism, the movement associated with T. S. Eliot and his American followers. E. J. Pratt published his first collection, *Newfoundland Verse*, in 1923, and followed it with three more volumes during the decade. Though Pratt, like the Confederation Poets, relied heavily on descriptions of the Canadian landscape, he was a modernist in his increasing willingness to experiment with new forms. In 1928, another new poet, Dorothy Livesay, published *Green Pitcher*, her first poetry collection. Though in these poems she does not touch on the feminist issues that would become so important in her later works, her extensive use of imagery indicates that even at the beginning of her literary career, Livesay was strongly influenced by the modernists.

McGill University was the home of what came to be called the Montreal Group: a circle of writers, most of whom had been undergraduate students there, whose intention was to introduce literary modernism to Canada. They began by publishing a literary supplement to McGill's student newspaper, which evolved into an independent journal, *The McGill Fortnightly Review*, appearing from 1925 to 1927. This was followed by *The Canadian Mercury*, produced from 1928 to 1929 and ultimately ceasing publication due to the stock market collapse. Nevertheless, these publications had succeeded in their purpose. Writers such as A. J. M. Smith, F. R. Scott, E. J. Pratt, A. M. Klein, Leo Kennedy, John Glassco, and Leon Edel would ensure that modernism had a permanent place in Canadian poetry.

Francophone Literature

Like the McGill publications, the French magazine *Le Terroir* (1909; *The Soil*) had a long-lasting influence. Its purpose was to discourage poets from using French models for their literary works and encourage them instead to write poetry that reflected the scenery and the lifestyle of their native region. Blanche Lamontagne-Beauregard, the first major female poet of French Canada, was influenced by the *Terroir* movement. In the 1920s, she published several collections of lyric poetry focusing on the Gaspé Peninsula, as well as a volume of Gaspesian legends in prose. Another important member of the *Terroir* group was Nérée Beauchemin, whose collection *Patrie intime* (1928; *Intimate Homeland*) reflects his love of Quebec and his dedication to his Catholic faith. Alfred Desrochers published his first volume of poetry in 1928; his flair for combining myth and reality, the lyrical and the actual, would lead to his being ranked as one of the finest poets of the twentieth century. Some French Canadian writers, such as René Chopin and Paul Morin, still clung to the neoclassical forms of their continental French predecessors. Though these poets were admired for their elegant diction, proponents of modernism considered them more European than Canadian in style.

While some writers limited their efforts to one genre, others proved to have a wide range of talents. In 1926, Robert Choquette of Montreal won the Prix David for his first collection of poems, published when he was just twenty. He released his first novel the following year, and in the 1930s, he began a long, successful career in radio as a scriptwriter and producer, but he continued to publish award-winning poetry throughout his life.

Another French Canadian writer who exhibited skills in a variety of areas was Georges-Charles-Jules Bugnet, who wrote under the pseudonym of Henri Doutremont. A native of France, in 1905, he brought his young wife to a farm in Alberta, where he worked the land, developed new strains of roses, and wrote novels, stories, and poems. Though his fiction usually falls into the prairie category, dealing with the problems of immigrants unfamiliar with the demands of their natural surroundings, his first novel, *Nipsya* (1924), focuses on the plight of the Métis, the mixed-blood descendants of French settlers and Native Americans.

Maurice Constantin-Weyer was another immigrant who was drawn to the western provinces. In 1903, he arrived in Manitoba, where he is said to have acquired a Métis wife and become the father of three children. When World War I broke out, Constantin-Weyer returned to France and remained there, writing novels set in western Canada. Among them is *La Bourrasque* (1925; *The Half-Breed*, 1930), based on the life of the Métis leader Louis Riel. In 1928, Constantin-Weyer was awarded the Prix Goncourt.

Impact

Though they wrote in different languages, the anglophone and the francophone Canadian writers of the 1920s shared the same goal: to develop a literary tradition worthy of the country they loved. Much of what they wrote did not stand the test of time, for they were trying out new ideas and new forms in which to express them. However, by the middle of the twentieth century, they were well on the way toward achieving their goal. They came to see that Canadian literature would inevitably be as varied as the land itself and, just as inevitably, would reflect new ideas, as befitted so new a country.

Rosemary M. Canfield Reisman

Further Reading

Atwood, Margaret, ed. *The New Oxford Book of Canadian Verse in English.* New York: Oxford University Press, 1996. A collection of Canadian poetry, with an introductory survey by well-known Canadian author Atwood.

Benson, Eugene, and William Toye, eds. *The Oxford Companion to Canadian Literature.* 2d ed. Toronto: Oxford University Press, 2005. Contains essays on major literary movements and issues. Unlike the later *Concise Oxford Companion*, also includes entries on francophone writers not published in English.

Hammill, Faye. *Canadian Literature.* Edinburgh: Edinburgh University Press, 2007. Views the subject both historically and thematically.

Harrison, Dick. *Unnamed Country: The Struggle for a Canadian Prairie Fiction.* Edmonton: University of Alberta Press, 1977. A major study of western Canadian writing and writers.

Kröller, Eva-Marie, ed. *The Cambridge Companion to Canadian Literature.* Cambridge, England: Cambridge University Press, 2004. Contains twelve essays by leading scholars that cover a wide range of subjects, plus an introduction dealing with some major issues in the study of Canadian literature.

New, W. H. *A History of Canadian Literature.* 2d ed. Ithaca, N.Y.: McGill-Queen's University Press, 2003. A standard historical and critical study with an extensive chronology.

See also: Fitzgerald, F. Scott; Hemingway, Ernest; Literature in the United States; Poetry; Theater in Canada

■ Literature in the United States

The 1920s represents the first full decade of what can rightly be called twentieth-century American literature. The difference between American literature published before World War I and that of the 1920s is the difference between nineteenth- and twentieth-century literary values and expression. In the postwar era, American literature of every genre finally burst free of Victorian restraint and sensibility to move into modern forms and perspectives.

The literature of the 1920s is bookended neatly by the official end of World War I in 1919 and the beginning of the Great Depression of the 1930s, signaled by the stock market crash in October 1929. In those ten years, U.S. literature evolved from provincial expressions that looked to Europe for guidance to a body of literature that Europe watched for signs of innovation. This change was reflected by the presentation of the 1930 Nobel Prize in Literature to novelist Sinclair Lewis, the first writer from the United States to be so honored. This decade witnessed innovation and experimentation in every literary field, challenges to previous assumptions about the very forms and functions of literature, and assaults on ideals and institutions on every front.

Poetry and Drama

The literary renaissance started first in poetry, which by the 1920s had already begun its transition into modern forms. Two Chicago-based magazines—*Poetry*, founded in 1912 by Harriet Monroe, and *The Little Review*, founded in 1914 by Margaret Anderson—helped introduce readers to a two-pronged revolution in American poetry: a native strain that bucked nineteenth-century restrictions in favor of American material and idiom, as seen in the work of Carl Sandburg and Robert Frost, and a European-inspired strain that drew on the literary and cultural advances of the Continent, where both T. S. Eliot and Ezra Pound lived during the decade. *Poetry* published the work of poets such as Eliot, Pound, Frost, Sandburg, Vachel Lindsay, Wallace Stevens, and Hart Crane, while *The Little Review*, of which Pound was foreign editor, notably featured the work of Eliot, Sandburg, Stevens, Crane, and William Carlos Williams (as well as that landmark work of modernism, James Joyce's *Ulysses*, serialized in its pages between 1918 and 1920; the finished version was published in 1922).

Poets of the native strain were well established by the early 1920s, with Edwin Arlington Robinson's *Collected Poems* winning the Pulitzer Prize in 1922. Additional significant publications of the decade include Williams's *Spring and All* (1923), Robinson Jeffers's *Roan Stallion* (1925), E. E. Cummings's *Is 5* (1926), and Frost's *New Hampshire* (1923) and *West-Running Brook* (1928). One of the best-selling volumes of 1928 was Stephen Vincent Benét's verse narrative of the Civil War, *John Brown's Body*. With regard to the more European symbolist strain, Eliot's *The Waste Land* was poetry's version of *Ulysses*, a poem of complex mythological and symbolic references, also published in 1922. Other symbolist works of the 1920s include Stevens's *Harmonium* (1923), Pound's first sixteen *Cantos* (1925), and Crane's *White Buildings* (1926). The differences between these two types of poetry can be exaggerated, with one regarded as direct and reader-friendly, the other dense and opaque (William Carlos Williams hated *The Waste Land*, and he was not the only American writer to feel that way), but the two schools shared a similar goal of reinventing the very subjects, language, and attitudes of poetry. Of the major pre-1920s poets, only the works of Walt Whitman and Emily Dickinson would survive the almost total reconstruction of the American poetic canon during the decade, while those who rose to prominence in the 1920s—Eliot and Pound, Frost and Williams—would dominate the poetic scene, not just through World War II but for the rest of the twentieth century.

Drama in the 1920s followed a similar trajectory. Before World War I, theater was noteworthy mainly for its famous players, not its plays. Great actors like the Booth brothers and the Barrymore family drew theatergoers into the twentieth century, especially well-known actors in much-loved roles such as Joe Jefferson in *Rip Van Winkle*. The change came with George Pierce Baker, who inspired dramatists and directors in drama workshops at Harvard University before going on to help establish the Yale School of Drama, and with George Cram Cook, who founded the Provincetown Players on Cape Cod in 1915 (and later in Greenwich Village), a workshop company that spawned early work by Susan Glaspell and Paul Green.

The major figure to come out of this renaissance was Eugene O'Neill, who wrote his early plays for the Provincetown Players, including *Bound East for Cardiff* (1916), and who would dominate the theater in the 1920s. He won three Pulitzer Prizes during the decade, for *Beyond the Horizon* (1920), *Anna Christie* (1921), and *Strange Interlude* (1928), and also saw the performance of his plays *The Emperor Jones* (1920), *The Hairy Ape* (1922), and *Desire Under the Elms* (1924). Playwrights of the 1920s like O'Neill rejected the melodramas of the past and pioneered new dramatic approaches such as symbolism and expressionism, new subjects such as Freudian psychology, and new forms of stagecraft. Elmer Rice's *The Adding Machine* (1923), George Kaufman and Marc Connelly's *Beggar on Horseback* (1924), and the works of other playwrights such as S. N. Behrman, Philip Barry, and Robert E. Sherwood reflected the new literary attack on American mores and institutions, especially middle-class materialism and the excesses of American capitalism.

Fiction

American fiction of the 1920s produced similar critiques of American values and traditions. The break with the nineteenth century may be regarded as starting with the publication of Sherwood Anderson's short story collection *Winesburg, Ohio* in 1919, which uncovered lives of quiet desperation in a small midwestern town. Incorporating the tools of Freudian psychology, Anderson reveals the repressiveness of small-town life, as evidenced by the alienation and estrangement of its residents. American realism in the second half of the nineteenth century had tackled larger themes, as seen in the work of Mark Twain, Henry James, and William Dean Howells; Edith Wharton's *The Age of Innocence* would win the Pulitzer Prize in 1921, but its upper-class characters and settings recalled an earlier time. The social realism of the 1920s focused more on inner lives and the average experience. Sinclair Lewis's five best-sellers in the 1920s—*Main Street* (1920), *Babbitt* (1922), decadence; *Arrowsmith*, Lewis's critique of medicine and science; and perhaps the most iconic novel of the 1920s, F. Scott Fitzgerald's *The Great Gatsby*, with its brilliant, poetic depiction of the decadent life of the Jazz Age rich and the end of the American Dream. Likewise, fiction published in 1929 includes *Look Homeward, Angel*, Thomas Wolfe's epic and romantic coming-of-age novel; Ernest Hemingway's *A Farewell to Arms*, a romantic but ultimately defeatist view of World War I; and William Faulkner's first major novel, *The Sound and the Fury*, a technical tour de force and a powerful dissection of the decline of one southern family. The American literary renaissance of the 1920s was less experimental than its European counterpart, in which Joyce and Virginia Woolf revolutionized the novel, but Faulkner and Dos Passos are remarkable for their technical advances. The revolution in the American novel tended to concentrate more on subject and theme, and on expanding the range of realism.

One indication of the breadth and energy of this literary awakening is the number of populations that gained new voices in the 1920s. As noted above, a number of new writers during the decade came out of the Midwest: Lewis (born in Minnesota), Anderson (Ohio), Dreiser (Indiana), Hemingway (Illinois), Sandburg (Illinois), and Fitzgerald (Minnesota). The literary dominance of New York and the East Coast was being challenged by writers from other areas of the country who wrote about their own special geographies and regional mores. A distinct southern resurgence also began in this decade: Faulkner's is the most prominent name, but other writers who used the American South as setting and anchor include Thomas Wolfe (North Carolina), Ellen Glasgow (*Barren Ground*, 1925, set in Virginia), and DuBose Heyward (*Porgy*, 1925, set in South Carolina). Nashville, Tennessee, was the home of the literary group known as the Southern Agrarians, centered at Vanderbilt University, which published *The Fugitive* magazine from 1922 to 1925 and whose members included the poets John Crowe Ransom, Robert Penn Warren, and Allen Tate. In 1930, the Agrarians published their manifesto, *I'll*

F. Scott Fitzgerald published his masterpiece The Great Gatsby *in 1925.* (Hulton Archive/Getty Images)

Arrowsmith (1925), *Elmer Gantry* (1927), and *Dodsworth* (1929)—are a catalog of the ills of American life at every level and in every profession, capturing the nation's growing sense of postwar disillusionment. The end of the war seemed to have freed American novelists to examine every corner of the country and find what was missing. The works of Anderson and Lewis exposed what had previously been a sacred tenet of the American ideal, the strength and intimacy of small-town life, revealing these communities to be often spiritually empty and chronically unhappy.

Every year of the 1920s witnessed another literary assault on American values and institutions, on literary conventions and gentility. For example, 1925 saw the publication of Theodore Dreiser's *An American Tragedy*, with its epic analysis of the failures of American capitalism and social class; John Dos Passos's *Manhattan Transfer*, a story of urban defeat and

Take My Stand, a defense of the South's agricultural way of life in the face of northern industrialism.

The literary movement of the 1920s that had the greatest impact on the future of American literature was the Harlem Renaissance. Begun before the end of World War I, this explosion of African American literary talent was promoted throughout the 1920s by such patrons of the arts as Alain Locke and Carl Van Vechten. The decade saw the publication of such significant works as *The Book of American Negro Poetry* (1922), edited by James Weldon Johnson; Jean Toomer's novel *Cane* (1923), an ambitiously structured series of vignettes; *The New Negro* (1925), an anthology of poetry, fiction, and essays edited by Locke; Langston Hughes's first book, the poetry collection *The Weary Blues* (1926); Claude McKay's novel *Home to Harlem* (1928), winner of the Harmon Gold Award for Literature; and Nella Larsen's first novel, *Quicksand* (1928).

Part of the reason for the emergence and greater prominence of African American artists in the 1920s was the media revolution that opened culture to wider audiences and broader participation, from radio (the popular *Amos 'n' Andy* show, for example, began in 1928) to the proliferation of magazines, book clubs, and publishing houses. In addition to the birth of such magazines as *Time* (1923), *The New Yorker* (1925), and *The Saturday Review* (1924), a wide range of smaller publications started in the 1920s to capture the literary outpouring of the decade, including *Contact* (1920), *The Double Dealer* (1921), *Broom* (1921), *The Fugitive* (1922), *This Quarter* (1925), *Hound and Horn* (1927), and *transition* (1927). Both the Book-of-the-Month Club (1926) and the Literary Guild (1927) were established in order to reach a broader audience of readers. Similarly, a number of important publishing houses had their start in the 1920s, including W. W. Norton (1923), Simon & Schuster (1924), Viking Press (1925), and Random House (1927). The titles listed under just one important publishing imprint of the 1920s, Charles Scribner's Sons, reads like a 1920s-era literary winners' circle: Fitzgerald, Hemingway, Ring Lardner, George Santayana, Edith Wharton, Thomas Wolfe, and Edmund Wilson. The energy generated by all this media and publishing activity helped to draw new readers and writers into the literary spotlight of the decade.

Expatriates and the Lost Generation

A superficial reading of the literature of the 1920s finds the predominant Jazz Age images—the Charleston, coonskin coats, and bootleg liquor—that readers associate with early F. Scott Fitzgerald works such as *This Side of Paradise* (1920), *Flappers and Philosophers* (1920), and *Tales of the Jazz Age* (1922). However, the important literature of the decade was both richer and darker than that. In drama and fiction, American realism confronted the multiple failures of the American Dream and catalogued those areas of life where reality never touched the promise. Writers were sketching out the images that readers would soon come to associate with 1920s literature: the trope of the wasteland, for example, so prominent in Eliot's 1922 poem, which would surface three years later in the form of the "Valley of Ashes" in Fitzgerald's *The Great Gatsby*.

Nowhere is this truer than in the expatriate experience of the 1920s. A number of American writers lived in Europe in the 1920s. Some, like Eliot and Pound, had been there during World War I, while others, including Hemingway and Cummings, returned after the armistice, and still others went there searching for the excitement and artistic freedom missing in the United States. Although their motivations were partly practical—the collapse of European economies after World War I meant that American dollars could support writers far longer in Paris or Berlin than in New York or Boston—what mostly drew these writers was the cultural excitement of a city like Paris, which they associated with Joyce, Gertrude Stein, and Marcel Proust. They were part of what Stein (an expatriate in France since 1903) came to call "the lost generation," a phrase Hemingway would use as one epigraph for *The Sun Also Rises* (1926), his portrait of the expatriates drinking and bedding their way across Europe. Hemingway's second epigraph, a long quotation from Ecclesiastes, hints at the more serious themes of the novel, among them the personal and spiritual impact of the war and the search for meaning and honor in a postwar world seemingly devoid of it. Like *The Great Gatsby*, *The Sun Also Rises* must be read beneath its glittering surface to reach the deeper diagnosis of American malaise.

Impact

When Sinclair Lewis was awarded the Nobel Prize in Literature in 1930, it was a signal that major writers and literary movements could now be seen emerging from the United States as well as from Europe. Over the next twenty-five years, O'Neill, Eliot, Faulkner, and Hemingway would all join the ranks of the Nobel laureates as well. During the 1920s, American literature became a force in the world, and it would remain so for the rest of the century. In the lecture he gave at the Nobel award ceremony in Stockholm, Lewis summarized the literary accomplishments of the decade. He decried the timidity and gentility of nineteenth-century literature and praised those writers who had first carved out a new way, including Dreiser, Anderson, O'Neill, and Willa Cather. He then went on to name Hemingway, Wolfe, Dos Passos, and Faulkner as being among those writers who were creating in the United States "a literature worthy of her vastness." Lewis's address capped a decade of literary achievement and pointed ahead to the continuing influence of this decade's literature on American life.

David Peck

Further Reading

Carpenter, Humphrey. *Geniuses Together: American Writers in Paris in the 1920s.* Boston: Houghton Mifflin, 1987. An account of Hemingway, Anderson, Pound, Kay Boyle, Djuna Barnes, and other expatriates in Paris.

Cowley, Malcolm. *Exile's Return: A Literary Odyssey of the 1920s.* New York: Viking Press, 1951. A firsthand account of the expatriate experience and the literary movements of the time.

French, Warren, ed. *The Twenties: Fiction, Poetry, Drama.* Deland, Fla.: Everett/Edwards, 1975. Thirty essays on significant writers of the 1920s, both famous and obscure.

Gregory, Horace, and Marya Zaturenska. *A History of American Poetry, 1900–1940.* New York: Harcourt, Brace, 1969. An account of the poetic renaissance in the first decades of the twentieth century.

Hoffman, Frederick J. *The Twenties: American Writing in the Postwar Decade.* Rev. ed. New York: Free Press, 1965. A comprehensive study of the literature of the 1920s, including analyses of important 1920s texts.

Murphy, Brenda. "Plays and Playwrights: 1915–1945." In *The Cambridge History of American Theatre,* edited by Don B. Wilmeth and Christopher Bigsby. Vol. 2. New York: Cambridge University Press, 1999. A comprehensive overview of American drama during a crucial period in its development.

See also: Anderson, Sherwood; Eliot, T. S.; Faulkner, William; Fitzgerald, F. Scott; Fugitive Poets; Hemingway, Ernest; Lewis, Sinclair; Lost Generation; Poetry; Pound, Ezra; Theater in the United States

---

■ Little Blue Books

Before widespread college education and mass media provided almost universal access to information and entertainment, publisher Emanuel Haldeman-Julius's Little Blue Books, selling for just a few cents each, put great novels, plays, works of history and philosophy, and an enormous variety of other books into the hands of millions of ordinary American readers.

Working from a small printing company in Girard, Kansas, publisher Emanuel Haldeman-Julius created a nationwide sensation in popular culture by producing what came to be known as Little Blue Books, which were affordable editions of literary works that many working Americans might otherwise never have read or encountered. Haldeman-Julius's experience working as a journalist for many years gave him helpful tools and contacts when he launched his own publishing venture. He was purportedly inspired to create the Little Blue Book series because he had been deeply moved by an inexpensive edition of an Oscar Wilde poem when he was a teenager.

Starting in 1919 with the publication of books priced at ten to twenty-five cents, Haldeman-Julius did such successful business that he was able to drop his price to five cents per copy by the early 1920s. A single day's press run was 24,000 copies. Printed on low-grade "pulp" paper, wrapped in light blue covers, and bound with staples, the pocket-sized books measured just 3.5 by 5 inches. Volumes ranged in thickness from 32 to 128 pages. Haldeman-Julius advertised Little Blue Books in mainstream newspapers and magazines, sometimes offering coupons and subscription opportunities to facilitate ordering.

Although Haldeman-Julius was a socialist, only a small number of his titles dealt with socialism or other subjects considered controversial during the 1920s. Little Blue Books included editions of Shakespeare's plays, volumes of fiction and poetry by some of the world's most acclaimed authors, biographies of literary and historical figures, dictionaries, and books on Christianity and other religions. Among the Little Blue Books disseminating American culture were songbooks, collections of jokes and riddles, instructional books on topics as diverse as candy making and golf, and volumes on such popular themes as marriage, pregnancy, and child care.

Impact
Haldeman-Julius intended his Little Blue Books to make exposure to history, literature, and culture easy and inexpensive for the American public. During the 1920s and 1930s, Little Blue Books disseminated knowledge and culture to vast numbers of readers. They also provided important early reading experiences for later authors as diverse as Western adventure writer Louis L'Amour and Nobel Prize–winning novelist Saul Bellow.

Karen Manners Smith

Further reading
Dean, Virgil, ed. *John Brown to Bob Dole: Movers and Shakers in Kansas History.* Lawrence: University Press of Kansas, 2006.

Mordell, Albert, ed. *The World of Haldeman-Julius*, by Emanuel Haldeman-Julius. New York: Twayne, 1960.

See also: Book publishing; Literature in the United States

■ Lloyd, Harold

Identification: American actor, writer, and film producer
Born: April 20, 1893, Burchard, Nebraska
Died: March 8, 1971, Beverly Hills, California

Harold Lloyd's silent comedies, often filmed on location and featuring more realistic characters than those created by his contemporaries, provide a glimpse into middle-class life in the 1920s. In Lloyd's best films, the camera follows an ordinary young man through a series of extraordinary mishaps. Lloyd's films reflect traditional American values and the optimism and energy of the Jazz Age.

In the 1920s, silent comedies evolved from two-reel filler pieces driven by gags into feature films of increasing complexity. Lloyd was the first of the leading comic actors of his time to make a feature-length movie in the tradition of the gag film, paving the way for such contemporary entertainers as Charlie Chaplin, Roscoe "Fatty" Arbuckle, and Buster Keaton to do the same. Lloyd's film *A Sailor-Made Man* (1921),

followed quickly by *Grandma's Boy* (1922), combined comic routines, intricate plotlines, and the theme of transformation. Much of his films' success is attributed to Lloyd's everyman character, which he called a "glasses-character" because of the horn-rimmed eyeglasses he wore.

The Glasses-Character
Lloyd developed his persona of a typical young man in deliberate contrast to Charlie Chaplin's signature character known as the Little Tramp. Unlike the Little Tramp, the glasses-character is always a respectable member of society, sometimes wealthy, but more often a sincere, industrious member of the middle class. Usually, the glasses-character must overcome some personal weakness or inadequacy in order to win the hand of a young woman. In *A Sailor-Made Man*, he is rich but lazy, and he must demonstrate a willingness to work. In *Grandma's Boy*, he is a coward who acquires courage with the assistance of his clever grandmother.

In many ways, the glasses-character is an extension of his creator. In his autobiography, Lloyd describes himself as an average person from a typical midwestern family. He makes no claims for possessing innate talent and insists he is not by nature a funny person. He does, however, credit himself with ambition, persistence, and a firm work ethic.

Stunts, Previews, and Sound Films
Lloyd balanced his "story films" with "thrill films" driven by risky stunts. *Safety Last* (1921), one of Lloyd's best-known films, required him to scale a skyscraper in a stunt providing a visual metaphor for the notion of climbing to success. In an incredible stunt sequence, he dangles over a city street, clutching a clock face that has sprung open with his weight. This segment was filmed on a platform erected on the roof of a tall building in Los Angeles. A facade made to look like the building's top two stories was set a few yards in from the roof's edge, with precisely established camera angles creating the illusion of great height. The shot was a dangerous one, yet Lloyd insisted on performing it himself, in spite of his fear of heights and his wounded right hand. Lloyd believed that his anxieties would transfer convincingly on the screen.

Much of Lloyd's success derives from how closely attuned he was to his audiences. He drew on contemporary fads and interests for gags and plots, and he made extensive use of previews. He also edited scenes that failed to draw laughs from test audiences. Although Lloyd was not the first filmmaker to use previewing, he was one of the first to recognize and exploit its value, typically holding five or six previews for each production and reworking scenes between each showing.

In 1929, Lloyd released his first sound film, *Welcome Danger*, which was shot as a silent picture and reedited to incorporate sound. In spite of this film's popularity, Lloyd's subsequent movies failed to attract significant crowds. Presumably this was because his character's example of the American work ethic paying off no longer reflected the spirit of the times after the Great Depression descended on the country.

Impact

Harold Lloyd is credited with shaping the development of the modern romantic comedy. By rerouting slapstick from the realm of the clown into the everyday life of an average fellow, Lloyd created a comedy of embarrassment that allowed audiences to laugh with rather than at his character. The influence of his "story films," melding plot, theme, and gags can be seen in the work of his contemporaries, Chaplin and Keaton, in the screwball comedies of the 1930s and 1940s, and in the genre of television situation comedy. His legacy is also evident in Blake Edwards's film *The Great Race* (1965) and in the Pink Panther cartoon series. Lloyd's climactic chase scene in *Girl Shy* (1924) was copied for the iconic chariot race in the film *Ben-Hur: A Tale of the Christ* (1925).

K. Edgington

Further Reading

Bengtson, John. *Silent Visions: Discovering Early Hollywood and New York Through the Films of Harold Lloyd.* Solano Beach, Calif.: Santa Monica Press, 2011. An examination of American cultural history through silent films.

D'Agostino, Annette M. *The Harold Lloyd Encyclopedia.* Jefferson, N.C.: McFarland, 2004. A comprehensive reference work by an established film historian and Lloyd scholar.

Lloyd, Harold. *An American Comedy.* Edited by Wesley Winans Stout. New York: Dover, 1971. Stresses Lloyd's work ethic, developed in his childhood.

Reilly, Adam, ed. *Harold Lloyd: The King of Daredevil Comedy.* New York: Macmillan, 1977. A filmography including photos, reviews, and essays by noted critics.

Vance, Jeffrey, and Suzanne Lloyd. *Harold Lloyd: Master Comedian.* New York: Harry N. Abrams, 2002. An informative book illustrated with photographs, cowritten by Lloyd's granddaughter.

See also: Arbuckle, Fatty; *Ben-Hur;* Chaplin, Charlie; Film; Keaton, Buster; *Safety Last*

■ Lodge, Henry Cabot

Identification: American senator
Born: May 12, 1850, Boston, Massachusetts
Died: November 9, 1924, Cambridge, Massachusetts

Henry Cabot Lodge was a Republican senator from Massachusetts who chaired the powerful Senate Foreign Relations Committee. Lodge successfully prevented the United States from signing the Versailles Treaty to end World War I and from joining the League of Nations; instead, he led the United States to sign a separate peace treaty during the administration of President Warren G. Harding.

Henry Cabot Lodge was descended from two New England families, the Cabots and the Lodges. Lodge received a Harvard law degree and the first Ph.D. in political science granted by Harvard University. Lodge served in the U.S. Congress for six years as a congressman and thirty years as a senator. He was an early advocate for the expansion of the U.S. Navy and entry into World War I on the side of the Allies. In his speeches, Senator Lodge criticized President Woodrow Wilson's policy of neutrality, his inattention to U.S. military preparedness, and, later, his perceived failure to be firm enough against a defeated Germany. Lodge countered Wilson's Fourteen Points to guide peace talks with his own plans to oppose the United States signing any of the Paris peace treaties or joining the League of Nations. Lodge believed that League membership would prevent the United States from freely pursuing its own international objectives, while U.S. military forces would have to be commanded by an international body. As chairman of the Foreign Relations Committee, Lodge crafted separate armistices with Germany, Austria, and Hungary in 1921, formally ending American engagement in the war without further European entanglements. Lodge successfully maneuvered the Senate's ratification of the 1921 Four-Power Treaty, signed by the United States, Great Britain, France, and Japan,

Henry Cabot Lodge. (Getty Images)

ending the Anglo-Japanese Alliance. The four signatories agreed to respect one another's territorial rights and to consult one another if any one of the four was attacked. In 1922, Lodge also prevented the United States from joining the World Court. Lodge died from a stroke in 1924 and was succeeded as leader of the Senate by Kansas senator Charles Curtis.

Impact

Lodge contributed to the withdrawal of the United States from an active foreign policy and to the nation's increasing isolationism. Lodge and Curtis worked against President Wilson's plan to end World War I and helped propel Warren G. Harding to the Republican presidential nomination in 1920. The withdrawal of the United States from a more assertive role in world affairs in the interwar era, in which Lodge played an important role, had a large but unknowable impact on the road to World War II.

William A. Paquette

Further Reading

Cooper, John Milton. *Breaking the Heart of the World: Woodrow Wilson and the Fight for the League of Nations.* New York: Cambridge University Press, 2011.

Miller, William J. *Henry Cabot Lodge: A Biography.* New York: Heineman, 1967.

Widenor, William C. *Henry Cabot Lodge and the Search for an American Foreign Policy.* Berkeley: University of California Press, 1980.

See also: Curtis, Charles; Foreign policy, U.S.; Harding, Warren G.; Isolationism; League of Nations; Wilson, Woodrow

---

■ *Look Homeward, Angel*

Identification: Intensely autobiographical novel about a young man's coming of age
Author: Thomas Wolfe
Date: 1929

The publication of Look Homeward, Angel *was hailed by critics and such literary luminaries as William Faulkner and Sinclair Lewis as the first appearance of a major new voice in American letters. Because of this auspicious beginning, Thomas Wolfe was, for the remainder of his relatively short life, the object of considerable critical and popular interest. So closely identified was the author with his novel's protagonist, the Romantic egoist Eugene Gant, that each new work by Wolfe was perceived as a further chapter in the life of an individual whose hunger for experience appeared insatiable.*

Set in a thinly disguised small town in the mountains of North Carolina (Wolfe's Altamont is actually Asheville), *Look Homeward, Angel* is peopled with a host of vividly depicted characters, all modeled after real-life personages, especially the Wolfe family, who are given the fictional surname Gant. In addition to the author's alter ego Eugene, characters include Eugene's mother, Eliza Gant, an ambitious businesswoman modeled after Julia Elizabeth Wolfe; his father, W. O. Gant, a frustrated artist patterned after William Oliver Wolfe; and his closest sibling, Ben (Benjamin Harrison Wolfe), whose premature death from pneumonia serves as the novel's climax. This pivotal event releases the precocious protagonist from any lingering ties he might have to his birthplace and frees him fully to engage in his personal quest to unlock the mysteries of the world beyond Altamont.

Immediately following publication of the book, Wolfe's minimally fictionalized portraits of his relatives and other townspeople caused considerable consternation and even outrage among some members of his family and the general citizenry. For eight years after the novel's release, the author did not feel comfortable returning to Asheville.

Wolfe's obsessive need to register the daily minutiae of his internal and external experiences proved to be both a blessing and a curse. Some critics gave credit to his editor, Max Perkins, for reining in Wolfe's natural verbosity and severely cropping the manuscript; others extolled the lengthy impressions and often overwrought emotionalism of Wolfe's protagonist as embodying the essence of youthful idealism.

Impact

As both a concrete and emotional rendering of a young man's experience of himself and his engagement with the larger world, *Look Homeward, Angel* has been compared to other coming-of-age narratives such as *A Portrait of the Artist as a Young Man* by Irish writer James Joyce. Indeed, it may be that *Look Homeward, Angel* is the archetypal American bildungsroman, as it captures what many perceive to be an integral part of the American national identity: an all-encompassing longing for some transformative experience that will make it possible for each individual to achieve his or her full potential.

S. Thomas Mack

Further Reading

Ensign, Robert Taylor. *Lean Down Your Ear upon the Earth, and Listen: Thomas Wolfe's Greener Modernism.* Columbia: University of South Carolina Press, 2003.

Holman, C. Hugh. *The Loneliness at the Core: Studies in Thomas Wolfe.* Baton Rouge: Louisiana State University Press, 1975.

Idol, John Lane. *A Thomas Wolfe Companion.* New York: Greenwood Press, 1987.

See also: Faulkner, William; Literature in the United States

■ Los Angeles Aqueduct dynamiting

The Event: A California water rights controversy involving several dynamite attacks on an aqueduct that was diverting water from Owens Valley to Los Angeles

Also known as: California Water Wars

Dates: May 21, 1924; April 4 and 12, 1926; May 26, 27, and 28, 1926; June 5, 19, and 25, 1926; July 16, 1927; November 7, 1931

Place: Owens Valley, California

The diversion of water for industrial and residential developments in Los Angeles threatened the prosperity of landowners in Owens Valley, California. Both the building of the aqueduct and its vandalizing by Owens Valley property owners played a formative role in the historical development of balancing environmental, business, and residential priorities.

The nineteenth-century settlers of Los Angeles had access to plenty of community water. Wineries even developed along the banks of the Los Angeles River. The warm and sunny climate of the area began to attract many new residents toward the end of the nineteenth century. In 1890, there were around 51,000 persons in Los Angeles; the population had doubled by 1900 and had nearly doubled again by 1904. Limited local water sources were the sole obstacle to continued population growth.

The Search for Water

In 1902, the City of Los Angeles purchased the Los Angeles City Water Company. William Mulholland was the superintendent of the company, which was later renamed the Los Angeles Department of Water and Power (LADWP). Aware that Los Angeles needed more water as the city grew, Los Angeles mayor Fred Eaton realized that the best potential water sources were the Owens River and Owens Lake, some two hundred miles to the north. In 1905, when he was no longer mayor, he began to buy land in the more arid southern part of Owens Valley, along with the accompanying water rights.

After being assured that the water was for a cattle farm in Owens Valley, most residents sold their property and water rights, eager to move to more prosperous areas to the south. They were unaware that Eaton intended the water for eventual irrigation of the San Fernando Valley just north of Los Angeles.

After the City Council agreed to build an aqueduct from Owens Valley to Los Angeles, voters in 1905 approved a bond to buy some Owens Valley land. A bond to finance construction was approved in 1907, and the aqueduct was completed by 1913, though Owens Valley land purchases continued until 1934. Meanwhile, several unincorporated areas of San Fernando Valley voted to join Los Angeles in the years between 1915 and 1932.

Protests

In 1923, there was a water shortage in California, and Owens Valley residents blamed the aqueduct for pumping out their groundwater. On May 21, 1924, forty men dynamited the Lone Pine aqueduct spillway gate. On November 16 of that year, between sixty and one hundred protesters occupied the Alabama Gates. Between 1926 and 1927, there were about ten more instances of dynamiting. On May 26, 1926, ranchers blasted a ten-foot section of concrete-lined pipe one mile south of the Alabama Hills head gate. They dynamited the No Name Siphon area and another 475 feet of the aqueduct on May 27, 1927. The next day, the intake structure of the Big Pine powerhouse was also destroyed. Incidents reportedly continued until 1931, presumably because protesters intended to drive up the price of the remaining land that the City of Los Angeles wished to buy.

The two principal perpetrators of the protests were arrested for embezzlement and fraud in their banking business during August 1927, after which the protests petered out. They were later convicted and served prison sentences of ten years each.

Impact

The Los Angeles Aqueduct was claimed as the longest since the Roman aqueducts were constructed some two thousand years earlier. The original aqueduct proved insufficient for the needs of Los Angeles, so the city extended the aqueduct north toward tributaries of Mono Lake and also sought and obtained water from the Colorado River. In 1970, LADWP completed a second Owens Valley aqueduct. Water rationing continued to be put in effect during times of drought.

Because the aqueduct projects were completed without environmental impact reports, Inyo County, the Mono Lake Committee, and the National Audubon society sued the state of California during the 1970s and 1980s. Compromise settlements were reached, but Owens Valley and Mono Lake were left with troubled ecosystems. Much of the history of the development of the first aqueduct is the basis for the film *Chinatown* (1974), directed by Roman Polanski.

Michael Haas

Further Reading

Erie, Steven P. *Beyond Chinatown: The Metropolitan Water District, Growth, and the Environment in Southern California.* Stanford, Calif.: Stanford University Press, 2006. Discusses the coordination of water delivery to nineteen million residents in twenty-six cities and water districts in six counties.

Hoffman, Abraham. *Vision or Villainy: Origins of the Owens Valley–Los Angeles Water Controversy.* College Station: Texas A&M University Press, 1981. Scholarly history attempting to debunk various conspiracy theories.

Mulholland, Catherine. *William Mulholland and the Rise of Los Angeles.* Berkeley: University of California Press, 2000. A biography of the Irish immigrant by his granddaughter.

Reisner, Mark. *Cadillac Desert.* Rev. ed. New York: Penguin, 1993. An exposé of the government agencies that have sought to bring water to people in the arid parts of the West.

Sauder, Robert A. *The Lost Frontier: Water Diversion in the Growth and Destruction of Owens Valley Agriculture.* Tucson: University of Arizona Press, 1994. Examines the impact of the Los Angeles aqueduct on the people of Owens Valley.

Starr, Kevin. *Material Dreams: Southern California Through the 1920s.* New York: Oxford University Press, 1990. Establishes the context of population growth in Los Angeles, also dealing with the water wars.

Walton, John. *Western Times and Water Wars: State, Culture, and Rebellion in California.* Berkeley: University of California Press, 1992. Interprets the water wars in the context of rising populism against money politics, also discussing the dynamiting of the aqueduct.

See also: Cities; Natural resources, exploitation of; Science and technology

■ Los Angeles Memorial Coliseum

Upon its completion in 1923, the Los Angeles Memorial Coliseum was the largest sports stadium in the country, with

a seating capacity of over seventy-five thousand. Its construction provided much-needed promotion for the city of Los Angeles and played a prominent role in the city's being accepted to host the tenth Summer Olympic Games in 1932.

Football game at the Los Angeles Memorial Coliseum. (Getty Images)

The idea for the Los Angeles Memorial Coliseum began in the difficult economic climate following World War I, when an elite group of Los Angeles citizens known as the Community Development Association (CDA), led by *Los Angeles Times* publisher Harry Chandler, proposed the construction of a major sporting arena. At the time, the city had no outdoor sports facility, and the association felt that such a facility would encourage tourism and raise the national profile of the city. The association also decided that the stadium would memorialize World War I veterans.

Groundbreaking began on December 21, 1921. The CDA chose to place the stadium in Exposition Park due to its proximity to the University of Southern California, whose football team was to use the stadium for its home games. Architects John and Donald Parkinson modeled the east entrance, with its long, arcaded peristyle, on the ancient stadiums of Greece and Rome. Built in two years at a cost of $800,000, the coliseum was one of the most expensive arenas in the nation, second only to Yankee Stadium in New York City. The Parkinsons agreed to waive their profits to keep the project under budget and built the stadium over an existing gravel pit, saving on excavation costs.

Voters rejected a bond to fund the stadium, but the CDA created a funding arrangement to see their

project to completion: Using local bank loans, the CDA built the stadium and retained control of it for ten years, during which time it leased the building to the city of Los Angeles. The rental money paid back the loans, and the contract stipulated that after ten years the city would take over control of the arena. The transfer did not actually occur until after the 1932 Olympic Games.

Impact

October of 1923 saw the much-anticipated opening football game at the Los Angeles Memorial Coliseum. At the end of its first decade, the stadium was renovated in order to add an additional twenty-five thousand seats for the 1932 Summer Olympics. The Los Angeles Memorial Coliseum remains significant in the twenty-first century as the only U.S. stadium to have hosted two Olympic Games, two Super Bowls, and a World Series. Home to the University of Southern California Trojans football team, the coliseum joined the list of National Historic Landmarks on July 27, 1984.

Katie S. Greer

Further Reading

Epting, Chris. *Images of America: Los Angeles Memorial Coliseum.* Chicago: Arcadia, 2002.

Riess, Steven A. "Power Without Authority: Los Angeles' Elites and the Construction of the Coliseum." *Journal of Sport History* 8, no. 1 (Spring, 1981): 50–65.

See also: Architecture; Chandler, Harry; Football; Sports

■ Lost generation

Dubbed a "lost generation" by American writer Gertrude Stein, expatriate American writers living in Paris, France, after World War I benefited from the freedom of their surroundings and were mutually inspired with creative energy. Living far from the United States and being immersed in Parisian life allowed these writers to reexamine national values and to write from a fresh perspective and in a new style.

By the outbreak of World War I, Paris had become Europe's leading cultural center, attracting writers, artists, and musicians from the all over the continent. A small number of American writers and publishers established homes in the city, including

Edith Wharton, Gertrude Stein, Sylvia Beach, and Natalie Barney. Aspiring writers E. E. Cummings, John Dos Passos, Ernest Hemingway, Malcolm Cowley, Harry Crosby, and Dashiell Hammett, who had driven ambulances during World War I, returned to Paris in the early 1920s, soon to be joined by other talented Americans. Writers arrived from such literary circles as the Chicago Renaissance group, the Algonquin Round Table, and the Harlem Renaissance. Many were drawn not only by the presence of other creative people but also by the freedoms France offered: African Americans generally experienced less racial discrimination in Paris than in the United States, and unlike America, France had no laws prohibiting the consumption of alcohol or homosexual intimacy between consenting adults. Paris offered many opportunities for artistic and sensual experimentation. Economically, the city was especially affordable for writers because American newspapers paid for articles about Parisian life.

Café Society and Salons

Most of the expatriates clustered in Paris's Latin Quarter and the Montparnasse section of the city, living cheaply on the strength of the dollar as compared to the franc. They encountered one another at bookstores such as Sylvia Beach's Shakespeare & Company, as well as in restaurants such as the Rotonde and the Café du Dôme. Wealthy Americans Gerald and Sara Murphy opened their Riviera estate, Villa America, for frequent parties. Not surprisingly, the lost generation became notorious for its excesses, episodes of which have been chronicled in memoirs or thinly camouflaged in fictional accounts, such as F. Scott Fitzgerald's short story "Babylon Revisited" or his novel *Tender Is the Night*.

The literary salons hosted by writers Stein and Barney provided more sophisticated gatherings. Stein, whose literary experiments were considered as revolutionary as paintings by Spanish artist Pablo Picasso, mentored both Hemingway and Sherwood Anderson. Barney, known for the gatherings she held for her lesbian friends, was an influential supporter of the arts. She hosted weekly events that brought together Europeans and Americans, unpublished writers and potential publishers, and struggling artists and wealthy patrons. She established an academy for women writers and maintained close friendships with male authors such as Ezra Pound, Thornton Wilder, and Sinclair Lewis.

Hemingway's *The Sun Also Rises* (1926)

Ernest Hemingway's The Sun Also Rises *(1926) evoked the lives of disillusioned "lost generation" expatriates in a novel of brilliant dialogue and understated style. The novel's main characters, devastated by World War I, leave behind the modern world to travel to a seemingly more innocent, rural Spain. However, they are unable to escape a postwar world in which all traditional values seem abandoned. Hemingway's protagonist and alter ego Jake Barnes finds himself caught between his cynicism and his struggle to make sense of it all:*

I thought I had paid for everything. Not like a woman pays and pays and pays. No idea of retribution or punishment. Just exchange of values. You gave up something and got something else. Or you worked for something. You paid some way for everything that was any good. I paid my way into enough things that I liked, so that I had a good time. Either you paid by learning about them, or by experience, or by taking chances, or by money. Enjoying living was learning to get your money's worth and knowing when you had it. You could get your money's worth. The world was a good place to buy in. It seemed like a fine philosophy. In five years, I thought, it will seem just as silly as all the other fine philosophies I've had.

Literary Journals and Small Presses

The writers of the lost generation published in literary journals that were often financed and managed by Americans. Pound helped secure funding for *The Transatlantic Review* from American lawyer John Quinn, who had unsuccessfully defended *The Little Review*, founded by writers Margaret Anderson and Jane Heap, against charges of censorship for publishing segments of James Joyce's controversial novel *Ulysses* in the United States. Anderson and Heap moved *The Little Review* to Paris, where Beach published *Ulysses* through her bookstore, Shakespeare & Company. The publishing company Three Mountain Press, operated by Bill Bird, released Pound's poetry collection *A Draft of Cantos XVI*, Hemingway's first collection of short stories, and William Carlos Williams's work *The Great American Novel*. Author and publisher Robert McAlmon ran Contact Press, another small publishing house. In 1927, writers and patrons Harry and Caresse Crosby founded the influential Black Sun Press. In the same year, writer and critic Eugene Jolas launched the literary journal *transition*, which published works by European surrealists, as well as innovative poetry by Stein and Hart Crane.

Impact

The body of writing produced by the lost generation, while varied in theme and style, formed the basis of American literary modernism and influenced the direction of American literature in succeeding decades. The presses and literary journals of the period not only gave voice to aspiring writers and their unconventional work but also advanced the role of the cottage publishing industry in the literary world.

K. Edgington

Further Reading

Fabre, Michel. *From Harlem to Paris: Black American Writers in France, 1840–1980.* Urbana: University of Illinois Press, 1993. Contains chapters on lost generation writers Countee Cullen, Jessie Fauset, Gwendolyn Bennett, and Langston Hughes.

Fitch, Noel Riley. *Sylvia Beach and the Lost Generation: A History of Literary Paris in the Twenties and Thirties.* New York: W.W. Norton, 1983. Provides a clear account of the role Beach and her bookstore played in the development of American literature, also commenting on Beach's relationship with Irish author James Joyce, as well as her struggle to publish his novel *Ulysses.*

Hemingway, Ernest. *A Moveable Feast: Sketches of the Author's Life in Paris in the Twenties.* New York: Charles Scribner's Sons, 1964. A collection of anecdotes and profiles of major figures of the 1920s.

Kennedy, J. Gerald, and Jackson R. Bryer, eds. *French Connections: Hemingway and Fitzgerald Abroad.* New York: St. Martin's Press, 1998. Places the two writers and their major works in the context of post–World War I France.

Monk, Craig. *Writing the Lost Generation: Expatriate Autobiography and American Modernism.* Iowa City: University of Iowa Press, 2008. Examines seventeen lost generation autobiographies as critical texts that shaped American modernist literature.

Vaill, Amanda. *Everybody Was So Young: Gerald and Sara Murphy, a Lost Generation Love Story.* New York: Houghton Mifflin, 1998. A study of the wealthy

young couple that inspired the main characters of F. Scott Fitzgerald's novel *Tender Is the Night.*

See also: Fitzgerald, F. Scott; Harlem Renaissance; Hemingway, Ernest; Literature in the United States; Stein, Gertrude

■ Loudspeakers

Loudspeakers, devices that convert electrical impulses to acoustic waves, developed over many decades and communicated sound in 1920s motion picture theaters, radios, telephones, and television sets. Loudspeaker sound quality varied in importance, depending on the type of sound communication desired.

The first loudspeakers were installed in telephones by German inventor Johann Philipp Reis in 1861 and developed further by American inventor Alexander Graham Bell in 1876. Loudspeaker patents and ongoing developments in loudspeaker technology can be traced back to the work of other nineteenth-century inventors such as Ernst Siemens, Nikola Tesla, Thomas Edison, and Oliver Lodge. Lodge invented the "moving-coil" loudspeaker in the late nineteenth century. Although this later proved to be the best approach, it was not immediately successful. It was not until 1924 that the moving-coil loudspeaker, combined with direct radiator technology, took hold. The patents covering this device were attributed to American engineers Chester W. Rice and Edward W. Kellogg.

Sound is produced by vibrating air molecules that translate their frequency to the ear. The question for 1920s loudspeaker technicians was how to efficiently produce this vibration. Rice and Kellogg did so by attaching a thin, paperlike cone to a ring of rigid metal. This ring was made part of the loudspeaker enclosure and was therefore itself quite rigid. The center of this cone, however, had to be made to vibrate under the influence of electric waves, thus causing the paperlike cone to vibrate. This was called the direct radiator principle.

Attached to the center of this cone was a tiny coil of wire. This coil was placed between two permanent magnets (in some cases electromagnets were used), and the wires of the coil were attached to the output of whatever device was being used, such as a television or a radio. When a coil of wire was placed in a magnetic field, and the electrical current in the coil was varied, the coil itself vibrated up and down. Hence, an electrical wave fed to the tiny coil caused a small current to flow with varying frequency and amplitude. This vibration was transferred to the paper-like cone, producing sound.

Impact

Throughout the remainder of the 1920s, improvements were made in the moving-coil speaker, although none were dramatic. Although alternative designs have since been developed, the moving-coil direct radiator loudspeaker continues to be the most common form throughout the world in the twenty-first century.

Robert E. Stoffels

Further Reading

Beranek, Leo. *Acoustics.* New York: McGraw-Hill, 1954.

Davis, Don, and Eugene Patronis. *Loudspeakers and Loudspeaker Arrays: Sound System Engineering.* 2d ed. Boston: Elsevier Focal Press, 2006.

Eargle, J., and M. Gander. "Historical Perspectives and Technology Overview of Loudspeakers for Sound Reinforcement." *Journal of the Audio Engineering Society* 52, no. 4 (2004): 412–432.

See also: Electrical recording; Inventions; Science and technology; Talking motion pictures; Telephone technology and service; Television technology

■ Lowell, Amy

Identification: American poet
Born: February 9, 1874, Brookline, Massachusetts
Died: May 12, 1925, Brookline, Massachusetts

One of the leaders of the Imagist movement, Amy Lowell dominated the American poetry scene of the 1920s, publishing several volumes of verse, essays, and book-length studies. A dynamic public lecturer, she attracted a large following, not only to her own work, but also to the poetry of her contemporaries.

Amy Lowell was born into a distinguished and wealthy New England family of merchants, industrialists, scholars, poets, and educators. Growing up in the genteel surroundings of Brookline, Massachusetts, she was not expected to go to college or have a career, as most young women of her class married early and devoted themselves to their homes and families. By her late teens, however, Lowell had developed an abiding interest in literature, especially nineteenth-century poetry. She began writing early, though originally without any intention of publishing her work.

Early Career

As she entered her thirties, Lowell became more serious about her poetry. Critics deemed her first published book, *A Dome of Many-Coloured Glass* (1912), to be derivative and heavily influenced by the English Romantics, especially John Keats. Dissatisfied with her debut, Lowell was eager to learn about a new movement, Imagism, which abandoned much of the ornate style of nineteenth-century poetry in favor of a direct, stripped-down style in which the imagery was the focus of the poem. She soon became friends with the leading Imagists, including Richard Aldington and H. D. (Hilda Doolittle), and effectively acted as the group's business manager and promoter, even as her own poetry began to demonstrate increasing vigor. By the end of World War I, Lowell had established herself as a leading talent of, and proselytizer for, the new poetry.

Maturity

By the early 1920s, Lowell had become a controversial figure, appearing on public platforms to debate new forms of poetry with audiences that still esteemed traditional forms such as the sonnet and believed that poetry should rhyme. A champion of free verse, Lowell argued that modern life was more attuned to poems that followed broader rhythms and emulated natural speech patterns, rather than those measured by the number of syllables per line. At the same time, she pioneered what she called "polyphonic prose," a style that brought to prose the intensity of poetry, especially in terms of its images and internal rhymes. Yet she was also an admirer of more traditional writers like Robert Frost, a poet she hailed in journals such as *The New Republic* and *The Bookman* as one of the great writers of the 1920s.

Keenly aware of the energy driving other artistic movements of the decade, Lowell sought to make poetry an essential element of American culture. In her effort to dispel her compatriots' provincialism, she also brought to 1920s America an appreciation of modern French poetry. Poets like Ezra Pound and

T. S. Eliot attacked her for what they saw as a dilution of poetry's power, believing that it would—and should—always appeal only to a minority of aesthetes. The idea that poetry could be an important element in democratic culture seemed preposterous to certain modernist writers whose sense of exclusivity was part of an authoritarian temperament. Lowell's more capacious sense of what poetry could be won her many followers, although her tendency toward frequent publication produced much writing of middling quality that obscured her best work.

Lowell's many books include verse narratives, translations of Chinese poetry, and biographical and literary criticism. She returned to her roots in nineteenth-century poetry with her biography of John Keats and was one of the first Keats biographers to do justice to his love for Fanny Brawne, presenting her in much more rounded and sympathetic terms than previous biographies. However, it is her lyric poems of the 1920s that have continued to interest contemporary critics. Her love poems addressed to her companion, the actress Ada Dwyer Russell, express an intensity akin to that found in the novels and poetry of D. H. Lawrence—another writer with whom she frequently corresponded and whose work she publicized, despite the scandal it caused in conservative American literary circles. In 1926, a year after her death, Lowell was posthumously awarded the Pulitzer Prize in poetry.

Impact

As biographers and her fellow Imagists attest, Amy Lowell was a key figure in American poetry during the 1920s. A flamboyant performer, known for smoking cigars and traveling in high style in her Pierce-Arrow automobile, she could draw audiences in the hundreds to her readings and lectures. While she retained many of her family's conservative convictions—she refused, for example, to support the feminists of the 1920s—her unorthodox lifestyle and poetry nevertheless contributed significantly to the changing manners and styles of the decade.

Carl Rollyson

Further Reading

Damon, S. Foster. *Amy Lowell: A Chronicle, with Extracts from Her Correspondence.* Boston: Houghton Mifflin, 1935. An extensive biography written by a friend of Lowell's, supplemented by primary documents.

Gould, Jean. *Amy: The World of Amy Lowell and the Imagist Movement.* New York: Dodd, Mead, 1975. A candid and intimate biography.

Gregory, Horace. *Amy Lowell: Portrait of the Poet in Her Time.* New York: Thomas Nelson & Sons, 1958. A broad sketch that places Lowell in the context of the contemporary literary scene.

Munich, Adrienne, and Melissa Bradshaw, eds. *Amy Lowell, American Modern.* New Brunswick, N.J.: Rutgers University Press, 2004. A collection of essays discussing Lowell's work.

Ruihley, Glenn Richard. *The Thorn of a Rose: Amy Lowell Reconsidered.* Hamden, Conn.: Archon Books, 1975. A biography of Lowell that includes a critical defense of her poetry.

See also: *Bookman, The;* Doolittle, Hilda; Frost, Robert; *John Keats;* Literature in the United States; Poetry

---

■ Luce, Henry R.

Identification: American magazine publisher and editor
Also known as: Father Time
Born: April 3, 1898, Tengchow, China
Died: February 28, 1967, Phoenix, Arizona

With the initial publication of Time *magazine in 1923, Henry Luce launched the first national weekly news magazine in the United States. Luce had a reputation for being a tough editor and a visionary manager and publisher. With his strong interest in politics and world events, Luce became a dominant figure in journalism and spent his career building the vast Time Inc., later home to* Fortune *(1930),* Life *(1936),* Sports Illustrated *(1954), and* People *(1974).*

Henry Robinson Luce's interest in journalism and international affairs could be traced to his childhood as the son of Presbyterian missionaries. He was born in 1898 in China and spent most of his childhood there. His parents emphasized a solid education, and Luce was an avid reader of newspapers and magazines. He later honed his journalism skills as a college staff member of the *Yale Daily News.*

Luce's professional career began in 1921, when he worked as a reporter for the *Chicago Daily News.* In late 1921, he joined the staff of the *Baltimore News,* where he was reunited with college friend and former journalism rival Briton Hadden. The two decided to start their own weekly publication with content that would be radically different from what they considered the dry, formulaic writing of the large daily newspapers. They preferred news articles that were structured like a story with a beginning, middle, and end and not written in the inverted pyramid style (with the main facts first) of most newspapers.

Time Magazine

In February 1922, the two men resigned from the Baltimore paper to work on the new magazine, initially called *Facts*. They changed the name to *Time: The Weekly News Magazine*, believing that their publication would inform busy readers about major world events in less time than a newspaper. Luce and Hadden began their venture—incorporating as Time Inc.—with $86,000 collected from various sources.

True to the original vision, *Time* magazine's first issue offered news analyses and a subjective point of view on world issues. The stories were compartmentalized into news sections, and the writing was crisp, light, and laced with adjectives, inverted sentence structure, and opinionated observations that were to become known among journalists as "Timestyle." Luce did not believe that anyone, even a trained journalist, could be objective. The content of *Time* reflected this belief.

When the first issue launched on March 3, 1923, Luce and Hadden were counting on the magazine to appeal to an educated, middle-class audience. Both men shared duties at first, but eventually Luce took over as business manager and Hadden as editor. The first editorial staff was all male and included many of the publishers' friends and former college classmates. All were well educated, but few had extensive journalism experience.

Time often focused on individuals rather than events and would offer detailed stories about the personal interests of political and social figures of the era. The magazine lost money its first year and had fewer than 20,000 subscribers. After several years of shaping the style and content of the magazine, however, the two men began to enjoy success. By 1925, subscription rates began to rise, and by 1930, circulation has risen to 300,000.

Luce, prompted by his strong interest in business and the lack of space for financial stories in *Time*, launched a second major magazine, *Fortune*, in 1929. Hadden died during the planning stages

Henry R. Luce. (Time & Life Pictures/Getty Images)

of the magazine, and Luce bought his partner's stock share. *Fortune* was the first magazine devoted exclusively to business. The stock market crashed in October 1929, three months before the first copy of *Fortune* was published. The magazine survived, primarily by devoting its first several issues to investigating business methods and the reasons behind the financial collapse.

Personal Life

Luce married his first wife, Lila Hotz, on December 22, 1923. They had two sons. The couple divorced in 1935, the same year Luce met and married his second wife, Clare Boothe, who had one daughter from a previous marriage. Boothe was famous in her own right as a playwright, journalist, ambassador, and U.S. congresswoman. Luce, a Republican and devout Presbyterian, always remained active in the promotion of Christianity and philanthropy, particularly in China.

In 1964, Luce retired from what had become one of the world's largest and most successful publishing companies. Luce enterprises made $503 million in 1966. Luce died in 1967 at the age of 64.

Impact

Editors at more "serious" magazines such as the *New Yorker*, the *Nation*, and *Literary Digest* initially criticized *Time* for editorial bias and its unusual style of long, descriptive news stories, but by 1938, *Literary Digest* had ceased publication, and by the mid-1930s, many major newspapers across the country had begun adding Sunday news magazines to compete with the *Time* format. With the success of *Time*, Henry Luce created the first news magazine and what would become one of the world's largest media companies, Time Inc. The company's magazines, books, broadcast media, and other outlets would dominate journalism and reach millions of news consumers in the ensuing decades. As a strong believer in capitalism and an outspoken conservative, Luce was more than a publisher; he was a media giant who left a lasting influence on journalism, world politics, and economics.

Sherri Ward Massey

Further Reading

Baughman, James L. *Henry R. Luce and the Rise of the American News Media.* Baltimore, Md.: Johns Hopkins University Press, 2001.

Brinkley, Alan. *The Publisher: Henry Luce and His American Century.* New York: Alfred A. Knopf, 2010.

Herzstein, Robert E. *Henry R. Luce: A Political Portrait of the Man Who Created the American Century.* New York: Charles Scribner's Sons, 1994.

See also: Hearst, William Randolph; Magazines; *New Yorker, The;* Newspapers, U.S.

■ Lynching

Lynching was most prevalent in the southern United States from the late nineteenth century through the early twentieth century and was used primarily as a form of social and racial control of African Americans by whites. Although lynching was still practiced in the South during the 1920s as a means of punishment and control, several factors contributed to its decline during that decade.

Lynching is the mob killing of a person without legal authorization. Hanging has been the most common method in the United States, but it has also included beating, burning, castration, and dismemberment. Many believe the term originated

Ku Klux Klan's Use of Lynching

By the early 1920s, the Ku Klux Klan had some three million members, many of them prominent representatives of the middle class, and the group successfully influenced the election of public officials in Indiana, Oregon, Oklahoma, and other states. In Tulsa, numerous judges, lawyers, doctors, teachers, entertainers, bankers, and businessmen were Klan members. The Klan and its sympathizers enforced their views through violence and intimidation, particularly lynching. The actions of lynch mobs are often thought of as spontaneous outbreaks of violence, but in fact many were planned events, with newspapers announcing their time and place, agents selling train tickets to the sites, and families packing picnic lunches to watch the gruesome spectacles.

during the American Revolution with Colonel Charles Lynch, who with several others took unauthorized actions to punish suspected Loyalists. During the 1800s, lynching was a form of punishment and intimidation used in the West against cattle rustlers and horse thieves. However, lynching became most common in the South and the southern border states following the Civil War to maintain white authority after the emancipation of the slaves.

Lynchings increased dramatically in the late 1860s after the founding of the Ku Klux Klan, a southern white supremacy group intent on enforcing segregationist Jim Crow laws and codes of conduct. African American males were lynched more than any other race or gender, and individuals needed only to be accused of a crime to become victims of lynching. Murder or rape were common provocations for lynching, but a black man arguing with a white person, living with a white woman, or demanding respect from a white person could also incur the wrath of white mobs. Since there was no formal arrest or trial, crimes were often fabricated to justify the violence, which was sometimes attended by hundreds of spectators.

Migration and Resistance

A noticeable decline in lynching occurred in the early 1900s, partly due to the Great Migration of the

1920s, during which approximately one million southern blacks moved north to escape white violence and in pursuit of jobs created by the labor shortage due to World War I. African Americans were also beginning to resist mob violence in the 1920s, despite the fact that such resistance often resulted in greater violence. In 1921, for example, a group of African American World War I veterans gathered to protect a young black man in Tulsa, Oklahoma, who had been accused of assaulting a white female elevator operator and arrested. In a scuffle at the jail, a gun was fired, and a white mob member was killed. Whites retaliated by setting fire to and destroying over one thousand homes and two hundred businesses in the segregated Greenwood district of Tulsa. The Tulsa race riot killed thirty-nine individuals, twenty-six of them black; some reports claim the number of blacks killed was much higher.

Antilynching Legislation

In June of 1920, six African American men were accused of raping a young white woman at a circus in Duluth, Minnesota. A mob of several thousand whites forced itself into the jail where they were being held, pulled the six men from their cells, and beat and lynched three of them. After national and local reports decried the lynching, activists pushed for a state antilynching bill, which was signed into law on April 21, 1921. The bill provided for the firing of police officers deemed negligent in protecting people in their custody from lynch mobs and for damages to be paid to the families of any person lynched.

The National Association for the Advancement of Colored People (NAACP) aggressively campaigned for federal antilynching legislation in the early part of the twentieth century. In addition to the numerous state-level lawsuits brought in defense of black civil rights, the NAACP lobbied Congress to pass the Dyer antilynching bill, first introduced by Representative Leonidas Dyer of Missouri in 1918. The bill classified lynching as a federal crime and authorized jail time and/or stiff fines for individuals involved in a lynching. Additionally, the county where a lynching took place would pay remunerations to the victim's family. The Dyer bill, initially passed by the House of Representatives in 1922, was defeated in the Senate by southern Democratic senators, who argued that it was unconstitutional and a violation of state's rights.

Impact

Through the efforts of resistance, migration, and legislation, lynchings of African Americans throughout the southern United States in the 1920s declined significantly from previous decades. According to records kept by the Tuskegee Institute, the lynchings of 281 African Americans were reported nationwide from 1920 through 1929—about half as many as in the preceding decade. By the 1920s, Minnesota and several other states had passed antilynching laws, but lynching was not addressed on the federal level until the civil rights laws of the 1960s. In 2005, the U.S. Senate approved a resolution formally apologizing for failing to pass antilynching legislation in the late nineteenth and early twentieth centuries.

Richard L. McWhorter

Further Reading

Berg, Manfred. *Popular Justice: A History of Lynching in America.* Lanham, Md.: Ivan R. Dee Publishers, 2011. Provides a history of lynching from colonial times in America through the early twenty-first century.

Fedo, Michael. *The Lynchings in Duluth.* St. Paul: Minnesota Historical Society Press, 2000. Account of the 1920 lynching of three black men in Duluth, Minnesota, which spurred the state's antilynching law.

Ginzburg, Ralph. *One Hundred Years of Lynchings.* Baltimore, Md.: Black Classic Press, 1988. Collection of newspaper articles describing incidents of lynching in the United States from the 1860s through the 1960s.

Lightweis-Goff, Jennie. *Blood at the Root: Lynching as American Cultural Nucleus.* Albany: State University of New York Press, 2011. Examines the geographical and cultural history of lynching through a focus on cultural, visual, and literary texts.

Madigan, Tim. *The Burning: Massacre, Destruction, and the Tulsa Race Riot of 1921.* New York: St. Martin's Press, 2001. Recounts the Tulsa, Oklahoma, race riot of 1921, using taped interviews with survivors and witnesses.

See also: African Americans; Dyer antilynching bill; Jim Crow in the U.S. South; Ku Klux Klan; National Association for the Advancement of Colored People (NAACP); Racial discrimination

■ MacLeish, Archibald

Identification: American poet, playwright, and public
official
Born: May 7, 1892, Glencoe, Illinois
Died: April 20, 1982, Boston, Massachusetts

*Throughout the 1920s, Archibald MacLeish sought to un-
derstand and express his relationship to America through
poetry. A member of the lost generation writers, MacLeish's
efforts during this period led to literary works that later won
him three Pulitzer Prizes.*

As a young man, Archibald MacLeish pursued a legal
career, but in 1923, he turned his attention to writing
poetry. His experiences of World War I and its aftermath prompted him to take his family to France,
where other American expatriate authors such as Ernest Hemingway, F. Scott Fitzgerald, and Gertrude
Stein were also living. There, MacLeish published
three collections of verse: *The Happy Marriage* (1924),
The Pot of Earth (1925), and *Streets in the Moon* (1926),
in which two poems, "The Silent Slain" and "Memorial Rain," are dedicated to the memory of his brother
Kenneth, who had perished in the war. Other poems
of this period reflect the expatriate's sense of loss of
traditional values. Originally published in *Streets in the
Moon*, MacLeish's poem "Ars Poetica," with its famous assertion that a poem "should not mean, but
be," became an almost inevitable part of later American poetry anthologies.

Return from France
After returning from Europe in 1928, MacLeish
bought a farm in Conway, Massachusetts, which remained his primary home for the next fifty years.
That same year, MacLeish published the poem "The
Hamlet of A. MacLeish" and the following year "Einstein," which both illustrate the extent to which expatriate poetic contemporaries Ezra Pound and T. S.
Eliot had influenced his work.

MacLeish's second most celebrated poem, "You,
Andrew Marvell," appeared in his 1930 volume *New
Found Land.* It alludes to British writer Andrew Marvell's seventeenth-century poem "To His Coy Mistress" and its theme to live each day to its fullest.
"You, Andrew Marvell," which is MacLeish's eerie
response to Marvell's injunction, describes a person
continuing to lie facedown in the sun as night's
shadow sweeps across the world. The poem can be
read as a pessimistic disavowal of Marvell's message,
but it could also be understood as a warning to anyone
who does not rise to the opportunity that each day
provides.

Reconciliation with America
In the late 1920s, MacLeish wrote the poem "American Letter," which also appeared in *New Found Land*
and signified an emotional return to his native land
and the need to reestablish his connection with it.
The poem demonstrates MacLeish's urge to recapture the American Dream and is inscribed "For
Gerald Murphy," an American artist living in southern
France. It reiterates MacLeish's discomfort at being
American, dreaming of foreign places and finding it
difficult to realize the great possibilities available in
one's native land. Many believe MacLeish implies in
this poem the need to serve and understand one's
country.

From 1928 to 1929, MacLeish traveled through
Mexico on foot and mule to retrace the route of
Spanish explorer Hernán Cortés's army as it conquered Mexico in the sixteenth century. Using this
research, MacLeish would write the epic poem *Con-
quistador* that, in 1933, would earn him the first of his
three Pulitzer Prizes. The poem is based on a history
of the Spanish conquest of Mexico and is told from
the perspective of Bernál Díaz, a Spanish foot soldier
in Cortés's army. Many believe the theme of conquest
in this poem is meant to be a metaphor for the European conquest of North America, the land that would
become the United States.

Impact

In addition to writing poems that have persisted as anthology favorites, MacLeish's career illustrates the attitude of American intellectuals who feared the nation's failure to understand that the postwar extravagance of society posed threats of continuing disorder. MacLeish's dissatisfaction with the United States was transformed during this period with attempts to come to terms with it. Committed to his country as he was, MacLeish rejected the Marxist philosophy that began to compel many American intellectuals in the 1920s and grew stronger after the 1929 stock market crash. The essentially positive evolution of his thinking in the late 1920s prepared him for a later distinguished career in American government and public service to such international bodies as the United Nations Educational, Scientific, and Cultural Organization (UNESCO).

Robert P. Ellis

Further Reading

Donaldson, Scott, and R. H. Winnick. *Archibald MacLeish: An American Life*. Boston, Mass.: Houghton Mifflin, 1992. Covers MacLeish's expatriate life, Harvard professorship, *Fortune* magazine editorship, and political work in the United States.

Drabeck, Bernard A., and Helen E. Ellis, eds. *Archibald MacLeish: Reflections*. Amherst: University of Massachusetts Press, 1988. A biography drawn from conversations recorded the last four years of MacLeish's life, including MacLeish's commentary on his poetry, prose, and the writings of his contemporaries.

MacLeish, Archibald. *Collected Poems, 1917–1982*. Boston, Mass.: Houghton Mifflin Company, 1985. A collection of poems, some found in manuscript form after MacLeish's death.

MacLeish, William H. *Uphill with Archie: A Son's Journey*. New York: Simon & Schuster, 2001. Juxtaposes the lives of MacLeish and his youngest son and includes recollections of time spent with noted poets and authors of the 1920s.

Smith, Grover. *Archibald MacLeish*. Minneapolis: University of Minnesota Press, 1971. A study of MacLeish's life and work.

See also: Eliot, T. S.; Fitzgerald, F. Scott; Hemingway, Ernest; Lost Generation; Poetry; Stein, Gertrude

■ Macy's Thanksgiving Day Parade

The Event: Launch of the annual parade in New York City
Date: November 27, 1924
Place: New York, New York

What began as the Macy's Christmas Parade on November 27, 1924, has become an annual Thanksgiving Day tradition with millions of spectators nationwide. The 1924 parade was a huge success for Macy's Department Stores and was so popular with parade-goers that it has been held every year since.

Now known as the Macy's Thanksgiving Day Parade, the Macy's Christmas Parade was first held on November 27, 1924. The idea for the parade came from Macy's employees, many of whom were European immigrants and were accustomed to large, outdoor Christmas celebrations in their homelands. When they approached Macy's president Herbert Strauss, he approved the idea and placed ads in local newspapers claiming that Macy's would provide "a surprise New York will never forget."

The first parade began at 9 A.M., was six miles long, and was watched by approximately 250,000 spectators along the parade route. Early floats featured well-known characters such as the Old Lady in the Shoe, Little Miss Muffet, and Little Red Riding Hood. The parade also included live animals borrowed from the Central Park Zoo. The current tradition of musical entertainment started with the first parade when four bands performed along the route.

In 1927, the parade changed its name to the Macy's Thanksgiving Day Parade and featured four giant character balloons: Felix the Cat, a dinosaur, a toy soldier, and an elephant. These early balloons were inflated with pure helium, which exploded when the balloons were released at the end of the parade. The following year, the balloons were mixed with helium and air, and from 1929 to 1932, the balloons were affixed with a return address and Macy's presented a cash reward to whoever returned the balloon.

Celebrities became a traditional part of the parade in 1934, and the parade was first televised in 1945. From 1942 to 1944 the parade was canceled because of a shortage of helium and rubber during World War II.

Impact

Since its launch in 1924, the Macy's Thanksgiving Day Parade has become an annual holiday event for families to attend in New York City. The parade has grown more spectacular every year as additional giant balloons have been added to the lineup and big-name celebrities have agreed to perform. With the advent of television, millions of people nationwide now watch the parade from their homes, and it continues to be a favorite family holiday tradition.

Stephanie Hines

Further Reading

Grippo, Robert M. *Macy's: The Store, the Star, the Story.* Garden City Park, N.Y.: Square One Publishers, 2009.

Grippo, Robert M., and Christopher Hoskins. *Macy's Thanksgiving Day Parade.* Charleston, S.C.: Arcadia Publishing, 2004.

See also: Felix the Cat

■ Magazines

Magazines increased in popularity in the 1920s, with many beginning publication during the decade and many already in existence experiencing an increase in circulation. Through their widespread sale and distribution, magazines served to spread fashions and other trends through articles and advertisements, popularize a great number of influential authors, and give a voice to the activists and underrepresented groups of the period.

The development of the magazine industry in the United States began in the mid-eighteenth century, when the relationship between magazines and advertisers was largely nonexistent. However, the two industries soon became interdependent, and by the early twentieth century, this fusion resulted in the creation of the popular magazine, a commercial publication intended to be read by a large, general audience. This change, along with cheaper methods of publishing, ultimately led to an increase in circulation, especially within the middle class. This increase continued throughout the 1920s as new and existing magazines achieved widespread popularity and both reflected and shaped the culture of the decade.

New Magazines

Many magazines that would become prominent and influential in later decades were first published in the 1920s. Among the more significant was *The Saturday Review*, a Saturday supplement to the *New York Evening Post* that began publication in 1920 and became a separate magazine in 1924. *Better Homes and Gardens*, originally titled *Fruit, Garden and Home*, was founded in 1922 by publisher Edwin T. Meredith, a former United States secretary of agriculture. *Better Homes and Gardens* became an extremely prosperous magazine, achieving a circulation of one million by the end of the decade. Another important title first published during the decade was *Reader's Digest*, founded by DeWitt and Lila Wallace. First circulated in 1923, it published reprinted and abridged articles featuring useful information. Also established in 1923, *Time*, founded by Henry Luce and Britton Hadden, was conceived as a concise news report intended for busy businesspeople. In its first issue, it covered many different areas of news in only thirty-two pages and introduced the magazine's signature writing style. In 1928, the magazine began its yearly recognition of the year's most influential person, naming aviator Charles Lindbergh its first "Man of the Year."

The American Mercury, founded in 1924 by journalist and social critic H. L. Mencken and his editorial partner George Jean Nathan, was in some ways a continuation of an earlier magazine, *The Smart Set* (1900–1930, edited by Mencken and Nathan from 1914 to 1923). Seeking a readership of intellectuals and skeptics and gaining a circulation of seventy thousand by the late 1920s, its articles were generally short and iconoclastic or satirical, emphasizing American topics. *Commonweal*, founded in 1924 by Michael Williams, was the first independent Catholic journal in the United States and would go on to take controversial positions on a number of religious and political issues. *The New Yorker*, founded by Harold Ross in 1925, mixed humor, fiction, nonfiction, and news aimed at a sophisticated audience. The illustrations, sketches, and satirical drawings included in the early issues soon became a distinguishing feature of the magazine. Also in 1925, *Arizona Highways* was founded by the Arizona Highway Department as a publication dedicated to Arizona road construction and maintenance; however, it would go on to become a magazine filled with travelogues and artistic photographs, including some by noted photographer Ansel Adams.

Cofounder of Time *magazine Briton Hadden is pictured here at his desk.* (Time & Life Pictures/Getty Images)

The short-lived magazine *Fire!!* was created in 1926 by such noted Harlem Renaissance figures as Langston Hughes and Zora Neale Hurston and featured a variety of literary works by its creators and others. Although only one issue was released, the magazine served to further define the artistic goals of the Harlem Renaissance, shaping the legacy of the period. Also in 1926, the *New York Enquirer*, which would eventually became the *National Enquirer*, was founded by William Griffin. *Parents* was founded that same year by George J. Hecht; edited by Clara Savage Littledale, the magazine reported on health and nutrition in a manner easily understood by the average reader. *BusinessWeek*, first published several weeks before the stock market crash in 1929, also focused on providing valuable information in lay terms.

Other important magazines founded during the 1920s included *Architectural Digest* (1920), *The Freeman* (1920), *PGA Magazine* (1920), *Scott Stamp Monthly* (1920), *Writer's Digest* (1920), *Barron's* (1921), *The Hunter's Horn* (1921), *Elks Magazine* (1922), *Foreign Affairs* (1922), *The Fugitive* (1922), *Harvard Business Review* (1922), *Antiques* (1922), *Outdoor America* (1922), *Science News* (1922), *The Ring* (1922), *The Golden Book Magazine* (1925), *Camping Magazine* (1926), *Dance Magazine* (1926), *Flying* (1927), *Flying Models* (1928), and *Model Airplane News* (1929).

Established Magazines

In addition to the foundation of many influential magazines and journals, the 1920s also brought about a circulation increase for many existing magazines, with some experiencing newfound national popularity. *The American Magazine* (1876) focused on human interest stories, social issues, and fiction; the February 1922 cover reported that circulation had reached 1.75 million. *The Delineator* (1873) had more than one million subscribers by 1920; it enjoyed much success due to its focus on the changing roles of women during the early decades of the twentieth century. Founded in 1883, *The Ladies' Home Journal* also appealed to the new key readership demographic of women, who played an essential role in the success of magazines and the advertisements during the 1920s. *House Beautiful* (1896) not only appealed to female readers but also named a number of female editors, with Ethel B. Power editing throughout much of the 1920s. *Good Housekeeping* (1885) had been acquired by the Hearst Corporation in 1911, and its decision to publish literature written by its readers and offer publication contests resulted in increased dissemination. Another Hearst title, *American Weekly* (1896), featured sensationalist stories and illustrations of beautiful women. *The Crisis*, the magazine founded by W. E. B. Du Bois for the National Association for the Advancement of Colored People (NAACP) in 1910, continued to publish fiction, essays, and news related to African American interests throughout the decade.

Small literary magazines also accounted for a portion of the periodical readership during the decade, as numerous influential writers of the period wrote short fiction and first published their works in magazines, frequently while living abroad. *The Little Review*, founded by Margaret Anderson in 1914, published such famous transatlantic modernists and experimental writers as Ezra Pound and James Joyce. The magazine was published throughout the decade, as were *The Midland* (1915), the *Southwest Review* (1915), and *The Dial* (1840).

Impact

Magazines have made significant contributions to culture throughout their history, and the magazines of the 1920s were no exception. Many of the authors published in literary magazines during the period, such as Ernest Hemingway and Langston Hughes, continued to grow in fame in later decades, and the trends promoted within magazines and their advertisements shaped the popular perception of the period. Despite economic hardship, many magazines first published in the 1920s survived the Great Depression and endured into the subsequent decades, with the publication of some continuing into the next century.

Anthony J. Fonseca

Further Reading

Brown, Bruce W. *Images of Family Life in Magazine Advertising: 1920–1978*. Edited by Suzanne K. Steinmetz. New York: Praeger, 1981. Chronicles how female consumers became a key demographic for magazine advertisers.

Kitch, Carolyn. *Pages from the Past: History and Memory in American Magazines*. Chapel Hill: University of North Carolina Press, 2005. Explores the role of magazines in shaping and recording the culture and history of the United States.

Mott, Frank Luther. *A History of American Magazines*. 5 vols. Cambridge, Mass.: Harvard University Press, 1968. Includes detailed discussions and photos, as well as informative bibliographic histories, of various U.S. magazines.

Sumner, David E. *The Magazine Century: American Magazines Since 1900*. New York: Peter Lang, 2010. Chronicles American magazines published between 1900 and 2000, noting the reading public's habits and the growth of magazines by decade.

Wood, James Playsted. *Magazines in the United States*. 3d ed. New York: Ronald Press, 1971. Discusses American reading habits, women's magazines, muckraking magazines, and farm magazines, with emphasis on major titles and literary magazines.

See also: Advertising in the United States; *American Mercury, The; Dial, The;* Hearst, William Randolph; Mencken, H. L.; *New Yorker, The;* Wallace, DeWitt

---

■ Mah-Jongg

The Chinese game of Mah-Jongg became popular in the United States in the 1920s as part of a broader fad for both games and Asian-inspired goods. First standardized for *American players early in the decade, the tile-based game proved to be an inexpensive form of socialization that appealed to players from a wide range of socioeconomic backgrounds.*

Mah-Jongg was originally developed in China, likely arising from a combination of tile and card games played for money in peasant villages. The origin of the Chinese game's modern form is similarly uncertain, but one theory credits imperial army officer Chen Yumen with combining elements of these peasant games in the mid-nineteenth century. Both Chinese and American styles of Mah-Jongg are similar to the card game rummy. Each player starts with thirteen or fourteen tiles and draws or discards tiles in order to assemble a legal hand. In American Mah-Jongg, hands may be made up of specific number patterns, matching pairs or groups, or other configurations of tiles.

Standard Oil representative Joseph Park Babcock introduced a simplified version of the game to the United States in the 1920s, standardizing the rules and westernizing the tile symbols to make them accessible to American players. Babcock's modified rules were detailed in his 1920 book *The Rules of Mah-Jongg*, which would be included in many game sets later in the decade. Babcock also formed the Mah-Jongg Sales Company and trademarked the spelling "Mah-Jongg" (generic variant spellings such as "mah-jong" and "mah jong" have also been in wide use since the game was introduced). The game was modestly popular at first but became a major hit by the mid-1920s. Other game and toy manufacturers, including Milton Bradley and Parker Brothers, produced cheap wooden and luxurious ivory sets. Demand for Mah-Jongg sets was so high that Chinese-made tiles were at times manufactured from cow bones from the United States, as ivory was more difficult to obtain in large quantities.

The Mah-Jongg craze continued throughout the 1920s. Songs such as Eddie Cantor's "Since Ma Is Playing Mah Jong" satirized the game's popularity, while making racially stereotyped comments about its origins. Nevertheless, enthusiasts founded Mah-Jongg clubs that would continue to operate even after the end of the initial fad. Members often played in rooms elaborately decorated with Chinese furniture, silks, and fans, as well as Asian-inspired Art Deco pieces.

Impact

Mah-Jongg's popularity waned by the end of the 1920s, but the game continued to be played by dedicated groups throughout the subsequent decades. One such group, the National Mah Jongg League, formed in 1937 and produced a rule book outlining new standardized rules for American Mah-Jongg. The widespread growth and use of the Internet has spurred new interest in the game and its variants, including computer-based Mah-Jongg solitaire.

Alexandra Carter

Further Reading

Cavallero, Christina, and Anita Luu. *Mah-Jongg: From Shanghai to Miami Beach*. San Francisco: Chronicle Books, 2005.

Rep, Jelte. *The Great Mah-Jong Book: History, Lore, and Play*. North Clarendon, Vt.: Tuttle Publishing, 2007.

See also: Asia; Fads; Hobbies and recreation

■ *Main Currents in American Thought*

Identification: A three-volume study of American intellectual history
Author: Vernon Louis Parrington
Date: 1927 to 1930

In its three volumes, Main Currents in American Thought *presented the first full-scale history of ideas in America, discussing key thinkers from early colonial times through the beginning of the 1920s. Viewing ideas as instruments of change, author Vernon Louis Parrington presented his pessimistic assessment of the decline of liberalism through the numerous intellectual portraits included in his work.*

Historian Vernon Louis Parrington published *Main Currents in American Thought* in three volumes between 1927 and 1930, with the third volume published posthumously. Inspired by populist political theory and the works of such progressive historians as James Harvey Robinson and Charles Beard, Parrington set out to showcase the development of American ideas from the seventeenth through the early twentieth centuries in the writings of scholars, statesmen, and authors such as Roger Williams, Anne Hutchinson, Thomas Jefferson, Thomas Paine,

Andrew Jackson, Abraham Lincoln, Frank Norris, and William Dean Howells. Fearful of big government and big business, he also sought to critically assess the tension between American democratic theory as articulated by its most important exponents and the actual historical experience of American democracy.

In *Main Currents in American Thought*, Parrington describes the conflicts between the forces of progress and reaction that have shaped American ideology. He describes the progress of ideas as a bitter struggle between democratic optimism and rationality, marked by intellectual freedom, and pessimism, characterized by aristocratic inflexibility and religious intolerance. In the first volume, *The Colonial Mind, 1620–1800*, he represents the religious ideas of the Massachusetts Bay Colony leaders as dogmatic and inflexible. In *The Romantic Revolution in America, 1800–1860*, he continues his pessimistic analysis when describing the development of the West, chronicling the displacement of an older, genteel agrarianism with a new philosophy of economic progress marked by business consolidation and corporate profit. *The Beginnings of Critical Realism in America, 1860–1920* completes the historical narrative, with Parrington expressing dissatisfaction with the emergence of a business-oriented middle class and its dominance of all aspects of democratic liberal thought. He attributes what he sees as social and political decline to the consolidation of big business and scientific determinism.

Impact

In the 1920s, an era marked by intolerance and postwar disillusionment despite its seemingly widespread prosperity, *Main Currents in American Thought* was a sobering reminder of corporate America's effects on the agrarian, rural way of life and on American politics. For its contributions to the field of history, Vernon Louis Parrington's intellectual history of the United States was awarded the Pulitzer Prize in 1928 and exerted a profound influence on American historiography for a generation or more.

Charles F. Howlett

Further Reading

Hall, H. Lark. *V. L. Parrington: Through the Avenue of Art*. Piscataway, N.J.: Transaction, 2011.

Hofstadter, Richard. *The Progressive Historians: Turner, Beard, Parrington*. New York: Random House, 1968.

Skotheim, Robert Allen. *American Intellectual Histories and Historians.* Princeton, N.J.: Princeton University Press, 1966.

See also: *Frontier in American History, The;* Historiography

■ *Main Street*

Identification: A novel about a young woman frustrated by small-town life
Author: Sinclair Lewis
Date: 1920

Main Street challenged the predominant view of midwestern life by dissecting the mediocrity and cultural sterility of the fictional but typical small town of Gopher Prairie, Minnesota. One of Sinclair Lewis's first novels, Main Street *achieved both commercial and critical success during the 1920s, contributing to Lewis's overall popularity.*

Sinclair Lewis was born and raised in Sauk Centre, Minnesota, but his experiences at Yale University led him to view small-town life from a more critical perspective. He conceived the idea for what would eventually become *Main Street* while home for the summer in 1905, and he was reminded of his disillusionment while revisiting Sauk Centre in 1916. He began work on the novel in earnest two years later, basing its setting on his own hometown.

Published in 1920 and set in the previous decade, *Main Street* recounts the experiences of Carol Milford, a former librarian who marries Will Kennicott, a doctor from Gopher Prairie, Minnesota. Several years older than Carol but much less sophisticated, Will describes Gopher Prairie as an up-and-coming community that his bride can help beautify. Nevertheless, the young woman is stunned by the town's drabness and squalor. The novel goes on to describe Carol's modest attempts to introduce culture to the community and the hostility she faces. She comes to realize that her husband, like most of Gopher Prairie's citizens, is crude and unthinkingly conventional; Will cannot understand his wife's interests in art, literature, and Progressive politics.

The birth of a son provides Carol with only a temporary respite, and she increasingly finds herself spending time with men other than her husband. Will arranges a diverting trip through the West, but

Carol's unhappiness resumes the moment they return to Gopher Prairie. Taking her son with her, Carol leaves town and begins working for the Bureau of War Risk Insurance in Washington, D.C. However, when Will comes to see her after a year, she agrees to return to Gopher Prairie with him. Finding herself somewhat more comfortable with the town, she believes that with time and patience she can still effect change there.

Impact
Main Street became a popular and critical success, selling 180,000 copies in little more than six months. The book continued to sell throughout the decade, remaining a best seller for several years after its initial publication. Although the decision to award Lewis the 1921 Pulitzer Prize for *Main Street* was overruled, Lewis would go on to win the Nobel Prize in Literature in 1930, the first American author to do so.

Grove Koger

Further Reading
Bucco, Martin. *Main Street: The Revolt of Carol Kennicott.* New York: Twayne, 1993.
Grebstein, Sheldon Norman. *Sinclair Lewis.* New York: Twayne, 1962.
Lingeman, Richard R. *Sinclair Lewis: Rebel from Main Street.* St. Paul, Minn.: Borealis Books, 2005.

See also: *Babbitt;* Lewis, Sinclair: Literature in the United States; Rural life

■ **Man o' War**

Identification: American racehorse
Born: March 29, 1917, Lexington, Kentucky
Died: November 1, 1947, Lexington, Kentucky

One of the most successful racehorses of the 1920s, Man o' War won nearly every race he entered. His athleticism boosted morale and attendance at races and helped the U.S. racing industry recover from the effects of World War I and the antigambling sentiment of the previous decade.

Foaled at Nursery Stud in Lexington, Kentucky, Man o' War was the progeny of the successful racehorses Fair Play and Mahubah. Samuel Riddle purchased Man o' War in 1918, and his racing career began the next year. He won his debut race at Belmont Park in

Man o' War. (AP Photo)

Kenilworth Park in Windsor, Ontario, Canada. After defeating Sir Barton, Man o' War was retired from racing and began a career as a stud. His offspring sired during the 1920s included Belmont Stakes winners American Flag and Crusader, as well as the 1929 Kentucky Derby victor, Clyde Van Dusen.

Impact

Over the course of two decades, Man o' War sired more than three hundred foals, many of which became successful racehorses in later years and produced noteworthy offspring such as Seabiscuit. In 1957, Man o' War was inducted into the National Thoroughbred Racing Hall of Fame in recognition of his achievements on the racetrack, and in 1959, a race at Belmont Park was named in his honor.

Elizabeth D. Schafer

Further Reading

Bowen, Edward L. *Man o' War: Racehorse of the Century.* Lexington, Ky.: Eclipse Press, 2008.

Cooper, Page, and Roger L. Treat. *Man o' War.* Yardley, Pa.: Westholm, 2004.

Ours, Dorothy. *Man o' War: A Legend Like Lightning.* New York: St. Martin's Press, 2006.

See also: Horse racing; Sports

New York, finishing six lengths ahead of his competitors. He continued to dominate races that year, only being defeated once.

In 1920, Man o' War ran eleven races, winning all of them. He began the season by winning the Preakness Stakes and went on to set the U.S. speed record for one mile at the Withers Stakes. Finishing twenty lengths ahead of the second-place horse, he achieved a world record running the Belmont Stakes. Man o' War set another world record at the Dwyer Stakes. Returning to Belmont Park, he won the Lawrence Realization with a lead of one hundred lengths, setting an additional world record. He achieved another U.S. record at the Jockey Club Stakes. Man o' War's other races included the Stuyvesant Handicap, the Miller Stakes, and the Travers Stakes. Although Man o' War never entered the Kentucky Derby, he defeated the 1920 winner, Paul Jones, at the Potomac Handicap, setting a track record.

Man o' War ran his final race on October 12, 1920, finishing seven lengths ahead of Sir Barton at

■ Marathon dancing

A fad with staying power, marathon dancing encapsulated the daring, shady ambiance of the Roaring Twenties. Competitions drew business, as well as gamblers, hustlers, and other unsavory types, to communities. They brought drama into the lives of ordinary Americans and gave participants a chance at fame and fortune. After the 1929 stock market crash, marathons provided cheap refuge for the unemployed and an engaging challenge for competitors.

Dance marathons were an extension of the late-nineteenth- and early-twentieth-century craze for endurance events: automobile, six-day bicycle, and long-distance foot races. Before World War I, ballroom dancers Vernon and Irene Castle gave exhibitions, helping make dancing more socially acceptable in a culture emerging from Victorian repression. After the war, the booming economy and the popularity of jazz music made dancing part of everyday life.

Unlike most endurance fads of the 1920s, such as

rocking chair marathons, flagpole sitting, kissing contests, and aviation feats, marathon dancing regularly drew large, paying crowds. The trend began in 1923 when a pair of English dance instructors whirled without interruption for seven hours. Within months, the continuous dancing record rose to twenty-five hours. The United States became captivated when an American woman, using several partners, raised the mark to twenty-seven hours.

By the mid-1920s, dance marathons were common throughout the United States. Within five years, they were well-received community events, often advertised on local radio. More than twenty thousand amateur and professional dancers, musicians, entertainers, announcers, judges, and support personnel were employed in the industry. Every sizable town hosted marathons. Cash awards of up to five thousand dollars drew contestants, though winners were often chosen in advance. Audiences by the thousands paid twenty-five cents to watch men and women dance for hours in hopes of gaining records, money, and recognition. To keep marathons interesting, promoters added progressively difficult challenges, like blindfold dancing or sprints. One of the most famous dance marathons of the 1920s took place at Madison Square Garden in New York City in June 1928. The competition was hosted by publicist Milton Crandall, who called it the Dance Derby of the Century.

During the Depression, dance marathons became more of a source of income than a lighthearted activity. For the unemployed, it meant temporary shelter. For contestants, it meant food; they received twelve snacks every day and a cot for ten minutes every hour. The dance marathon record, set in the mid-1930s, stood at 3,780 hours, or 157.5 days.

Impact

Actor June Havoc, comedian Red Skelton, and writer Horace McCoy all gained experience in the dance marathon industry. The fad faded in the late 1930s as the United States prepared for World War II. In the 1970s, twenty-four-hour dance marathons were revived for charitable purposes, and many colleges and high schools carried the 1920s marathon dancing tradition into the twenty-first century.

Jack Ewing

Further Reading

Kyvig, David E. *Daily Life in the United States, 1920– 1940: How Americans Lived Through the Roaring*

Twenties and the Great Depression. Chicago: Ivan R. Dee, 2004.

Martin, Carol. *Dance Marathons: Performing American Culture in the 1920s and 1930s.* Jackson: University Press of Mississippi, 1994.

See also: Charleston, The; Dances, popular; Fads; Flagpole sitting; Lindy Hop; Music, popular; Unemployment

■ Marin, John

Identification: American modernist artist
Born: December 23, 1870, Rutherford, New Jersey
Died: October 1, 1953, Cape Split, Maine

John Marin was one of the first American painters to express an individual modern style synthesized from contemporary European art movements.

First exposed to modern art in Paris, France, in 1920, Marin developed his abstract expressionist painting style in the following years. During summers with his family in Maine, the artist began exploring less urban landscapes and focusing on the coastline. His watercolors *Maine Islands* (1922) and *Red and Green and Blue Autumn* (1921) maintain the structural fragmentation of earlier cityscape paintings but exhibit a new organic rhythm with vivid color.

Marin's early professional education included architectural studies and practice, followed by formal art training at the Pennsylvania Academy of the Fine Arts in Philadelphia from 1899 to 1901. A more significant influence to his 1920s painting style was his six-year journey throughout Europe, beginning in 1905. Marin's distinctive watercolor style soon emerged, which especially featured translucent color washes. His compositions and subject matter became abstract forms with opaque linear elements that would later be the foundations of his signature style.

While in Paris, Marin met photographer Edward Steichen, who would prove to be instrumental to the artist's future success in the United States. Steichen returned to New York with several Marin watercolors and showed them to fellow photographer Alfred Stieglitz, whose Photo Secession Gallery was an important venue for early American modernists. In 1910, Stieglitz exhibited Marin's first show. His reputation as a leading American painter was established in 1913 when he was included in the Armory Show, an exhibition credited with introducing twentieth-century Parisian art movements to the American public.

Watercolor paintings dominated Marin's work in the 1920s. *Movement in Brown with Sun* (1928) was part of a series depicting various views of the Brooklyn Bridge with the inclusion of the sun and its surrounding aura. This painterly style was reminiscent of the natural and organic rhythms found in Marin's earlier coastline paintings.

In 1929 and 1930, Mabel Dodge Luhan, an important collector and patron of the arts, invited Marin to Taos, New Mexico. He completed approximately one hundred paintings inspired by the new geography and cultures he encountered during this time. *Dance of the San Domingo Indians* (1929) and *Entrance to Hondo Canyon* (1930) reflect the focus of many of his New Mexico watercolors.

Impact

Marin was an established American abstract expressionist in the 1920s, portraying landscapes and city scapes with direct brushstrokes and conveying an emotional experience to the viewer. By the end of the decade, his distinctive style paved the way for a new generation of artists known as Taos Moderns.

Michael and Patricia Coronel

Further Reading

Curry, Larry. *John Marin, 1870–1953: A Centennial Exhibition.* Los Angeles: Los Angeles County Museum of Art, 1970.

Fine, Ruth Eileen. *John Marin Collection of the Colby College Museum of Art.* Waterville, Me.: Colby College, 2003.

Reich, Sheldon. *John Marin: A Stylistic Analysis and Catalogue Raisonné.* Tucson: University of Arizona Press, 1970.

See also: Art movements; Stieglitz, Alfred

■ Marriage and dating

Marriage remained an important and enduring feature of American society, but the advent of dating during the 1920s replaced chaperoned "calling" at home or at community events as the major activity of courtship. In tandem with the rise of the automobile, mass communication, and youth culture, dating weakened the influence of a couple's parents and helped change the traditional model of marriage into one based on personal fulfillment rather than social duty.

The late Victorian era, which shaped the ideas of the parents of 1920s youth and teenagers, had idealized marriage and family and promoted a sharp distinction between domestic life and the outside world. The former was the realm of women's interests, the latter the arena in which men were to carry out their responsibilities as breadwinners. Although marital love was valued, other interpersonal ties, such as same-sex friendship or the mother-child bond, frequently claimed marriage partners' most intense emotional ties.

Dating and Courtship

By 1920, the United States had undergone enormous social, political, and economic changes. Young men had served overseas in World War I and widened their horizons. The first generation of young women with an undisputed right to vote had just come of age. Leisure time increased as the economy boomed. A great variety of amusements sprang up, automobiles became a more affordable means of independent transportation, and the concept of "dating," first mentioned in 1914, quickly took hold.

Besides movies, amusement parks, restaurants, and other commercial activities, college life included sporting events and on-campus parties and dances. These were glamorized in magazines and newspaper accounts, and high school students and out-of-school youths imitated these attractive parts of campus life. The iconic image of the 1920s short-skirted flapper kicking up her heels with a similarly exuberant dancing partner expresses how compelling dating was to the young and unattached, and how sexually provocative it appeared to older generations.

Social historians claim that, unlike the pairing-off practices of previous decades, dating in the 1920s was not necessarily part of courtship but done primarily to boost a young person's popularity. The material goods associated with dating, particularly automobiles and money, helped confer popularity on the young men who possessed them. The more popular men a young woman could be seen with, the more popular she would become. Women who had the most dates also tended to marry younger, so dating certainly played some role in courtship.

By this time, premarital "petting"—physical exploration short of sexual intercourse—became socially acceptable among the young, even inspiring "petting parties" in colleges, and as many as half of young women are believed to have had intercourse with their future marriage partners.

The New Marriage

By the 1920s, the idea of marriage demanding extraordinary self-sacrifice on the wife's part was falling into disrepute. As in earlier periods of American history, marriage was envisioned as a partnership, but during the 1920s, both partners explicitly expected to attain personal and sexual happiness from their marriage. Increasingly widespread understanding of birth control methods and Freudian psychology made these goals seem attainable.

The average age at marriage dropped during the decade, and a greater percentage of the population married than in the late nineteenth century. Middle-class men tended to marry younger, with one-third marrying before age twenty-four, and fewer than 20 percent of young women had to choose between a college education and marriage. Even so, after marriage, few middle-class women worked outside the home; the general prosperity of the decade made stay-at-home mothering possible for the majority of American families.

Married partners tended to replay the dating pattern by socializing together as a couple more than their parents had done. Although married men and women might continue to participate in same-sex social groups, it was generally assumed that their emotional center was firmly in the family.

Divorce became more common as the expectations of marriage changed and its realities did not always keep pace. In contrast to the economic considerations or abuses that were the historical grounds for divorce, those petitioning for divorce during the 1920s often cited emotional or sexual dissatisfaction.

Impact

The 1920s saw more frank discussion of sexual and interpersonal issues than ever before. Paradoxically, this seems to have led both to happier marriages and to more conscious dissatisfaction with the realities of marriage. Numerous doomsayers predicted that marriage would disappear, interpreting the rapid changes in social mores as a fatal assault on the

institution. Rather, marriage continued to be central in most people's lives, but with a stronger emphasis on the couple bond.

Emily Alward

Further Reading

Bailey, Beth. "From Front Porch to Back Seat: A History of the Date." *OAH Magazine of History* 18, no. 4 (July, 2004): 23–26. Presents the theory of dating as a popularity ritual.

Coontz, Stephanie. *Marriage, a History: From Obedience to Intimacy, or How Love Conquered Marriage.* New York: Viking Penguin, 2005. An extensive survey of marriage through the ages. The chapter on the 1920s describes how the era's customs elevated the pair bond.

Fass, Paula S. *The Damned and the Beautiful: American Youth in the 1920s.* New York: Oxford University Press, 1977. A study of collegiate life and mores during the decade.

Finlay, Barbara. *Before the Second Wave: Gender in the Sociological Tradition.* Upper Saddle River, N.J.: Pearson Prentice Hall, 2007. Includes essays on gender roles in the 1920s and on rating-and-dating.

Heitmann, John Alfred. *The Automobile and American Life.* Jefferson, N.C.: McFarland, 2009. Explores the relationship between the automobile and courtship customs, among other topics.

See also: Birth control; Flappers; "Roaring Twenties"; Sex and sex education; Women in college; Women in the workforce; Women's rights

---

■ Marx Brothers

The Marx Brothers were one of the biggest comedy acts in vaudeville, starring in three hit shows on Broadway during the 1920s. As a result of the decade's innovations in film sound, the Marx Brothers also starred in their first feature film with sound in 1929.

Born to Jewish immigrants Samuel and Minnie Marx in New York City, the Marx Brothers were Leonard (stage name Chico), Adolph (Harpo), Julius Henry (Groucho), and Herbert Manfred (Zeppo). However, Zeppo did not join the act until 1918, when he was called on to replace the second youngest brother, Milton (Gummo) Marx, who left show business to join the Army during World War I. In the years

Marx Brothers. (Hulton Archive/Getty Images)

thousand-dollar budget. The two-reel film *Humor Risk* was shot in Fort Lee, New Jersey, with players from the *N' Everything* cast. However, the comic characters Chico and Groucho had developed on stage did not translate well to silent film, because they relied heavily on humorous dialogue and wordplay. The resulting film was a disaster for which no distributor could be found.

Afterward, the Marx Brothers returned to vaudeville, where their show *The Twentieth Century Revue* went bankrupt in 1923. The Brothers found themselves unemployed and without prospects; before their plans to dissolve the act could be realized, however, Chico brokered a deal with theater producer Joseph M. Gaites. With Gaites's help, the Marx Brothers compiled two recently failed musicals by playwrights Will and Tom Johnstone into a revised show entitled *I'll Say She Is!*

I'll Say She Is! opened in Philadelphia on May 29, 1923. The show made the Brothers extremely wealthy, also garnering them the approval of New York's intellectual elite. Within a year of touring with *I'll Say She Is!*, the Brothers had bounced back from financial ruin and were headed for Broadway. When the show opened at the Casino Theatre on Broadway on May 19, 1924, drama critic Alexander Woollcott was in attendance. He became instantly enamored with the shenanigans of Harpo, praising his performance in a review for the *Sun* newspaper. Woollcott met Harpo after the show the next night and subsequently invited the performer to join the literary and intellectual group known as the Algonquin Round Table.

From Stage to Screen

The Marx Brothers' next show, *The Cocoanuts*, was a satire of the Florida land boom of the 1920s, written by Algonquin Round Table member George S. Kaufman with coauthor Morrie Ryskind, also featuring songs by Irving Berlin. *The Cocoanuts* opened on Broadway on December 8, 1925, and ran for 377 performances. The Brothers took the show on tour in 1927, and it ran through much of 1928. This production was significant in its addition of entertainer

leading up to the 1920s, the four Marx Brothers became one of the most widely recognized acts in vaudeville, under the management of their mother. The Marx Brothers toured extensively between 1914 and 1918 in the musical comedy *Home Again*, written by Minnie's brother, Al Shean. The show was renamed *N' Everything*, and it opened as *The Marx Brothers Revue* on February 7, 1919, in Chicago and ran through December 1920.

Financial Setbacks and Broadway Success

Inspired by former vaudevillian Charlie Chaplin's success in film, the Marx Brothers attempted to launch their own film careers in 1920 with a self-financed short film. Chico, Groucho, and Zeppo each contributed one thousand dollars to the six-

Margaret Dumont to the Marx Brothers' ensemble of performers. Dumont, who portrayed a dignified lady of society, was the ideal contrast for the Brothers. She would play their foil in two stage productions and seven films, and she was sometimes referred to affectionately as the fifth Marx Brother.

Animal Crackers, the second Marx Brothers collaboration with writers Kaufman and Ryskind, opened at the Forty-Fourth Street Theatre on Broadway on October 23, 1928, and ran for 171 performances. Again the Brothers were joined by Margaret Dumont. For a period during the show's run, the Brothers spent their free time on Long Island, filming the screen adaptation of *The Cocoanuts*. With the Warner Bros. sound picture *The Jazz Singer* (1927), film had finally developed enough to communicate the Marx Brothers' verbal comedy. The motion picture studio Paramount Pictures, scrambling to match the output of talking pictures by film studio Warner Bros., optioned the commercially proven *The Cocoanuts* performance on film for $100,000. The film premiered in New York on May 3, 1929.

The Cocoanuts was an enormous financial success for Paramount, yet the decade ended with great losses for the Marx Brothers. Minnie Marx suffered a stroke and died in the early hours of September 14, 1929, and Groucho and Harpo went into debt after losing more than $250,000 each in the stock market crash of October 1929. Fortunately for the Marx Brothers, *The Cocoanuts* had established them as Hollywood stars, and they continued making successful films.

Impact

With the popularization of talking motion pictures, the Marx Brothers escaped the waning medium of vaudeville to pursue a career in film. The Brothers received top billing in twelve feature-length films between 1930 and 1950, and they were awarded an Honorary Academy Award in 1974. The comedic style of the Marx Brothers influenced many later screen comedians, paving the way for such comedies as the film *M*A*S*H* (1970) and the early works of actor and film director Woody Allen.

Jeff Burnham

Further Reading

Ellis, Allen W. "Yes, Sir: The Legacy of Zeppo Marx." *Journal of Popular Culture* 37, no. 1 (2003): 15–27. Explores Zeppo's contribution to the Marx Brothers's act.

Louvish, Simon. *Monkey Business: The Lives and Legends of the Marx Brothers*. New York: Thomas Dunne Books, 2000. Debunks many myths and rumors surrounding the Marx Brothers' personal lives and careers, showcasing lengthy passages from their film scripts.

Kanfer, Stefan. *Groucho: The Life and Times of Julius Henry Marx*. New York: Alfred A. Knopf, 2000. Links Groucho Marx's difficult personal life to his trademark comedic style.

Marx, Groucho. *Groucho and Me*. 1959. New York: Da Capo Press, 1995. The story of the Marx Brothers as related by Groucho through a series of anecdotes.

Marx, Harpo, and Rowland Barber. *Harpo Speaks!* 1962. New York: Limelight Editions, 2010. Details Harpo's childhood, his time with the Algonquin Round Table, and his experiences as a bachelor.

See also: Algonquin Round Table; Chaplin, Charlie; *Cocoanuts, The;* Talking motion pictures; Theater in the United States; Vaudeville

---

■ McFadden Act of 1927

The Law: Federal law prohibiting national banks from branching across state lines
Date: Enacted on February 25, 1927

The McFadden Act of 1927 prohibited national banks from opening branch offices across state lines, instead confining their operations to the states where they were headquartered. The act was named after Pennsylvania representative Louis Thomas McFadden, a Republican who also served as the chair of the House Committee on Banking and Currency.

The McFadden Act permitted national banks (that is, banks chartered by the federal government) to make real estate loans with terms of up to five years, and it also codified the authority of national banks to buy and sell investment securities as defined by the Comptroller of the Currency. Its major provision, however, involved prohibiting national banks from branching across state lines, a ban that lasted until 1994. Prior to the passage of the McFadden Act, some type of interstate branching by commercial banks was allowed in eighteen states. Smaller banks were fearful of the competitive advantage this provided to larger, out-of-state banks. National banks were also dissatisfied with the status quo, particularly since the National Banking Act of 1864, which created the national bank system, made no mention of branching, implying that branching was not allowed at all. The McFadden Act was introduced to address all of these concerns.

Specifically, the act forbade national banks from operating outside of their home state, yet they could branch within their home state in accordance with state branching regulations. Earlier in the decade, McFadden had introduced legislation that permitted branching by national banks, but the concept was opposed by state banks that did not welcome the competition and by the Federal Reserve Board, which wanted to prohibit both national and state banks from branching. In 1923 and 1924, Comptroller of the Currency Henry May Dawes, long opposed to branching in general, collaborated with a committee of national bankers to support removing branching restrictions for national banks. Their recommendations, along with the need for some kind of reform following extensive bank failures in 1926, proved to be the impetus for McFadden's bill. It passed both houses of Congress and was signed into law by President Calvin Coolidge in February of 1927.

Impact

While the branching restrictions of the McFadden Act lasted for nearly seventy years, many economists and historians blame these provisions for the harshness of the banking collapse during the Great Depression, pointing to Canada's system—which allowed nationwide branching and had no bank failures during that time—to prove their point. Later, large banks would get around the interstate branching ban by forming bank holding companies that controlled separate banks in more than one state. Despite an initial explosion in the number of national banks, the total number of banks dropped from roughly thirty thousand in 1920 to around eleven thousand in 1995, one year after the McFadden Act ended.

Brian D. Hendricks

Further Reading

Burton, Maureen, and Bruce Brown. *The Financial System and the Economy: Principles of Money and Banking.* 5th ed. Armonk, N.Y.: M. E. Sharpe, 2009.

Markham, Jerry W. *From J. P. Morgan to the Institutional*

Investor. Vol. 2 in *A Financial History of the United States.* Armonk, N.Y.: M. E. Sharpe, 2002.

See also: Banking; Congress, U.S.; Coolidge, Calvin

■ McKinsey, James Oscar

Identification: American accountant and management consultant
Born: June 4, 1889, Mexico, Missouri
Died: November 30, 1937, Chicago, Illinois

James Oscar McKinsey was a certified public accountant (CPA) and professor of accounting at the University of Chicago. In 1926, he established a firm that would later become McKinsey & Company, the largest consulting firm in the world. McKinsey also wrote the first book on business budgeting and the first textbook on management accounting.

McKinsey received his first bachelor's degree from the Missouri State Teachers' College in Warrensburg, Missouri, in 1912 and his law degree from the University of Arkansas in 1913. He then continued his studies, first at St. Louis University and then at the University of Chicago's School of Commerce and Administration, earning a second bachelor's as well as a master's degree. McKinsey became a member of the University of Chicago's accounting faculty in 1916, three years before receiving his graduate degree and passing his CPA examination in 1919.

Also in 1919, McKinsey began writing on the subject of business. He wrote the revolutionary work *Budgetary Control* (1922), the first book to apply the concept of budgeting to private industry rather than government, and then went on to write the first managerial accounting textbook in 1924. The latter reflected his increasing interest in managerial accounting and management in general, and he soon left his academic position to found McKinsey & Company.

McKinsey worked hard to make his firm a success. He put his clients first in all things, working seven days a week and on holidays, and he expected no less from his employees, even making his secretary come to work on Christmas Day. McKinsey claimed to have eaten over half of his meals with clients.

In 1935, the directors of Chicago department store Marshall Field's hired McKinsey's firm to study their company, which was still struggling in the midst of the Depression. Upon receiving McKinsey's recommendations, they were so impressed that they offered him the position of chairman of the board. He managed to make the company profitable again by drastically cutting personnel. His health suffered during this time, however, and two years after taking the job, he died of pneumonia at age forty-eight.

Impact

The firm that bears his name still lives on, as do many of the principles and strategies that McKinsey introduced to the fields of budgeting, managerial accounting, and management consulting. Programs that he developed while working at the University of Chicago still see practical application in education as well as industry. In his short lifetime, McKinsey revolutionized the way American companies did business.

Dale L. Flesher

Further Reading

McKinsey, James O. *Budgetary Control.* New York: Ronald Press, 1922. Reprint. Memphis, Tenn.: General Books, 2009.

Wolf, William B. *Management and Consulting: An Introduction to James O. McKinsey.* Ithaca, N.Y.: Cornell University, 1978.

See also: Business and the economy

Aimee Semple McPherson. (Getty Images)

■ McPherson, Aimee Semple

Identification: Pentecostal evangelist and faith healer
Born: October 9, 1890, Salford, Ontario, Canada
Died: September 27, 1944, Oakland, California

As a celebrated but controversial Pentecostal leader, Aimee Semple McPherson helped to shape American Protestantism and its engagement with politics and popular culture by promoting a conservative message through modern means in the early decades of the twentieth century.

Aimee Semple McPherson began her career as an itinerant evangelist in the late 1910s. She attracted both interest and criticism as a single mother and female preacher. Widowed as a young missionary in China and later estranged and divorced from her second husband, McPherson embodied the shifting notions of gender and sexuality prevalent in American culture in the years between World Wars I and II. Her marital status and profession signaled a radical departure from most women's roles as wives and mothers. McPherson's preaching, however, tended to affirm the very social conventions that she transgressed.

Born in Canada, McPherson settled in Los Angeles in 1918 and began constructing what would become a religious empire. Dedicated in 1923, Angelus Temple formed the center of this empire. The strikingly modern church became a popular attraction for locals and tourists who flocked to Los Angeles to see the evangelist they called "Sister Aimee." Although capable of seating 5,300 people, Angelus Temple often lacked the capacity to contain the vast crowds the preacher drew to the church. McPherson's Hollywood-style drama, combined with her conservative religious messages, proved wildly popular. She established a Bible college to train aspiring evangelists in 1923 and launched her own radio station in 1924, bringing her preaching into homes across the United States and even around the globe through regular broadcasts.

During the early 1920s, McPherson promoted a

moderate faith she labeled the "Foursquare Gospel." She sought to diminish interdenominational differences and broaden her religious appeal by avoiding the most controversial aspects of Pentecostalism in her preaching. McPherson discouraged, for example, speaking in tongues and other forms of ecstatic worship. Her tendency to embrace moderate theological positions allowed McPherson to form alliances with other Protestant groups in the early years of her Los Angeles ministry. As the modernist-traditionalist theological controversies of the 1920s progressed, however, McPherson's Foursquare Gospel assumed a more militant fundamentalist orientation and tended to blur the lines between Protestantism and American nationalism.

McPherson became involved in a series of scandals from the mid-1920s to the early 1930s. Her 1926 alleged kidnapping shocked her followers and captured the attention of the nation. Presumed drowned after disappearing while swimming on May 18, McPherson reappeared on June 23 in Douglas, Arizona. McPherson told authorities she had been kidnapped, taken across the border to Mexico, and held for ransom by three captors in a shack for several weeks. McPherson said that she cut through her restraints with a tin can and fled the shack, walking through the desert for several hours before collapsing in Agua Prieta, Mexico, where locals assisted her across the U.S. border. Although McPherson returned to immense fanfare, critics scoffed at her story. Rumors circulated that McPherson had disappeared with Kenneth Ormiston, her former radio station engineer, for a romantic tryst at Carmel-by-the-Sea, California. After months of controversy, Los Angeles district attorney Asa Keyes brought charges of perjury against McPherson and her mother for fabricating the kidnapping story and lying to a grand jury. The trial was highly publicized, and McPherson's medical history, weight, dress, and hair style became fodder for sensational news accounts and fictional narratives like Sinclair Lewis's novel *Elmer Gantry*. Keyes's case against McPherson unraveled when his star witness changed her testimony. The district attorney asked the court to dismiss all charges.

McPherson emerged from her ordeal as a national celebrity; however, her reputation suffered in other scandals. In the late 1920s, McPherson embraced Hollywood culture as never before. This transformation was physical as well as spiritual, marked by McPherson's dramatic weight loss, lavish wardrobe, and bobbed hair. The "bride of Christ" persona for which McPherson was famous took on overtly sexual overtones during this period as she tried to reach Hollywood's elite with her religious message. McPherson's actions drew sharp criticism, and critics accused her of abandoning the gospel.

The evangelist's 1931 marriage to Angelus Temple member David Hutton aggravated these problems. After the marriage ended in 1934, McPherson sought to rehabilitate her image by affirming her Pentecostal roots and aligning herself more closely with the movement. Her reputation was restored, and her popularity and influence increased during the remainder of her life. She died of a mysterious drug overdose in 1944.

Impact

McPherson achieved tremendous fame and cultural influence as a Pentecostal evangelist during the 1920s. As the founder of the Angelus Temple in Los Angeles and the International Church of the Foursquare Gospel, McPherson challenged conventional notions of gender and sexuality through her religious leadership, even as she affirmed conservative Protestant values and sought to solidify conservative Protestant cultural dominance. Blending modern innovations with conservative impulses, McPherson's ministry profoundly shaped American evangelicalism, and the Foursquare Church remains an international denomination with millions of members. As a dynamic evangelist and religious leader, McPherson's career reflected and influenced the relations among gender, sexuality, mass media, and Protestant religion in American culture.

Tammy Heise

Further Reading

Barfoot, Chas H. *Aimee Semple McPherson and the Making of Modern Pentecostalism, 1890–1926.* Oakville, Conn.: Equinox, 2011. Provides information on McPherson's life with the help of church documents and statements by McPherson's friends and relations.

Blumhofer, Edith. *Aimee Semple McPherson: Everybody's Sister.* Grand Rapids, Mich.: Eerdmans, 1993. Examines McPherson's religious upbringing, her use of promotional strategy in church development, and the continued success of the International Church of the Foursquare Gospel.

Epstein, Daniel Mark. *Sister Aimee: The Life of Aimee Semple McPherson.* Orlando: Harcourt, Brace, 1993.

Discusses McPherson's popularity among her contemporaries, her role in twentieth-century church history, and the financial success of the Foursquare Church.

McPherson, Aimee Semple. *The Story of My Life.* Waco, Tex.: Word Books, 1973. McPherson's autobiography.

Sutton, Matthew Avery. *Aimee Semple McPherson and the Resurrection of Christian America.* Cambridge, Mass.: Harvard University Press, 2007. Examines McPherson's life against the backdrop of California history and the development of Pentecostal Christianity in the United States.

See also: Evangelism; Religion in Canada; Religion in the United States; Women's rights

---

■ Mead, Margaret

Identification: American anthropologist
Born: December 16, 1901, Philadelphia, Pennsylvania
Died: November 15, 1978, New York, New York

Margaret Mead was renowned for her studies of culture, human development, child rearing, responses to authority, and sex roles. She produced over twenty books and numerous articles, many of which have been translated into many languages. She was also active in the feminist movement.

Margaret Mead's father, Edward Sherwood Mead, had a Ph.D. in political economics and was a professor of finance at the University of Pennsylvania's Wharton School. Her mother, Emily Fogg, was a sociologist who earned her postgraduate degree with an anthropological study of Italian immigrants. Mead would later use this research as the foundation for her own master's thesis in psychology. Emily was an unconventional mother for her time, advocating progressive ideals such as feminism and women's rights, healthy living, and active participation in social causes. Margaret's paternal grandmother, Martha Meade, lived with the family throughout Margaret's childhood and was her early teacher and confidant. Having worked in child psychology, Martha often encouraged Margaret to make and record observations of those around her.

The first of five children, Mead was raised with the expectation that she would attend college, which she did shortly after the end of World War I. She spent her first year at DePauw University in Indiana, but was unhappy there and left to continue her education at the all-female Barnard College in New York City. She would eventually be married three times, to Luther Cressman, Reo Fortune, and Gregory Bateson. All three marriages ended in divorce. Mead and Bateson had a daughter, Mary Catherine Bateson, who also became an anthropologist.

Mead's Life as an Anthropologist
Mead became interested in anthropology after taking a course at Barnard College. While at Barnard, she met anthropologist Franz Boas, who would later be her mentor at Columbia University, Barnard's parent school. She graduated from Barnard with a degree in psychology in 1923; completed her master's degree in psychology at Columbia University in 1924; and went on to pursue her doctorate in anthropology, also from Columbia. During this time, she became friends with fellow future anthropologist Ruth Benedict, who further encouraged her to pursue anthropology. Mead became an assistant curator at the American Museum of Natural History in 1926 and would continue to work there in one capacity or another until her death in 1978.

Her work in the South Pacific began with her research for her dissertation, conducted in Samoa over a nine-month period from 1925 to 1926. Mead's choice of region and subject matter (the experience of adolescents in Samoan culture) was a calculated career decision, as her male counterparts were usually not interested in child and adolescent topics. To answer the question of whether Samoan girls experienced the same adolescent stresses as Western girls or whether culture has a greater impact than biology, she collected data on fifty Samoan girls, most of whom were between eight and twenty years old. She later published her results in her first book, *Coming of Age in Samoa* (1928), in which she concluded that adolescence was less stressful for Samoan girls than for Western girls due to the less complicated demands of the former's culture, including the lack of sexual prohibitions.

After completing her doctorate in 1929, Mead continued to work at the American Museum of Natural History as curator. She would have preferred a university faculty job, but such positions were difficult for women to obtain in the 1920s. Over the course of her career, she went on to study the cultures of peoples in

Bali, New Guinea, and the Admiralty Islands, as well as American Indians in Omaha, Nebraska.

Impact

Margaret Mead was one of the world's foremost anthropologists and feminists. _Coming of Age in Samoa_ became a best seller and remains the world's most widely read anthropological study, though since the 1980s it has been the center of significant controversy. Mead gave commentary in the media, communicated with presidents, and helped to shape a sexual revolution for women. Her work after the 1920s included time spent with the National Research Council's Committee on Food Habits during World War II. She also became an adjunct professor at Columbia University (1954), president of the American Anthropological Association (1960), and president of the American Association for the Advancement of Science (1975). She was elected to the National Academy of Sciences in 1973 and was posthumously awarded the Presidential Medal of Freedom in 1979.

Camille Gibson

Further Reading

Banner, Lois W. _Intertwined Lives: Margaret Mead, Ruth Benedict, and Their Circle._ New York: Alfred A. Knopf, 2003. A joint biography of Mead and Benedict, their relationship with each other, and their work.

Bowman-Kruhm, Mary. _Margaret Mead: A Biography._ Westport, Conn.: Greenwood Press, 2003. A detailed account of Mead's life.

Howard, Jane. _Margaret Mead: A Life._ New York: Ballantine Books, 1984. Based largely on interviews and Mead's autobiography.

Mead, Margaret. _Blackberry Winter: My Earlier Years._ New York: William Morrow, 1972. An autobiography covering Mead's life up to World War II.

_____. _Coming of Age in Samoa: A Psychological Study of Primitive Youth for Western Civilization._ New York: William Morrow, 1928. Mead's first book, describing the experience of Samoan girls in the 1920s.

_____. _Letters from the Field, 1925–1975._ New York: Harper & Row, 1977. A collection of Mead's letters to family, friends, and colleagues.

See also: _Coming of Age in Samoa;_ Sex and sex education; Social sciences; Women in the workforce

■ Medicine

At the beginning of the 1920s, medical practice was still largely palliative. While the germ theory of disease and the importance of aseptic surgery and medical care had been firmly established, the ability of physicians to do more than ease discomfort was limited. Infectious diseases such as diphtheria and typhoid fever still had a high mortality rate, especially among children. Improvements in public health practices and the development of vaccines helped bring under control the most common of these diseases.

The relief that ensued in the United States after World War I soon evolved into what became known as the Roaring Twenties, and its impact was felt in medicine as well as most other aspects of society. Loosening morals allowed for a simmering epidemic of sexually transmitted diseases, while, ironically, improvements in public health set the stage for an annual increase in the incidence of polio. The appalling number of deaths due to infection during the war set in motion research into the isolation of agents capable of treating such infections. Other areas of research resulted in the beginnings of technology that would later prove essential for the noninvasive diagnosis of disease and other pathologies.

Development of Antimicrobials

The discovery and development of "magic bullets," drugs specifically targeted at infectious agents, had long been a dream of physicians and scientists. The first significant drug of this type was arsphenamine, an arsenic-containing compound developed by German scientist Paul Ehrlich, which proved effective in treating syphilis. Scientists at the Rockefeller Institute in New York used the principle underlying the synthesis of arsphenamine in an attempt to produce drugs effective against other agents.

By 1919, Rockefeller Institute researchers Walter Jacobs and Michael Heidelberger had developed tryparsamide for treatment of African sleeping sickness, a disease caused by the protozoan _Trypanosoma_. In 1920, the institute sent Drs. Wade Hampton Brown and Louise Pearce to what was then the Belgian Congo in order to carry out the first field trial of the drug. The study confirmed its effectiveness, with the doctors curing most of the seventy patients they treated, and tryparsamide served as a primary treatment for sleeping sickness for nearly four decades. Pearce was awarded the Ancient Order of the Crown

Researchers Discover Importance of Iron

In 1923, George Hoyt Whipple and Frieda S. Robscheit-Robbins began an extensive series of dietary administration experiments on artificially anemic dogs. In 1925, Whipple and Robscheit-Robbins discovered that the most effective mineral that could stimulate hemoglobin regeneration was iron. They also discovered that beef liver was the most effective dietary treatment for pernicious anemia, causing hemoglobin and red blood cell regeneration to go from one-third of normal levels to normal levels in as little as two weeks' time. Other effective dietary supplements included chicken gizzard smooth muscle, pig kidney, and beef kidney. Whipple and Robscheit-Robbins continued this research into the 1930s and 1940s.

of Belgium and was elected to the Belgian Society of Tropical Medicine for her work. She subsequently demonstrated that the drug was also useful in the treatment of syphilis, which is caused by the spirochete *Treponema*.

A large proportion of bacterial illnesses in the United States was associated with infections by either *Staphylococcus* or *Streptococcus* bacteria, organisms resistant to the effects of known drugs. In 1928, a series of serendipitous events led Scottish bacteriologist Alexander Fleming, working at St. Mary's Hospital in London, England, to discovered penicillin, a chemical with antibacterial properties. Penicillin is produced by members of the genus *Penicillium*, a mold commonly found on citrus fruits. Six years earlier, while suffering from a cold, Fleming had discovered an enzyme named lysozyme that could break down bacteria when drippings from his nose happened to fall on a culture of staphylococci. While it was useful in the laboratory, lysozyme seemed to have no obvious application in treatment of disease. Fleming's discovery of penicillin likewise stemmed from an accidental contamination of his cultures: while he was away on vacation, *Penicillium* spores happened to enter an open window in his laboratory and settled on a culture of *Staphylococcus*. When he returned some days later, he observed that in the region of the culture where the mold had grown, it had killed the bacteria. The following year, he carried out a crude clinical test, effectively treating a man's sinus infection with penicillin. However, Fleming lacked the knowledge or expertise to produce the drug on a scale large enough for testing on humans, and it would take over a decade and the catalyst of war before others could apply his discovery.

Poliomyelitis and Its Aftermath

Poliomyelitis had been a rare and largely unknown disease prior to the twentieth century. Cases that did develop appeared random and generally involved young children, as reflected by the alternative name "infantile paralysis." At the time, nobody knew that most infections occurred early in life and were generally mild, resulting in lifelong immunity. As conditions in the cities were improved and the proper disposal of sewage became common, polio infections started to occur later in life, when they would be more severe. The first major epidemics in the United States took place in New York City, first in 1907 and then again in 1916. Once these outbreaks subsided, however, the disease was forgotten by most of the public.

In the summer of 1921, another major outbreak of polio took place in New York. It is likely that Franklin D. Roosevelt, the recent candidate for vice president on the Democratic ticket, was exposed to the virus at this time. While vacationing on Campobello Island with his family in August, Roosevelt developed an infection characterized by chills and fever, which quickly progressed to paralysis of his legs. He recovered from the initial illness but remained paralyzed for the remainder of his life. The fact that a wealthy, prominent thirty-nine-year-old man could develop polio surprised the public and set in motion events that would eventually help fund research into the cause of the disease.

Roosevelt's colleague George Peabody brought to his attention the therapeutic warm waters at a resort located in Warm Springs, Georgia. Poor management and loss of tourism had left the resort in a dire financial situation. Roosevelt was intrigued by the possibility of using the waters to provide hydrotherapy to polio survivors, and in 1926, he purchased the property and turned it into a nonprofit institution, the Georgia Warm Springs Foundation. Roosevelt frequently visited the resort, which provided treatment to polio patients, who would continue to visit the resort even after Roosevelt's death in 1945.

Outbreaks of polio occurred on an annual basis during the 1920s, with each year seeing about four cases of infection for every 100,000 people. Little could be done beyond minimal palliative treatments. If paralysis affected the patient's ability to breathe, he or she would die from suffocation. This changed in 1927, when Philip Drinker, a medical engineer at Harvard, developed what became known as the iron lung. The principle was straightforward: Drinker attached discarded vacuum cleaners to an airtight chamber, which forced air in and out of the patient's lungs via an alternating push-pull mechanism. The so-called Drinker respirator was first used in October 1928 on a young patient at Children's Hospital in Boston. Although the iron lung was simply intended to keep the patient alive until respiratory mechanisms could recover, it would often be used to sustain his or her life indefinitely, sometimes for several decades.

Medical Technology

In 1925, at Beth Israel Hospital in Boston, Physician-in-Chief Hermann Blumgart and his student Otto Yens developed a means to measure blood flow using radium, a radioactive tracer. They tested the tracer by injecting it first into Blumgart's own arm and then into a patient. Using a modified cloud chamber to detect the radiochemical, Blumgart and Yens were able to follow the movement of blood through the circulatory system. Previous methods for measuring blood flow had been unsuccessful, as instruments were often inaccurate or unstable. The success of the experiment resulted in the establishment of nuclear medicine as a diagnostic tool, with Blumgart regarded as the father of the discipline.

Blumgart's work was also timely, as cardiovascular disease (CVD) surpassed tuberculosis as the leading cause of death among Americans early in the 1920s, if not before. CVD would account for over 14 percent of all deaths by the end of the decade, a proportion that would later increase to nearly 40 percent. This was partly the result of significant decreases in the incidence of infectious disease during this same period. The mortality rate of diphtheria was one-third of what it had been at the beginning of the century, while that of influenza and pneumonia, with the exception of the 1918 influenza epidemic, had been reduced by more than half.

Diabetes remained a major cause of death. Though it was thought at first to be an infectious disease, Cana-dian researchers Frederick Banting and Charles Best demonstrated that diabetes was in fact the result of a deficiency of the pancreatic hormone they called "isletin." Later renamed "insulin," this hormone was shown to control the blood sugar levels at the heart of the illness. Banting and his laboratory director, John McLeod, were awarded the Nobel Prize in Physiology or Medicine in 1923 for their discovery.

Impact

Penicillin represented only the first of many antimicrobials effective in the treatment of bacterial and, later, viral diseases. Sulfa drugs would start to be developed and produced soon after, in the early 1930s, but penicillin proved to be the more effective agent, capable of killing most major pathogenic bacteria. As a result of World War II, British scientists came to the United States, where the industrial manufacture of seemingly unlimited amounts of what was later termed antibiotics was instrumental in saving the lives of both service personnel and civilians. The fact that penicillin was produced by a common mold resulted in extensive research into the isolation of dozens of similar antimicrobials during future decades. Physicians were no longer helpless in treating most bacterial infections.

While the Roosevelt family was wealthy enough to initially fund the Warm Springs Foundation, the endeavor was far too costly to be maintained without other sources of funds. During the 1930s, a series of annual Birthday Balls and the establishment of the National Foundation for Infantile Paralysis (later renamed the March of Dimes Foundation) helped raise money to fund both the Warm Springs resort and research into the cause, treatment, and prevention of polio. In the 1950s, physicians and researchers Jonas Salk and Albert Sabin developed vaccines capable of immunizing children against the disease. By the end of the twentieth century, polio had been largely eradicated from the world.

The nonprofit basis of the Warm Springs Foundation was unique for its time. When the 1920s began, patients either paid for their own medical procedures or depended on charity. In 1929, however, the first health insurance program was established by Justin Ford Kimball, an administrator at Baylor University Hospital in Dallas, Texas, under the name Blue Cross. Local teachers paid a monthly fee that allowed them twenty-one days of free use of a semi-private room at the hospital. By 1935, Blue Cross had enrolled over 500,000 members. Five years later, medical societies established Blue Shield, an insurance program for covering surgery.

Richard Adler

Further Reading

Brown, Kevin. *Penicillin Man: Alexander Fleming and the Antibiotic Revolution.* Stroud, England: Sutton, 2005. Recounts Fleming's discovery of penicillin, which set the stage for a revolution in health care.

Cooper, Thea, and Arthur Ainsberg. *Breakthrough: Elizabeth Hughes, the Discovery of Insulin, and the Making of a Medical Miracle.* New York: St. Martin's Press, 2010. Describes the discovery of insulin and its impact on the life of fifteen-year-old Elizabeth Hughes, one of the earliest recipients.

Cunningham, Robert. *The Blues: A History of the Blue Cross and Blue Shield System.* DeKalb: Northern Illinois University Press, 1997. Details the founding and evolution of the first private health insurance program, established in 1929.

Grob, Gerald N. *The Deadly Truth: A History of Disease in America.* Cambridge, Mass.: Harvard University Press, 2002. A history of ailments and evolving health care in the United States, addressing the change in perception of disease after World War I.

Oshinsky, David M. *Polio: An American Story.* New York: Oxford University Press, 2005. Describes the appearance of poliomyelitis in epidemic form in the United States during the twentieth century.

See also: Banting, Frederick Grant; Cancer; Health care; Insulin; Iron lung; Polio; Sex and sex education; Sexually transmitted diseases; Vitamin D discovery

■ Meighen, Arthur

Identification: Canadian politician
Born: June 16, 1874, Anderson, Ontario, Canada
Died: August 5, 1960, Toronto, Ontario, Canada

Arthur Meighen served as leader of the Conservative Party in Canada from 1920 to 1926 and as prime minister from July 10, 1920, to December 29, 1921, as well as from June 29 to September 25, 1926. He is also remembered for his role in the Canadian constitutional crisis of 1926, commonly called the "King-Byng affair."

During the years from 1908 to 1920, Arthur Meighen rose to a position of leadership in the Conservative Party in Canada, serving in the House of Commons from 1908 to 1913, holding several cabinet posts under the Robert Borden administration between 1913 to 1920 and becoming Conservative Party leader and prime minister following Borden's retirement in July 1920. As prime minister, Meighen attempted to maintain the "Unionist Party" alliance of Liberals and Conservatives that his predecessor had forged during World War I, but in the post–World War I years, the alliance quickly dissolved. Key political differences between the previously aligned parties, along with the rise of new Liberal Party leader Mackenzie King, served to accelerate this dissolution. Despite a strong effort by Meighen in the election held in September 1921, the Conservative Party (still calling itself the National Liberal and Conservative Party) suffered a major defeat, and King replaced Meighen as prime minister.

In the aftermath of the electoral defeat, Meighen remained Conservative Party leader and led the opposition to the policies of King and the Liberals. The two parties especially differed in their views on Canadian support for Great Britain in its defense of the Dardanelles strait in 1922. A bitter struggle over tariff policy in the 1924 by-election in Quebec ended in favor of the Liberals and significantly undercut Conservative Party power. In response to his electoral successes, King called a federal election for October 1925. The election, however, resulted in a Conservative Party resurgence. Due at least in part to Meighen's vigorous campaigning and oratorical skills, the party stood just seven seats away from the number needed to assume control of the government. Energized by these results, Meighen continued to work to strengthen Conservative support, focusing his efforts on obtaining a no-confidence vote against the Liberals and King in the next year's parliamentary session.

King-Byng Affair

In June 1926, a scandal in the Department of Customs further weakened the Liberal government. Seeking to avoid the prospect of parliamentary censure, King asked Governor-General Lord Byng to dissolve parliament and call an election. When Byng refused, King resigned, and Byng responded by asking Meighen, the opposition leader, to form a government. The ensuing constitutional debate was one of the most contentious events in Canadian politics during the decade.

Realizing the volatile nature of the situation, Meighen requested that his new cabinet be appointed in an "acting" capacity only, but this did little to reduce the controversy. Although precedent seemed to support the governor-general's refusal to dissolve parliament, especially when a debate over censure was underway, popular opinion tended to see the refusal as an unwarranted intrusion of British government into Canadian dominion affairs. In a vote taken in parliament on the issue, Meighen and his government lost by a single vote, forcing Meighen to ask the governor-general for dissolution and a new election. King focused the attention of voters on the constitutional issue and managed to divert attention from the Customs Department scandal, leading his party to victory.

After the election, Meighen resigned from his leadership position and returned to private life. Although he would later be appointed to the Senate in 1932 and attempted a brief political comeback in the early 1940s, his period of effective leadership was over.

Impact

Meighen's two brief periods as Canadian prime minister, from July 1920 to December 1921 and from June to September of 1926, belie his true influence and importance. As leader of the Conservative Party during the first half of the 1920s, he was known for his skills in oratory and debate as well as his uncompromising support of Conservative Party principles. Unfortunately, the circumstances that arose in the summer and early fall of 1926, for which he is most often remembered, placed him in a no-win situation and consequently brought an untimely end to his political career.

Scott Wright

Further Reading

English, John. *Arthur Meighen*. Don Mills, Ont.: Fitzhenry & Whiteside, 1977. Presents biographical information about Meighen, addressed to a juvenile audience.

Esberey, J. E. "Personality and Politics: A New Look at the King-Byng Dispute." *Canadian Journal of Political Science* 6, no. 1 (1973): 37–55. Provides a psychological perspective on the 1926 event that marked the turning point in Meighen's career.

Graham, Roger. *Arthur Meighen: A Biography.* Toronto: Clarke, Irwin, & Co, 1965. Covers the events of Meighen's career in the 1920s and beyond.

Granatstein, J. L., and Norman Hillmer. *Prime Ministers: Ranking Canada's Leaders.* Toronto: Harper-Collins, 1999. Contains a brief overview and assessment of Meighen's political career, placing him in the context of other Canadian prime ministers of the period.

Meighen, Arthur. *Unrevised and Unrepented II: Debating Speeches and Others by the Right Honourable Arthur Meighen,* edited by Arthur Milnes. Montreal: McGill-Queen's University Press, 2011. Contains Meighen's public addresses as well as a selection of tributes and articles to and about him.

See also: Canadian nationalism; Elections, Canadian; King, William Lyon Mackenzie

---

■ Mellon, Andrew

Identification: American banker, industrialist, and secretary of the treasury
Born: March 24, 1855, Pittsburgh, Pennsylvania
Died: August 26, 1937, Southampton, New York

Andrew William Mellon's contributions to American economics and society ranged from banking to philanthropy to income tax policy. He became secretary of the treasury in 1921 under President Warren Harding, continuing in that role under his successors, Calvin Coolidge and Herbert Hoover. His 1924 book on tax policy is considered a classic. He was one of the most famous public officials of the 1920s and appeared on the cover of Time magazine twice between 1923 and 1928.

Mellon was the son of a wealthy Pittsburgh banker, Thomas Mellon, and a graduate of the University of Pittsburgh, which was then called Western University. He followed his father into banking. In 1921, he was selected by President Harding to become secretary of the treasury, a position he held until 1932. His objectives as secretary were to reduce the national debt that had accumulated during World War I and to reduce individual income tax rates, which had been raised as high as 90 percent during the war. Mellon's theory of taxation was that lower rates would result in greater tax collections by the government. He argued that when tax rates were too high, consumers had little incentive to earn more income. But with lower tax rates, consumers would work harder because they would be able to keep more of their incremental income. His tax policy was outlined in his 1924 book, entitled *Taxation: The People's Business.* Congress did not immediately lower the rates to the levels he suggested, but by 1929, he had accomplished his goals through a series of tax bills. He also succeeded in reducing the national debt; the lower rates did bring in increased tax revenues.

In 1932, Texas representative Wright Patman threatened Mellon with impeachment due to a conflict of interest. Before the impeachment proceedings came to a vote, however, Mellon resigned to become the American ambassador to Great Britain.

Impact

Mellon had great influence over American tax policy during the formative years of income tax legislation. His tax philosophy of not overtaxing the rich took several years to enact, but it eventually became law. However, much of his work was abandoned under the administration of President Franklin D. Roosevelt, who immediately raised tax rates in opposition to Mellon's tax policies. Mellon's tax policy of easing tax burdens on corporations and the very wealthy was resumed in the 1980s under the administration of President Ronald Reagan.

Dale L. Flesher

Further Reading

Cannadine, David. *Mellon: An American Life.* New York: Vintage Books, 2008.

Love, Philip H. *Andrew W. Mellon: The Man and His Work.* Baltimore: F. H. Coggins & Company, 1929.

Mellon, Andrew W. *Taxation: The People's Business.* New York: Macmillan, 1924.

See also: Banking; Coolidge, Calvin; Harding, Warren G.; Hoover, Herbert; National debt, U.S.; Revenue Acts of 1924, 1926, and 1928; Stock market crash

---

■ Mencken, H. L.

Identification: American journalist and social critic
Also known as: Henry Louis Mencken
Born: September 12, 1880, Baltimore, Maryland
Died: January 29, 1956, Baltimore, Maryland

In his day, H. L. Mencken was one of the foremost commentators on American life and is credited with writing essays, satires, and news reports that captured the social and cultural tensions in 1920s American society.

Mencken composed scores of essays, satires, and books that criticized what he saw as American culture's tendency toward mediocrity. For more than fifty years, Mencken wrote works discussing topics from evangelism to medicine. He was an outspoken critic of American democracy; more particularly, he questioned whether the average person had the capacity for the kind of informed and rational decision making necessary for democracy to work effectively. Mencken is therefore often portrayed as antidemocratic, although his central concern was more with the ability of American democracy to live up to the ideals of exceptionalism that, in his view, it was built upon.

Mencken's writings reflect a man with an elitist

H. L. Mencken. (Getty Images)

view of society. He often directed his most pointed attacks against the middle classes, whom he considered poorly educated and intolerant. In this way, Mencken's works often demonstrate the fundamental tension in the 1920s between rural populations' attitudes toward society and culture and the more progressive ideas of urban intellectuals. Although he often attacked the American South as a hotbed of ignorance and intolerance, he married Sara Haardt, an English professor from Alabama. The two met in 1923 and were married in 1930 after an extended courtship.

In part because of his role at two prominent magazines—*The Smart Set*, where he served as literary critic, and later *The American Mercury*, which he cofounded in 1924 and edited until 1933—Mencken developed close relationships with many of the most prominent literary figures in the United States. He supported novelist Ayn Rand in her early attempts at publication and often engaged in fierce written and verbal sparring with other prominent authors, such as Theodore Dreiser and Sinclair Lewis. A prolific writer in his own right, Mencken composed multivolume works of essays as well as *The American Language*, a book analyzing the way English was spoken in the United States. In 1928, Mencken even collected various writings by other people denouncing himself and published the set as *Menckeniana: A Schimpflexikon*. He was also a regular contributor to the *Baltimore Sun* newspaper from 1906 until he suffered a stroke in 1948.

The Scopes Trial

In his capacity as a contributor to the *Sun*, Mencken traveled to Dayton, Tennessee, in the summer of 1925 to cover the trial of John Scopes, a biology teacher charged with teaching evolution to his high school class in violation of Tennessee statute. The trial became a media sensation. In Mencken's coverage of the proceedings, he often referred to the town's inhabitants in derogatory terms, while suggesting that anyone who supported prosecutor William Jennings Bryan was little more than a backward imbecile. It was Mencken who dubbed the proceedings the "monkey trial."

Banned in Boston

One of the most famous incidents in Mencken's professional life came in 1926, when *The American Mercury* magazine fell out of favor with Frank J. Chase,

the head of the New England Watch and Ward Society in Boston. Chase was a minister and worked as a self-appointed censor in the city. When the *Mercury* published "Hatrack," a story by Herbert Asbury about a small-town prostitute struggling and ultimately failing to find religious and social redemption, Chase had a Harvard Square peddler arrested for selling the magazine. Mencken traveled to Boston and deliberately sold a copy of the offending magazine directly to Chase, perhaps intending to create a highly publicized examination of free speech rights in America. He was arrested and charged with violating local obscenity laws. Although he was acquitted, the trial cost Mencken more than twenty thousand dollars in court and legal fees, as well as lost revenue.

Mencken then decided to sue Chase. A federal judge sided with Mencken and declared that only state-sanctioned officials, not private citizens, had the power to determine a community's obscenity and censorship regulations. Despite the ruling, United States Post Office solicitor Horace J. Donnelly pursued legal action against the *Mercury*, invoking the Comstock Law that banned obscene material from being transported through the U.S. mail. Mencken took up the challenge, but because the relevant issue of the *Mercury* had already been mailed, the case went nowhere.

Impact

H. L. Mencken was perhaps the most important and influential critic of American life since Mark Twain. During the 1920s, he stood in the vanguard of intellectuals who rejected America's emphasis on business, as well as those who worried about what they saw as the unrefined nature of American culture. His involvement helped start or enhance the careers of writers throughout the decade, including Joseph Conrad, Theodore Dreiser, and Sinclair Lewis.

Shawn Selby

Further Reading

Hobson, Fred. *Mencken: A Life.* New York: Random House, 1994. Discusses Mencken's autobiography, private and public life, and posthumous reputation and publications.

Manchester, William Raymond. *Disturber of the Peace: The Life of H. L. Mencken.* New York: Collier Books, 1962. Offers biographical information about Mencken, his perspective on American society, and his rise to prominence as a critic.

Mencken, H. L. *A Mencken Chrestomathy: His Own Selection of His Choicest Writing.* New York: A. A. Knopf, 1949. Presents a collection of essays, articles, and eulogies selected by Mencken from his life's work.

Rodgers, Marion Elizabeth. *Mencken: The American Iconoclast.* New York: Oxford University Press, 2005. Provides insight into Mencken's views on media censorship, Prohibition, and religion, also discussing his anti-Semitism and work for *The American Mercury* magazine.

Teachout, Terry. *The Skeptic: A Life of H. L. Mencken.* New York: Harper Collins, 2002. Examines Mencken's life and work against the backdrop of the 1920s, following his development as a writer, editor, and journalist.

See also: *American Mercury, The;* Newspapers, U.S.; Scopes trial

---

■ Menuhin, Yehudi

Identification: American violinist and conductor
Born: April 22, 1916, New York, New York
Died: March 12, 1999, Berlin, Germany

Yehudi Menuhin's extraordinary musical career began in San Francisco in the 1920s, when he made his first public appearances and established a solid reputation as a first-class violinist in spite of his young age.

Menuhin was a child prodigy, beginning his violin education as a four-year-old. His career as a violinist took off in the early 1920s under the mentorship of violinist Sigmund Anker and, most notably, Louis Persinger, concertmaster and violin soloist with the San Francisco Symphony. Persinger was also Menuhin's main accompanist throughout the 1920s and beyond. As a young boy, Menuhin was already giving public recitals and concerts in Oakland, San Francisco, and New York, before he traveled to Europe in late 1926.

In Paris, he studied with Romanian-born virtuoso George Enescu, who was to remain a significant figure in Menuhin's life. After spending the summer of 1927 with Enescu in Romania, Menuhin returned to the United States to perform two concerts at Carnegie Hall with the New York Symphony Orchestra under conductor Fritz Busch. At the age of twelve, Menuhin was already an established performer. In 1928, he made his first gramophone recordings and embarked on a fifteen-week tour that took him through Los Angeles, Minneapolis, Chicago, Cleveland, and Pittsburg. The following year, he played again at Carnegie Hall. In recognition of his talent, a supporter presented him with a monetary gift facilitating the purchase of a Stradivarius violin, which remained his instrument of choice for the following two decades. Menuhin's performances throughout the 1920s were described as phenomenal. Although some critics noted occasional imperfections in intonation, the consensus was that his playing was that of an artistic genius.

Soon afterward, the young prodigy left for Europe for the second time, and in April 1929, just a few days before his thirteenth birthday, he played violin concertos by Johann Sebastian Bach, Ludwig van Beethoven, and Johannes Brahms in Berlin under the direction of conductor Bruno Walter. According to Menuhin, this event marked the start of his adult career.

Impact

Yehudi Menuhin was one of the most complex musical personalities of the twentieth century. As a violinist, he toured the United States, Europe, South America, Australia, New Zealand, and India. He was widely recorded as a solo instrumentalist and conductor, and later in life, he dedicated much of his energy to the running of music festivals, establishing music academies for the young in England and Switzerland, and founding the Menuhin International Violin Competition for musicians under the age of twenty-two.

Luminita Florea

Further Reading

Burton, Humphrey. *Yehudi Menuhin: A Life.* Boston, Mass.: Northeastern University Press, 2001.

Menuhin, Yehudi. *Unfinished Journey.* New York: Alfred A. Knopf, 1977.

Menuhin, Yehudi, and Catherine Meyer. *Violin: An Illustrated History.* New York: Rizzoli International, 2009.

See also: Classical music

■ *Merry Widow, The*

Identification: A silent film adaptation of the operetta by Viktor Leon and Leo Stein, with music by Franz Lehar
Director: Erich von Stroheim
Date: 1925

The filming of The Merry Widow *was marked by controversies among producers, stars, and von Stroheim, one of the finest directors of the period. Nevertheless, the film became immensely popular and influential to later adaptations of the operetta.*

Von Stroheim, who cowrote the screenplay with Benjamin Glazer, retained little of the operetta's original comedy. His title character is Sally O'Hara, a touring American dancer portrayed by Mae Murray. Sally attracts the amorous attentions of rival cousins Prince Danilo (John Gilbert) and Prince Mirko (Roy D'Arcy), heir to the throne of the fictitious European country of Ruritania. Considered unsuitable as a prospective addition to the royal family, Sally chooses to take revenge on those who have snubbed her and marries the repulsive but wealthy Baron Sadoja, the true power behind the throne. Fortunately for Sally, Sadoja soon suffers a seizure and dies. Sally, now a rich widow, goes to Paris, where she again encounters the rival princes. Danilo, who has a title but no money, declares his love, but Sally believes he only seeks her fortune. In the ensuing duel between the cousins, Danilo gallantly fires his pistol into the air instead of shooting his cousin, but Mirko seriously wounds him. While Danilo is recovering, a crippled doorman assassinates Mirko. In short order, Danilo becomes king, Sally's money is no longer an impediment, and the story ends happily.

Production aspects of *The Merry Widow* are noteworthy as well. The lavish coronation scene is notable for having been filmed in an early Technicolor process. In another deviation from the original operetta, the film score provides organ music merely as background for the action.

Impact

The Merry Widow of 1925 was hailed as an opulent and entertaining film, but it bears little resemblance to the original operetta. Rather, it is a testimony to the creative independence of a strong-willed film director. In fact, the filming of the 1934 sound remake was delayed for four years because von Stroheim insisted that many elements of the plot belonged to Glazer and himself. The film also shows that, by the 1920s, Hollywood studios making film adaptations were more interested in the work's title and prestige than in creating a close copy of the original story.

Patrick Adcock

Further Reading

Carey, Gary. *All the Stars in Heaven: Louis B. Mayer's MGM*. New York: Dutton, 1981.
Fountain, Leatrice Gilbert. *Dark Star: The Untold Story of the Meteoric Rise and Fall of Legendary Silent Screen Star John Gilbert*. New York: St. Martin's Press, 1985.
Koszarski, Richard. *Von: The Life and Films of Erich von Stroheim*. New York: Limelight Editions, 2001.

See also: Film; Gilbert, John; Goldwyn, Samuel; Metro-Goldwyn-Mayer (MGM)

■ Metro-Goldwyn-Mayer (MGM)

Identification: Motion picture studio
Date: Incorporated in April 1924

The formation of Metro-Goldwyn-Mayer Pictures Corporation (MGM) brought together three established film companies, marking the most important show business merger of the 1920s and the birth of the most financially successful motion picture studio of Hollywood's Golden Age.

In the late 1910s and early 1920s, film entrepreneur Marcus Loew made a series of business moves culminating in the MGM merger. After the establishment of Loew's, Inc. in 1919, he acquired a controlling interest in Metro Pictures Corporation. Then, in 1924, Loew added Louis B. Mayer Productions and Goldwyn Pictures as partners to form MGM. Loew acted as president of the parent company and distribution arm until his death in 1927, while Mayer served as head of the Culver City studio until 1951. Mayer's keen business sense meshed with the artistic brilliance of the new MGM production head, Irving Thalberg, who was only twenty-three at the time of the merger.

Although Samuel Goldwyn, head of Goldwyn Pictures, owned the facility that housed the new MGM studio, he distanced himself from it and started the autonomous company Samuel Goldwyn Productions. MGM retained Goldwyn's corporate logo, Leo the Lion, whose head was encircled by the motto *Ars Gratia Artis* (art for art's sake).

MGM's first production, *He Who Gets Slapped* (1924), capitalized on the popularity of actor Lon Chaney and was an important initial success for the studio. Along with new productions, MGM had to deal with some costly projects left over from before the merger, most significantly *Greed* and *Ben-Hur*. Director Erich von Stroheim, who had shot over forty thousand feet of film for *Greed*, refused to shorten the picture. MGM took over the film and released a ten-thousand-foot version in December 1924. *Ben-Hur*, which had begun filming in Rome in late 1923, had stagnated because of cost and creative difficulties. After a change of director and a second filming attempt in Rome and Los Angeles, *Ben-Hur* premiered in December 1925. While the final production cost was almost $4 million an enormous sum by 1920s standards, *Ben-Hur* eventually grossed nearly $11 million, setting a record MGM success until well into the 1940s.

Although MGM was slow to embrace change, *The Broadway Melody* (1929), the studio's first all-talking musical film, was a huge success and won an Academy Award for Best Picture.

Impact

MGM produced over 160 films through 1930, among them *The Big Parade, Min and Bill, The Big House*, and *Anna Christie*, and their impressive roster of contract actors included Greta Garbo, John Gilbert, Joan Crawford, Norma Shearer, Buster Keaton, and Marie Dressler. MGM became synonymous with lavish budgets, glamorous acting stars, and box-office successes from the 1920s to the early 1950s.

Patricia King Hanson

Further Reading

Eyman, Scott. *Lion of Hollywood: The Life and Legend of Louis B. Mayer.* New York: Simon & Schuster, 2005.

Hay, Peter. *MGM: When the Lion Roars.* Atlanta: Turner, 1991.

Vieira, Mark A. *Hollywood Dreams Made Real: Irving Thalberg and the Rise of MGM.* New York: Abrams, 2008.

See also: *Ben-Hur;* Film; Goldwyn, Samuel; *Greed;* Talking motion pictures

Postcard showing Metro-Goldwyn-Mayer Studios. (Getty Images)

■ Mexico

Mexico has played an important role in the economy of North America as a source of both labor and natural resources, especially oil. During the 1920s, Mexican labor and oil filled significant needs in the economy of the United States.

During the 1920s, relations between Mexico and the United States were marked by tension and difficulty. Mexico had just undergone a long and bloody revolution, established a new constitution, and was engaged in bringing about social reform and freeing itself from foreign influences within its borders. Consequently, Mexico was not welcoming foreign investment, especially in land. Meanwhile, the United States was pursuing a foreign policy of isolationism and protectionism, with the U.S. government's main concern in Mexico being to protect the investments of American oil companies. In addition, Mexican laborers were no longer being freely admitted into the United States.

Mexico as a Labor Source

At the beginning of the 1920s, the United States was suffering from a labor shortage in agriculture, mining, and railroad construction. World War I had severely reduced the preexisting workforce, while the Immigration Act of 1917 had virtually eliminated Asia as a source of inexpensive manual labor. In order for the agricultural, mining, and railroad sectors of the economy to recover, the government agreed to waive certain provisions of the Immigration Act, such as literacy, so that employers could bring Mexican laborers into the United States. Due to unrest and the difficulty of earning a living in Mexico during the revolution, a large number of Mexican men entered the United States to work and soon came to rely on this work as a major source of income to support their families.

By 1921, following the return of American soldiers from the war and the completion of much railroad construction, the need for immigrant labor was severely reduced. As a result of legislation in 1921 and again in 1924, legal immigration became more difficult, and illegal immigration increased. In order to deal with the increase in illegal entry, the United States established the U.S. Border Patrol on May 28, 1924.

The Mexican Constitution of 1917 and the United States

In 1917, Mexico adopted a new constitution that implemented important internal reforms, some of which impacted Mexico's relations with other countries. The new constitution included provisions for changes in the educational system, anticlerical policies designed to roll back the influence of the Catholic Church, and redistribution of land with limitations on foreign ownership. Article 27, which effectively prohibited foreign ownership of natural resources, was the most troubling to the United States, as several large American companies held titles and had major capital invested in Mexican oil. When Álvaro Obregón became president of Mexico in 1920, U.S. president Woodrow Wilson refused to recognize his government, fearing that Article 27 would be applied retroactively.

During the presidency of Warren G. Harding, the relationship between the United States and Mexico became more strained, with concern deepening in the United States over the future of American oil and land holdings in Mexico. The United States' refusal to recognize Obregón's administration was causing problems for both countries. Obregón was well aware of the importance of American political and economic support for his presidency. Negotiations had been ongoing between the two countries since Harding's election, but virtually no progress had been made.

Among the issues causing problems were accusations by groups in the United States that the Mexican regime was following the doctrines of Soviet-style communism. The Mexican government insisted that land reform and distribution did not constitute communism, as private businesses still operated in Mexico, the new constitution had established freedom of speech and the press, and overall, the Mexican system of government was similar to that of the United States. From May to August of 1923, negotiators for the two countries met in Mexico City and formulated the Bucareli agreements, by which the United States would recognize Obregón's government and extend formal diplomatic relations to Mexico in exchange for no retroactive revocation of oil titles. The Mexican government also expressed a desire to encourage foreign exploitation of resources as long as their laws and authority were respected.

On November 30, 1924, Plutarco Elías Calles was inaugurated as president of Mexico. Although Calles had served as Obregón's secretary of the interior and was chosen by Obregón to succeed him, his election led to radical changes in government policy. While Obregón had been conservative in his reforms, Calles immediately began to implement major changes, including increased redistribution of land, enforcement of anticlerical constitutional provisions, and rejection of the Bucareli agreements in order to retroactively enforce the nationalization of natural resources. These changes once again brought about American accusations that the Mexican regime was embracing communism. The Mexican government passed two laws that significantly affected American interests, limiting foreigners' rights to oil exploitation to fifty-year concessions and severely limiting foreign land ownership.

With the possibility of war erupting between the two countries, the Coolidge administration opted for negotiation, designating Dwight Whitney Morrow as the new ambassador to Mexico. Morrow dealt with Calles on a very personal basis, bringing aviator Charles Lindbergh to Mexico on a goodwill tour and accompanying Calles on trips. His influence helped resolve the issues regarding oil and land. The Mexican Supreme Court eliminated time limits on foreign oil concessions, and the government agreed to recognize foreign oil concessions that had been developed before 1917.

Anticlericalism Under Obregón and Calles

In addition to questions of oil rights and land ownership, the issue of anticlericalism caused conflict both within Mexico and between Mexico and the United States. Obregón had judiciously imposed the anticlerical provisions of the constitution in parts of Mexico where the Roman Catholic Church had little influence, and he refrained from doing so in areas where the Church enjoyed enormous power and prestige. In contrast to the moderate Obregón, Calles was determined to rid Mexico of the influence of the Catholic Church. Upon becoming president, he insisted on enforcing the anticlerical laws of the constitution throughout Mexico, including the prohibition of religious processions, the nationalizing of Catholic schools and hospitals, and the deportation of foreign-born priests and nuns. He also signed the Law for Reforming the Penal Code, informally called the Calles Law, which set specific fines and prison sentences for violations of the anticlerical laws.

The immediate reaction of the Church and its followers was suspension of all worship services and an economic boycott. When these measures failed to produce results, disillusioned Catholics throughout Mexico began to resort to violence. The movement, known as the Cristero Rebellion or the Cristero War, lasted from 1926 to 1929. The rebellion was disastrous for Mexico, both economically and politically, and had a serious effect on issues related to American control of oil and land. Ambassador Morrow's office worked on a proposal for ending the conflict. With the assistance of Father John J. Burke, head of the U.S. National Catholic Welfare Conference, Morrow presented draft proposals to interim president Emilio Portes Gil, who lacked Calles's fanatical hatred of Roman Catholicism, as well as to the Vatican and other interested parties. On June 21, 1929, an agreement known as the *arreglos* was reached, and Catholic worship services resumed on June 27.

Impact

The relationship between the United States and Mexico evolved in the 1920s, becoming one in which parties could resolve conflict and disagreement via negotiation rather than military intervention. Ambassador Dwight Morrow played a major role in U.S.-Mexico relations, using diplomatic channels to influence internal Mexican affairs and bring about accord between the two countries. The policies of negotiation in the 1920s made an important contribution to the developing positive relationship between the United States and Mexico, which would eventually lead to such collective ventures as the North American Free Trade Agreement and the Commission for Environmental Cooperation.

Shawncey J. Webb

Further Reading

Buchenau, Jürgen. *Plutarco Elías Calles and the Mexican Revolution.* Lanham, Md.: Rowman & Littlefield, 2007. A study of Calles's role in the revolution, his presidency, and his influence on modern-day Mexico.

Hall, Linda B. *Álvaro Obregón: Power and Revolution in Mexico, 1911–1920.* College Station: Texas A&M University Press, 2000. Provides information on the revolution's goals and ideals, as well as Obregón's role in the revolution and his subsequent presidency.

Meyer, Jean A. *The Cristero Rebellion: The Mexican People Between Church and State, 1926–1929.* Cambridge, England: Cambridge University Press, 2008. A study of the religious conflict, its connection to the Mexican Revolution, and its importance in the government's establishing of its authority.

Nicolson, Harold. *Dwight Morrow.* New York: Arno Press, 1975. Provides background on Morrow and the many roles he played in business, politics, and diplomacy.

Spenser, Daniela. *The Impossible Triangle: Mexico, Soviet Russia, and the United States in the 1920s.* Durham, N.C.: Duke University Press, 1999. Provides context for the policies of the Mexican government during the period.

See also: Border Patrol, U.S.; Coolidge, Calvin; Foreign policy, U.S.; Harding, Warren G.; Latin America and the Caribbean

---

■ *Meyer v. Nebraska*

The Case: U.S. Supreme Court ruling on a state statute prohibiting foreign language instruction for schoolchildren

Date: Decided on June 4, 1923

Arguing for a broad interpretation of the "liberty" guaranteed by the Constitution, the Supreme Court struck down a Nebraska law that forbade the teaching of foreign languages to schoolchildren.

After the United States entered World War I in 1917, significant prejudice arose against German Americans, particularly against unassimilated German immigrants living in German communities in the Great Plains. In Nebraska, where approximately ten thousand parochial students received part or all of their education in German, state legislature adopted an Americanization program. One element in this program was a statute sponsored by Senator Harry E. Siman that prohibited the teaching of foreign languages to children who had not yet completed eighth grade. The statute was adopted on April 9, 1919, after the conclusion of World War I, reflecting

residual resentment against foreign immigrants, especially those of German descent.

Robert T. Meyer, a teacher in Hampton, Nebraska, openly flouted the law, as did many other German-language teachers. The Hamilton County attorney visited Meyer's school on May 25, 1920, and found Meyer's pupil, ten-year-old Raymond Parpart, reading aloud from a German Old Testament. Meyer was charged with violating the Siman Act and fined twenty-five dollars. He appealed to the Nebraska Supreme Court, but it upheld the law by a vote of 4 to 2. Meyer's Canadian-born attorney, Arthur Mullen, then made an appeal to the U.S. Supreme Court.

The Supreme Court heard arguments on February 23, 1923, and reached a decision on June 4, 1923. Justice James McReynolds, writing for a majority of seven justices, struck down the Nebraska law as an unconstitutional violation of the due process clause of the Fourteenth Amendment. According to McReynolds, the "liberty" protected by the Constitution included an expansive series of rights that encompassed rights to marry, to raise children, and to educate those children in a foreign tongue. Only Justices Oliver Wendell Holmes Jr. and George Sutherland dissented.

Impact

The *Meyer* decision was one of the first instances in which the Supreme Court used the due process clause, which prevents governments from depriving residents of certain liberties, to uphold substantive personal liberties rather than merely procedural rights or economic liberties. This same expansive view of liberty was used during the 1920s by a conservative Supreme Court to strike down economic regulations, including minimum wage laws in *Adkins v. Children's Hospital* (1923). It also provided the precedent for rulings upholding a right to contraception within marriage in *Griswold v. Connecticut* (1965), as well as the right to have an abortion in *Roe v. Wade* (1973).

Jacob M. Appel

Further Reading

Finkleman, Paul. "German Victims and American Oppressors: The Cultural Background and Legacy of *Meyer v. Nebraska.*" In *Law and the Great Plains*, edited by John R. Wunder. Westport, Conn.: Greenwood Press, 1996.

Ross, William G. *Forging New Freedoms: Nativism,*

Education, and the Constitution, 1917–1927. Lincoln: University of Nebraska Press, 1994.

_____. *"Meyer v. Nebraska."* In *The History of Nebraska Law,* edited by Alan G. Gless. Athens: Ohio University Press, 2008.

See also: Education; Holmes, Oliver Wendell, Jr.; Immigration to the United States; Supreme Court, U.S.

■ Micheaux, Oscar

Identification: African American author and film-maker

Born: January 2, 1884

Birthplace: Murphysboro, Illinois

Died: March 25, 1951, Charlotte, North Carolina

Oscar Micheaux was the first African American film director to make full-length feature movies and the first to release a talking picture. A pioneer in the creation of "race films," he came into prominence during the 1920s. Using all-black casts and innovative techniques, Micheaux created complex cinematic depictions of African American society.

Oscar Devereaux Micheaux was the fifth of thirteen children and grew up in Metropolis, Illinois. He was an eager reader and was particularly enamored of educator Booker T. Washington's work. After working for his family's farm, he left home at sixteen to live with an older brother in Chicago. Micheaux worked in stockyards and steel mills and owned his own shoeshine stand before becoming a Pullman railway porter. In 1905, he bought land and began homesteading in South Dakota. He also started writing and sold articles to the *Chicago Defender,* an African American newspaper. In 1913, he finished the first of his seven self-published novels, a thinly disguised autobiography entitled *Conquest: The Story of a Negro Pioneer.* He sold his book door-to-door, earning enough to found the Western Supply Book Company, later called Micheaux Film and Book Company, in Omaha, Nebraska.

Early Filmmaking Career

After his homestead failed in 1915 following a drought, Micheaux moved his company's operations to Sioux City, Iowa. Just after the conclusion of World War I, he relocated to Chicago to raise funds to make films. His first project, released in 1919, was the silent movie *The Homesteader,* based on his own 1917 novel.

A critical and commercial success, the movie financed his second silent feature, *Within Our Gates* (1920), which depicted lynching and other injustices based on prejudice and served as a counterbalance to D. W. Griffith's racially denigrating film *The Birth of a Nation* (1915). *Within Our Gates* caused a sensation and established the pattern of Micheaux's moviemaking career. As screenwriter, director, producer, and occasionally as an actor, he continued to release feature films showcasing the African American experience. Between 1920 and 1929, he released a total of fifteen silent movies. Though the films were low-budget one-takes using mostly amateur talent (often involving Micheaux's second wife, Alice Burton Russell), borrowed costumes, found locations, and improvised lighting, they demonstrated Micheaux's storytelling skills. His mysteries, comedies, and socially relevant melodramas emphasized the humanity of protagonists and antagonists alike. He explored controversial subjects such as the effects of discrimination, the difficulty of assimilation for those of mixed races, and the moral aspects of denying one's heritage to try to pass as white. A highlight of Micheaux's filmmaking career during the 1920s was the film *Body and Soul* (1925), one of his few surviving silent films. Based on one of Micheaux's own novels, the movie features athlete, actor, and singer Paul Robeson in his cinematic debut.

Later Years

Over the course of his filmmaking career, Micheaux perfected crosscutting, or switching from one scene to another to heighten suspense, and he virtually invented soft-focus dream sequences incorporating flashbacks. Because of the fragile nature of early celluloid film, which turned brittle and disintegrated as it aged, most of Micheaux's silent movies have been lost over time.

Micheaux continued making movies throughout the 1930s and into the 1940s, first experimenting with sound in the musical comedy short *Darktown Revue* (1931). Later that year, he produced the first African American feature-length talking picture, *The Exile,* loosely based on his debut novel. Micheaux suffered financial setbacks during World War II, returned to writing novels, and made his final movie, *The Betrayal,* in 1948. He died of a heart attack three years later.

Impact

Oscar Micheaux's movies, primarily due to budgetary constraints, are considered crude productions by modern standards, and he has been criticized for casting light-skinned actors as heroes and dark-skinned actors as villains. However, his film work collectively offers a powerful alternative to the standard depictions of African Americans as maids, butlers, or porters during the early years of the twentieth century. Micheaux's characters are shown as real people who are not confined by race to traditional roles.

Micheaux received a number of posthumous honors. He gained a star on the Hollywood Walk of Fame in 1987 and a special award from the Directors Guild of America in 1989. He was also recognized with an award by the Black Filmmakers Hall of Fame. An organization at Duke University and an annual South Dakota film festival are named for him, and in 2010, the United States Postal Service issued a commemorative stamp with his portrait.

Jack Ewing

Further Reading

Bogle, Donald. *Toms, Coons, Mulattoes, Mammies, and Bucks: An Interpretive History of Blacks in American Films.* 4th ed. New York: Continuum, 2010. An overview of how African Americans have been portrayed in domestic cinema, from the earliest silent films to the modern era.

Bowser, Pearl, Jane Gaines, and Charles Musser, eds. *Oscar Micheaux and His Circle: African American Filmmaking and Race Cinema of the Silent Era.* Bloomington: Indiana University Press, 2001. Includes analyses of Micheaux's films, examinations of African American acting troupes, and other subjects integral to early black filmmaking.

Green, J. Ronald. *With a Crooked Stick: The Films of Oscar Micheaux.* Bloomington: Indiana University Press, 2004. Examines fifteen of Micheaux's films in terms of technique, autobiographical elements, and themes, discussing his influence on later African American filmmakers.

McGilligan, Patrick. *Oscar Micheaux, The Great and Only: The Life of America's First Black Filmmaker.* New York: HarperCollins, 2007. A life story from the biographer of filmmakers George Cukor and Alfred Hitchcock.

Micheaux, Oscar. *The Homesteader: A Novel.* Sioux City, Iowa: Western Book Supply Company, 1917. Micheaux's novel that served as the basis for his first silent film.

See also: African Americans; Civil rights and liberties; *Emperor Jones, The;* Harlem Renaissance; Jim Crow in the U.S. South; Lynching; Racial discrimination; Robeson, Paul; Talking motion pictures

■ Migrations

The United States has been a major destination for international migrants since the country's founding. Along with the economic and social developments of the 1920s, the United States also experienced waves of extensive internal migration with significant social, political, and economic consequences.

In the 1920s, several factors were responsible for the widespread internal migration that characterized the decade. Economic opportunity was one major pull factor causing people to migrate from one part of the country to another. Areas undergoing rapid economic growth held strong attraction for migrants in the 1920s; people were more motivated to move to any part of the country where their job skills were more likely to attract higher wages. Some Americans were compelled to move to a new place to escape ethnic or racial prejudice, along with oppressive religious or political policies and practices.

Westward Migration

The first major wave of internal migration in America was the migration of European settlers from the East to the West. The earliest European immigrants to America settled on the East Coast. Over the years, mostly due to population growth and decreased economic opportunities in the East, a significant number of them moved westward to take advantage of the inexpensive and fertile land available there. Governmental policies such as the offer of free land to soldiers also encouraged migration to the West. Similar offers were made to homesteaders as an incentive to farm and improve the land. Besides land, the emergence of the ever-growing Hollywood movie industry in California spurred westward migration during the first decades of the twentieth century. The nascent oil industry in Texas also attracted a considerable number of people interested in the abundantly available jobs.

Great Northern Migration

The demographic shift known as the Great Northern Migration, during which many African Americans left southern states for the Midwest and Northeast, occurred roughly between the end of World War I and the onset of the Great Depression. In all, over 1.1 million African Americans migrated from the South during the period. The reasons for the migration are various. W. E. B. Dubois believed that the South's Jim Crow laws drove African Americans to seek better conditions in the North. Northern factories' need for additional workers during World War I also offered new opportunities to African Americans. Those who migrated to northern cities, like Chicago and New York, established their own communities within those cities in which African American culture flourished.

African American Migration

The migration pattern of African Americans was slightly different from that of the dominant Caucasian and European immigrant population. Millions of African Americans who were born in the southern parts of the country began migrating north after the Civil War, a trend that accelerated throughout the 1920s. Around 1900, more than 90 percent of African Americans lived in the southern states. Following the great migration, however, their population grew by more than 40 percent in the North. Many educated African Americans moved to the North because of available economic opportunities. Among the push factors for African American migration to the North were the mandated racial segregation and general racism prevalent in the South at the time. Other push factors included crop failures and natural disasters such as floods and droughts. The mechanization of farm labor also reduced job opportunities on farms. Many African Americans also moved to reunite with their partners and family members who had already traveled north.

The movement of African Americans away from the South proved to be one of the most notable waves of migration during the 1920s. Northern factories suffered an extreme labor shortage as the number of foreign immigrants was drastically reduced by the National Origins Acts, which were also known as the Immigration Acts of 1924 and 1926. Taking advantage of the job opportunities newly available in northern factory cities, many African Americans left the South to begin new lives in the North.

Transportation for Migrants

Although internal migration in 1920s America was not limited to the extremely poor, most of the people moving were in search of work and ways to survive. This meant that many migrants could not afford their own automobiles or passenger train tickets. Hitchhiking became a common means of transportation during the 1920s, and many itinerant workers and even entire migrant families could be seen walking along roads with their thumbs extended to appeal for rides. Many people also snuck onto freight trains for free transportation.

Impact

Internal American migration flourished during the 1920s for economic, political, religious, and social reasons. Residents crowding on or near the eastern seaboard were officially encouraged to move west to seek new opportunities and inexpensive land. Itinerant casual workers traveled railroads in search of labor. Most of these were men and boys, although by some accounts, women and girls riding the rails may have accounted for up to 20 percent of itinerant workers. Finally, many African Americans migrated to the North to escape the harsh living conditions in the southern states. Further causes of migration included the free land being offered to homesteaders and the reuniting of families separated in their search for work. The 1920s was a time of major population shifts from rural to urban areas throughout the United States. For African Americans, the shift was even more drastic. Their population was almost entirely rural prior to 1920, but by the second half of the twentieth century, more than 90 percent of African Americans lived in urban areas.

O. Oko Elechi and Rochelle E. Cobbs

Further Reading

Cresswell, Tim. *The Tramp in America.* London: Reaktion Books, 2001. Discusses the experiences of traveling homeless people in the United States during the early twentieth century.

Gregory, James N. *The Southern Diaspora: How the Great Migrations of Black and White Southerners Transformed America.* Chapel Hill: University of North Carolina

Press, 2005. Examines the factors sparking the mass migration from the South to the North and West between 1900 and 1970, noting the resulting developments in religion, society, and popular culture.

Nugent, Walter. *Into the West: The Story of Its People.* New York: Vintage Books, 2001. Presents a chapter focusing on Americans' westward migration during the 1920s.

Reitman, Ben L. *Sister of the Road: The Autobiography of Boxcar Bertha, As Told to Dr. Ben Reitman.* New York: Amok Press, 1988. An autobiography detailing Boxcar Bertha's experiences traveling with itinerant casual workers along railroads in 1920s America.

Wilkerson, Isabel. *The Warmth of Other Suns: The Epic Story of America's Great Migration.* New York: Random House, 2010. Follows the lives of three African Americans migrating from the South to the North in search of safety and work.

See also: African Americans; Anti-Semitism; Asian Americans; Civil rights and liberties; Demographics; Great Migration; Immigration to the United States; Jim Crow in the U.S. South; Racial discrimination; Transportation; Travel; Unemployment

■ Millay, Edna St. Vincent

Identification: American poet
Born: February 22, 1892, Rockland, Maine
Died: October 19, 1950, Austerlitz, New York

Edna St. Vincent Millay epitomized a generation of women poets, along with Elinor Wylie and Amy Lowell, who achieved popular and critical success. Millay caused a sensation in New York literary circles with poems that heralded an independent voice that readers and critics alike found irresistible. She was also a superb public performer in the New York theater of the 1920s.

Millay came from quite modest circumstances as one of three daughters raised by a hardworking and ambitious mother, who became a single mother in 1899 when she ordered her husband out of the house. From then on, the family learned to be self-sufficient and focused on the writing that would make Millay, called "Vincent" as a young girl, both prominent and prosperous.

Edna St. Vincent Millay. (Time & Life Pictures/Getty Images)

Millay seemed to burst onto the literary scene in 1912. Her poem "Renascence" was published in an anthology, *The Lyric Year,* impressing critics with its mature meter and contemporary freshness. The traditional tetrameter of the poem and its theme of death and resurrection seemed an especially impressive achievement for a twenty-year-old poet. Millay moved her family to New York City and soon became a fixture of the Greenwich Village literary scene. Her poetry collection *A Few Figs From Thistles* (1920) expressed her forthright feminism and sensuality. Another collection, *Second April* (1921), demonstrated her command of free verse at a time when many American poets were still experimenting with new forms of poetry.

A Poet of the 1920s

In addition to her successful poetry collections, Millay wrote the well-received antiwar play *Aria Del Capo* (1921) and won the Pulitzer Prize in 1923 for her book *The Harp Weaver and Other Poems.* References to smoking cigarettes, jazz, bisexual love, and other lifestyle choices studded poems that the public and her colleagues read as autobiographical, although Millay was reticent about her life in public print. In his novel *I Thought of Daisy* (1929), writer Edmund Wilson drew on Millay's life in the creation of his heroine.

Millay married Dutch entrepreneur Eugen Boissevain in 1923. He created a comfortable country home for her, taking care of the business of daily life and managing her career while she was free to roam the grounds and write, leaving periodically for her celebrated speaking tours. Although she vowed never to leave her husband, Millay became involved with a poet fourteen years her junior, George Dillon, who became the subject of some of her love sonnets.

Millay also took advantage of her position as public figure to become involved in politics, promoting Progressive causes and protesting the conviction of Nicola Sacco and Bartolomeo Vanzetti, two Italian anarchists executed in 1927 for the alleged murder of two men during an armed robbery. Like many other writers of her generation, she deemed the court verdict unjust and prejudiced against immigrants.

Later Career

In 1931, Millay published the acclaimed *Fatal Interview*, a collection of fifty-two sonnets, many of them written to Dillon and a few to her husband. Not bound by the conventions of society, Millay typified the carefree spirit of the 1920s, experimenting with nude photography and conducting romantic affairs with women as well as men. The grimmer period of the Depression and World War II seemed less suitable to her temperament, although she continued publishing her work, including the volume *Collected Lyrics* (1943) and poems about World War II. But her energy was fading, especially after a car crash in 1936 and a nervous breakdown in the mid-1940s. Her husband died in 1949, and she died the following year after a fall at her home in Austerlitz, New York.

Impact

Millay's life and career are synonymous with what has sometimes been called the Jazz Age or the Roaring Twenties. Her famous line about "burning the candle at both ends" is often used to capture her vibrant, defiant pose as poet, public figure, and feminist. She insisted that for herself, as for her female contemporaries, no distinctions should be made between the sexes when evaluating works of art. Although her work is no longer considered as prestigious as it was in the 1920s, Richard Wilbur and other, later poets

have praised her for writing some of the most beautiful sonnets in the English language.

Carl Rollyson

Further Reading

Brittin, Norman A. *Edna St. Vincent Millay*. New York: Twayne, 1967. Presents a biography of Millay, along with a critical study of her poetry.

Epstein, Daniel Mark. *What My Lips Have Kissed: The Loves and Love Poems of Edna St. Vincent Millay*. New York: Henry Holt, 2002. Offers insights into Millay's family relationships, her romantic life, and her literary accomplishments.

Mattson, Francis O. *Edna St. Vincent Millay, 1892–1950*. New York: New York Public Library, 1991. A catalog of the New York Library's 1992 exhibition of Millay's letters, poetry, and photographs.

Meade, Marion. *Bobbed Hair and Bathtub Gin: Writers Running Wild in the Twenties*. Orlando, Fla.: Harcourt, 2005. Presents a discussion on the lives and careers of women writers, including Millay and her contemporaries Dorothy Parker, Zelda Fitzgerald, and Edna Ferber.

Milford, Nancy. *Savage Beauty: The Life of Edna St. Vincent Millay*. New York: Random House, 2004. Discusses Millay's public and private life, also addressing her addiction to morphine and her role in cosmopolitan society.

See also: *Harp Weaver, and Other Poems, The*; Poetry; "Roaring Twenties"; Sacco and Vanzetti case; Theater in the United States; Wilson, Edmund

---

■ Millikan, Robert Andrews

Identification: American physicist
Born: March 22, 1868, Morrison, Illinois
Died: December 19, 1953, San Marino, California

During the 1920s, Robert Millikan was the face and voice of American science. He became the leader and driving force of the California Institute of Technology (Caltech), won the 1923 Nobel Prize in Physics for his work on determining the charge of the electron, and did a great deal of early research into cosmic rays.

Robert Andrews Millikan received the first Ph.D. from the physics department of Columbia University in 1895. He then became a professor at the University

The Compton Effect

In 1929, a decisive experiment made by Nobel laureate Arthur Holly Compton challenged Millikan's theory that photons are the primary constituents of cosmic rays. Reexamining the question of whether Earth's magnetic field has an effect on the intensity of cosmic rays, Compton organized a massive survey of the globe. His experiment sought to detect a difference between the intensity of the rays, which varied according to latitude. By September 1932, the results of the survey showed that there was, indeed, a "latitude effect," leading Compton to conclude that cosmic rays were composed at least partly of charged particles, a theory that Millikan had previously rejected.

of Chicago, where he worked with physicist Albert A. Michelson, the United States' first Nobel Prize winner in science. Millikan began looking for a line of research that could help establish his name in physics.

Oil Drop Experiment and Nobel Prize

Beginning in 1909, Millikan began a series of experiments that sought to measure the charge on an electron. Working first with droplets of water and then with droplets of oil, he was able to determine the charge with a greater degree of accuracy than had previously been attainable. The experiments also provided experimental proof of the physical reality of electrons. For his efforts, Millikan would receive the Nobel Prize in Physics in 1923, becoming the second American to do so.

California Institute of Technology

In the years leading up to World War I, Millikan had become involved with the National Research Council (NRC), an offshoot of the National Academy of Sciences, created under the direction of astronomer George Ellery Hale and chemist Arthur A. Noyes. The NRC sought to assist the government in scientific matters and played a significant role in the United States' war effort. Both Hale and Noyes were impressed with Millikan, who served as vice chair of the NRC during the war, and Millikan was impressed with

their vision for developing science. Hale and Noyes were also trying to establish the Throop College of Technology, a small school in Pasadena, California, as a major scientific research institution. They changed the name to the California Institute of Technology (Caltech) and convinced Millikan to leave Chicago for Pasadena to become chair of the university's executive council.

Millikan proved to be a superb administrator and fundraiser, attracting such distinguished faculty members as physicists J. Robert Oppenheimer and Carl Anderson, geneticist Thomas Hunt Morgan, and chemist Linus Pauling to Caltech. His vision extended beyond physics to biology, geology, and engineering, and he sought funds from private citizens, foundations, and business, hoping to avoid too many entanglements with the federal government and its stricter oversight. This vision served the university well in the 1920s, but the Depression of the 1930s forced the government to take a larger role in all things scientific. Still, with help from Hale, Noyes, and others, Millikan had built one of the country's great research institutions almost overnight.

Cosmic Ray Research

While Millikan was working to build up Caltech, he was also embarking on what would be the last phase of his career in scientific research. Beginning in 1921, he turned his attention to the study of what he would term "cosmic rays." Discovered by Austrian scientist Victor Hess before the war, cosmic rays were radiation that seemed to emanate from the reaches of outer space. In a series of balloon flight experiments performed throughout the 1920s, Millikan eventually came to the conclusion that cosmic rays were composed of high-energy photons emitted when higher elements such as helium, oxygen, and silicon were created in stars from hydrogen atoms. A religious man, he saw this as evidence that God was continually creating new atoms in order to forestall the universal heat death predicted by the laws of thermodynamics, in which the universe would continue to lose energy until it could no longer sustain life. Millikan often spoke of the compatibility of science with religion, delivering a series of lectures on the subject at Yale University in 1926 and 1927.

Impact

Robert Millikan reached the zenith of his scientific and public career in the 1920s. In 1927, his picture even appeared on the cover of *Time* magazine, and he was widely regarded by the public and many fellow scientists as the leading voice of American science. However, toward the end of the decade, his scientific work began to come under criticism. First, new experiments challenged Millikan's figure for the electron charge (although the new figure was within Millikan's range of error, only about one-half of 1 percent higher). Then his cosmic ray theory was disputed by Arthur H. Compton, winner of the 1927 Nobel Prize in Physics, who correctly proposed that cosmic rays were charged particles rather than photons. Millikan reacted poorly to these developments, and his reputation began to suffer. Still, Caltech continued to flourish and grow under his leadership, and while his other achievements may have been challenged over time, this aspect of his legacy remains undiminished.

George R. Ehrhardt

Further Reading

Crease, Robert P., and Charles C. Mann. *The Second Creation: Makers of the Revolution in Twentieth-Century Physics.* Rev. ed. New Brunswick, N.J.: Rutgers University Press, 1996. A history of particle physics, containing a chapter on the cosmic ray research of Millikan and others.

Goodstein, David. "In Defense of Robert Andrews Millikan." *Engineering and Science* 63, no. 4 (2000): 30–38. Detailed discussion of the oil drop experiment and recent attempts to discredit Millikan.

Goodstein, Judith R. *Millikan's School: A History of the California Institute of Technology.* New York: W. W. Norton, 2006. A study of the founding and development of Caltech.

Kargon, Robert H. *The Rise of Robert Millikan: Portrait of a Life in American Science.* Ithaca, N.Y.: Cornell University Press, 1982. Describes Millikan's ascendancy to the top of the American science establishment.

Kevles, Daniel J. *The Physicists: The History of a Scientific Community in Modern America.* Cambridge, Mass.: Harvard University Press, 1995. An extensive overview of the development of modern physics in the United States.

Millikan, Robert A. *The Autobiography of Robert A. Millikan.* New York: Prentice-Hall, 1950. Informative, but subjective and at times self-serving.

See also: Astronomy; California Institute of Technology (Caltech); Compton, Arthur Holly; Education; Nobel Prizes; Physics; Science and technology

■ Miss America pageants

Identification: An annual beauty contest
Date: 1921 to 1927
Place: Atlantic City, New Jersey

Established in September 1921, the Miss America pageant became the best-known example of female beauty contests in the United States. Often imitated in later years, the Miss America pageant set the example for dignified beauty pageants all over the world, after a somewhat chaotic beginning occasionally tinged with scandal.

Seeking a way to keep tourism alive in Atlantic City after Labor Day, a group of officials and entrepreneurs came up with a beauty pageant. In 1920, trying to extend the tourist season, the owner of Atlantic City's Monticello Hotel, H. Conrad Eckholm, convinced the Businessmen's League to hold a "Fall Frolic" in September after Labor Day. The event was successful enough to warrant holding it, or something similar, again in 1921.

Miss America

It was decided that a beauty contest would be part of the festivities for 1921. On the spur of the moment, a newspaper reporter named Herb Test came up with the title of "Miss America." Pictures of attractive girls were submitted from various U.S. cities. The selected winner was sixteen-year-old Margaret Gorman. Despite Test's winning title suggestion, Gorman was called the "Inter-City Beauty Contest Winner." Her prize was a golden trophy in the shape of a mermaid.

In 1922, sensing that they were headed in the right direction, the organizers doubled the budget. They introduced a new central character to the festivities: King Neptune, also known as His Oceanic Majesty, played by inventor Hudson Maxim. Because he was sensitive to smells, the sixty-nine-year-old was surrounded by young women called his "Scent Guard." Their bathing costumes became part of the festival attractions.

Sixteen-year-old Mary Katherine Campbell won the 1922 beauty competition. By the time of the 1923 pageant, there were seventy-five contestants, as the pageant surged in popularity. Every state east of the Mississippi River, except Mississippi, was represented. Campbell won this year as well; her second win brought concern that one popular girl could dominate the pageant for years, and so three wins was determined the limit for anyone.

The 1924 pageant was extended to five days and featured eighty-three contestants. The bathing suit competition was judged in a building so hot and packed with spectators that many people fainted. The winner of this year's contest was Philadelphian Ruth Malcolmson, although some saw her win as the competition's attempt to reward Philadelphia for providing a majority of the Atlantic City tourist trade. Another contestant showed up married and with a baby, leading to the pageant finally barring married women. Californian contestant Fay Lanphier, who became Miss America in 1925, was the first winner from a western state.

A Touch of Scandal

As the competition became increasingly popular, audiences grew to 300,000 people watching the pageant's annual rolling chair parade on the boardwalk. One of the contestants was found to be a professional showgirl, not an "amateur" beauty contestant. Two months later, another scandal erupted when a series of newspaper articles claimed that 1925 winner Lanphier had been contracted to star in a movie for Paramount, entitled *The American Venus*, before running in the 1925 Miss America pageant, thus eliminating her from the "amateur" category of contestants. However, the articles were later retracted.

Norma Smallwood was the 1926 winner and received an enormous prize estimated at $100,000, which contributed to many people's disillusionment with the pageant. Shortly before the 1927 pageant, Smallwood demanded an additional $600 for her appearance at it to crown the new Miss America. Denied the money, she went to North Carolina and crowned the queen of a country fair instead.

The 1927 pageant was the last Miss America pageant held during the 1920s. In March 1928, hotel operators canceled it out of concern that the pageant was harming the reputation of Atlantic City with too many scandals, too many women using the pageant as a career stepping-stone, too many professional actors and models getting involved, and too many questionable judging decisions being made.

Impact

The Miss America pageant became the gold standard for every other beauty pageant held in the United States, apart from a brief period between 1928 and 1935, when the competitions were canceled. Beginning in the late 1930s, the Miss America pageant improved its reputation and gradually developed a humanitarian emphasis, with winners spending their year of victory traveling the world and raising support and awareness for various causes.

Russell Roberts

Further Reading

Deford, Frank. *There She Is: The Life and Times of Miss America*. New York: The Viking Press, 1971. A history of the Miss America pageant through 1970.

Levi, Vicki Gold. *Atlantic City: 125 Years of Ocean Madness*. 2d ed. Berkeley, Calif.: Ten Speed Press, 1994. A volume chronicling all of the entertainment madness in Atlantic City during its heyday.

McMahon, William H. *So Young … So Gay!* Atlantic City, N.J.: Atlantic City Press, 1970. Examines the development of Atlantic City as the nation's premier resort.

Miller, Fred, and Susan Miller. *Atlantic City, 1854–1954: An Illustrated History*. Atglen, Pa.: Schieffer, 2009. An illustrated history of Atlantic City's heyday.

Riverol, Armando. *Live From Atlantic City*. Bowling Green, Ohio: Bowling Green State University Popular Press, 1992. Another volume about the history of the Miss America pageant, drawing heavily on Deford's book.

Roberts, Russell, and Richard Youmans. *Down the Jersey Shore*. New Brunswick, N.J.: Rutgers University Press, 1993. Discusses different cultural aspects of the New Jersey shore, including the Miss America pageant.

See also: Bathing suits; "Roaring Twenties"

■ Mitchell, Billy

Identification: U.S. Army general
Born: December 28, 1879, Nice, France
Died: February 19, 1936, New York City, New York

Billy Mitchell, considered the architect of the U.S. Air Force, campaigned relentlessly for the recognition of the importance of military air power. While his efforts were quashed at the time, many of his ideas and predictions would later be vindicated, and the Air Force eventually became an independent and equal branch of the U.S. armed services.

Billy Mitchell. (Getty Images)

William "Billy" Mitchell, the son of a U.S. senator, joined the U.S. Army in 1898. At the end of World War I, he was recognized as a leading aviation commander; by 1920, he was serving as assistant chief of the U.S. Army Air Service and battling to establish a separate air force.

Mitchell argued that military aviation would make battleships useless, but his ideas were largely ignored. In 1921, in order to prove to the U.S. War and Navy Departments that aerial bombings could sink a battleship, he created the First Provisional Air Brigade and arranged several test bombings, most notably of the captured German dreadnought *Ostfriesland.* In defiance of all expectations, the bombers sank the ship. Navy officials were outraged by what they saw as an attack on naval capabilities, although the demonstration did spur them to develop the aircraft carrier, which would prove essential to the United States' Pacific victory in World War II.

Mitchell suffered a setback in 1923 and 1924 when the Navy refused to cooperate with a War Department proposal to jointly expand the Air Service. He appeared before Congress in early 1925 to criticize both Army and Navy leadership for their failure to

compromise. In response, when his term in the Air Service expired, he was demoted to colonel and transferred.

On September 3, 1925, the Navy dirigible *Shenandoah* crashed in a thunderstorm. Mitchell blamed the War and Navy Departments for the loss of life and accused them of criminal negligence and action bordering on treason. He was court-martialed for his statement, and in December 1925, he was convicted of insubordination and suspended from active duty. Mitchell resigned his commission on February 1, 1926. As a civilian, he continued to campaign for an independent U.S. Air Force until his death in 1936.

Impact

Anticipating the future of warfare, Billy Mitchell tried to convince the U.S. government and military of the importance of developing and utilizing air power. While his campaign was largely blocked during his lifetime, it came to fruition in 1941 with the establishment of the U.S. Army Air Forces, later the U.S. Air Force. In 1942, Congress voted to restore Mitchell's previous rank of major general, and he was posthumously awarded a Congressional Gold Medal in 1946.

Peggy E. Alford

Further Reading

Davis, Burke. *The Billy Mitchell Affair.* New York: Random House, 1967.

Hurley, Alfred F. *Billy Mitchell: Crusader for Air Power.* Rev. ed. Bloomington: Indiana University Press, 1975.

Maksel, Rebecca. "The Billy Mitchell Court-Martial: Courtroom Sketches from Aviation's Trial of the Century." *Air and Space Smithsonian* 24, no. 2 (July, 2009): 46–49.

See also: Airships; Aviation; World War I veterans

■ Mix, Tom

Also known as: Thomas Hezikiah Mix
Identification: American film actor
Born: January 6, 1880, Mix Run, Pennsylvania
Died: October 12, 1940, Florence, Arizona

Known as Hollywood's first Western superstar and "King of the Cowboys," Tom Mix was one of the most recognized actors of the silent film era and greatly influenced genera-tions of subsequent cowboy actors, including John Wayne.

After serving in the United States Army during the Spanish-American War, Tom Mix gained experience in the fields of ranch work and rodeo horsemanship. He began his movie career with the film studio Selig Polyscope Company in 1910. In 1917, he signed with the Fox Film Corporation.

Mix appeared as the hero in the white hat in over 160 matinee cowboy silent films during the 1920s. He also wrote and directed many of these films, be-coming so successful that his weekly Fox salary grew to $7,500. One of Mix's goals was to provide his fans with at least equal entertainment value for the money they spent at the box office to see his films. He threw himself into acting, performing his own stunts and often sustaining injuries.

Mix built his own frontier town at the Fox studio lot, complete with Western props and furnishings. Known as Mixville, it covered twelve acres. It included dusty streets lined with typical Western houses and shops, as well as an American Indian village and a simulated desert. He finished his silent film career with work at the Film Booking Office of America in 1929. In the early 1930s, he performed in nine talking movies for the Universal Pictures film studio.

Impact

Mix is credited with making over three hundred films, although not all of them were released to movie theaters, and some have been lost over the de-cades. One of the top box-office stars of the 1920s, he was a great showman who defined the evolution of Western films with his character's heroism. After his sudden death in an automobile accident in 1940, a Ralston-Purina radio show and comic books based on Mix's film character remained popular for well over a decade. For his contributions to the motion picture industry, he was honored with a star on the Holly-wood Walk of Fame and, in 1958, was inducted as a charter member of the Western Performers Hall of Fame of the National Cowboy and Western Heritage Museum.

Alvin K. Benson

Further Reading

Jensen, Richard D. *The Amazing Tom Mix: The Most Fa-mous Cowboy of the Movies.* New York: iUniverse, 2005.

Mix, Paul E. *Tom Mix: A Heavily Illustrated Biography of the Western Star, with a Filmography.* Jefferson, N.C.: McFarland, 2001.

See also: Film; Radio; Talking motion pictures

■ Model A Fords

The introduction of the Model A Ford in 1927 marked a major shift in the philosophy of automobile manufacturing at the Ford Motor Company. For decades, the Ford Motor Company had been committed to maintaining one automo-bile model and stressing low prices. The emphasis on style and new technological improvements in the Model A sig-naled the company's entry into mainstream automobile manufacturing.

In 1920, the Model T, introduced by Henry Ford in 1908, was one of the most popular automobiles in America, coming at a price many Americans could afford. The Model T accounted for nearly two-thirds of the cars on American roads at that time, and the Ford Motor Company's share of the automobile market was 54 percent. No other automobile manu-facturing company came close to challenging the Ford Motor Company's position as industry leader. Nevertheless, advances in the automobile industry, particularly innovations in styling, expansion in the range of options made available to buyers, and op-portunities to buy on credit began to erode Ford's market dominance.

Rationale for the Model A

As early as 1920, Edsel Ford, who had been named president of Ford Motor Company in 1919, had been trying to get his father, Henry, to develop a new Ford model. In 1920, the Ford Motor Company manufac-tured nearly one million Model T automobiles; four years later, that figure soared to approximately two million. By 1926, however, sales had declined notably as innovations at General Motors (GM) drew cus-tomers away from the Model T Ford.

In the spring of 1927, Henry Ford reluctantly agreed to shut down production of the Model T and allow his staff to develop a replacement car. On May 25, 1927, Edsel Ford publicly announced the deci-sion. With the Ford Motor Company out of the com-petition for the time being, Chevrolet sales in 1927 reached one million; this was the first time since 1908 that a company other than the Ford Motor Company led automobile sales in the United States.

Production and Reception
When Edsel Ford announced the company's decision to discontinue the Model T, its potential replacement was still a dream. Ford Motor Company executives and engineers spent the next six months discussing aspects of design and production, while manufacturing plants were shut down and retooled. Not only did the main assembly plants at places like River Rouge outside Detroit need to be refitted to produce a new model, but so did dozens of other facilities that produced parts for the car. The cost of retooling, including profits lost while the company sat idle for six months with no new product to offer, was estimated at $250 million.

As it turned out, the losses would be made up once the Model A was available for sale. Between May and November, speculation about what the new Ford automobile would look like kept the public interested in Ford products. In late November, the company staged a series of showings around the country before sending cars to dealerships. Estimates place the number of people viewing the Model A at 10 million in the first week the car was on display.

The Model A had many innovations, making it appealing to car buyers and a competitive success for Ford executives. Unlike the Model T, the Model A came in several styles and price points, accomplishing in a single model what GM and Chrysler were trying to do by having different nameplates for different price points. It featured a more stylish body modeled on the Lincoln, which was a line Ford bought in 1922. It also offered a greater choice of colors, a new transmission, a more powerful engine, and various safety features not present in the Model T. Competitively priced in a range of five hundred dollars to twelve hundred dollars, it became tough competition for Chevrolet automobiles. By 1929, the Ford Motor Company had returned to its first-place ranking among automotive dealers, capturing nearly one-third of the market.

Impact
Compared to the lasting popularity of the Model T, the Model A had a relatively short life span. The automobile was only offered for sale between 1927 and 1931. Nevertheless, its production revolutionized the way Ford Motor Company did business. No longer would the company stick with one model for years with price representing the sole selling point; instead, styling, technological innovations, and personal-image-driven marketing became part of the Ford Motor Company sales plan. The company also began providing credit to dealers to help pay for inventory as well as to buyers who wished to purchase an automobile in installments.

Laurence W. Mazzeno

Further Reading
Alvarado, Rudolph, and Sonya Alvarado. *Drawing Conclusions on Henry Ford.* Ann Arbor: University of Michigan Press, 2001. Includes a chapter on the development and marketing of the Model A, focusing on Ford's efforts to capitalize on public interest in the new model.

Bak, Richard. *Henry and Edsel: The Creation of the Ford Empire.* Hoboken, N.J.: Wiley, 2003. Describes the development of the Model A, listing its many innovations and discussing its impact on the car-buying market.

Batchelor, Ray. *Henry Ford: Mass Production, Modernism, and Design.* New York: Manchester University Press, 1994. Discusses Henry Ford's decision to design the Model A as a means of remaining competitive with other automobile manufacturers.

Brinkley, Douglas. *Wheels for the World: Henry Ford, His Company, and a Century of Progress, 1903–2003.* New York: Penguin Books, 2003. Describes Ford's efforts to develop the Model A and recapture market share lost due to declining Model T sales.

Watts, Steven. *The People's Tycoon: Henry Ford and the American Century.* New York: A. A. Knopf, 2005. A comprehensive examination of Henry Ford's influence on American society, including a discussion of the company's struggles to produce the Model A.

See also: Automobiles and auto manufacturing; Chrysler, Walter P.; Transportation

■ **Montessori method**

The Montessori method sprang from an educational philosophy valuing children's psychological development, their independent exploration of educational materials, and their sensory engagement in study.

The Montessori method can be traced back to the early twentieth century and the work of Italian physician Maria Montessori. She observed the development of children with intellectual disabilities and noticed that they excelled in self-teaching educational settings. Next, she began to apply her educational approach to children without disabilities. In 1907, Montessori established a day care institution for low-income families, called the Children's House, in Rome, Italy. There, she implemented her educational theory and noticed that the children became more peaceful and organized when they were given blocks of uninterrupted time to interact independently with their learning environment and educational materials.

In 1915, a glass-encased Montessori classroom containing twenty-one children pursuing their self-guided educational initiatives was shown in the Panama-Pacific exposition in San Francisco. Spectators had the opportunity to view the interactions and learning activities of the Montessori method. The Montessori classroom won both of the exposition's education awards.

Key supporters of the Montessori method in the United States during the 1910s and 1920s included inventor Alexander Graham Bell and educators Anne E. George and Frank Arthur Vanderlip. American pedagogue John Dewey also explored self-teaching systems in early childhood education around the beginning of the twentieth century. However, his research focused on the supervision of children's intellectual growth, whereas the Montessori method relied entirely on children's self-guided development. Although the Montessori method declined in popularity in the United States for some decades, it was revived in the 1960s and spread to thousands of American schools by the twenty-first century.

Impact

From its introduction to the United States shortly before the 1920s to its popularity in the twenty-first century, the Montessori method has been shown to be a successful educational approach. Children learn from the carefully prepared educational environment and from one another. The role of the Montessori teacher is to prepare the classroom environment to facilitate the growth and development of each child and to observe when each child is ready for a new challenge. In the twenty-first century, the Montessori method has become the basis of developmentally focused pedagogical practice in many early childhood programs throughout the United States.

Melinda Swafford

Further Reading

Lillard, Angeline Stoll. *Montessori: The Science Behind the Genius.* New York: Oxford University Press, 2008.

Standing, E. M. *Maria Montessori: Her Life and Work.* Reprint. New York: Plume, 1998.

Wentworth, Ronald A. Lubienski. *Montessori for the New Millennium: Practical Guidance on the Teaching and Education of Children of All Ages, Based on a Rediscovery of the True Principles and Vision of Maria Montessori.* Mahwah, N.J.: L. Erlbaum Associates, 1999.

See also: Dewey, John; Education; Social sciences; Women in the workforce

■ Moody, Helen Wills

Identification: American tennis player
Also known as: Helen Newington Wills, Helen Wills Moody Roark
Born: October 6, 1905, Centerville, California
Died: January 1, 1998, Carmel, California

Helen Wills Moody dominated women's tennis beginning in the 1920s, drawing large crowds to her matches and generally inspiring Americans by her athleticism. She became a role model for aspiring tennis players, who learned the game in record numbers.

When Moody won the U.S. Open in 1923, while still a teenager, she became the first female American tennis star, setting sportsmanship standards on the court and modeling poise off-court. Critics of her technique agree that while her strokes were sometimes imperfect and her footwork was slow, the strength of her racquet swing was unparalleled until the 1990s. Her lack of early formal lessons were remedied by coaching from William "Pop" Fuller of the Berkeley Tennis Club and Hazel Hotchkiss Wightman, the latter of whom became her doubles partner.

Moody won the National Girls Championship at Forest Hills, New York, in 1921. By the end of 1922, she was ranked third in the United States. In 1923, Moody entered the University of California at Berkeley to study art, but she also played on the

Helen Wills Moody. (Getty Images)

national women's team and defeated her competitor Molla Mallory for the title. She practiced against male players at Berkeley to prepare for her 1924 season, debuting at Wimbledon and on the U.S. Olympic Team in Paris, France. Moody lost the Wightman Cup competition and Wimbledon singles title, but she became the first American woman to win a major international title in almost two decades when she defeated the French player Didi Vlasto in Paris, winning a singles gold medal as well as a gold medal for her doubles work with Wightman. On her return home, Americans cheered for her at train stations, parades, and public events. Over the next seven years, Moody won six U.S. Championship titles, three Wimbledon titles, and two French Championship titles, in a record that stood for five decades.

Impact

As a pioneer of women's tennis, Moody broke gender barriers and worked against restrictive notions about female athletic attire, opening better opportunities for women in sports, especially in tennis. Male and female opponents wilted under the power of her volleys; her power and strength provided evidence of women's athleticism to those who insisted that their proper place was in the home.

Rebecca Tolley-Stokes

Further Reading

Moody, Helen Wills. "My Life on the Courts." *Saturday Evening Post,* June 17, 1933, p. 24.

_____. *Fifteen-Thirty: The Story of a Tennis Player.* New York: Charles Scribner's Sons, 1937.

See also: Olympic Games of 1924 (Summer); Sports; Tennis; Women's rights

∎ *Moore v. Dempsey*

The Case: U.S. Supreme Court ruling on due process of law

Date: Decided on February 19, 1923

In Moore v. Dempsey, *the Supreme Court ruled that a mob-dominated series of trials had denied the African American defendants their constitutional right to due process of law. The ruling established that in such cases, federal courts were obliged to protect the defendants from discrimination and unfair trials, reviewing cases and releasing defendants when appropriate.*

Moore v. Dempsey emerged from a violent conflict that occurred in Phillips County, Arkansas, in 1919. A political gathering of African American sharecroppers was disrupted by gunfire from white residents, triggering days of violence and the murder of five whites and as many as two hundred blacks. More than one hundred black men were arrested. In the ensuing trials, the defendants were given little opportunity to defend themselves, testimony was obtained through threats and physical violence, and mobs called for the conviction and execution of the defendants. One trial lasted less than an hour, with the all-white jury deliberating for less than five minutes. Twelve men were eventually sentenced to death. Six of the verdicts were overturned at the state level, and with legal aid from the National Association for the Advancement of Colored People (NAACP), the remaining defendants appealed their case before the U.S. Supreme Court.

Although the state of Arkansas insisted that the men's rights had not been infringed, the Court determined that according to the 1915 case *Frank v. Mangum*, mob-dominated trials that interfered with proper legal proceedings violated the defendants' right to due process of law, as protected in the Fourteenth Amendment to the Constitution. Thus, in a decision of six to two, the Court reversed the original rulings and sent the case back to the Arkansas courts, which eventually freed all those convicted. In the majority opinion, Justice Oliver Wendell Holmes Jr. acknowledged that while states should generally be allowed to consider appeals based on specific procedural irregularities without federal intervention, the federal judiciary must intervene when, as in this case, a trial is a simply a spectacle influenced by overwhelming public sentiment. This decision therefore applied not only to the specific case of *Moore v. Dempsey* but also to the propriety of federal intervention in state matters.

Impact

Moore v. Dempsey established the right of federal courts to review claims of violation of due process in state criminal proceedings, countering a history of deference to states on such matters. The case represents an important step toward the eventual barring of a variety of practices aimed at denying constitutional rights to African Americans, contributing to the progress of the civil rights movement in the United States.

Francine S. Romero

Further Reading

Cortner, Richard C. *A Mob Intent on Death: The NAACP and the Arkansas Riot Cases*. Middletown, Conn.: Wesleyan University Press, 1988.

Whitaker, Robert. *On the Laps of Gods: The Red Summer of 1919 and the Struggle for Justice that Remade a Nation*. New York: Crown Publishers, 2008.

See also: African Americans; Dyer antilynching bill; Lynching; Racial discrimination

■ Morgan, Thomas Hunt

Identification: American scientist
Born: September 25, 1866, Lexington, Kentucky
Died: December 4, 1945, Pasadena, California

One of the founders of modern genetics, Thomas Hunt Morgan revolutionized the understanding of chromosomes through his work with the common fruit fly. Publishing numerous books and papers throughout the 1920s, Morgan defined several basic concepts of heredity and introduced the fruit fly as a model system for the study of genetics and development.

Thomas Hunt Morgan attended the State College of Kentucky and Johns Hopkins University before being appointed associate professor of biology at Bryn Mawr College late in the nineteenth century. In 1904, Morgan left Bryn Mawr for Columbia University.

At Columbia, Morgan began breeding the common fruit fly, *Drosophila melanogaster*, for use in genetic experiments. He and his colleagues isolated different eye-color mutations found in male flies and determined that the recessive genes causing the mutations were passed on to offspring via the X chromosome. From the data collected, Morgan further discerned that genes are arranged on individual chromosomes in a linear fashion. While the theory that chromosomes carry genetic material had been proposed by scientists Theodor Boveri and Walter Sutton early in the century, Morgan's research confirmed it.

Throughout the 1920s, Morgan's lab remained highly productive and attracted many famous scientists, and Morgan continued to explore his interest in such topics as animal development, genetics, and evolution. He published a number of landmark books and papers over the course of the decade, including *Embryology and Genetics* in 1924 and *Evolution and Genetics* in 1925. The next year, he released *The Theory of the Gene*, and in 1927, *Experimental Embryology*. In 1924, Morgan was awarded the Darwin Medal in recognition of his work. Morgan left Columbia in 1928 to establish the Division of Biology at the California Institute of Technology (Caltech), where he would remain until his retirement.

Impact

Thomas Hunt Morgan's discoveries made it possible for geneticists to map genes and construct detailed

Thomas Hunt Morgan. (AP Photo)

recombination maps of chromosomes. He popularized the research of *Drosophila melanogaster*, which would later be used to study genomic evolution, cancer, neurodegenerative diseases, alcoholism, learning and memory, and genetic diseases. For his work in the field of genetics, Morgan was awarded the Nobel Prize in Physiology or Medicine in 1933.

Michael A. Buratovich

Further Reading

Allen, Garland E. *Thomas Hunt Morgan: The Man and His Science.* Princeton, N.J.: Princeton University Press, 1978.

Carlson, Elof Axel. *Mendel's Legacy: The Origin of Classical Genetics.* Cold Spring Harbor, N.Y.: Cold Spring Harbor Laboratory Press, 2004.

Shine, Ian, and Sylvia Wrobel. *Thomas Hunt Morgan: Pioneer of Genetics.* Lexington: University of Kentucky Press, 2009.

See also: California Institute of Technology (Caltech); Science and technology; Sturtevant, Alfred H.

■ Morton, Jelly Roll

Identification: American jazz composer and pianist
Also known as: Ferdinand Joseph LaMothe, Ferdinand Joseph La Menthe, Ferdinand Joseph Lemotte
Born: October 20, 1890 (sources vary), New Orleans, Louisiana
Died: July 10, 1941, Los Angeles, California

Jelly Roll Morton is widely credited as one of the first important jazz composers to lay the foundation of modern American jazz. His works combine composed music, improvised sections, ragtime, blues, and the New Orleans style of collective improvisation.

Morton grew up in New Orleans, the birthplace of jazz in the early twentieth century. New Orleans was a melting pot for musical styles popular in nearby states, including ragtime from Missouri and the blues from Mississippi. During his years touring the eastern United States from 1904 to 1917, Morton started combining blues, spirituals, and ragtime with popular songs to create the style that would become American jazz. Morton settled in Los Angeles from 1917 to 1922, where he enjoyed popular success. In 1922, he moved to Chicago, the new center of jazz activity and a common destination for musicians from New Orleans.

During the 1920s, sheet music and the piano roll were still popular, but the phonograph record emerged as the primary medium for selling music. Morton's short pieces were well suited to the three-minute length of phonograph records. Morton began recording with his group, the Red Hot Peppers, in 1926. The resulting recordings are among the finest examples of Morton's achievements as composer, arranger, and pianist. The innovations of Morton's Red Hot Peppers are contemporary with those of jazz trumpeter Louis Armstrong and his groups, the Hot Five and the Hot Seven. In 1928, Morton moved to New York City, where he continued to record his music for Victor Records. During the second half of the 1920s, Chicago declined as the center of jazz activity, while the thriving New York City music industry drew talented musicians such as Duke Ellington and Fats Waller.

Impact

The Great Depression brought about a decline in Morton's career. In May and June of 1938, Morton recorded interviews and performances for ethnomusicologist Alan Lomax for the Archive of Folk Songs at the United States Library of Congress. This comprehensive record documents Morton's legacy as the first significant jazz composer and a transitional figure between ragtime and jazz piano styles. Morton's highly refined performances and compositions combined the simultaneous improvisation of the New Orleans style and the simpler style of Midwestern ragtime into a new jazz style. He is often credited with combining sections of individual improvisation and rehearsed group arrangements, which later became the standard format for jazz music. Morton's contribution to the history of rock and roll was marked in 1998, when he was inducted into the Rock and Roll Hall of Fame as an early influence.

David Steffens

Further Reading

Lomax, Alan. *Mister Jelly Roll: The Fortunes of Jelly Roll Morton, New Orleans Creole and Inventor of Jazz.* Berkeley: University of California Press, 2001.

Ward, Geoffrey C., and Ken Burns. *Jazz: A History of America's Music.* New York: A. A. Knopf, 2000.

See also: Ellington, Duke; Jazz; Music, popular; Waller, Fats

■ Motels

Also known as motor hotels or motor courts, motels emerged as a vital component of the burgeoning travel industry of the 1920s, providing motorists with relatively inexpensive and convenient lodging during long journeys and becoming a familiar part of the rapidly changing North American landscape.

An essential support system to North American transportation and commerce, the lodging industry underwent dramatic changes during the 1920s due to increases in leisure time, disposable income, and the frequency and distance of business travel. With the arrival of the automobile at the turn of the twentieth century and the development of a federal highway system beginning in the 1910s, demand grew for accommodations that would cater to motorists traveling long distances and seeking convenient places to stay overnight. This demand was exacerbated by the economic growth of the 1920s and the spread of affordable automobiles, such as the Ford Model T.

In response, many entrepreneurs began to open lodging establishments along well-traveled highways. Rooms in these establishments tended to be both smaller and less numerous than those of urban and resort hotels, often with exterior entrances. Amenities were few and limited in scope. Their most typical locations, on newly constructed highways or in the outskirts of towns, often made them inconvenient to restaurants, tourist attractions, and business destinations. Nevertheless, their numbers and revenue increased steadily during the 1920s as more highways and cheaper automobiles brought about a rapid rise in the number of motorists. The 1925 opening of the Milestone Mo-Tel, later the Motel Inn, in San Luis Obispo, California, coined a term that would signify roadside lodging for decades to come.

The quality of motels, most of which were locally owned and operated, varied widely in the 1920s. Industry standards regarding cleanliness, room size, and amenities were nonexistent. Some loosely organized motel federations emerged, but these operated primarily as referral networks and exercised no control over the operation of their member motels. Although conditions eventually brought about demands for standardization, most motorists of the 1920s proved willing to endure such inconveniences for the sake of traveling with greater speed and facility than had previously been possible.

Impact

The emergence of motels during the 1920s combined with other factors, most notably the construction of new highways and the availability of affordable automobiles, to revolutionize travel in the United States and Canada. Although the Great Depression impeded their growth in the 1930s, motels rebounded in the latter half of the twentieth century to become the preferred mode of lodging for many Americans and Canadians. Following World War II, the continued construction of new highways and ongoing demand for greater standardization led to a decline in the "mom-and-pop" motels of the 1920s and the emergence of nationwide and global motel chains.

Michael H. Burchett

Further Reading

Jakle, John A., Keith A. Sculle, and Jefferson S. Rogers. *The Motel in America.* Baltimore: Johns Hopkins University Press, 1996.

Sandoval-Strausz, A. K. *Hotel: An American History.* New Haven, Conn.: Yale University Press, 2009.

Witzel, Michael Karl. *The American Motel.* Osceola, Wis.: Motorbooks International, 2000.

See also: Automobiles and auto manufacturing; Federal highway system; Transportation; Travel

■ Mount Rushmore

Designed and constructed by sculptor Gutzon Borglum, the memorial at Mount Rushmore was first proposed early in the 1920s, with construction beginning late in 1927. Carved into a granite mountainside in South Dakota, the memorial depicts the faces of four United States presidents: George Washington, Thomas Jefferson, Theodore Roosevelt, and Abraham Lincoln.

In 1923, South Dakota state historian Doane Robinson proposed the construction of a massive outdoor carving of western heroes among the granite pillars known as the Needles in South Dakota's Black Hills. Robinson believed that such a monument would boost the state's economy through increased tourism. Senator Peter Norbeck and Congressman William Williamson supported the plan in Washington, D.C., securing partial federal funding for the project. In 1924, the renowned sculptor Gutzon Borglum was hired to design and create the monument. Borglum rejected the proposed site at the Needles, as the rock was not sturdy enough for his purposes, as well as the original concept of western heroes, choosing instead to sculpt the heads and torsos of Presidents George Washington, Thomas Jefferson, Theodore Roosevelt, and Abraham Lincoln into the granite face of Mount Rushmore.

The site was dedicated on August 10, 1927, and work began on October 4. The initial phase of the project focused on removing excess rock from the surface of the mountainside, with the construction of Washington's head the next major step. Workers used

Mount Rushmore in 1927. (Time & Life Pictures/Getty Images)

dynamite to remove large chunks of granite from the mountain and also used tools such as jackhammers and chisels for more precise work. Construction continued throughout the remainder of the decade.

Impact

Mount Rushmore came under the jurisdiction of the National Park Service in 1933, becoming a national memorial. The head of George Washington was completed in 1934, followed by that of Jefferson in 1936, Lincoln in 1937, and Roosevelt in 1939. Funding ran out in October of 1941, several months after Borglum's death, preventing the carving of the planned torsos and causing the memorial to be declared complete. In the subsequent decades, the site became the subject of an ongoing dispute with the Lakota people, a Native American group that considers the Black Hills to be sacred land illegally seized by the United States government. Despite this controversy, Mount Rushmore has become one of South Dakota's most popular tourist attractions.

Scot M. Guenter

Further Reading

Larner, Jesse. *Mount Rushmore: An Icon Reconsidered.* New York: Nation, 2003.

Smith, Rex Alan. *The Carving of Mount Rushmore.* New York: Abbeville Press, 1994.

Taliaferro, John. *Great White Fathers: The True Story of Gutzon Borglum and His Obsessive Quest to Create Mount Rushmore.* 2d ed. New York: PublicAffairs, 2004.

See also: National Parks of the United States; Native Americans

■ Movie palaces

The magnificent movie palaces of the 1920s were visible symbols of the decade's widespread prosperity and conspicuous consumption. Such elaborate theaters allowed audiences from all socioeconomic classes to view films in sophisticated and luxurious settings that contrasted sharply with the nickelodeons and vaudeville theaters of earlier decades.

Early in the twentieth century, films appeared primarily in vaudeville theaters, amusement parks, and small storefront theaters known as nickelodeons. As films became increasingly more sophisticated, so too did their venues, culminating in the development of the large, elaborate theaters known as movie palaces. One of the first movie palaces was the Regent Theatre, which opened in Harlem in February of 1913 but did not achieve renown until it came under the supervision of Samuel L. Rothafel later in the year. Rothafel believed in providing audiences with a level of comfort and sophistication far greater than the low ticket price would suggest. Accordingly, Rothafel glamorized the presentation of silent films by embellishing the Regent's decor, orchestra, screen, seats, staff, and stage. He did the same for a number of theaters throughout the 1910s and 1920s, including the Roxy Theatre in New York, which opened in 1927. The early movie palaces of the 1910s set a standard for luxury and extravagance that became apparent in those of the next decade.

During the 1920s, deluxe movie palaces opened in cities throughout the United States. Notable theaters included the Paramount in New York, opened in 1926, and Grauman's Chinese Theatre in Los Angeles, opened in 1927. Movie palaces were built and decorated in a variety of styles, including Art Deco, Baroque, Chinese, Egyptian, Gothic, Mayan, Moorish, neoclassical, Persian, Spanish Mission, Renaissance, rococo, and eclectic combinations thereof. Inside were colossal rotundas and lobbies, large-scale paintings and sculptures, elaborate mirrors and chandeliers, massive marble columns, and monumental staircases. The theaters bore names such as Avalon, Majestic, Regal, Rialto, Riviera, Rivoli, Tivoli, or simply the Palace, reinforcing their royal grandeur and reputations for opulence.

Impact

As the prevalence of movie palaces during the 1920s had largely relied upon the prosperity of the period, the onset of the Great Depression generally halted the construction of new venues. One of the last major movie palaces built was Radio City Music Hall, which opened in midtown Manhattan in December of 1932. However, although many movie palaces of the 1920s were torn down in later decades to make way for multiplex theaters, several palaces remained open to the public, serving as testaments to a golden age of moviegoing.

James I. Deutsch

Further Reading

Hall, Ben M. *The Best Remaining Seats: The Story of the Golden Age of the Movie Palace.* New York: Bramhall House, 1992.

Naylor, David. *American Picture Palaces: The Architecture of Fantasy.* New York: Van Nostrand Reinhold, 1981.

Waller, Gregory A., ed. *Moviegoing in America: A Sourcebook in the History of Film Exhibition.* Malden, Mass.: Blackwell, 2002.

See also: Architecture; Art Deco; Film; Grauman's Chinese Theatre; Talking motion pictures; Vaudeville

■ Museum of Modern Art (MoMA)

Identification: American art museum
Date: Founded in November 1929

The Museum of Modern Art (MoMA) was the first American museum to focus its collection solely on works of art created in the late nineteenth and early twentieth centuries. In displaying works by such artists as Vincent Van Gogh and Paul Cézanne, the museum played a key role in defining modern art and its relationship to society.

The Museum of Modern Art (MoMA), originally located in a rented space in the Heckscher Building in Manhattan, was envisioned by wealthy collectors Lillie P. Bliss, Mary Quinn Sullivan, and Abby Aldrich Rockefeller. The founders sought to call attention to modern artists and works largely neglected by American museums, which typically focused on art from earlier eras. The former president of the Albright Art Gallery board of trustees, A. Conger Goodyear, became president of the new museum. Other additions to the board of trustees included philanthropist

Josephine B. Crane, *Vanity Fair* magazine editor Frank Crowninshield, and Paul J. Sachs, associate director of Harvard's Fogg Museum.

Despite his youth and relative inexperience, art historian Alfred H. Barr Jr. was made the first director of MoMA upon Goodyear's suggestion. Barr and the museum's founders envisioned establishing a multi-departmental institution that would unite twentieth-century fine and applied art under one roof, creating a fluid body of exhibits capable of changing as modern art changed and articulating the significance of modern art within its contemporary context.

The museum's first show, a loan exhibition of late nineteenth-century paintings, was held on November 7, 1929, and included works by Cézanne, Van Gogh, Paul Gauguin, and Georges Seurat. Despite opening to the public less than two weeks after the stock market crash that would mark the beginning of the Great Depression, MoMA proved to be an immediate success and continued to build its collection, paving the way for future groundbreaking exhibitions.

Impact

In the 1920s, the impact of modern art on the overall field and history of art had yet to be determined. The founders of MoMA sought to change that, placing modern art in the public eye, and this effort greatly shaped the development of the field. In later decades, the museum would display works created during the 1920s by artists such as Claude Monet, Pablo Picasso, and Georgia O'Keeffe, as well as collecting more than 100,000 additional works of art.

Ellen Lippert

Further Reading

Bee, Harriet Schoenholz, and Cassandra Heliczer. *MoMA Highlights: 350 Works from the Museum of Modern Art, New York.* New York: Museum of Modern Art, 2004.

Hunter, Sam. *The Museum of Modern Art, New York: The History and the Collection.* New York: H.N. Abrams, 1997.

Lynes, Russell. *Good Old Modern: An Intimate Portrait of the Museum of Modern Art.* New York: Athenaeum, 1973.

See also: Art movements; O'Keeffe, Georgia; Photography

■ Music, popular

A pivotal decade for popular music in the United States, the 1920s marked the coming of age of the record industry as recorded music became popular and profitable. Reflecting the cultural changes of the period, new styles of music such as jazz and blues entered the mainstream consciousness, with several variations developing throughout the decade, while musical comedies introduced songs and dances that would become popular both on and off the Broadway stage.

The popular music of the 1920s was largely influenced by the social climate of the United States during the period. American culture in the 1920s was shaped by several unprecedented historical, political, and social events, including the end of World War I, Prohibition and the associated wave of organized crime, and the economic boom and urban migration of the era. A time of great change, progress, and disillusionment, the decade was marked by the rejection of tradition. Recovering from the devastation of World War I, many Americans embarked on an escapist search for lost happiness by presenting themselves as optimistic and carefree.

The popular music of the era appealed to such sentiments, expressing a sense of urgency and change, rejecting the melodic qualities that dominated music prior to the turn of the century, and introducing atonality and new rhythms. It also reflected the tongue-in-cheek overtones of popular culture, especially in the songs written for musical comedies. The era was further marked by the transition from the ragtime music of the previous decades to jazz, the popularity and cultural influence of which caused writer F. Scott Fitzgerald to dub the entire decade the Jazz Age.

Jazz

Although jazz had existed in the previous decade, it did not enter the mainstream until the 1920s. Several factors contributed to the rising popularity of jazz, a style generally characterized by its use of syncopated rhythms and improvisation. World War I was a major factor, as African-American troops had traveled in North America and Europe, in some cases bringing jazz music with them. In addition, numerous African Americans migrated from the rural South to the urban North throughout the period, forming communities in major cities such as Detroit, Chicago, and New York, where the sounds of jazz and the blues spread.

Brothers George (left) and Ira Gershwin. (Getty Images)

In New York, jazz flourished as part of the African American cultural and artistic movement later known as the Harlem Renaissance. New Yorkers flocked to the Hollywood Club, renamed Club Kentucky later in the decade, to listen to the Washingtonians, the band led by Duke Ellington. Harlem's Cotton Club, a whites-only club featuring black performers, opened its stage to numerous jazz musicians as well as to the blues singers Bessie Smith and Ma Rainey. Many major jazz musicians and singers of the era appeared onstage at the Cotton Club at some point, with Ellington and his band providing regular entertainment starting in 1927. Meanwhile, the Dixieland style of jazz took root in Chicago, brought to the city by musicians from New Orleans such as Louis Armstrong. Widely popular, Dixieland introduced the saxophone as the band's focal instrument, thus differentiating its style from that of standard jazz.

Concurrently with the rise of African American musicians, the orchestra led by Paul Whiteman successfully targeted white, middle-class audiences and became a popular dance band. Whiteman, a classically trained musician, created a modified jazz style that was carefully orchestrated, performed by a larger ensemble, and did not include much improvisation. The band's music blended symphonic textures with simpler harmonies and jazzy rhythms.

In 1924, Whiteman invited composer George Gershwin, among others, to write jazz-inspired pieces for a concert, aiming to combine modern and classical styles and forms. Unlike most jazz performances, this concert was to take place in a concert hall rather than a nightclub. Whitman's experiment was unprecedented, as jazz had never before been performed in a traditional setting or combined with classical forms. In addition, Gershwin's music was typically "jazzy"—that is, jazz-influenced—but not jazz per se. Nevertheless, Gershwin composed *Rhapsody in Blue,* a popular symphony of sorts and the first example of symphonic jazz. Following its performance on February 12, 1924, the piece received mixed reviews from critics, many of whom were confused by its mixing of genres. Audiences, however, embraced it immediately and enthusiastically, and it was performed numerous times throughout the decade and since.

The experiment was pivotal for Gershwin's oeuvre, as it motivated him to create a second jazz-influenced composition, *An American in Paris* (1928), and subsequent orchestral pieces, including the popular American opera *Porgy and Bess* (1935). Such orchestral work had a profound impact on American and European music in the 1920s and later decades. Whiteman's and Gershwin's music was not considered "real" jazz, as it differed from traditional jazz in several ways, generally by eliminating improvisation and combining jazz influences with classical styles. Nevertheless, such music served to introduce jazz to audiences during a time when pure jazz remained outside the mainstream.

Technological Developments

Developments in technology and marketing affected the ways music was experienced by and distributed to its audiences. During the 1920s, the number of public and commercial radio stations grew rapidly. Radio shows devoted to music became popular, with some even broadcasting from nightclubs and other music venues. Performances at the Cotton Club by Duke Ellington and his band, among other performers, were broadcast to a nationwide listening audience. This model of distribution allowed a wide audience to become familiar with the musicians and listen to a live performance without having to leave their homes.

Sound recording, which had begun in the second

half of the previous century, had evolved into a booming industry by the early 1920s, with approximately 100 million records sold each year. A substantial number of these records were "race records," recordings by and for African Americans. These records featured blues and jazz, as well as ragtime, gospel, and other genres of music. While race records existed as a result of the widespread segregation in U.S. society, they called attention to African American artists and styles of music, bringing such music into the mainstream. At times, they also influenced songwriters to compose music that mainstream audiences found more appealing.

By the 1920s, music was available through the radio and records as well as in films, which were typically silent except for musical accompaniment. Previously, music had mostly been disseminated in the form of sheet music, which required the consumer to be able to read music, play an instrument, and often read lyrics in order to perform it. With the new availability of recorded music, consumers could listen to and enjoy music without needing musical training. This created a passive audience more accustomed to listening to music than playing it. With the new technologies available, songs were published en masse and widely distributed, increasing the popularity of the songs as well as the dances that frequently went with them.

This new way of experiencing and consuming music brought about another significant shift, placing focus upon the performer of the song rather than the composer. In the past, music was recreated at home from sheet music, employing instruments and amateur musicians available in the household, so each performance would vary in quality and sound. With the advent of records and radio broadcasts, the consumer could purchase and listen to an expert rendition of any given song. During the 1920s, consumers became attached to the versions of songs recorded by particular performers, rather than the intentions of their composers. Consumers began to care more about the voices and looks of favorite performers than the work or reputation of composers.

Musical Comedy

Another major source of popular songs in the 1920s was musicals. Musicals of the era greatly differed from their romantically influenced predecessors, focusing instead on lively, comical plots about everyday people. Two such musicals, *Funny Face* (1927) and *Lady, Be Good* (1924), featured songs by George Gershwin and his lyricist brother, Ira. Live musical comedies were consistently popular throughout the 1920s despite the prevalence of technological advancements such as records and the radio.

Since the market for musicals continued to be strong, songwriters such as the Gershwins and Irving Berlin wrote songs intended for the Broadway stage. The popularity of the songs they produced was only underscored by the dances choreographed to their music. The 1920s showcased the dancing of siblings Adele and Fred Astaire in memorable performances to songs such as "Fascinating Rhythm" in *Lady, Be Good.* In addition, several popular dances of the period originated in stage productions, most notably the Charleston, which was popularized by the song of the same name featured in the 1923 show *Runnin' Wild.*

Impact

The 1920s produced numerous influential figures who would continue to shape the field of popular music in later decades, including Duke Ellington and George and Ira Gershwin. Styles of music popularized during the period, such as jazz and the blues, grew in popularity over time and branched out into various subgenres, leading to the eventual development of rock and roll. The advancements in mass distribution of live and recorded music made during the 1920s would further shape the field, allowing for the establishment of a record industry that would dominate American popular music for much of the century.

Yiorgos Vassilandonakis

Further Reading

Cox, Jim. *Music Radio: The Great Performers and Programs of the 1920s through Early 1960s.* Reprint. Jefferson, N.C.: McFarland, 2005. Discusses the popular-music-based radio programs of the 1920s and later decades.

Gioia, Ted. *The History of Jazz.* New York: Oxford University Press, 1997. Recounts the development of jazz, with several chapters describing the events of the 1920s.

Harrison, Daphne Duval. *Black Pearls: Blues Queens of the 1920s.* Reprint. New Brunswick, N.J.: Rutgers University Press, 2000. Describes the influence of the blues, as sung by African American women, on the music and society of the 1920s.

Oja, Carol J. *Making Music Modern: New York in the 1920s.* New York: Oxford University Press, 2003. Explores the significance of modernist composers in shaping the decade's music.

Oliver, Paul. *Songsters and Saints: Vocal Traditions on Race Records.* Cambridge: Cambridge University Press, 1984. Details the various genres of music, other than the blues, that appeared on race records in the 1920s.

Shaw, Arnold. *The Jazz Age: Popular Music in the 1920s.* New York: Oxford University Press, 1989. Chronicles the musical developments of the 1920s, including sections on specific songs and performers.

Tick, Judith, and Paul Beaudoin, eds. *Music in the USA: A Documentary Companion.* New York: Oxford University Press, 2008. Examines the history of music in the United States and features several sections on the 1920s.

See also: Armstrong, Louis; Berlin, Irving; Cotton Club; Ellington, Duke; Gershwin, George; Jazz; *Rhapsody in Blue*; Smith, Bessie; Whiteman, Paul

■ *Nanook of the North*

Identification: A documentary film about an Inuit family
Director: Robert J. Flaherty
Date: 1922

Often described as the first feature-length documentary film, Nanook of the North *capitalized on the increasing interest in the 1920s in so-called primitive societies. Audiences were fascinated by exotic locales and ways of life that seemed simpler and, in some ways, more admirable than the hectic, competitive world of 1920s America.*

Director Robert Flaherty first set out simply to record the lives of the Inuits in northern Quebec. By his own account, he knew almost nothing about filmmaking, and his first efforts resulted in an undistinguished collection of scenes with no discernible plot or narrative. A fire that destroyed much of this early film proved a boon to Flaherty, who realized he needed to shape his film into an aesthetic whole and impose a structure on the raw footage he shot.

What Flaherty created is not a pure documentary, as it contains fictional elements. It focuses on a hero, Nanook, and his effort to feed and entertain his family. When viewed in the context of 1920s silent film, *Nanook* has much in common with the adventure films of directors such as Douglas Fairbanks Sr. Nanook performs great feats of strength and endurance, hunting sea lions and building an igloo for his family in a single day. He must live by his wits and physical prowess, but he is also a family man, playing with his young son and teaching him the rudiments of hunting. Thus, the film became a crowd pleaser, appealing to 1920s audiences who had never seen this austere Arctic world in which every day was a struggle for existence. Indeed, one of this silent film's titles informs the audience that Nanook later died of starvation.

Perhaps because Flaherty had no precedents to follow, he did not consider the ramifications of his approach to documentary filmmaking. Many of his scenes were staged or manipulated for the camera. For example, he had his subjects hunt only with spears or harpoons, even though in reality they used guns. Nanook's real name was Allakariallak, and his "wife" was recruited from the local population to play the part. Although Flaherty has been severely criticized for this distortion of reality, he believed that he could take certain liberties in his quest to portray a way of life that was rapidly disappearing.

Impact

Nanook of the North was a worldwide sensation, demonstrating to audiences the capacity of film to bring distant and far-flung cultures within reach. While his methods have since come under scrutiny, Flaherty is still considered to be a founding father of the documentary film genre, having been the first to establish that low-cost nonfiction films could be entertaining and profitable.

Carl Rollyson

Further Reading

Barnouw, Eric. *Documentary: A History of the Non-Fiction Film.* 2d rev. ed. New York: Oxford University Press, 1993.

Hockings, Paul, ed. *Principles of Visual Anthropology.* 3d ed. Berlin: Mouton de Gruyter, 2003.

McGrath, Melanie. *The Long Exile: A True Story of Deception and Survival Amongst the Inuit of the Canadian Arctic.* New York: Harper Perennial, 2007.

See also: Canadian minority communities; *Coming of Age in Samoa;* Film

■ National Association for the Advancement of Colored People (NAACP)

Identification: American civil rights organization
Date: Founded on February 12, 1909

Established to secure the rights of all Americans guaranteed in the Thirteenth, Fourteenth, and Fifteenth Amendments to the Constitution, the National Association for the Advancement of Colored People (NAACP) sought to bring an end to lynching, among other forms of racial injustice. Its legal and educational efforts in the 1920s changed the political landscape of the country and laid the groundwork for later successes in the Civil Rights movement.

Since its inception in 1909, the NAACP has been a racially inclusive organization. The original founders of the NAACP included Caucasian Americans Mary White Ovington, Oswald Garrison Villard, William English Walling, and Henry Moskowitz. African American leaders W. E. B. Du Bois, Ida B. Wells-Barnett, and Mary Church Terrell were also instrumental in the organization's founding. In 1912, the NAACP established its first national office in New York City. Moorfield Storey, the former president of the American Bar Association, became the NAACP's first president. Scholar and civil rights activist W. E. B. Du Bois was the only African American on the NAACP's executive committee at that time. After being named director of publications and research, he founded the NAACP magazine, *The Crisis*, in 1910.

The Dyer Anti-Lynching Bill

The 1920s was a time of growing prosperity, new ideas, technological developments, and a heightened demand for increased personal freedoms and social change. Many Americans supported the NAACP because they were uncomfortable with the enforcement of racial segregation in Jim Crow laws and the influence of right-wing conservatives on political and social discourse. The organization therefore seized the opportunity to pressure the federal government to enact a law against lynching, which was primarily done to African American men as a means of racial intimidation. The NAACP's effort to pass the anti-lynching legislation became one of the organization's major legislative battles in the 1920s.

Leonidas C. Dyer, a Republican representative from Missouri, introduced the Dyer anti-lynching bill in 1921. The bill's main objective was to give the federal government legal authority to dissolve lynch mobs. This was deemed necessary when law enforcement failed, neglected, or refused to hold lynch mobs accountable for violating the equal protection law. The bill proposed that state officers who failed to enforce the anti-lynching law would be fined or

The NAACP and the Brotherhood of Sleeping Car Porters

The Brotherhood of Sleeping Car Porters was the first national union of any profession to be organized by African Americans. The brotherhood worked to oppose racism and class prejudice in hiring practices, both within and outside the transportation industry. The interstate mobility of the brotherhood's members allowed them to use the rails as a network over which information and strategies could be widely shared. The union helped create local chapters of the NAACP and distributed copies of the *Chicago Defender* across the South to educate prospective migrants seeking jobs in the North and Midwest about the job markets they would find in those regions.

subjected to prison terms; the county where the lynching occurred was also to pay fines. To support and promote the bill, the NAACP prepared a map that exposed the extent of lynching in the United States by region and state.

The anti-lynching bill ultimately failed, despite its passing in the House of Representatives and the favorable report it received from the Senate Judiciary Committee. The bill faced opposition from Democratic senators from the South and a prominent Republican senator from Idaho, William Borah. The bill may also have failed because it was not supported by President Warren Harding. The controversy over the anti-lynching bill marked the beginning of a widespread African American disillusionment and disassociation with the Republican Party. After this time, African Americans tended to support the Democratic Party instead of the Republican Party. However, the NAACP continued its anti-lynching campaign for several more decades until the number of cases decreased significantly in the 1960s.

During the rest of the 1920s, the NAACP initiated lawsuits challenging policies that promoted disenfranchisement and racial segregation. The organization also lobbied politicians and policy makers, organizing many campaigns to educate the American public about the dangers, immorality, and injustice of racial oppression and segregation.

Impact

The Dyer anti-lynching bill may have failed to pass in the U.S. Senate, but it did lead to a dramatic decrease in the incidence of lynching. Many historians credit the NAACP with exposing the horrors and prevalence of lynching in the United States and spearheading the anti-lynching movement. The NAACP's political and legal campaigns from the 1920s and early 1930s also laid the foundation for other major civil rights victories, such as the Supreme Court cases *Murray v. Pearson* (1936), *Gaines v. Canada* (1938), and *Brown v. Board of Education* (1954). Although the organization's initial and primary goal was the elimination of lynching and of racial discrimination, it also campaigned for the promotion of educational, political, social, and economic rights for all Americans. Arguably the longest-running civil rights organization, the NAACP remains active in the twenty-first century, with a registered membership of over 500,000 people.

Edward J. Schauer
O. Oko Elechi

Further Reading

Gabbidon, Shaun L. *W. E. B. Du Bois on Crime and Justice: Laying the Foundations of Sociological Criminology.* Burlington, Vt.: Ashgate, 2007. Discusses Du Bois's writings and theories on crime, his experiences with the criminal justice system, and his influence on later criminologists.

Greene, Helen Taylor, and Shaun L. Gabbidon. *African American Criminological Thought.* Albany: State University of New York Press, 2000. Presents information on the influence of African American criminologists including Du Bois, Wells-Barnett, and E. Franklin Frazier.

Gross, Kali N. *Colored Amazons: Crime, Violence, and Black Women in the City of Brotherly Love, 1880–1910.* Durham, N.C.: Duke University Press, 2006. Examines the experiences of African American women prosecuted for crimes in Philadelphia in the early twentieth century, noting the relations among gender, race, and criminal justice.

Jonas, Gilbert. *Freedom's Sword: The NAACP and the Struggle Against Racism in America, 1909–1969.* New York: Routledge, 2007. Presents a discussion on the first sixty years of the NAACP, discussing the activities of NAACP leaders Du Bois, Thurgood Marshall, and James Weldon Johnson.

Sullivan, Patricia. *Lift Every Voice: The NAACP and the Making of the Civil Rights Movement.* New York: New Press, 2009. A history of the NAACP and its impact on American civil rights activism.

See also: African Americans; American Civil Liberties Union (ACLU); Civil rights and liberties; Du Bois, W. E. B.; Dyer antilynching bill; Jim Crow in the U.S. South; Johnson, James Weldon; Ku Klux Klan; Negro History Week; Racial discrimination

---

■ National Broadcasting Company (NBC)

Identification: Commercial radio broadcasting network
Date: Established September 9, 1926

The creation of the National Broadcasting Company (NBC) by the Radio Corporation of America (RCA) was a significant milestone in broadcasting history, as it marked the beginning of the network era of commercial radio and television broadcasting. NBC's Red and Blue Networks were the first two major commercial radio networks in the United States.

The roots of NBC lay in the manufacture of radio sets by RCA. David Sarnoff, the general manager of RCA, decided that the best way to sell more radios would be to create new radio programming that would appeal to consumers. In 1922, RCA shareholder Westinghouse established a radio station in the New York market, WJZ. The promise of WJZ was that its programming could be carried by other stations linked to it via telephone wires, thus broadcasting its content to a larger audience. The gatekeeper to these crucial telephone wires was another one of RCA's shareholder firms, American Telephone and Telegraph (AT&T).

Building a Network

AT&T used its telephone wires, with their state-of-the-art sound quality, to link stations together to create a "chain broadcast." The company refused to lease its telephone wires to RCA, wanting to maintain its monopoly on toll broadcasting, in which advertisers would pay for fifteen-minute chunks of airtime. In 1922, AT&T established its own radio station in New York, WEAF.

After repeated legal pressures on AT&T by RCA,

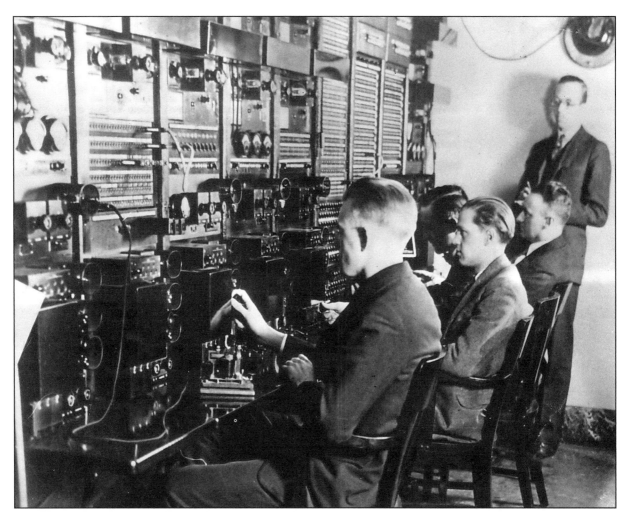

The signal to put the first NBC show on the air is given inside the main control room in 1926. (Getty Images)

the two companies reached an agreement in 1925, with AT&T deciding to focus on its telephone business instead of broadcasting. In July of 1926, Sarnoff purchased WEAF from AT&T for $1 million. With the gate to the network finally open and the profitable WEAF in tow, the first president of NBC, Merlin Aylesworth, announced the establishment of his new company on September 9, 1926. The company's name, National Broadcasting Company, was a statement of intent: RCA fully expected NBC to become the premier destination for radio programming and felt that the term *national* signified such prestige and quality.

In January of 1927, with twenty-three affiliate stations, NBC began operation of dual networks: the Red Network, initially broadcast on WEAF, and the Blue Network, broadcast on WJZ. News of these new networks traveled fast, and the United Independent Broadcasters (UIB) soon emerged as a rival to NBC Red and Blue. After securing considerable funding and political connections from the Columbia Phonograph Company, UIB was granted pay access to AT&T's wires and started broadcasting as the Columbia Phonograph Broadcasting System on September 18, 1927.

Programming

NBC had twenty-eight affiliates by the end of 1927. Its Red Network carried primarily popular entertainment programming, which was mainly commercial—that is, sponsored by advertisers—while its Blue Network consisted of lower-powered stations and featured cultural and educational programming. This latter programming largely consisted of sustaining programs, produced either by nonprofit organizations or by the networks themselves, which, unlike commercial programs, did not rely on advertising sponsors for funding. NBC would pay its affiliates to accept commercial programming and receive payment from the sponsors in turn, but the affiliates paid NBC directly for the sustaining programming, which they might broadcast in order to fulfill public service requirements or simply to appeal to a greater audience.

As radio became increasingly popular, NBC carried a wide variety of programming to satisfy the appetites of listeners. Sports programming was popular, and early NBC sports broadcasts included boxing, college football, and baseball's World Series. Two of NBC's most successful programs of the 1920s, *The Chase and Sanborn Hour* and *Amos 'n' Andy*, debuted in 1929.

Impact

At the end of the 1920s, the three dominant networks—NBC Red, NBC Blue, and CBS—were broadcasting approximately 350 hours of national programming per week. In 1930, the U.S. Census Bureau reported that 45 percent of American households owned radios. By this time, however, most Americans were listening to NBC programming on Philco radio sets, not RCA. NBC's dominance of radio broadcasting would continue until 1943, when the Federal Communications Commission, formed in 1934, would force the company to sell its Blue Network, which later became the American Broadcasting Company or ABC.

Jane E. Turk

Further Reading

Barnouw, Erik. *A History of Broadcasting in the United States.* 3 vols. New York: Oxford University Press, 1968. Chronicles the development of broadcasting in the United States.

Douglas, Susan. *Inventing American Broadcasting, 1899–1922.* Baltimore: Johns Hopkins University Press, 1987. Describes the period leading up to the establishment of network broadcasting, in which amateur operators and commercial broadcasters struggled for dominance of the airwaves.

Gomery, Douglas. *A History of Broadcasting in the United States.* Malden, Mass.: Blackwell, 2008. A detailed history of American broadcasting from radio to the digital era.

Hilmes, Michele, ed. *NBC: America's Network.* Berkeley: University of California Press, 2007. A collection of essays on the history of NBC, from its origins in radio broadcasting to the digital age.

MacDonald, J. Fred. *One Nation Under Television: The Rise and Decline of Network TV.* New York: Pantheon, 1990. Examines the dominance of network television from the 1950s through the 1970s and the subsequent emergence of cable television.

Robinson, Marc. *Brought to You in Living Color: Seventy-Five Years of Great Moments in Television and Radio from NBC.* New York: Wiley, 2003. An overview of significant programs and individuals that shaped the history of NBC.

See also: Advertising in the United States; Federal Radio Commission (FRC); Radio; Radio Act of 1927; Radio Corporation of America (RCA); Sarnoff, David

■ National Conference on Street and Highway Safety

The Event: First efforts to address American motor vehicle safety on a national scale
Date: December 1924; March 1926

Automobiles entered a world without traffic safety infrastructure, resulting in a high rate of traffic deaths and injuries in the early twentieth century. By the end of the 1920s, the fatality rate for automobile accidents had increased to about 30,000 deaths per year. The National Conference on Street and Highway Safety sparked an ongoing safety movement that reduced U.S. traffic fatalities by about 90 percent per vehicle mile traveled by the end of the twentieth century.

After its inception, the automobile was expected to take its place among pedestrians, bicycles, horse-drawn vehicles, and street railways on city streets with no traffic signals, lane markings, or speed limits, as well as on unpaved rural highways. After the introduction of the Model T Ford in 1908 made automobile travel affordable for an increasing number of Americans, it became clear that new kinds of traffic regulation and infrastructure were necessary. A patchwork of local jurisdictions formulated and enforced traffic laws in urban areas; however, the traffic environment was almost entirely unregulated elsewhere.

In early 1924, insurance expert Ernest Greenwood made a proposal for a national conference on traffic safety that received immediate support from engineer and future president Herbert Hoover, who was then U.S. Secretary of Commerce. The proposal advocated for "waste elimination," meaning it sought to avoid the waste of lives and property associated with traffic accidents. Hoover gathered support for the conference from the nascent American Automobile Association (AAA), the International Association of Chiefs of Police, the Accident Committee of the Highway Research Board, and the American Association of State Highway Officials.

The group that met in 1924 and 1926 drafted the Uniform Motor Vehicle Code, which they proposed as a measure to be adopted by all jurisdictions, including what came to be the federal highway system. It proposed the licensing of drivers, rational insurance plans, driver financial responsibility, state regulation of the traffic environment, automobile registration and inspection, gated railroad crossings, and dozens of other innovations that were gradually adopted by local and state jurisdictions over the next fifty years. By the mid-1970s, most of these reforms were in place.

Impact

The National Conferences on Street and Highway Safety set in motion first a nationwide, and later a global, movement to reduce traffic fatalities and injuries. Their legacy continued well into the twenty-first century, improving traffic safety and further developing the governmental regulation of American traffic.

Rachel Maines

Further Reading

Flink, James J. *The Automobile Age.* Cambridge, Mass.: MIT Press, 1988.

Norton, Peter D. 2008. *Fighting Traffic: The Dawn of the Motor Age in the American City.* Cambridge, Mass.: MIT Press, 2008.

World Health Organization. *World Report on Road Traffic Injury Prevention.* Geneva, Switzerland: World Health Organization, 2004.

See also: Automobiles and auto manufacturing;

Cities; Federal Aid Highway Act of 1921; Federal highway system; Hoover, Herbert; Transportation

■ National debt of the United States

Due to the deficit spending associated with World War I, during which the federal government's expenditures exceeded its revenues, the national debt of the United States reached a record level by 1920. During the 1920s, however, the federal government reduced its expenditures and steadily lowered the national debt.

The United States government increased its expenditures to record levels in financing World War I, at times borrowing money from institutions and even citizens through the sale of war bonds and stamps, which could be redeemed for the purchase value plus interest after the war. As a result, the national debt had risen to $25 billion by June of 1919. Much of the debt took the form of interest-bearing securities, with the goal of keeping the government's expenditures lower than its revenues and using the surplus to reduce the national debt. However, the economy experienced a severe economic downturn early in the 1920s. Tax rates were reduced, which helped the economy to recover rapidly. Despite declining tax revenue, the government was able to repay some of the national debt every year in the decade, reducing the overall debt from $24 billion in 1920 to $16 billion in mid-1930.

The Federal Reserve

There was a close connection between the national debt and the Federal Reserve system, which had been established in 1913. The Federal Reserve banks were authorized to engage in open-market operations, meaning they could buy or sell government securities, such as bonds, in transactions with private investors. In the 1920s, Federal Reserve officials discovered that buying securities tended to increase bank reserves and thus expand bank lending power. They developed a countercyclical approach, buying securities during recessions and either selling during boom periods or letting the investments reach maturity

Between 1923 and 1924, and again between 1926 and 1927, both recession periods, the Federal Reserve pumped more than $300 million into the banking system through open-market purchases. They significantly reduced their holdings of Treasury securities as prosperity returned. After increasing their holdings to over $600 million in 1927, they reduced their holdings by nearly $400 million as the economy boomed in 1928.

The national debt also affected the Federal Reserve's ability to lend to banks. As long as the Treasury was issuing securities, the Federal Reserve could make loans available to banks at interest rates lower than those the Treasury was paying on its new bonds. By June of 1920, commercial banks held $3.7 billion of Treasury securities, mostly financed by borrowing from the Federal Reserve. In combination, the Reserve's lending and securities purchases brought about a sizeable increase in the money supply and contributed strongly to the severe inflation of the beginning of the decade.

Refunding

Even though the U.S. Treasury was no longer a net borrower, it still needed to repay maturing short-term securities, which made up a significant portion of the national debt. This would prove difficult because as of 1921, more than $7 billion of its debt was due to be repaid within the next two years. In a process known as refunding, many of the securities maturing in 1921 were repaid in further Treasury notes that would mature in three to five years.

In 1922, the Treasury issued about $764 million of bonds that would mature in twenty-five to thirty years, paying 4.25 percent interest. In contrast, long-term bonds maturing in 1927 and 1928 were refunded with short-term securities. In 1929, the Treasury began to issue short-term Treasury bills, the first batch of which matured in three months. These bills, which would become a mainstay of federal finance for the remainder of the twentieth century, were issued at a discount from their redemption value. A very active market developed for buying and selling Treasury bills.

Impact

The repayment and refunding of the U.S. national debt throughout the 1920s channeled funds into private capital markets, stimulating both growth and speculation. The remaining government securities became a valuable part of the national financial system, considered stable in price, low in risk, and easy to buy and sell. However, this policy of reducing the national debt became a handicap during the Great Depression, as President Herbert Hoover implemented a major increase in federal tax rates in 1932 to reduce the federal deficit, despite severe unemployment.

Paul B. Trescott

Further Reading

Cannadine, David. *Mellon: An American Life.* New York: Vintage Books, 2008. A biography of Andrew Mellon, who was secretary of the treasury between 1921 and 1933.

Chandler, Lester Vernon. *Benjamin Strong, Central Banker.* Washington, D.C.: Brookings Institution, 1958. A biography of Strong, who was president of the Federal Reserve Bank of New York from its creation until 1928 and worked closely with the U.S. Treasury.

Dewey, Davis Rich. *Financial History of the United States.* 12th ed. New York: Augustus M. Kelley, 1968. A history of U.S. finances, featuring two chapters on debt policies during and after World War I.

Friedman, Milton, and Anna Jacobson Schwartz. *A Monetary History of the United States, 1867–1960.* Princeton, N.J.: Princeton University Press, 2008. A history of money in the United States that provides details of the interaction between the Federal Reserve and the Treasury.

Meltzer, Allan H. *A History of the Federal Reserve, Volume 1: 1913–1951.* 3 vols. Chicago: University of Chicago Press, 2003. Chronicles the important interactions between the Federal Reserve and the Treasury concerning the national debt.

See also: Banking; Credit and debt; Mellon, Andrew; Recession of 1920–1921

■ National Football League (NFL)

Identification: First and most successful professional football league in the United States
Also known as: American Professional Football Association (APFA); American Professional Football Conference; NFL
Date: Established on August 20, 1920

Founded in 1920, the National Football League was the first American professional football organization. Although initially far less popular than sports such as college football and baseball, professional football increased in popularity throughout the decade as enduring NFL teams such as the New York Giants and Green Bay Packers joined the league.

First played in 1869 in a game between Rutgers University and Princeton University that barely resembled the modern sport, American football evolved over the next several decades, becoming incredibly popular in colleges and universities. Many cities and towns also established semiprofessional teams, often made up of former college players, but such teams operated with very little organization or regularity. Hoping to control player salaries and establish consistent rules, representatives from four Ohio-based semiprofessional teams met on August 20, 1920, in Canton, Ohio, to discuss forming a professional league. Originally named the American Professional Football Conference, the league consisted of the Cleveland Indians, the Akron Pros, the Dayton Triangles, and Canton's home team, the Bulldogs. On September 17, the four Ohio teams, along with six from other states, agreed to form a larger league, renaming it the American Professional Football Association (APFA). The organization was renamed the National Football League (NFL) in 1922.

Franchises

Throughout the 1920s, the NFL featured teams from a wide array of locations, many of which were not major metropolitan areas. Towns such as Rock Island, Illinois, and Green Bay, Wisconsin, fielded teams that often equaled or surpassed the success of teams such as the Chicago Bears and the New York Giants. Professional football teams received little attention due to the popularity of the well-established college teams as well as that of professional baseball, and many newspapers in cities with NFL teams devoted little space to game results. Teams often struggled financially due to this lack of public interest, but many small towns, most notably Green Bay, developed a powerful base of support for their professional teams, which were perceived as drawing national attention to previously unknown parts of the country. In such towns, an NFL team was a source of community identity and pride. However, most of the teams founded in the 1920s were short lived, as the typically low ticket sales were often insufficient to maintain a competitive roster. Teams such as the New York Giants survived only because their owners were devoted fans determined to maintain their franchises even as they lost money, while Green Bay, unlike most small-town teams, survived by offering public ownership of the team to raise the necessary funds to continue competing.

Players

During the 1920s, most NFL players maintained regular jobs while not on the field, partly because salaries tended to be relatively low. Most professional players were former college athletes, but even the more famous collegians struggled to draw crowds at the professional level. One notable exception in the 1920s was University of Illinois standout Harold "Red" Grange, whose 1925 debut in the NFL with the Chicago Bears generated an unprecedented amount of national attention as well as increased ticket sales. However, his impact was short lived, as he and his manager, C. C. Pyle, tried to capitalize on his newfound notoriety by forming a rival league, the American Football League (AFL), in 1926. The AFL lasted only one season, and Grange, despite his prowess on the field, failed to draw consistently large crowds upon returning to the NFL. Although they often created an initial boost in ticket sales and media coverage, star players such as Grange ultimately had little effect on a given team's long-term success in the 1920s.

Impact

Despite the hardships of the 1920s, professional football began to gain popularity over the course of the next several decades, taking advantage of the new medium of television beginning in the late 1940s. In 1958, the NFL championship game between the Baltimore Colts and New York Giants became the first to end in sudden-death overtime, marking the beginning of the league's meteoric rise as the most popular and lucrative sports league in the United States. By the 1980s, the NFL had surpassed all other professional sports leagues in North America in television ratings and financial revenues.

Aaron D. Horton

Further Reading

Coenen, Craig R. *From Sandlots to the Super Bowl: The National Football League, 1920–1967.* Knoxville: University of Tennessee Press, 2005. A comprehensive study of the origins and development of the NFL from its founding in 1920 to the first Super Bowl in 1967, with an abundance of tables and statistics.

Neft, David S., Richard M. Cohen, and Rick Korch. *The Football Encyclopedia: The Complete History of Professional Football from 1892 to the Present.* New York: St. Martin's Press, 1994. An exhaustive resource that includes results from every game since 1920, as well as complete historical rosters and player statistics.

Peterson, Robert W. *Pigskin: The Early Years of Pro Football.* New York: Oxford University Press, 1997. A general history of professional football from its beginnings at the turn of the twentieth century to the 1958 NFL championship game.

Whittingham, Richard. *What a Game They Played: An Inside Look at the Golden Era of Pro Football.* Lincoln: University of Nebraska Press, 2001. An oral history of the first few decades of the NFL, featuring recollections by players such as Red Grange and Sammy Baugh.

Ziemba, Joe. *When Football Was Football: The Chicago Cardinals and the Birth of the NFL.* Chicago: Triumph Books, 1999. A detailed study of the Chicago Cardinals, one of the founding franchises of the NFL.

See also: Football; Four Horsemen of Notre Dame; Gipp, George; Grange, Red; Rockne, Knute; Sports; Thorpe, Jim

---

■ National Parks of the United States

With the increasing ubiquity of the automobile during the 1920s and the consequent upswing in mobility of the American people, national parks became more popular than ever. The U.S. national park system embarked on a decade of incredible growth, with more effective administration, a growing number of parks, and many more people coming to visit them.

The 1920s was a vital decade in the history of national parks in the United States. The National Park Service (NPS) had just come into existence in 1916 and would spend the following decade professionalizing its operations. At its inception, the NPS was charged with the care of thirteen national parks; by 1920, that number had increased to seventeen.

Drawing People to the Parks

The first director of the NPS, Stephen Mather, was determined to do whatever was necessary to make the national parks into viable tourist destinations. To accomplish this, he relied on one of the technological factors that helped revolutionize American life and

Entrance sign for Shenandoah National Park. (Time & Life Pictures/Getty Images)

mobility during the 1920s: the automobile. Mather sought congressional funding to improve the roads to and throughout the parks. With the completion of the Park-to-Park Highway, a 5,000-mile loop that linked twelve parks in eleven Western states, in 1920, national parks began to draw over one million visitors per year. That amount continued to grow as Americans took to the roadways in ever-increasing numbers, reaching two million by 1925.

The influx of automobiles into some of the nation's most pristine wilderness areas did present a problem: Prominent naturalist and national park enthusiast John Muir recognized that while the automobile could be a potential boon to the parks in terms of drawing more visitors, it could also lead to pollution. However, since the management of the parks was still very much in a nascent stage, Mather's road-building campaign and other proposals faced little opposition from park superintendents, who had mostly worked in isolation from one another prior to the formation of the NPS.

Professionalizing and Defending the National Park System

One of Mather's many accomplishments during the 1920s was the establishment of a cadre of park superintendents, rangers, and other leaders who shared his visions of conservationism and promotion. He was aided in this endeavor by Horace M. Albright, his assistant and the man who would succeed him as NPS director, and the two handpicked many of the leaders who would work closely with them to achieve a common goal. Mather chose superintendents on the basis of their professional abilities, competence, and integrity, and established high standards for all positions within the service, from superintendent to park ranger. He appointed Albright as superintendent of Yellowstone, the NPS's flagship park.

Even though the parks were increasingly popular with the American public, support was by no means universal. Business interests, reclamation officials within the same government department that was home to the NPS, and other pro-development forces saw the NPS as a threat. Following passage of the Federal Water Power Act in 1920, which allowed dams to be built within national parks, a fight broke out over the proposed construction of a mine and two hydroelectric dams in Grand Canyon National Park. Secretary of the Interior Franklin K. Lane was in favor of the project, but Mather rallied public support against it, which was enough to halt all development within the park.

New Parks and More Visitors

During the 1920s, five new national parks were authorized or established by Congress: Hot Springs in Arkansas (1921), Shenandoah in Virginia (1926), Mammoth Cave in Kentucky (1926), Bryce Canyon in Utah (1928), and Grand Teton in Wyoming (1929). Grand Teton had been a project of special interest to Albright, and he secured its national park status with Mather's support and the assistance of Standard Oil scion and philanthropist John D. Rockefeller Jr., who had bought up much of the land in 1927 to thwart the construction of proposed dams in the area. When Congress did establish the park, however, the land Rockefeller purchased was not a part of it and would not become federal land until the creation of Jackson Hole National Monument in 1943.

Impact

By the end of the 1920s, the enlarged, professionalized, and more accessible system of national parks was drawing over three million visitors per year, three times as many as when the decade began. Congress, sensing the public support, increased appropriations to build more roads for even greater access to the parks. That road-building effort was opposed by many, notably conservationists such as National Parks Association head Robert Sterling Yard. However, it did result in the creation of some of the most breathtaking scenic drives in the United States, such

as Going-to-the-Sun Road, which spans Montana's Glacier National Park.

Steven L. Danver

Further Reading

Albright, Horace M., and Robert Cahn. *The Birth of the National Park Service: The Founding Years, 1913–33.* Salt Lake City: Howe Brothers, 1985. A first-hand account of the beginnings of the NPS.

Miles, John C. *Guardians of the Parks: A History of the National Parks and Conservation Association.* Washington, D.C.: Taylor & Francis, 1995. Describes the National Parks Conservation Association, an independent advocacy organization for the NPS, and its role in helping to preserve national parks.

Runte, Alfred. *National Parks: The American Experience.* 4th ed. Lanham, Md.: Taylor Trade, 2010. A history of the national parks and their significance in American cultural identity.

Sellars, Richard West. *Preserving Nature in the National Parks: A History.* Rev. ed. New Haven, Conn.: Yale University Press, 2009. A detailed history of national parks in the United States, largely based on primary sources.

_____. "Manipulating Nature's Paradise: National Park Management Under Stephen T. Mather, 1916–1929." In *A Sense of the American West: An Anthology of Environmental History*, edited by James E. Sherow. Albuquerque: University of New Mexico Press, 1998. A look at the first thirteen years of the NPS.

See also: Air pollution; Automobiles and auto manufacturing; Federal highway system; Travel

■ Native Americans

Government policies seeking to force Native American assimilation into Anglo-American culture persisted during the 1920s. However, the decade was also marked by the first stirrings of a movement that would change that focus.

During the prior decade, the United States' participation in World War I had been seen by many Native Americans as a chance to cement their loyalty to the country and to demonstrate that they were full participants and thus entitled to full equality with Anglo-Americans. However, many Native Americans wondered whether they should fight and die for a country that had done nothing positive for them. Others viewed fighting for the United States as a diminution of their own tribes' sovereignty.

In spite of their opposing viewpoints, Native Americans began to work together during the 1920s, recognizing that they were much more effective in collaboration than as individuals or as separate tribal groups. On a national level, the Society of American Indians (SAI) began to pay attention to the ramifications of federal Indian policies. On a more regional basis, groups such as the All Indian Pueblo Council in New Mexico, made up of representatives from nineteen different tribal groups, worked together on problems related to everyday aspects of Native American life.

Although Native Americans worked together to assert their own interests, their views did not significantly influence federal policy makers during the decade; Commissioner of Indian Affairs Charles H. Burke and Secretary of the Interior Albert B. Fall still held to the idea that the only possible future for American Indians was full assimilation into Anglo-American culture. The passage of the Indian Citizenship Act in 1924 was seen as simply the next step in this process. Agents from the Bureau of Indian Affairs (BIA) still spoke against the practice of Native American dances and religious rituals, and boarding schools still operated with the stated goal of "kill the Indian, and save the man." Often working closely with BIA agents, Christian missionaries sought to replace Native American religions with American Protestantism. Even some Native American groups, such as the Indian Rights Association (IRA), fought for total assimilation into Anglo-American society. The IRA tended to demonize Native American cultures, calling attention to what the association considered the immoral aspects of Native American ceremonies. However, it was the more "mundane" issue of the theft of Native American land and water that catapulted Native American issues into the national media and led to the first positive changes in federal Indian policy.

Native Activists and Allies

Although many Native American groups advocated for their rights during the 1920s, no group was more successful at gaining the national spotlight than the Pueblos of New Mexico. The Pueblos had advocated for themselves for centuries in dealing with the governments of Spain, Mexico, and the United States; these dealings took on both a new approach and a new urgency during the early twentieth century. The nineteen Pueblo tribes had long been unhappy that non-Indian squatters were allowed to live on Indian lands. However, in 1921, New Mexico senator Holm O. Bursum introduced a bill into Congress designed to provide the squatters with a way to legitimize their land claims and gain title to what, by the 1848 Treaty of Guadalupe Hidalgo, was Pueblo land, without any compensation to the tribes. The IRA protested the legislation directly to Secretary Fall, who convinced Bursum to rework the bill to be fairer to the Pueblos. However, the overall impact of the Bursum bill would have meant the transfer of a large part of the Pueblos' land base into non-Indian hands.

By 1922, the situation facing the Pueblos drew the attention of a social activist by the name of John Collier. Working with Pueblo leaders, Collier helped their newly formed group, the All Indian Pueblo Council (AIPC), to get coverage in local and national newspapers and magazines. Collier made it his mission to inform the American public of the land rights issues at stake and to help organize the Pueblos to fight the bill. Although the group was initially formed to deal with the immediate emergency posed by the Bursum bill, the AIPC grew into an organization that would help coordinate Pueblo efforts in land, water, educational, religious, and cultural issues for years to come. Although Collier exercised a profound influence on the activities of the AIPC throughout the 1920s, the council sought to maintain a distinctly Indian identity in its organization, leadership, and goals.

After Collier became involved in the AIPC in 1922, the group's meetings set a new precedent for council activities and tactics. What set this new council apart from the traditional council was the idea, encouraged by Collier, that they could organize to directly influence the federal government's legislative and judicial decisions that affected the Pueblos. The initial passage of the Bursum bill seemed to many Pueblo leaders to constitute another in a long line of attempts to deprive the Pueblos of their land. Although they knew little of the outside world, some of the early AIPC leadership had learned to be skeptical of government offers of assistance. Many supposed that governmental assistance came at the price of land cessions and cultural changes. Collier's influence on the AIPC and his insistence that only through organization could the Pueblos overcome this skepticism was vital. Although the Pueblos saw the need to organize to fight the Bursum bill, it was Collier who helped direct many of the early activities of the AIPC. Collier was especially instrumental in orchestrating a successful campaign against the Bursum bill.

In place of the defeated Bursum bill, U.S. Congress passed the Pueblo Lands Act of 1924, which established the Pueblo Lands Board to determine the validity of the competing Anglo-American and Native American land claims and establish the true boundaries and landholdings of each Pueblo community. The board was made up of the secretary of the interior, the attorney general, and a member to be appointed by the president. The Pueblo Lands Board was given the power of subpoena, the power to take testimony, and the power to make determinations on the validity of Anglo-American land claims. If the board decided that an Indian title was to be extinguished, it had to be by unanimous vote.

The knowledge and experience Collier gained while working with the Pueblos during the 1920s proved pivotal in the future of Native American rights protection, as Collier went on to become commissioner of Indian affairs in the early 1930s. During his years as commissioner, Collier implemented the Indian New Deal, which involved the returning of communal Indian land and supported Native American self-determination. Along with the Johnson-O'Malley Act that Collier helped pass, the Indian New Deal was one of the largest fundamental changes to the way that the United States viewed and treated Native American individuals and tribes.

Reforming Indian Policy

Collier was by no means the only reformer interested in bringing Native American issues to public attention, and land rights were not the only issue facing Native Americans in the 1920s. Inadequate health care on Native American lands was another area of increasing concern during the decade. Secretary of the Interior Hubert Work was under pressure from reformers to address health care, education, treaty rights, and many other areas of Indian policy. To assess these areas in 1926, Work commissioned the Committee of One Hundred, also known as the Advisory Council on Indian Affairs, which was made up of Native American activists, government officials, and reformers like Collier, to study the issues. Although the group catalogued many problems, the diverse group members could not come to a consensus on how best to address them.

In order to better focus on concrete suggestions for solutions, Work commissioned the Brookings Institution to survey the problems pointed out by the Committee of One Hundred and to come up with actionable reforms that would address the problems. Lewis Meriam, a staff member at Brookings, headed up the effort, which led to the production of a lengthy report in 1928, called *The Problem of Indian Administration* (also known as the Meriam Report). This report examined government policy in areas ranging from education and health care to the religious and cultural lives of Native Americans. The evidence provided by the report was devastating and placed the blame squarely on the federal government.

The Meriam Report detailed the poor living conditions faced by Native Americans across the country. Federal policies designed to transfer Native American lands into Anglo-American hands had resulted in the location of Native Americans onto an ever-shrinking amount of land, most of which was unsuitable for cultivation. Deprived of any hope of economic viability, Native Americans became dependent on minuscule federal payments in a system that fostered extreme poverty. This poverty led to poor nutrition, which, in combination with substandard housing and poor sanitation facilities, led to widespread health problems. The BIA and the Indian Health Service did not deal effectively with these health problems, with the result that Native Americans developed a very short life expectancy.

Impact

Although Native Americans did not end the 1920s in substantially better conditions than they began the decade, the activism of Native American groups such as the IRA and AIPC, the influence and public relations expertise of reformers like Collier, and growing calls for federal Indian policy reform set the stage for radical changes to take place during the following decade. During the 1930s, one of Collier's activities as commissioner of Indian affairs was to implement the Indian Reorganization Act, which attempted to deal with the specific problems outlined in the Meriam Report.

Steven L. Danver

Further Reading

Deloria, Vine, Jr. *American Indian Policy in the Twentieth*

Century. Norman: University of Oklahoma Press, 1992. Presents a series of essays on various aspects of twentieth century U.S. policy involving Native Americans.

Hoxie, Frederick E. "The Curious Story of Reformers and American Indians." In *Indians in American History: An Introduction*, edited by Peter Iverson. Wheeling, Ill.: Harlan Davidson, 1998. Examines the pseudo-reformers who led the call for assimilation before and during the 1920s, along with the emergence of reformers like Collier, who sought a fundamental shift in Indian policy.

_____. *Talking Back to Civilization: Indian Voices From the Progressive Era.* Boston, Mass.: Bedford/ St. Martins, 2001. Discusses the experiences of Native Americans in the early twentieth century, including a selection of primary historical sources, illustrations, and a chronology of significant dates.

Iverson, Peter. *"We Are Still Here": American Indians in the Twentieth Century.* Wheeling, Ill.: Harlan Davidson, 1998. Deals with the situation faced by Native Americans in the early 1920s and the fundamental changes portended by developments in the later part of the decade.

Philp, Kenneth R. *John Collier's Crusade for Indian Reform, 1920–1954.* Tucson: University of Arizona Press, 1977. Discusses John Collier's work with the Pueblos and his role in bringing the Pueblo land issue to a national forum.

See also: Education; Health care; Housing; Indian Citizenship Act of 1924

▪ Natural disasters

Natural disasters of the 1920s claimed many lives and inflicted large amounts of property damage. There were no early warning systems in place to alert people to oncoming storms, and the lack of building code regulations meant that structures were prone to collapse under the weight of snow or the force of hurricane-strength winds.

The natural disasters of the 1920s included some of the worst weather in U.S. recorded history. Record snowfalls hit North Dakota and Washington, D.C., and floods inundated Wyoming, Vermont, and states along the Mississippi River. Severe tornadoes swept the mid-Atlantic and Midwest states, while hurricanes wreaked havoc in Florida and the Gulf Coast.

Hurricanes and Tornadoes

On March 28, 1920, the Palm Sunday tornado outbreak brought devastation to states in the Midwest and the South. It included at least thirty-eight separate tornadoes, the first of which touched down in Springfield, Missouri. Nearly four hundred people lost their lives, and twelve hundred more sustained injuries. This tornado outbreak was allegedly the inspiration for scenes in the 1939 film *The Wizard of Oz.*

On April 20, 1920, seven tornadoes struck the southeastern United States, including a severe cyclone in Mississippi that stayed on the ground for a record 130 miles. In Alabama, Mississippi, and Tennessee, over 220 people were killed by these spring storms.

The Tampa Bay hurricane of 1921 formed southwest of Jamaica on October 20. It was at category 4 strength when it passed west of the Florida Keys but did little damage. The hurricane then weakened slightly, becoming a category 3 storm before hitting the mainland on October 25. It made landfall with wind speeds of around 125 miles per hour, causing a storm tide of 10.5 feet that flooded the Tampa Bay area and killed six people.

An outbreak of at least twenty-six tornadoes moved through the states of Alabama, Arkansas, Georgia, Louisiana, North and South Carolina, Oklahoma, and Virginia on April 29 and 30, 1924. The twisters ranged from F2 to F4 in intensity and left over one hundred people dead.

On June 28, 1924, Ohio was struck by the deadliest tornado in its history. It formed over Sandusky Bay, just south of Lake Erie, and followed an eastward course that took it through the town of Sandusky around 4:30 P.M. The tornado then tracked out over the lake before hitting the town of Lorain. The Lorain-Sandusky tornado caused eighty-five deaths, seventy-eight of which took place in Lorain, and fifteen of these were caused when the town's State Theater collapsed. It is estimated to have been an F4 storm. Three other nearby tornadoes also took their toll on that day.

On March 18, 1925, the Tri-State tornado hit the southern areas of Missouri, Illinois, and Indiana. It was rated an F5, with wind speeds of over three hundred miles per hour. The tornado traveled through thirteen counties, was an average of three-quarters of a mile wide, and left a continuous track of more than 219 miles, the longest ever recorded in the world.

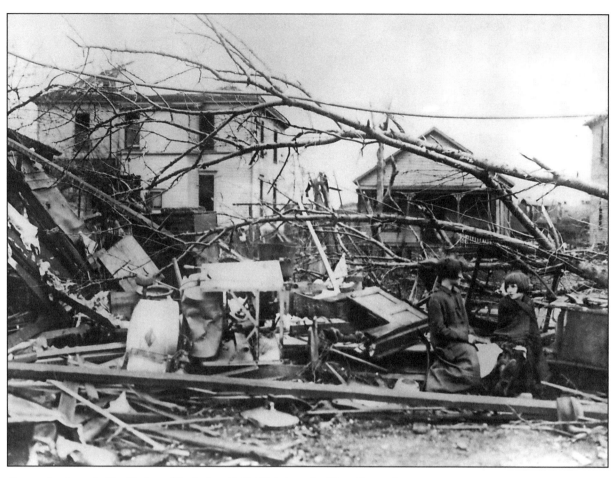

Damage to a house in Murphysboro, Illinois, from the Tri-State tornado. (Getty Images)

The deadliest U.S. tornado on record, it was responsible for at least 695 deaths and destroyed around fifteen thousand homes.

A hurricane that hit Florida on December 1, 1925, is the latest ever hurricane to make landfall in the United States in recorded history. Miami received 14 inches of rain, and gale-force winds were reported as far north as New Jersey. The storm was responsible for over fifty deaths in Florida and in the waters off the East Coast, including the crews of several ships.

The Great Miami Hurricane, another category 4 storm, made landfall just south of Miami, Florida, on September 18, 1926, with wind speeds of up to 150 miles per hour. The storm, which killed over 240 people and caused $100 million worth of damage, is credited with ruining the Florida land boom and causing the state's early slide into the Great Depression.

On May 9, 1927, ten separate tornadoes swept through Arkansas, Oklahoma, Texas, Kansas, and Missouri. The worst hit was Poplar Bluff, Missouri, where one tornado leveled forty city blocks, leaving only a handful of buildings in the town still standing. Around one hundred people were killed, making the Poplar Bluff tornado one of the twenty-five deadliest in U.S. history.

The Okeechobee Hurricane of 1928 formed on September 6 and lasted for two weeks. It hit several islands in the Atlantic Ocean at category 5 strength, including Puerto Rico, before making landfall as a category 4 storm in Florida, where it caused the worst damage in West Palm Beach and the heavily populated Lake Okeechobee area. The hurricane caused an estimated twenty-five hundred fatalities in the United States alone. Sixteen hundred of those victims were buried in a mass grave in Port Mayaca Cemetery, on the eastern side of Lake Okeechobee.

On May 1 and 2, 1929, a tornado outbreak swept

through the Appalachian Mountains from Alabama to Maryland, affecting six states along the way. The deadliest of these tornadoes struck Rye Cove, Virginia, where it destroyed a school and killed thirteen people. The Rye Cove tornado ranks as the most lethal tornado in the history of Virginia.

Rain and Floods

On June 23, 1925, a rockslide caused by heavy rains dammed a portion of the Gros Ventre River in western Wyoming. The dam remained stable for nearly two years, but on May 18, 1927, a heavy spring snowmelt accompanied by torrential rains caused the dam to collapse. The flood continued for at least 25 miles downstream and was up to 6 feet deep in places. Most of Kelly, Wyoming, was destroyed, and six people lost their lives.

The year 1927 saw a number of devastating floods. In Vermont, a flash flood caused by 9 inches of rainfall occurred on November 3 and 4 in the Winooski and White River Valleys, claiming eighty-four lives. During this same storm, rainfall reached a state record of 9.65 inches in Somerset, Vermont, while 14 inches fell on Kinsman Notch, New Hampshire, and Westerly, Rhode Island, recorded 9.4 inches.

The Great Mississippi Flood of 1927 took place in mid-April when the Mississippi River overflowed its banks and flooded to depths of 30 feet. The river swelled, in places growing to 50 miles wide. The flood spread over 27,000 square miles in eleven states, killing 246 people and leaving 700,000 homeless. It is still considered the most destructive river flood in United States history.

Snowstorms and Blizzards

On March 15, 1920, a blizzard began in central North Dakota that lasted for three days, with wind speeds reaching up to 70 miles per hour. The snowstorm took the lives of thirty-four people, including sixteen-year-old Hazel Miner, who died saving her younger brother and sister from freezing to death. The 1920 blizzard is considered one of the worst in North Dakota history.

In 1922, the blizzard that would become known as the Knickerbocker Storm hit the Atlantic seaboard states from the Carolinas through Pennsylvania. The area hardest hit was from Richmond, Virginia, through Baltimore, Maryland. On January 27 and 28, 1922, the storm deposited 28 inches of snow on Washington, D.C., and 26.8 inches on Baltimore, Mary-

land. The weight of the snow caved in the roof of the Knickerbocker Theatre in Washington, D.C., killing ninety-eight people.

Impact

The immense destruction and loss of life caused by natural disasters during the 1920s led to government efforts to minimize or eliminate the dangers associated with extreme weather, among them the adoption of building codes designed to prevent buildings from being severely damaged by storms or the weight of snow. The Great Mississippi Flood of 1927 led directly to the Flood Control Act of 1928, which tasked the Army Corps of Engineers with building a new, more extensive system of levees and floodways to contain the river, as the previous system had failed. The act also authorized an emergency fund for rescue work. The flooding of the Mississippi River Valley created extreme hardship, primarily for the poor and African Americans. Race relations in the southern states, already unpleasant, were exacerbated by the disaster, which led many African Americans to migrate to northern cities.

Karen S. Garvin

Further Reading

Ambrose, Kevin, Dan Henry, and Andy Weiss. *Washington Weather: The Weather Sourcebook for the D.C. Area.* Fairfax, Va.: Historical Enterprises, 2002. Includes historical accounts of blizzards, heat waves, and other weather phenomena over the last three hundred years.

Barry, John M. *Rising Tide: The Great Mississippi Flood of 1927 and How It Changed America.* New York: Simon & Schuster, 1997. Describes the flood, the events leading up to it, and the problems it caused.

Burt, Christopher C., and Mark Stroud. *Extreme Weather: A Guide and Record Book.* Rev. ed. New York: W. W. Norton, 2007. Discusses the impact of weather extremes and freak weather incidents such as pink snow. Includes precipitation and temperature records for U.S. cities.

Emanuel, Kerry A. *Divine Wind: The History and Science of Hurricanes.* New York: Oxford University Press, 2005. Explains how hurricanes are formed and how they move and includes information about the 1928 Okeechobee hurricane.

Felknor, Peter S. *The Tri-State Tornado: The Story of America's Greatest Tornado Disaster.* Lincoln, Nebr.:

iUniverse, 2004. Draws from both archival research and eyewitness accounts.

Mykle, Robert. *Killer 'Cane: The Deadly Hurricane of 1928.* Lanham, Md.: Taylor Trade, 2006. Details the events of the Okeechobee hurricane and its impact on people in the Lake Okeechobee area.

See also: Castle Gate, Utah, mining disaster; Great Mississippi Flood of 1927; Knickerbocker Storm; Okeechobee Hurricane of 1928; St. Francis Dam disaster

---

■ Natural resources, exploitation of

The economic growth experienced by the United States during the 1920s was based significantly on the exploitation of natural resources. As the nation established a presence in the global economy, the mining of coal and drilling of oil allowed for a new degree of political autonomy and individual financial freedom that would drive national economic expansion. However, this ongoing use of resources had negative effects on the country's environment.

In the years following World War I, the United States emerged as an industrial world leader. Economic expansion increased dramatically as the United States began to produce and manage natural resources that would ensure political and economic freedom throughout the decade. Coal mining and oil drilling, among other industries, boosted the country's gross domestic product throughout the decade. Despite the positive economic results of such practices, the exploitation of natural resources throughout the decade made pollution, deforestation, and industrial accidents and the related loss of human life significant areas of concern.

Water Resources

Seeking to exert more control over the various natural resources available in the United States, Congress enacted the Federal Water Power Act of 1920. This act granted the federal government jurisdiction over waterways throughout the United States, including rivers and reservoirs, for the purpose of producing hydroelectric power through the creation of artificial dams and hydroelectric plants. While hydroelectric power was a relatively clean and efficient form of energy, producing far less pollution than

coal, it was not without risks. In 1928, the St. Francis Dam in California collapsed, flooding several towns and killing at least four hundred people.

Coal Mining

During the 1920s, coal was a major source of energy in the United States, and as the economic expansion of the decade continued, the mining of coal became an increasingly crucial industry. Between 1920 and 1929, the U.S. coal industry greatly increased its production in order to meet consumer demand. While the primary purpose of coal was to generate electricity, it was also used to fuel various forms of transportation throughout the period, particularly trains and ships.

The exploitation of coal reserves across the United States led to a number of problems related to both the use and the extraction of the resource. The burning of coal released pollutants into the air and water, while the pollutants within the mines caused life-threatening health problems for workers. In addition, the underground location of many mines and the flammability of coal and various underground gasses contributed to several mine collapses and explosions, including the Stag Canyon mine disaster of 1923, the Castle Gate disaster of 1924, and the Coal Glen disaster of 1925. A reported 22,461 coal miners died as a result of underground and surface accidents between the years of 1920 and 1929, and such reports did not take into account deaths from black lung and other ailments caused by coal dust and related pollutants.

Steel Production

A significant rise in steel production contributed to the United States' overall economic growth during the 1920s. In the final months before the stock market crash of 1929, which signaled the beginning of the Great Depression, steel production had risen 34 percent from 1920. Increases in building construction and railway expansions contributed greatly to the increased demand for steel, and the automobile industry's total steel consumption more than doubled by the end of the decade. The production of steel required the use of a number of resources, including iron, the primary component of the alloy, and coal and coal by-products, used to fuel the furnaces in which iron was extracted from ore and impurities removed from the resulting metal.

Mineral Leasing Act of 1920

On February 25, 1920, President Woodrow Wilson signed the Mineral Leasing Act, giving statutory effect to the policy of leasing government lands containing mineral deposits such as coal, gas, oil, oil shale, phosphates, potassium, and sodium to private parties for development. The act established the principle that the government would retain ownership of public lands containing mineral deposits and would lease those lands and their resources to private developers. In so doing, the federal government became permanently involved in managing the mineral resources of the nation.

Oil Drilling

The increase in automobile production also spurred further exploitation of oil throughout the United States, which led the world in oil productivity at the beginning of the decade. However, an oil shortage in the early 1920s forced the United States to seek alternative drilling locations—both overseas and domestic—to replenish the nation's dwindling oil supplies.

In 1920, the Mineral Leasing Act was passed, granting the U.S. government the power to lease public lands to facilitate the location and extraction of coal, oil, and various other minerals as outlined by the act. The only federally owned lands excluded from this broad-reaching effort to further exploit oil reserves were those protected under the 1911 Appalachian Forest Act, national parks, and other lands specifically protected by the government. This act in effect gave the United States government ownership of any mineral deposits located within public lands and control over which companies could lease the land and extract natural resources.

While oil production created immediate wealth and urban development during the 1920s, numerous oil workers were killed or injured, and the effects of drilling did long-lasting damage to the ecosystem. Air, water, and land pollution caused by oil extraction and production affected crops, vegetation, and water supplies. Water pollution in particular became a federal concern, as the practice of dumping oil into waterways had negatively affected fish populations and migration and spawning patterns, as well as those of waterfowl. In 1924, the Oil Pollution Act was passed to prohibit the dumping of oil into coastal U.S. waters. However, the act was ineffective in protecting the waterways, and the United States would continue to suffer the effects of improper oil dumping.

Farmland and Forests

Technological advances by companies such as John Deere and the creation of new crop varieties prior to the 1920s allowed for an increase in agricultural output during the decade. The rise of commercial farming created a surplus of crops that in turn created reduced crop prices, allowing for increased consumption by the people of the United States. However, the farming practices of the period were often damaging to the land, particularly in the southern plains, where the soil became greatly eroded. In the next decade, this erosion would combine with a severe drought to produce massive dust storms throughout the region, which would come to be known as the Dust Bowl.

The U.S. Forest Service was established in 1905 to protect the nation's forests, but by the 1920s, concerns regarding forest conservation were again mounting. Prior to the 1911 passage of the Weeks Act, which allowed for the federal purchase and protection of forests, fires and logging had devastated woodlands throughout the United States. In 1924, the Clarke-McNary Act was passed to facilitate further purchases of forests for federal protection. The act also tasked the Forest Service with preventing forest fires and established programs to reforest cleared areas in an attempt to renew the resources that had been used by the lumber industry. In 1928, the McNary-Woodruff Act secured additional funding for the purchase of forested land.

Impact

The exploitation of natural resources throughout the United States led to economic expansion both at home and abroad. However, the nation's reliance on such resources would become a burden in later decades, with the depletion of domestic oil supplies creating a dependency on foreign oil. Nevertheless, some of the conservation efforts made during the 1920s, such as the purchase of national forests, would continue to benefit the nation into the next century.

Tina Marie Forsythe

Further Reading

Andrews, Richard N. L. *Managing the Environment, Managing Ourselves: A History of American Environmental Policy.* New Haven, Conn.: Yale University Press, 2007. Chronicles the development of American environmental policy and includes information on relevant 1920s policies.

Merchant, Carolyn. *American Environmental History: An Introduction.* New York: Columbia University Press, 2007. Surveys the environmental history of the United States and includes sections on both the exploitation of resources and the conservation efforts of the 1920s.

Rogers, Robert P. *An Economic History of the American Steel Industry.* New York: Routledge, 2009. Outlines the steel industry in the United States from the 1830s to 2001, offering passages on the historical, economic, environmental, and political importance of steel production in America.

Steen, Harold K. *The U.S. Forest Service: A History.* 1976. Reprint. Seattle: University of Washington Press, 2004. Details the history of the Forest Service from its foundation to the modern day, including discussion of the events and issues of the 1920s.

Yergin, Daniel. *The Prize: The Epic Quest for Oil, Money, and Power.* 1991. Reprint. New York: Free Press, 2009. Explores the underpinnings of the rise of the oil industry and the global and domestic conflicts and environmental issues related to it.

See also: Agriculture in the United States; Air pollution; Castle Gate, Utah, mining disaster; Federal Power Act of 1920; Gila Wilderness Area; Halibut Treaty of 1924; Labor strikes; Oil Pollution Act of 1924; Railway Labor Act of 1926; Transportation

---

■ Negro History Week

The Event: Celebration commemorating the place of African Americans in U.S. history.
Date: Established February 1926

Negro History Week was created as an annual celebration to increase awareness and interest in African Americans and their contributions throughout history. Established by African American scholar Carter G. Woodson, Negro History Week focused on the significant achievements and accomplishments of an underrepresented population.

Noted historian, educator, and author Carter G. Woodson created Negro History Week in response to what he observed was an absence or exclusion of information about the historical contributions of Africans and peoples of African descent in America. As a historian, Woodson believed strongly in the need to establish a body of literature based on the academic study of black history. Toward this end, he had established the Association for the Study of Negro Life and History (ASNLH) in 1915. The next year, the association began publishing the *Journal of Negro History* as a regular forum for African American scholarship.

The first Negro History Week celebration took place in the second week of February 1926. Woodson chose the second week of the month because it encompassed the birthdays of Abraham Lincoln and Frederick Douglass, whose roles in shaping the history of African Americans were well known. As the popularity of Negro History Week celebrations grew, the ASNLH became a permanent sponsor of the annual event.

Preparations for Negro History Week began months in advance. Woodson, through the association, distributed pamphlets and brochures to state departments of education, elementary and secondary schools, colleges and universities, civic organizations, and black news publications. Woodson included literature and programs emphasizing the achievements and contributions of African Americans, as well as suggestions for how to celebrate the week. To support communities in their educational efforts during Negro History Week, the association produced promotional materials including bibliographies, photographs, and posters. The popularity of Negro History Week continued to increase through the 1920s with outreach to libraries, museums, and educational institutions. Woodson chronicled the yearly successes of Negro History Week celebrations in the *Journal of Negro History.*

Impact

Negro History Week created a collective focus on black history and facilitated an appreciation for and awareness of the significant roles that African Americans have played in the development of American culture. The annual celebration allowed people of different races, ethnicities, and social backgrounds to come together and participate in learning about the black experience. Woodson, the driving force behind the event, established a successful mechanism through which to disseminate information about black history and culture. In 1976, the ASNLH—itself now the ASALH, or Association for the Study of African American Life and History—expanded and renamed Negro History Week, and it became Black History Month.

Kelly R. McBride

Further Reading

Battle, Thomas C., and Donna M. Wells., eds. *Legacy: Treasures of Black History.* Washington, D.C.: National Geographic, 2006.

Goggin, Jacqueline. *Carter G. Woodson: A Life in Black History.* Baton Rouge: Louisiana State University Press, 1993.

Woodson, C. G. "Negro History Week." *Journal of Negro History* 11, no. 2 (1926): 238–242.

See also: African Americans; Historiography

■ Negro League Baseball

Negro League Baseball, a form of the organized black baseball tradition also known as blackball, was African Americans' national pastime from roughly 1920 to 1955. No fewer than four separate leagues formed during the 1920s, starting with the Negro National League (NNL) at the beginning of the decade.

The Negro League was formed in the twentieth century in response to African Americans being barred from Major League Baseball. Institutional segregation in professional baseball dates back to 1867, when, in the aftermath of the Civil War, the National Association of Base Ball Players banned black ballplayers from the league, as well as any club that included black players. Its 1871 successor, the National Association of Professional Base Ball Players, did not explicitly continue the ban, but it remained in place by an implicit understanding popularly known as the "gentleman's agreement."

Early Blackball

Black ballplayers who broke the color line before 1898 were few, and included Moses Fleetwood "Fleet" Walker and John W. "Bud" Fowler. They represented the rise and subsequent decline of African Americans from organized baseball in the 1880s and 1890s,

the latter precipitated by the refusal of such white superstars as Adrian Constantine "Cap" Anson to play opposite a team fielding black players. By 1898, professional baseball reflected the "separate and unequal" sentiment toward African Americans that had been enshrined in American culture following the Supreme Court ruling *Plessy v. Ferguson* (1896).

Race relations in the United States worsened in the 1920s, amplified by the Ku Klux Klan, urban race riots, white nativism, and economic instability. Despite these restrictions, baseball became a staple in black leisure culture, the growth of which was enabled by the large-scale migration of African Americans to the metropolitan areas of the North. There, they found increased economic opportunities as laborers, domestics, service employees, and factory workers, whereby they could earn unprecedented amounts of disposable income and thus enjoy greater leisure time than before.

The driving force behind blackball's adoption of a successful organized structure was Chicago American Giants owner-manager Andrew "Rube" Foster. Born in 1879 in Kankakee, Illinois, Foster was raised during a period in which professional blackball teams and leagues were created and folded on a seasonal, and sometimes monthly, basis. Early attempts to form a blackball league prior to the 1920s include the Southern League of Base Ballists (1886), which collapsed after several months because of financial difficulties; the League of Colored Base Ball Clubs (1887), which folded after several weeks due to low attendance and the league's failure to attract the biggest black baseball team of the late nineteenth century, the New York Cuban Giants; and the integrated International League of Independent Professional Base Ball Clubs (1906), which dissolved after a season as a result of disorganization and low attendance. In 1910, four years after the failure of the International League, another attempt was made to organize a national blackball league but was aborted before a single game could be played.

The Negro Leagues

Despite the difficulties they faced in organizing, many great independent clubs formed between 1900 and 1920, including the Baltimore Black Sox, the Brooklyn Royal Giants, the Chicago American Giants, the Homestead Grays (based near Pittsburgh), and the Indianapolis ABCs. These teams were early participants in the first long-lasting Negro Leagues, the

The Negro League Chicago American Giants in 1922. (Getty Images)

Negro National League (NNL) and the Eastern Colored League (ECL). After the collapse of the ECL in 1928, several of its teams would become part of the American Negro League (ANL), established the following year.

From 1920 to 1926, Rube Foster served as president and secretary of the NNL's governing body, the National Association of Colored Professional Base Ball Clubs. He invested his own money in faltering franchises, often paying the teams' transportation costs and hotel bills. Foster was also the league's booking agent, scheduling the games himself in an effort to avoid the disorganization that had brought financial and structural instability to many earlier blackball clubs in that era. Foster's original conception of the Negro Leagues was based on Major League Baseball; in his vision, the NNL would be one of two leagues whose teams competed for the Negro League title. However, a second league, projected to be made up of ball clubs on the East Coast, never fully merged with the NNL during Foster's lifetime.

The most feasible league to bring in was the ECL, established in 1923, but they remained independent after merger negotiations ended in 1924 over irresolvable issues. This failure to amalgamate arguably resulted in both leagues remaining structurally and financially weak until the NNL and ANL merged in 1933 under Gus Greenlee, owner of the Pittsburgh Crawfords and the founder and president of the second Negro National League.

The first teams to play in the NNL were located in the urban Midwest: the Chicago Giants, the Chicago American Giants, the Cincinnati Cuban Stars, the Dayton Marcos, the Detroit Stars, the Indianapolis ABCs, the Kansas City Monarchs, and the St. Louis Giants (later the Stars). The only NNL teams to win a pennant before the reorganization in 1933 were the Monarchs, the American Giants, and the St. Louis Stars. In 1923, the Atlantic City Bacharach Giants and the Hilldale Club of Darby, Pennsylvania, associate NNL teams that were ineligible to compete for the championship, broke from the league to form the ECL with four other East Coast teams. This kicked off a battle between the two leagues for the top players, as not all teams made their players sign written contracts, and among those that did, these contracts were rarely respected and never legally enforced. Players commonly exploited this system by jumping from one team or even league to another if they felt they were not being fairly compensated.

While the 1940s is widely regarded as the golden era of Negro League Baseball, the 1920s also fielded some of the league's greatest players, including National Baseball Hall of Famers James Thomas "Cool Papa" Bell, Leroy "Satchel" Paige, John Henry "Pop" Lloyd, and William Julius "Judy" Johnson. Cool Papa Bell is regarded as one of the fastest baseball players of all time; Satchel Paige once said of him, "One time, he hit a line drive right past my ear. I turned around and saw the ball hit his rear end as he slid into second." Players would perform in front of crowds ranging from hundreds of spectators in coal mining towns to over ten thousand people at Major League fields such as Chicago's Comiskey Park.

The Negro League World Series, for which blackball is popularly known, started in 1924 and was played until 1927. Pennant winning teams such as the ECL's Homestead Grays and the NNL's Kansas City Monarchs annually battled one another for Negro League supremacy, a tradition given long life after the resurrection of the NNL in 1933 and the revival of the World Series in 1942.

Impact

Ultimately, the Negro Leagues speak to the resilience of black culture and the drive of African Americans to establish their own, equally significant leisure traditions during the Jim Crow era. As a parallel institution, the Negro Leagues were not equal to Major League Baseball in terms of ownership, crowd size, marketing, discretionary income, and access to professional ballparks. On the field, however, Negro League teams performed exceptionally well, often beating white professional and semiprofessional teams. The integration of the Major Leagues in 1947, while a landmark step in terms of social progress, sounded the death knell of the Negro Leagues. The NNL played its last game in 1948, while its opponent league in the World Series, the Negro American League, held on until 1958, and the last annual Negro League all-star game was played in 1962.

Herbert G. Ruffin II

Further Reading

Heaphy, Leslie A. *The Negro Leagues, 1869–1960.* Jefferson, N.C.: McFarland, 2003. A history of organized blackball.

Hogan, Lawrence D. *Shades of Glory: The Negro Leagues and the Story of African American Baseball.* Washington, D.C.: National Geographic, 2006. A detailed history that includes important historical and socioeconomic context.

Peterson, Robert. *Only the Ball Was White: A History of Legendary Black Players and All-Black Professional Teams.* New York: Gramercy Books, 1999. A tribute to the great players of the Negro Leagues.

Rhoden, William C. *Forty Million Dollar Slaves: The Rise, Fall, and Redemption of the Black Athlete.* Louisville, Ky.: Broadway, 2007. A critical look at the treatment of black athletes in American society.

Rogosin, Donn. *Invisible Men: Life in Baseball's Negro Leagues.* Lincoln: University of Nebraska Press, 2007. A history of the Negro Leagues and their social significance, including firsthand accounts from surviving players.

See also: African Americans; Baseball; Bell, James "Cool Papa"; Johnson, Judy

■ *Newberry v. United States*

The Case: U.S. Supreme Court ruling on the constitutionality of federal campaign finance regulations affecting primary and general elections
Date: Decided on May 2, 1921

In Newberry v. United States, *the Supreme Court struck down part of a law enacted by Congress limiting the amount candidates could spend on primary and general election campaigns for Congress. In particular, the court ruled that the federal government can only regulate general elections, not the party nomination process of which primaries are a part.*

During the 1920s, the Supreme Court shaped the authority of Congress by declaring many of its laws unconstitutional. In the case of *Newberry v. United States,* the Supreme Court struck down parts of the Federal Corrupt Practices Act (FCPA) of 1910. While the original law limited campaign spending on general elections, a 1911 amendment extended these limits to primary elections as well, stipulating that no candidate could spend more than $5,000 total on a campaign for the House of Representatives, more than $10,000 on a campaign for the Senate, or more than any provisions in state law, whichever was less.

The state of Michigan passed a law in 1913 limiting federal campaign spending to a percentage of the salary of the office the candidate was seeking. In 1918, during his campaign for the Senate, Truman Handy Newberry was therefore limited to spending $3,750 toward the Republican Party nomination, and the same amount on the general election. He won the nomination, and went on to win the general election, but spent on the order of $100,000 in the process. Newberry was investigated for violating federal campaign finance law, tried, and convicted in 1921. He appealed his conviction, contending parts of the FCPA was unconstitutional.

By a vote of five to four, the Supreme Court agreed with Newberry, reversing his conviction and striking down the 1911 amendment to the FCPA. The Court stated that while Article I, Section 4 of the Constitution grants Congress the power to regulate congressional elections, that power did not extend to primary elections, which are not elections to Congress but part of the party nomination process.

Impact

Newberry v. United States was an early setback to federal efforts to control the role of money in U.S. elections. Ironically, the man who led the charge against Newberry was famed industrialist Henry Ford, whom Newberry had beaten in the Senate election. Himself one of the country's wealthiest men and no stranger to exercising the power of money, Ford was nonetheless happy to draw on campaign finance law and progressive sentiments to attack his opponent. Following the Supreme Court decision, the Senate conducted its own contentious investigation, eventually finding Newberry entitled to his seat. However, in the face of ongoing political headwinds, Newberry resigned in 1922. In 1925, the FCPA was amended again to correct some of its defects, establishing, among other provisions, the practice of quarterly campaign finance reports.

Eric T. Bellone

Further Reading

Corrado, Anthony, et al., eds. *Campaign Finance Reform: A Sourcebook.* Washington, D.C.: Brookings Institution, 1997.

Ervin, Spencer. *Henry Ford vs. Truman H. Newberry: The Famous Senate Election Contest.* Reprint. New York: Arno Press, 1974.

See also: Civil rights and liberties; Congress, U.S.; Corrupt Practices Act of 1925; Political parties; Voting rights

■ New Criticism

First articulated in the 1920s and 1930s, the principles of New Criticism became the dominant approach to the study of literature and poetry in the post–World War II era, focusing on the structure and form of the work itself rather than on its cultural, historical, or social context or its author. Although New Criticism fell out of favor toward the end the twentieth century, it introduced a new, and some argue more pure, approach to reading and studying literature and poetry.

During the 1920s, a number of U.S. critics, the majority of whom taught at southern colleges and universities, began to express dissatisfaction with the then-current impressionistic and moralistic approaches to literature. They began using the term "criticism" as a mode of inquiry into the structure of literary works, believing that literature, particularly poetry, should be examined and critiqued objectively, striving to exclude from the analysis the author's point of view, the cultural context of the work, and the reader's own feelings about the work. Most scholars resisted this new approach at first, but several southern academics embraced it.

At Vanderbilt University in Nashville, Tennessee, for example, professors John Crowe Ransom, Allen Tate, Cleanth Brooks, and Robert Penn Warren rejected traditional approaches to the study of literature and turned instead to the "new" critics who seemed to offer a more modern approach. Calling themselves the Fugitive Poets and then the Southern Agrarians (to emphasize their separation from both northern industrialism and southern parochialism), individuals such as Ransom, Tate, Brooks, and Warren were inspired by poet T. S. Eliot's essay "Tradition and the Individual Talent" (1919), in which he stressed that poetry should be read and analyzed closely, without emotion, and apart from the personality of the poet or writer.

Many of the Southern Agrarians later established creative writing programs at new colleges and universities and wrote several books and textbooks intended to reduce the complex social, cultural, and economic issues raised by New Criticism to more user-friendly tools for reading and interpreting literature. In general, these strategies were meant to help readers and critics avoid various errors of interpretation and to analyze poetry and fiction independent of one's emotions or the culture and history surrounding the work.

Impact

New Criticism taught a method of literary analysis to students from the 1920s through the 1970s and became the dominant pedagogical approach in American high schools and colleges, with Brooks and Warren's *Understanding Poetry* (1938) and *Understanding Fiction* (1943) becoming standard textbooks for millions of students. Although New Criticism is no longer taught as the preferred approach to reading literature, elements of it continue to be used as tools of literary criticism.

Tyrone Williams

Further Reading

Brooks, Cleanth. *The Well Wrought Urn: Studies in the Structure of Poetry.* New York: Harcourt Brace, 1975.

Davis, Garrick. *Praising It New: The Best of the New Criticism.* Athens, Ohio: Swallow Press, 2008.

Graff, Gerald. *Professing Literature: An Institutional History.* Chicago: University of Chicago Press, 2007.

See also: *Dial, The;* Education; Eliot, T. S.; Fugitive Poets; *Fugitive, The; I'll Take My Stand;* Literature in the United States; Poetry; Southern Agrarians

---

■ Newspapers, U.S.

Newspapers prospered in the 1920s as advertising revenues and readership grew. Chain ownership expanded, causing newspapers to become more concentrated through mergers. The first tabloid, or half-sheet, newspapers were published in cities as the nation's population shifted from rural to urban areas.

The newspaper industry in the 1920s reflected the economic and demographic changes taking place in the United States. The decade was one of industrial expansion and business mergers, and it was a boom period for newspaper chains. For the first time, more people were living in cities than in small towns, and the urbanization of the country and rising literacy rates meant growing numbers of subscribers and advertisers. New types of machines improved the production quality and distribution of newspapers. The consolidation trend affecting businesses also influenced newspapers, which became more concentrated, resulting in a decline in the number of papers even as subscription rates grew.

Boom in Chain Ownership

The first newspaper chains were established before World War I, but the period between 1918 and 1929 saw a rapid increase in chain ownership. This was the second such growth period, the first having taken place between 1896 and 1907. The Hearst Corporation bought 28 papers during this period, while the Gannett Company acquired 16. Thirty-one chains owned 153 newspapers in 1923; by 1929, fifty-nine chains owned 325 dailies. This rapid industry growth can be attributed to the availability of investment capital thanks to a prosperous economy, as well as the desire of corporations to buy out their competitors. The 1920s also capped an eighty-year period of growth in daily newspaper circulation, which peaked at 42.9 million in 1929. This growth had become particularly rapid after 1880 due to increased industrialization, the rise of literacy, and the mechanization of newspaper production.

While readership grew during the 1920s, the total number of papers shrank, as newspapers in many cities succumbed to mergers, continuing a trend that had begun at the turn of the century. The number of cities with only one newspaper grew from 686 in 1920 to 913 in 1930. One factor driving this consolidation was increased production costs: Combining morning and evening papers was more economical, as newspapers could devote all their resources to a single edition. For advertisers, placing ads in one newspaper was cheaper than advertising in two. Businessman Frank Munsey was widely known as a killer of newspapers due to the sheer number of papers that he closed or merged, sometimes simply in order to remove competition. As some newspapers were absorbed by their competitors, however, a new type of newspaper was making its debut in New York: the modern tabloid.

Front page of the tabloid New York Daily News *on November 3, 1925.* (NY Daily News via Getty Images)

The First Tabloids

The U.S. Census of 1920 found that, for the first time, people living in cities outnumbered those living in rural areas. This shift to the cities provided a growing readership for tabloid newspapers, whose smaller size and generous use of pictures found an audience among immigrants who could not read English. The first regularly published tabloid in the United States was the *Illustrated Daily News*, later simply the *Daily News*, in New York. It was started in 1919 by cousins Robert McCormick and Joseph Medill Patterson, managers of the *Chicago Tribune*, who were inspired by the English *Daily Mirror* tabloid. In 1924, feeling the heat of competition, Hearst Corporation owner William Randolph Hearst launched the *New York Daily Mirror* tabloid, while former bodybuilder Bernarr Macfadden started a third tabloid, the *New York Evening Graphic*, that same year. By the mid-1920s, tabloids had begun to appear in other U.S. cities as well, as publishers started new papers or converted traditional papers to the half-sheet format.

The tabloids' smaller paper size, big headlines, and more numerous pictures set them apart from the older, text-heavy broadsheet newspapers. Sensational stories about sex scandals, murders, trials, and gangsters filled their pages. Walter Winchell wrote a show-business column for the *Evening Graphic* and later the *Daily Mirror*, the first of its kind and the forerunner of modern celebrity gossip columns.

A series of famous trials made for sensational news. In search of a story, the staff of the *Daily Mirror* uncovered new evidence in the unsolved 1922 double murder of pastor Edward Wheeler Hall and church choir leader Eleanor Reinhardt Mills in New Jersey, causing the case to be reopened and go to trial in 1926. Hall's widow and two of her brothers were accused of committing the murders, having assumed Hall and Mills were lovers. One highlight was the testimony of pig farmer Jane Gibson, known as the "pig woman," who said she had been present on the night of the murders. At the time of the trial, she was reported to be on her deathbed in a hospital and had to be wheeled into the courtroom on a stretcher. The trial was covered by as many as two hundred reporters, including James Mills, the murdered choir leader's widower. Also reporting on the case was sportswriter Damon Runyon, who wrote a syndicated column for the Hearst papers. The trial ended without a conviction.

Hearst regularly paid people for their stories. In 1926, when fifty-one-year-old millionaire Edward West Browning married fifteen-year-old Frances Belle "Peaches" Heenan, whose mother wanted Browning's money, Hearst paid Heenan to report on her marriage to Browning. Heenan later sued for separation, and the courtroom drama made more headlines, first in the tabloids and then in the national newspapers. One infamous example of the *Evening Graphic*'s "composographs"—faked photos made by pasting pictures of faces onto posed actors—depicted Browning and Heenan in their bedroom. Images such as these, and others featuring nearly nude women, earned the tabloid its nickname, the "*Pornographic.*" The tabloid's reputation hurt its ability to attract advertising, and it folded in 1932.

The tabloids distinguished themselves by their emphasis on photographs, especially in the *Daily News*, the masthead of which declared the paper to be "New York's Picture Newspaper." Pictures of corpses were common in tabloid photojournalism; perhaps the most famous example of the tabloids' use of pictures of the dead was the *Daily News*'s 1928 coverage of Ruth Snyder's execution by electric chair, consisting of a front page that screamed "DEAD!" next to a full-page picture of her final moments in the chair. Snyder had been convicted of the 1927 murder of her husband, along with coconspirator Judd Gray, who was also executed. The two had been having an affair and had plotted the murder in an attempt to cash in on an insurance policy that Snyder had taken out on her husband. Photographers were barred from her execution, but photographer Tom Howard, an employee of the *Chicago Tribune* working with the *Daily News*, used a camera strapped to his leg to secretly photograph the event.

Stories of the Decade

Sex scandals and murder trials were not the only courtroom dramas that made headlines in the 1920s. In 1921, in the wake of the Red Scare, two Italian anarchists were tried for the murder of two men during an armed robbery in Massachusetts. Nicola Sacco and Bartolomeo Vanzetti were executed in 1927, despite the contention of their defense attorneys that they had been convicted on weak evidence. The clear bias of Judge Webster Thayer against the defendants was additional fodder for the newspapers; an article in the now-defunct *New York World* attacked Thayer's behavior as unethical, while an editorial in the *Boston Herald* condemned the judge's refusal to grant Sacco and Vanzetti a new trial.

In 1925, journalists from across the country reported on the trial of high school biology teacher John Scopes in Dayton, Tennessee. The state of Tennessee was prosecuting Scopes for breaking a state law that prohibited the teaching of evolution in school. William Jennings Bryan was counsel for the prosecution and Clarence Darrow argued for the defense. The jury voted to convict, although the Tennessee Supreme Court later reversed the conviction on a technicality. Journalist and satirist H. L. Mencken covered the trial for the *Baltimore Evening Sun*, referring to it for the first time as the "monkey trial."

While these and other famous trials received a lot of coverage, the biggest story of the decade was Charles Lindbergh's 1927 nonstop solo flight from New York to Paris. The *St. Louis Globe-Democrat* helped finance the flight, and news of Lindbergh's safe landing broke newspaper sales records. The *New York Times* bought Lindbergh's story and provided a reporter to write it. Other major stories of the 1920s, in terms of the amount of coverage received, include the Paris Peace Conference that ended World War I (and formally concluded in 1920), the attendant debate over whether the United States should join the League of Nations, and the various attempts throughout the decade to enforce Prohibition.

Professionalization

In the 1920s, journalists continued a movement begun in the early 1900s toward improving educational and professional standards for their trade. In 1922, newspaper editors formed their first national professional association, the American Society of Newspaper Editors. The following year, the association adopted seven principles to which they would aspire, known as the canons of journalism: responsibility; freedom of the press; independence; sincerity, truthfulness, and accuracy; impartiality; fair play; and decency. Also in 1923, journalism educators organized the Council on Education for Journalism, which set forth a statement of principles and standards. By the end of the decade, around two hundred colleges and universities would offer courses in journalism, with more than fifty having established separate schools or programs.

Impact

Newspapers were Americans' main source of news and an important source of entertainment in the 1920s. The first U.S. tabloid newspapers were launched during this decade, leading to the greater use of graphics in newspapers, a trend made possible by improvements in printing technology. Newspaper circulation peaked in 1929, and advertising increased. Newspapers' household penetration was higher in the 1920s than it would be again; although circulation held steady after the crash of 1929, newspaper advertising declined as radio advertising grew more popular. In subsequent decades, the rise of radio, television, and online news would compete for Americans' attention, diminishing the impact of newspapers.

Lisa Kernek

Further Reading

Lee, Alfred McClung. *The Daily Newspaper in America: The Evolution of a Social Instrument.* New York: Mac-Millan, 1937. An economical and sociological look at the American newspaper industry from 1710 to 1936.

Miller, Nathan. *New World Coming: The 1920s and the Making of Modern America.* New York: Scribner, 2003. An overview of the social and economic trends of the decade, including the role played by newspapers and tabloids.

Mott, Frank Luther. *American Journalism: A History, 1690–1960.* 3d ed. New York: MacMillan, 1962. A general survey and historical reference text.

Stephens, Mitchell. *A History of News.* 3d ed. New York: Oxford University Press, 2007. Chronicles the development of news transmission throughout human history.

Wallace, Aurora. *Newspapers and the Making of Modern America: A History.* Westport, Conn.: Greenwood Press, 2005. Includes a chapter focused on the New York tabloids.

See also: Cities; Hall-Mills murder case; Hearst, William Randolph; Mencken, H. L.; Sacco and Vanzetti case; Scopes trial

Harold Ross, founder of The New Yorker *magazine.* (Getty Images)

■ New Yorker, The

Identification: Literary and news magazine
Founding editor: Harold W. Ross
Date: 1925 to present

As the United States was becoming increasingly urbanized in the 1920s, with its cultural capital in New York City, The New Yorker *magazine set a national standard for journalistic quality and style through its sophisticated articles, stories, poems, and cartoons.*

In his prospectus to potential investors for a new weekly magazine, journalist Harold Ross explained that *The New Yorker* would be written for a metropolitan audience and would not be "edited for the old lady in Dubuque." Ross moved to New York City six years before launching the magazine in 1925, and though *The New Yorker* became popular with America's educated elite, its founder never finished high school. However, Ross excelled at recruiting, encouraging, and editing many of the most talented writers

and artists in the United States at the time. He would continue as editor of *The New Yorker* until his death in 1951. The print run of the magazine's first issue was 30,000 copies, but it grew by the end of the decade to 105,000 copies, with approximately 30 percent of its readers living outside New York City.

Early Writers and Artists

Several members of the Algonquin Round Table, a group of celebrated New York writers and critics of the 1920s—including Dorothy Parker, Robert Benchley, Alexander Woolcott, Franklin Pierce Adams, and Ross himself—helped ensure the success of the new magazine. One of Ross's most important employees was Rea Irvin, the art director who would give the magazine its unique visual style. Designed by Irvin, the cover of the first issue was a portrait of a man holding a monocle and wearing top hat; he was given the name Eustace Tilley. The signature image would continue to appear periodically on the cover of the magazine, notably every year in late February, the anniversary of the first issue, published on February 21, 1925.

Hired as a manuscript reader in 1925, Katharine Angell became chief literary editor by the end of the decade. Under the guidance of Angell, who became Katharine White after marrying fellow staffer E. B. White in 1929, the magazine would help to introduce some of the leading writers of the time. John O'Hara, who published more than fifty pieces of fiction in *The New Yorker* during the 1920s, was one of the first well-known "*New Yorker* authors," and frequent contributors such as John Cheever, Marianne Moore, John Updike, J. D. Salinger, Vladimir Nabokov, Alice Munro, and Richard Wilbur would help the magazine establish its literary reputation—as it helped establish theirs.

Staff writers and artists established the tone of the magazine in its first few years. Humorist James Thurber developed his trademark style while writing for the "Talk of the Town" section, which contained pointed vignettes of life in the city. As "Reporter at Large," Morris Markey pioneered immersion journalism and helped to show the magazine's serious and lighter sides. E. B. White produced the "Notes and Comment" section, and Janet Flanner regularly sent in a "Letter from France" that she signed "Genêt." Lois Long wrote the fashion column "On and Off the Avenue," and A. J. Liebling wrote regularly about the press. George T. Ryall's racetrack column, published under the pseudonym "Audax Minor," continued to appear until 1978. The signature cartoons by Peter Arno, Helen Hokinson, and others, which poked fun at conventional attitudes, became one of the magazine's most popular and recognizable features.

Financing

Initial funding for *The New Yorker* was provided by Raoul Fleischmann, a yeast magnate who served as the magazine's publisher for several decades. During the early years, when commercial success proved elusive and debts mounted, Fleischmann poured several hundred thousand dollars into the publishing enterprise. By 1930, *The New Yorker* had become one of the top three American magazines in the nation, and Fleischmann recouped his investment many times over.

Insisting on an impermeable wall between the business and editorial operations of the magazine, Ross refused to allow advertising to influence the material that he published. He insisted that ads in his magazine reflect a refined sensibility and that they represent products and services that appealed to his affluent readership—or at least to those who, by reading glamorous ads, could partake in the fantasy of being affluent.

Impact

By the end of the 1920s, most of its features and departments were in place, and *The New Yorker* had developed the essential elements of an institutional personality that would endure into the twenty-first century. The magazine originally specialized in humor, particularly parodies and puns, but its tone varied as it offered savvy commentary on the wide spectrum of contemporary experience.

Steven G. Kellman

Further Reading

Davis, Linda H. *Onward and Upward: A Biography of Katharine S. White.* New York: Harper & Row, 1987. Biography concentrating on White's marriage, family, and relationships with contributing writers at *The New Yorker.*

Kunkel, Thomas. *Genius in Disguise: Harold Ross of "The New Yorker."* New York: Carroll & Graf, 1996. Biography examining Ross's childhood, military career, three marriages, and clashes with business partner Raoul Fleischmann.

_____, ed. *Letters from the Editor: "The New Yorker's" Harold Ross.* New York: Modern Library, 2001. Compilation of letters written by Ross beginning with his service in France during World War I until his death in 1951.

Lee, Judith Yaross. *Defining "New Yorker" Humor.* Jackson: University Press of Mississippi. 2000. Covers the first five years of *The New Yorker* and examines the writing, cartoons, and business aspects of the magazine.

Thurber, James. *The Years with Ross.* 1957. New York: Perennial, 2001. Memoir of Thurber's time working with Harold Ross at *The New Yorker*, from the 1920s through Ross's death.

Yagoda, Ben. *About Town: "The New Yorker" and the World It Made.* Cambridge, Mass.: De Capo Press, 2001. Examines the workings of *The New Yorker* magazine through archival records such as interoffice memorandums, edited manuscripts, and correspondence. Concentrates on the Harold Ross years and touches briefly on more recent years at the magazine.

See also: Algonquin Round Table; Literature in the United States; Magazines; Parker, Dorothy; Ross, Harold

■ New York Yankees

Identification: American professional baseball team
Date: Established in 1901

During the 1920s, talented players and strong team managers established the New York Yankees as one of the most successful teams in major-league baseball. Winning its first American League pennant in 1921, the team claimed five more league championships and three World Series titles before the end of the decade. Meanwhile, the opening of the first Yankee Stadium in 1923 gave the team a new home.

Known as the Highlanders until 1913, the New York Yankees was one of the least successful teams in the American League for much of its early history. This changed in 1921, when the Yankees won the first of three consecutive American League championships. After losing the World Series to the National League's New York Giants in 1921 and 1922, the Yankees beat the Giants in 1923, winning the team's first World Series. The Yankees won an additional three consecutive league championships between 1926 and 1928, losing the World Series to the St. Louis Cardinals before sweeping the Pittsburgh Pirates in 1927 and the Cardinals the following year.

The Yankees dominated the American League throughout the 1920s, ranking below second place only twice during the decade. Three other teams won league championships during the period—the Cleveland Indians in 1920, the Washington Senators in 1924 and 1925, and the Philadelphia Athletics in 1929—but no team won as consistently as the Yankees did.

Players and Managers

The New York Yankees comprised a number of talented players during the 1920s, the most notable of which was George Herman "Babe" Ruth. Ruth, whose contract was purchased from the Boston Red Sox for $125,000, joined the Yankees at the start of the decade. He had been a successful pitcher with the Red Sox, but with the Yankees, Ruth became a full-time outfielder known for his powerful batting skills. Ruth set multiple home run records, establishing his reputation as one of the greatest power hitters of all time by the end of the decade. In 1925, another strong hitter, Lou Gehrig, became a fixture in the Yankees' lineup and would go on to play in more than two thousand consecutive games. Sluggers Bob Meusel, Tony Lazzeri, Earle Combs, and Mark Koenig further strengthened the team's offense and, along with Ruth and Gehrig, became one of the most feared batting orders in baseball history, known as "Murderers' Row." The Yankees' notable pitchers of the decade included Bob Shawkey, Herb Pennock, and Waite Hoyt, the latter two having joined the Yankees through trades with Boston early in the decade.

Two others who played important roles in the team's success were field manager Miller Huggins and business manager Ed Barrow. Hired in 1918, Huggins devised a new baseball strategy to take full advantage of the team's power hitters. Prior to the 1920s, teams employed the "inside game" strategy, which emphasized a tight defense, speed on the bases, and discipline at the plate. Huggins instead introduced a strategy that played on the strengths of power hitters such as Ruth and Gehrig, placing more emphasis on home runs. This new focus on batting spread to numerous other teams by the end of the decade. Ed Barrow, like several Yankee star players, came to New York from Boston. Known as a hardnosed negotiator, Barrow orchestrated player trades and purchases and organized the Yankees' farm system, which became a major source of talented new players.

Yankee Stadium

In 1923, the New York Yankees moved into a new facility, the first Yankee Stadium. For the previous decade, the Yankees had played home games in the Polo Grounds, also the home of the New York Giants. After conflicts with the Giants and amid growing competition for the New York fan base, team owner Jacob Ruppert purchased a lumberyard in the Bronx, located across the Harlem River from the Polo Grounds. There, he built the venue that would play host to the Yankees' home games for more than eighty years. The stadium had three tiers of seating that could accommodate as many as seventy thousand spectators, more than double the capacity of some other ballparks. Yankee Stadium hosted its first game on April 18, 1923, during which the Yankees beat the Red Sox by a score of four to one.

Impact

Having been established as one of the most successful baseball teams in the United States during the 1920s, the New York Yankees continued to build upon this reputation in the subsequent decades. A number of talented players of the 1920s, such as Babe Ruth and Lou Gehrig, continued to play for the Yankees into the 1930s, and new star players joined the team and contributed to its ongoing success over the years. During the remainder of the twentieth century, the New York Yankees went on to win more than twenty World Series titles.

Paul E. Doutrich

Further Reading

Levitt, Daniel R. *Ed Barrow: The Bulldog Who Built the Yankees' First Dynasty.* Lincoln: University of Nebraska Press, 2008. A biography of the business manager who led the Yankees throughout the 1920s.

Rader, Benjamin G. *Baseball: A History of America's Game.* 3d ed. Chicago: University of Illinois Press, 2008. Explores the development of the game of baseball, including discussion of the events of the 1920s.

Reisler, Jim. *Before They Were the Bombers: The New York Yankees' Early Years, 1903–1915.* Jefferson, N.C.: McFarland, 2002. Chronicles the early years of the team, prior to the 1920s.

Seymour, Harold. *Baseball: The Golden Age.* New York: Oxford University Press, 1989. A history of baseball focusing on the early twentieth century through the 1920s.

Stout, Glenn, and Richard A. Johnson. *Yankees Century: One Hundred Years of New York Yankees Baseball.* Boston: Houghton Mifflin, 2002. A retrospective on the Yankees' long history, featuring several sections related to the 1920s.

See also: Baseball; Gehrig, Lou; Landis, Kenesaw Mountain; Ruth, Babe; Sports

---

■ Nightclubs

Nightclubs of the 1920s reflected the cultural, economic, and societal changes occurring during the decade. They allowed Americans to drink illegal alcohol and to listen to jazz, which many regarded as "devil's music." Nightclubs provided a venue for women to flaunt new fashions that exposed more skin, and integrated nightclubs enabled whites and blacks to mix socially.

The United States experienced substantial economic, technological, and cultural change during the 1920s. The country was transforming from a rural to an urban nation, and nightclubs were becoming a popular and integral part of the new urban nightlife.

Prohibition and the First Nightclubs

The Eighteenth Amendment went into effect in January 1920, and with it the manufacture, transportation, and sale of alcohol became illegal. Most Americans found ways to drink in spite of the law, and members of organized crime (who were then referred to as "gangsters") provided illegal alcohol to patrons in establishments called speakeasies. Many believe the term "speakeasy" came about because people needed to keep their voices low and "speak easy" when ordering alcohol.

Speakeasies were often hidden in basements, rooming houses, and attics, and patrons would need a password, a special knock, or a special handshake to get in. Once inside, alcohol was often served in teacups in case of a police raid, and the first cocktails were invented when the mostly homemade and harsh-tasting liquor, sometimes referred to as "bathtub gin," was mixed with fruit juices or soft drinks. It is estimated that in 1927, there were over thirty thousand speakeasies, which was about twice the number of legal bars and saloons before Prohibition.

The increased risk of police raids prompted gangsters to begin referring to their speakeasies as "nightclubs" and to issue membership cards that provided the illusion of legality. In the early part of the decade, nightclubs afforded Americans with a fashionable and elegant environment where they could listen and dance to live jazz played by the decade's great jazz performers. The Cotton Club in Harlem, New York, launched the careers of many 1920s jazz legends such as pianist Duke Ellington and trumpeter Louis Armstrong. The Cocoanut Grove in the Ambassador Hotel in Los Angeles, California, attracted Hollywood celebrities and was an integrated venue where white and black patrons could dance and be entertained under the same roof.

Jazz, Race, and Gender

The Jazz Age was gaining momentum in the early 1920s, and with the influx of African American musicians who migrated north during and after World War I, nightclub owners were able to offer live jazz, which was frequently played by black musicians to primarily white audiences. Segregation between races was still prevalent in 1920s America, and many nightclubs, such as New York City's The Cotton Club, had a "whites-only" policy. All-black nightclubs also existed, and some nightclubs called "black-and-tan clubs" admitted both white and nonwhite customers who enjoyed jazz, alcohol, and the opportunity to socialize and mingle together. The Savoy Ballroom in New York City and The Black and Tan Club in Seattle, Washington, are famous examples of these integrated clubs.

The Nineteenth Amendment, ratified in 1920, gave women the right to vote, and with it, a new sense of freedom to drastically relax their dress, hairstyles, and behavior. With shorter hair and skirts and a new sense of independence, flappers felt free to visit speakeasies and nightclubs, smoke cigarettes, drink hard liquor, listen to jazz, and dance the Charleston or the Lindy Hop.

Nightclubs encouraged changing sexual dynamics as well. These venues became popular locations for dating, then a newly emerging form of social interaction between young men and women. Meanwhile, other underground nightclubs and speakeasies in metropolitan areas such as New York City provided social interaction, entertainment, and a degree of safe haven for homosexuals, who continued to experience widespread homophobia in mainstream society and even criminalization.

Impact

Many Americans during the 1920s believed that nightclubs were a symbol of the decay of respected institutions and values. Modern historians, however, view nightclubs as instrumental in the evolution of race and gender relations in the United States and offering a setting for Americans to not only evade but to challenge the cultural and societal restrictions of the era. Speakeasies and nightclubs allowed Americans to simultaneously ignore and reject the policies of Prohibition. Jazz music, with its focus on improvisation, was unconventional and atypical of the popular music that came before. Whites and blacks began socializing together openly in integrated nightclubs and with a greater sense of equality than ever before; women were afforded the opportunity to exercise their growing independence by smoking, drinking, and dancing; and homosexuals found community within the relative safety of nightclubs. Nightclubs in many ways mirrored the drastic shift among many facets of American life during the 1920s.

Derk R. Babbitt

Further Reading

Bjorn, Jars, and Jim Gallert. *Before Motown: A History of Jazz in Detroit, 1920–1960*. Ann Arbor: University of Michigan Press, 2001. Presents a history of Detroit, jazz, and jazz nightclubs.

Giordano, Ralph G. *Satan in the Dance Hall: Rev. John Roach Straton, Social Dancing, and Morality in 1920s New York City*. Lanham, Md.: Scarecrow Press, 2008. Focuses on the social debate surrounding the morality of social dancing and jazz music in the 1920s, with dance halls in New York City highlighted.

Kenney, William Howland. *Chicago Jazz: A Cultural History, 1904–1930*. New York: Oxford University Press, 2009. Examines the evolution of jazz in Chicago, Illinois, during the early twentieth century, including discussion of Chicago nightclubs and cabarets.

Lerner, Michael A. *Dry Manhattan: Prohibition in New York City*. Cambridge, Mass.: Harvard University Press, 2007. An account of life in Prohibition-era New York City, with several chapters devoted to speakeasies and nightclubs that served alcohol during the 1920s and 1930s.

Lewis, David Levering. *When Harlem Was in Vogue*. New York: Penguin Books, 1997. A detailed account of Harlem Renaissance participants and includes an examination of nightclubs, cabarets, and speakeasies of the 1920s.

Sagert, Kelly Boyer. *Flappers: A Guide to an American Subculture*. Westport, Conn.: Greenwood Press, 2010. Provides insight into women's changing role in the 1920s and examines their foray into speakeasies and dance clubs as patrons, not performers.

See also: Bathtub gin; Black-and-tan clubs; Cocoanut Grove; Cotton Club; Dances, popular; Flappers; Jazz; Organized crime; Prohibition; Speakeasies; Urbanization

■ Nineteenth Amendment

The Law: Constitutional amendment making it illegal to deny a citizen the right to vote based on sex
Also known as: Susan B. Anthony Amendment; Women's Suffrage Amendment
Date: Ratified on August 18, 1920

The Nineteenth Amendment to the United States Constitution, ratified in 1920, ensured that women could not be denied the right to vote by the federal government or the states based on their sex. Although American women did not emerge as a united voting bloc during the 1920s, this reform gave them more political influence and a better vantage point from which to pursue social and economic equality.

Although the Fifteenth Amendment, ratified in 1870, prohibited the federal government and the individual states from denying citizens the right to vote based on race, sex-based voting discrimination was not yet prohibited by the beginning of the 1920s. Women could vote in some states, particularly in the western half of the country, but the majority prohibited women from voting or restricted female voters to specific kinds of elections, such as those for municipal offices. The ratification of the Nineteenth Amendment to the Constitution in 1920 granted women the right to vote in all elections throughout the United States.

Suffrage Movements
The successful ratification of the Nineteenth Amendment occurred after more than seventy years of organization and demonstration by women's rights activists throughout the United States. The first formal call for American women's suffrage occurred at the Seneca Falls Convention in 1848. Hosted by Elizabeth Cady Stanton and Lucretia Mott, two antislavery reformers who had met at an 1840 conference that barred both from participation because of their sex, the Seneca Falls Convention produced the "Declaration of Sentiments," which listed women's grievances with their position in society, including their exclusion from the ballot box.

Although early women's rights activists did not initially focus the majority of their efforts on winning the vote for women, the cause took on more importance by the mid-1860s, largely due to congressional actions following the Civil War. Throughout the United States' early history, voting requirements were considered a state matter; however, in 1868, the Fourteenth Amendment to the Constitution linked the number of a state's representatives in Congress explicitly to the voting rights of male citizens. Likewise, the Fifteenth Amendment, ratified in 1870, made it illegal to deny the right to vote to any citizen based on race or prior servitude but did not reference discrimination in suffrage rights based on sex.

These amendments suggested two things to women's rights reformers: first, that an expansion of voting rights could be obtained through the passage and ratification of a constitutional amendment, and second, that women had been deliberately excluded from the categories of voters identified and protected by the Fourteenth and Fifteenth Amendments. Two separate women's rights organizations were founded and mobilized in light of these realizations. The American Woman Suffrage Association (AWSA), founded by Lucy Stone and her husband, Henry Blackwell, in 1869, concentrated on trying to attain women's suffrage on a state-by-state basis. The National Woman Suffrage Association (NWSA), founded the same year by Elizabeth Cady Stanton and Susan B. Anthony, pursued a broader agenda for women's rights that included attaining women's suffrage through a constitutional amendment.

In spite of opposition, the NWSA orchestrated the introduction of a women's suffrage amendment in Congress in 1878; however, it was not voted on until 1887, when it was defeated. The NWSA united with the AWSA in 1890, creating the National American Woman Suffrage Association (NAWSA), and the organization continued to work toward state- and amendment-based suffrage. Between 1869 and 1919, fifteen states granted women full suffrage: Wyoming, Colorado, Utah, Idaho, Washington, California, Arizona, Oregon, Kansas, Montana, Nevada, Oklahoma, South Dakota, Michigan, and New York. Limited suffrage was granted in twenty-five others. This meant that women from such states could exert political pressure on elected officials to pass an amendment to the Constitution granting the right to vote to women nationwide.

The unification of the women's suffrage organizations also brought new women into the leadership of the movement, including Alice Paul and Carrie Chapman Catt, whose approaches to activism differed radically. As president of the NAWSA between 1915 and 1920, Catt initially focused on winning the support of President Woodrow Wilson and other political leaders for the cause. When the United States entered World War I in 1917, she urged NAWSA members to lend their efforts to supporting war work, whether that meant knitting bandages, selling victory bonds, or entering the workplace. Such efforts, she believed, would not only demonstrate that women were capable of performing necessary social services in times of national emergency but also

"The Negro Woman and the Ballot"

In 1927, the writer, educator, and activist Alice Moore Dunbar-Nelson published an article titled "The Negro Woman and the Ballot" in the African American magazine *The Messenger*, in which she posed the question "What have black women done with their vote?" Dunbar-Nelson believed that black women had accomplished not nearly enough following their enfranchisement in 1920, and she encouraged them to start exercising their power as voters without bowing to pressure from their male peers or from forces in the Republican Party. She noted that African American women had already demonstrated their power as a group in the congressional elections of 1922, in which their votes had helped oust Republican legislators who had failed to support the anti-lynching legislation known as the Dyer bill. Dunbar-Nelson's work, although popular among African American publishers at the time, did not attract the attention of white publishers.

convince national politicians, including President Wilson, that women's wartime labors should be rewarded with the vote.

In contrast, Alice Paul established the National Woman's Party (NWP), which sought to pressure political leaders directly. The NWP held President Wilson, as leader of the party in power, responsible for women's lack of voting rights. In protest, members of the NWP picketed the White House, frequently holding signs suggesting that the United States was no more democratic than Germany. When NWP picketers were eventually arrested and imprisoned, they went on sensationalized hunger strikes that turned the protestors into martyrs for the cause of women's suffrage.

Passage and Ratification

The combination of strategies employed by the NWP and NAWSA successfully pushed the House of Representatives to pass a women's suffrage amendment in 1918 with the necessary two-thirds majority. The Senate failed to support the amendment that year, but when the House again passed the measure in the summer of 1919, the Senate followed suit. Women's rights activists immediately turned their attention toward convincing the requisite thirty-six states to ratify the amendment by the fall of 1920 so women could participate in the November presidential election. Although a few states ratified the amendment almost immediately, women's suffrage advocates had to persuade several governors to call special sessions of their state legislatures to secure ratification. Tennessee ratified the amendment on August 18, 1920, becoming the thirty-sixth state to do so. The necessary number of ratifications having been obtained, the Nineteenth Amendment was certified six days later and went into effect. Little more than two months later, the 1920 presidential election became the first in which all women in the United States were eligible to vote.

Impact

In the immediate years following the ratification of the Nineteenth Amendment, Congress passed legislation supported by female activists, including the Sheppard-Towner Act, which provided funding for infant and prenatal care. However, once it became clear that women did not vote as a bloc, legislation promoting women's issues received no more attention than did other reform measures. In addition, women's access to the ballot box did not result in a profound change in the political leadership of the United States. Although the number of female voters and politicians increased significantly after 1920, women continued to constitute a minority of both elected and appointed governmental officials into the early twenty-first century.

Christy Jo Snider

Further Reading

Baker, Jean H. *Sisters: The Lives of America's Suffragists.* New York: Hill and Wang, 2005. Explores how the private lives of Lucy Stone, Susan B. Anthony, Elizabeth Cady Stanton, Frances Willard, and Alice Paul affected their efforts to obtain women's suffrage.

Camhi, Jane Jerome. *Women Against Women: American Anti-Suffragism, 1880–1920.* Brooklyn, N.Y.: Carlson, 1994. Examines the arguments and efforts of anti-suffragists to prevent the passage of the Nineteenth Amendment.

Cott, Nancy F. "Feminist Politics in the 1920s: The National Woman's Party." *Journal of American His-*

tory 71, no. 1 (June, 1984): 43–68. Briefly examines the role of the National Woman's Party in the passage of the Nineteenth Amendment and then focuses on the actions of that organization in the 1920s to continue the fight for women's political equality.

Flexner, Eleanor, and Ellen Fitzpatrick. *Century of Struggle: The Woman's Rights Movement in the United States.* Cambridge, Mass.: Harvard University Press, 2000. Provides a detailed survey of how female activists attained the right to vote with the passage of the Nineteenth Amendment in 1920.

Wheeler, Majorie Spruill, ed. *One Woman, One Vote: Rediscovering the Woman Suffrage Movement.* Troutdale, Oreg.: NewSage Press, 1995. Contains more than two dozen essays on specific individuals, events, and subjects related to the women's suffrage movement of the nineteenth and early twentieth centuries.

See also: Elections of 1920, U.S.; Equal Rights Amendment; League of Women Voters; Paul, Alice; Sheppard-Towner Act of 1921; Wilson, Woodrow; Women's rights

---

■ *Nixon v. Herndon*

The Case: U.S. Supreme Court ruling on the constitutionality of a state statute forbidding blacks from participating in the Texas Democratic primary
Date: Decided on March 7, 1927

Citing the Fourteenth Amendment, the Supreme Court found that the right to vote in a state primary cannot be affected on the basis of race by a state statute. Thus, the statute was found to be in violation of the Fourteenth Amendment and declared unconstitutional.

Dr. L. A. Nixon, an African American physician and member of the Democratic Party, attempted to vote in the 1924 Democratic primary in El Paso, Texas. His attempt was rebuked by the election judges, who cited a state statute that prohibited blacks from participating in any statewide Democratic Party primary election. Nixon sued, arguing that this prohibition violated Fourteenth and Fifteenth Amendment principles. In a unanimous vote, the Supreme Court ruled that the Texas statute was unconstitutional.

Writing for the majority, Justice Oliver Wendell Holmes Jr. declared the Texas statute to be so clearly in violation of Nixon's Fourteenth Amendment equal protection rights that analysis of the Fifteenth Amendment was unnecessary. Holmes noted that one of the specific intents of the Fourteenth Amendment was to protect blacks from discrimination. The statute in question was deemed to be in clear violation of this intent as well as the literal wording of the amendment. Furthermore, Holmes declared that it made no difference that the statute affected participation in a primary rather than a final election, since a primary election could very well determine the final election result.

Impact

Nixon v. Herndon was the first of a group of Supreme Court cases that has come to be known as the "white primary" cases, all of which were supported by the National Association for the Advancement of Colored People (NAACP) and involved white communities in southern states attempting to disenfranchise blacks. The *Herndon* decision set the precedent by which the Court struck down these discriminatory practices. Expanding on *Herndon*, the Court declared in *Nixon v. Condon* that when private parties act under a state grant of power, they must be considered state actors and thus subject to the Fourteenth Amendment. This principle was further expanded in *Terry v. Adams*, where a pre–primary candidate nominating process was considered to be an integral part of the election process and thus subject to the Fourteenth Amendment.

The precedent set in *Herndon* ultimately led to the landmark case of *Smith v. Allwright*, in which all-white primaries were abolished.

Ramses Jalalpour

Further Reading

Hine, Darlene Clark. *Black Victory: The Rise and Fall of the White Primary in Texas.* Columbia: University of Missouri Press, 2003.

Zelden, Charles L. *The Battle for the Black Ballot: Smith v. Allwright and the Defeat of the Texas All-White Primary.* Lawrence: University Press of Kansas, 2004.

See also: African Americans; American Civil Liberties Union (ACLU); Civil rights and liberties; Jim Crow in the U.S. South; National Association for the Advancement of Colored People (NAACP); Voting rights

■ Nobel Prizes

The Nobel Prizes are yearly awards that honor the achievements of living individuals, pairs, or trios whose scientific, literary, or diplomatic or humanitarian efforts have most benefited humankind. In the 1920s, a number of individuals and pairs from North America were awarded Nobel Prizes in various fields.

First awarded in 1901, the Nobel Prizes are international awards that recognize the achievements by individuals or groups in five fields: chemistry, physics, physiology or medicine, literature, and promotion of peace. Funded by the estate of Swedish inventor and entrepreneur Alfred Nobel, the prizes consist of a diploma, a medal, and a monetary award that may be awarded to an individual or shared by two or three recipients. In some cases, individuals sharing a prize are honored for collaborative work; in other cases, the prize is awarded to multiple individuals in recognition of separate achievements.

In the 1920s, relatively few North Americans became Nobel Prize winners compared to the number in later decades. European scientists tended to dominate the fields of chemistry, medicine, and physics, and in fact, no North American would win the prize for chemistry or literature until the next decade. In addition, a number of prizes were not awarded for various years: the Peace Prize was not awarded in 1923, 1924, or 1928; the Nobel Prize in Chemistry was not awarded in 1924; and the Nobel Prize in Physiology or Medicine was not awarded in 1921 or 1925. Nevertheless, six individuals from the United States and Canada were recognized for their noteworthy contributions during the decade.

Peace
The 1925 Nobel Peace Prize was shared by Charles G. Dawes of the United States and Sir Austen Chamberlain of the United Kingdom for unrelated achievements. Then serving as vice president of the United States, Dawes was awarded the prize in recognition of his role in mediating the German reparations crisis and establishing the Dawes Plan in early 1924. After World War I, the Treaty of Versailles established that Germany must pay reparations to a number of European countries, particularly France. When Germany failed to make the payments of money and natural resources, French and Belgian troops occupied a region of Germany known as the Ruhr. Dawes, a

successful banker and politician, led the negotiations to resolve this crisis and ease hostilities in the region. The resulting Dawes Plan called for the withdrawal of troops from the Ruhr and established a payment plan that featured lower, more stable payments that would increase only after five years. Dawes did not receive the prize until December 1926 and was not present in Oslo to give an acceptance speech.

American diplomat Frank B. Kellogg was awarded the Nobel Peace Prize for 1929, although he did not receive the prize until the following year. He was honored for his work on the Kellogg-Briand Pact of 1928, signed while Kellogg was serving as secretary of state in the Coolidge administration. Also known as the Pact of Paris, the treaty began as an agreement of friendship between the United States and France proposed by French foreign minister Aristide Briand. The pact evolved under Kellogg's direction, becoming a multilateral agreement that outlawed war as a means of national policy. Representatives of various nations and territories signed the pact on August 27, 1928, with more than thirty additional nations signing within a year. In subsequent years, the pact would prove ineffective in preventing war, particularly World War II; however, it established the concept that military action for reasons other than self-defense was in violation of international law and served as part of the basis for the prosecution of war criminals.

Physiology or Medicine
The sole Nobel Prize in Physiology or Medicine awarded to North Americans in the 1920s was shared in 1923 by the Canadian surgeon Frederick Banting and Professor John J. R. Macleod of the University of Toronto. The two were jointly recognized for the discovery of insulin, a hormone secreted by the pancreas that plays a vital role in metabolism, especially of carbohydrates. Banting and Macleod's discovery, which included a complex extraction process that produced safe and effective material for clinical use, was used to treat diabetes, an insulin-deficiency disorder that was then fatal.

The awarding of the prize to Banting and Macleod in particular caused considerable controversy, as a number of other individuals were considered at least partially responsible for the discovery. Charles Best, a medical student, worked closely with Banting from the beginning, while trained biochemist James Collip joined the efforts later and made important advances in the purification of pancreatic extracts. In addition, while Macleod had supplied Banting and his colleagues with laboratory space and funding, he had not played an active role in the research. Banting initially considered refusing the prize due to these circumstances, but he eventually accepted and gave half of his monetary award to Best; Macleod likewise shared his prize money with Collip. Further controversy would develop in later years alongside allegations that a European scientist had discovered insulin before Banting and his colleagues.

Physics

The Nobel Prize in Physics for 1923 was awarded to Robert A. Millikan, then chair of the executive council at the California Institute of Technology (Caltech), for his determination of the constant charge of electrons and work on the photoelectric effect. A skilled experimentalist, Millikan worked for many years to determine the electrical charge of the electron by studying individual charged oil drops suspended in an electrical field. His "oil-drop experiment" eventually yielded a reasonably accurate value for the charge of the electron. In addition, Millikan's experiments dealing with the photoelectric effect served to support theories articulated by European physicists Albert Einstein and Niels Bohr, who received the Nobel Prizes for 1921 and 1922, respectively.

The 1927 Nobel Prize in Physics was shared by American professor Arthur Holly Compton and Scottish researcher Charles T. R. Wilson for separate accomplishments. Working at Washington University in St. Louis, Missouri, at the time of his discovery, Compton demonstrated the scattering of x-rays by electrons. Some of the scattered x-rays were found to have longer wavelengths than the incident rays, and this increase in wavelength indicated a corresponding decrease in energy. Known as the Compton Effect, this discovery contradicted aspects of multiple existing theories.

Impact

The scientific and diplomatic achievements by North Americans honored with Nobel Prizes during the 1920s would continue to shape their respective fields in the subsequent decades. While the Dawes Plan would be replaced by the Young Plan by the end of the decade and the Kellogg-Briand Pact would be broken on several occasions prior to the start of World War II, the two agreements represented the spirit of international cooperation that would in many ways mark the twentieth century, despite the conflicts of the period. Likewise, the discovery of insulin would serve as the foundation for further developments in the field of medicine, while the increasingly detailed understanding of the nature of electrons would lead to the creation of such technology as the atomic bomb.

John R. Phillips

Further Reading

Bliss, Michael. *The Discovery of Insulin*. Reprint. Chicago: University of Chicago Press, 2007. Contains many details of Banting's experiments and analyzes the conflict that developed among Macleod, Banting, Best, and Collip over credit for the discovery of insulin.

Ellis, Lewis Ethan. *Frank B. Kellogg and American Foreign Relations, 1925–1929*. Reprint. New Brunswick, N.J.: Rutgers University Press, 1974. Details Kellogg's diplomatic work and the complex negotiations that led to the Kellogg-Briand Pact.

Feldman, Burton. *The Nobel Prize: A History of Genius, Controversy, and Prestige*. New York: Arcade, 2000. Lists Nobel Prize winners by year and country and includes stories of some controversial awards.

Nobel Foundation. *Nobel Lectures: Physics, 1922–1941*. Amsterdam: Elsevier, 1965. Contains the biographies and Nobel lectures of rival American physicists Robert A. Millikan and Arthur Holly Compton.

Schuker, Stephen A. *The End of French Predominance in Europe: The Financial Crisis of 1924 and the Adoption of the Dawes Plan*. Chapel Hill: University of North Carolina Press, 1988. Analyzes the impact of the Ruhr crisis, the Dawes Plan, and the realignment of power in Western Europe.

See also: Banting, Frederick Grant; California Institute of Technology (Caltech); Compton, Arthur Holly; Dawes Plan; Dawes, Charles G.; Insulin; Kellogg, Frank B.; Kellogg-Briand Pact of 1928; Millikan, Robert Andrews

■ Normand, Mabel

Identification: American silent film star
Also known as: Amabel Ethelreid Normand
Born: November 9, 1892, New Brighton, New York
Died: February 23, 1930, Monrovia, California

Between 1909 and 1926, Mabel Normand made at least 167 comic shorts and 23 full-length feature films. Known for her beauty, comic timing, and physical agility, Normand is one of the only women typically included in the pantheon of silent movie comedians.

Although she would later claim a birth date of 1895 and her gravestone bears that, Normand was actually born in 1892. As a child, Mabel played backstage while her father built sets and props for the Snug Harbor Music Hall. Her education remains a mystery; she told conflicting stories of homeschooling, a Boston art school, and a convent.

At sixteen, Mabel headed to New York City with only fifty cents. She supported herself by modeling for artist Charles Dana Gibson, who created a famous series of "Gibson girls." Drawings of the beautiful teenager appeared on the covers of magazines such as *The Saturday Evening Post* and *Life*. Since she was both pretty and funny, Mabel was encouraged by friends to apply for a position in the exciting new movie business. At the Biograph Company film studios, she met motion picture directors D. W. Griffith and Mack Sennett, with whom she began a relationship.

Hollywood Career

When Sennett moved from New York to California, he took Normand with him. Sennett built his successful Keystone Studios on physical comedy. Normand's zest for life and fearlessness made her a perfect heroine for Sennett; she quickly became an audience favorite as well. She recognized the talents of Roscoe "Fatty" Arbuckle and Charlie Chaplin early on and acted in several films with them. Arbuckle and Normand were featured in thirty-six comedies together. Chaplin only stayed a year at Keystone, but he appeared in eleven films with Normand, some of which she directed. Their collaboration culminated in *Tillie's Punctured Romance* (1914), the first feature-length Keystone comedy. By 1915, Normand and Chaplin were among the most popular stars in Hollywood. The slapstick romance *Mickey* (1916), starring Normand as a Western roustabout, was the first and only film produced by the Mabel Normand Feature Film Company.

Normand left Sennett after their planned wedding was canceled and began work for filmmaker Samuel Goldwyn in 1918, at the peak of her acting success. Although she tried to add glamour to her image, she was most successful in playing some variation of the spunky tomboy, a role that was increasingly difficult to sustain as Normand aged and experienced failing health. *Molly O'* (1921) was a box-office hit, but its success was soon overshadowed by two scandals: Normand's costar and friend Fatty Arbuckle was accused of rape and manslaughter, and Normand's companion, director William Desmond Taylor, was killed. Arbuckle was acquitted, but his films were banned; Taylor's murder was never solved. Press coverage probed the lives of movie stars, and Normand's excessive drinking and drug use became public knowledge. Fearful of government censorship, the Hollywood film industry tried to disassociate itself from stars with questionable lifestyles. By thirty, Normand had lost her good name, and her career never fully recovered. She starred in a comeback film, *Suzanna* (1923), and acted in *The Extra Girl* (1923), but soon after their release, another murder, committed by Normand's chauffeur, made headlines. Some states banned her films. Normand fled to

Mabel Normand. (Hulton Archive/Getty Images)

Europe, later appearing unsuccessfully on Broadway. Disillusioned and ill, Normand returned to Hollywood and appeared in several short films. She married actor Lew Cody in September 1926. Normand's final screen appearance was in *Should Men Walk Home?* (1927), the last of five shorts she made with director Hal Roach. In 1930, Normand died of tuberculosis at age thirty-seven.

Impact

In contrast to many other silent actors who had previous stage careers, Mabel Normand began her acting career in the movies. Normand was unique in silent films for combining beauty and physical abandon. Moving adroitly between romantic interludes and physical comedy, Normand paved the way for generations of American women comedians. In addition to her great popularity and influence as a performer, Normand also wrote, directed, and produced films, pioneering as a woman in the male-dominated motion picture industry.

Carolyn Anderson

Further Reading

Basinger, Jeanine. *Silent Stars.* New York: A. A. Knopf, 2000. Analyzes Normand's and 1920s feature comedies and includes black-and-white photographs.

Brownlow, Kevin. *The Parade's Gone By….* Berkeley: University of California Press, 1997. An illustrated study of American silent film.

Citron, Stephen. *Jerry Herman: Poet of the Showtune.* New Haven, Conn.: Yale University Press, 2004. Includes a discussion of *Mack & Mabel*, a musical based on the lives of Mack Sennett and Mabel Normand.

Fussell, Betty Harper. *Mabel.* New York: Limelight Editions, 1992. A biography containing correspondence between Normand's grandnephew and her nurse, along with a collection of black-and-white photographs.

Jacobs, Lea. *The Decline of Sentiment: American Film in the 1920s.* Berkeley: University of California Press, 2008. Analyzes the shifts in popular taste that encouraged the transition from slapstick to sophisticated comedy in 1920s American movies.

See also: Censorship; Chaplin, Charlie; Film; Goldwyn, Samuel; Griffith, D. W.; Sennett, Mack; Taylor, William Desmond

■ Novarro, Ramón

Identification: American film star
Also known as: José Ramón Gil Samaniego
Born: February 6, 1899, Durango, Mexico
Died: October 30, 1968, Hollywood, California

Ramón Novarro was a Mexican-born film star during the silent era of Hollywood film. The film production company Metro-Goldwyn-Mayer (MGM) selected him as a romantic actor rivaling Italian-born heartthrob Rudolf Valentino. Novarro's greatest film performance may have been his starring role in the 1925 film Ben-Hur.

Ramón Novarro's sensuality, physicality, and exceptional good looks gained him the attention of Hollywood movie stars and directors. His persistence and patience eventually earned rewards with a starring role in the 1922 MGM film *The Prisoner of Zenda*. Both he and the film were overnight box-office successes.

Novarro reputedly appeared as an extra in over one hundred films between 1916 and 1921. He also played small parts in nine films before 1921, moving on to larger roles in *The Prisoner of Zenda* (1922) and director Cecile B. DeMille's *Ben-Hur* (1925). Novarro was recruited for leading roles in silent film classics, including *Scaramouche* (1923), *The Arab* (1924), *The Student Prince in Old Heidelberg* (1927), and *The Pagan* (1929).

The film industry's transition from silent to talking films initially concerned Novarro, who had an accent. However, his musical skills, along with his considerable acting talent, kept him a much sought-after actor, although he was typically cast as a foreigner from an exotic country. The year 1929 was seminal for Novarro, who had became increasingly bored with his acting career and had frequent conflicts with MGM producer Louis B. Mayer. The stock market crash of 1929 wiped out his fortune, and the death of his younger brother increased Novarro's dependence on alcohol. His personal life was complicated by deep devotion to his Roman Catholic faith, which conflicted with his homosexuality.

Impact

Ramón Novarro never denied his Mexican origins, but Hollywood's directors and studio executives created foreign roles for him, representing many nations with the exception of Mexico. Novarro is remembered as one of Hollywood's most talented actors who brought to the screen some of the greatest charismatic images of the silent film era.

William A. Paquette

Further Reading

Berumen, Frank Javier Garcia. *Ramon Novarro: The Life and Films of the First Latino Hollywood Superstar.* New York: Vantage Press, 2001.

Ellenberger, Allan R. *Ramon Novarro: A Biography of the Silent Film Idol, 1899–1968.* Jefferson, N.C.: McFarland, 1999.

Soares, André. *Beyond Paradise: The Life of Ramon Novarro.* Jackson: University Press of Mississippi, 2010.

See also: *Ben-Hur;* DeMille, Cecil B.; Film; Metro-Goldwyn-Mayer (MGM)

■ Oil Pollution Act of 1924

The Law: Federal law making it illegal to purposely spill oil into coastal navigable waters and authorizing detention and fines for those in violation
Date: Enacted on June 7, 1924
Also known as: Federal Oil Pollution Act

The Oil Pollution Act of 1924 was one of the earliest federal laws passed during the twentieth century to address the effects of pollution on wildlife, the environment, human health, public safety, and commerce.

Inspired by the concerns of Secretary of Commerce Herbert Hoover, legislation for the Oil Pollution Act of 1924 was first introduced in Congress by New Jersey representative Thomas Frank Appleby in 1921. The bill sought to address the growing concerns of citizens and businesses regarding water pollution caused by oil spilled from cargo ships and factories. The tourism and seafood industries were losing money, and the health and well-being of the public was at risk from oil fires, contaminated water, and dying marine animals.

To prove the necessity of the Oil Pollution Act, hearings were held during the sixty-seventh and sixty-eighth sessions of Congress. Testimony and evidence given by scientists, health officials, and business leaders convinced Congress to move forward in making the law. However, the original version presented was very strict: Any form of water pollution in any waterway would be prohibited. Consequently, this early draft met with disapproval from the oil industry, prompting lawmakers to revise and loosen most of the act's restrictions, thereby weakening its power and enforceability.

During the first session of the Sixty-Ninth Congress, the Oil Pollution Act finally passed both the House and the Senate and was signed into law by President Calvin Coolidge on June 7, 1924. In final form, the law prohibited oil-burning vessels from intentionally dumping oil or related debris into coastal

Oil Pollution in the 1920s

Public concern over conservation problems associated with oil pollution began to surface after World War I, when the shipping industry began using oil rather than coal to power ships. This shift added to the oil pollution problem, which was further exacerbated by vessel accidents, non-marine accidents, and operations that dumped automobile waste oil into water systems. About 70 percent of the world's oil traveled by sea. The establishment of oil pollution laws motivated the oil industry to develop the technology to prevent excess discharge of oil in the cleaning of tanks and in the handling of dirty ballast water.

waterways and empowered the secretary of war and Army Corps of Engineers to detain and arrest those in violation of the law. Violators could be fined as much as $2,500 or be imprisoned for up to a year.

Impact

Despite inadequate resources for enforcement, the Oil Pollution Act of 1924 paved the way for future legislation protecting the nation's people and its rivers, streams, lakes, and other waterways from the harmful effects of environmental pollution. The act was repealed in 1970, but subsequent laws in the late twentieth century incrementally broadened the applications of antipollution law and increased its penalties, raising maximum fines and allowing for license revocations.

Michele T. Fenton

Further Reading
"Federal Oil Pollution Act." *Public Health Reports* 39, no. 51 (December, 1924): 3206–3208.
Speight, James G. *Environmental Analysis and Technology for the Refining Industry.* Hoboken, N.J.: Wiley-Interscience, 2005.

U.S. Congress. House. Committee on Rivers and Harbors. *Pollution of Navigable Waters*. Washington, D.C.: Government Printing Office, 1921.

See also: Natural resources, exploitation of; Science and technology

■ Okeechobee Hurricane of 1928

The Event: North Atlantic hurricane that caused massive damage and loss of life in Florida
Date: September 16, 1928
Place: South Florida

In 1928, the Okeechobee Hurricane resulted in the second greatest loss of life of any hurricane to hit the United States during the twentieth century. Nearly two thousand people died when Lake Okeechobee in south Florida overflowed, and thousands of homes and acres of cropland were destroyed. As a result, federally approved flood protection was implemented, building codes were improved, and the Herbert Hoover Dike was built to prevent such floods in the future.

It would not be until the late 1940s that hurricanes were given human names. In the 1920s, hurricanes were instead named for the place they did the most damage or the date on which they made landfall. The Okeechobee Hurricane was named for the south Florida lake it crossed in 1928, devastating the communities surrounding it.

The first warning of the hurricane's approach was on September 10, from a ship 900 miles east of the island of Guadeloupe in the Caribbean. The storm hit Guadeloupe on September 12, killing approximately a thousand people and destroying nearly every building on the island. After hitting Puerto Rico on September 13, the storm crossed the Bahamas and made landfall on the southeastern coast of Florida on September 16 as a category 4 storm with sustained winds of 130 to 155 miles per hour.

Coastal South Florida
Thanks to early warnings, residents of coastal Florida were prepared for the storm, and loss of life was minimal, at twenty-six recorded dead. Miami, Fort Lauderdale, and Hollywood suffered minor damage to homes and businesses, but the area surrounding West Palm Beach witnessed the destruction of over seventeen hundred homes and several million dollars in

damage. Reports claim that houses in the city were blown off their foundations, and Clematis Street, the main thoroughfare, resembled a lumber yard. Many city buildings were completely flooded or swept away. The greatest damage, however, occurred fifty miles inland along the southern shores of Lake Okeechobee.

Lake Okeechobee
Lake Okeechobee has an area of 720 square miles, and in 1928 had several residential and farming communities established around its perimeter. The lake's water level was already three feet higher than normal on September 16 due to heavy rains in previous weeks. Residents were notified of the approaching storm that day and left, but it was late arriving, so many returned to their homes, thinking it had missed the area. As the northerly winds strengthened during the evening, the lake began to rise. At least ten inches of rain fell throughout the night as hurricane-force winds blew. A levee that protected the area south of the lake broke, washing away thousands of acres of farmland and the dikes used to protect them. Because the lake was in an isolated area in 1928, it would be three days before government aid would arrive. Due to the difficult terrain, the vast area involved, and the slowly receding floodwaters, it would be six weeks before the search for bodies was ended. Over two thousand residents of the communities surrounding Lake Okeechobee were killed, but the exact number is unknown. Three-quarters of the inhabitants were migrant farm workers, many of whom were swept deep into the Everglades when the dikes broke, and their bodies were never recovered.

Impact
To prevent future flooding disasters, the Florida state legislature created the Okeechobee Flood Control District, which was authorized to cooperate with the U.S. Army Corps of Engineers. After an assessment visit by President Herbert Hoover in 1929, the Corps drafted a plan to construct floodway channels, major levees, and control gates along the shores of Lake Okeechobee. Building codes in the state were improved, and the Herbert Hoover Dike was constructed in 1930 to further protect the area.

Donald W. Lovejoy

Further Reading
Barnes, Jay. *Florida's Hurricane History*. Chapel Hill: University of North Carolina Press, 2007. Chrono-

logical descriptions of Florida hurricanes and detailed accounts of the Okeechobee Hurricane using eyewitness reports and numerous photographs.

Elsner, James B., and A. Birol Kara. *Hurricanes of the North Atlantic: Climate and Society.* New York: Oxford University Press, 1999. Compares North Atlantic hurricanes, especially those that have hit the United States, and describes how they have affected people and property.

Lodge, Thomas E. *The Everglades Handbook: Understanding the Ecosystem.* 3d ed. Boca Raton, Fla.: CRC Press, 2010. An overview of the Florida Everglades with a description of the topography and the water features of Lake Okeechobee; includes numerous color photographs.

Sheets, Bob, and Jack Williams. *Hurricane Watch: Forecasting the Deadliest Storms on Earth.* New York: Vintage Books, 2001. A general hurricane reference book, describing the history of the important storms, how they were caused, and the methods used to forecast them.

Simpson, Robert H., and Herbert Riehl. *The Hurricane and Its Impact.* Baton Rouge: Louisiana State University Press, 1981. An overview of hurricanes and the destruction they can cause. Includes a section that provides suggestions for protecting oneself from injury and property damage during these storms.

Will, Lawrence E. *Okeechobee Hurricane and the Hoover Dike.* 3d ed. St. Petersburg, Fla.: Great Outdoors Publishing Company, 1971. An account written by an Okeechobee Hurricane survivor describing the progress of the hurricane across the lake with eyewitness reports and previously unpublished photographs.

See also: Hoover, Herbert; Knickerbocker Storm; Natural disasters

---

■ O'Keeffe, Georgia

Identification: American artist
Born: November 15, 1887, Sun Prairie, Wisconsin
Died: March 6, 1986, Santa Fe, New Mexico

Known for her highly original approach to painting, Georgia O'Keeffe was ranked as one of the most celebrated women artists in the twentieth century, both nationally and internationally.

Georgia O'Keeffe. (Getty Images)

The decade of the 1920s marked a period of significant growth for Georgia O'Keeffe. By the beginning of the 1920s, she had given up her teaching job at West Texas Normal College in Canyon, Texas, and moved to New York City. She was encouraged in her art by well-known photographer Alfred Stieglitz, who greatly admired her work and exhibited it in his gallery at 291 Fifth Avenue, which was a gathering place for much of New York's artistic community. In New York, O'Keeffe began a period of intense artistic experimentation.

The O'Keeffe-Stieglitz Relationship

Although he was twenty-three years older than O'Keeffe, Stieglitz quickly became a major factor in O'Keeffe's personal and professional life. Before long, the two were living together, and Stieglitz began the process of divorcing his first wife, Emmeline Obermeyer Stieglitz so he would be free to marry O'Keeffe.

Stieglitz was consistently supportive of Georgia's work and worked hard to promote it. In 1923, he organized an extensive exhibition of her work that was highly successful and led to O'Keeffe's being viewed as a major figure in the American art world, which had previously been dominated by men. The success of the 1923 exhibition encouraged Stieglitz to make it an annual event. In 1927, the first O'Keeffe exhibition was held at the Brooklyn Museum, organized by Stieglitz. This exhibition established O'Keeffe's international reputation as an important artist, regardless of gender. On December 11, 1924, Stieglitz married O'Keeffe, who had been the model for hundreds of Stieglitz photographs, many of which were overtly sensual or nude. The two lived in a suite in New York City's Shelton Hotel. O'Keeffe soon fell into her husband's pattern of living most of the year in New York City but spending the summers at the Stieglitz family's summer home near Lake George in the Adirondack mountains.

O'Keeffe Broadens Her Subject Matter

Whereas early in the decade, O'Keeffe was doing a great deal of abstract and nature painting, her style expanded after moving to New York. There, she painted views from the Stieglitz suite at the Shelton Hotel, producing some of her best-known painting, including *The Shelton with Sunspots* (1926) and *Radiator Building—Night, New York* (1927).

She became intrigued by the architecture of New York City's tall buildings. At this stage in her artistic development, she also produced complex paintings depicting the industrial areas that she saw from her windows at the Shelton.

Northern New Mexico

By the summer of 1929, O'Keeffe had wearied of spending her summers at Lake George. Accompanied by her friend, Rebecca Strand, she traveled by train to New Mexico in May 1929. Shortly after their arrival in New Mexico, O'Keeffe and Strand were invited to spend the summer on a ranch outside Taos, owned by art patron Mabel Dodge Luhan. Located in the high desert, surrounded by dramatic landscapes and towering mountains, this part of northern New Mexico ignited in O'Keeffe a sense of having discovered her true home. She explored the area relentlessly, painting pictures of much that she was seeing and experiencing. She also visited the D. H. Lawrence Ranch, where she stayed for several weeks and painted one of her most celebrated canvases, *The Lawrence Tree* (1929). Stieglitz resisted any notion that he might travel to the West with his wife. It was clear that the summer spent in Taos marked the most significant turning point in O'Keeffe's artistic and personal life.

The couple began to grow apart and pursued separate romantic affairs, although they maintained a regular correspondence and never divorced.

Impact

Georgia O'Keeffe became one of the most influential painters in the art world during the 1920s and continued to have significant impact on later generations of artists. Whereas many artists of her day looked to Europe for ideas and subject matter, O'Keeffe became an American artist to whom contemporary major painters, both national and international, looked for artistic inspiration.

R. Baird Shuman

Further Reading

Castro, Jan Garden. *The Art and Life of Georgia O'Keeffe.* New York: Three Rivers Press, 1995. Presents images of O'Keeffe's paintings, along with photographs of the artist, personal documents, and excerpts from interviews.

Cowart, Jack, and Juan Hamilton. *Georgia O'Keeffe: Art and Letters.* Washington, D.C.: National Gallery of Art, 1989. Features photographs and letters associated with O'Keeffe's life and work.

Drohojowska-Philp, Hunter. *Full Bloom: The Art and Life of Georgia O'Keeffe.* New York: W. W. Norton, 2006. A comprehensive biography of O'Keeffe, discussing her artistic career, relationship with photographer Alfred Stieglitz, and her later years.

Eldredge, Charles C. *Georgia O'Keeffe: American and Modern.* New Haven, Conn.: Yale University Press, 1996. Examines O'Keeffe's work as an American artist, noting her development toward abstraction and her aesthetic vision.

Morgan-Griffiths, Lauris. *Georgia O'Keeffe: An American Perspective.* London: Quercus, 2011. Includes images of O'Keeffe's works, along with commentary on her life, artistic development, and most popular paintings.

See also: Art movements; Photography; Stieglitz, Alfred

■ Oliver, Joe "King"

Identification: American jazz musician, bandleader, and composer
Also known as: Joe Oliver; Joseph Nathan Oliver

Born: May 11, 1885, Aben, Louisiana
Died: April 10, 1938, Savannah, Georgia

Joe "King" Oliver helped define early jazz in the 1920s. Despite a relatively short career, he influenced the transition from collective improvisation to individual solos. Oliver also popularized the use of mutes such as plungers and derby hats to alter the sound and create special tonal effects.

Joe Oliver was raised in New Orleans and earned the nickname "King," due to the powerful tone he produced on the cornet. Throughout the first decade of the twentieth century, he performed with various orchestras and dance bands throughout New Orleans and performed in the Storyville district, which many believe to be the birthplace of jazz. From 1916 to 1919, Oliver teamed with popular trombonist Edward "Kid" Ory and his successful jazz orchestra.

In 1919, Oliver moved to Chicago, played with various bands, and then traveled to California, where he teamed with jazz pianist Jelly Roll Morton. By 1922, Oliver was back in Chicago and had started the Creole Jazz Band with a two-year engagement at the popular jazz club Lincoln Gardens. Louis "Satchmo" Armstrong, Oliver's protégé, joined the band, introducing Armstrong to the Chicago jazz scene. The Creole Jazz Band compiled a prolific body of work, producing over thirty recordings in two years. "Dippermouth Blues," recorded during this period, is one of Oliver's most famous songs.

The Creole Jazz Band disbanded after wage and royalty disagreements in 1924. The following year, Oliver led the Dixie Syncopators and performed at the Plantation Café in Chicago, a position he held until 1927 when he moved to New York City and made what many believe was a career-ending decision. Offered steady employment as a performer and bandleader at the newly opened Cotton Club, Oliver

Joe "King" Oliver playing the cornet with members of the Creole Jazz Band. (Getty Images)

turned down the position after salary negotiations broke down. Oliver was never to see the same level of popularity again.

By 1930, Oliver was in failing health and suffering financially from several bad investments. His style of New Orleans jazz was no longer as popular, and he spent the next several years touring throughout the South with various bands. In 1937, unable to play his cornet due to gum disease, Oliver worked at menial jobs in Savannah, Georgia, until his death.

Impact

The center of Dixieland activity shifted from New Orleans to Chicago during the 1920s. Innovative musicians such as Joe "King" Oliver introduced significant stylistic changes that were central to the evolution of jazz. Oliver placed more emphasis on improvisational solos, infused ragtime elements, and included piano and string bass in his bands. He spread the sound of the new, aggressive style of Dixieland from California to New York, performing and recording with the giants of the Jazz Age.

Douglas D. Skinner

Further Reading

Hardie, Daniel. *Exploring Early Jazz: The Origins and Evolution of the New Orleans Style.* Lincoln, Nebr.: Writers Club Press, 2002.

Kirchner, Bill, ed. *The Oxford Companion to Jazz.* New York: Oxford University Press, 2005.

See also: Armstrong, Louis; Beiderbecke, Bix; Cotton Club; Jazz; Morton, Jelly Roll; Music, popular

---

■ *Olmstead v. United States*

The Case: U.S. Supreme Court's ruling on the application of the Fourth and Fifth Amendments to wiretapping private telephone conversations
Date: Decided on June 4, 1928

The Supreme Court's ruling in Olmstead v. United States *held that the Fourth Amendment guarantee against unreasonable searches and seizure did not apply to the government's wiretapping of private telephone conversations. The Court also ruled that since the Fourth Amendment had not been violated, the Fifth Amendment protection against self-incrimination could not apply.*

Roy Olmstead, the suspected ringleader of an extensive bootlegging operation, was convicted of conspiring with about fifty other people to unlawfully import, possess, transport, and sell alcohol in violation of the National Prohibition Act. Federal officers gathered incriminating information against the defendants via wiretaps from the streets near the defendants' homes and in the basement of Olmstead's office. The placement of the wiretaps did not involve physical entry onto the defendants' property. Olmstead challenged the conviction on the grounds that the wiretapped private telephone conversations recorded by federal officers without a warrant had been admitted in his criminal trial in violation of his Fourth and Fifth Amendment rights. The Ninth Circuit Court of Appeals upheld Olmstead's conviction, and he appealed to the U.S. Supreme Court.

In *Olmstead v. United States*, the specific issue before the Court was whether the introduction into evidence of private telephone conversations intercepted by means of a wiretap violated the defendant's Fourth and Fifth Amendment rights. By a vote of five to four, the Court held that listening to communications passing over telephone wires did not constitute a search or seizure under the Fourth Amendment, because the evidence was simply a conversation and no physical entry of the defendants' houses or offices had taken place. In upholding Olmstead's conviction, the Court reasoned that the Fourth Amendment prohibition against unreasonable searches and seizures only applied to material things such as persons, houses, and papers, and did not apply to voluntary conversations that were overhead. The Court further held that since the Fourth Amendment did not apply, the Fifth Amendment argument had to be dismissed.

Impact

The *Olmstead* decision was the first case to consider the legality of wiretaps. The Communications Act of 1934 made unauthorized wiretapping a federal crime. Nevertheless, the federal law did little to deter wiretapping and eavesdropping by government officials. The *Olmstead* decision was overturned in *Katz v. United States* in 1967, whereby the U.S. Supreme Court held that the Fourth Amendment applied to eavesdropping, including wiretapping, even when it occurs without physical entry, because the amendment protects people's right to privacy anytime there is a reasonable expectation of privacy.

LaVerne McQuiller Williams

Further Reading

Charns, Alexander. *Cloak and Gavel: FBI Wiretaps, Bugs, Informers, and the Supreme Court.* Urbana: University of Illinois Press, 1992.

Kuhn, Betsy. *Prying Eyes: Privacy in the Twenty-First Century.* Minneapolis, Minn.: Twenty-First Century Books, 2008.

See also: Prohibition; Supreme Court, U.S.

■ Olympic Games of 1920 (Summer)

The Event: First post–World War I Olympic Games
Date: April 20–September 12, 1920
Place: Antwerp, Belgium

In June 1914, the International Olympic Committee convened to finalize plans for the 1916 and 1920 Olympic Games. Later that month, Austrian Archduke Franz Ferdinand was assassinated. World War I began shortly thereafter, and the 1916 Olympics were canceled. Following the war, world athletic leaders and Olympic officials met in Lausanne, Switzerland, to plan the 1920 Olympic Games, hoping also to provide a morale boost to the world following the devastation of the war.

Antwerp, Belgium, was chosen to host the 1920 Olympic Games as a way to honor the city for the destruction it endured during the war. Although not banned from the 1920 Games, wartime aggressors Germany, Austria, Hungary, Bulgaria, and Turkey were not invited to participate and did not attend.

With a relatively short time to prepare for the Games, Belgium had to construct athletic venues despite a lack of postwar funding and materials. When athletes first arrived in Antwerp in 1920, some venues had not been completed, and many athletes were housed in cramped quarters and slept on folding cots.

Olympic Firsts

The opening ceremony occurred on August 14, 1920, and was officiated by Belgian King Albert and his wife, Queen Elizabeth. During the opening ceremony, the Olympic flag, designed in 1914, was raised for the first time ever. The five interconnecting rings in the flag symbolize the five continents of the world that are unified through participation in the Games.

The colors of the rings were chosen because at least one color appears in every national flag of every country in the world.

The Olympic oath was also recited for the first time at the 1920 Games. First written in 1914 by Frenchman Pierre de Coubertin, considered by many the father of the modern Olympics, the oath is taken by an athlete of the host country, who, while holding a corner of the flag, promises on behalf of all the athletes to respect and abide by the rules that govern the Olympics. Belgian fencer Victor Boin recited the first Olympic oath, swearing to participate "in a spirit of chivalry, for the honor of our country, and for the glory of sport."

Also at the 1920 opening ceremonies, hundreds of white homing pigeons were released for the first time in modern history. The birds were used in 1920 to commemorate those who had died on the side of the victors in World War I, but the tradition has come to symbolize peace among all nations.

American Olympic Committee Controversy

Considerable controversy emerged between American athletes and the American Olympic Committee (AOC). In November 1919, the president of the AOC, Gustavus Towne Kirby, announced the team that would be representing the United States in Antwerp. Due to time constraints, there were several transportation and lodging setbacks for the Americans. Postwar transportation, for example, was hindered by the availability of adequate ships that could cross the Atlantic Ocean. Olympic athletes who were in the military sailed to Belgium aboard a military cruiser and were accorded first-class accommodations, but the remaining 254 members of the U.S. Olympic team were transported onboard an aging transport ship, and the athletes felt the ship lacked adequate accommodations and training facilities.

Controversy ensued between the athletes and the American Olympic officials, and to express their dissatisfaction, almost all of the athletes onboard the ship signed a petition expressing their grievances about crowded sleeping quarters, poor ventilation, inadequate training facilities, and a rodent infestation.

Once in Antwerp, the American athletes were housed in a local YMCA and in a rundown primary school with folding cots to sleep on. Several athletes soon decided to move to a local hotel, despite a warning from American officials that the move would be considered an act of insubordination. Triple jumper Dan Ahearn was suspended from the team after moving to a hotel, and many other American athletes threatened to boycott the Games if they did not receive better living conditions and if Ahearn was not reinstated. The Olympic Committee eventually reinstated Ahearn, but the living quarters remained the same. None of the athletes refused to compete.

Medal Standings

At the time of the 1920 Olympics, winter and summer sports were combined into one Olympiad. (The first separate Winter Olympics was held in 1924 in Chamonix, France.) A total of 2,626 athletes (2,561 men and 65 women) from 29 countries participated in the Games, with the United States winning the most medals (95) and the most gold medals (41). Sweden compiled 63 medals; Great Britain, 44; Belgium and France, 42 each; and Finland received 34. Figure skating and ice hockey were introduced in 1920, with the United States winning the silver medal in ice hockey.

Athletic Achievements

Athletes from the United States dominated the 1920 Olympic Games. American runner Charles Paddock was expected to win both the 100-meter and 200-meter events, though he was upset in the 200-meter by fellow American Allen Woodring, a last-minute addition to the team. Paddock won a team gold medal for the 4 × 100 meter relay. Although American athletes had dominated the field events in the 1912 Olympics, their performance in 1920 was not as stellar, giving way to Finnish athletes who received gold medals in the decathlon, pentathlon, and shot put. Paavo Nurmi of Finland made his Olympic debut in 1920 by winning the gold in the 10,000-meter run and 8,000-meter team cross country events, as well as the silver in the 5,000-meter run. His countryman Johannes Kolehmainen set a world record in the marathon. Americans received gold medals in pole vault and high jump that year.

In swimming, the United States won 11 of 15 events, led by triple gold medalists Norman Ross and Ethelda Bleibtrey, who became the first American woman to win an Olympic swimming title. Duke Paoa Kahanamoku of Hawaii led an American sweep of the 100-meter swimming event, and American women swept the 400-meter freestyle and won gold in the 4 × 100 meter freestyle relay. American men and women won the springboard diving events, with fourteen-year-old

Aileen Riggin winning a gold medal. In rowing, John Kelly Sr. won gold in single and double sculls, and the men's teams received a gold medal in the eight oars with coxswain event.

Nedo Nadi of Italy won five gold medals in fencing, and Belgium won the gold medal in football (soccer) before 40,000 spectators. At age seventy-two, Swedish shooter Oscar Swahn earned a silver medal in team double-shot running deer event to become the oldest medalist in Olympic history.

Impact

Although the 1920 Olympic Games were organized within a short amount of time and the austere facilities were criticized by the American team, the Games provided the opportunity to revive the Olympic spirit with new traditions such as raising the Olympic flag, reciting the Olympic oath, and the releasing of white birds to symbolize peace among all nations during the Games.

Alar Lipping

Further Reading

Espy, Richard. *The Politics of the Olympic Games.* Berkeley: University of California Press, 1979. Historical account of the political, economic, social, and philosophical forces that have influenced the Olympic Games.

Guttmann, Allen. *The Olympics: A History of the Modern Games.* 2d ed. Urbana: University of Illinois Press, 2002. A study of the history of the modern Olympic Games.

Lucas, John. "American Preparations for the First Post World War Olympic Games, 1919–1920." *Journal of Sport History* 10, no. 2 (1983): 30–44. Provides an account of the organizing of the American athletic representation at the 1920 Olympic Games.

Mallon, Bill, and Anthony Th. Bijkerk. *The 1920 Olympic Games: Results for All Competitors in All Events, with Commentary.* Jefferson, N.C.: McFarland, 2009. Results with commentary of every event in the 1920 Games.

Spivey, Nigel. *The Ancient Olympics.* New York: Oxford University Press, 2005. Researches the first Olympics of ancient Greece by exploring the events, rules, and athlete training and diet of the time.

See also: Kahanamoku, Duke; Olympic Games of 1924 (Summer); Olympic Games of 1924 (Winter); Olympic Games of 1928 (Summer); Olympic Games of 1928 (Winter); Paddock, Charles; Scholz, Jackson; Sports; Thorpe, Jim

■ Olympic Games of 1924 (Summer)

The Event: International athletic competition showcasing over three thousand athletes from forty-four countries
Also known as: Games of the VIII Olympiad
Date: May 4–July 27, 1924
Place: Paris, France

The 1924 Summer Olympics testified to the growing worldwide appeal of the Olympic Games. These were the first Olympic Games to use an Olympic motto and to conclude with a closing ceremony and the raising of three flags, those of the International Olympic Committee (IOC), the host country, and the next host country.

The Games of the VIII Olympiad were held in 1924 in Paris, France. Paris was chosen to host the Games over the bids of cities including Amsterdam, Berlin, Los Angeles, Rio de Janeiro, and Rome. Paris was the home of Pierre de Coubertin, founder of the International Olympic Committee (IOC), the organization responsible for reviving and running the Olympic Games in the twentieth century. The 1924 Summer Olympics were de Coubertin's last as president of the IOC. The Paris Games attracted 3,089 athletes from forty-four countries to compete in 126 events. As Europe was still recovering from the devastating effects of World War I, a strong political shadow still lingered, as neither Germany nor Russia was invited to participate; even France's occupation of the Ruhr area was unsettling to many. France's financial problems and a devastating spring flood only added to the tensions as the Games neared. However, the popularity of the Games smoothed over international conflict and indicated the widespread appeal of sports and the Olympic ideal.

The Games
In order to better accommodate the large number of visiting athletes, a number of temporary structures were erected around the city's Olympic Stadium, called the "Stade Olympique Yves-du-Manoir," giving rise to the first use of the term "Olympic Village." The Games were officially opened on May 4, 1924, by

Paavo Nurmi during the 1924 Olympic Games. (Gamma-Keystone via Getty Images)

Gaston Doumergue, the prime minister of France, who would soon afterward become president of France. The Olympic Oath was taken by athlete Georges André of France, who was competing in his fourth Olympic Games since 1908. The opening ceremonies were held in the stadium known as the Stade de Colombes, which held forty-five thousand spectators. The Games featured 126 events in nineteen sports on the program, along with seven demonstration sports, including volleyball. The events were staged in seventeen venues in and around Paris. Concurrent arts competitions in architecture, literature, music, painting, and sculpture were held along with the sporting events, and medals were awarded in most of them.

Notable Performances
The highlights of the Games were in the athletic events. William Dehart Hubbard became the first African American to win an Olympic gold medal in an individual event, the running long jump. Finnish runner Paavo Nurmi won gold medals in each of his

five events, and his fellow Finn Ville Ritola won four gold and two silver medals for races. These "Flying Finns" were two in a long line of athletes to share that nickname. Harold Abrahams and Eric Liddell of Great Britain had their gold medal wins in the 100-meter and 400-meter race memorialized in the 1981 motion picture *Chariots of Fire*. French fencer Roger Ducret also won five medals, including three gold medals. Legendary Hawaiian swimmer Duke Kahanamoku was defeated in the 100-meter freestyle race by fellow American swimmer Johnny Weissmuller, who won three gold medals in swimming, along with a bronze medal in water polo. Future pediatrician Benjamin Spock, along with future founder of First National City Bank of New York (later Citibank) James Stillman Rockefeller, won gold medals in rowing for the United States. Future Washington Redskins coach Dudley DeGroot anchored the gold medal–winning U.S. rugby team. American athlete Gertrude Ederle won three medals in swimming, while American teammates Helen Mills and Helen Wightman each won two gold medals in tennis. In fact, of the eight double-medal winners in women's competitions, seven were from the United States.

Summary of Competition

These Games exhibited some of the political tensions that the world was attempting to forget. Controversy accompanied some of the sports, such as the host country's negative reaction to American competitors' success. Fencers from Hungary and Italy fought a duel four months after the Games had ended, reflecting issues of national pride. Despite the difficulties the IOC would have dealing with international sports federations, the 1924 Summer Olympics were the first Olympic Games to set a standard distance for the marathon (26.2 miles) and to use a 50-meter swimming pool with marked lanes. The national anthems of the victorious athletes accompanied the awarding of medals. The United States won forty-five gold medals, which amounted to more than the total medal count of any of the remaining forty-three nations. Finland and France, with fourteen and thirteen gold medals, respectively, were the only other countries to secure more than nine gold medals. In the track and field events, the United States won thirty-two of its total ninety-nine medals. In fact, the United States, Finland, and Great Britain won a collective sixty of the eighty-one total medals awarded in the twenty-seven men's events. American divers won eleven of the fifteen medals awarded in the five diving events. Uruguay outscored its five football opponents, winning the gold before an estimated sixty thousand people and promptly initiating the victory lap tradition by running around the stadium thanking the crowd. Czechoslovakian gymnasts won nine of the twenty-eight medals in that sport; France and Switzerland captured all but six of the remaining gymnastics medals. Sweden won all three medals in the modern pentathlon, while American tennis players swept the medals in their discipline. American swimmers, both men and women, won nineteen of thirty-three total medals awarded in their discipline. Finland was dominant in freestyle swimming and Greco-Roman wrestling.

Impact

International sporting events like the British and French Open in golf and tennis were already extremely popular, so when over one thousand journalists descended on Paris to report on the Olympic Games, it was a further sign that the Olympic Games had matured and that de Coubertin's ideals of international athletic competition had gained widespread acceptance. Despite the concerns expressed by London's *The Times* newspaper that such sport competitions only served to further nationalistic pride and divisiveness, going so far as to suggest that the Games should be abolished or at least that Great Britain should withdraw, countries from around the world sent their best athletes to test the idea that sport could transcend politics. The Paris Games were the first to return to a previous host city and debuted the Olympic motto *Citius, Altius, Fortius* (Faster, Higher, Stronger).

P. Graham Hatcher

Further Reading

Beck, Peter. "Politics and the Olympics: The Lesson of 1924." *History Today* 30, no. 7 (July, 1980): 7–9. Details the political climate after World War I and its lingering effect on the competitions at the Paris Games.

Dabney, Wendell Phillips. *Cincinnati's Colored Citizens: Historical, Sociological, and Biographical.* Reprint. Cincinnati, Ohio: Ohio Book Store, 1988. Provides background and biographical information about Cincinnati athlete William Dehart Hubbard, the first African American to win an Olympic gold medal in an individual event, in this case the running long jump at the 1924 Summer Games.

Guttmann, Allen. *The Olympics: A History of the Modern Games.* 2d ed. Urbana: University of Illinois Press, 2002. A chronologically organized study of the Olympic Games' political and social significance, written for an undergraduate audience.

Johnson, William Oscar. *The Olympics: A History of the Games.* New York: Bishop Books, 1996. Provides an overview of the Olympic Games, including statistics, surrounding issues, and impact.

Phillips, Ellen. The *VIII Olympiad: Paris 1924, St. Moritz 1928.* New York: Firefly Books, 1996. Details the events and the stories behind the 1924 Summer Games in Paris, France.

The Olympic Games: Athens 1896–Athens 2004. New York: Dorling Kindersley, 2004. Provides a visual history of the modern Olympic Games, discussing background information and a chronology of events and medalists.

See also: Ederle, Gertrude; Kahanamoku, Duke; Olympic Games of 1920 (Summer); Olympic Games of 1924 (Winter); Olympic Games of 1928 (Summer); Olympic Games of 1928 (Winter); Soccer; Sports; Tennis; Weissmuller, Johnny

---

■ Olympic Games of 1924 (Winter)

The Event: International athletic competition retroactively designated as the first Winter Olympics
Also known as: I Olympic Winter Games
Date: January 25–February 5, 1924
Place: Chamonix, France

Originally known as the "International Winter Sports Week," the events in Chamonix highlighted winter sports in their own venue and not as a part of the more popular Summer Olympics. In 1926, the International Olympic Committee (IOC) designated the competitions at Chamonix as the first Winter Olympics.

Before the 1921 decision to proceed with competitions at Chamonix, there had been a growing desire to provide more visibility for winter sports, which until that time were severely limited in scope due to the Summer Games' schedules. Originating as a partnership with the organizers of the 1924 Paris Summer Olympics, the resort town of Chamonix at the base of Mount Blanc prepared to stage a week of international competition in a variety of winter sports. Despite resistance from the founder of the IOC, Pierre de Coubertin, and some Scandinavian countries, 258 athletes from sixteen countries gathered to participate in competitions that became more than a supplement to the quadrennial Summer Games. Some ten thousand spectators attended the sixteen events of the Winter Games.

The Games

The Games were officially opened by Gaston Vidal, the French undersecretary of physical education, and the Olympic Oath was taken by French biathlete Camille Mandrillon. According to the traditions of the time, during the opening ceremonies the athletes paraded in their sports's uniforms, even carrying their sports's equipment, such as ski poles and hockey sticks, with them. Events took place at three venues: a specially designed bobsleigh run, a ski jump, and the Olympic Stadium in Chamonix. The weather warmed as the Games opened, causing many venues to melt and become slushy. However, before the end of the Games, the temperature dropped to –25 degrees Fahrenheit, causing thick layers of ice to impede the ski jump and skiing events. The sixteen events held included men's bobsleigh; men's curling; figure skating for men, women, and pairs; men's ice hockey; military patrol; Nordic skiing (including two cross-country events for men, ski jumping for men, and the Nordic combined, featuring skiing and ski jumping in one event); and five events in men's speed skating. Interestingly, curling had previously been considered a demonstration sport and would not be played as a full-medal Olympic sport again until 1998.

Notable Performances

American athlete Charles Jewtraw's victory in the men's 500-meter skating event made him the first gold medal recipient in Winter Games history. Austria's Herma Szabo became the first female to win an individual gold medal in women's figure skating. Thorleif Haug of Norway captured three gold medals in the 18-kilometer and 50-kilometer cross-country skiing events and the Nordic combined. Finnish skater Clas Thunberg won medals in all five men's skating events, winning three gold medals, along with a silver and a bronze medal, while Norway's Roald Larsen won two silver and three bronze medals in those same events. Sweden's Gillis Grafström became the first athlete to win a gold medal in both the

Summer and Winter Olympics when he successfully defended his 1920 gold medal performance in men's figure skating at the 1924 Winter Games. The Canadian ice hockey team won a gold medal in their event, followed by the United States ice hockey team with a silver medal. Like Grafström, the Canadians defended their 1920 Summer Games gold medal performance at Chamonix. D. G. Astley of Ireland won both gold and silver medals in curling, as he played one match for Sweden while also playing for the champion team from Great Britain. Eleven-year-old Norwegian Sonja Henie made her Olympic debut in figure skating, winning the support of the crowd but finishing eighth. In an unusual conclusion to the Games, de Coubertin recognized British explorer Charles Bruce with an alpinism prize for his leading of an expedition to scale Mount Everest in 1922.

Summary of Competition
Athletes from Finland and Norway won four gold medals each, and Norway's seventeen total medals easily outdistanced Finland's eleven medals. Great Britain and the United States each won four medals overall, ranking third place among the sixteen countries competing at the Games. Competitors from Austria and Switzerland won two gold medals each and Canada, Great Britain, Sweden, and the United States each won one gold medal.

Impact
The 1924 Games at Chamonix proved that a separate winter venue would best highlight an expanded schedule of events displaying the talents of athletes competing in winter sports. In 1925, the IOC endorsed subsequent independent Winter Games in the same year as the Summer Games, awarding the hosting of the 1928 Winter Games to St. Moritz, Switzerland. That practice continued until 1992, when a two-year interval was created between the Summer and Winter Olympics.

P. Graham Hatcher

Further Reading
Guttmann, Allen. *The Olympics: A History of the Modern Games.* 2d ed. Urbana: University of Illinois Press, 2002. A chronologically organized study of the Olympic Games' political and social significance, written for an undergraduate audience.

The Olympic Games: Athens 1896–Athens 2004. New York: Dorling Kindersley, 2004. Provides a visual history of the modern Olympic Games, discussing background information and a chronology of events and medalists.

Searle, Caroline, and Bryn Vaile, eds. *The Official Olympic Games Companion: The Complete Guide to the Olympic Winter Games.* London: Brassey's Sports, 1998. An anthology of the Winter Games from 1924 to 1998, endorsed by the IOC.

U.S. Olympic Committee. *Chamonix to Lillehammer: The Glory of the Olympic Winter Games.* Colorado Springs: U.S. Olympic Committee, 1994. Highlights the participation and achievement of American athletes at the Winter Games held between 1924 and 1994.

Wallechinsky, David, and Jaime Loucky. *The Complete Book of the Winter Olympics.* London: Aurum Press, 2009. Provides complete details on all statistical aspects of the 1928 Games at St. Moritz as well as subsequent Games for comparison purposes.

See also: Hockey; Olympic Games of 1920 (Summer); Olympic Games of 1924 (Summer); Olympic Games of 1928 (Summer); Olympic Games of 1928 (Winter); Sports

■ Olympic Games of 1928 (Summer)

The Event: International athletic competition
Also known as: Games of the IX Olympiad
Date: May 17–August 12, 1928
Place: Amsterdam, Netherlands

The 1928 Summer Games at Amsterdam were the first to incorporate the lighting of the Olympic flame into the opening ceremonies. Representatives from Greece led the parade of nations, while the host country entered the stadium last. These Games witnessed an expanded program of events for women and were also the only Summer Games held in a country other than the one hosting that year's Winter Games until 1948, when St. Moritz, Switzerland, hosted the Winter Games and London, England, hosted the Summer Games. The 1928 Summer Games were also noteworthy for their broad range of medal-winning nationalities: Athletes from twenty-eight countries were awarded gold medals, while five other countries captured at least one silver or bronze medal.

Amsterdam had sought to host the 1920 and 1924 Games, but the cities of Antwerp and Paris were chosen first. After competing with Los Angeles for the

Runners exiting the Olympic stadium in 1928. (© Underwood & Underwood/Corbis)

next opportunity to host, Amsterdam's selection as host city was announced in 1923 by Pierre de Coubertin, the founder of the International Olympic Committee (IOC), after which the Netherlands Olympic Committee set about the task of preparing for the Games. Of the sixty-two countries invited, forty-six accepted and sent 2,883 athletes, of whom almost 10 percent were female. Germany was invited to return to the Games for the first time since having been banned from Olympic competition in 1920. Concurrent with the Games were art competitions, sports congresses, and reports on physiological research, including the first gathering of a sports medicine group.

The Games

Dutch nobleman Prince Hendrik, representing Queen Wilhelmina, officially opened the 1928 Summer Olympics. Dutch athlete Henri Denis took the Olympic

Oath. The Amsterdam Olympics were the first Summer Games to initiate symbolic practices that became rituals performed at all later Olympic Games. These included the lighting of the Olympic flame at the Olympic stadium, the selection of Greece as the first country in the parade of nations, with the host country as the final entrant into the stadium, and a public releasing of doves. It was in the marketing for the 1928 Summer Olympics that posters first displayed the Olympic design of five interlocking rings. These Games were also the first to be officially designated the "Summer" Olympics, as well as the first to be conducted in a separate country from the same year's Winter Games.

The 1928 Summer Games consisted of 109 competitions in sixteen sports, plus three demonstration sports. Early competition in football and field hockey occurred in May and June, with the majority of the competition taking place over the final two to three weeks of the Games. Women's events were extended to include track-and-field competitions and gymnastics, despite the various objections of de Coubertin and the Vatican.

Notable Performances

Official attendance at the Games' events amounted to 251,747 spectators, over half of whom were believed to have come for the football (soccer) competition alone. Swiss gymnasts Georges Miez and Hermann Hänggi each won four medals, totaling five gold medals between them. Paavo Nurmi of Finland won the last of his nine gold medals in the 10,000-meter race, along with two silver medals. India initiated a streak of six consecutive Olympic gold medal performances in field hockey by winning its initial gold medal at the 1928 Summer Games. American swimmer and future film star Johnny Weissmuller won gold medals in the 100-meter freestyle swim and the 4 × 200-meter relay events. Then a major general, Douglas MacArthur served as president of the United States Olympic Committee (USOC) during these Games and led the American team presence. In all, athletes from five continents won gold medals, and the Games featured eleven multiple gold medal winners, led by Swiss gymnast George Miez, who received three.

The 1928 Summer Games also featured the first expanded Olympic program for women, offering competition in gymnastics and five track-and-field events. However, German runner Lina Radke's visible exhaustion after winning the 800-meter race contributed to the future limiting of women's Olympic races to distances of 200 meters or less until 1960.

Summary of Competition

The United States won fifty-six total medals, including twenty-two gold medals, easily outdistancing Germany's thirty-one medals and ten gold medals. Finland and Sweden each totaled twenty-five medals. The Dutch won nineteen medals, six of which were gold. In men's athletics, British and Canadian competitors tended to dominate the short distances, while the Finns performed better in longer races. Americans were strongest in relays and field events. American and Canadian women took eight of the fifteen track-and-field medals. Italian and Argentine athletes excelled at boxing, while the Danes and Dutch took cycling honors. American divers received gold medals in the four diving events, winning nine of the twelve overall medals. French and Italian athletes won almost half of the fencing medals. Swiss male gymnasts won gold medals in five of their sport's seven events, while the Dutch women's gymnastics team won a gold medal in their discipline.

Uruguay received a gold medal in football, defeating Argentina in a second game after the first had ended in a tie. Due to the rising popularity of Olympic competition in this sport and conflicts between the international football group Fédération Internationale de Football Association (FIFA) and the Olympic concept of amateurism, FIFA formed its own World Cup tournament for 1930. That event was hosted by Uruguay, who defeated Argentina again. With football removed from the program of events at the 1932 Los Angeles Olympic Games, Olympic football became secondary to the World Cup in the eyes of FIFA fans.

India won a gold medal in field hockey without allowing any of its competitors to score a goal, while northern European countries completely dominated the sailing competition. American swimmers, both men and women, won eleven of the thirty-three total medals in their events, including six gold medals. Finnish and Swedish athletes were preeminent in both freestyle and Greco-Roman wrestling.

Impact

The Summer Games of 1928 further reinforced the universal appeal of the Games with their record attendance, new traditions in the opening ceremonies, and expanded women's competitions. Outstanding individual and team performances ushered in an era of Olympic fame after the IOC presidency of de Coubertin. As the Games welcomed Germany's return, political issues that would embroil the Games in subsequent years were minimized, likely due to the year's overall prosperity and efforts to communicate international goodwill. The Amsterdam Games provided a financial model that future host countries would study as they prepared for the Games. The Coca-Cola Company, a frequent Olympic sponsor, was first involved in the financing of the Olympic Games at the 1928 Summer Games.

P. Graham Hatcher

Further Reading

Guttman, Allen. *The Olympics: A History of the Modern Games.* 2d ed. Urbana: University of Illinois Press, 2002. A chronologically organized study of the

Olympic Games' political and social significance, written for an undergraduate audience.

Johnson, William Oscar. *The Olympics: A History of the Games.* New York: Bishop Books, 1996. Provides an overview of the Games, including statistics, surrounding issues, and impact.

The Olympic Games: Athens 1896–Athens 2004. New York: Dorling Kindersley, 2004. Provides a visual history of the modern Olympic Games, discussing background information and a chronology of events and medalists.

Van Rossem, G., ed. *The Ninth Olympiad: Being the Official Report of the Olympic Games of 1928 Celebrated at Amsterdam.* Amsterdam: J.H. de Bussy, 1928. Provides the official details of the preliminary organizing efforts, conduct, and administration of the 1928 Summer Games.

Wels, Susan. *The Olympic Spirit: One Hundred Years of the Games.* San Francisco: Collins, 1996. Offers a general overview of the Games, including a summary of the 1928 Summer Games.

See also: Olympic Games of 1920 (Summer); Olympic Games of 1924 (Summer); Olympic Games of 1924 (Winter); Olympic Games of 1928 (Winter); Soccer; Sports; Weissmuller, Johnny

---

■ Olympic Games of 1928 (Winter)

The Event: International winter athletic competition consisting of fourteen events in eight sports, with two demonstration sports

Also known as: II Olympic Winter Games

Date: February 11–19, 1928

Place: St. Moritz, Switzerland

The 1928 Winter Olympics were the first Winter Games to be held in a separate country from the Summer Games of the same year, as well as the first to include Asian and South American athletes, attesting to the global popularity of the Games during the period between World Wars I and II.

When the International Olympic Committee (IOC) considered the success of the 1924 Winter Games at Chamonix, France, it moved quickly to adapt to the growing popularity of winter sports being showcased in their own venues. In 1925, the IOC awarded the II Olympic Winter Games to St. Moritz, Switzerland, in a decision that signaled the true independence of the winter sports competitions from their summer counterparts.

The Games

Edmund Schulthess, president of the Swiss Confederation and successor to Pierre de Coubertin as IOC president and Games organizer, officially opened the Games on February 11, 1928; Swiss skier Hans Eidenbenz spoke the Olympic oath. Events took place at five venues, including a setting for the bobsleigh skeleton, an event in which participants would sled headfirst down an icy track. The St. Moritz Games are considered the birthplace of this fast-paced event, which became very popular. While fifteen events were originally scheduled, the 10,000-meter men's speed skating competition was eventually canceled in the fifth heat, due to warm weather that affected the integrity of the ice. In fact, some figure skating events were moved to a nearby hotel because of thawing outdoor ice. Events held included men's bobsleigh; men's speed skating; men's, women's, and pairs' figure skating; men's ice hockey; skiing; and tobogganing. Two demonstration sports were included: military patrol, which later evolved into the biathlon, and skijoring, in which competitors wearing skis are pulled across the ice by horses or dogs.

Notable Performances

Returning from her debut at Chamonix, Norway's fifteen-year-old figure-skating sensation Sonja Henie became the youngest gold medalist in history, a title she maintained through the next two Winter Games. Her fellow Norwegian Bernt Evensen won three medals in speed skating, one in each distance category. Finnish speed skater Clas Thunberg won two gold medals in the 500-meter and 1,500-meter events as a thirty-five-year-old, finishing with five gold medals, leaving him with seven gold medals in total for his Olympic career. Sweden's Gillis Grafström won his third consecutive gold medal in men's figure skating, despite a leg injury. Per-Erik Hedlund of Sweden won the 50-kilometer cross-country ski competition in spite of a sharp temperature spike over the course of the event.

As they had for the previous four years, Canada's ice hockey team dominated their event, winning three games without allowing an opposing goal scored. Sixteen-year-old American Billy Fiske was the driver on his country's gold-medal-winning bobsleigh team; he would later be remembered as the second American aviator killed in World War II. Argentina's two bobsleigh entries finished just out of medal contention in fourth and fifth places, which were the best performances for athletes representing countries outside Europe and North America at the 1928 Winter Games.

Summary of Competition

Athletes from Norway dominated the 1928 Winter Olympics, winning six of the fourteen gold medals awarded and accumulating fifteen medals in total; the nearest competitors were the United States with six total medals and Sweden with five. Finland and Austria won four medals each, but none of the other countries received more than one medal, and athletes from some participating countries, such as Argentina, did not win any medals.

Impact

The Winter Olympic Games of 1928 bore witness to the growing appeal of participating in and observing the world's premier athletes in a separate setting from the Summer Games. They were also the last before the Great Depression and the tumultuous years that would follow through World War II. However, with budding stars such as skater Sonja Henie and broader participation from Asia and South America, the popularity of the 1928 Winter Games convinced the IOC that their decision to highlight winter sports in separate venues was wise.

P. Graham Hatcher

Further Reading

Guttmann, Allen. *The Olympics: A History of the Modern Games.* 2d ed. Urbana: University of Illinois Press, 2002. A chronologically organized study of the Olympic Games' political and social significance, written for an undergraduate audience.

Phillips, Ellen. *The VIII Olympiad: Paris 1924, St. Moritz 1928.* New York: Firefly Books, 1996. Details the events and stories behind the 1928 Winter Olympic Games at St. Moritz.

Searle, Caroline, and Bryn Vaile, eds. *The Official Olympic Games Companion: The Complete Guide to the Olympic Winter Games.* London: Brassey's Sports, 1998. An anthology of the Winter Games from 1924 to 1998, endorsed by the IOC.

U.S. Olympic Committee. *Chamonix to Lillehammer: The Glory of the Olympic Winter Games.* Colorado Springs: U.S. Olympic Committee, 1994. Highlights the participation and achievement of American athletes at the Winter Games held between 1924 and 1994.

Wallechinsky, David, and Jaime Loucky. *The Complete Book of the Winter Olympics.* London: Aurum Press, 2009. Provides complete details on all statistical aspects of the 1928 Games at St. Moritz, as well as subsequent Games for comparison purposes.

See also: Olympic Games of 1920 (Summer); Olympic Games of 1924 (Summer); Olympic Games of 1924 (Winter); Olympic Games of 1928 (Summer); Sports

---

■ O'Neill, Eugene

Identification: American playwright
Born: October 16, 1888, New York City, New York
Died: November 27, 1953, Boston, Massachusetts

Eugene O'Neill emerged from obscurity to write an estimated forty-five plays, for which he was awarded four Pulitzer Prizes and a Nobel Prize in Literature. O'Neill was the driving force behind American theater's movement away from melodrama and entertainment toward realistic drama.

O'Neill's early life was aimless and unfulfilling. The son of a distinguished actor, O'Neill was enrolled in various schools in New York and Connecticut and spent one year at Princeton. He lived a bohemian life in New York, married, fathered a child, was divorced, went to sea, traveled to South America and then to South Africa, returned to an inexpensive apartment in New York City, and attempted suicide. He developed tuberculosis and was sent to a sanatorium for six months. There, he decided to write a play. In 1916, he went with friends to Provincetown, Massachusetts, with a copy of his one-act play *Bound East for Cardiff* (1914) and made plans to produce it with the theatrical group known as the Provincetown Players.

O'Neill and the American Theater

The Provincetown Players relocated to New York in 1916. In their resolution to remain an amateur organization relying primarily upon O'Neill's plays, they began an experimental theater to perform plays exploring issues considered inappropriate for Broadway. They also sought to initiate a kind of American theater that provided an alternative to the melodramatic

Eugene O'Neill. (AP Photo)

plays and shows popularized on Broadway. O'Neill's plays tended to contain painful autobiographical content or themes and experiences inspired by his family life.

His first full-length play, *Beyond the Horizon*, noted for its sense of tragic realism that seemed to narrow character options, was produced on Broadway. O'Neill sought other forms of expression that would allow a greater range of experiences and began experimenting with theatrical devices. In *The Emperor Jones*, O'Neill's depiction of a man's regression from civilized behavior into irrational fears is indicated by drumbeats of increasing tempo. This production, the Players' first hit, was followed by *The Hairy Ape* (1921), which employs expressionistic elements, masks, soliloquies, and spoken asides that indicate the depth of the characters' minds.

O'Neill also began to experiment with the lengths of his plays, one of the most popular being *Anna Christie*, for which he received a Pulitzer Prize in 1922. His first full-length play to suggest the tragic inevita-

bility that he saw in his own life was *Desire Under the Elms* (1924), which connects incest, infanticide, and retribution into a powerful tragedy ranking among the most prominent American plays of the twentieth century.

Beyond the 1920s

Toward the end of his major productive cycle in the 1920s, O'Neill began experimenting with bolder techniques, such as his use of masks in *The Great God Brown* (1926). He also explored the effect of longer plays, such as *Strange Interlude* (1926–1927) and *Mourning Becomes Electra* (1929–1931), the latter of which requires seven hours to perform. Established as a major dramatist, O'Neill continued his writing success throughout the 1930s. He was awarded the Nobel Prize in Literature in 1936, but his plays were not being widely produced; experimental theater was not always received enthusiastically by theatergoers. He stopped writing for a time.

When he resumed his work, he omitted expressionistic experimentation and returned to more realistic frameworks with everyday settings. *The Iceman Cometh* (1939), one of the most complex and incisive of his tragedies, was not produced until 1946. In *Long Day's Journey Into Night* (1939–1941), O'Neill continued working through the guilt and rage addressed so many times in his plays. It became the definitive drama of his family and its legacy, but he requested it be withheld from publication for twenty-five years.

Impact

During the 1920s, American theater developed into a cultural medium through which serious issues and ideas could be explored. O'Neill's Pulitzer Prize–winning play *Beyond the Horizon*, produced in 1920, interrupted the Broadway mainstays of melodrama, musical theater, and theatrical farce, replacing them with plays portraying a realistic and often tragic view of life. O'Neill conceived of a contemporary theatrical style based on Greek drama and capable of reaching significant emotional highs and lows. O'Neill used events from his own family's history to reflect his view that individual needs and fears set into motion an inevitable chain of tragic events.

Mary Hurd

Further Reading

Black, Stephen A. *Eugene O'Neill: Beyond Mourning and Tragedy.* New Haven, Conn.: Yale University

Press, 2002. Argues that O'Neill's writing was self-therapy for grief.

Gelb, Arthur, and Barbara Gelb. *O'Neill: Life With Monte Cristo.* New York: Applause, 2002. Traces O'Neill's life through 1918.

O'Neill, Eugene. *Early Plays.* Foreword by Jeffrey H. Richards. New York: Penguin Books, 2001. Includes seven one-act plays written between 1914 and 1921, along with five full-length plays.

_____. *Four Plays.* Foreword by A. R. Gurney. New York: Signet Classics, 2007. A collection of O'Neill plays including *Anna Christie, The Hairy Ape, The Emperor Jones,* and *Beyond the Horizon* as examples of his theatrical devices.

_____. *Long Day's Journey Into Night.* Foreword by Harold Bloom. New Haven, Conn.: Yale University Press, 2002. A play with autobiographical references to O'Neill's family.

See also: *Desire Under the Elms; Emperor Jones, The;* Literature in the United States; *Strange Interlude;* Theater in the United States

---

■ Organized crime

In the United States, criminal organizations had been in existence for many years prior to the 1920s, although the term "organized crime" was not in use before this decade. The passing of the Eighteenth Amendment in 1919 and the institution of Prohibition in the United States completely changed the shape of organized crime, turning fragmented and poorly managed criminal gangs into highly structured and well-organized criminal enterprises.

Until 1919, organized crime in the United States had primarily consisted of loosely coordinated groups of men whose criminal activities were mostly restricted to gambling and theft. The ratification of the Eighteenth Amendment in this year set the stage for major changes in the structure of organized crime in America. In concert with the National Prohibition Act, also known as the Volstead Act, the amendment prohibited virtually all things associated with the creation and consumption of alcohol, setting in motion what is now known as the Prohibition era. It was not until 1933 that Congress passed the Twenty-First Amendment, which repealed the Eighteenth Amendment and left control of alcoholic beverages to the authority of individual states.

Saint Valentine's Day Massacre

When seven members of George "Bugs" Moran's gang were executed by a group of men dressed as police officers on Valentine's Day, 1929, Al Capone was believed to be behind the hit, and the event marked the beginning of the end of Capone's reign as Chicago's crime czar. The massacre sparked a wave of reforms that helped to dismantle Capone's empire. Although no one was ever tried for the killings, the incident brought Capone's illegal activities under the scrutiny of the Federal Bureau of Investigation, eventually leading to his 1931 conviction for tax evasion.

The driving force behind the Prohibition era was the temperance movement, a social movement that was closely associated with religious conservatism. Beginning in the late eighteenth to early nineteenth centuries, the temperance movement argued that alcohol consumption was a major cause of immoral and criminal behaviors, such as prostitution and domestic abuse. One of the most influential organizations behind the movement was the Women's Christian Temperance Union (WCTU), members of which believed that behaviors caused by alcohol consumption were destroying the American family and thus advocated for legislation that would make the sale and use of alcohol illegal in the United States. If alcohol were made illegal, they believed, women and children would be better protected from the negative effects associated with alcohol use, and crimes associated with alcohol abuse would decrease. Instead, Prohibition actually led to the increase of criminal behavior in the United States, as organized crime started to become a significant problem.

Organizing Crime

At the beginning of the 1920s, the U.S. economy was showing signs of distress, with increasing unemployment rates causing many citizens to struggle financially. Immigration rates were also on the rise, and new immigrants were finding it difficult to earn a living in their new country of residence. With jobs being scarce and people looking for new ways to provide for their families, many turned to illegal activity as a way of producing income.

Prior to the 1920s, organized crime generally consisted of undersized and disorganized gangs that fought over small, poorly valued territories. These gangs earned their money through the control of crime markets such as drugs, prostitution, gambling, and theft, none of which were very profitable. All this would soon change, however.

While the federal government could make most things associated with the production and consumption of alcohol illegal, it was unable to control and eliminate consumer demand for the product, and prior to Prohibition, consumer demand had been high. The popularity of alcohol was not diminished by the passing of the Eighteenth Amendment; if anything, making alcohol illegal made it even more popular, especially among young people. Prohibition created a natural market for organized crime, as groups of men who had long fought one another over territory suddenly became united in their efforts to supply Americans with alcohol. The success and growth of organized crime were aided by the fact that the federal government did very little to actually enforce the newly created laws against alcohol.

The Effects of Organized Crime in the 1920s

The lack of enforcement of these new laws, the tremendous demand for alcohol, and the growth of organized criminal enterprises all led to severe increases in crime throughout the country. During the 1920s, across all fifty states, alcohol-related crimes dramatically increased over the course of the decade: Arrests for law violations associated with Prohibition increased by 102 percent; the arrest rate of individuals for public drunkenness and disorderly conduct increased by 41 percent; arrests for driving while under the influence of alcohol increased by 81 percent; the crimes of residential burglary and theft of personal property increased by 9 percent; and personal violence and violent crimes, such as homicide, assault, and battery, increased by a total of 13 percent. The total number of federal convictions increased by 561 percent, and the federal prison population increased by 366 percent, which entailed an increase in the operating costs of federal prisons of over 1,000 percent. All of this led to an increase of $11.4 million in funding for police agencies, which placed a tremendous burden on American citizens, especially during the economic recession of 1920 and 1921.

During the 1920s, violent acts became part of the

normal operating procedure for members of criminal organizations, most often directly related to disputes over distribution areas. Countless organized crime gangs would fight to establish dominance over a particular geographical area and control the illegal markets there; Chicago alone saw over four hundred gang-related murders per year. The decade's most widely publicized act of violence that can be directly linked with organized crime is Chicago's Saint Valentine's Day Massacre in 1929, which was partially in retaliation for previous crimes and partially the result of a struggle for control of illegal enterprises such as gambling and alcohol distribution. On February 14, Al Capone's South Side Italian gang lured members of the North Side Irish gang, controlled by George "Bugs" Moran, into an ambush that resulted in the deaths of seven people.

Another by-product of the growth of organized crime was that members of criminal organizations became power brokers in the affairs of mainstream society and legitimate businesses. While members of organized crime supplied the demand for alcohol, they also established strong and powerful ties to the community. These ties were enhanced by the development and control of speakeasies, underground establishments that dealt in illegal activity and were owned and operated by members of organized crime. Speakeasies primarily flourished as a place to buy alcohol, but they often provided patrons with easy access to gambling and prostitution as well and became centers of social gatherings for many of the wealthy and powerful individuals of a particular community. Having social access to these individuals allowed criminal organizations to develop political connections in their communities, which eventually led to widespread political corruption throughout many of the urban communities in the United States.

The Location of Organized Crime

In the 1920s, most of the activity associated with criminal organizations was located in large urban communities throughout the United States. Cities such as Chicago, New York, and Boston became centralized hubs for the illegal markets affiliated with organized crime. Urban areas were ideal environments in which criminal enterprises could flourish, providing access to a large pool of potential members as well as a sizeable consumer base for illegal goods and services.

Within these urban communities, organized crime

gangs were highly segregated from mainstream society. Members of these gangs usually resided in ethnically homogeneous neighborhoods and remained virtually unidentifiable to community members who were not part of the local culture. Living within an insulated structure provided safety to gang members and allowed them to develop strong social ties within their neighborhood.

The Demographics of Organized Crime
During the 1920s, members of organized crime were primarily young males who had recently immigrated to the United States. Most organized crime gangs were Italian, Irish, Jewish, or African American; in the late 1920s in Chicago, for example, 31 percent of all leaders of organized crime gangs were Italian, 29 percent were Irish, 20 percent were Jewish, and 12 percent were African American.

Typically, when coming to the United States, these immigrants relocated to one of the large, urban communities located either in the Midwest or on the East Coast, where they lived in ethnically segregated neighborhoods and usually struggled to find employment. The inability of new immigrants to find lawful work was an important component in the longevity and growth of organized crime. Most of these men arrived in the United States with little education and few marketable skills, which made it difficult to secure a legitimate occupation and forced many of them to turn to organized crime simply in order to earn a decent living.

Impact
The 1920s was a unique time in the history of organized crime, marking the beginning of many aspects now associated with organized criminal enterprises. Much of the success that criminal organizations experienced during this decade came as a direct result of the passing of the Eighteenth Amendment. The Prohibition era was the catalyst for the growth and prosperity of these enterprises, the activities of which both encompassed and evolved beyond criminal behavior during this decade. Criminal organizations were influential in corporate and political affairs as well, with many high-ranking leaders of organized crime crossing over into legitimate business. This blurred the lines between criminal and noncriminal behavior and provided social acceptance to many organized crime leaders, who then had the political power necessary to influence both local and national elections.

The public prominence of organized crime began to fade in 1933 with the passing of the Twenty-First Amendment, which repealed the ban on alcohol, thereby rendering unnecessary the primary service that gangs had been providing throughout the United States. When citizens no longer had to turn to bootleggers for their supply of alcohol, the criminal gangs were forced to seek other opportunities to generate income. Not surprisingly, in the decades to come, these gangs would turn to the illegal drug market as their primary source of revenue.

Jay Gilliam

Further Reading
Finckenauer, James O. *Mafia and Organized Crime: A Beginner's Guide.* Oxford, England: Oneworld, 2007. An introduction to the phenomenon of organized crime and its economical and societal effects.

Haller, Mark H. "Organized Crime in Urban Society: Chicago in the Twentieth Century." *Journal of Social History* 5, no. 2 (Winter, 1971–1972): 210–234. Discusses the role played by organized crime in Chicago.

_____. *History of Organized Crime, 1920–1945.* Washington, D.C.: United States National Institute of Law Enforcement and Criminal Justice, 1976. Studies how gambling operations combined with bootlegging operations to create new criminal organizations.

Lyman, Michael D., and Gary W. Potter. *Organized Crime.* 5th ed. Upper Saddle River, N.J.: Prentice Hall, 2010. An extensive overview of the history of organized crime, as well as its social, political, and economic aspects and what can be done to control it.

Woodiwiss, Michael. *Organized Crime and American Power: A History.* Toronto: University of Toronto Press, 2003. Examines the nature of organized crime and its interplay with the major power structures of American society.

See also: Bathtub gin; Capone, Al; Crimes and scandals; Gambling; Prohibition; Saint Valentine's Day Massacre; Speakeasies

■ *Orphans of the Storm*

Identification: A silent film about two orphaned sisters during the French Revolution
Director: D. W. Griffith
Date: 1921

Orphans of the Storm was the last commercially successful film by director D. W. Griffith, the last film actor Lillian Gish made with Griffith, and the last film the Gish sisters appeared in together.

Orphans of the Storm is based on a popular nineteenth-century French play, *Les deux orphelines* (1874; *The Two Orphans*), by Adolphe d'Ennery. After silent screen star Lillian Gish took director D. W. Griffith to an Italian production of the play in New York City, he decided to adapt it into a film and give it more scope by changing the setting to eighteenth-century France, with the French Revolution as a backdrop. Griffith also added factual material to the original storyline by taking material from Thomas Carlyle's history *The French Revolution: A History* (1837) and Charles Dickens's novel *A Tale of Two Cities* (1859).

The film opens with an impoverished man about to leave his infant daughter on the steps of a church, where he sees another abandoned baby girl. The man has second thoughts and takes both babies home to raise together. The girls (Louise, played by Dorothy Gish, and Henriette, played by Lillian Gish) grow and soon lose their parents, and Louise's eyesight, to the plague. Henriette takes Louise to Paris to seek a cure but is abducted by a lecherous French aristocrat (Morgan Wallace). A noble aristocrat (Joseph Schildkraut) soon saves Henriette and becomes her lover. Meanwhile, an evil beggar (Lucille La Verne) exploits Louise. As the French Revolution erupts around them, Henriette and her aristocrat-lover are sentenced to die at the guillotine but are rescued at the last moment by revolutionary leader Georges Danton (Monte Blue). The girls are reunited, and Louise's eyesight is restored.

Griffith was known for his conservative political and social views, and opening titles in the film warn of the dangers of Bolsheviks and anarchists. The director wanted to be certain viewers did not mistakenly see parallels between his film and the recent Russian Revolution.

Impact

D. W. Griffith is often credited as having either invented or refined the language of cinema (including camera movement, cutting between scenes, close-ups), and *Orphans of the Storm* exemplifies many of his techniques. Critics have praised Griffith's use of period details in the film and his expert handling of crowd scenes, as well as the performances of Dorothy and Lillian Gish. The sisters began their film careers with Griffith a decade earlier, and *Orphans of the Storm* was the last time Griffith would direct either sister and would also be the last film they would star in together.

Michael Adams

Further Reading

Affron, Charles. *Lillian Gish: Her Legend, Her Life.* Berkeley: University of California Press, 2002.
Schickel, Richard. *D. W. Griffith: An American Life.* New York: Limelight Editions, 1996.
Simmon, Scott. *The Films of D. W. Griffith.* New York: Cambridge University Press, 1993.

See also: Film; Gish, Dorothy; Gish, Lillian; Griffith, D. W.

■ Ott, Mel

Identification: American baseball player and manager
Also known as: Master Melvin; Melvin Thomas Ott
Born: March 2, 1909, Gretna, Louisiana
Died: November 21, 1958, New Orleans, Louisiana

At 5 feet 9 inches, Mel Ott was considered too short to play professional baseball effectively. In his eighteen-year career for the New York Giants, however, he led the team in home runs, was the youngest major-league player to hit 100 home runs, and was the first in the National League to hit 500 home runs.

As a youth, Melvin Thomas Ott learned the game of baseball from his father Charles, who once pitched for a semiprofessional team. By 1925, at the age of sixteen, Ott was playing for a semiprofessional team in Patterson, Louisiana. The owner soon recommended Ott to New York Giants manager John McGraw. After a tryout in September 1925, McGraw

Mel Ott. (Getty Images)

decided to apprentice Ott with the Giants rather than send him to the minor leagues for development. McGraw did not want a minor-league manager to change Ott's unorthodox batting style, which involved lifting his front foot before hitting the ball.

Playing his first major-league game in 1926, Ott demonstrated tremendous power and became the Giants regular right fielder in 1928. In 1929, at twenty years old, Ott became the youngest major-league player to hit during the regular season. He also set a National League record for number of walks in a doubleheader (six) and later tied his own record in 1944.

Ott was not only a tremendous hitter but also a premier outfielder. In 1929, he set a major-league record as an outfielder for completing twelve double plays in one season. During his twenty-two-year professional career, Ott's batting average was .304, and he hit 511 home runs, collected 488 doubles, scored 1,859 runs, and had 1,860 runs batted in (RBIs).

Impact

A versatile, power-hitting, and very popular player, Mel Ott set impressive standards for future major-league players. He is on the select list of players who hit 500 or more home runs, 400 or more doubles, scored 1,000 or more runs, and had 1,000 or more RBIs. Garnering 87 percent of the votes, Ott was elected to the Baseball Hall of Fame in 1951. At the time of his death in an automobile accident in 1958, he held fourteen major-league records. Ott's legacy was honored in 2006 when his image was featured on a U.S. postage stamp.

Alvin K. Benson

Further Reading

Martin, Alfred M. *Mel Ott: The Gentle Giant.* Lanham, Md.: Scarecrow Press, 2003.

Stein, Fred. *Mel Ott: The Little Giant of Baseball.* Jefferson, N.C.: McFarland, 1999.

See also: Alexander, Grover Cleveland; Baseball; Cobb, Ty; Gehrig, Lou; Grove, Lefty; Hornsby, Rogers; Ruth, Babe; Sports

■ Ouija boards

The Ouija board became a fad in the early 1920s, finding its way into the music and movies of the decade. It was connected with Spiritualism, the nineteenth-century religious movement in which mediums claimed to speak to the dead. Various Christian groups denounced the game, considering it demonic.

The most popular version of talking board games, the Ouija board was invented in the late 1890s and was owned by the Ouija Novelty Company of Baltimore, Maryland. Over the next twenty years, assorted versions of the board were patented and copyrighted. Ownership and manufacturing rights changed hands frequently, and numerous lawsuits were brought to determine rights.

By 1919, William Fuld obtained full ownership of the Ouija board copyright in addition to the patent for the version of the heart-shaped planchette still in use in the early twenty-first century. While the Ouija board was popular prior to the 1920s, it was only after Fuld obtained full ownership of the game and launched an aggressive marketing campaign that the board became an American fad. Fuld licensed the

Baltimore Talking Board Company to manufacture and sell the boards, and he placed ads in mail-order catalogs and in a variety of magazines, including *Popular Science*.

In 1920, the Internal Revenue Service (IRS) levied a tax against the Baltimore Talking Board Company for the sale of the Ouija board. In response, the company sued the IRS for reimbursement. It claimed that the boards were not games but instead were religious objects and were thus exempt from taxes. In *Baltimore Talking Board Co. Inc. v. Miles, Collector of Internal Revenue*, the court ruled that the Ouija board was a game, not a religious device, and was therefore taxable. Despite the court's ruling, the Ouija board became a popular tool for professional Spiritualist mediums and anyone interested in communicating with the dead.

Impact

The Ouija board became a popular cultural icon beginning in 1919 and was featured in many movies, plays, and songs of the 1920s. By the mid-1920s, the popularity of the Ouija board had waned significantly. Nevertheless, after William Fuld's death in 1927, the Ouija board continued to be manufactured under the supervision of the Fuld family until it was sold to Parker Brothers in 1966.

Its popularity and the controversy surrounding its connection to the supernatural have continued well into the twenty-first century. Parker Brothers released a glow-in-the-dark version of the game in 1999, and numerous Christian leaders continue to claim the game as evil and a tool of the devil.

John L. Crow

Further Reading

Cornelius, J. Edward. *Aleister Crowley and the Ouija Board*. Los Angeles: Feral House, 2005.

Hunt, Stoker. *Ouija: The Most Dangerous Game*. New York: HarperCollins, 1992.

See also: Fads; Spiritualism

■ Our Gang comedies

Identification: Short comedy films starring children
Director: Hal Roach Sr.
Date: 1922–1944

This long-running and immensely popular film series centered on children being themselves, a quality not typically seen in films of the 1920s. The equal treatment in storylines of girls and boys as well as whites and nonwhites was also revolutionary for the period.

Hal Roach created the Our Gang series concept while auditioning an overly made-up and rehearsed child actor. Contrasting the child he had just auditioned with a group of children playing outside his window, he realized that watching children participating in childlike activities was more entertaining than watching a child imitate adult acting styles.

The Early Years

Roach began producing short, two-reel silent "Hal Roach's Rascals" series in 1922, with the title "Our Gang" being added to the pilot of the first short film. The series would be called by both titles until 1932 when "Our Gang" became the exclusive name of the series. In 1927, he changed distributors from Pathé to Metro-Goldwyn-Mayer (MGM) Studios, and the series was converted to sound in 1929.

The directorial approach of the early films was to focus on the natural behavior and unaffected reactions of the child actors. Although scripts were written by Roach's staff, the children did not memorize lines. Instead, they were given the overall plot and an explanation of the scene they would be shooting. Both Roach and the directors believed the best performances would come from natural behavior, not acting, so improvisation was encouraged. For silent productions, direction was given via megaphone as the children played out the scenes.

The themes and concepts of the Our Gang films were unusual for the 1920s. They featured the adventures of a group of children, the majority of whom were poor, who where often put at odds with wealthier children, interfering adults, and parents. The early silent films frequently centered on the children engaged in seemingly carefree activities that soon took an unexpected twist and ended with them in trouble with annoyed adults. Many popular plots had the children modeling adult actions that led to trouble, which was resolved by the group working together. In *Love My Dog* (1927), for example, the children put on a dog show for the neighborhood. When a dogcatcher takes one of the dogs and threatens to euthanize it, the group raises money together and saves the animal.

Scene from Our Gang comedy in 1929. (CBS via Getty Images)

Cast Members

Many of the first cast members in the series were recommended by studio employees or were the children of Roach's friends. Original cast member Ernie "Sunshine Sammy" Morrison was an established child actor with another Roach series and is believed to be the first African American actor signed to a long-term Hollywood contract.

The Our Gang films are noted for including African Americans and girls, both of whom were presented in storylines as equals to white male characters. Although there were many racial and gender stereotypes that would be considered unacceptable today, the integration of females and nonwhite char-

acters into major roles was revolutionary for the era. Many have cited the importance Roach placed on presenting a world in which everyone had an equal share in childhood innocence and adventures.

Cast turnovers were commonplace as the children grew to adolescence. Roach often had six or seven lead characters, with several new and younger secondary characters who would replace main characters as they grew older. Of the six original cast members, Allen "Farina" Hoskins appeared most often in the short films, with one hundred total appearances. Hoskins was the only original cast member to make the transition from silent to sound films in 1929, and he was considered the most popular original Gang member and the most popular black child star of the 1920s. His last Our Gang film, *Fly My Kite*, was released in 1931.

From the beginning, Roach incorporated a menagerie of animals into the films. Cows, monkeys, cats, mules, and horses had roles in the storylines, but the animal many remember best is the pit bull terrier named Pete the Pup, better known as Petey. Petey's signature ring around one eye was added by then-unknown Hollywood makeup artist Max Factor. Different dogs were used as Petey throughout the years, and the ring often changed sides or would sometimes not be in place at all. Petey was eventually removed from the series in the late 1930s.

Impact
The Our Gang series was a hit from the beginning and did well at the box office throughout the 1920s and early 1930s. Many believe that Roach's move to MGM in 1927 helped with the success of the series because it afforded him larger budgets and the opportunity to have the short films packaged with MGM feature films to the Loews Theatres chain. By 1934, however, many theater owners stopped showing film shorts and began running double-feature programs instead. Roach considered dropping the Our Gang series, but he instead developed short (ten-minute) Our Gang films with his first, *Bored of Education* (1936), winning the Academy Award for Best Short Subject (One Reel) in 1936. The series ended in 1944 with 221 single episodes released.

R. L. Smith

Further Reading
Bond, Tommy, and Ron Genini. *Darn Right It's Butch: Memories of Our Gang*. Wayne, Pa.: Morgin Press, 1994. An autobiography by 1930s Our Gang cast member, also providing information on other cast members of that era.

Browne, Ray B., and Pat Browne, eds. *The Guide to United States Popular Culture*. Bowling Green, Ohio: Bowling Green University Popular Press, 2001. Supplies synopses, background information, and analysis on significant entries in American cultural history, including the Our Gang series.

Gulick, Rebecca. *Those Little Rascals: The Pictorial History of Our Gang*. Avenel, N.J.: Crescent Books, 1993. A pictorial history of the series, with information on cast members.

Maltin, Leonard, and Richard W. Bann. *The Little Rascals: The Life and Times of Our Gang*. New York: Crown, 1992. Includes information on original and subsequent cast members and photographs of scenes and actors.

Ward, Richard Lewis. *A History of the Hal Roach Studios*. Carbondale: Southern Illinois University Press, 2005. An illustrated history supplemented with financial information and synopses of the studio's films and television series.

See also: Academy Awards; Film; Metro-Goldwyn-Mayer (MGM); Roach, Hal, Sr.; Talking motion pictures

■ Ozawa v. United States

The Case: U.S. Supreme Court ruling on whether American residents born in Japan were eligible for citizenship

Date: Decided on November 13, 1922

While white people had been eligible for American citizenship since the founding of the country, and all black persons became citizens upon adoption of the Fifteenth Amendment to the Constitution, the Supreme Court decided in Ozawa v. United States *whether Japanese people could be included in the definition of "white."*

Born in Japan, Takao Ozawa came to the United States in 1894; graduated from high school in Berkeley, California; petitioned with intent to naturalize in 1902; and was a junior at the University of California at the time of the initial court case. His children attended American schools, and the family attended church and spoke English at home. Under U.S. law, he was qualified to be a citizen in every respect but one: his race.

Starting in 1875, Congress had passed a series of laws restricting Asian immigration to the United States. In 1906, Congress passed an immigration act that was perceived as vague regarding those eligible to become American citizens on the basis of race. Ozawa therefore petitioned for citizenship on the ground that Japanese people should be considered "white."

Noting that citizenship was limited to white persons at the founding of the United States, the Supreme Court defined "whites" as members of the Caucasian race. Those born in Japan were deemed non-Caucasians, thus not "white," and therefore ineligible to become citizens.

Impact

The Supreme Court's decision occurred in the midst of an ongoing debate about immigration and a rising tide of anti-Asian sentiment on the West Coast. During the first half of the twentieth century, fears that immigrants were taking jobs away from native-born citizens and changing the character of the nation drove the passage of starkly racist legislation designed to keep out newcomers from Asia as well as from southern and eastern Europe.

The Supreme Court ruling in *Ozawa* fueled the argument that some immigrants, particularly those from Asia, were "unassimilable," or not able to adapt successfully to American culture. Just before this decision, the Immigration Act of 1921 had imposed a national origins quota system as the basis for immigration policy, and these provisions were strengthened in 1924. Under these laws, nearly all immigration from independent Asian countries was halted until 1952.

Michael Haas

Further Reading

Higham, John. *Strangers in the Land: Patterns of American Nativism, 1860–1925*. 2d ed. New York: Atheneum, 1963.

Tichenor, Daniel J. *Dividing Lines: The Politics of Immigration Control in America*. Princeton, N.J.: Princeton University Press, 2002.

Zolberg, Aristide R. *A Nation by Design: Immigration Policy in the Fashioning of America*. Cambridge, Mass.: Harvard University Press, 2006.

See also: Asian Americans; Demographics; Immigration Act of 1921; Immigration Act of 1924; Immigration to the United States; Racial discrimination

P

■ Paddock, Charles

Identification: American athlete
Born: August 11, 1900, Gainesville, Texas
Died: July 21, 1943, Sitka, Alaska

In the early 1920s, Charles William Paddock proved himself to be the world's best sprinter, winning Olympic medals and setting records. While he supported himself financially through journalism and film, he continued to rank among the world's best short-distance runners until his retirement from athletics in 1929.

Concerned about his frailty as a baby, Paddock's parents, Charles H. and Lulu Robinson Paddock, moved with him to Pasadena, California, hoping that the new climate would be beneficial to his health. In 1918, Paddock left high school to join the U.S. Marines. Following the end of World War I, he made an international name for himself at the Inter-Allied Games in France, winning the 100-meter and 200-meter dashes and running on the winning American team in the 4 × 200-meter relay.

In 1919, Paddock enrolled at the University of Southern California, where he lettered in track-and-field from 1920 to 1923 and was captain of the team as a senior. During this time, he also competed internationally. At the 1920 Olympics in Antwerp, Paddock placed first in the 100-meter and second in the 200-meter dash, and he teamed with fellow American runners Jackson Scholz, Loren Murchison, and Morris Kirksey to set a world record of 42.2 seconds in the 4 × 100-meter relay. On April 23, 1921, at an athletic meet in Redlands, California, Paddock ran 100 meters in 10.4 seconds, setting an individual world record. On June 18, 1921, in Pasadena, he did something even more remarkable: He ran 110 yards, slightly more than 100 meters, in 10.2 seconds. While not an official time, he unofficially established a new world record.

In the 1924 Paris Olympics, Paddock placed fifth in the final of the 100-meter and second in the

Charles Paddock at the 1920 Olympic Games. (Popperfoto/Getty Images)

200-meter dash, losing the latter race to Scholz. In 1928, Paddock again won a place on the U.S. Olympic team but won no medals in Amsterdam. He retired from competition the following year.

Having previously worked in both silent film and reporting, Paddock relied on journalism for a living after retiring from track-and-field. He rejoined the Marines at the age of forty-one when the United States entered World War II. On July 21, 1943, he died in a military airplane crash near Sitka, Alaska.

Impact

Known for his well-timed leaps across finish lines, Charles Paddock played a major role in athletics from 1919 until 1929. His official record for the 100-meter dash, 10.4 seconds, remained unbroken until 1930, while his unofficial record of 10.2 seconds would not be bettered until 1956. During this time, among sprinters, Paddock was indeed (as the title of his 1932 book describes him) "the fastest human."

Victor Lindsey

Further Reading

Paddock, Charles W. _The Fastest Human._ New York: T. Nelson & Sons, 1932.

Wallechinsky, David. _The Complete Book of the Summer Olympics._ Wilmington, Del.: Sport Classic Books, 2004.

See also: Olympic Games of 1920 (Summer); Olympic Games of 1924 (Summer); Olympic Games of 1928 (Summer); Scholz, Jackson; Sports; World War I veterans

---

■ Palmer raids

The Event: The arrest of thousands of American resident aliens, including anarchists and prominent leftist leaders, in raids authorized by Attorney General A. Mitchell Palmer

Date: November 7, 1919, and January 2, 1920

Place: Thirty-three cities and towns in twenty-three states

The Palmer raids marked the first massive roundup, incarceration, and, in some cases, deportation of individuals in response to the Red Scare. Fearing that the United States might face a violent overthrow of the government similar to Russia's Bolshevik Revolution in 1917, authorities began to target foreign residents believed to hold dangerous views.

The large influx of immigrants into the United States in the early twentieth century, the aftermath of World War I, and the events of the Russian Revolution created an atmosphere of suspicion and distrust of foreign-born residents, especially advocates of anarchism and communism. A general strike in Seattle in February 1919 further roused fears of a labor-backed uprising. Then, in June, an anarchist group set off bombs in eight American cities, one of which detonated in the home of Attorney General Palmer.

Under the Immigration Act of 1918, only the secretary of labor could issue arrest warrants and sign deportation orders for violations of the Immigration Act. Palmer hired attorney J. Edgar Hoover to investigate and identify known radical groups and their members and used the information Hoover provided to convince the Department of Labor that the Union of Russian Workers posed a threat to the state. The first Palmer raids took place on November 7, 1919, when federal agents arrested hundreds of people in twelve different cities, many of whom had no association with the Russian Workers. On December 21, 249 foreign-born residents were deported to the Soviet Union, 199 of whom were union members arrested during the raids.

After informally persuading some junior Department of Labor officials to expand the list of targets, Hoover organized a new round of raids larger in scope. On January 2, 1920, over four thousand people were arrested at Communist Party and Communist Labor Party meetings. Most were seized without warrants and illegally detained in overcrowded holding facilities. The raids encompassed thirty-three cities in twenty-three states.

Impact

Once the detainees were under the authority of the Department of Labor, the new acting secretary of labor canceled over two thousand deportation warrants on the grounds that they violated due process. Palmer's prediction of a mass antigovernment uprising on May 1, 1920, proved to be false, and the fallout damaged his credibility. A report released by the American Civil Liberties Union, detailing illegal acts committed by the Department of Justice during the raids, was endorsed by prominent lawyers and law professors. Many cases were subsequently dismissed, and of the thousands arrested, only 556 individuals were ever deported. Palmer lost the Democratic nomination for president later that year.

Michael Haas

Further Reading

Hagedorn, Ann. _Savage Peace: Hope and Fear in America, 1919._ New York: Simon & Schuster, 2008.

Murray, Robert K. _Red Scare: A Study in National Hysteria, 1919–1920._ Reprint. Westport, Conn.: Greenwood Press, 1980.

Pietrusza, David. *1920: The Year of the Six Presidents.* New York: Basic Books, 2008.

See also: Civil rights and liberties; Communism; *Gitlow v. New York* (1925); Hoover, J. Edgar; Immigration to the United States; Red Scare, The

■ Parker, Dorothy

Identification: American writer and critic
Also known as: Dorothy Parker Campbell; Dorothy Rothschild
Born: August 22, 1893, West End, New Jersey
Died: June 7, 1967, New York, New York

Known for her acerbic wit, Dorothy Parker was a founding member of the legendary Algonquin Round Table, a daily lunch meeting where writers of the day would exchange witticisms and barbs. Her poetry, critical reviews, and fiction appeared in such prominent publications as The New Yorker, Vanity Fair, *and* Vogue *and made her one of the most important writers of the 1920s. Her outspokenness and independence embodied the "New Woman" ideal of the decade.*

Initially a journalist and drama critic, Dorothy Parker became one of the most quoted of humorous writers. In one famous rhymed quip of the 1920s, she asserted, "Men don't make passes at girls who wear glasses." Parker has sometimes been dismissed as a clever but troubled self-promoter, but scholars and academics recognize her for penning a significant body of work across a variety of literary genres. Her books of poetry were best sellers, and in 1929, she won the O. Henry Award for the best short story for "Big Blonde." She later saw success as a Hollywood screenwriter with then-husband Alan Campbell, winning an Academy Award for the screenplay *A Star Is Born* (1937).

As one of the few female members of the Algonquin Round Table, Parker was a celebrity during the age of the flapper. Her short hair, slim lines in dress, and rejection of Victorian ideas about drinking and casual sex typified the flapper style and attitudes of the decade, yet she also poked fun at the fad in her poem "The Flapper."

During the Round Table years of 1919 to 1929, Parker was an intimate of critic Alexander Woollcott, humorist Robert Benchley, and others, and her sar-

donic wit was often quoted and published in newspaper columns written by members of the group.

Impact
Dorothy Parker is known as a pioneer in women's humor, revealing a sharp and witty perspective on American society. Her writing is marked by irreverence, and she mocks restrictive gender roles, male privilege, and social privilege. In her writing, female characters often judge themselves as lacking in some way, but in reality, Parker was critiquing a society that places women in stultifying roles. In the late 1960s, she became an icon among feminists for her take on women's societal roles. Although much of her poetry was dismissed as "flapper verse," Parker's writing is still published and studied in the early twenty-first century.

Charlotte Templin

Further Reading
Hans, Julia Boissoneau. "Whose Line Is It Anyway? Reclamation of Language in Dorothy Parker's Polyphonic Monologues." *Studies in American Humor,* n.s. 3, no. 17 (2008): 99–116.

Parker, Dorothy. *Complete Stories.* Edited by Colleen Breese and Regina Barreca. New York: Penguin Books, 2003.

Pettit, Rhonda S. *The Critical Waltz: Essays on the Work of Dorothy Parker.* Madison, N.J.: Fairleigh Dickinson University Press, 2005.

See also: Algonquin Round Table; Flappers; Literature in the United States; *New Yorker, The;* Newspapers, U.S.

■ Parrish, Maxfield

Identification: American artist and illustrator
Also known as: Frederick Parrish
Born: July 25, 1870, Philadelphia, Pennsylvania
Died: March 30, 1966, Plainfield, New Hampshire

Maxfield Parrish was an enormously popular artist during the first third of the twentieth century. His talents and techniques coincided with the great age of magazine and book illustration, so his images became known and admired by most literate Americans.

The son of an engraver and landscape painter, Parrish showed artistic talent at an early age. He attended

Haverford College, where he first studied architecture. He later studied at the Pennsylvania Academy of the Fine Arts. One of Parrish's first professional opportunities came in 1897 with a commission to illustrate author L. Frank Baum's book *Mother Goose in Prose*. The turn of the century brought a great surge of popularity for illustrators with the emergence of many new magazines. Color reproduction was refined during this era, making possible a new standard of artistry in print. Parrish illustrated magazine covers for such popular publications as *Hearst's Magazine*, *Collier's Weekly*, and *Life*, among others. He also provided advertisement artwork for manufacturers such as Colgate and Oneida.

In 1920, at age fifty, he was able to retire from most commercial work and focus on painting, living on royalties from his calendar and poster illustrations. Some of his best-known works come from this time, including *Daybreak* (1922), a painting with a luminous, neoclassical setting and partially clothed androgynous figures. During his later career, Parrish turned exclusively to painting landscapes.

Although Parrish produced memorable art for almost his entire adult life, his name is most often associated with the 1920s. This is partly because his popularity peaked then, with an estimated one out of every four households owning a Parrish print. The 1920s was a decade of experimentation in art, and Parrish was a master innovator. His androgynous nudes matched the era's ideal of the slim female figure.

Impact

Parrish's influence on the visual arts was immense, especially during the 1920s. He was highly praised for his method of layering oil color and varnish to create startling colors and an almost three-dimensional effect. The popularity of his subject matter and paintings has endured far beyond his lifetime. Notable musical and literary artists who have used Parrish's concepts or art to enhance their work include Michael Jackson, Elton John, and Kurt Vonnegut.

Emily Alward

Further Reading

Ludwig, Coy L. *Maxfield Parrish*. Atglen, Pa.: Schiffer, 1993.

Wagner, Margaret E. *Maxfield Parrish and the Illustrators of the Golden Age*. San Francisco: Pomegranate, 2000.

See also: Advertising in the United States; Art movements; Book publishing; Home furnishings; Magazines

■ Paul, Alice

Identification: American suffragist, feminist, and activist
Also known as: Alice Stokes Paul
Born: January 11, 1885, Mount Laurel Township, New Jersey
Died: July 9, 1977, Moorestown Township, New Jersey

Alice Paul was an influential figure in the American campaign for women's suffrage and equal rights for women. Known for her militant activism and emphasis on working at the federal level, she was a key figure involved in some of the most significant political achievements for women's rights during the early twentieth century.

Alice Paul toasting the ratification of the Nineteenth Amendment in Tennessee. (Getty Images)

After playing a prominent role in the women's suffrage movement that resulted in the passage of the Nineteenth Amendment to the Constitution in 1920, Paul continued her activism on behalf of women's rights. Though women had obtained the right to vote, Paul pressed for federal legislation that explicitly guaranteed the legal equality of the sexes. The National Woman's Party (NWP), founded and led by Paul, hosted a national convention in 1921 to celebrate suffragist pioneers, discuss the future of the movement, and marshal support for Paul's agenda; however, a significant portion of the convention participants favored more traditional interactions with state legislation, so Paul and the NWP largely pursued their own path. Paul authored several states' equal rights bills and drafted the Equal Rights Amendment (ERA), a proposed constitutional amendment to outlaw discrimination based on gender. The ERA was introduced to Congress in 1923, but it would not be approved until 1972, after which the amendment failed to obtain ratification by two-thirds of the states as required by the U.S. Constitution.

Motivated by her experiences with the nation's political and legal systems, Paul continued her education in the 1920s. Having already completed her doctorate in economics in 1912, Paul earned a series of law degrees during the 1920s, focusing on common law traditions that prevented women's full participation in the workforce. She also traveled extensively, both nationally and abroad, in an attempt to galvanize support among like-minded individuals and organizations.

Impact

Alice Paul influenced several generations of activists organized for the advancement of women's rights. She successfully lobbied for the United Nations to include references to gender equality in the United Nations Charter and for gender discrimination to be included as a category of discrimination addressed in the U.S. Civil Rights Act of 1964.

Brad Stoddard

Further Reading

Adams, Katherine H., and Michael L. Keene. *Alice Paul and the American Suffrage Campaign.* Urbana: University of Illinois Press, 2008.

Butler, Amy E. *Two Paths to Equality: Alice Paul and Ethel M. Smith in the ERA Debate, 1921–1929.* Albany: State University of New York Press, 2002.

Lunardini, Christine A. *From Equal Suffrage to Equal Rights: Alice Paul and the National Woman's Party, 1910–1928.* New York: New York University Press, 1986.

See also: Equal Rights Amendment; Nineteenth Amendment; Voting rights; Women in college; Women's rights

■ Peanut butter and jelly sandwiches

Many technological advances of the 1920s made life easier for Americans. Two such changes were the invention of the automatic bread slicer and the patent for churning peanuts into nonseparating butter, which made the peanut butter and jelly sandwich possible. Peanut butter and jelly sandwiches could be easily and cheaply prepared while still being flavorful and nutritious, and many Americans embraced the new combination.

The ingredients of the peanut butter and jelly sandwich came from different regions of the world and from varying eras. The peanut, a legume, was a staple of Brazil for centuries and was later cultivated in the Carolinas and Georgia during American colonial times. Dr. John Kellogg of Battle Creek, Michigan, served peanut butter in the 1890s as a dietary supplement for the sick and elderly in his sanatorium. Early peanut butters were not initially popular among consumers, however, because of their bitter taste and because the ingredients separated easily, which required constant remixing.

Jelly, on the other hand, had been a common food in Europe and Great Britain since the Middle Ages. Cooks discovered they could preserve fruit and fruit juice by boiling it and combining it with sugar, so jams and jellies were popular as desserts and spreads. Bread, the "staff of life," was an ancient household staple. The loaves were cut as needed with slices often varying in thickness or width.

The year 1928 was a landmark for all the ingredients required for peanut butter and jelly sandwiches. Joseph Rosenfield, a California food entrepreneur, had obtained a patent for the process for churning roasted peanuts into a paste that retained the natural oil and could be stored without refrigeration for up to a year; in 1928, Rosenfield licensed that spread to Pond Company, which began selling it under the brand name Peter Pan. The Chillicothe Baking Company of Chillicothe, Missouri, sold the first commercially presliced loaf of bread in 1928 after Otto Rohwedder introduced his invention, a machine that evenly sliced bread and then wrapped it. Not surprisingly, sandwich bread soon became a staple in most American lunches. That same year, Florence Cowles published the cookbook *Seven Hundred Sandwiches*, which had recipes for several kinds of peanut butter sandwiches combined with other ingredients, one of which was jelly.

Impact

Peanut butter and jelly sandwiches were the result of two 1920s innovations: nonseparating peanut butter and the bread slicing machine. The new sandwiches provided Americans with a quick and nutritious meal that remains a staple in American households even in the early twenty-first century.

Julia Meyers

Further Reading

Liberman, Sherri, ed. *American Food by the Decades.* Santa Barbara, Calif.: Greenwood Press, 2011.

Smith, Andrew F., ed. *Oxford Encyclopedia of Food and Drink in America.* 2 vols. New York: Oxford University Press, 2004.

Tannahill, Reay. *Food in History.* New York: Crown Trade, 1995.

See also: Agriculture in the United States; Bread slicer; Inventions

■ Pershing Map

The Pershing Map, created in 1922, was the first systematic attempt to survey existing U.S. roads and to establish a unified national policy for interstate routes. The plan emphasized military preparedness and favored heavy industry and development along the coasts. Roads identified as military priorities would receive preference for federal highway funding.

The United States' entry into World War I brought into focus the primitive condition of most U.S. roads and their inadequacy in meeting defense needs. Wartime also provided a convenient platform for promoting commercial development. The lack of transportation infrastructure that hindered the movement of troops and supplies also increased manufacturing costs, inhibited growth outside of cities, and contributed to regional isolation.

In 1919 and 1920, the U.S. Army organized two motor convoys across the United States to identify barriers to transcontinental military operations. At the time, most defenses were based on the East Coast, while the threat of invasion from Mexico and Asia was an increasing concern. The 1919 convoy left Washington, D.C., on July 7 and arrived in San Francisco on September 6. Following the route of the Lincoln Highway, more than half of which was unimproved dirt road, it averaged 57 miles per day. The 1920 convoy, which followed a more southerly route to San Diego, averaged fewer than 30 miles per day.

In 1921, as part of a general plan to establish a national highway system, Bureau of Public Roads director Thomas MacDonald asked the Army to supply a prioritized list of those routes most critical to national defense. The United States Geological Survey sent out teams to do a detailed survey of these routes, and the results were summarized in a massive, 32-foot-long map, which General John Pershing presented to Congress in 1922. Priority roads were concentrated on the East and West Coasts, along the Mexican border, and around the Great Lakes, while little attention was paid to the South. No separate legislation funded these specific roads, but the map did influence later decisions regarding funding.

By the time the Pershing Map appeared before Congress, war fever and concern for defense had ebbed. The growth of civilian automobile culture and the current needs of rapidly expanding industries and population centers would dictate the nation's road-building trajectory instead.

Impact

The degree to which the Pershing Map contributed to overall highway policy in the 1920s is difficult to assess, since the nation's taste for war and preoccupation with military concerns had already begun to wane. Future president Dwight D. Eisenhower, who participated in the 1919 convoy and was subsequently involved in drawing up the plans for the map, would become a strong supporter of the U.S. interstate highway system, and many of the superhighways established during his administration follow the routes originally outlined in 1922.

Martha Sherwood

Further Reading

Batchelder, A. G. "The Immediate Necessity for Military Highways." *National Geographic* 32 (December, 1917): 477–499.

Gutfreund, Owen D. *Twentieth Century Sprawl: Highways and the Reshaping of the American Landscape.* New York: Oxford University Press, 2005.

Kaszynski, William. *The American Highway: The History and Culture of Roads in the United States.* Jefferson, N.C.: McFarland, 2000.

See also: Automobiles and auto manufacturing; Federal Aid Highway Act of 1921; Federal highway system; National Conference on Street and Highway Safety (1924, 1926); Route 66; Transportation; Travel

■ Phillips, C. Coles

Identification: American artist and illustrator
Born: October 3, 1880, Springfield, Ohio
Died: June 13, 1927, New Rochelle, New York

C. Coles Phillips was a prolific artist and illustrator of the 1910s and 1920s. He was known primarily for his illustrations of sensual yet innocent young women, which were featured on the covers of many popular magazines.

By the 1920s, C. Coles Phillips was already one of the most successful illustrators in the United States. His watercolor images graced the covers of magazines such as *Life, Ladies' Home Journal, Saturday Evening Post*, and *Good Housekeeping*, and frequently appeared in successful advertisements and popular books. Phillips's specialty was images of young women, often in their underwear or nightgowns, sometimes dressed in the latest fashions. His women, whom he always painted from life, were all-American beauties: wholesome and beautiful, sexy without being naughty. He was the creator of the "fade-away girl," a kind of image in which the clothing of the woman in the foreground matched the color of the background so that she seemed to be fading away, distinguished only in places where fine lines detailed buttons or hems. These intriguing and eye-catching images had the added benefit of being less expensive, as magazines could print them in only one or two colors, unlike the four-color images created by other artists.

In the 1920s, Phillips continued to expand his repertoire and to draw critical and popular attention.

He won a competition to portray the "Spirit of Transportation" in 1920 and created the mildly scandalous "Miss Sunburn" for a suntan lotion advertisement in 1924. In 1921 and 1922, Phillips contributed some illustrations to the yearbook of the U.S. Naval Academy, the *Lucky Bag.* The original paintings for his illustrations were highly sought after by collectors, and he created several images directly for the art market.

Phillips was diagnosed with kidney disease in 1924, and ill health forced him to give up his art shortly before his death in 1927. One of the last books he illustrated was Temple Bailey's best-selling novel *Peacock Feathers*, published in 1924 and made into a movie in 1925.

Impact

Phillips's illustrations were wildly popular, capturing the new sense of freedom that women felt in the years after World War I. His use of Art Deco design elements in advertising and his creation of the fade-away girl influenced later artists, and the increasing sensuality of his images of women opened the door for the more provocative illustrations that would follow.

Cynthia A. Bily

Further Reading

Ermoyan, Arpi. *Famous American Illustrators.* Edison, N.J.: Chartwell Books, 2002.

Platnick, Norman I. *The Fade-Away Lady: A Collector's Guide to Coles Phillips and Valentine Sandberg.* Bay Shore, N.Y.: Enchantment Ink, 2007.

Schau, Michael. *All-American Girl: The Art of Coles Phillips.* New York: Watson-Guptill, 1975.

See also: Advertising in the United States; Art Deco; Art movements; Fashions and clothing; Magazines; Parrish, Maxfield

■ Philosophy and philosophers

During the 1920s, philosophy in America transitioned between focusing on broad social philosophical concerns, such as the nature of democracy, citizenship, and the role of public education, to primarily more technical, academic concerns, such as the nature of knowledge and fundamental claims about reality as a whole. Philosophy as a discipline became less central to public discussions and policy making, instead becoming more technical and professionalized as an academic endeavor.

Beginning in the late eighteenth century and continuing throughout much of the history of the United States, philosophy was part of the broad intellectual and social life of the country. The political philosophy of the Enlightenment was openly and explicitly woven into foundational documents in American history, such as the Declaration of Independence and the U.S. Constitution. Some of the country's Founding Fathers, including Thomas Jefferson and Benjamin Franklin, were acknowledged by their contemporary philosophers in Europe as serious academic thinkers as well as political and social activists. The movement that came to be known as American Transcendentalism was widely influential in the first half of the nineteenth century, due in large part to the writings of intellectuals Henry David Thoreau and Ralph Waldo Emerson. By the beginning of the twentieth century, however, philosophy in America had become less public and more academic, technical, and specialized, as had other intellectual fields of study.

Pragmatism

Throughout the 1920s, the predominant and most influential school of philosophical thought in America was pragmatism. Beginning as far back as the late 1860s with the works of philosophers Charles Sanders Peirce and William James, pragmatism had become the tradition most associated with American intellectual life during the early twentieth century. Pragmatism was in part a response to, and rejection of, much of the history of western European philosophical thought. In particular, pragmatism rejected much of what was seen as abstract philosophical problems. The term *pragmatism* can be traced to the Greek word for "deed" or "action." Pragmatists thus emphasized the practical effects and consequences of holding some philosophical view. For example, a long-standing philosophical question had been whether people's actions were determined by external causes or were the result of the person's free will. James posited that what mattered were the practical consequences of accepting one or the other of these views. Underlying this attitude was the notion that a belief or claim is empty and meaningless unless there are some practical consequences that result from holding that belief or making that claim.

Professor John Dewey was a prominent pragmatist philosopher during the 1920s, although he called his philosophical perspective "instrumentalism," not pragmatism. His writings were voluminous and spanned most areas of philosophy: metaphysics, epistemology, ethics, aesthetics, and political philosophy, among others. Among his important works during this decade were *Experience and Nature* (1925), *The Public and Its Problems* (1927), and *The Quest for Certainty* (1929). Dewey argued that people in general seek simple answers to questions and problems, which they tend to portray in an either-or approach. According to Dewey's pragmatic philosophy, thinking in terms of binary opposition is mistaken. For Dewey, inquiry is the result of interaction between people, other organisms, and their often-changing environments. He posited that action is based on responses to those environments. Dewey also argued that natural and social science reveal the workings of the world and that scientists can generate testable hypotheses based on their observations. Knowledge, including moral knowledge, is a matter of interactive experience, according to Dewey, not a matter of acquiring absolute certainty about eternal, unchanging truths. Dewey saw the quest for certainty as not only mistaken but a source of intolerance and conflict as it promotes the view that there is a single, correct description of the world and a single, correct view about things, so all other descriptions or views are wrong and must be rejected. This did not mean, for Dewey, that all descriptions and views were equally valid. His understanding was that knowledge is a matter of interactive experience during which one learns what works and what does not. Truth, he claimed, is not a matter of latching onto some eternal reality but rather of having justification to act on the basis of a belief.

This pragmatist conception of truth and knowledge found practical application in social arenas. Supreme Court justice Oliver Wendell Holmes Jr. openly identified his view of the nature of law as legal pragmatism. Based on the pragmatist notion that how something functions is the nature of that thing, Holmes claimed that what really makes something a law and thus has the power of regulating people's behaviors is what the courts actually enforce. If Congress passes some piece of legislation but no court ever makes a ruling that is consistent with that legislation, then, according to Holmes, that legislation is not really law; it has no impact or consequence on anyone's actions. Holmes referred to this pragmatist view of the law as the "bad man theory" of law, meaning law is simply what can be expected to happen to people who misbehave in certain ways.

Process Philosophy

Dewey and pragmatism were heavily influenced by the understanding of the world that was part of biological evolutionary theory. Charles Darwin and other biologists had also rejected views of the world as eternal and unchanging. Dewey saw evolutionary biology as dovetailing with the pragmatist view of interactive experience and responses to changing environments. In the Scopes trial of 1925, which challenged the teaching of evolution in American schools, social critic H. L. Mencken noted connections between pragmatist philosophy and evolutionary science. Just as evolutionary science had an impact on philosophy, he argued, so did contemporary physics. This was especially true of the scientific revolution brought about by the theories of physicist Albert Einstein as they related to the philosophical thought and work of philosopher Alfred North Whitehead and what came to be called "process philosophy."

Einstein had argued that when thinking of the basic nature of the universe, it was important to note that things exist in and must be understood in four dimensions: three dimensions of space and one dimension of time. According to Einstein, space and time are so closely connected that the world should be thought of as being in space-time. That is, space and time are not absolute facts or features about the universe but rather they are relative systems we use to make sense of our experiences.

Whitehead drew on this notion of four-dimensionality and claimed that reality should be conceived of as an event-based ontology. Ontology is the study of what makes up the world. Usually people think the world is made up of actual things, such as physical objects, animals, and so forth. However, Whitehead argued that events actually constitute the basic elements of the world. The facts of nature, he claimed, must be understood in terms of their spatial and temporal relations—that is, how they relate to other facts of nature in terms of space and time. As he put it, "Nature is known to us in our experience as a complex of passing events." This view applies easily to discussing events, or occurrences, such as the ringing of a bell or the barking of a dog. The event of a bell ringing is not the same thing as the bell itself, Whitehead argued, nor is it the same thing as the sound that is made by the bell. He concluded that the event of the bell ringing is distinct from the things involved in that event. Whitehead went so far as to claim that what we usually think of as "things" are in

Philosopher Alfred North Whitehead (Hulton Archive/Getty Images)

fact events. For example, a bell might be seen as an event because it came into existence at some point and will go out of existence at some point. Its very nature is a set of space-time relations, just as the ringing of a bell is a set of space-time relations. For Whitehead, then, what we normally consider objects are really events, although from our perspective they are "frozen" events.

Given his view that the fundamental facts of nature are not things but events, Whitehead noted that the basic concepts of nature used in modern science are concepts like energy and interactions and processes. He sometimes spoke of this as the view of "nature alive." What he meant was that the world is not simply a collection of objects but is instead processes, interconnections, and transformations. It is creative development and transition, not permanent structures, which are fundamental to nature and to experience. This view of process philosophy was spelled out in a number of Whitehead's writings during the

1920s, including *The Concept of Nature* (1920), *Science and the Modern World* (1925), and *Process and Reality* (1929).

Impact

Some philosophers of the 1920s made important contributions to American culture broadly, especially Dewey, who had a significant impact on public education and political life, as well as nonprofessionals, such as African American intellectual leaders W. E. B. Du Bois and Alain Locke, who were very influential in promoting racial equality and civil rights. Lesser-known academic thinkers, such as Whitehead, wrote on fundamental concerns regarding the nature and function of education as well as the relations between philosophy and the natural and social sciences. The decade saw an increased professionalization of philosophy that continued throughout the rest of the twentieth century. A serious revival of "public" philosophy did not take place until toward the end of the century, with the social and political writings of philosophers John Rawls and Richard Rorty.

David Boersema

Further Reading

Harris, Leonard, Scott L. Pratt, and Anne S. Waters, eds. *American Philosophies: An Anthology*. Malden, Mass.: Blackwell, 2002. Offers a history of philosophical movements in the United States.

Hollinger, David A., and Charles Capper, eds. *The American Intellectual Tradition, Volume II: 1865 to the Present*. 6th ed. New York: Oxford University Press, 2010. Presents information on developments in American philosophy, psychology, social history, and other types of intellectual history. Also features chronologies, notes, and suggestions for further reading.

Kuklick, Bruce. *A History of Philosophy in America, 1720–2000*. New York: Clarendon Press, 2007. Discusses American philosophy in three periods, including the pragmatic period of philosophy predominant between 1859 and 1934.

Lachs, John, and Robert B. Talisse, eds. *American Philosophy: An Encyclopedia*. New York: Routledge, 2008. A scholarly examination of trends in American philosophy, including an analytical index, cross-references, and definitions of key terms.

Marsoobian, Armen T., and John Ryder, eds. *The Blackwell Guide to American Philosophy*. New York: Blackwell, 2007. Features essays on American phil-osophical movements such as pragmatism, including bibliographies.

See also: Dewey, John; Du Bois, W. E. B.; Education; Holmes, Oliver Wendell, Jr.; Mencken, H. L.; Physics; Science and technology; Scopes trial (1925); Social sciences

■ Photography

In the 1920s, photography was becoming more widely appreciated as a fine art and beginning to prove its value as a news and advertising medium. In everyday life, camera images grew to be an enduring aspect of Americans' understanding of society and themselves.

In the early 1920s, the leading American art photographer of the preceding two decades, Alfred Stieglitz, emerged from a period of personal retrenchment that had culminated in the closing of his New York gallery, 291, in 1917. It had been a modest and largely noncommercial venture that nonetheless earned lasting renown as a fulcrum of modernism in the arts in the United States. Stieglitz marked his reemergence as a creative artist with a 1921 solo exhibition that represented the scope of his work over more than three decades. The show also included a series of recent photographs of his companion, American painter Georgia O'Keeffe, whom he would marry in 1924. The photographs of O'Keeffe, the beginnings of a "collective portrait" of her that would occupy Stieglitz into the 1930s, included intimate views of her face and body that provided a conclusive challenge to conventions of portraiture and the nude, which still had limited currency in the photographic salons of the time.

Edward Steichen had been a close associate of Stieglitz for over two decades, first as cofounder of 291 and then as the gallery's talent scout in Europe. After serving in World War I as a specialist in photography with the American Expeditionary Forces, he remained in France for several years and then returned to the United States in order to reestablish his photographic career. Steichen was soon drawn into the fields of fashion and advertising photography, serving as a highly paid chief photographer for Condé Nast Publications and becoming one the most prolific and celebrated photographers of the twentieth century.

Eastman Kodak Company

For nearly half a century following its initial conviction under the Sherman Act in 1913, and for more than twenty years after its 1927 conviction by the Supreme Court, the Eastman Kodak Company continued to maintain an estimated 90 percent share of its market, with no measurable change. It remained America's largest manufacturer of cameras, photographic and motion-picture film, and supplies. Its branches were international. If antitrust prosecutions had any effect on it, they were most discernible in what experts defined as the medium ease of entry by others into Eastman's fields of enterprise. By most criteria, Eastman's advantages were enormous, muted only by litigation.

Pictorialism and Straight Photography

Steichen's penchant for creating stylish, accessible images and his aggressive marketing of his talents and personality created a rift between himself and Stieglitz that embodies some of tensions and complexities in photographic practice and history. Yet both men's photographs from the 1920s typify the growing ascendance of straight photography, a style that increasingly characterized the medium during that decade and after. In broad terms, straight photography is the successor to pictorialism, the more classical artistic style that Stieglitz and Steichen had practiced and promoted years earlier. Pictorialism retained a popular following in the 1920s through the support of such groups as the Pictorial Photographers of America, which had been founded in 1916. While pictorialism stressed the kinship of photography to the graphic arts of the time, emulating the appearance of paintings and etchings by consistently pursuing soft focus and muted tonality, straight photography embraced the clarity of camera optics and exploited the dynamic tonal range of contemporary photographic materials.

The transition from soft-focus pictorialism to straight photography was apparent on the West Coast as well as in the East. In California, photographers such as Edward Weston and Imogen Cunningham, who by the early 1920s had developed successful careers based upon a refined pictorialist aesthetic, were beginning to embrace a new, precise way of composing and printing photographs that paralleled not only the work of their contemporaries in the East but also that of advanced photographers in Europe. The 1920s saw increasing cross-fertilization in photography between Europe and North America by means of exhibitions, publications, and travel. In 1921, the avant-garde painter and photographer Man Ray left New York for Paris, followed by advertising photographer and graphic designer Paul Outerbridge in 1925. Both had been frequent visitors to Stieglitz's 291 gallery, and each moved away from the elder artist's purist approach to photography by maintaining dual identities as both artists and commercial photographers.

Among the leading modernist photographers of the 1920s were Paul Strand and Charles Sheeler, both also associated with Stieglitz. Strand's wide-ranging interests included filmmaking, and in 1921, he collaborated with Sheeler on *Manhatta*, a short experimental film that was closely tied to their own still photography of New York and has since been entered into the U.S. National Film Registry. Sheeler, also a painter, went on to produce work that would integrate his photography and his painting to an unprecedented degree, as can be seen in his varied series of images from 1927 depicting the Ford Motor Company's River Rouge plant.

Photography and Society

It can be difficult to draw a line between photography as an art form and photography that serves social processes and needs, particularly when assessing the work of documentary photographers. Early in her career, pictorialist Doris Ulmann produced a series of portraits of literary, artistic, and intellectual figures, among them American educator John Dewey, Russian ballerina Anna Pavlova, and British poet William Butler Yeats. Later, however, she applied her signature portrait style to the documentation of the residents of remote rural communities in the southern Appalachians, thus anticipating the major government-sponsored photographic projects of the 1930s that were conceived as instruments of social change. In the Southwest, Laura Gilpin's work in the 1920s evolved from romantic, soft-focus pictorialism toward an eloquent engagement with the landscapes and native peoples of the region. The later work of sociologist and photographer Lewis Hine includes not only themes of poverty but also images that celebrate labor, such as *Powerhouse Mechanic Working on*

Steam Pump (1920), one of the most admired photographs of the twentieth century.

Other photographers who are popularly associated with the 1930s achieved substantial mastery in the previous decade, notably Walker Evans and Margaret Bourke-White. After spending a year in Paris studying literature, Evans returned to New York, where he soon established a distinctive photographic style. Among his tools was the Leica camera, introduced in Germany in 1925, which Evans employed as if it were a photographic notebook. Bourke-White began photography as a hobby, but after obtaining a bachelor's degree in biology from Cornell University in 1927, she opened a studio and began to specialize in industrial photography. Her photographs for the Otis Steel Company in 1929 achieved a drama rare in documentary and industrial photography and doubtless contributed to her being hired as a staff photographer for Henry Luce's *Fortune* magazine, which first appeared in February of 1930.

As wide-ranging as Bourke-White's photography was to become, it was a British photographer, E. O. Hoppé, who first succeeded in producing a comprehensive photographic presentation of the United States. German-born, of French ancestry, but ultimately British by choice, Hoppé was perhaps the most famous photographer of his time. His first visit to the United States, in 1919, was for the purpose of photographing New York and some of its celebrities, as well as sounding out the prospects for a branch of his London studio, which he would return to establish in 1921. In 1925 and 1926, he traveled across the United States several times, taking hundreds of photographs of cities and towns, landscapes, and everyday people; his book *Romantic America*, published in 1927, asserted on its title page that it was "The First Popular Pictorial Presentation of Our Country." The extraordinary acuity of his social vision and the technical quality of his camera work make *Romantic America* a landmark of photographic modernism.

Photographic representation of the nation's Native American, African American, and other ethnic groups was offered by practitioners both from within and without these communities. From his studio in New York's Harlem district, African American photographer James Van Der Zee chronicled daily life and noted personalities, including those associated with the Harlem Renaissance. Japanese American amateur photographers in Los Angeles, San Francisco, Seattle, and elsewhere on the West Coast formed camera clubs that met to exchange ideas and stage exhibitions. Edward Curtis, who had begun photographing native peoples in the American and Canadian West as early as the mid-1890s, was able to finance the publication of the final volumes of his twenty-volume *The North American Indian* only after taking work in 1920 as a still photographer and movie camera operator in Hollywood film studios.

Impact

Although daguerreotyping, the first widely used photographic process, had been introduced to the public in 1839, it was only during the 1920s that photography became integral to journalism and advertising. The long-anticipated practical transmission of photographs by telephone and telegraph began in earnest in the early 1920s, forever changing the fundamental requirements of daily journalism. In advertising, photographs began to overtake illustrations as a successful means of selling both products and ideas, thereby contributing substantially to the rise of consumerism.

Within the fine arts, photography came to be seen as an indispensable means of interrogating and understanding the social and physical worlds, and it also afforded artists new forms of vision and expression. By the end of the decade, photography had begun to participate fully in the advanced cultural currents of the time and would soon come to be regarded as an essential art form, rather than a peripheral or auxiliary one. The contributions of such notable art photographers as Stieglitz, Steichen, Weston, Strand, Evans, and Bourke-White helped establish photography as an artistic medium unto itself.

Clyde S. McConnell

Further Reading

Davis, Keith F. *An American Century of Photography: From Dry Plate to Digital.* 2d ed. Kansas City, Mo.: Hallmark Cards, 1999. A survey that includes chronological essays alongside reproductions of infrequently seen photographic works.

Greenough, Sarah, ed. *Modern Art and America: Alfred Stieglitz and His New York Galleries.* Washington, D.C.: National Gallery of Art, 2000. Presents 350 reproductions of the art that Stieglitz exhibited and fostered over four decades, alongside essays on the individual artists.

Guimond, James. *American Photography and the American Dream.* Chapel Hill: University of North Carolina Press, 1991. A guide to the themes and effects of documentary photography in America, including an appraisal of the work of Lewis Hine during the 1920s.

Johnson, Patricia. *Real Fantasies: Edward Steichen's Advertising Photography.* Berkeley: University of California Press, 2000. A comprehensive scholarly study of Steichen's work and career that also addresses major issues in the evolution of advertising in the 1920s and later.

McEuen, Melissa A. *Seeing America: Women Photographers Between the Wars.* Lexington: University Press of Kentucky, 2000. A collection of essays on five canonical women photographers, all but one of whom were producing important images in the 1920s.

Prodger, Philip. *E. O. Hoppé's Amerika: Modernist Photographs from the 1920s.* New York: W. W. Norton, 2007. Includes an introductory essay that compares Hoppé's 1920s-era photographs with those of later leading American photographers.

Tsujimoto, Karen. *Images of America: Precisionist Painting and Modern Photography.* Seattle: University of Washington Press, 1982. An exhibition catalog that explores the unparalleled alignment of photography with painting that emerged in the 1920s, featuring comprehensive illustrations and biographies of thirty-four artists.

See also: Advertising in the United States; Architecture; Art movements; Harlem Renaissance; Museum of Modern Art (MoMA); O'Keeffe, Georgia; Stieglitz, Alfred; Van Der Zee, James

■ Physics

The physics community in the United States made a number of breakthroughs in the 1920s, including definitively establishing the particle nature of electromagnetic radiation and the wave nature of elementary particles. Such accomplishments, along with the increasing number of physics degrees earned throughout the decade, allowed the United States to establish a foundation for further scientific breakthroughs.

Throughout the 1920s, physics took on a new significance in the United States. Nearly one thousand Americans earned Ph.D.'s in physics in that time, twice as many as in the previous fifty years. European physicists were frequent visitors to American colleges and universities during the decade, and Albert Einstein and Marie Curie toured the country to popular acclaim, inspiring many young men and women to study physics. A number of these students studied abroad with noted scientists and research institutions, while others remained in the United States to study at developing institutions such as the California Institute of Technology.

Pure Physics

The great unsolved problems of physics in the 1920s centered on the nature of the atom and the mysteries of the quantum nature of energy. Many of the decade's discoveries built upon earlier work: Near the beginning of the twentieth century, Max Planck of Germany had resolved a long-standing paradox of heat radiation by postulating that energy could only be emitted or absorbed in discrete packets called quanta. Albert Einstein used Planck's insight to explain the photoelectric effect—the ability of light to eject electrons from certain metals—while Niels Bohr of Denmark used Planck's theory to explain the emission and absorption of light by hydrogen atoms. For these discoveries, the two were awarded the Nobel Prize in Physics for 1921 and 1922, respectively, and their work inspired further research. American physicist Robert A. Millikan performed experiments dealing with the photoelectric effect and also worked to determine the electrical charge of the electron. His discoveries validated Einstein's and Bohr's theories, and his measurement of the charge of the electron through his oil-drop experiment resulted in a reasonably accurate value. For his contributions to the field, Millikan received the Nobel Prize in Physics in 1923.

By the 1920s, atoms were known to be made up of a positively charged nucleus surrounded by electrons. Likewise, x-rays were known to be electromagnetic waves of very short wavelength. As classical waves, they were expected to scatter off of the electrons in a metal without experiencing a change in wavelength. In 1920, Arthur Holly Compton of Washington University in St. Louis, Missouri, discovered that in fact the scattered x-rays were of a longer wavelength, and thus lower in energy, than the x-rays striking the material—a phenomenon dubbed the "Compton effect." Einstein's photoelectric theory suggested that light could interact with electrons as particles, called photons, instead of as waves. Compton studied interactions between x-rays and electrons as particle collisions and was able to precisely explain the relationship between x-ray scattering angle and wavelength, determining that x-rays scattered from charged electrons as though they were particles instead of waves. This confirmed the existence of photons, and Compton shared the Nobel Prize in Physics in 1927 for the discovery.

In 1924, French physicist Louis de Broglie suggested that if electromagnetic waves could act as particles, then perhaps particles could also act as waves. This theory was confirmed by American physicist Clinton J. Davisson and his colleagues at Bell Laboratories, who were engaged in the study of how electrons scatter from metals. They discovered a scattering pattern incompatible with the particle nature of electrons, but exactly what would be expected from waves of the type predicted by de Broglie, thus confirming his theory.

In previous decades, the spontaneous ionization of gases in sealed containers had been explained as the effect of intense radioactivity of unknown origin. Victor Francis Hess of Austria had measured the intensity of this radiation at various altitudes and discovered that it initially declined with altitude but then increased at very high altitudes to intensities many times higher than surface values. Based on the data collected, he concluded that the radiation was of extraterrestrial origin. In 1925, Millikan embarked on a series of experiments to test Hess's hypothesis. He measured radiation on airplanes and balloons at various altitudes and determined the intensity of the radiation at different elevations on land and at different depths below the surface. His results conclusively proved Hess's theory to be correct. Millikan named the radiation "cosmic rays" and theorized that the rays were high-energy photons created by the fusion of hydrogen atoms in interstellar space.

However, many physicists were skeptical of Millikan's explanation of cosmic rays. According to Millikan's theory, cosmic rays should not be deflected by Earth's magnetic field and should instead bombard Earth uniformly from all directions. If the cosmic rays were charged particles, however, they would be deflected by Earth's magnetic field, and this deflection would be affected by latitude-based variations in the strength of the field. In the late 1920s and the following decade, numerous scientists, including Compton, who believed the rays to be composed of charged particles, continued to perform research in this area.

Near the end of the 1920s, quantum mechanics began to blur the distinction between physics and chemistry. Richard C. Tolman investigated the properties of molecules in excited quantum states, while P. M. Morse applied the theory of wave mechanics developed by Erwin Schrödinger in 1927 to diatomic molecules. Linus C. Pauling traveled to Europe on a Guggenheim Fellowship to study quantum mechanics under various scientists, including Niels Bohr and Arnold Sommerfeld of Germany. After returning to the United States in 1927 and taking a position at the California Institute of Technology, Pauling began to develop a quantitative theory of chemical bonding based on the theory of quantum mechanics, building upon the work of Tolman and Morse.

Applied Physics

In 1921, Joseph Valasek discovered a new class of crystals that exhibit a spontaneous electric polarization. Valasek christened them "ferroelectrics," because their polarization behavior in variable electric fields strongly resembles the behavior of ferromagnetic materials such as iron in variable magnetic fields. Ferroelectrics would go on to be used in infrared cameras and as nonvolatile memory in computers. The same year, Walter G. Cady developed the first quartz crystal oscillator based on his studies of piezoelectric crystals, which become electrically polarized when mechanically deformed. Cady discovered that they will also vibrate when polarized with an external electric field oscillating at one specific frequency. This extremely stable vibration would lead to the use of piezoelectrics in high-precision clocks and radios.

Despite the expectations of many physicists that radio waves would not follow the curvature of the earth, transatlantic radio communication had proved possible, leading scientists to theorize the existence of conducting layers high in the atmosphere that refracted radio signals and allowed them to "bounce" to their destinations. In 1926, A. Hoyt Taylor and E. O. Hulburt of the Naval Research Laboratory in Washington, D.C., published a theory that postulated a reflecting layer of free electrons in the atmosphere; meanwhile, Merle A. Tuve and Gregory Breit of Johns Hopkins University used pulse-echo techniques to measure the altitude of one such ionized layer of atmosphere, which would later become known as the ionosphere. The development of communications technology was further carried out by Vladimir Zworykin of the Westinghouse Corporation, who worked to develop primitive television systems based on the cathode ray tube, a device that uses a scanning electron beam to draw pictures on a fluorescent screen. Philo Farnsworth pursued a parallel line of development with private funding in California.

Physics in U.S. Society

Physics in the 1920s was somewhat hampered by restrictions on international cooperation established after World War I. Institutions such as the National Academy of Sciences (NAS) and the National Research Council (NRC) actively discouraged the participation of German physicists in scientific meetings and congresses. Despite this, many American physicists circumvented the NRC and NAS by meeting with their German counterparts independently.

The social changes of the 1920s further shaped the field of physics as women, who had entered the workforce in significant numbers during World War I and been granted the right to vote in 1920, took on a larger role in the sciences and in academia in general. Many women looked to college for new opportunities, and half of all undergraduates during the 1920s were female. The number of scientific Ph.D.'s awarded to women increased during the decade, although the percentage of female physics Ph.D.s recipients remained steady at little more than 3 percent. After completing their studies, some women found work in the new industrial laboratories, which needed technical workers and were open to hiring women. In 1921, the U.S. Civil Service Commission abandoned sex-based restrictions on qualifying examinations for scientific positions.

Two of the nation's most successful scientific institutions rose to prominence in the 1920s. Throop Polytechnic Institute, established late in the previous century, was renamed the California Institute of Technology, or Caltech, in 1921. Caltech attracted numerous influential scientists during the 1920s, including Millikan, who took on the position of chairman of the executive council, becoming the effective president of the institute. In the realm of research and development, the research laboratories of the Western Electric Company and the American Telephone and Telegraph Company (AT&T) were con-solidated into Bell Telephone Laboratories in 1925. Bell Labs was responsible for a number of technological achievements during the late 1920s, including the invention of a synchronous-sound system for talking motion pictures.

Impact

Many physicists of the 1920s, including Clinton Davisson and Linus Pauling, would go on to win the Nobel Prize for the research they performed during the decade. In addition, further research would be conducted based on the period's discoveries, including additional groundbreaking research into the nature of cosmic rays that would lead to the discovery of such new elementary particles as the positron and the muon. The increased understanding of the nature of the atom gained during the 1920s would lead to the development of the atomic bomb and nuclear power in later decades.

Billy R. Smith Jr.

Further Reading

Gamow, George. *Thirty Years That Shook Physics: The Story of Quantum Theory.* New York: Dover Books, 1966. Discusses the development of atomic and nuclear physics between 1895 and 1945.

Heilbron, John L. ed. *The Oxford Guide to the History of Physics and Astronomy.* New York: Oxford University Press, 2005. Provides a thorough account of the history of physics, including the developments of the 1920s.

Kevles, Daniel J. *The Physicists: The History of a Scientific Community in Modern America.* Cambridge, Mass.: Harvard University Press, 1995. Covers the history of physics in the United States from 1800 to 1995, with four chapters devoted to the 1920s.

Pais, Abraham. *Inward Bound: Of Matter and Forces in the Physical World.* New York: Oxford University Press, 1986. Places the discoveries of the 1920s within a contemporary and historical context.

_____. *Niels Bohr's Times, in Physics, Philosophy and Polity.* Oxford: Clarendon Press, 1991. Explores Niels Bohr's influence over the field of physics during the 1920s.

See also: Bell Labs; California Institute of Technology (Caltech); Compton, Arthur Holly; Einstein, Albert; Millikan, Robert Andrews; Nobel Prizes; Science and technology; Zworykin, Vladimir

■ Pickford, Mary

Identification: Canadian American film star
Also known as: Gladys Louise Smith; Gladys Marie
Smith
Born: April 8, 1892, Toronto, Ontario, Canada
Died: May 29, 1979, Santa Monica, California

*Canadian-born actor Mary Pickford became "America's
sweetheart" in the silent films of the 1920s. A pioneer of early
Hollywood, she was a cofounder of United Artists and one of
the thirty-six original founders of the Academy of Motion Picture Arts and Sciences, home of the Academy Awards. Her
active film career extended from 1905 to 1933.*

Though she always claimed her middle name was
Marie, Mary Pickford was born Gladys Louise Smith
to John Charles Smith and Charlotte Hennessy. She
had two younger siblings, Jack and Lottie. After their
father died in 1898, the Smith children began to appear on stage. At age seven, Gladys acted in *The Silver
King* at Toronto's Princess Theatre and soon thereafter joined Toronto's Valentine Company, where she
starred as Little Eva in the company's 1901 production of *Uncle Tom's Cabin*. She spent most of the decade touring the United States with her mother and
siblings, acting in numerous plays and trying to break
into Broadway. Eventually she was cast in the Broadway
play *The Warrens of Virginia* (1907), for which, at the
producer's insistence, she changed her name to
Mary Pickford.

Mary Pickford in 1922. (AP Photo)

Early Film Career
In 1909, Pickford joined the Biograph Company
under film director D. W. Griffith, where she inspired
a huge following as "the girl with the golden curls."
She briefly worked with the Independent Moving
Pictures Company in 1911 but returned to Biograph
in 1912; then, after appearing on Broadway later that
year, she returned to film for good in 1913, joining
Adolph Zukor's Famous Players Film Company (later
Paramount Pictures). Pickford starred in numerous
comedy dramas, earning the nickname "America's
sweetheart," and soon achieved sufficient popularity
to demand quality control over her film productions, forming the Pickford Film Corporation within
Famous Players. In 1919, she partnered with Griffith
and actors Charlie Chaplin and Douglas Fairbanks
Sr. to form United Artists film studio. Through this
joint venture, Pickford could produce and star in her
own movies, thus ensuring top quality and favorable
distribution.

Fame
By the 1920s, Mary Pickford had reached the pin-
nacle of her success and film career and had been
called the most popular and recognizable woman
in the world. She divorced her first husband in
1920 and married Fairbanks less than a month later.
Fairbanks was at the height of his own film career,
acting in swashbucklers such as *The Thief of Bagdad*
for United Artists, and the two attracted large crowds
of fans whenever they appeared in public together.
They lived in Beverly Hills at their estate, Pickfair, a
wedding gift from Fairbanks to Pickford.

Pickford's career blossomed in 1920 with *Pollyanna*,
her first film for United Artists, which made over $1
million. Other notable early productions include the
similarly successful *Little Lord Fauntleroy* (1921) and
Rosita (1923). During the 1920s, she appeared in seventeen silent films, the last one opposite actor and

bandleader Charles "Buddy" Rogers in *My Best Girl* (1927). In 1929, she starred in *Coquette,* her first sound film and her first onscreen appearance without her trademark golden curls, which she had cut off following her mother's death the year before. She won an Academy Award for the role.

Behind the scenes, Pickford's business sense and skills in contract negotiation became legendary. She attained creative rights to her movies, shared in the profits, and helped lay the foundation for the modern film industry. She organized the Motion Picture Relief Fund in 1921 to aid actors experiencing financial hardship and cofounded the Academy of Motion Picture Arts and Sciences in 1927, which, in addition to creating the Academy Awards to recognize achievement in film, also acted as a forum for conflict resolution within the industry.

With the advent of sound films, Mary Pickford's career and influence soon faded. She appeared in three more sound films—*The Taming of the Shrew* (1929), *Kiki* (1931), and *Secrets* (1933)—before retiring from acting. Pickford and Fairbanks divorced in 1936; the following year, Pickford married former co-star Buddy Rogers, with whom she later adopted two children. She was presented with an Academy Award for Lifetime Achievement in 1976.

Impact

Mary Pickford helped shape Hollywood and the American motion picture industry as it exists today. She oversaw every aspect of the production and distribution of her films, established several Hollywood institutions and philanthropic organizations, and encouraged independent filmmakers through her work with United Artists. The Library of Congress houses a collection of her films, and the Mary Pickford Theater there is named in her honor. She is further memorialized by the Pickford Center for Motion Picture Study in Hollywood, the ornate Mary Pickford Theatre in Cathedral City, California, and the traditions of the Academy of Motion Picture Arts and Sciences.

Barbara Bennett Peterson

Further Reading

Brownlow, Kevin, and Robert Cushman. *Mary Pickford Rediscovered: Rare Pictures of a Hollywood Legend.* New York: Harry N. Abrams, 1999. An overview of Pickford's film career.

Herndon, Booton. *Mary Pickford and Douglas Fairbanks: The Most Popular Couple the World Has Ever Known.* New York: Norton, 1977. Describes Pickford's marriage to Fairbanks and their foreign travels.

Leavey, Peggy Dymond. *Mary Pickford: Canada's Silent Siren, America's Sweetheart.* Toronto: Dundurn Press, 2011. A biography detailing Pickford's early life, acting career, and lasting impact on the film industry.

Pickford, Mary. *Sunshine and Shadow.* Garden City, N.Y.: Doubleday, 1955. Pickford's autobiography, including her philosophy of life.

Whitfield, Eileen. *Pickford: The Woman Who Made Hollywood.* Lexington: University Press of Kentucky, 2007. Describes Pickford's life and financial skills.

See also: Academy Awards; Chaplin, Charlie; Fairbanks, Douglas, Sr.; Film; Grauman's Chinese Theatre; Movie palaces; Talking motion pictures; Theater in the United States; *Thief of Bagdad;* United Artists

■ *Pierce v. Society of Sisters*

The Case: U.S. Supreme Court decision holding that the government may not force students to attend government schools
Date: Decided on June 1, 1925

In Pierce v. Society of Sisters, *the Supreme Court ruled against an Oregon law, motivated largely by anti-Catholic prejudice, mandating that children be educated only at public schools. Through amicus curiae briefs, the Pierce case marked the beginning of American Catholics, Jews, and Protestants working together to defend religious freedom.*

On November 7, 1922, Oregon voters enacted a ballot initiative by a vote of 115,506 to 103,685. Scheduled to take effect on September 1, 1926, the Compulsory Education Act, informally known as the "School Bill," required all children aged eight to sixteen years to attend public, government-run schools. Exemptions would be provided for disabled children, eighth-grade graduates, those living far from public schools, and those whose parents obtained a permit for private instruction. The initiative was supported by the Ku Klux Klan (then a powerful political force in Oregon), the Masons, nativists, populists, and Progressive reformers alike.

Lawsuits against the School Bill were brought by the Society of the Sisters of the Holy Names of Jesus and Mary, which operated several parochial schools, and by the nonsectarian Hill Military Academy in Portland. After hearing the cases, the federal district court issued an injunction against the bill, and the cases then went before the Supreme Court.

The 1923 Supreme Court decision in *Meyer v. Nebraska*, holding that a state cannot outlaw the teaching of foreign languages in private schools, provided the key precedent for *Pierce*. Writing for a unanimous court, Justice James McReynolds declared the School Bill unconstitutional. Although the Society of Sisters based their case primarily on the First Amendment protection of the freedom of religion, the Court's ruling was made on the basis of parents' civil liberties and on the economic rights of the schools and their customers. The Court explicitly rejected the notion that the state could compel children to go to a particular kind of school. The *Pierce* decision fit comfortably with many prior Supreme Court cases, including *Adkins v. Children's Hospital* (1923), in upholding Americans' right to freedom of choice in making contracts and exercising other liberties protected by the due process clause of the Fourteenth Amendment.

Impact

Cited in more than one hundred subsequent Supreme Court cases, *Pierce* became a core precedent for decisions protecting family, personal, and religious life from government interference. *Pierce* also advanced the now well-established principles that corporations such as schools are protected by the Fourteenth Amendment, that plaintiffs can file suit against an allegedly unconstitutional law before the law goes into effect, and that businesses have standing to sue based on the legal rights of their customers.

David B. Kopel

Further Reading

Abrams, Paula. *Cross Purposes:* Pierce v. Society of Sisters *and the Struggle over Compulsory Public Education.* Ann Arbor: University of Michigan Press, 2009.

Seid, Richard. "Seventy-Five Years After *Pierce v. Society of Sisters.*" *University of Detroit Mercy Law Review* 78, no. 3 (Spring, 2001): 373–546.

See also: *Adkins v. Children's Hospital;* Civil rights and liberties; Education; Ku Klux Klan; *Meyer v. Nebraska;* Religion in the United States; Supreme Court, U.S.

■ Piston, Walter

Identification: American composer
Born: January 20, 1894, Rockland, Maine
Died: November 12, 1976, Belmont, Massachusetts

Walter Piston influenced generations of American composers throughout his lifetime, both during his career as a professor of music at Harvard University (1926–1960) and as a composer of his own chamber and orchestral works.

In his early twenties, Piston performed as a violinist and pianist with various dance bands around Boston. After the United States entered World War I, he enlisted in the U.S. Navy as a member of the Navy Band, for which he arranged popular music and taught himself to play several different instruments. While still serving in the Navy, Piston also played violin for the MacDowell Club, under the direction of French musician Georges Longy. In 1919, once the war had ended, he enrolled in his first formal composition class at Harvard.

The following year, Piston became a full-time student at Harvard, where he studied under such renowned composers as Archibald Davison, E. B. Hill, and Walter Spalding. Upon graduation, he won the prestigious John Knowles Paine Traveling Fellowship, which supported his travel to Paris for further composition studies. From 1924 to 1926, he studied with Nadia Boulanger, a prominent teacher who instructed many other American composers during the 1920s, including Roy Harris and Aaron Copland. After returning to Boston in 1926, Piston accepted a faculty position at his alma mater, teaching music theory and composition.

Though Piston composed many pieces during the 1920s, he published just two. The first, *Three Pieces for Flute, Clarinet, and Bassoon* (1925), was influenced by his studies with Boulanger and was well received in Boston. The second, *Suite for Orchestra* (1929), is stylistically similar to *Three Pieces* but also incorporates some elements of jazz and popular music. Piston began publishing works more frequently after 1929, beginning with his *Sonata for Flute and Piano* (1930), now a standard in the solo flute repertory.

Impact

Piston remained on the Harvard faculty until his retirement in 1960 and continued to compose music throughout the remainder of his life. Among his most notable works are his Symphony no. 3 (1947) and Symphony no. 7 (1960), for which he won Pulitzer Prizes. Several of his students during the 1920s and 1930s would later achieve critical acclaim as composers of American music, including Elliott Carter, Leroy Anderson, Irving Fine, and Leonard Bernstein. He wrote several books that would become seminal textbooks in the field of music theory, most notably *Harmony* (1941), *Counterpoint* (1947), and *Orchestration* (1955).

Natalie L. Cherwin

Further Reading

Pollack, Howard. *Harvard Composers: Walter Piston and His Students, from Elliott Carter to Frederic Rzewski.* Metuchen, N.J.: Scarecrow Press, 1992.

_____. *Walter Piston.* Ann Arbor: UMI Research Press, 1982.

Tawa, Nicholas E. *From Psalm to Symphony: A History of Music in New England.* Boston, Mass.: Northeastern University Press, 2001.

See also: Classical music; Copland, Aaron; Jazz; World War I veterans

---

■ Player pianos

The production of player pianos in the United States started at the end of the nineteenth century, around the same time that mass-produced pianos for home use became popular. By the early 1920s, these self-playing pianos had become a major form of home entertainment.

One of the earliest player pianos sold in the United States was the Pianola, developed by inventor Edwin Scott Votey in Detroit, Michigan, in 1895 and manufactured by the Aeolian Company. Due to a successful advertising campaign, the Pianola trademark became synonymous with player pianos. In 1904, the piano manufacturing company M. Welte & Sons introduced the Welte Mignon piano, which could reproduce not only notes but also dynamics and pedaling. This new type of player piano came to be known as a reproducing piano.

American companies soon started to develop their own reproducing pianos such as the American Piano Company's Ampico piano and the Aeolian Compa-

ny's Duo-Art piano. For these instruments, many major pianists of the early twentieth century made piano rolls to record their performances: Pianist and composer Sergei Rachmaninoff recorded thirty-four pieces for Ampico piano rolls between 1919 and 1929, for example.

During the 1920s, player pianos became a major medium of home entertainment and changed the way music was disseminated in American society. With the rise of jazz music and dance trends such as the foxtrot, player pianos and piano rolls were employed to reproduce popular music, but they were also used in the classical music industry. Some composers began releasing piano rolls along with their sheet music publications. For example, George Gershwin composed his piece *Rhapsody in Blue* for solo piano and jazz orchestra in 1924, and in the same year, he published the two-piano version of his composition, also recording it for Duo-Art piano rolls. Player piano sales peaked around 1923, when about 194,000 player pianos were sold in the United States, representing more than 50 percent of all piano sales at that time.

Impact

Player piano sales declined significantly around the time the U.S. stock market crashed in October 1929. Additional factors in the declining popularity of player pianos included the technological improvement of phonograph recordings and the advancement of radio technology. A revival of the instrument's popularity came in the 1960s, when collectors started to restore antique player pianos and the Aeolian Company began manufacturing a new range of Pianolas. American composer Conlon Nancarrow even wrote fifty studies for player piano, some of which were published in 1977.

Fusako Hamao

Further Reading

Dolan, Brian. *Inventing Entertainment: The Player Piano and the Origins of an American Musical Industry.* Lanham, Md.: Rowman & Littlefield, 2009.

Holliday, Kent A. *Reproducing Pianos Past and Present.* Lewiston, N.Y.: E. Mellen Press, 1989.

Reblitz, Arthur A. *Player Piano: Servicing and Rebuilding.* Vestal, N.Y.: Vestal Press, 1997.

See also: Gershwin, George; Jazz; Music, popular; *Rhapsody in Blue*

■ Poetry

American poets introduced a number of literary innovations during the 1920s in order to comment on a world that they considered both intellectually and spiritually bankrupt.

The period between the early twentieth century until the end of World War II is generally considered the modernist period in American literature. It was one of the most robust periods in American poetry. Some early experimentalists in modernism included poets Carl Sandburg, Sara Teasdale, Edna St. Vincent Millay, Vachel Lindsay, and Edgar Lee Masters. These writers published their works in the journal *Poetry: A Magazine of Verse*, which had been founded in Chicago by Harriet Monroe in 1912. Concurrent with modernist poets, a circle of talented African American writers published poetry as part of the intellectual and artistic movement known as the Harlem Renaissance.

Modernism

Although American poets had a significant impact on its development, modernism began as a primarily European movement. In addition to influences from the French Symbolists, modernist poets were keenly aware of advancements made in psychology. Issues related to the unconscious—as defined by psychologists Sigmund Freud and Carl Jung—helped modernist poets examine the self in their poetry, as organized religion began to lose some of its authority in their eyes.

Several other artistic movements emerging during the early twentieth century have been linked to modernism, including Dadaism, Imagism, and Surrealism. The supporters of these movements strongly believed in the need for poetic experimentation. They rejected traditional modes of expression as being useless in the modern world. Refusing to be party to the past, writers sought to create something new and separate from previous poetic movements. Poetry became increasingly abstract and devoid of clarity, reflecting poets' belief that the world was a chaotic place.

The American expatriate poets Ezra Pound, T. S. Eliot, H. D. (Hilda Doolittle), and Gertrude Stein were prominent modernist writers. Poets E. E. Cummings, Archibald MacLeish, and John Peale Bishop were also connected to the literary circle of Eliot, Stein, and Pound. Eliot's first poetry collection, *Prufrock and Other Observations*, was published in 1917.

This collection included his first great poem "The Love Song of J. Alfred Prufrock." It has been argued that this collection ushered in modernist poetry to the English-speaking world.

Eliot was initially influenced by the writing of nineteenth-century French Symbolists, especially the poetry of Charles Baudelaire. After traveling widely for a time, Eliot settled in London during World War I. While in London, he struck up a collaborative relationship with Pound, who had been a proponent of Imagist poetry. Although Pound and Eliot were very different in their approach to both life and writing, they contributed positively to each other's literary careers. Pound was involved in the editing and shaping of Eliot's groundbreaking work *The Waste Land*, which was published in *The Dial* magazine in 1922. Eliot became one of the most important poets of his age after the publication of this poem, which came to represent the crumbling of Western civilization. By the late 1920s, Eliot had become a more conservative proponent of traditional religious values, but in *The Waste Land*, he expresses a modernist disillusionment with the human condition, with the literary and social traditions of the nineteenth century, and even with the concept of progress. Like Eliot, many other American modernist poets struggled to capture the instability of the age in their poetry.

Pound was connected not only to Eliot but also to the Irish poet William Butler Yeats. In his early twenties, Pound moved to London, arriving in 1908. He was determined to learn from Yeats, whom he considered the most accomplished poet writing in English. In addition to Yeats and Eliot, Pound's Imagist circle included the poet Hilda Doolittle, who later came to be known as H. D. Other women poets who made their imprint on the world of modernist poetry included Marianne Moore, Amy Lowell, and Mina Loy.

For much of the 1920s, American modernist poet Hart Crane worked on his tribute to New York City's Brooklyn Bridge. His resulting epic poem, *The Bridge*, was published in 1930. It is composed of fifteen separate lyric poems. Taking inspiration from fellow American poet Walt Whitman, Crane attempted to merge the many mythologies of America into a unified whole. He had visions of constructing a poem that could counterbalance the pessimism that he believed characterized Eliot's *The Waste Land*. Where Eliot and Pound saw modern life in the 1920s as troubled at best, Crane saw a future that was full of

Poet William Carlos Williams. (Time & Life Pictures/Getty Images)

The Fugitives

The Fugitive poets were members of a literary circle based in Nashville at Vanderbilt University. Member poets included John Crowe Ransom, Merrill Moore, and Allen Tate. The group published a short-lived but influential literary magazine known as *The Fugitive* between 1922 and 1925. Other prominent members of the circle included Pulitzer Prize–winning writer Robert Penn Warren and poet Donald Davidson, who was one of the founding members of the Fugitives. The group is best remembered for its dedication to the school of literary criticism and textual analysis known as New Criticism.

The dissolution of the Fugitives gave rise to the Southern Agrarians in the latter 1920s. This group of writers, many of whom had been part of the original literary circle, was ardent and vocal in its support of traditional Southern values and ways of life in response to the social, political, and economic changes of the 1920s.

potential for growth and believed that the search for a better America and for a better person was a worthy cause.

Wallace Stevens, another American poet of the modernist era, released a poetry collection titled *Harmonium* in 1923, revealing himself to be a master of many styles. He incorporated several avant-garde modes of expression into his poetry, which allowed him to layer his writing with emotional and intellectual depth. While Stevens worked at creating his own poetic language, contemporary poet William Carlos Williams focused on capturing the pulse of American speech in his writing, releasing poetic works such as *Spring and All* (1923) and the epic poem *Paterson* (1946–1958).

While many important American poets of the 1920s incorporated some aspect of modernism into their work, Robert Frost was not one of them. Frost did not reject traditional poetic forms; instead, he used them to explore themes to which ordinary Americans could relate. Frost did not escape reality through abstraction or an inward examination of the self; rather, he employed a down-to-earth identification with the reader. As a result, his poetry resonated greatly with the American public.

Harlem Renaissance

African American poets such as Langston Hughes, Claude McKay, and Countée Cullen contributed to the literary, artistic, and intellectual movement of the Harlem Renaissance. The Harlem Renaissance traces its beginnings to the end of World War I, when many Southern black veterans decided to move to the large Northern cities in order to find gainful employment. The cities of the North provided many opportunities to work in factories, whereas the rural South remained tied to farming. The new economic opportunities brought forth an energy that manifested itself in the arts as well.

Harlem Renaissance writers developed an emphasis on promoting African American heritage. Langston Hughes became a highly influential African American writer as part of the Harlem Renaissance. His first poetry collection, *The Weary Blues*, published in 1926, represented a new portrayal of African American life. While Hughes was criticized at the time for his use of dialect in his poems and for his portrayal of everyday African American life, he eventually came to be considered a brilliant stylist.

Cullen was another major figure of the Harlem Renaissance. His poetry was forceful and spoke to issues related to discrimination. He gained recognition for his ability to paint pictures of a strong people who suffered great hardships yet still persevered. In such collections as *Color* (1925), *Copper Sun* (1927), and *The Black Christ, and Other Poems* (1929), Cullen became a prominent voice of the Harlem Renaissance.

Although he was born in Jamaica, the poet Claude McKay spent time living in a variety of countries, as well as in the United States. His most important collection of poetry, *Harlem Shadows*, was published in 1922. McKay has been considered one of the first modern poets of African descent to express his anger over racial discrimination in his writing.

In 1924, African American writer Alain Locke edited the anthology *The New Negro*. This volume presented works by many of the most significant African American poets to a larger audience.

Impact

The decade of the 1920s saw many dramatic changes in American poetry. As an outgrowth of the chaotic times, American poets employed various new literary approaches during the 1920s in order to comment on the world around them. It seemed as if the nineteenth century had no relevant answers for the new world of poetry, and it was difficult for American poets, especially expatriate American poets, to adjust to what World War I had done to Western civilization. These poets gave voice to the disjointed nature of modern life. Their approach did not soothe a weary public, however, and some readers felt distanced by the increasing complexity of modernist poetry.

African American poets also found their literary voice during the 1920s, in the framework of the Harlem Renaissance. They expressed a pride in who they were and hoped for a better future for those who had been brutalized by racial discrimination.

The American poets of the 1920s have had a lasting impact on the American literary landscape. Maturing as poets during a tumultuous decade, poets such as Eliot, Pound, Crane, Stevens, Williams, Frost, and Hughes became giants in the history of American poetry.

Jeffry Jensen

Further Reading

Bogan, Louise. *Achievement in American Poetry, 1900–1950*. Chicago: H. Regnery, 1951. Discusses signifi-

cant developments of American poetry in the first half of the twentieth century.

Feinstein, Sascha. *Jazz Poetry: From the 1920s to the Present*. Westport, Conn.: Greenwood Press, 1997. An examination of how African American poetry has evolved since the Harlem Renaissance.

Gray, Richard J. *American Poetry of the Twentieth Century*. New York: Longman, 1998. Presents a study of the major changes and innovations that shaped American poetry during the twentieth century.

Hirsch, Edward. "Helmet of Fire: American Poetry in the 1920s." In *A Profile of Twentieth Century American Poetry*, edited by Jack Elliott Myers and David Wojahn. Carbondale: Southern Illinois University Press, 1991. Provides insights into how American poetry was made new during the 1920s.

MacGowan, Christopher J. *Twentieth Century American Poetry*. Malden, Mass.: Blackwell, 2004. Offers an introduction to twentieth-century American poetry.

Stead, Christian K. *Pound, Yeats, Eliot, and the Modernist Movement*. New Brunswick, N.J.: Rutgers University Press, 1986. Examines the significance of poets like Pound, Eliot, and Yeats to the development of twentieth-century poetry.

See also: *Dial, The;* Fugitive Poets; *Fugitive, The;* Harlem Renaissance; *Harp Weaver, and Other Poems, The;* Literature in the United States; Lost Generation; New Criticism; Southern Agrarians; Williams, William Carlos

■ Polio

Polio was an epidemic disease that crippled or killed thousands of people annually between the 1910s and 1950s, before the development of effective prevention and treatment.

Poliomyelitis, more commonly known as polio, is a viral disease that causes an inflammation of the spinal cord, which can lead to temporary or permanent paralysis. Polio viruses have likely infected humans for millennia, but the disease did not emerge as an epidemic public health threat until the late nineteenth century. Scholars believe there are references to polio, or at least to its effects, documented in ancient Egypt, but serious cases involving paralysis were apparently rare. Up through the eighteenth century, general documentation of polio-like illnesses was sparse, until the improving sanitation of the industrial age reduced early childhood exposure to the virus. Polio is an enteric infection, meaning that the infection is transmitted through pathogens in feces. People contract the virus by eating or drinking something that has been contaminated through contact with an infected person. Virologists believe that for thousands of years the virus was so widespread in the environment that most people were exposed to it as infants, experienced a mild infection, and gained lifetime immunity. As modern plumbing systems became more widespread, sources of contamination became fewer.

Outbreaks in the 1920s

By the early twentieth century, polio outbreaks had emerged in northern Europe and the United States. Annual epidemics became commonplace, while patient age crept steadily upward. Polio had long been referred to as "infantile paralysis" because initially the cases noticed mostly occurred in very young children. By the 1920s, however, patients were more likely to be teenagers or young adults. The older the patient, the more likely it was that the effects of the disease would be severe. While the death rate for young children was under 5 percent, adult patients developed a 24 percent chance of dying from the illness. Paralysis rates were also higher in adult patients than in children. Some scholars believe the total number of cases of polio decreased in the 1920s, while others believe the overall incidence remained about the same for many years. In either event, the proportion of cases that progressed to paralysis increased.

Scientists were baffled in determining how the disease spread. The polio virus had been discovered in 1908, but researchers could not determine how it spread from one person to another. The common belief was that it was airborne—that is, patients became infected when they breathed in the virus. This is why the disease was believed to be related to filthy living conditions; the realization that it was enteric would not happen until the 1930s. When an outbreak occurred, the blame was placed on recent immigrants or the urban poor living in slums. When researchers pointed out that all spectrums of society were touched by the disease, it was suggested that the infection was spread by flies. The fact that polio tended to be a seasonal disease, with many outbreaks occurring in the summer months, reinforced the notion that flies were in some way responsible. Efforts to control the disease included quarantines and sending children away from the city for the summer

months. The latter technique was not particularly successful, as outbreaks often struck youth camps.

In 1921, polio struck its most famous victim, future president Franklin Delano Roosevelt. Roosevelt was thirty-nine years old, physically fit and athletic, and a rising star in the Democratic Party when he fell sick while on vacation at his family's summer home in Canada. After going for a swim, he became ill with what was initially thought to be a simple cold but was later recognized as polio. Roosevelt had planned a life in politics and refused to allow the disease to derail his ambitions. Although he was open about having contracted polio, he downplayed the fact that the disease had left him permanently paralyzed when he sought and won the governor's office in New York in 1928. Concealing the full extent of his disability from the public, Roosevelt became a voice for expanded research into improved treatments and the development of a vaccine. A wealthy man, he directed a large portion of his personal fortune toward finding treatments and a cure for polio. In 1924, he began traveling regularly to Warm Springs, Georgia, to bathe in the hot springs there. In 1927, Roosevelt purchased the property and established the Roosevelt Warm Springs Institute for Rehabilitation, a hydrotherapy center for polio patients, which would remain in operation even after Roosevelt's death.

Impact

Unfortunately, the 1920s ended with no advances in the search for a vaccine. Physicians were becoming better at treating the symptoms and helping patients cope with paralysis, but they were still limited in preventing the illness.

One of the worst polio epidemics in the United States occurred in 1952. Hospitals developed respiratory care centers for those whose paralysis made them unable to breathe on their own. These centers eventually became the intensive care units common to many twenty-first-century hospitals. In April 1955, ten years after the death of President Roosevelt, an effective polio vaccine developed by researcher Jonas Salk was released. By the end of the twentieth century, polio had been virtually eliminated throughout the United States and the world.

Nancy Farm Männikkö

Further Reading

Daniel, Thomas M., and Frederick C. Robbins, editors. *Polio.* Rochester, N.Y.: University of Rochester

Press, 1999. A collection of essays that includes a general history of polio, along with descriptions of specific outbreaks and responses within the United States.

Nathanson, Neal, and Olen M. Kew. "From Emergence to Eradication: The Epidemiology of Poliomyelitis Deconstructed." *American Journal of Epidemiology* 172, no. 11 (December, 2010): 1213–1229. A concise description of the history of polio as a modern epidemic disease along with an explanation of twenty-first-century efforts to eradicate the virus globally.

Oldstone, Michael B. A. *Viruses, Plagues, and History: Past, Present, and Future.* Rev. ed. New York: Oxford University Press, 2010. An overview of viruses and virology that explains technical material in language aimed at the average reader.

Oshinsky, David M. *Polio: An American Story.* New York: Oxford University Press, 2005. Discusses the history of the polio vaccine.

Rogers, Naomi. *Dirt and Disease: Polio before FDR.* New Brunswick, N.J.: Rutgers University Press, 1992. A history of polio and societal responses to it in the early decades of the twentieth century.

See also: Iron lung; Medicine

■ Political parties

The Democratic and Republican Parties dominated American politics in the 1920s, with Republicans controlling the presidency throughout the majority of the decade. Nevertheless, several minor parties challenged the mainstream political platforms and argued for political, social, and economic reform during the period.

Marked by urbanization and accelerated industrialization following the end of World War I, the 1920s saw rapid social, economic, and technological advancement. The Progressive Era of the previous decades had been characterized by reforms in response to rampant political corruption, including efforts to undercut political bosses and their domineering political machines. The Progressive reform movement significantly influenced American politics and political parties, introducing major reforms to the American political system. One such reform was the advent of the direct primary, which weakened the ability of parties and political bosses to manipulate the nomination process and afforded candidates the opportunity to campaign directly to voters. Although the major parties of the 1920s contained both Progressive and conservative factions, the American political consciousness after World War I leaned toward somewhat more conservative ideology. The major parties did not facilitate radical policies and change during this time, and political lethargy and positive rhetoric were prevalent. Nevertheless, a number of smaller parties continued to challenge the mainstream political system of the United States.

Major Political Parties

As in previous decades, U.S. politics of the 1920s was dominated by the Republican Party and the Democratic Party. Founded in the era of Jacksonian democracy, the Democratic Party originally espoused an ideology that emphasized political equality among eligible voters, who at that time were white men. The Democrats experienced political dominance from the party's inception until the Civil War. The party experienced a steady decline in popularity in the early twentieth century, with a brief period of success and international dominance during World War I and the presidency of Woodrow Wilson, whose role in the creation of the League of Nations established the Democratic Party's new reputation for interventionism.

In the 1920s, the Democratic Party was largely overshadowed by Republican political success and was further weakened by the inability to consolidate and unite the fragmented Progressive factions in the party. This left the party itself vulnerable to the influence of minor parties, which appealed to the desire to change and develop political strategy to regain political salience and competitiveness. In an attempt to differentiate itself from the Republican Party, the Democrats incorporated tenets that favored agrarian constituents and the organized interests of farmers into its basic political strategies. Perceived as antibusiness, the strategy backfired, driving many party loyalists to the Republican Party.

The Republican Party was founded in response to the expansion of slavery in western territories, which its leaders opposed. Historically, the party was associated with post–Civil War constitutional amendments granting emancipated slaves citizenship and suffrage as well as favorable business policies that aided Reconstruction in the southern states. In the early twentieth century, the Republican Party successfully

Republican Resurgence Ends America's Progressive Era

The Republican resurgence of 1918–1920, which stemmed from voter dissatisfaction with Progressivism, Wilson, and the Democrats, led to a decade of Republican electoral dominance. Harding's scandal-ridden administration ended with his death in 1923, and then Republican Calvin Coolidge assumed the presidency, easily winning election in his own right in 1924. Both Coolidge and his successor as president, Herbert Hoover, led strongly probusiness and antiprogressive administrations. It was not until the 1930s that the Democratic Party regained dominance in U.S. politics, as Hoover's insufficient measures to repair the economy during the Great Depression contributed to Franklin D. Roosevelt's election to the presidency in 1932.

established itself as the party of rapid industrialization, catering to business interests in the age of urbanization. During the 1920s, the party's political platform and business-friendly policies secured its political dominance. The Republican Party won major victories in the elections of 1920, 1924, and 1928, which saw Republicans Warren G. Harding, Calvin Coolidge, and Herbert Hoover take the presidency, respectively. The party would control the White House and Congress into the early 1930s.

The concept of normalcy was a key theme in American politics after the end of World War I, as many Americans longed to return to a carefree, peacetime lifestyle. Republican politicians and party leaders understood this national attitude and capitalized on it with their political rhetoric and strategy. Warren G. Harding coined the phrase "return to normalcy" in his 1920 campaign, characterizing normalcy as "a regular steady order of things." The Republican Party's policies supported this steady return to normalcy by initiating economic growth through such efforts as the Revenue Act of 1924, which lowered federal tax rates.

Minor Political Parties

Although the Republican Party dominated U.S. politics throughout the 1920s, a number of minor political parties emerged or further developed during the

decade as various groups sensed little interest in their concerns and issues within the two major parties. Minor parties were also motivated by the desire to reform the nation's society or political and economic systems. However, since minor-party issues or political platforms were often nominally incorporated into the platforms of the major political parties in attempts to sway voters, it was difficult for minor parties to grow into larger and more significant political organizations. Federal opposition to ideologies espoused by some minor parties further hindered their progress toward national recognition.

Despite these obstacles, some minor parties experienced successful campaigns and became formidable political forces. One of the active minor parties that experienced short but significant popularity was the Socialist Party of America. Founded in 1901 on a leftist political platform, the party expressed much opposition to the American government and the capitalist economic system. While the party had experienced some success in the previous decade, the 1920s proved to be a difficult era for socialism. The widespread prosperity of the period convinced many Americans of the benefits of capitalism and made labor organizing difficult, while the Russian Revolution of 1917 caused an ideological split within the party. Those who remained after this split did not consider the Russian Revolution an appropriate model for social change in the United States. Furthermore, numerous party members and leaders had been arrested under laws such as the Espionage Act of 1917, which restricted the expression of anti-American sentiment, including speeches denouncing the United States' participation in World War I. Prominent Socialist Party leader Eugene V. Debs, who had run for president on several occasions in the previous two decades, ran his 1920 campaign while in prison and was once again unsuccessful in obtaining a significant percentage of votes. Party membership experienced a significant decline throughout the rest of the decade.

After the ideological split, the former members of the Socialist Party of America who supported the Russian Revolution formed two major organizations in 1919: the Communist Party of America and the Communist Labor Party. These organizations merged to form the Workers Party of America in 1921. In 1929, the consolidated party was renamed the Communist Party USA. The party was politically active throughout the decade and received international support from the newly formed Soviet Union and the Third Communist International, or Comintern. However, it did not experience political success on a national scale.

A short-lived political party of the 1920s was the Progressive Party. The party, which was separate from the earlier Progressive Party of 1912, was founded on principles of reform that echoed those of the Progressive Era. Focused on agrarian political issues and opposing corporate monopolies, the party primarily appealed to Midwestern farmers and organized laborers. The Progressive Party was active during the 1924 presidential election, with the party's founder, Robert M. La Follette, campaigning as its candidate. While La Follette had sufficient support to obtain the thirteen electoral votes from his home state of Wisconsin, as well as a significant percentage of the popular vote, he was an otherwise unsuccessful candidate. La Follette died the following year, thus marking the end of the party's organized political efforts.

One of the most formidable single-issue parties of the 1920s was the Prohibition Party. Founded in 1869, it had been one of the few single-issue political parties to successfully sustain its organizational longevity on a single political platform: the prohibition of alcohol. The Prohibition Party had achieved its goal with the 1919 ratification of the Eighteenth Amendment to the Constitution, which outlawed the sale and consumption of alcohol. The decade following the passage and ratification of the Eighteenth Amendment was marked by active campaigning in defense of the status quo. Both Republicans and Democrats had supported the prohibition platform in the previous decades, but Republican support outlasted Democratic support in the 1920s.

Political Parties and American Culture
Political parties of the 1920s displayed a propensity to align with constituents on specific issues. While the decade was marked with little political competition as the Democratic Party rebuilt its weakened political platform, both political parties made alignments that would be further galvanized in the 1930s under the politics of the New Deal. The Republican Party, more attuned to the industrial sector than the Democrats, called for labor reforms such as shorter workdays, wage increases, and collective bargaining. The Democratic Party continued to appeal to the traditions of rural politics during the 1920s, but as more

Americans migrated to urban areas throughout the decade, the Democratic message seemed antiquated. When the Democrats were successful in recruiting voters from the urban working class, they did so based on ethnocultural appeals rather than economic ones. Ethnic, racial, and religious divisions had historically played a role in political parties and campaigns, and this trend continued during the 1920s. Neither party actively sought to increase the diversity of its membership, convention delegations, or elected officials. Thus, despite the Progressive policies of the previous decades and the widespread social change of the period, the political parties of the 1920s continued to further the social obstacles to equal suffrage and equitable elected representation among minority groups in the United States.

Impact
While some of the minor political parties of the 1920s dissolved during the decade, the Socialist Party of America and the Communist Party USA experienced a resurgence in popularity during the Great Depression, as the devastating economic downturn prompted some Americans to seek alternative economic and political solutions. The Prohibition Party remained active long after the repeal of Prohibition in 1933, promoting various socially conservative causes in addition to alcohol prohibition. Despite the ongoing appeal of these parties and the development of other minor political parties in later decades, such as the Green Party and the Libertarian Party, American politics continued to be dominated by the Democratic Party and Republican Party throughout the twentieth century.

Heather E. Yates

Further Reading
Adkins, Randall E. *The Evolution of Political Parties, Campaigns, and Elections: Landmark Documents, 1787–2008.* Washington, D.C.: CQ Press, 2008. Demonstrates the development of political parties in the United States through primary source documents.

Hagedorn, Ann. *Savage Peace: Hope and Fear in America, 1919.* New York: Simon & Schuster, 2007. Explores the political climate that shaped the beginning of the 1920s.

Salmore, Barbara G., and Stephen A. Salmore. *Candidates, Parties, and Campaigns: Electoral Politics in America.* 2d ed. Washington, D.C.: CQ Press, 1989. Explains the electoral process in the United States, focusing on the importance of political parties in campaigns.

Sundquist, James L. *Dynamics of the Party System: Alignment and Realignment of Political Parties in the United States.* Rev. ed. Washington, D.C.: Brookings Institution, 1983. Chronicles the ways in which American political parties have changed throughout history and the reasons for such changes.

Timberlake, James H. *Prohibition and the Progressive Movement, 1900–1920.* New York: Atheneum, 1970. Explores the development of a movement that would shape both American politics and culture in the 1920s through the prohibition of alcohol.

See also: Corrupt Practices Act of 1925; Debs, Eugene V.; Elections, U.S., of 1920; Elections, U.S., of 1924; Elections, U.S., of 1928; Harding, Warren G.; Hoover, Herbert; La Follette, Robert M.; Smith, Alfred E.; Wilson, Woodrow

■ Polygraph

The polygraph, also known as a lie detector, changed the way police interrogation and criminal investigation was conducted in the United States, replacing questionable methods such as the use of narcotics ("truth serum" drugs) and hypnosis.

Throughout history, countless techniques have been employed to reveal whether an individual is lying. However, it was not until the late nineteenth century that scientific methods for detecting deception began to be developed. During the 1910s, American psychologist William Marston and Italian psychologist Vittorio Benussi separately created machines that measured a subject's blood pressure or breathing during interrogation.

In 1921, medical student John Larson created the first polygraph at the University of California at Berkeley; his device was adapted from British cardiologist James Mackenzie's "ink polygraph" and Marston's device. Initially called the "cardio-pneumo-psychogram," Larson's polygraph simultaneously recorded blood pressure, respiratory rates, and pulse rates through a continuous reading from tubes attached to the machine and the subject. These physiological results were scratched by two metal needles onto a strip of smoked black paper fed between two cylinders.

There were some drawbacks to Larson's polygraph, however. For one, the smoked black paper required a special treatment of shellac in order to preserve the information that was recorded on it. This procedure was not always successful, and many recordings would later become damaged in storage.

Larson's colleague Leonarde Keeler further refined his model into a briefcase-sized machine that also monitored galvanic skin response by recording electrodermal activity (the resistance of the subject's skin to electric current). In 1926, Keeler patented this version, which would be refined several times over the following decades as technology improved.

Impact

Working with Berkeley police, Larson and Keeler became the first to successfully solve crimes using a lie detector device. The Marston lie detector was front and center in the landmark Supreme Court case *Frye v. United States* (1923) when the Court dismissed the scientific validity of the then-new polygraph test and deemed the polygraph results inadmissible. This ruling was made on the basis that expert testimony could only be admitted from "a well-recognize scientific principle or discovery," which would become the precedent for future expert testimony. Despite this, the modern polygraph would go on to be used by large police agencies throughout the world as well as employers concerned about security, and in the late twentieth century, polygraph results began to be admitted in some state courts.

Amber Freitas

Further Reading

Block, Eugene B. *Lie Detectors, Their History and Use.* New York: D. McKay, 1977.

Larson, John A. *Lying and Its Detection: A Study of Deception and Deception Tests.* Chicago: University of Chicago Press, 1932.

Tilstone, William J., Kathleen A. Savage, and Leigh A. Clark. *Forensic Science: An Encyclopedia of History, Methods, and Techniques.* Santa Barbara, Calif.: ABC-CLIO, 2006.

See also: Inventions; Science and technology; Supreme Court, U.S.

■ Pornography

The idea of labeling a creative product "pornography" as a tactic of censorship began to be successfully questioned in the 1920s as part of the social experimentation of the decade, and the power of the courts to ban books began to diminish.

Coined during the mid-nineteenth century to refer to materials describing prostitution, the word "pornography" was likely unfamiliar to many average Americans in the early 1920s. Rather, the designations "immoral" or "obscene" were commonly applied to sexually explicit and stimulating materials. The core of opposition to pornography during the 1920s lay in the belief that community moral standards were threatened by any dissemination of creative products promoting eroticism and "obscenity," and that such works should therefore be barred through obscenity laws. Such prohibitions became more problematic, however, as veterans of World War I returned from Europe with more liberal attitudes toward sexuality and as American women gained greater freedom of expression, both politically and socially. The growth of U.S. cities also brought increased access to obscene materials in a variety of venues, ranging from bookstores to drugstores.

Obscene Materials

Literature and the arts saw the most charges of obscenity. While mainstream novels such as D. H. Lawrence's *Lady Chatterley's Lover* (1928) and Radclyffe Hall's *The Well of Loneliness* (1928) were potential targets, accusations of obscenity were more often leveled against publications focused on borderline erotic subjects, including reprints of older popular textual materials and new social scientific works such as Bronislaw Malinowski's anthropological study *The Sexual Life of Savages in North-Western Melanesia* (1929). Popular magazines such as *True Confessions*, begun in 1922, offered female audiences accounts of scandalous behavior along with sentimentality, a combination that proved very popular.

In the visual arts, the underground trade in erotic materials flourished. Most nude and sexually explicit photographs, produced in both the United States and Europe, continued to be anonymously produced images sold either singly or in sets, though fine art photographers such as Edward Steichen and Alfred Stieglitz began experimenting with provocative nude images as well. A bridge between these and print media was sexually oriented comics, a genre crystallized during the 1920s in the form of eight-page, pocket-sized booklets popularly known as "Tijuana bibles." While their content was sexually explicit, Tijuana bibles also mocked prominent political figures and cultural icons, providing a form of social satire. Privately produced single-reel celluloid movies depicting explicit sex, popularly known as "stag films," were first created around the turn of the century and continued to circulate in a limited fashion, shown to private, all-male audiences throughout the 1920s. Obscenity charges also arose against the stage shows sponsored by major burlesque houses and Broadway theaters, which pushed the limits of social acceptability regarding nudity.

Suppression and Control

During the 1920s, pornographic materials were regulated through the legal classification of a book or image as "obscene," meaning the item in question brought into public view subjects that were both indecent and sexually stimulating. This dual quality of obscenity gave the concept a breadth of scope that could be applied equally to what modern audiences would consider serious works of art and literature as well as to plainly pornographic materials. The fact that federal law did not explicitly define obscenity gave state and local authorities leeway to interpret the concept according to their communities' moral standards.

Local antivice organizations that had emerged in previous decades continued their moral crusades against all works they considered unsuitable, though with diminishing degrees of success. The widely used Hicklin standard, developed in nineteenth-century English law and adopted in the United States, had permitted discrete passages from a work to be identified as obscene and used as grounds for suppression of the entire work. However, this standard began to lose ground in U.S. courts in the twentieth century; in the early 1920s, the New York Society for the Suppression of Vice failed in its attempt to suppress James Branch Cabell's mythological novel *Jurgen* because the court considered the work in its entirety and deemed it not obscene. In another case, *Halsey vs. New York Society for the Suppression of Vice*, a judge ruled that a challenged work should always be considered in its entirety.

However, legal attacks on obscenity were in many other cases successful. The targets were frequently publishers and booksellers, as well as librarians who allowed members of the public to borrow copies of an offending book. Publishers were also subject to a prohibition on the mailing of any book, print, pamphlet, or publication judged to be obscene. The penalties for violators could be quite severe: a fine of up to five thousand dollars, imprisonment for up to five years, or both.

To safeguard their creations, film studios set up their own regulatory body, founding the Motion Picture Producers and Distributors of America (MPPDA) in 1922. Having lost a Supreme Court case over state censorship, the industry hoped the MPPDA would help ease the local and state distribution restrictions it faced.

Impact

In the 1920s, questions surrounding the definition of obscenity collided with deep cultural resistance to graphic depictions of sexuality. Nevertheless, the absence of absolute and unchanging criteria invited high-profile legal challenges by writers and other artists defending their creative works, thus highlighting the issue in the public consciousness. Widely publicized court cases such as *Halsey* laid the foundations for later landmark judgments against censorship in the early 1930s, and antivice societies began to diminish in strength and numbers.

Robert B. Ridinger

Further Reading

Ernst, Morris Leopold, and William Seagle. *To the Pure . . . A Study of Obscenity and the Censor.* New York: Viking Press, 1928. Outlines the component issues in and venues for the ongoing cultural struggle with pornography in the 1920s.

Friedman, Andrea. *Prurient Interests: Gender, Democracy, and Obscenity in New York City, 1909–1945.* New York: Columbia University Press, 2000. An overview of antiobscenity activism in New York for several decades and the changing landscape of the cultural debate regarding pornography.

Gertzman, Jay A. *Bookleggers and Smuthounds: The Trade in Erotica, 1920–1940.* Philadelphia: University of Pennsylvania Press, 2002. A detailed account of the business of publishing pornography during the interwar period and the associated political and moral issues.

Mencken, H. L., and Carl Bode. *The Editor, the Bluenose, and the Prostitute: H. L. Mencken's History of the*

"Hatrack" Censorship Case. Boulder, Colo.: Roberts Rinehart, 1988. A previously unreleased account written in 1926 by the editor of the *American Mercury* newspaper describing his battle with attempts to block the paper's distribution on grounds of indecency.

Wheeler, Leigh Ann. *Against Obscenity: Reform and the Politics of Womanhood in America, 1873–1935.* Baltimore: Johns Hopkins University Press, 2004. An in-depth case study of women's organizations in Minneapolis and St. Paul, Minnesota, and their role in local crusades against vice.

See also: *American Mercury, The;* Book publishing; Censorship; Film; Literature in the United States; Photography

■ Post, Emily

Identification: American author and etiquette expert
Born: October 27, 1872, Baltimore, Maryland
Died: September 25, 1960, New York City, New York

Emily Post's name became synonymous with etiquette in the 1920s. Her etiquette rules provided the ultimate standard of behavior in polite American society for men and women of the era to follow.

Emily Post's literary career began after her divorce in 1905, when she started writing magazine articles and serialized stories as a means to support herself. She found moderate success as a novelist, but it was her book *Etiquette in Society, in Business, in Politics, and at Home* (1922) that brought her national recognition. At over six hundred pages long, it was the most comprehensive list of etiquette rules that had ever been published. *Etiquette* provided rules for the upper class of the 1920s on how to interact with one another, including instructions on writing letters, introducing people, setting the dinner table, hosting guests, being a guest, writing thank you notes, and directing servants in the household. Post's main philosophy of etiquette was for people to strive to please the greatest number of people while offending the least.

In 1927, Post released a new edition of *Etiquette.* This updated version took into account the changes in American society in the past five years and included rules for those of the middle classes who, for

Emily Post. (© Bettmann/Corbis)

example, could not afford the servants that Post had originally assumed her audience would have. The new additions covered topics such as how to be an attentive host while preparing a meal for guests and how to dress for formal affairs on a limited budget.

Impact

After the release of her books, Emily Post became a household name. Countless people sought out her answers to their etiquette questions, which she answered in a weekly newspaper column. Over the following decades, she continued to update *Etiquette* in addition to writing many more books on the subject. Post founded the Emily Post Institute in 1946; when she retired, her work was continued by her granddaughter-in-law, Elizabeth Post, who was in turn succeeded by daughter-in-law Peggy Post in 1995. Members of the Post family still remain the leading experts on etiquette and manners in the United States.

Kristen Pavka

Further Reading

Claridge, Laura P. *Emily Post: Daughter of the Gilded Age, Mistress of American Manners.* New York: Random House, 2009.

Kolbert, Elizabeth. "Place Settings." *The New Yorker,* October 20, 2008, 88–92.

Post, Emily. *Etiquette in Society, in Business, in Politics, and at Home.* New York: Funk & Wagnalls, 1922.

See also: Fashions and clothing; Marriage and dating; Roaring Twenties

■ Postage stamps

Several notable commemorative stamp designs were issued throughout the 1920s. Technological advances during this period improved efficiency and security in postal service.

In the American colonies, formalized mail delivery began during the early seventeenth century, with Founding Father Benjamin Franklin as the first postmaster general. The first paper stamps were issued in the United States on March 3, 1847, but the stamps were not available for sale until July 1, 1847, in New York City, with other cities following shortly afterward.

Originally, people who sent mail did not have to pay, and there were no size or weight restrictions for mail. The letter carrier would collect payment when the mail reached its destination. As part of a general reform, the United States Postal Service (U.S.P.S.) changed its practice and introduced paid postage, revolutionizing and improving mail delivery.

Stamps of the 1920s

During the 1920s, stamps were increasingly manufactured by machine. Among the definitive stamps of regular issue in the 1920s were the Pilgrim Tercentenary set, issued in 1920. This set of three stamps commemorated the three hundredth anniversary of the Pilgrims' landing at what would become Plymouth, Massachusetts. They depict the *Mayflower,* the landing of the Pilgrims, and the signing of the settlers' compact. These high-quality engravings were the first U.S. stamps issued without the name of the country appearing.

The most definitive stamps of the 1920s were the Series of 1922, also known collectively as the Fourth Bureau Issue. The stamps in this series were sold for over ten years. While these designs were being developed, stamp printing procedure changed from flat plate printing, a technique that required cutting, to a rotary press that created perforations that could be torn, making it easier to separate and distribute the stamps efficiently.

Since 1908, only Benjamin Franklin and President George Washington had appeared in profile on definitive stamps; however, the Series of 1922 appeared in a two-part sequence that introduced twenty-three new designs depicting the faces of a number of U.S. presidents and other celebrated figures. Lower-value stamps included the half-cent stamp with American Revolutionary War soldier Nathan Hale, the four-cent stamp showing George Washington's wife, Martha, and the five-cent memorial stamp for President Theodore Roosevelt. Higher-value stamps featured cultural icons, such as the Brule Sioux warrior known as Hollow Horn Bear, the Golden Gate Bridge, Niagara Falls, a bison, and the Lincoln Memorial, and a five-dollar stamp depicted Liberty personified. Many of these stamps appeared in their own distinctive colors, making it easier for postal employees to identify values quickly. The half-cent Nathan Hale stamp and many others in the series had no particular usage at the time. Only four of the stamps saw widespread usage: the one-cent Franklin stamp for postcards, the one-and-a-half-cent Harding stamp for third-class mail, the two-cent Washington stamp for first-class mail, and the three-cent Lincoln stamp for first-class mail, beginning in 1932 after the U.S.P.S. issued a price increase.

A new ten-cent special delivery stamp was also issued during the 1920s. This stamp features a mail delivery motorcycle parked against the curb of a private residence. The special delivery stamp reflected two hallmarks of the 1920s American attitude for the future, optimism and new technology. The U.S.P.S. issued the stamp to highlight the spirit of patriotism, giving advance notice of the specific date of issue. This set a precedent for first day covers, also known as first day of issue covers, which are postage stamps used in the mail on the first day of their issue.

Stamp Collecting

Stamps became a collectable item during the 1920s, which promoted philately, the study of stamps and their use. From 1926 to 1932, the Two-Cent Red Sesquicentennial Issues were released in commemoration of the 150th anniversary of the American

Revolutionary War. This commemorative issue featured more than twelve stamps, generally known as "Two-Cent Reds." The set included representations of Revolutionary War sites, battles, and military leaders, such as Valley Forge, the Battle of White Plains, and General von Steuben. Other stamp images depicted objects and events in American history, such as the Liberty Bell, the Ohio River Canalization, and the Massachusetts Bay Colony. Ten million of the stamps received an overprint of the words "Molly Pitcher," after a woman who reportedly fought in the Battle of Monmouth.

Impact

The U.S.P.S. was concerned about stamp theft and efficient mail processing. To prevent forgery, early stamps had been produced from small engravings etched into the steel die used to press stamps. A machine affixing stamps to envelopes, postcards, and wrappers as a security measure had been introduced in 1850. Machine-stamped metered mail had become a popular method of theft prevention. The postage meter idea had been redesigned in 1912 by Arthur Pitney, who went into business with Walter Bowes in 1920 to manufacture and market the machine. Pitney's Model M Postage Meter made the process more efficient. The machine did not replace paper stamps, but it remains in use by twenty-first-century businesses sending out bulk mail.

R. L. Smith

Further Reading

Garfield, Simon. *The Error World: An Affair with Stamps.* Boston: Houghton Mifflin Harcourt, 2009. A memoir describing the author's collection of misprinted stamps, known as errors.

Juell, Rodney A., and Steven J. Rod, eds. *Encyclopedia of United States Stamps and Stamp Collecting.* Minneapolis, Minn.: Kirk House, 2006. Presents a comprehensive overview of U.S. postage stamp history, including notes on technological progress in stamp manufacturing, suggestions for collecting, and a glossary for terms related to stamp production.

Klug, Janet, and Donald J. Sundman. *One Hundred Greatest American Stamps.* Atlanta: Whitman, 2007. Contains information about U.S. history, along with images of one hundred selected stamps representing important historical events or developments in postage stamp manufacturing.

Mackay, James. *The Guinness Book of Stamps: Facts and Feats.* 2d ed. Enfield, England: Guinness Books, 1988. Discusses the history of stamps and collecting.

Wozniak, Maurice D. *Warman's U.S. Stamps Field Guide: Values and Identification.* Iola, Wis.: Krause, 2011. A pocket guide to postage stamp prices, featuring color photographs, pricing for used and unused stamps, and suggestions for beginning a collection.

See also: Airmail; Hobbies and recreation

■ Pound, Ezra

Identification: American poet
Born: October 30, 1885, Hailey, Idaho
Died: November 1, 1972, Venice, Italy

Ezra Pound established himself as one of the most important literary figures of the 1920s, but his move to Italy and his attraction to Italian fascism led to his marginalization as a poet and spokesman.

Born in Idaho and raised in Pennsylvania, Ezra Pound had visited Europe several times before he moved to London in 1908. There, he worked on his poetry and translations, made important contacts in the literary world, and met his future wife, Dorothy Shakespear. He published several collections of poetry, among them *Lustra* (1916), the sharp, dramatic tone of which signaled a break with the archaic diction of his earlier poems.

One of Pound's most important works, *Hugh Selwyn Mauberley*, was published in London in 1920. A series of short poems about a writer much like Pound himself, it expresses disillusionment with Great Britain and disgust with the slaughter of World War I. Shortly afterward, Pound and Dorothy left London for Paris, where Pound again befriended a number of important literary, musical, and artistic figures, including lost generation writer Ernest Hemingway.

During this period, Pound championed the work of avant-garde American composer George Antheil, who assisted Pound in developing his opera *Le Testament de Villon* (1926), and met Antheil's frequent collaborator, Olga Rudge, a concert violinist with whom he would carry on a lifelong affair. He also edited T. S. Eliot's long poem *The Waste Land*, which

Ezra Pound. (Time & Life Pictures/Getty Images)

first appeared in the literary magazine *The Dial* in 1922, carrying a dedication to Pound. In addition, it was through Pound's efforts that a small press published Hemingway's collection of prose vignettes, *in our time*, in 1924.

However, Pound was growing impatient with Paris. He had written prolifically and campaigned tirelessly on behalf of his friends, but he had made little money and felt unappreciated. He and Dorothy moved to the port town of Rapallo, Italy, in 1924, a move that coincided with Pound's growing enthusiasm for the Italian fascist movement. By this time, he had already embarked on a long series of difficult, if frequently dazzling, poems that he called *The Cantos*. The first three had appeared in the American magazine *Poetry* in 1917; by 1928, Pound had published two dozen more. The project would occupy him off and on for the rest of his life.

Impact

Ezra Pound played a key role in the development of twentieth-century literature through both his own innovative poetry and his frequent promotion of other writers. However, his anti-Semitic radio broadcasts for Italy during World War II, along with his subsequent arrest for treason and incarceration in a psychiatric hospital, damaged his reputation and continue to make evaluation of his work problematic.

Grove Koger

Further Reading

Ackroyd, Peter. *Ezra Pound and His World.* New York: Scribner, 1980.

Carpenter, Humphrey. *A Serious Character: The Life of Ezra Pound.* Boston, Mass.: Houghton Mifflin, 1988.

Nadel, Ira Bruce. *The Cambridge Introduction to Ezra Pound.* Cambridge, England: Cambridge University Press, 2007.

See also: Anti-Semitism; *Dial, The;* Eliot, T. S.; Hemingway, Ernest; Literature in the United States; Lost Generation; Poetry; *Waste Land, The*

■ President's Conference on Unemployment

The Event: A conference convened in response to the 1921 recession and the resultant high rate of unemployment
Date: September 26–October 13, 1921
Place: Washington, D.C.

Upon taking office in 1921, President Warren G. Harding was faced with an economic recession and growing unemployment. At the behest of Secretary of Commerce Herbert Hoover, Harding convened the President's Conference on Unemployment. Though the conference emphasized voluntary measures by business and communities, it marked the first time the federal government had undertaken direct action to reduce unemployment.

When President Warren G. Harding took office in early 1921, he inherited an economic recession with steep unemployment rates, which rose to 11.9 percent that same year. Harding's predecessors had maintained a primarily laissez-faire economic policy, rejecting the idea of government intervention in an economic downturn in favor of market-generated recovery. By contrast, Harding's secretary of commerce, Herbert Hoover, argued that the federal government should take action to alleviate unemploy-

ment. Hoover recommended holding a national conference to address the issue, and the president agreed.

On September 26, 1921, Harding gathered over three hundred leaders in labor, business, and academia to focus on proposing new measures to decrease unemployment. President Harding and Secretary Hoover emphatically maintained that they would not fight unemployment by opening the public treasury and directly providing monetary aid. Instead, they intended for the conference to emphasize voluntary and cooperative action by businesses, individuals, and local communities.

Once approved by President Harding, the conference's final recommendations were issued to the public. These included encouragement for businesses and individuals to move ahead with any plans for construction or repairs, rather than waiting for market improvement, and for businesses and their employees to voluntarily rotate individual jobs with unemployed workers. It also called for an increase in, and acceleration of, public works projects and encouraged the creation of voluntary state and local committees tasked with assisting individuals in finding employment. Secretary Hoover used independent labor organizations and facets of the Department of Commerce to disseminate reports of communities that successfully implemented the recommendations, encourage the public to help the unemployed through individual good works, and bolster an optimistic attitude throughout the country.

Impact

By the end of 1922, the market had improved significantly, and the immediate unemployment crisis had abated. The extent to which the economic upturn is attributable to the Conference on Unemployment is unclear. However, although it emphasized voluntary measures, the federal government's unprecedented policy of taking direct action to fight unemployment laid the foundation for the more expansive New Deal policies ushered in by President Franklin D. Roosevelt during the Great Depression of the 1930s.

Jenny L. Evans

Further Reading

Murray, Robert K. *The Harding Era: Warren G. Harding and His Administration.* Newtown, Conn.: American Political Biography Press, 2000.

Rothbard, Murray N. *America's Great Depression.* 5th

ed. Auburn, Ala.: Ludwig von Mises Institute, 2000.

Wilson, Joan Hoff. *Herbert Hoover: Forgotten Progressive.* Reprint. Prospect Heights, Ill.: Waveland Press, 1992.

See also: Agricultural Marketing Act of 1929; Elections, U.S., of 1920; Harding, Warren G.; Hoover, Herbert; Income and wages; Roosevelt, Franklin D.; Unemployment

---

■ President's Daughter, The

Identification: Memoir alleging President Warren G. Harding fathered an illegitimate child
Author: Nan Britton
Date: 1927

The President's Daughter is noteworthy as the first sensational, tell-all political autobiography in the United States, claiming that Harding fathered a child in 1919 with author Nan Britton (1896–1991) while he was a U.S. senator. In the immediate wake of the book's publication, commentators focused on whether they could believe Britton. While no conclusive evidence of Harding's paternity was ever established, the story further tarnished Harding's reputation, already beset by talk of extramarital affairs and the corruption scandals of his presidency.

It is believed that Britton wrote her memoir to provide money for her child, Elizabeth Ann, whom she alleged Harding had fathered. Britton had longstanding ties to Harding: She grew up near Harding's hometown of Marion, Ohio, and attended school with his sister Abigail. Britton's father occasionally wrote articles for the newspaper Harding owned. Upon moving to New York City and training to be a secretary, Britton contacted Harding, then the U.S. senator from Ohio, for help in finding a job. As the two corresponded, Britton claimed to see romantic interest. Biographers have noted that Harding's letters seemed friendly yet professional.

Britton was in many ways a contrast to Harding's wife, Florence, an older woman who had been unable to produce a child with Harding. Throughout the book, Britton claims that she was better able to meet Harding's needs and thus served as a better partner. According to Britton, she and Harding had their first tryst in a New York hotel room. Harding

then gradually became a patron of the Britton family. Britton claims that Harding fathered her daughter in his Senate office. She defends the absence of love letters from Harding by writing that she and Harding agreed to destroy such letters. She claims to have gone through a ceremony with a ring, similar to a marriage ceremony, and alleges that Harding provided for the child. However, since Britton struggled financially to keep the child, arrangements were made for Britton's sister and her husband to adopt the girl.

After Harding entered the White House in 1921, Britton visited him several times. She wrote that they had an encounter in a closet on one occasion to avoid being discovered by Florence. The president sent Britton to Europe, where she learned of Harding's death. His will did not mention Britton or Elizabeth Ann. When she proved unable to produce any evidence supporting her claims of an affair, Harding's circle refused to give her any aid.

Impact
The President's Daughter dealt a further blow to Harding's already wobbling reputation. For a time after the release of the book, Harding's legacy was dominated by questions of whether he produced an illegitimate child rather than his impact on political matters. While Harding's relationship with Britton remains questionable, the scandal caused by the book has contributed to Harding's consistent historical evaluation as one of the worst U.S. presidents.

Caryn E. Neumann

Further Reading
Britton, Nan. *The President's Daughter.* New York: Elizabeth Ann Guild, 1927.
Payne, Phillip G. *Dead Last: The Public Memory of Warren G. Harding's Scandalous Legacy.* Athens: Ohio University Press, 2009.

See also: Crimes and scandals; Harding, Warren G.

■ Progressive Party of 1924

Identification: American political party
Date: Founded in 1924

The Progressive Party was a third political party that emerged during the 1924 presidential campaign, organized around U.S. senator Robert La Follette of Wisconsin. The party pro-

vided a voice for those unhappy with the major political parties, including midwestern populists and unionists.

In 1924, several political forces dissatisfied with the two-party system amassed around the campaign efforts of Wisconsin senator Robert La Follette, a former Republican. They hoped to offer a challenge to the Republican and Democratic parties, or, if they could not replace one of the major parties, at least force one or both to shift in a more liberal direction. Although La Follette would only win Wisconsin in the presidential election, his campaign carried a number of Midwest precincts and accounted for over 16 percent of the popular vote.

The Birth of a Campaign

The party and its platform developed out of the Conference for Progressive Political Action (CPPA), a coalition of left-wing and progressive interest groups that first met in February 1922. On July 4, 1924, at the CPPA national convention in Cleveland, Robert La Follette Jr. appeared to announce his father's intention to run as an independent Progressive candidate. The CPPA elected to back La Follette's candidacy and adopted a platform that mirrored the senator's own ideas. The Progressive Party mainly existed in name only, as La Follette did not want a third party to interfere in the election of Progressive Republicans and Democrats at the state and local level, and thus La Follette was the only candidate on the party's ticket. Joining him as running mate was Montana senator Burton K. Wheeler, a Democrat, who had broken with his party when they nominated John W. Davis to challenge Republican incumbent Calvin Coolidge.

The central tenet of the Progressive Party's platform was the guarding of freedom from corporate and industrial interests. In an effort to curb the rise of big business and unfair control of resources, the party continued to push for traditional progressive values, such as the use of government to break private monopolies, the election of all federal judges for limited terms, conservation of all natural resources, and public ownership of utilities, railroads, and major industries. They wanted the government to provide public works programs during depressions and institute a progressive tax on large incomes, estates, and inheritances. Their platform also called for the protection of collective bargaining rights for labor and agriculture, ratifica-

tion of the Child Labor Amendment, an end to the influence of commercial interests on foreign policy, and revision of the Treaty of Versailles to bring it more in line with the terms of the armistice, among other measures.

Party Support

Supporters of the Progressive Party grew to include trade unions, populists, the Socialist Party, and African American groups. The Steuben Society, a German American organization, joined La Follette's campaign with the promise to deliver six million votes, and the American Federation of Labor also voiced its support for La Follette and Wheeler, although the group refrained from endorsing the party itself.

Of all the Progressive Party supporters, western and midwestern farmers were the most loyal. Their support was so widespread and locked in that the Progressives did not see the need to campaign to them. Ultimately, farmers turned out to be the most effective of La Follette's supporters at the ballot box, delivering over half of his votes.

Election Day

As the election neared, the Progressive Party found itself mired in complications. Without a preexisting party infrastructure, La Follette had to coordinate his campaign from scratch, relying on inexperienced supporters and organizations with often conflicting interests. As the Progressives attempted to organize and unite local efforts and campaigns, questions of what issues would dominate, who would control the flow of campaign contributions, where to direct the money, and which geographic areas to focus on added friction to the party machinery. In addition, La Follette had to use up much of his campaign's resources simply to get on individual states' ballots.

La Follette campaigned mainly in the East and the Midwest, while Wheeler started by touring heavily in his native New England and later campaigned in the western states that La Follette did not visit. Their efforts resulted in the Progressive Party receiving over 4.8 million votes, a total of 16.6 percent of the popular vote. They only won the electoral votes of one state, Wisconsin, although they made a strong showing in the Midwest and the West, finishing second behind the Republicans in eleven other states.

Impact

At a time when both major parties were fielding conservative candidates, La Follette and Wheeler provided a more progressive option. Although they captured over 16 percent of the popular vote, demonstrating significant support, they could not translate those numbers into victory. Organizational problems, the lack of a national party to provide centralized control, and insufficient funding prevented the Progressives from making a stronger showing. While there had been talk of making the Progressive Party a genuine third party after the election, La Follette's death in 1925 caused the party to lose what little momentum remained. The movement would be briefly resurrected by La Follette's sons as the Wisconsin Progressive Party in 1934.

James G. Downhour

Further Reading

Cooper, John Milton, Jr. "Why Wisconsin? The Badger State in the Progressive Era." *Wisconsin Magazine of History* 87, no. 3 (Spring, 2004): 14–25. Discusses why Wisconsin became the leader of the American Progressive movement.

MacKay, Kenneth Campbell. *The Progressive Movement of 1924.* New York: Columbia University Press, 1947. Charts the rise and fall of the 1924 movement and addresses the difficulties faced by third parties in the United States.

Miller, John E. "Fighting for the Cause: The Rhetoric and Symbolism of the Wisconsin Progressive Movement." *Wisconsin Magazine of History* 87, no. 4 (Summer, 2004): 14–25. Examines the tactics that helped the Progressive movement command public attention.

Nye, Russel B. *Midwestern Progressive Politics: A Historical Study of Its Origins and Development, 1870–1950.* East Lansing: Michigan State College Press, 1951. A narrative of Progressivism in the Midwest and its relationship to local regionalism.

Shideler, James H. "The La Follette Progressive Party Campaign of 1924." *Wisconsin Magazine of History* 33, no. 4 (June, 1950): 444–457. An overview of the campaign and why it ultimately collapsed.

See also: Agriculture in the United States; Coolidge, Calvin; Davis, John W.; Elections, U.S., of 1924; Foreign policy, U.S.; La Follette, Robert M.; Political parties; Unionism

■ Prohibition

The Prohibition era, spanning from 1919 to 1933, was one of the most controversial periods in U.S. history, partly because of criminal responses to the banning of alcohol and partly because many people saw the Eighteenth Amendment as an encroachment on individuals' constitutional rights.

During the fourteen years between the passage of the Volstead Act in October 1919, its ratification as the Eighteenth Amendment, and its repeal in 1933, the manufacture, sale, transportation, importation or exportation, and consumption of alcoholic beverages were officially considered illegal in the United States. The practical repercussions of this legislation during the 1920s were numerous, involving extreme acts of criminality as well as socially damaging tendencies that produced effects quite contrary to the presumed intentions of Prohibition.

A Growing Trend

Many historians have noted a strong undercurrent of opposition to the consumption of alcohol, generally referred to as temperance movements, surfacing periodically throughout U.S. history. During the eighteenth century and into the nineteenth century, local taverns maintained an important position in American society. A change in attitude in the late nineteenth century was tied in part to the governmental decision to allow individual states to issue licenses that transformed general gathering places into competing businesses whose main function was to sell alcoholic beverages. Fairly soon, the image of the tavern gave way to that of the saloon or the bar. In time, these terms took on meanings in American culture that no longer corresponded to the original colonial institutions.

Whatever might have been intended by the creation and spread of licensed, tax-producing premises, various studies show that levels of alcohol consumption rose at a higher rate than population growth by the 1890s. Almost all social histories of the United States, beginning with early descriptions of raucous conditions during the California gold rush, include references to the drinking habits associated with saloons, especially in industrial urban settings or railway towns. By the 1890s, temperance movements had developed into seriously organized anti-drink campaigns, as Americans noticed an increase in drunkenness, prostitution, drug use, violence, and theft, often located in close proximity to bars and saloons.

A major turning point that would contribute directly to the enactment of formal Prohibition came with the founding of the Women's Christian Temperance Union (WCTU) in Cleveland, Ohio, in 1874. The WCTU encouraged full abstinence through educational efforts. By the turn of the century, the WCTU's Department of Scientific Temperance Instruction had obtained legislative action in all states requiring classroom instruction on the negative effects of alcohol. From here, it was a relatively short step, via the efforts of the Anti-Saloon League (founded in 1893), for proponents of legal Prohibition to obtain the national legislation that became the Eighteenth Amendment in January 1920.

The Volstead Act and the Eighteenth Amendment

A key factor leading Congress toward a Prohibition law came with the nation's entry into World War I in 1917. Legislators feared that military personnel's discipline and health would be menaced by the widespread availability of liquor. They also feared that processes involved in alcohol manufacturing would consume vital foodstuffs needed for the war effort. Thus, well before the Volstead Act itself was drafted, several wartime laws, particularly the Food and Fuel Control Act (August 1917), began to extend federal control over the liquor industry. Prior to passage of the Volstead Act in 1919, over half of the United States had adopted some form of control over alcohol, the most extreme being "dry state" laws that either banned or strictly limited the sale of liquors.

Congress passed the Volstead Act in October 1919, and the legislation was ratified by two-thirds of the individual states. Prohibition became a constitutionally binding law in all of the United States, rather than a matter for individual states to determine. The Volstead Act would undermine itself, however: The law contained wording that set the stage for loose interpretations and loopholes, such as the use of the word "intoxicating" instead of "alcoholic" to describe beverages.

Nearly all historians agree that instead of curbing consumption, the Volstead Act opened the door to a wide range of illegal activities supplying alcohol for the black market. "Bootlegging" was the term applied to activities associated with the production and sale of illegal alcohol. Illegal distilleries developed inside the United States. The alcohol-smuggling industry began to flourish as well, either beyond the sight of law enforcement agents or, in cases involving bribery, while the latter chose to overlook illegal alcohol transportation and distribution. At the same time, "speakeasies," or businesses willing to risk the penalty for serving alcohol, provided perfect targets for organized crime syndicates eager to collect "protection money." Many such establishments were run by organized crime leaders. Although speakeasies could be found nearly everywhere, those in larger metropolitan areas such as New York City, Chicago, or Pittsburgh became major landmarks. Some, like the Mayflower Club in Washington, D.C., attracted respectable members of society. Whereas the common saloon had generally attracted customers from the same social class, Prohibition-era speakeasies tended to cater to a variety of clients, diversifying their activities with auxiliary attractions such as gambling.

Conflicting Opinions For and Against Continuing Prohibition

Several different organizations called for repeal of, or at least revisions in, the Eighteenth Amendment during the 1920s. One of the most strident of these was the Association Against the Prohibition Amendment (AAPA), established in 1918 under the leadership of former naval officer William H. Stayton. Many of the AAPA's arguments opposed Prohibition as an encroachment on constitutional rights. The group particularly highlighted the fact that persons charged could be prosecuted under both state and federal law, which, although upheld in the *U.S. v. Lanza* Supreme Court decision in 1922, seemed contrary to the Fifth Amendment outlawing double jeopardy. AAPA membership was reported to have grown from 100,000 in 1921 to over 700,000 in 1926. Its ranks came to include some prominent figures of the 1920s, including two former mayors of New York City, a retired federal judge, and the nationally recognized publisher Charles Scribner.

Critics of Prohibition made slight gains as early as 1923, when the New York legislature repealed its own specific laws for the enforcement of the Eighteenth Amendment. Although some anti-Prohibition campaigns called for the total repeal of the legislation, other Prohibition modification campaigns focused on specific issues. American Federation of Labor chief Samuel Gompers was among a series of witnesses who testified before a 1924 joint congressional hearing to consider possible modification of the Prohibition

Men pouring alcohol down a drain. (Hulton Archive/Getty Images)

laws, such as making low-alcohol-content beer legal again. The joint committee's legal counsel was Julian Coleman, head of the Constitutional Liberty League. Some activists strongly opposed to Prohibition were called to testify, especially members of the Molly Pitcher Clubs, which were women's clubs closely associated with the AAPA, although they largely disbanded by the late 1920s. A second round of Senate hearings in 1926 followed calls on the Senate floor in 1925 from New Jersey senator Walter Edge. The modifications under consideration by this date included suggestions to change the definition of "intoxicating beverages" to allow individual states to make their own decisions on Prohibition, to permit the use of alcohol for medicinal purposes, and to organize a national referendum to either repeal Prohibition or make serious changes in its provisions.

Over the next few years, issues relating to the Eighteenth Amendment appeared in the political platforms of a number of politicians. Very vocal Prohibition opponents included politicians such as Senator James W. Wadsworth Jr., who was a member of a prominent colonial family and married to the daughter of Secretary of State John Hay. As he sought reelection in 1926, Wadsworth likely calculated that supporting the repeal of Prohibition could strengthen his chances for nomination to the presidential elections in 1928. His calculation was wrong, however, even though his successful opponent in the Senate race, Judge Robert F. Wagner, the future mayor of New York City, championed similar but less extreme "pro-wet" convictions. In the end, "pro-dry" Secretary of Commerce Herbert Hoover received the Republican presidential nomination and won the 1928 election over New York's Democratic governor and anti-Prohibitionist Al Smith Jr. in a loss attributed by many to Smith's Roman Catholic background, rather than his position on Prohibition.

In 1928, Wadsworth became actively involved in efforts to reorganize the AAPA and redirect its efforts to put an end to Prohibition by expanding research into its controversial practical effects, negative economic influences, and comparisons with temperance programs that appeared to work better in other countries. Among its findings in the 1929 pamphlet "Scandals of Prohibition Enforcement" were alarming statistics showing widespread corruption within police agencies and revealing that, in ten years, about thirteen hundred employees of the Federal Prohibition Bureau had been fired for illegal conduct. By the end of the 1920s, it seemed clear that, if progress toward ending or substantially modifying the Volstead Act were to come, as it eventually did in 1933, it would be with support from Democratic legislators.

Impact

In many ways, the era of Prohibition in the United States was a lesson in social balance and constitutional procedure. As many of its initial opponents had argued, it was more harmful than beneficial to make the production, distribution, and consumption of alcohol illegal. A prime example of this was the involvement of organized crime in breaches of Prohibition. Beyond practical repercussions, making the Volstead Act a formal amendment to the Constitution had the effect of solidifying the 1919 legislation. Any measures to alter the Eighteenth Amendment were therefore extremely complicated. Finally, many could and did argue from the outset that prohibiting the consumption of alcoholic drinks was itself unconstitutional, since it limited individual freedoms legally protected in the country's founding documents. As the American public became increasingly opposed to Prohibition, Congress passed a number of legislative acts intended to mollify opposition, ending with the Blaine Act that initiated the repeal of Prohibition and became the basis for the Twenty-First Amendment ratified in December 1933.

Byron Cannon

Further Reading

Clark, Norman H. *Deliver Us from Evil: An Interpretation of American Prohibition.* New York: Norton, 1976. An overview of the historical developments resulting in Prohibition, from the nineteenth century through the 1920s to its repeal.

Homan, J. A. *Prohibition, The Enemy of Temperance: An Exposition of the Liquor Problem.* Cincinnati, Ohio:

Christian Liberty Bureau, [c. 1910]. A twentieth-century argument against Prohibition, showing its negative effects on society as a whole.

Kyvig, David E. *Repealing National Prohibition.* 2d ed. Kent, Ohio: Kent State University Press, 2000. Describes the processes of opposition leading to the repeal of the Eighteenth Amendment in 1933.

Sinclair, Andrew. *Era of Excess: A Social History of the Prohibition Movement.* New York: Harper Colophon Books, 1962. A general history of Prohibition in the United States.

Warner, Harry S. *Prohibition, An Adventure in Freedom.* Westerville, Ohio: World League Against Alcoholism, 1928. A statement by defenders of the Eighteenth Amendment, referred to in this book as "The Great Experiment."

See also: Bathtub gin; Capone, Al; Flappers; Nightclubs; Organized crime; Speakeasies

---

■ *Prophet, The*

Identification: Inspirational book of twenty-six prose poems or poetic essays
Author: Kahlil Gibran
Date: 1923

The Prophet investigates aspects of human life and growth. Admired by readers but ignored by critics, the book has been consistently popular since its initial publication in 1923.

Kahlil Gibran was born in Bsharri, Lebanon (then Syria) and brought by his mother to the United States with his siblings at age twelve. After settling with his family in Boston, Gibran moved to New York City. Gibran was not widely known as a writer or artist when *The Prophet* was published. However, the book became a hit; after modest sales in its first year, sales doubled the year after the book's publication, only to double again the following year. By 1931, it had already been translated into more than twenty languages. Along with his literary colleagues during the 1920s, Gibran was instrumental in developing the Mahjar, or immigrant, school of Arab American writing, building bridges between Eastern and Western thought and expression. Illustrated with twelve drawings by the author, *The Prophet* is Gibran's best-known work and his third book written in English.

The Prophet is an extended conversation between Almustafa, a holy man, and inhabitants of Orphalese, a distant land where he has lived in exile for twelve years. Awaiting the ship that will bring him back home, Almustafa encounters a group of residents and a seer named Almitra, who asks Almustafa to explain what has been revealed to him about the interval between birth and death. His response is structured in twenty-six short chapters, each a discourse on some facet of life. Among the best-known sections are "On Love," "On Marriage," and "On Children." In a letter to his benefactor, Mary Haskell, who encouraged him to write in English rather than in translation, Gibran summed up the book by saying that humans are more significant than they know and that "all is well." The book is generally thought to be partly autobiographical, with Almustafa representing Gibran, Almitra representing Haskell, and Orphalese representing New York City, where Gibran had been living for twelve years before the book's publication.

Impact

Many see *The Prophet* as a beloved classic that offers sustenance; others consider it trite and overly sentimental. In either case, its words have lasted across generations, cultures, and societal changes, with themes that reflect wisdom from disparate spiritual traditions without requiring beliefs, practices, or erudition. Seemingly old-fashioned for its Roaring Twenties audience, the book continued to sell, even during the economic downturn of the Great Depression. In the 1960s, it became a staple of the counterculture movement in the United States. Into the twenty-first century, passages from *The Prophet* are still recited at weddings and funerals, and there is some discussion about the book becoming a Hollywood film.

Jean C. Fulton

Further Reading

Acocella, Joan. "Prophet Motive: The Kahlil Gibran Phenomenon." *The New Yorker*, January 7, 2008, 72–77.

Waterfield, Robin. *Prophet: The Life and Times of Kahlil Gibran.* New York: St. Martin's Press, 2000.

See also: Book publishing; Literature in the United States; Poetry; Roaring Twenties

■ Psychology, psychiatry, and psychoanalysis

Concepts from psychiatry, psychoanalysis, and psychology spoke to the concerns of Americans in the 1920s, as they tried to cope with the social consequences of better mobility, increased personal independence, and awareness of diversity. Simplifications of theories from these fields promoted more open attitudes toward sex, legislation to control immigration and fertility, and environmental manipulations attempting to shape behavior and improve society.

In the 1920s, psychology, psychiatry, and psychoanalysis functioned as separate and independent disciplines. Psychology was an academic discipline that was no longer taught as a part of moral philosophy. Learning, sensation, memory, and the assessment of such traits as intelligence were major areas of psychological focus. Psychiatrists viewed their mission as the treatment of mental illness, a category beginning to expand beyond identifiable brain diseases. Most psychologists and many psychiatrists were suspicious of psychoanalysis, the data of which was neither measurable nor clearly related to brain structures. Psychoanalysts, who had been trained as physicians, read their own academic journals and met with their own organizations instead of participating in scholarly discussion with psychologists or psychiatrists. During the 1920s, the concepts from each of these disciplines that filtered down to the public were usually simplified by enthusiastic advocates and molded to fit popular stereotypes. The general public took these simplifications as scientific truth.

Psychoanalysis

During the 1920s, psychoanalysis was a work-in-progress. Still dominated by the teachings of Austrian neurologist Sigmund Freud, this technique involved the guided exploration of a patient's unconscious mind. The goal of psychoanalytic therapy was for the patient to gain insight into unconscious emotional conflicts. According to Freud, the central driving force behind such conflicts was libido, or sexual energy. To Freud, libido represented a much broader motive than the desire for sexual fulfillment; rather, it fueled the entire range of human affections. Freud's writings during the 1920s further broadened his concept of libido and motivation. In his work *The Ego and the Id* (1923), Freud suggested that instinctual forces known as the *id* were often inhibited by a moral guide instilled in childhood that he called the *superego*. The reasoning part of human personality, the *ego*, was in Freud's view responsible for arbitrating between the opposing forces of the *id* and *superego*.

Psychoanalysis had only a modest influence on American psychiatry during the 1920s. This may have been partly due to the length, rigor, and distance of psychoanalytical training programs, which were still primarily located in Europe. Additionally, Freud was in the process of revising his theories. Although some American psychiatrists, such as A. A. Brill, objected to the internal contradictions they saw in psychoanalysis, the first generation of American psychoanalysts still reflected Freud's earlier views. Most American psychiatrists remained outside the psychoanalytic fold during the 1920s, perhaps because psychoanalysis was regarded as having only limited application. With no effective medication, psychoanalysis was not a viable treatment option for hospitalized patients who were inarticulate, mute, or incoherent, and it was too costly and time-consuming for most patients suffering from neuroses.

Popular interpretations of psychoanalytic ideas, however, had a dramatic effect on American society during the 1920s, bringing about a shift in manners and moral attitudes. Before and during World War I, dress styles and societal norms seemed directed toward the preservation of unmarried women's chastity. During the 1920s, society became more open about sexual matters. Makeup, revealing clothing styles, and shorter hair came to be seen as symptoms of women's growing sexual independence. Explicit accounts of erotic adventures could be found in magazines and in the novels of authors such as F. Scott Fitzgerald and Ernest Hemingway. Many cultural developments contributed to this change in mores: the mobility permitted by widespread automobile ownership, women's increasing economic independence and political participation, and some decline in the prestige and power of traditional religious institutions. Another important factor was the idea attributed to Freud that the suppression of sexual impulses results in repression and neurosis. Some people took Freud's teachings to mean that sexual restraint could be harmful to one's mental health. Few who thus cited Freud were aware that he viewed self-imposed control as necessary for civilization, even at the cost of personal anxiety.

Psychiatry

Most psychiatrists in the 1920s worked in large mental hospitals with patients so impaired they could not function in ordinary family and social interactions. Most of these patients were considered to suffer from an incurable brain disease and given only custodial care.

Experimental interventions were sometimes made during the 1920s. Some patients with terminal brain syphilis recovered after being inoculated with malaria; the high fevers malaria induced killed the syphilis bacteria. One group of patients who hallucinated or displayed incoherent speech or preposterous beliefs were called schizophrenic. Schizophrenics mostly remained hospitalized, although a small percentage of them experienced mysterious recovery. Deeply depressed patients would usually recover to a degree, although some would later experience a relapse. Despite such occasional successes, the number of patients in American mental hospitals increased to several hundred thousand by 1930.

By the end of the 1920s, about 30 percent of all psychiatrists had practices consisting of nonhospitalized patients. Some of these psychiatrists practiced in child guidance clinics and dealt with children's school and family problems. Other office psychiatrists were consulted by anxious and unhappy women who described their unsettled condition as "nerves." Many of these office psychiatrists adopted the commonsense psychology of Adolph Meyer, whose technique was to appraise every sphere of the patient's life—biological, family, work, and social adjustment—in order to identify the patient's faulty reaction pattern and encourage adaptive changes. Such changes were often effected through social workers' attempts to alter the patient's environment.

Psychology

Within academic psychology during the decade, no area of study was more important than learning, and no learning psychologist was more important than John Watson. Psychologists experimenting with learning behaviors studied improvements in the performance of laboratory rats that repeatedly overcame obstacles in a maze and thereby obtained a reward. Watson extrapolated from this research an integrated theory of learning with implications for improving society. Calling his theory "behaviorism," Watson was emphatic that scientific psychology should report only observable behavior and make no inferences

Sigmund Freud. (Getty Images)

about the workings of the mind. Watson's entire learning theory was based on the idea that learning is a simple process of linking stimuli with responses and that repeated stimulus responses become habits. Vocal sounds linked to particular objects become words, for example. According to Watson, thinking is a learned behavior as well, resulting from learned sequences of words. Watson further posited that emotions such as fear were internal visceral responses that had become conditioned to dangerous objects. His notion was that every person forms a unique personality because, over the course of a lifetime, responses are linked to a unique sequence of changing environmental stimuli.

Watson wrote articles for popular magazines and became one of the best-known psychologists of the 1920s. His ideas were easy for the public to understand. He argued that behavioral control achieved by the linking of desirable responses to positive environments would instill good habits and improve society. He freely offered parents advice on how to instill desirable habits in their children. Neurotic fears, according to Watson, were the product of bad

conditioning and could be eliminated by reconditioning. Critics argued that children differ in temperament and that Watson's universal rules for conditioning children were far too rigid. Watson nonetheless retained his popularity because his message of a better life through learning was a hopeful one that resonated with the public.

The issue of the 1920s that aroused the most intense controversy between psychologists and the general public concerned the nature of intelligence and the validity of the tests that purportedly measured it. A successful intelligence quotient (IQ) test was first devised by French psychologist Alfred Binet. Binet's test consisted of schoolbook questions carefully arranged in order of difficulty. The test had proven useful in identifying children who would have experienced difficulty coping with standard elementary school curricula. A group version of such a test had been successfully used in World War I to select U.S. Army recruits who could master complex military tasks.

Psychologists held differing views about the origins of intelligence. Psychologists Henry Goddard and Robert Yerkes held that IQ test scores measured a person's genetically inherited ability. These psychologists cited pedigree studies showing that brilliant achievers seem to cluster in some families. The genetic determination of intelligence was a significant factor in laws drafted by legislators concerned about declining national intelligence. Such legislators wrote the Immigration Law of 1924, reducing the quota of U.S. immigrants from southern Europe, where children were performing less well on IQ tests. Children who scored below 70 on IQ tests were classified as having mental disabilities. Many state eugenic laws were written authorizing the reproductive sterilization of people with mental disabilities to prevent the possibility of their procreating and transmitting their low IQ to progeny. In 1927, the U.S. Supreme Court upheld the constitutionality of sterilization legislation in the case of *Buck v. Bell*. A number of psychologists opposed such laws based on the inadequacy of the scientific evidence supporting the theory that IQ is entirely hereditary. They noted that such environmental antecedents as intellectually impoverished home environments and inadequate schooling were correlated with low IQ test scores just as strongly as ancestry. Joined by civil libertarians, moralists, and journalist Walter Lippmann, the opposition to sterilization laws had increased dramatically by 1930.

Psychologists during the 1920s adapted general ability tests to measure the aptitudes required in specific vocations. During the 1920s, managers attempted to improve morale and increase industrial productivity by making greater efforts to match workers with appropriate jobs. The demand for aptitude tests for placement decisions increased greatly. In 1921, the Psychological Corporation was founded to design and publish psychological tests.

Impact

Some of the social changes inspired by psychology, psychiatry, and psychoanalysis of the 1920s did not survive the test of time. Studies of adopted children and identical twins reared apart showed convincingly that a combination of both learning environments and inherited genes determine IQ scores. Compulsory sterilizations were ultimately deemed arbitrary and cruel. By the 1940s, state eugenic laws were falling into disuse and beginning to be repealed. The conditioning programs recommended by Watson were considered too rigid by later child psychologists. The emotional bonds established between parents and children were increasingly held to be more important than conditioning methods. Those who interpreted psychoanalytic theory as a sanction for unrestrained sexual expression found little fulfillment in the direction psychology and psychiatry took after the 1920s.

Certain aspects of 1920s psychology, psychiatry, and psychoanalysis did make enduring contributions to modern understandings of the mind. The new openness of the 1920s in discussing personal problems became the basis for the Sensitivity Training groups of the 1970s, which sought to make people better aware of others' sensitivity. Psychoanalysis became dominant in American psychiatry during the generation of the 1950s. While its direct importance in psychiatry and psychology has since faded, psychoanalytic concepts under other names have become a part of the mainstream. The refining of Watson's behaviorism by psychologist B. F. Skinner resulted in the development of an effective behavior-based therapy. IQ tests and aptitude tests are still consid-

ered sufficiently predictive of achievement potential to be used in selection decisions by colleges and employers alike.

Thomas E. DeWolfe

Further Reading

Burnham, John C. *Paths into American Culture: Psychology, Medicine, Morals.* Philadelphia: Temple University Press, 1988. Includes chapters dealing particularly with psychology and psychoanalysis in the 1920s.

Fancher, Raymond E. *The Intelligence Men: Makers of the IQ Controversy.* New York: W. W. Norton, 1987. Describes the IQ test and its history with special attention to the nature-nurture debate.

Gay, Peter. *Freud: A Life for Our Times.* New York: W. W. Norton, 1988. Discusses the turbulent period of the 1920s in Freud's life, including his revisions of his theories and his responses to dissenters.

Leahey, Thomas Hardy. *A History of Psychology: Main Currents in Psychological Thought.* 6th ed. Upper Saddle River, N.J.: Prentice-Hall, 2003. Contains chapter-long discussions of Freudian theory, behaviorism, and applied psychology.

Shorter, Edward. *A History of Psychiatry.* J. Wiley & Sons, 1997. Includes a chapter describing the concerns of psychiatrists during the 1920s.

Watson, John. *Behaviorism.* Rev. ed. New York: W. W. Norton, 1970. An examination of behaviorism written by its most famous early advocate.

See also: *Buck v. Bell;* Education; Eugenics movement; Health care; Immigration to the United States; Medicine; Racial discrimination; Sex and sex education

---

■ *Public Opinion*

Identification: A book about the role of public opinion in a democracy
Author: Walter Lippmann
Date: 1922

Written during a time of widespread disillusionment with government following World War I, Public Opinion *was the first book to apply twentieth-century developments in fields such as philosophy and psychology to the question of how public opinion is shaped and what role it should play in democratic decision making.*

In this book, Lippmann uses the concept of stereotypes, or mental images, to describe how individuals view the world around them, including the unseen world that exists outside their own immediate experience. Amplified across society, these stereotypes permit only an error-filled and imperfect basis for sound decision making. According to Lippmann, the public is composed of so many ill-informed, inattentive, and even neurotic citizens that it would be folly to place the decision-making process in their hands. He therefore urges that, in a democracy, the public cast their votes for individuals to represent them and then leave decision making entirely to these representatives, insiders whose knowledge goes beyond mere stereotypes.

In Lippmann's view, the news media, which still consisted mainly of newspapers in 1922, is inherently biased and incapable of adequately informing public opinion. Drawing on his own experience as a journalist and wartime government functionary, he makes a sharp distinction between news and truth, comparing the news to a searchlight that gives the public an intermittent glimpse of this or that aspect of the environment but never a clear picture of the whole. He also expresses the fear that propaganda, having been used on an unprecedented scale in World War I, would be employed in the future to produce a manufactured, rather than enlightened, consent of the governed. To cope with these defects in existing institutions, Lippmann recommends that intelligence bureaus, staffed by qualified experts, be relied on to provide timely and factual information to all government departments and that a similar intelligence system be used throughout society as a check against the press.

Impact

Public Opinion can be considered the founding book in the field of communication studies, having pointed the way to later scholarship on such topics as agenda setting. Beyond that, its ideas became the subject of much discussion among intellectuals during the 1920s, especially when educator John Dewey weighed in with his more optimistic view that improved methods of public discussion could lead to a more salutary role for public opinion. While some of Lippmann's views may now be considered naïve, his book became a classic by raising issues that will remain pertinent for as long as democracy itself exists.

Larry Haapanen

Further Reading

Adams, Larry Lee. *Walter Lippmann.* Boston: Twayne, 1977.

Blum, D. Steven. *Walter Lippmann: Cosmopolitanism in the Century of Total War.* Ithaca, N.Y.: Cornell University Press, 1984.

García, César. "Walter Lippmann and George Santayana: A Shared Vision of Society and Public Opinion." *Journal of American Culture* 29, no. 2 (June, 2006): 183–190.

See also: Dewey, John; Lippmann, Walter; Newspapers, U.S.; Political parties; Psychology, psychiatry, and psychoanalysis